CW01394996
Castello damina
Linha equinocialis:
Motes lune

OCEAN

John Haywood studied medieval history at the universities of Lancaster, Cambridge and Copenhagen. He has worked for many years as a lecturer in the educational travel industry, is a frequent speaker on cruise ships, and is the author of more than twenty books, including *Northmen: the Viking Saga, AD 793–1241*, *The New Atlas of World History*, *The Great Migrations*, *The Penguin Historical Atlas of the Vikings* and *Dark Age Naval Power*.

Also by Author

Northmen: The Viking Saga AD *793–1241*

The New Atlas of World History: Global Events at a Glance

Viking: The Norse Warrior's (Unofficial) Manual

The Historical Atlas of the Celtic World

The Celts: Bronze Age to New Age

The Penguin Historical Atlas of the Vikings

OCEAN

A History of the Atlantic Before Columbus

JOHN HAYWOOD

An Apollo Book

First published in the UK in 2024 by Head of Zeus,
part of Bloomsbury Publishing Plc

9 7 5 3 1 2 4 6 8

A catalogue record for this book is available from the British Library.

ISBN (HB): 9781801109901
ISBN (E): 9781801109888

Cover design: Meg Shepherd
Maps © Isambard Thomas at Corvo
Endpaper map: Cantino Planisphere, 1502, Biblioteca Estense, Modena
Typeset by DivAddict

Printed and bound in Great Britain by
CPI Group (UK) Ltd, Croydon CR0 4YY

Head of Zeus Ltd
First Floor East
5–8 Hardwick Street
London EC1R 4RG

WWW.HEADOFZEUS.COM

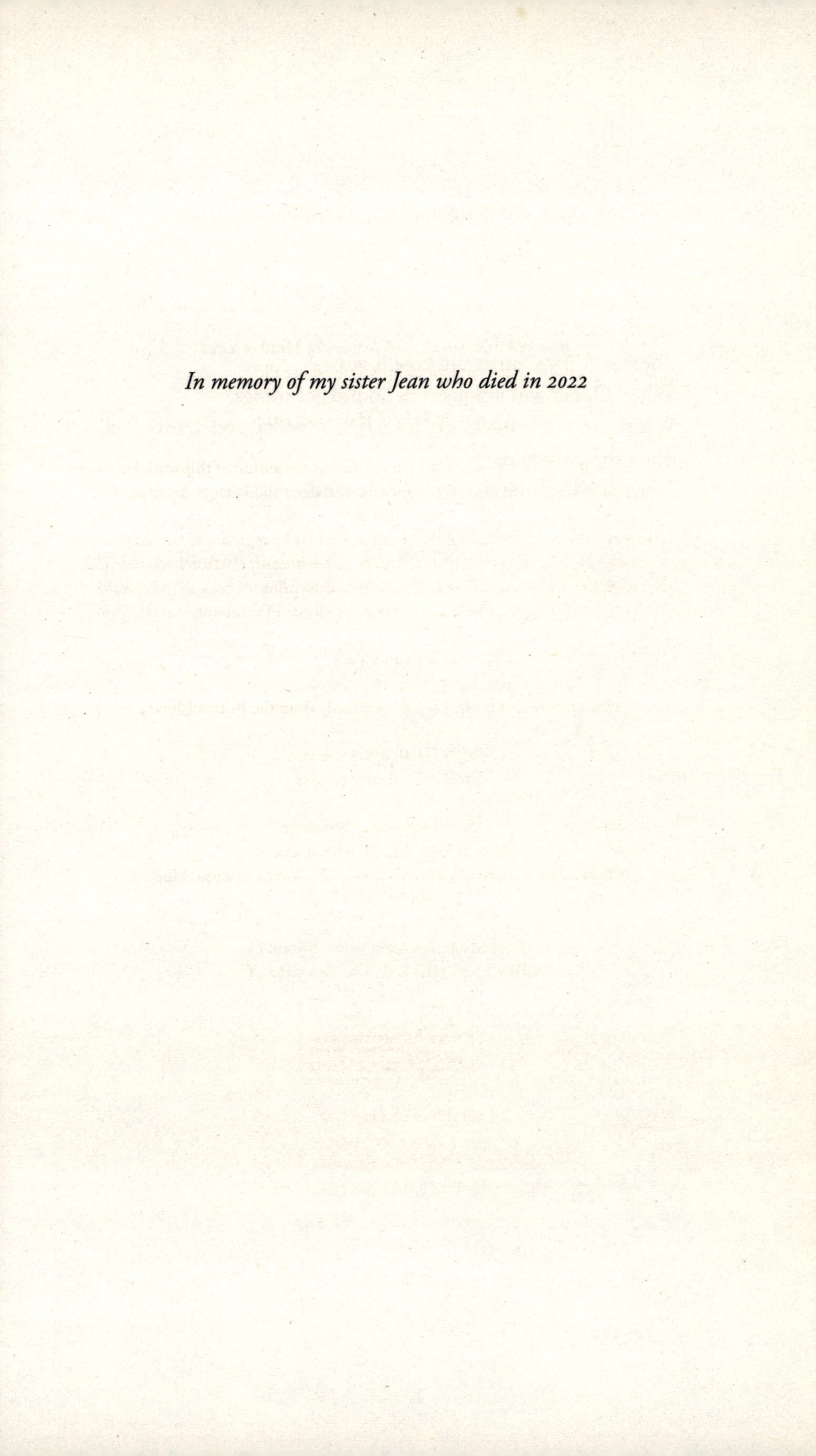

In memory of my sister Jean who died in 2022

There will come an age in far-off years,
When Ocean will unloose the bounds of things,
When the whole broad earth shall be revealed and Tethys shall disclose new worlds
Nor shall Thule be the limit of the land.

Seneca the Younger, *Medea*, lines 375–9

CONTENTS

Maps

Map 1 *Atlantic and marginal seas*

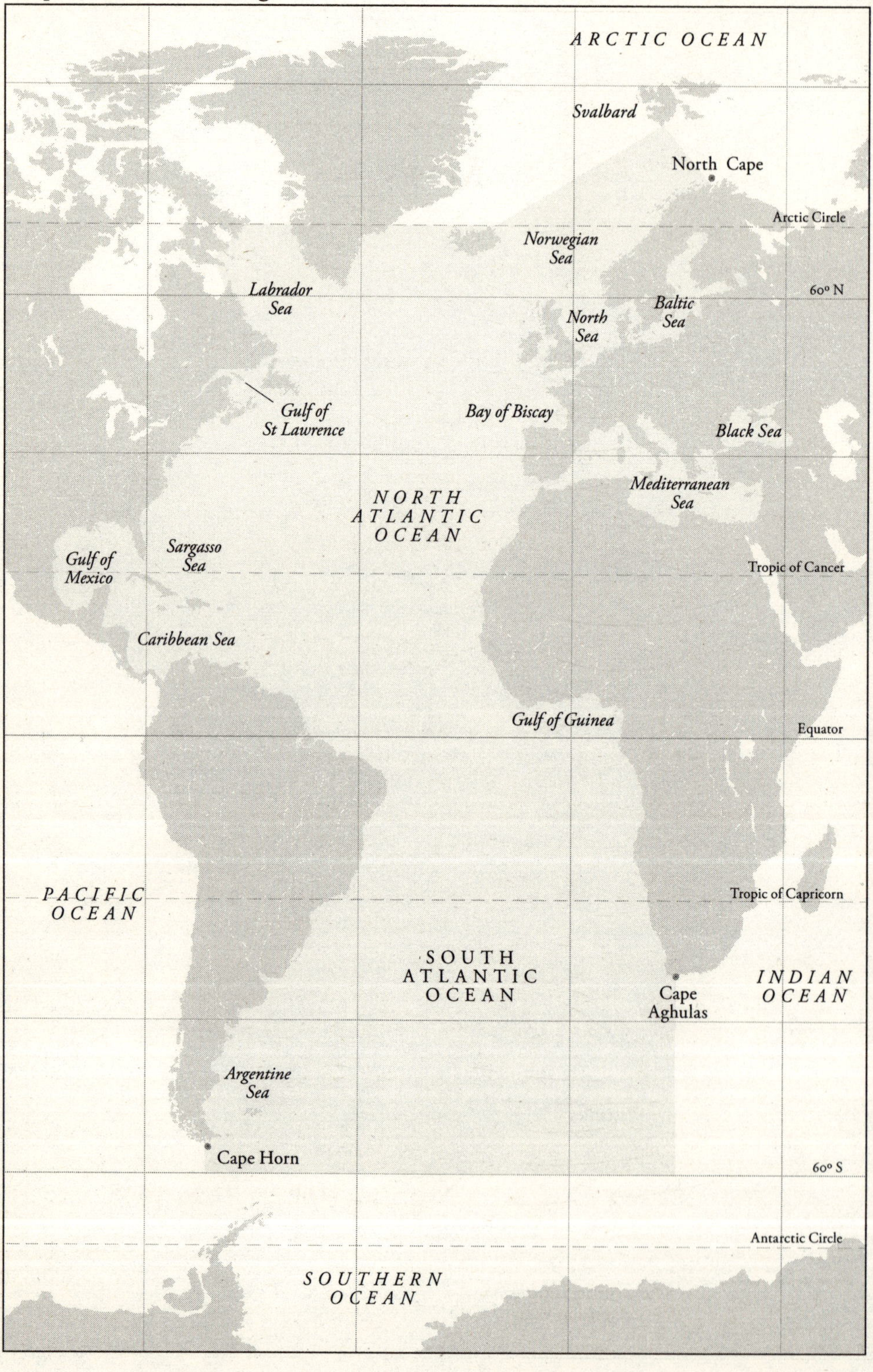

Map 2 *Atlantic winds and currents*

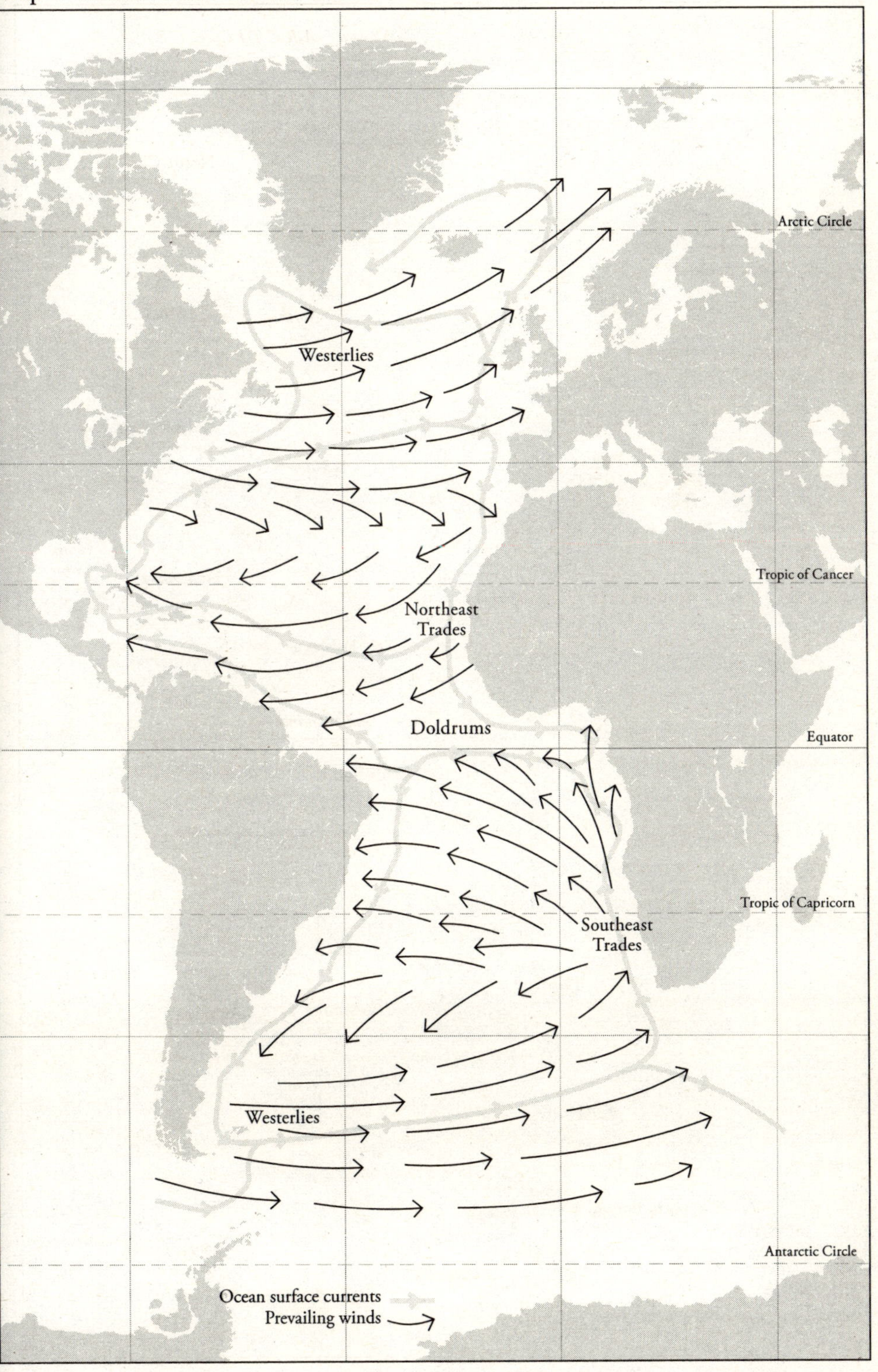

Map 3 *Atlantic Europe*

Barents Sea
North Cape
Alta
White Sea
Lofoten Islands
HÅLOGALAND
Arctic Circle
egian
ea
dheim
Gulf of Bothnia
Oslo
Stockholm
Novgorod
Tanumshede
SKÅNE
Baltic Sea
eby
ibeck
Gdansk
ice
me
Adriatic Sea
Constantinople (Istanbul)
malfi
Atlantic Europe

Map 4 *Greco-Roman oceans*

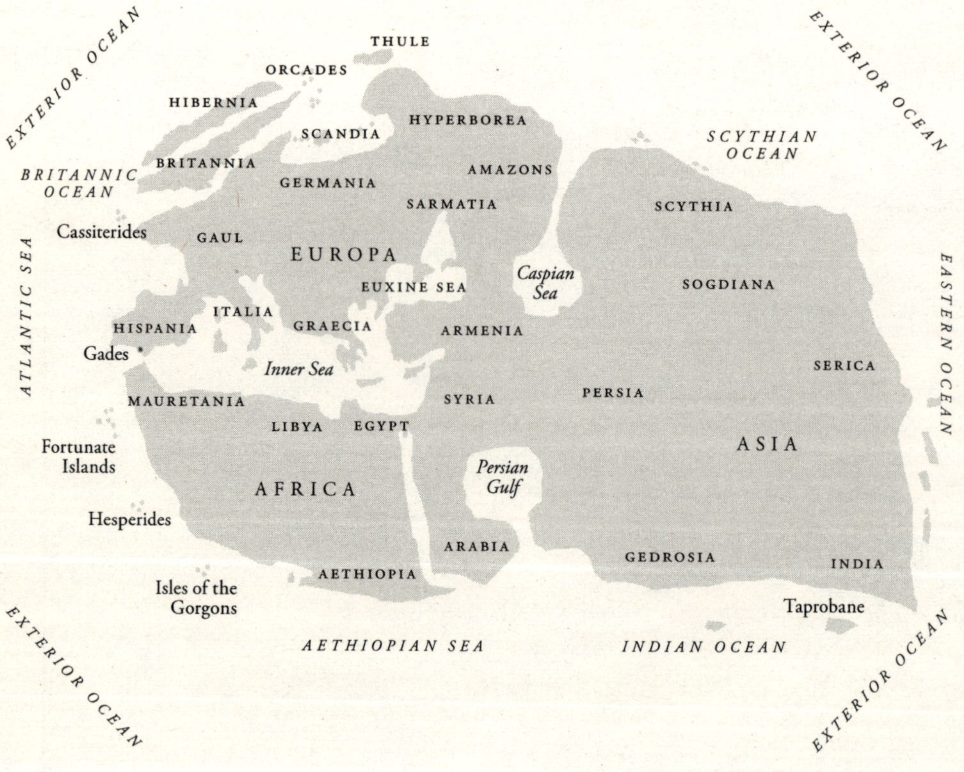

Map 5 *The Norse Atlantic*

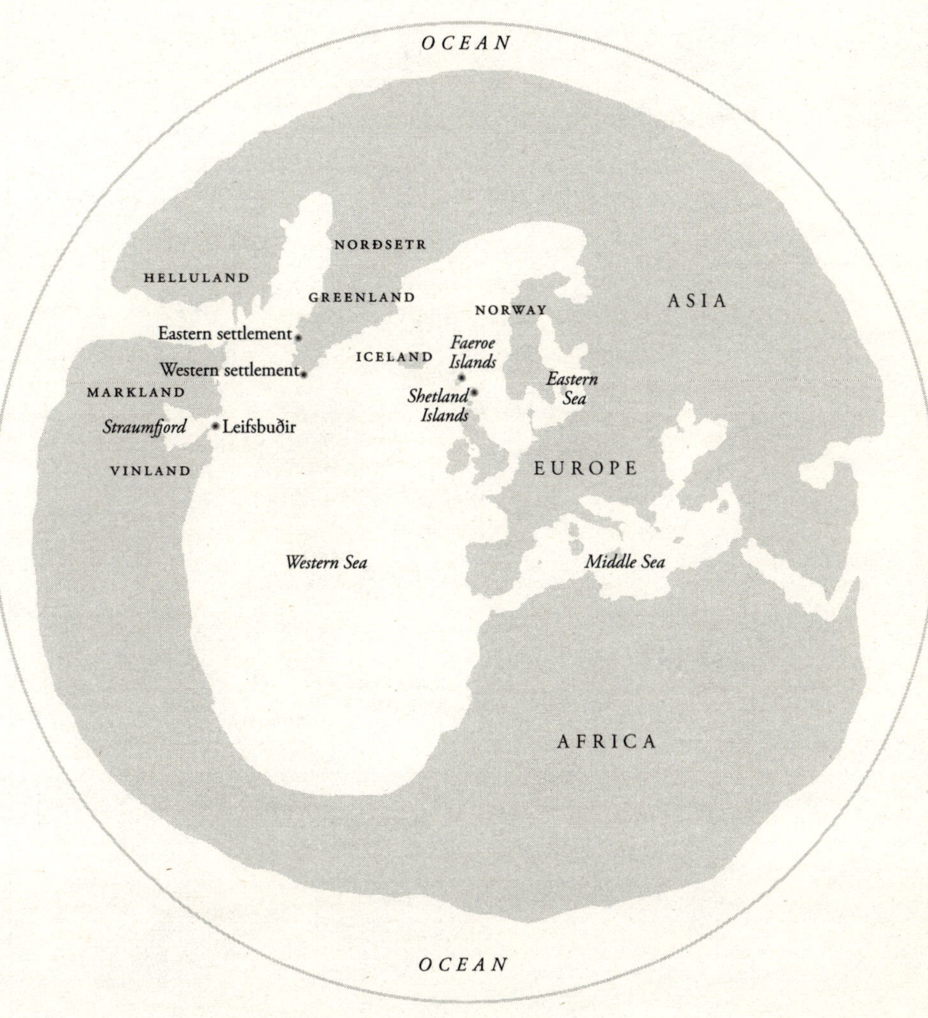

Map 6 *Exploration of the African coast, 1312–1488*

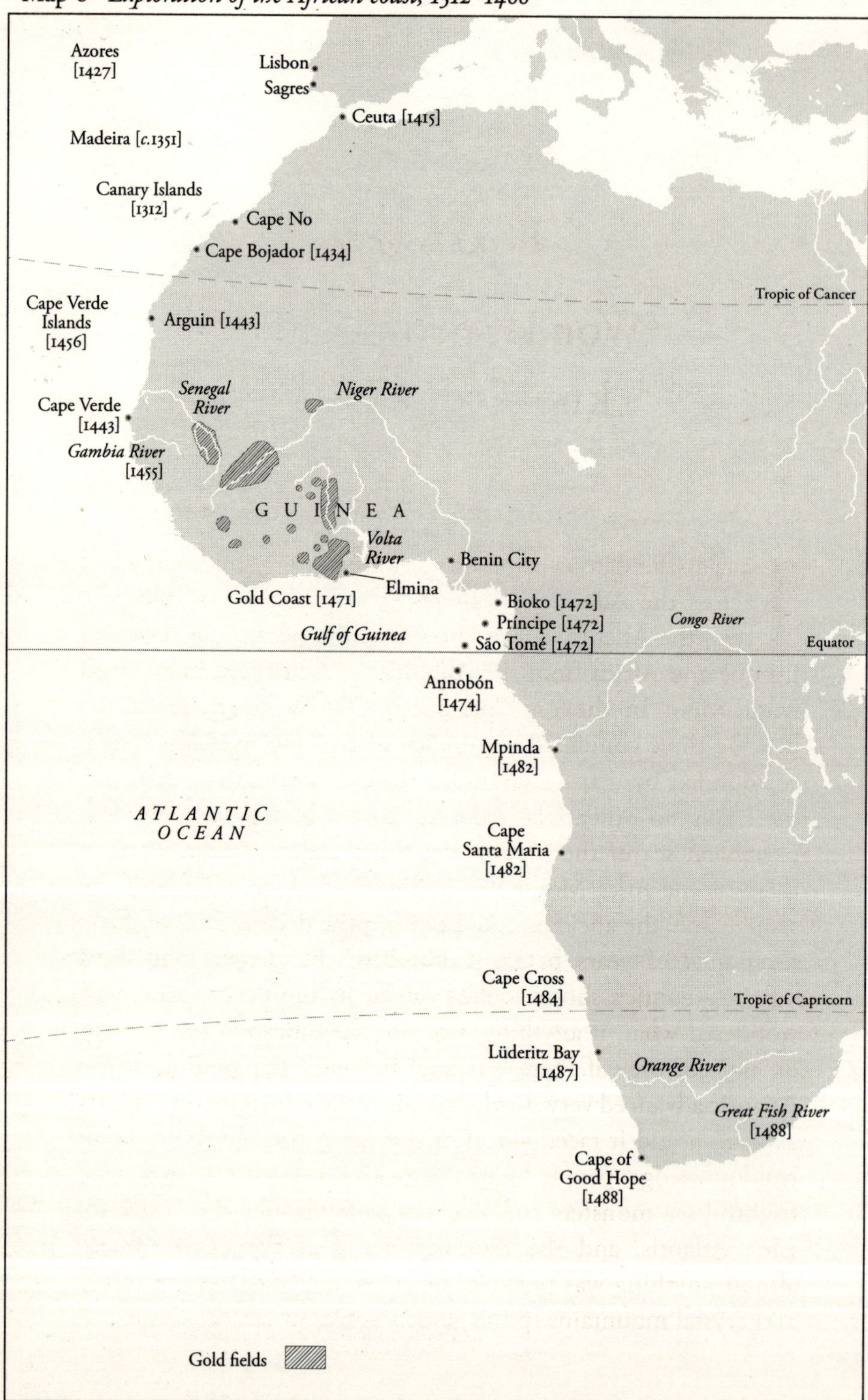

Foreword

'Wonder grows where knowledge fails'[1]

1492 is the date everyone knows, the year Columbus sailed across the Atlantic Ocean and changed geography. Before this, the Atlantic as we know it – the ocean that separates Europe and Africa from the Americas – didn't exist in anyone's world view. In the pre-Columbian Old World there existed just the three conjoined continents of Europe, Asia and Africa, surrounded by a truly boundless global ocean, *the* Ocean, for there was no other. The Atlantic existed but it was only as a peripheral sea of the Ocean, the sea of Atlas, though whether this was the Atlas Mountains or the mythological Titan of the same name, the ancients could never quite decide. For countless thousands of years before Columbus, the people who lived on the Atlantic's shores looked out at its limitless expanse and wondered what, if anything, was out there beyond the horizon or, indeed, even if there was any 'beyond'. Exploration of the Atlantic advanced very slowly but the human imagination abhors a vacuum and it raced ahead of the navigators. In the place of real knowledge, people imagined an Ocean filled with wonders, frightful sea monsters and legendary islands, like the Fortunate Isles, Atlantis, and the Promised Land of the Saints, where almost anything was possible, from talking birds, seas of blood and crystal mountains to the golden apples of eternal youth and the abodes of demons and the dead. These fantastic tales are as much part of the history of the Atlantic as developments in shipbuilding, navigation and trade. Before Columbus, the ocean was an idea as much as a place, and what seafarers believed, or imagined, they knew about it determined their expectations of what they might discover by voyaging on it. Advanced seafaring traditions don't develop where the sea offers only a watery grave; there has to be something achievable to aim for. Compared to the Pacific Ocean, the Atlantic is short of real islands to discover, but belief in legendary islands encouraged European navigators to go to sea in search of them: even Columbus never doubted their existence and expected to make landfall on some of them when he sailed west, as he thought, to Asia. In the process, they gained the confidence to leave their familiar coastal waters and learned how to sail the open ocean, discover the world and set bounds to the once boundless ocean. Today, Atlantic Studies is an academic discipline in its own right, but its focus is very much on the post-Columbian legacy of European colonialism, migration and the trans-Atlantic slave trade, and the long, myth-shrouded age that went before is all too often only briefly dealt with. An epic 168,000 years of human history on and around its shores has become little more than a footnote. The history of the pre-Columbian Atlantic is more important than this – it was the essential prelude to everything that happened afterwards. It was the where and when that Europeans served their apprenticeships in ocean navigation, commerce and colonialism, and that saw them formulate the ideologies they used to justify their territorial claims and their exploitation of colonized peoples. When Europeans finally broke out onto the world's oceans in the sixteenth century, they already had everything they needed to secure global domination.

Introduction

Birthing pains

Catastrophism – Plate tectonics – Making a monkey of Columbus – Geography is destiny – The wrong end of the world

When was the Atlantic born? The sixteenth-century Flemish cartographer Abraham Ortelius (1527–1598) thought he knew. Ortelius had mapped the world more accurately than any previous cartographer, and he was struck by how closely the Atlantic coasts of the Old and New Worlds seemed to fit together. Could this possibly be a coincidence, he asked? It seemed to him that 'the Americas had been torn away from Europe and Africa by earthquakes and sudden floods'. He argued that 'the vestiges of the rupture reveal themselves, if someone examines a map of the world and considers carefully how the eminences and bays of the coasts of the three continents attach to one another'.[2] Ortelius believed that this violent separation, which created the Atlantic Ocean, must have occurred as a result of the catastrophic overnight destruction of the legendary island of Atlantis, which in his day was believed to be a historical event. As births go, labour was agonizingly painful but mercifully brief.

Catastrophism

The matching fit of the opposite coasts of the Atlantic was obvious for all to see, and even more so after the continental shelves had been charted accurately in the nineteenth century, but how was it possible that great masses of solid land could roam freely over the Earth's surface? For Ortelius, a catastrophe of Biblical proportions was the only imaginable explanation. Catastrophism was very popular in early geological thought. In Ortelius's day, most Europeans accepted that the mythological Biblical account of the Creation was literally true and that the world was, therefore, only about 6,000 years old. Not only did all of human history have to be crammed into this narrow time frame, but all of geological history too. The Earth was simply not old enough for geological changes to have happened gradually; mountain ranges and oceans, if they had not been present since the Creation, could only have been the result of sudden cataclysmic events of unimaginable power, like Noah's Flood, which, like the destruction of Atlantis, was also then believed to be a historical event.

Catastrophism went out of fashion in the nineteenth century, as geologists steadily amassed evidence proving that the Earth was in reality many hundreds of millions of years old. That was more than time enough for continents to move, mountains to grow and oceans to open and close. And now, to support this, there was persuasive fossil evidence, such as the fossils of *Glossopteris*, a tropical tree that flourished in the Permian period (299–252 million years ago), which geologists were finding in South America, southern Africa, India, Madagascar, Australia and even in deep-frozen Antarctica. Evidence such as this led the German geologist Alfred Wegener (1880–1930) to formulate his theory of 'Continental Drift'. Wegener proposed that, around 300 million years ago, all of the Earth's continents had been joined in a single supercontinent he named Pangea ('all the Earth'), surrounded by a superocean, since called Panthalassa ('all the sea'). It was from the break-up of this supercontinent that the modern continents and oceans had been created as its fragments had 'drifted' apart. While other geologists could see merit in Wegener's theory, it struggled to find acceptance, because there were no known geological forces capable of moving continents around the globe.

Plate tectonics

Had Wegener not died during a geological expedition to the Greenland ice cap in 1930, he might conceivably have lived long enough to see himself vindicated. The breakthrough came in 1953, when the American oceanographer Marie Tharp mapped the ocean floor and discovered the Mid-Atlantic Ridge, a 16,000-kilometre-long chain of underwater mountain ranges and rift valleys running down the middle of the Atlantic Ocean from the Arctic to the Antarctic like the spine of some vast primeval sea serpent. This turned out to be only a part of a continuous 40,000-kilometre-long chain of ridges and rifts on the beds of all the world's oceans. These ridges, it was discovered, were volcanically active zones, creating and spreading new ocean floor. This discovery paved the way for the modern science of plate tectonics (the geological equivalent of Darwinism), which explains not only how continents can move and new oceans can be created and destroyed, but earthquakes, volcanism and mountain-building too.

The missing motive force that could move continents was convection currents rising from the Earth's hot core. The Earth's rocky crust is as solid as it feels, but the layer which underlies it, the mantle, is slightly plastic at geological scales, and it flows with the convection currents, stretching, tearing and fracturing the crust as it does so. The movement is infinitesimally slow, around 2.5 centimetres a year, the same rate that human fingernails grow, but it constantly creates and reabsorbs the ocean floor and rearranges the continents. For most of geological time, the continents have been scattered randomly over the globe, but on at least five, perhaps as many as ten, occasions, the continents have been welded together into vast supercontinents surrounded by superoceans: Wegener's Pangea was the last of these, but, some 200 million years in the future, another one will form. It's already got a name: Novopangea.

The same forces that create supercontinents also tear them apart again, scattering the continents over the globe once more.

It was from the break-up of Pangea that the Atlantic Ocean was born. That break-up began around 200 million years ago between what became North America and Africa. It was accompanied, and perhaps caused, by a catastrophically violent volcanic outburst of the sort that would not have disappointed Ortelius: it may have led to the mass extinction that marks the boundary between the Triassic and Jurassic periods. South America did not begin its divorce from Africa until about 117 million years ago, and it too was accompanied by a violent volcanic episode. Once South America's separation was complete, around 83 million years ago, it began to drift slowly west and north, towards North America. When the two continents met and joined, as recently as 2.8 million years ago, the Atlantic we know was fully born: it is the youngest of the Earth's oceans.

Making a monkey of Columbus

The plants and animals that were now stranded on their island continents took their own evolutionary paths, but, despite the widening oceans between them, there could still be some surprising contacts. It is now well established that the first human inhabitants of the Americas came from Asia via the Bering Strait land bridge during a period of low sea level during the Ice Age, and it was long believed that that the ancestors of today's South and Central American monkey species must have made the same journey only a few million years before them. Recently discovered fossil evidence from South America has turned that assumption on its head: they are all descended from African ancestors who arrived in South America between 32 and 35 million years ago. This was long after the two continents had fully separated, so these monkeys must have been the first primate oceanic seafarers, beating those other primate seafarers, Leif Eriksson and Christopher Columbus, across the Atlantic by a comfortable margin. It isn't credible that these monkeys were voluntary emigrants: they were most likely swept out to sea in a storm and survived on a natural raft of floating vegetation. It helped that at this time the Atlantic was only around 1,500 kilometres wide, about half its modern-day narrowest point between Liberia and Brazil, and also that, before South America linked up with North America, the winds and ocean currents were more favourable for east-to-west Atlantic crossings than they are today. What's even more surprising is that the fossil evidence shows that at least two different species of monkey made the crossing a few million years apart. Monkeys weren't the only land mammals to make the crossing; they were preceded by the ancestor of that pig-sized South American rodent, the capybara.

Geography is destiny

The human history of the Atlantic began in southern Africa well over 100,000 years ago, but it would be Europeans who would discover the ocean in the fullest meaning of the word. Almost all the coasts of the Atlantic had been discovered by someone by the time the last Ice Age came to an end around 12,000 years ago, but what they knew of the wider ocean was limited to their own coastal waters. Europeans were the first to learn how to sail the open Atlantic and explore and chart all of its coasts, the first to discover the ocean in its entirety and then use those skills to do the same in the rest of the world's oceans. This was no accident of history; it was largely determined by the geography of the Atlantic itself.

Where are the places in the world that advanced seafaring first began? For a start, none of them are on open ocean coasts. Almost everywhere in the world, humans who lived on sea coasts quickly learned to build rafts or canoes the better to catch fish offshore, but where the view out to sea was just an empty horizon, the technology rarely developed any further without some outside stimulus. Neither on Africa's long west coast, nor on South America's Atlantic or Pacific coasts. Our earliest primate ancestors probably already well understood that open water was dangerous, so, unless there was some obvious advantage to sailing far out to sea to compensate for the innate danger of drowning, humans rarely strayed far from the shore. Inevitably, some of those who ventured out to fish would have been blown far out to sea beyond the horizon. If this happened off the South American or West African coast, those who were lucky enough to make it back to the shore would have reported that there was nothing at all out there, only the ever-receding horizon where the sky met the sea.

What was needed for more advanced seafaring traditions to begin developing was attainable goals, such as offshore islands visible from the shore or the chance to save days of walking around a bay or inlet of the sea by paddling a boat directly across to the other side. Some parts of the world are particularly rich in such attainable goals. The Southeast Asian archipelago, with its thousands of intervisible islands, was one such place, a friendly nursery where the ancestors of the Malays, Polynesians, Melanesians and Micronesians learned the skills that enabled them to navigate the Indian and Pacific oceans in distant prehistory. In the Atlantic, the nursery seas with the attainable goals were, mostly, at least, around Europe. With its many peninsulas, bays and fjords, Europe has the longest coastline in relation to its area of any continent, over three times longer than Africa's, with only one third of the area. Europe also has inland seas, the Baltic Sea, the North Sea, the English Channel, the Irish Sea and, most of all, the Mediterranean Sea, which it shared with North Africa and Asia; these bounded seas offered manageable challenges, where seafarers could watch the land disappear over their sterns, confident in the knowledge that another landfall was never far away. This made them ideal environments for Europeans to learn the shipbuilding and navigation skills that allowed them, eventually, to master the Atlantic.

North America's coastline runs Europe's a close second when it comes to length in relation to land area, and, while much of it is ice-bound, the island-studded Caribbean looks full of potential to be a nursery sea. Yet, despite the apparently favourable environment, at the time Europeans arrived in the New World, in the fifteenth century, even in the Caribbean large dugout canoes were still the limit of seafaring technology. Sails and oars were unknown. This absence of more advanced seafaring technology was a consequence of environmental factors specific to the Americas which determined that the transition from hunting and gathering to farming took some thousands of years longer than it did in most of the Old World. In the Old World, farming, and the population growth that resulted, hastened developments such as metalworking, the growth of states and long-distance trade, all of which promoted advances in shipbuilding and navigation: it was, for example, the demand for tin, copper and silver in the Bronze Age Mesopotamian civilizations that first sent Mediterranean seafarers out into the distant Atlantic. In the fifteenth century, the Andean and Mesoamerican civilizations were just attaining the technological level of the Old World's Bronze Age, and elite demand for prestigious copper, bronze and gold objects was stimulating growth in long-distance trade, just as it had in the Old World. During his fourth voyage to the New World, in 1502, Columbus encountered a large Mayan trading canoe off the coast of Honduras. Among the cargo, he found that the traders carried 'hatchets resembling the stone hatchets used by the other Indians, but made of good copper; and hawks' bells of copper, and crucibles to melt it'. Mayan metalsmiths travelled with their products, spreading knowledge of metallurgy along maritime trade routes in much the same way that it had been spread by itinerant smiths in Bronze Age Atlantic Europe. The indigenous American civilizations were developing along the same trajectory as those in the Old World; plank-built boats with masts and sails would no doubt have come with time, but the arrival of Europeans in 1492 stopped the clock.

If geography fostered advanced seafaring in Europe, it also long delayed the moment when Europeans became true oceanic sailors. By the fourteenth century, when the Europeans were on the brink of their oceanic expansion, the Micronesians, Melanesians and Polynesians had already been sailing the open Pacific, a far larger ocean than the Atlantic, for at least 2,500 years. What the Pacific had in abundance and the Atlantic lacked was oceanic archipelagos, especially in the west. Most of the Atlantic archipelagos are on the continental shelves. There are only a handful of isolated volcanic islands and four oceanic archipelagos in the Atlantic: the Azores, Madeira, the Canaries and the Cape Verde Islands, collectively known as Macaronesia, a name derived from Greek, *makárōn nēsoi*, the 'islands of the fortunate', an allusion to the belief that the souls of the blessed went to dwell on paradisiacal islands in the west. Unlike the Pacific, with its hundreds of archipelagos, there was a severe shortage of attainable goals for apprentice ocean navigators and little chance of accidental discoveries by off-course mariners. Most of the lands such seafarers thought they sighted were mirages and phantoms. Only in its far northern limits is there an abundance of islands leading out into the ocean, and it is very telling that it was here, and only here, that any Europeans, in this case the Norse, crossed the Atlantic before Columbus in 1492, using the Shetland Islands, the Faeroes, Iceland and Greenland as convenient stepping stones to the Americas. Another geographical factor which drew European seafarers out onto these chilly northern Atlantic waters was their fish stocks. Fertilized by silt from Arctic glaciers and great continental rivers like the St Lawrence and the Rhine, these are among the world's richest fishing grounds.

Winds and currents also discouraged Europeans from straying too far from home waters. The prevailing westerlies which batter Europe's Atlantic coast stood in the way of mid-latitude ocean crossings, while the prevailing northeasterly winds and ocean currents along North Africa's Atlantic coast discouraged exploration in that direction because they made it so difficult to sail back again. It was only in the fourteenth or early fifteenth century, when the Portuguese discovered the phenomenon they called the *volta do mar* (the 'turn of the sea'; see Chapter 14, page 389), that European seafarers learned how to use these seemingly adverse winds to their advantage and break out into the wider world's oceans.

However, it was not only geography that held Europeans back;

there were cultural factors too. No, it was not the fear of sailing over the edge of the world: belief in the sphericity of the Earth was well established by the beginning of the Christian era. It was that medieval Europeans had a cultural inferiority complex that left them in awe of the achievements of the ancient world. This gave them an exaggerated respect for the learning of the ancient Greeks and Romans and a world view that told them that there was nowhere else to go beyond the bounds of the three continents of Europe, Asia and Africa that they had always known. Medieval Europeans understood that in principle it would be possible to sail west to Asia, but it was half a world away and no ship yet built could traverse so much empty ocean. Nor could Asia be reached by sailing around Africa, because they dared not pass Cape Bojador, the ancient point of no return on the coast of Western Sahara, beyond which the sea was believed to boil in the equatorial heat. Respect for the ancients kept Europeans bottled up in the northeast Atlantic for centuries, but all the while their ships steadily improved and their navigation became increasingly scientific. It took intellectual courage, as well as physical courage, to challenge their inherited wisdom, but when Europeans finally attained both, in the fifteenth century, they were more than ready for the challenges of the world's oceans.

The wrong end of the world

However, none of this was enough by itself to draw Europeans out onto the world's oceans; they also needed an economic incentive, and that too was related to geography. In terms of pre-Columbian geography, Europe was at the wrong end of the world. By the late Middle Ages, growing prosperity in Christian Europe was leading to rising demand for luxuries, like silk, spices, jewels, ivory and gold, which came either from east Asia or sub-Saharan Africa and could only be bought from Muslim middlemen in the Middle East or North Africa. Centuries of mutual hostility meant that Europeans objected to this, not only because they had to pay monopoly prices but because it felt like they were funding their enemy's armies and navies. Europeans, therefore, had a strong incentive to try to find trade routes that cut out the Muslim middlemen. This economic geography, too, explains why there was no attempt to enter the Atlantic from the east: the Muslim Middle East did not need new trade routes that might threaten its monopoly on east–west trade and, as for India and China, they did not need to discover the world; the world came to them.

I

Who ate the first oyster?

c.168,000 BP–5000 BC

The Atlantic refuge – The Neanderthal Atlantic – Out of Africa – Climate change brings new ways – The first boats – Doggerland – The limpet eaters – Picturing the Mesolithic – Archaic adaptations – The oyster empire – The 'Uttermost Part of the Earth' – In a state of nature – Killing with kindness

'He was a bold man who first ate an oyster,' wrote Jonathon Swift,[3] and anyone who can remember the first time they were offered a live oyster will readily agree with him – they look anything but appetizing. Shellfish are, for most people, either an acquired taste or one they never acquire. Thanks to archaeology, we may now know, roughly, when and where the adventurous beachcomber, man or, just as likely, woman, lived who first ate a shellfish: it was on the Western Cape coast in South Africa around 160,000 years ago. This was an event of more than culinary interest; it marked the evolution of behaviourally modern humans – that is, people like us. Whoever it was who ate it, that first meal of shellfish began the human history of the Atlantic Ocean.

Scatters of roughly worked stone cleavers and hand axes on sites as far apart as South Africa, Angola and Morocco tell us that archaic humans, most likely *Homo erectus* or its evolutionary successor *Homo heidelbergensis*, were already living on Africa's Atlantic coast over half a million years ago. Humans and the

Atlantic go back a long way. Similar tools from sites only slightly more recent in Spain and France show that the same archaic humans had found their way to Europe's Atlantic coast not long after that. What these pioneers thought, if indeed they thought anything at all, when they looked out to sea is un-guessable: the inner lives of archaic humans remain elusive. We do not even know if they possessed language; if they didn't, then they could not have told any stories or dreamed up any myths to explain what they were looking at. Whatever they thought, it seems that archaic humans did not see the sea as a source of food, because there is no evidence even from coastal occupation sites for the exploitation of marine resources. This is surprising, because there is good evidence that archaic humans did sometimes eat freshwater fish, at least. It is possible that evidence has been lost to changing sea levels, but it appears that archaic humans had not yet evolved the adventurous omnivorousness that is such a marked characteristic of modern humans: they were still too much creatures of instinct to be the first to eat shellfish. Though there is strong circumstantial evidence that archaic humans in the Southeast Asia archipelago had some seafaring capacity (even if it only involved a bamboo raft or swimming in the warm tropical waters while holding on to a floating log and hoping not to be eaten by a shark), there is no reason to believe that they ever went to sea in the Atlantic. Archaic humans lived on both sides of the Strait of Gibraltar, only 13 kilometres apart, but genetic studies prove that they never met and mingled. Both populations followed separate evolutionary pathways: those on the African side evolved into anatomically modern humans (*Homo sapiens sapiens*, i.e. us), those on the European side into the Neanderthals (*Homo sapiens neanderthalensis*).

The Atlantic refuge

Humans evolved during the Pleistocene Epoch, which lasted from around 2.5 million years ago to as recently as 11,700 years ago: it roughly coincides with the earliest period of human prehistory, known as the Palaeolithic or 'Old Stone Age'. Often called the 'Ice Age', the Pleistocene saw extreme climatic swings from very cold glacial periods, which saw enormous ice sheets accumulate in high latitudes, to milder interglacial periods with temperatures as high as or even higher than those of the present day: some climate scientists would argue that we are living in an interglacial period right now, one that is being artificially prolonged by human-induced global warming, and that, in the geological long term, a return to glacial conditions is inevitable. The environmental impact extended even into the tropics. During glacial periods, so much of the Earth's water was locked up in ice sheets that the climate became drier and sea levels fell temporarily by up to 100 metres below those of the present day. Forests retreated and deserts and grasslands – tundra, steppe and savannah – spread. In these periods, Africa became so arid that its rainforests almost vanished and deserts and semi-deserts covered around 70 per cent of its land. During the mild interglacial periods, sea levels rose, rainfall increased and the grasslands gave way to forests again.

These were testing times for both plants and wildlife and, it follows, for the early humans, who depended on them for their sustenance. It wasn't so much the cold that was the problem – not everywhere got cold – it was the instability. Some climate switches were so rapid that they took place within the span of a single human lifetime. Many species were pushed into extinction because they couldn't adapt quickly enough to the changing conditions. It's quite likely that we owe our own large brains to this environmental instability, because it created a strong selective pressure in favour of adaptability and intelligence. Despite this advantage, the evidence preserved in our DNA shows that the early human population went through several 'bottlenecks', when it may have been reduced to just a few thousand individuals. Humans were saved from extinction by retreating to a handful of areas, known as refugia, in the northeast and far south of Africa, where the environment remained relatively stable. Perhaps the most important of these for human evolution was the rocky coast of the Western Cape region, spanning the boundary between the Atlantic and Indian oceans.

Anatomically modern humans, *Homo sapiens sapiens*, evolved in Africa nearly 300,000 years ago, but though they may have looked just like us, they did not yet behave like us. There was no sudden leap to behavioural modernity; early modern humans continued to use the same tools and follow the same way of life as their archaic ancestors for another 200,000 years: the development of behavioural modernity was a process, not a sudden event like switching on a lightbulb. Minds, of course, don't fossilize, but the capacity for abstract and symbolic thought that enables modern human behaviour, including language and art, can be deduced from material culture, and it's from coastal caves in the Western Cape, at Diepkloof, Ysterfontaine, Mossel Bay, Blombos and the Klasies River Mouth, that the earliest archaeological evidence for behavioural modernity comes. Ground ochre that was probably used for body painting, dating to around 160,000 years, found at Pinnacle Point at Mossel Bay, is currently the oldest evidence hinting at the emergence of behavioural modernity. The occupants of this cave roasted stone in a fire pit to make it easier to flake into sharp tools and spearheads. This was a process that required several careful steps, and therefore, archaeologists argue, it should probably be seen as evidence that they were using language to pass on instructions for complex tasks: if so, they may have told the first stories about the ocean, too. They also produced tiny microblades, sharp stones too small to be useful tools by themselves, which must have been combined to make composite tools such as harpoons or barbed spears. Making complicated tools like these had been well beyond the mental capacities of earlier human species. What is currently claimed to be the oldest known drawing by human hands is a simple geometric pattern, drawn with red ochre, found on the walls of Blombos Cave, which has been dated to around 73,000 years ago. The oldest known portable art comes from Diepkloof Rock Shelter, about 150 kilometres north of Cape Town, where several hundred pieces of broken ostrich shells, engraved with geometrical patterns, were found. The shells, which the inhabitants used for carrying water, dated to around 60,000 years ago. It's far from clear what was being communicated by these repetitive patterns: one theory is that they represented an idea of group identity.

Early modern humans took refuge in these caves on the Western Cape during one of the coldest periods of the last Ice Age, when Africa was at its most desiccated. Luckily for *Homo sapiens*, the Western Cape was an exception, enjoying a fairly stable Mediterranean climate, with dry summers and rainy winters, that was not so different from that of the present day. Then, as now, the vegetation was dominated by the biodiverse *fynbos* ('fine bush') of shrubland, heath and patchy woodland. This environment offered a wide range of game, such as gazelles and antelope, tortoises and ostriches, and an exceptionally wide range of plants with edible bulbs and tubers that could be gathered easily with the aid of a simple digging stick. There was also the even more stable environment of the ocean. The seas off the Western Cape are particularly rich because of a convergence between the warm Indian Ocean Aghulas Current and the upwelling cold Atlantic Benguela Current, which brings nutrients from the ocean depths up to the surface, encouraging the growth of phytoplankton. These tiny organisms are the base of the marine food chain, so the area supports abundant stocks of shellfish, fish, seabirds and marine mammals. The sea, therefore, offered reliable and inexhaustible food resources, but only for those whose behaviour was flexible enough to exploit them. Shell middens at Ysterfontaine, a small harbour town around 90 kilometres north of Cape Town, and other sites, indicate that this profound dietary, and cultural, change took place between 120,000 and 164,000 years ago. Mussels and limpets, which were abundant on the rocky coastline, were the first shellfish to be exploited, but they were later joined by periwinkles and whelks. Despite the chance of being washed off the rocks and into the sea by breaking surf, the sheer abundance of molluscs made the risk worthwhile. This abundant food was also easy to prepare: charring on the shells is evidence that they were simply thrown into the embers of a fire to cook until they opened. Bones found in the middens are evidence that the Ysterfontaine people hunted Cape fur seals, cormorants and penguins along the shoreline, but, so far, no site on the Western Cape has produced convincing evidence for fishing. Whale barnacles that have been found in the middens probably should be seen as evidence for scavenging meat and blubber from beached whale carcasses. As for oysters, they don't seem to have been eaten at Ysterfontaine, and their shells are only rarely found in middens at other contemporary sites in the Western Cape: they were plainly not anyone's first choice of shellfish. So far, the earliest evidence for the routine consumption of oysters comes from that other African refugium, in the northeast, on Eritrea's Red Sea coast, where they were being collected along with clams and crabs as early as 125,000 years ago.

Dietary modernity didn't emerge all in one go; the quantities of marine food remains found are quite small, so it appears that the early modern humans of the Western Cape preferred terrestrial foods, perhaps only turning to the sea when they failed. There is an important caveat to this conclusion, however. For most of the period that these caves were occupied, sea levels were lower than they are today, so some of them would have been many kilometres inland. If their inhabitants preferred to eat their seafood fresh, close to the places where they found it, the evidence of their meals is now underwater.

The Neanderthal Atlantic

Anatomically modern humans first migrated out of Africa around 100,000 years ago, but they got no further than the Middle East and, after a few thousand years at most, they died out for reasons we don't understand. The definitive migration out of Africa took place about 30,000 years later, and by about 12,000 years ago modern humans had colonized every continent except Antarctica. In the Middle East, modern humans encountered the Neanderthals. Neanderthals had significant physical differences from modern humans; they were stouter, barrel-chested almost, and had shorter limbs; their brains were slightly larger than those of modern humans, but their craniums were longer and lower and they had low brows and prominent brow ridges, which helped give them their popular reputation for being dimmer than the literally high-browed modern humans. They also had prominent bulbous noses and we know from analysing remnants of their aDNA (ancient DNA) that they probably had reddish hair and light skins, unlike modern humans, who at this time were all dark-skinned. Many of their features can be explained as evolutionary adaptations to a cold climate. The short, stout physique is shared by many Arctic peoples today: it is much better at conserving body heat than a tall, slender body. The bulbous nose probably helped heat cold air before it got to the lungs and the fair skin helped them metabolize vitamin D from the limited sunlight of high latitudes. Those modern humans who remained in high latitudes evolved similar adaptations in time. When they were first discovered in the nineteenth century, the Neanderthals were believed to have been knuckle-dragging dimwits, the archetypal cartoon cavemen, armed with clubs and possessed of a limited monosyllabic vocabulary. In recent decades, new discoveries have been eroding steadily the supposed behavioural and cognitive differences between Neanderthals and modern humans. Though Neanderthals used a narrower range of tools than modern humans, they made art and wore body ornaments, manufactured complex tools, cooked their food, probably had some form of religious belief, buried their dead and almost certainly had language like their modern African cousins. Another sign of their modernity: Neanderthals also ate seafood.

The range of the Neanderthals fluctuated along with the climate, but at its greatest it extended from Europe's Atlantic coast east far into Central Asia and as far south as Israel. Across most of this range, Neanderthals ate a meat-rich diet. Because their only hunting weapon was the spear, Neanderthals needed to get close to their prey to make a kill. Probably for this reason, they only occasionally hunted large and dangerous animals like aurochs, woolly rhinoceros and mammoth, preferring smaller game such as red deer, in wooded areas, and reindeer, on open steppe and tundra. Analysis of tartar on fossilized teeth shows that Neanderthals supplemented their meaty diet with fungi, fruits and berries. However, in coastal areas, Neanderthals were notably more flexible about what they ate than earlier human species.

Probably, nowhere in Ice Age Europe had a more stable environment than Gibraltar, the rocky mountain-peninsula that marks the boundary between the Atlantic Ocean and the Mediterranean Sea. Here, through all the swings globally, the climate remained reliably temperate throughout. About 140,000 years ago, a group of Neanderthals moved into the Gorham's Cave complex at the base of the cliffs on the 'Rock's' east coast. The cave's entrance is only just above sea level today and is most easily accessed by boat, but in glacial periods it would have been about 2 kilometres from the sea, on the edge of a sandy coastal plain, and, so, much more sheltered and accessible. Butchered animal bones excavated from the cave show that the Neanderthals were active hunters of ibex, which would have flourished on the Rock, and their favourite red deer. However, instead of depending solely on terrestrial mammals, the Gorham's Cave people exploited a very wide range of other food sources. Large numbers of rabbits and birds were eaten, both of which they probably trapped, as well as tortoises. Part of the attraction of Gibraltar must have been that it is a major staging post in spring and autumn for birds migrating between Africa and Europe, while its cliffs made it an attractive nesting place for seabirds in the summer. Altogether, the Gibraltar Neanderthals ate 145 different bird species (about a quarter of the total number of bird species known to inhabit Europe). Pine nuts are the only plant food they can be shown to have eaten, but the Neanderthals took advantage of their coastal location to hunt basking monk seals and collect mussels, limpets and sea urchins in large quantities, which they took back to the cave to bake in the fire. Dolphins and tuna were also eaten in limited quantities, but it is not clear how these were caught, because there is no evidence for the specialist fishing gear, such as harpoons and fish spears, that some of their modern human contemporaries used; the dolphins were likely beached. The Gorham's Cave Neanderthals were so comfortable in their coastal niche that their descendants stayed on for 100,000 years, their way of life barely changing in all that time, so much so that one of their hearths was used continually for 8,000 years.

Coastal sites like Figueira Brava in Portugal, and others in Spain, Italy and Greece, have also provided evidence of the exploitation of marine food sources, so it seems likely that this foraging behaviour was as common among Neanderthals as it was among contemporary anatomically modern humans such as those who lived in the Western Cape. It's still an open question if Neanderthals built any kind of watercraft. They certainly never reached any of the major Mediterranean islands, despite the low sea levels in glacial periods, but tools identified as belonging to the Neanderthals' Mousterian culture have been found on a few of the smaller Greek islands, including Kephalonia, so they must have been able to make very short sea crossings by some means. Having said that, there is no evidence that modern humans were capable of doing anything more ambitious than that either until about 48,000 years ago, when the first humans arrived in Australia, a feat that required a sea crossing of at least 90 kilometres even when Ice Age sea levels were at their lowest.

The willingness of Neanderthals to exploit marine food sources challenges the idea that they were somehow less adaptable to different environments than anatomically modern humans. This, and other evidence of behavioural modernity, is making it increasingly difficult to explain why the Neanderthals eventually became extinct. There's now little reason to believe that they were not as clever as modern humans, and so, although competition with them for resources may be part of the explanation, it is very unlikely to be the whole story. The Neanderthals died out around 40,000 years ago. Those who lived in Gorham's Cave were among the last survivors, but modern humans cannot have been directly responsible for their extinction, because it was another 10,000 years before they arrived in southern Spain. Studies of surviving Neanderthal DNA show that they had low genetic diversity, best explained by a small population, perhaps as few as 5,000 across their whole immense range. Small, isolated groups like the Gorham's Cave Neanderthals may have suffered from inbreeding, with the accumulation of genetic imperfections leading to a collapse of fertility. A small population would also explain the slower pace of technological innovation among Neanderthals. Larger groups are more likely to have new ideas and more likely to find people willing to accept and build on them. This is why, in recorded human history, it is the crowded cities that have always been the main centres of cultural and technological innovation.

Neanderthals and anatomically modern humans may be scientifically classified as different species, but it is clear that when they encountered each other they saw other people. A bit ugly maybe, but people just the same, not animals or aliens. Conflict over territory was common among modern hunter-gatherers, so we shouldn't imagine that that their first instinct was to embrace one another as long-lost cousins, but embrace one another they certainly did sometimes. Neanderthals and modern humans interbred, and all non-African modern humans have inherited 2–4 per cent of their DNA from the Neanderthals. Rather than becoming literally extinct, the Neanderthals may simply have been genetically swamped by the far more numerous modern humans who kept pouring out of Africa.

Out of Africa

The Atlantic was the greatest obstacle to the human diaspora out of Africa. When, 70,000 years ago, anatomically modern humans left Africa for the Middle East, they split into two great branches. One branch headed west into Europe and by about 45,000 years ago had reached the Atlantic, and there it stopped, blocked by the ocean to the west and the vast ice sheet that covered almost all of the northern half of the continent. They had reached the edge of the world and would go no further in that direction for all of 44,000 years. The second branch of humanity headed east and, thousands of years later, some of its distant descendants crossed the Bering Strait from Asia into the Americas and had populated both coasts of the continents, south all the way to Tierra del Fuego, by about 11,000 years ago. It was only when Norse explorers met Native Americans in Vinland around a thousand years ago that these two branches met, and humanity finally completed its global circumnavigation.

On the face of it, at least, the first modern humans in Atlantic Europe specialized in hunting the vast herds of reindeer, horses and bison that roamed Ice Age Europe's tundras and steppes, changing camp often as they followed their seasonal migrations. Those migrations were predictable and reliable: the wildlife would follow the same routes, converge on the same river crossings, the same summer and winter pastures year after year, and their meat came in conveniently large packages. Even those hunters whose wandering took them close to the sea seem only occasionally to have turned to it for sustenance, relying on marine resources no more than their ancestors in the Western Cape had, or the Neanderthals they replaced. For example, at La Riera Cave in Asturias on Spain's Atlantic coast, which was occupied from around 23,000 years ago to around 13,000 years ago, some 26,600 shells were deposited but, spread over 10,000 years, that doesn't add up to a great reliance on shellfish. Shellfish may be rich in protein, vitamins and essential minerals, but they are low in calories and so probably would not have been first-choice foods for people living in the chilly sub-Arctic climate of Ice Age Europe. The same cannot be said of marine mammals, such as seals and walrus, with their thick layers of energy-rich blubber, valuable not only as food but also for heating and lighting. Nonetheless, evidence that marine mammals were actively hunted is slight, although it is likely that most of the coastal sites, where marine resources could have been exploited more intensively, have been submerged by the post-glacial rise in sea levels.

One group of marine mammals that certainly was exploited was whales. There is no evidence that late Palaeolithic Europeans possessed any seafaring technology, so they were most likely opportunistically scavenging the carcasses of beached whales rather than actively hunting them. A beached whale would have provided a hunter-gatherer band with a windfall of meat and blubber, but it would not have been without risk if bears got to it first: bears have a strong sense of ownership of their food, and they really don't like to share. All the same, it's hard to imagine that late Palaeolithic hunter-gatherers would have passed up such a feast had the opportunity arisen, though that is pure surmise. The only parts of whales that we actually know for certain they used are their bones, which they could have collected quite safely from the bleached skeletons of long-dead animals, and that was not for food but for tool-making. Although dozens of whalebone projectile points have been found, it was most commonly used to make woodworking wedges and chisels. Whalebone is not as dense as antler or the bones of terrestrial mammals, such as deer, making it easier to work, while it is also more impact resistant, making it well suited for hard use. Most of the tools so far discovered show signs of considerable use and repair, so they were obviously a valued part of the Palaeolithic toolkit and were kept for a long time. Their users probably valued whalebone tools because they were very durable and did not need to be replaced very often. The bones may also have been valued for their large size, which allowed larger tools to be made. Some whalebone tools were decorated with incised geometrical patterns and animals, while others have grooves to fit tiny microlithic flint blades which would have been held in place with resin glue.

During the Magdalenian period (*c.*18,000–12,000 bp) whales' bones were in great demand for toolmaking and were widely distributed. Whalebone artefacts have mostly been found in Cantabria and the Pyrenean region, straddling the modern border between Spain and France, where hundreds have been found spread across nearly forty cave sites. As very few of these sites are close to the sea, the occupants must have been acquiring them by trade. The pattern of distribution suggests that the bones were distributed via a 600-kilometre exchange network, the earliest known network for trading marine products, extending from the Cantabrian coast into the Pyrenees and beyond as far as the Ariège valley in southern France. It would probably be wrong to imagine that there were itinerant Palaeolithic whalebone merchants: the bones are most likely to have been distributed from one band to another as part of exchanges of useful commodities intended to cement mutually supportive social networks that could be called upon in hard times. Whalebone tools have been found as far from the Atlantic as Andernach in the German Rhineland, hinting that this network may have been even more extensive. Only finished whalebone tools have been found in caves, no whole bones or toolmaking waste, so the tools must have been made elsewhere, probably on the coast where the stranded whales were found, at sites that will now be deep underwater. Isturitz cave, close to the Atlantic at the western end of the Pyrenees, is where the largest concentration of Magdalenian whalebone artefacts has been found, so this may have been an exchange hub for the onward distribution of the artefacts to areas further inland.

The apparent unimportance of marine food resources to late Palaeolithic Europeans is mirrored in the spectacular cave art for which southwest France and northern Spain is justly famous. Far and away the majority of animals portrayed in the art of the period are terrestrial, deer, horses, aurochs and bison being the most common, while sea creatures make only a token appearance.

Perhaps the best-known example is found in Tito Bustillo Cave, at Ribadesella on the Cantabrian coast, where there is a two-metre-long 29,000-year-old drawing of a baleen whale. Even in the Ice Age Bustillo Cave was close to the sea, so the whale is almost certainly drawn from life, perhaps to commemorate a stranding and the feast that followed. Other caves and rock shelters in the region have drawings of seals, a salmon, a halibut (a large flatfish), a couple of flounders and two great auks, an extinct flightless seabird. Sea creatures also appear on a few portable items, such as a beluga whale incised on a pendant made from a sperm whale's tooth found at Las Caldas in Asturias and a bone pendant with an incised sperm whale from Arancou, not far from the Atlantic coast in Basse-Navarre. Add an incised sperm whale on a bone implement from Grotte de la Vache in Ariège and a seal on a slate plaque from Gönnersdorf in the Rhineland and that really is about it. There isn't a close correlation between the animals late Palaeolithic people chose to paint or draw and those they chose to hunt and eat, but it is still clear that sea creatures didn't loom very large in their imaginations, just as they don't seem to have loomed large in their diets.

Climate change brings new ways

As the last glaciation drew to its close around 10,000 years ago, hunter-gatherers everywhere were forced to adapt to rapidly changing environments as the climate warmed, and this brought much greater reliance on the sea for food for those who lived in coastal areas. Over the next 3,000 years, sea levels rose by an average 2 metres every century, twice the worst-case scenario for the twenty-first century as a consequence of human-induced climate change. As water flowed back to the oceans from the thawing ice sheets, sea levels rose, flooding familiar landscapes and campsites (along with all the evidence of Palaeolithic use of maritime resources). Open steppes, with their easily tracked herds of reindeer, horses and mammoths, gave way to dense woodlands inhabited by more elusive game. Food was abundant, it just came in smaller packages. Hunter-gatherers could no longer specialize. Instead they needed to become generalists, exploiting a much wider range of resources, including the sea. In Atlantic Europe, this period of adaptation is known as the Mesolithic or Middle Stone Age, and it is often seen as a transitional period between the Palaeolithic big game hunting way of life and the advent of settled farming around 4000 BC. In North America, the same period is known as the Archaic.

Mesolithic Europe was inhabited by two genetically distinct populations. Whole-genome analysis of their remains shows that the people of the Atlantic west still had the brown or black skin and the dark-brown or black hair of their African ancestors but that they also had strikingly blue eyes. They would have looked clearly different to the hunter-gatherers in eastern and far northern Europe, who, by this time, had evolved the light skins characteristic of modern Europeans.

Mesolithic hunter-gatherers favoured locations that offered a variety of habitats in a small area, especially wetlands, estuaries and coasts. The food resources of these highly productive environments were effectively limitless given the technology available at the time, and this allowed them to adopt more sedentary lifeways than their Palaeolithic ancestors, perhaps moving only between winter and summer camps. New technologies emerged, fishing nets, wickerwork fish traps, barbed harpoons and fishhooks for fishing, bows and arrows for hunting fast-moving small game and wildfowl, woven baskets for collecting shellfish, nuts, berries and fungi, and watercraft to increase access to aquatic resources. In contrast to Palaeolithic humans, Mesolithic Europeans made great use of marine resources when they had access to them. Just compare the size of the Mesolithic shell midden excavated at Ertebølle in Jutland, Denmark, which contained over 50 million shells, along with the bones of fish, seabirds, seals and deer, accumulated over just seven or eight hundred years with La Riera's meagre 26,600 accumulated over 10,000 years. The importance of seafoods in the Mesolithic diet is further demonstrated by the isotope analysis of a contemporary human burial from Tybrind Vig on the Danish island of Fyn, which showed that the young woman lived mainly on a diet of shellfish, fish and seal meat.

The first boats

In the new world of the Mesolithic, boats were essential to make the most of aquatic food sources, whether on salt or fresh water. On sheltered waters, Mesolithic Europeans used logboats (also called dugout canoes) which were fashioned simply by hollowing out a single tree trunk with adzes and fire. The oldest logboat found so far, dated to between 8040 BC and 7510 BC, found during road-building at Pesse in the Netherlands, looked so crude that it was thought to be an old feeding trough for livestock until radiometric dating proved that it was made millennia before anyone kept livestock in Europe. Experiments with a replica have shown that the Pesse logboat was a perfectly practical vessel for fishing and wildfowling on sheltered waters, but, with a freeboard of only a few centimetres, it would have foundered quickly if taken on the open sea. Some Mesolithic logboats have been found to contain heavy rocks, which were probably carried as ballast to make them more stable – they are quite easy to capsize, as I discovered when paddling a replica in Denmark – while others had clay hearths for small fires, probably as aids to torchlight fishing at night. Logboats might be an unspectacular beginning to the history of Atlantic seafaring, but they had great potential for refinement and expansion, for example, by adding planks to the sides to increase the freeboard, and, over thousands of years, as better woodworking tools and carpentry techniques developed, from these simple beginnings evolved the plank-built vessels of historical times. However, they weren't the boats Mesolithic people went to sea in, and go to sea they certainly did, the archaeology is quite clear about that.

Roughly as old as the Pesse logboat is a representation of an altogether more seaworthy kind of boat carved or engraved onto an ice-polished rock 72 metres above sea level near Valle, on Efjorden in Nordland in Arctic Norway. The land in northern Norway has been steadily rising since the end of the Ice Age as it rebounds from the vast weight of the Scandinavian sheet which had pressed it down into the mantle. If the ship was originally carved close to sea level, as later rock art was, the ship was probably carved around 10,000 years ago, which would make it the oldest representation of a boat anywhere in the world. The engraving is the barest outline of a boat – at 4.3 metres long, it may actually be life-size – but its profile is identical to hundreds of later and more detailed ship carvings from northern Norway. The boats depicted by these carvings have a distinctive profile, with steep prows and horizontal projections at both ends, which makes them look very similar to traditional Inuit umiaks, light, flexible and buoyant open boats, propelled by paddles, which were made by shaping greased hides around a wooden skeleton or wickerwork frame. Until the advent of outboard motors and fibreglass boats, the Inuit used their very seaworthy umiaks for hunting whales and for transporting family groups on seasonal migrations. As there is little timber in Arctic Norway suitable for building plank boats, it's likely that the boats in the carvings, some of which have animal-head figureheads, were built and used in a similar way. Hide boats must also have been used further south along Europe's Atlantic coast. Mesolithic hunter-gatherers settled in the Shetland Islands, which required a voyage of at least 80 kilometres across the North Atlantic from the nearest land, in the Orkney Islands: they certainly didn't do that in a logboat. Hide boats were made of highly perishable materials, so it's not likely that any prehistoric remains will be found, but their use around the coasts of Ireland, Britain and France is well documented from around the first century BC.

The post-glacial environmental changes in northwest Europe were particularly complex. As the last glaciation came to an end, water released by melting ice sheets poured back into the seas, bringing rapidly rising sea levels globally. However, in the areas that had been most heavily glaciated, northwest Europe and northern North America, the rising sea levels were cancelled out because the land was also rising due to a phenomenon known as isostatic uplift. The weight of the huge ice sheet centred on Scandinavia had pressed the Earth's crust down into the slightly plastic mantle by hundreds of metres. Then, much more slowly, the crust, freed of the vast weight of the ice sheets, began to rise as the mantle oozed back into place underneath it. Around the Gulf of Bothnia in the northern Baltic Sea, this rebound is still going on at a rate of nearly one centimetre a year, faster than the predicted rate of sea level rise from global warming. The gently sloping shores here make the consequences of uplift very obvious even within a human lifetime. If a young fisherman built a boatshed by the shore, it would be high and dry by the time he retired. Back in the Mesolithic, when these changes were going on at a faster rate and over a larger area than they are today, some hunter-gatherer bands would have returned to familiar hunting grounds and found them flooded by the sea, while others would have found that a convenient seashore fishing campsite was now lost in a forest. This must have induced a profound sense of insecurity in many people – could anything be relied upon?

Doggerland

The changes to sea level were at their most extreme around what is now the North Sea. At the end of the Ice Age, there was no North Sea. Britain and Ireland were both simply part of the European mainland, while the area now covered by the North Sea was a vast plain broken only by a range of low hills, which today form the Dogger Bank, a shallow area of the sea which is now an important fishing ground. During the later stages of the Ice Age, herds of reindeer, mammoths and woolly rhinoceros roamed this plain, christened Doggerland by archaeologists, and their remains are still there, littering the seabed. Fishermen regularly dredge up the teeth and tusks of mammoths, as well as the tools of the human hunters who followed them across the frigid landscape. As the ice sheets retreated and water began to flow back into the oceans, Doggerland was slowly submerged, but the process created the kind of richly varied landscape that was very attractive to Mesolithic hunter-fisher-gatherers: an ever-changing mix of terrestrial woodland, salt marsh, mudflats, tidal lagoons and estuaries, that offered a year-round buffet of wild foods such as deer and wild boar, nuts and berries, fungi, shellfish, fish, wildfowl and seals. Archaeologists believe that Doggerland could have been one of Mesolithic Europe's most densely populated regions.

This bountiful landscape was doomed by the warming climate. By around 7000 BC the rising seas had cut Britain and Ireland off from the continental mainland and turned the Dogger Bank into an isolated and fast-shrinking island. Doggerland's demise was hastened by one of the greatest natural disasters ever to strike the North Atlantic, the Storegga Slide. During the last glaciation, the Scandinavian ice sheets piled up enormous but unstable quantities of rock, sand and clays on the edge of the Norwegian continental shelf. Then, around 6225–6167 BC, the colossal weight of this rubble caused the continental shelf along a length of 290 kilometres to collapse, taking 3,500 cubic kilometres of rock with it into the depths of the North Atlantic and triggering a massive tsunami. The size and spread of the wave has been charted from the deposits it left behind onshore. In the Shetland Islands, the tsunami deposits have been found lying 20 metres above sea level, and it was still 4 metres high when it reached the Firth of Forth over 400 kilometres further south on Scotland's North Sea coast: flood deposits have been found almost 80 kilometres inland. The tsunami rolled on, taking with it a fair chunk of Doggerland before spending the last of its force battering the coast of the Low Countries. With no possibility of any warning of the tsunami's approach and no high ground to flee to, the consequences for the Mesolithic people living in Doggerland must have been catastrophic. Further north, the tsunami crossed the Atlantic to crash into the still uninhabited east coast of Greenland. It is not known if Doggerland was ever repopulated, but within a few hundred years of the tsunami, the last of it had been claimed by the sea.

The limpet eaters

Mesolithic hunter-gatherers trod very lightly on the landscape. Most of their campsites survive only as scatters of discarded stone tools and a few small post-holes marking the site of a brushwood hut or hide tent: most are discovered only by accident. However, in coastal areas, the locations of camps are often advertised by mounds of shells, up to a few metres high, perched on old shorelines. Oronsay is a small (just 5 square kilometres), fertile, Hebridean island which can be reached dry-shod from its larger neighbour Colonsay at low tide. Today, the island is mostly covered in *machair*, the delightfully springy, wildflower-rich pastureland which flourishes on the light soils of blown shell sand without which farming would hardly be possible in the Hebrides. Cattle, kept by the island's single farm, keep the *machair* neatly mowed and prevent it reverting to the low, dense woodland of birch and hazel which would be the island's natural state. This is what would have greeted the island's first inhabitants when they arrived about 7,000 years ago.

This small island has produced five large middens built up mostly from the discarded shells of limpets, oysters, whelks, periwinkles, scallops, cockles and razorshell clams. The middens also contained hazelnut shells, seal bones and large quantities of fishbones, especially those of young saithe (pollock), which favour inshore waters where they could easily be caught or trapped without the need to go to sea. The excavators conducted a detailed analysis of the ear bones (called otoliths) of the saithe. Saithe spawn in late winter and grow rapidly after hatching. Their ear bones grow in proportion, so by measuring them it was possible to estimate the time of year the fish were caught. From this, it was possible to deduce that each camp was occupied at a different time of year. This probably means that Oronsay was permanently inhabited by a single group who moved around the coast as the year progressed, although it is odd that the winter camp is on the more exposed west coast. The camps were sited hard up against what would have been the high tide line in the Mesolithic, so close that the inhabitants would have been exposed to sea spray in bad weather. However, sea spray was a small price to pay for the relief sea breezes would have given from the swarms of biting midges that plague the Scottish Highlands in summer.

Shellfish were eaten in enormous quantities not so much because people relished them (it is difficult to imagine that anyone really relished eating limpets, they are chewy and rather tasteless), but because they had to if they were not to starve. It has been estimated that to get the same quantity of calories as would be provided by a single red deer, it would be necessary to eat 50,000 oysters or 30,000 limpets. Some archaeologists have speculated that the Oronsay people did not eat the limpets but used them as bait for fishing for the much more appetizing and nutritious saithe, but this is unlikely, because they are so well protected by their shells that few fish are used to eating them.

Mesolithic people pursued similar lifeways further south, in Ireland, Brittany and the Iberian Peninsula. The people of the Asturian culture (9250–6500 bp) of northern Spain similarly exploited a wide range of terrestrial and marine food sources. The Asturians led relatively sedentary lives close to the sea, but they obtained most of their food from the land. Red deer, hunted in the heavily forested countryside, along with wild boar and aurochs (the wild ancestor of modern cattle), were their most important food source for most of the year, but in late winter and early spring, when wild animals were in poor condition, the Asturians spent their time on the seashore harvesting limpets, building up huge *concheros* (shell middens) in the process. Limpets have not become a byword for tenacity for nothing; they cling so tightly to their rocks that even the wildest winter storms cannot shift them. To stand any chance of removing them intact, limpets must be taken unawares, either by inserting a blade under the rim of the shell or by a sudden sharp blow. Mesolithic Asturians developed a unique tool, the Asturian pick-axe, specifically to harvest limpets. The pick-axes were made from hand-sized quartzite pebbles, a tough metamorphic rock that doesn't fracture easily, which were chipped away to create a sharp point at one end.

Picturing the Mesolithic

At the UNESCO World Heritage site at Alta in Arctic Norway, the people of the Mesolithic Komsa culture left a vivid pictorial record in over 3,000 petroglyphs, engraved on ice-smoothed rocks over a period of around 3,700 years (4200 BC–500 BC). The petroglyphs depict a way of life that was focused on hunting reindeer and elk (moose). The most elaborate scenes show great reindeer drives as teams of hunters, armed with bows and arrows, drive the herds into fenced traps where they can be killed more easily. There are many carvings of hide boats, some with figureheads that look like elk heads. Several of these scenes show hunters pursuing swimming reindeer: reindeer are strong swimmers and can migrate between islands. A few scenes show fishing for halibut with hook and line and for smaller fish with nets, and there are a few sea birds, porpoises and whales. It looks as if the sea was much less important to the carvers than reindeer hunting, but archaeological excavations of kitchen middens in their abandoned villages tell an entirely different story; they actually relied on the sea for between 60 per cent and 95 per cent of their food. What this tells us is that the carvings were not intended to be representative of everyday life (and a reason, perhaps, not to draw too many conclusions from the subjects of Palaeolithic art also). Reindeer must have had some importance, probably cultic, that went well beyond mere subsistence, for example as totemic animals in a shamanistic religion. Elks and bears also commonly appear in hunting scenes, and these two must be totemic animals because there is no evidence that they were eaten. The fish, on which the Komsa people really depended, were so commonplace that they gave only the huge, and delicious, halibuts cultic status.

The carvers were most likely among the ancestors of today's Sámi people* (but certainly not their only ancestors), who, in historic times, made special sacrifices to their gods for success in halibut fishing. Like the Komsa people, most Sámi have always lived on the coast and engaged in fishing much more than the reindeer herding for which they are popularly known, but reindeer have a special place in their myths and, when they look at the night sky, they see not the constellations named after Classical gods, but a cosmic reindeer hunt.

Archaic adaptations

The Atlantic Ocean has two sides, but for most of human prehistory the American side remained completely uninhabited by humans.

Where the first Americans came from, when they arrived and how they got there are probably the most contentious questions in world archaeology today. Despite the lingering uncertainties, one theory can be ruled out: this is the so-called Solutrean hypothesis, which argues that the Americas were first peopled by Palaeolithic Europeans of the Solutrean culture (22,000–17,000 years ago) of southwest France who crossed the Atlantic in umiak-like skin boats following the edge of the Arctic sea ice, which extended much further south than it does today, hunting seals along the way to survive. The main basis of the hypothesis is a perceived similarity between the stone projectile points of the Solutrean culture and those of the Palaeoamerican Clovis culture (13,500–12,800 years ago). Though the similarities are striking, most archaeologists dismiss the hypothesis on the grounds that the two cultures were not contemporaneous; there is a gap of over 3,000 years between them. Where were the Solutreans during the missing millennia? Critics of the hypothesis explain the similarities in the lithic technology as simply an example of convergent

* Still commonly known as Lapps: Sámi consider this name to be derogatory.

evolution – both types of projectile point were designed to do the same job – that is, kill large game animals. It is also thought improbable that the Solutreans could have survived on sea ice for long enough to cross to America, a journey which would have taken many months. Even the superbly adapted Thule Inuit, in historical times, did not ever live on sea ice for extended periods; they caught their seals and then went back to their camps on land. The Thule possessed a variety of watercraft and a highly specialized technology for hunting marine mammals. There is no evidence that the Solutreans had either, nor, indeed, that they ever hunted seals. And why would a band of hunters have headed out, threading their way through the sea ice for month after month, with no idea where they were going? For all they knew, the ice went on forever; they didn't know that America was there, waiting to be discovered. It makes no sense at all that they would have done such a thing. The Solutrean hypothesis is also incompatible with the genetic evidence: the DNA of all modern Native Americans shows that they came from northeast Asia and nowhere else. This absolutely rules out any possibility that Europeans or Africans migrated across the Atlantic and settled permanently in the Americas at any time before Columbus.

The exact timing of the arrival of humans in the Americas has not yet been settled, but it was at least 14,000 to 15,000 years ago, a time when, due to low glacial-period sea levels, the Bering Strait which now separates Asia from the Americas was then an open tundra. As for the 'how', there are two main theories: one is that the migrants walked across the Bering Strait following herds of prey animals; the other is that they used some sort of watercraft to migrate along the Pacific coast. Whichever route they used, the ancestral Native Americans found themselves in two vast and completely uninhabited continents full of naïve big game animals that, not having evolved alongside humans like wildlife in the Old World, did not instinctively regard them as a threat. It was a hunter's paradise. These pioneers flourished and expanded rapidly across their new found lands, probably reaching the Atlantic coast by around 14,500 years ago and the southern tip of South America by 14,000 years ago. The islands of the Caribbean were settled, from South America, somewhat later, between 6,000 and 7,000 years ago. The end of the last glaciation around 10,000 years ago ushered in dramatic environmental changes. Forests spread across the open Ice Age steppes and tundra and, stressed by the changing climate and by over-enthusiastic human hunting, many big game species became extinct. The ancestral Native Americans responded by adapting and diversifying their ways of life to the new environments and exploiting a wider variety of resources such as nuts, berries, fish and shellfish in ways that are analogous to those of Mesolithic Europeans.

The people of the Maritime Archaic culture (7000 BC–1000 BC), which flourished along North America's northeast coast from Maine north to Newfoundland and Labrador, developed a regular seasonal round. In the summer, the Maritime people lived on the coast, scavenging beached whales, hunting seals and fishing both from the shore and from large dugout canoes, spearing their prey with harpoons made of antler. Unlike so many other maritime hunter-gatherer-fisher cultures, shellfish were not exploited to any great extent. Perhaps because they were able to obtain as much high-quality meat and fish as they needed, they saw shellfish as emergency famine food to be eaten only when nothing better was on offer. In autumn, the Maritime people moved inland to riverbanks to take advantage of salmon runs before spending the winter hunting caribou in the forests. In the spring, they moved back to riverbanks for the spring salmon runs before moving on again to the coast for summer. This was a secure way of life, with a dependable and sustainable supply of food. Particularly in the north, it persisted until the arrival of European settlers in the seventeenth century, so it may have been descendants of the Maritime people who the Norse met in Vinland.

Further south along the coasts of North America, the Caribbean and South America maritime foragers made much greater use of shellfish and the tell-tale shell middens are a common sign of prehistoric occupation. The largest shell midden in North America is the Turtle Mound, near New Smyrna Beach, on Florida's east coast. Accumulated between 1000 BC and AD 1400, this mound originally stood about 23 metres high and was used by the Timucua people as a refuge from flooding during hurricanes. Today, despite mining for hardcore, it stands 15 metres high. Despite the vast numbers of shellfish collected, Native American shellfish fisheries were managed sustainably for thousands of years. One study of oyster shells from middens around Chesapeake Bay, some of which were used continuously for as long as 5,000 years, shows no reduction in size over time, something which would be expected if the oysters were being over-exploited. Early English settlers, such as Captain John Smith, were impressed by the huge oyster reefs in the Chesapeake, but those who followed him mined, rather than harvested, the oysters, and it is estimated that today stocks are a mere 1 per cent of their pre-colonial level. And the oysters are much smaller.

The development of hierarchical societies – societies with a class structure, ruled by chiefs or kings – is normally something that follows on from the adoption of farming. Hunter-gatherer populations are usually limited by the natural productivity of the environment and tend to have fairly egalitarian social structures. Even the earliest farmers could produce more food than they needed to support themselves and their families most years. That surplus food not only supported population growth, it was the first form of wealth: unevenly distributed, it led to the emergence of social classes and, ultimately, to the emergence of chiefdoms and kingdoms. There were a few places in the world, however, where the natural resources were so rich that, with Stone Age technology at least, they were effectively inexhaustible, and in those places very untypical hunter-gatherer societies emerged which had all the trappings of complex farming societies, including permanent settlements, monumental buildings and social classes. Coastal environments, for example the Pacific coasts of Peru and North America, were very favourable for this because of their abundant maritime resources. Most complex hunter-gatherer societies soon transitioned to agriculture but some survived into the modern age.

The oyster empire

One of the longest surviving of these complex hunter-gatherer societies was the Calusa, which flourished in southern Florida from around 1100 BC until the beginning of the eighteenth century, by which time their numbers had been catastrophically reduced by pandemics of European diseases such as smallpox. Spanish visitors described how the Calusa were divided into 'commoners' and 'nobles' and were led by a 'king' with the support of a 'high priest'. The nobles gained their status by being intermediaries between the people and their gods. Not surprisingly, the nobles strongly resisted all attempts by Spanish missionaries to convert them to Christianity, because it would have undermined their legitimacy. The Calusa had a permanent capital, which the Spanish called Calos, on Mound Key in Estero Bay. The king had a handsomely decorated palace which was comfortably large enough to accommodate gatherings of 2,000 people, although one hard-to-impress Christian missionary complained that the roof leaked. The palace was built atop a 10 metre-high artificial mound built with an estimated 18.5 billion discarded oyster shells, a tribute not only to the Calusa's organizational ability but to their appetites for shellfish. Overgrown with vegetation today, in Calos's heyday the mound would have been gleaming white, so that both it and the king's palace would have dominated the surrounding landscape and been visible far out at sea. This was not the only major construction project completed by the Calusa. Nearby were two large fishponds surrounded by dykes of shells and sediment. These were connected to the sea by a canal. The Calusa used nets to direct shoals of fish down the canal and into the ponds, where they could be trapped and kept alive until such time as they were needed for food. The effort was worthwhile because the ponds allowed the Calusa to smooth out seasonal variations in the availability of fish.

In their social complexity, the Calusa justify comparison with the near contemporary chiefdoms of the Mound Builder farming cultures of the Mississippi valley. However, unlike them, the Calusa did not practise farming at all, or even trade marine foods for farmed foods like maize. Analysis of food remains in Calusa middens indicates that, for those living on the coast, fish and shellfish (mostly oysters) made up 93 per cent of their diet. Only 6 per cent came from terrestrial animals like deer and the remainder of the diet was nuts and berries collected in the forest. The only crop grown by the Calusa was gourds, and this was not for food, it was because they could be hollowed out to make floats for fishing nets. Thanks to the great productivity of the fertile estuaries and mangrove swamps of the Gulf coast, which sustained vast numbers of oysters and provided sheltered environments for fish to breed and grow, safe from larger predators in the open sea, the Calusa simply did not need to toil in fields. The Calusan economy could not have functioned without boats. Spanish missionaries reported that they possessed a large fleet of canoes, including at least twenty special war canoes. No Calusa boats have been found yet, but they were no doubt made by hollowing out tree trunks as many other peoples around the Caribbean did. Some of these canoes could be very large. Columbus encountered Maya canoes off the coast of Yucatán that were nearly 30 metres long and had washstrake planks fitted to the sides to increase their freeboard and improve their stability and seaworthiness. The main means of propulsion were paddles: so far, no archaeological evidence has been found for the use of sails by Native Americans before European contact at the end of the fifteenth century, although they were adopted quickly after that.

At the beginning of the sixteenth century, the territory ruled directly by the Calusa extended along the southwest Florida coast from Charlotte Harbor to Cape Sable and the Florida Keys, but they controlled a small empire of tributary tribes which stretched across all of southern Florida to the Atlantic coast. In 1513, the Spanish explorer Juan Ponce de León became the first European to visit Florida. The Calusa twice attacked Ponce de León's ships with large fleets of canoes. Although they were driven off, the Spanish also withdrew. Ponce de León returned in 1521, intent, this time, on conquest, but the Spanish again withdrew after he was fatally injured in battle with the Calusa. Nearly 200 years of intermittent conflict followed, and all the while, epidemics of European diseases like smallpox whittled away at the Calusa. However, the final blow was struck not by the Spanish but by Creek and Yamasee slave raiders acting as allies of England in Queen Anne's War (1702–13). Those Calusa who escaped capture found refuge with other tribes, but they were never able to reform as a distinct group: they are now considered to be extinct, along with their remarkable way of life.

The 'Uttermost Part of the Earth'

The story of the Atlantic's shellfish age ends almost a full circle from where it began, in Tierra del Fuego, the archipelago at the very southern tip of South America. European contact spelled the end for the Archaic fisher-gatherer-hunter way of life all along the American Atlantic coast. The last survivors were the Yaghan (or Yámana) people of southeastern Tierra del Fuego, whose territory included Cape Horn, the southernmost point of South America, and spanned the boundary between the Pacific and Atlantic oceans. The Yaghan way of life was an unbroken tradition going back to the earliest days of human occupation in the Americas. Archaeological evidence gives good reason to believe that the ancestors of the Yaghan arrived in Tierra del Fuego at least 7,500 years ago having followed South America's Pacific coast south as the Ice Age glaciers of the southern Andes retreated back into the mountains. After Tierra del Fuego, there was nowhere else to go, so there they stayed, living further south than any other humans would do before the discovery of Antarctica in the nineteenth century, and that continent still has no truly permanent human inhabitants.

Travel overland in Tierra del Fuego's dense forests, full of fallen and rotting tree trunks, is very slow and arduous, so the Yaghan relied on canoes, made from the bark of evergreen beech trees, to move along the coasts. Fuegian canoes look both crude and fragile, yet they were tough and seaworthy enough for the Yaghan to brave the unpredictable weather and sail the notoriously hazardous waters around Cape Horn and make regular visits to the mountainous Isla de los Estados, 30 kilometres out in the Atlantic from the eastern tip of Tierra del Fuego. They may even occasionally have visited the Falkland Islands 480 kilometres further out in the Atlantic from Isla de los Estados. When Charles Darwin visited the Falklands in 1833, he speculated about how the islands' sole terrestrial mammal, the now extinct Falkland Islands' wolf or warrah, a relative of the extinct South American fox-like canid *Dusicyon avus*, could possibly ever have got there. Even at the height of the last Ice Age, sea levels were never low enough for the islands to have been linked to the mainland by a land bridge, so its introduction by the Yaghan, who kept domesticated wild dogs, is a distinct possibility. Archaeological surveys in 2020 discovered evidence – a barbed stone harpoon point, middens of seal and penguin bones, and indications of the use of fire – for an occasional human presence from around 1,000 years ago, but the warrah were there much earlier: the oldest sub-fossil remains found date to around 3,200 years ago.

Leaks are a constant problem in bark canoes, so the Yaghan tried to make their canoes from as few pieces of bark as possible, ideally, a single continuous piece up to 5 metres long for each of the sides sewn with seal sinews to a stiff bottom piece. The canoe was then reinforced from one end to the other with ribs made of saplings bent into a U shape and the hull was caulked with clay to make it watertight. This also allowed a small hearth to be carried without burning a hole through the hull. Despite everything, beech bark is brittle, and it frequently cracked and was easily holed, so an essential piece of every canoe's equipment was a small bucket for bailing. Bark also rotted quickly, so canoes needed to be replaced frequently: fortunately for both the trees and the Yaghan, stripping their bark did not kill them. Canoes were paddled: this was woman's work, freeing the men to hunt and fish from the canoe.

The Yaghan were almost exclusively dependent on the sea for their food. Their mountainous and densely forested territory, along both shores of the Beagle Channel and throughout the islands to its south, as far as Cape Horn, supports no large terrestrial animals other than the guanaco (a wild relative of the domesticated llama) and provides little in the way of edible plants beyond berries and the abundant *Cyttaria* fungus, which has the colour and texture of dried apricots but none of the flavour. The regular staple of the Yaghan diet was shellfish and mussels in particular, which could be collected in vast numbers along the shoreline at low tide. Sea urchins and crabs were collected by diving. This task was always left to the women, perhaps because they had more subcutaneous fat than men, meaning they could better withstand immersion in seawater that was rarely warmer than 8°C. The Yaghan trod very lightly on the earth and the only visible trace of their campsites today are the thousands of shoreline middens of shells discarded after their shellfish feasts. Because the Yaghan returned to the same sites again and again over thousands of years, many of these middens have reached heights of several metres. Now overgrown, they look at first glance to be natural grassy mounds. There aren't many places in the world where it is possible to get so close to the Stone Age in time as you can by visiting one of these old shoreline campsites: only three or four lifetimes ago, the shelly mounds were still growing a little taller, year on year, with the leftovers of Yaghan meals. The mounds are liminal places, where the fabric of time feels like it is folded so that the present and humanity's distant Stone Age past come almost within touching distance of one another.

Like other shellfish, mussels are rich in protein, vitamins and essential minerals, but they have very little carbohydrate: eating nothing but mussels soon induces something akin to 'rabbit starvation' (protein poisoning). Most of the Yaghans' carbohydrate intake came from the fat of sea lions and seals hunted by the men and from bird's eggs collected in the spring and the oily flesh of penguins. Fish were caught mostly using stone traps built in shallow bays. A beached whale was manna from Heaven, providing so much more blubber than a single band could use that the finders would light signal fires to invite other bands to join the feast. The Yaghan hunted with bows and harpoons, but they never developed the technology to hunt whales at sea. *Iacasi* (autumn, 'the time of plenty') was always the best time of year, because that was the season when their prey animals were at their fattest and most nourishing.

In a state of nature

When European explorers encountered hunter-gatherers around the world, they saw people who, in their eyes, lived in a state of nature. They had no kings or governments, social classes, organized religion (which, ideally, ought to be Christianity) or permanent homes, used only the simplest technology, grew no crops and frequently lacked all bodily shame, going about naked, or almost as good as. For good measure, they were almost always, and always wrongly, suspected of cannibalism. Lacking all the attributes of civilization, hunter-gatherers were seen as being just a small step above animals. Depending upon the inclinations of the beholder, savages were idealized as 'noble savages', unspoiled by corrupt civilization, considered to be dangerous vermin to be exterminated or enslaved, or were subjected to the well-meaning but often condescending paternalism of missionaries who sought to bring them the benefits of civilization and convert them to Christianity for their own good, whether they liked it or not.

In 1832–3, the British hydrographic survey ship HMS *Beagle* visited Tierra del Fuego in the course of a global circumnavigation. Sailing with the *Beagle* as the expedition's naturalist was the young Charles Darwin, whose discoveries on the voyage would inspire his theory of evolution by natural selection. Darwin's reaction on first meeting Yaghan in their homeland in 1833 was typical. 'These poor wretches were stunted in their growth,' he later wrote, 'their hideous faces bedaubed with white paint, their skins filthy and greasy, their hair entangled, their voices discordant, and their gestures violent. Viewing such men, one can hardly make one's self believe that they are fellow creatures, inhabitants of the same world. It is a common subject of conjecture what pleasure in life some of the lower animals can enjoy: how much more reasonably the same question may be asked with respect to these barbarians.'[4] Darwin compared their intelligence to 'the instinct of animals for it is not improved by experience'.

In the case of the Yaghan, Europeans' prudish disapproval of their nakedness was tempered to some extent by sheer astonishment – how on earth did they manage to survive in Tierra del Fuego's damp and cold climate, when they wore little or no clothing and even slept naked in the open? The Yaghan certainly could have made clothes from animal skins had they wanted to, and they did sometimes wear sealskins over their shoulders, so it is likely that at some point in their history they made a deliberate decision to go naked. The decisive factor was probably the difficulty of drying clothes made of skins in the region's humid climate. While total annual rainfall averages an unexceptional 770 millimetres, it rains, sleets or snows on about 300 days in an average year and, with summer temperatures rarely exceeding 9°C, evaporation is low. The Yaghan learned that wearing permanently wet clothing was more likely to induce hypothermia than going naked: bare skin dries a lot faster than wet clothing.

The Yaghan had a number of adaptations that enabled them to survive without clothing. One of these may have been physiological: Chilean researchers have claimed, on the basis of studies of DNA recovered from Yaghan skeletal remains, that their body temperature was 1°C higher than the human average. If true, this would have made them very hardy but, as there are now no full-blooded Yaghan left alive, the claim will be very hard to verify. The Yaghan certainly did have the short, stocky stature of other cold-adapted peoples such as the Inuit. Europeans saw their stunted appearance as a sign of degeneracy, but this body shape conserves heat much better than a tall, thin body, because it exposes a smaller surface area relative to weight. The Yaghan further reduced heat loss by customarily resting in the squatting position, huddled together, which further reduced the area of their bodies exposed to the cold. Another adaptation was to smear themselves thickly with seal fat as insulation against the cold. The Yaghan chose sheltered positions for their camps and built temporary beehive-shaped shelters thatched with grasses and leaves to keep out wind and rain, but their main protection against cold came from camp fires, which they kept burning constantly, even on the hearths in their canoes. Year-round, the Yaghan slept naked on the ground in front of their fires, but they were happy enough to have the extra warmth of a companion dog, their only domesticated animal. It was the sight of dozens of camp fires burning in the night that led Ferdinand Magellan, its first European visitor, to give Tierra del Fuego its name, 'the Land of Fires'.

Living literally at the end of the road, for thousands of years the Yaghan's outside contacts were limited to their immediate neighbours, the Kawésqar, who lived on the Pacific coast of Patagonia, and the Selk'nam (or Ona) and the closely related Haush, who lived in northern and eastern Tierra del Fuego. With the Kawésqar, the Yaghan had friendly relations. The two peoples shared a similar way of life based on canoe nomadism – the Yaghan name for the Kawésqar, the Alacaluf, means 'mussel eaters' – intermarriage was common and they sometimes shared resources, such as the iron pyrite crystals both used for striking sparks for fire lighting. In contrast, the Selk'nam and Haush shared a mainly terrestrial way of life based around hunting guanaco. Neither of these peoples used canoes in historical times, so it's far from clear how they managed to get to Tierra del Fuego in the first place. Although they were not directly competing for resources, there was a tradition of conflict between the Selk'nam and the Yaghan. The Selk'nam were the more proficient warriors, and the Yaghan generally feared them and tried to avoid them.

The Yaghan's long isolation began to come to an end in 1520 with Ferdinand Magellan's discovery of the strait – later named after him – that separated Tierra del Fuego from the South American mainland. For the next 300 years, contacts between the Yaghan and Europeans were infrequent and fleeting. The seas around Tierra del Fuego were dangerous and unpredictable and most seafarers who finished up there were on their way to somewhere else and wanted only to leave as soon as possible, so the Yaghan's traditional way of life continued unchanged.

Hoping that it might reduce the number of ships lost rounding Cape Horn, in 1826 the British Admiralty sent HMS *Beagle* on its first expedition to produce accurate navigation charts of the Tierra del Fuego archipelago. While there, the expedition's commander, Robert Fitzroy, abducted four Yaghan children, three boys and a girl, who he took back with him to Britain in 1830 to be 'civilized'. It was the custom at the time for Europeans to give members of the indigenous peoples they encountered infantilized names: the three boys were named Boat Memory, Jemmy Button and York Minster, and the girl Fuegia Basket. Boat Memory died of smallpox soon after arriving in Britain, but his companions were taught to speak English and converted to Christianity. Quick learners, after nine months training they were deemed civilized enough to be presented at court to Queen Victoria. Two years after their arrival in Britain, Jemmy Button, York Minster and Fuegia Basket were on their way back to Tierra del Fuego with Captain Fitzroy and Charles Darwin on the *Beagle*'s global circumnavigation. They were accompanied by a missionary, Richard Matthews, and it was hoped that they would help him convert the Yaghan to Christianity. In the event, Matthews' mission was a dismal failure, and his three converts quickly went back to their native ways.

Killing with kindness

The Yaghan were left in peace until the arrival of another hopelessly inept English missionary, Allen Gardiner, in 1848. He did not know a word of the Yaghan language, so it isn't at all obvious how he thought he would get his message across: perhaps he imagined that God would move their hearts. God didn't: the Yaghan chased Gardiner and his party away and, lacking any survival skills, they starved to death in the wilderness before they could be rescued. After another uninvited and unwanted missionary party was killed by the Yaghan in 1854, the mission was taken over by another Englishman, Thomas Bridges, who founded a mission station at Ushuaia in 1870, the first permanent European settlement in Tierra del Fuego. Bridges' life and work in Tierra del Fuego was recorded by his son Lucas in his book *Uttermost Part of the Earth* (1948), at once a great adventure story of frontier life and a moving elegy for the extinction of the Yaghan, the last vestige of the prehistoric Atlantic world. Bridges immersed himself in Yaghan culture, learning to speak their language, Yamána, fluently and even compiling a 32,000-word Yamána–English dictionary. There can be no doubting Bridges' sincere care for the welfare of the Yaghan, but neither he nor his son ever questioned whether converting them to Christianity was in their best interests. Bridges used his influence to protect the Yaghan from the genocide then being perpetrated by Argentinean ranchers against their Selk'nam neighbours, but the well-meaning but misguided activities of Bridges and his fellow missionaries proved just as fatal.

As was the case with so many other indigenous peoples, the encounter with European civilization had a shattering and demoralizing impact on the Yaghan. Conversion to Christianity and the powerful magic of European technology undermined their entire world view and left them de-cultured. The Yaghan were gathered at mission stations, destroying their traditional nomadic way of life. The Yaghan then became dependent on handouts or had to seek wage labour with ranchers. Frequent changes of campsite and an outdoor life had protected the Yaghan from epidemics and the gastrointestinal diseases contracted by contact with human sewage. The missionaries gave them permanent huts to live in, in which families lived in constant close contact, and made them wear clothes, which became damp, dirty and lice-infested. These were ideal conditions for the spread of epidemic diseases like measles and smallpox, contracted from Europeans, to which the Yaghan had no immunity. Thomas Bridges estimated that there were about 3,000 Yaghan before European contact, but that number was halved by a single measles epidemic in 1884. When Thomas Bridges died in 1898, 900 Yaghan still survived, but their hunter-fisher-gatherer way of life was completely extinct: the survivors worked as labourers for ranchers. The last full-blooded Yaghan, and last native speaker of the Yaghan language, was Cristina Calderón, who lived at Puerto Williams, on Navarino Island in Chilean Tierra del Fuego, until her death in February 2022, aged ninety-three. In 2003, she had been designated a Living Human Treasure under the UNESCO Convention for the Safeguard of Immaterial Heritage. While several hundred people still identify as Yaghan, the shell mounds are all that remains of their traditional way of life now, and even these are threatened by coastal erosion and the rising sea levels of a warming world.

2

The Book of Invasions

5000 BC–500 BC

The Tower of Hercules – Lebor Gabála Érenn – Megaliths and migrants – Neolithic seafarers – The Orkney 'Pompeii' – Technology and social change – The metal-rich west – Beakers and metalworkers – The Celts and the Atlantic – Plague and depopulation – Cultural conformity – The Great Orme copper mine – The amber route – Shipwrecks and trade – Ships of the Bronze Age metal traders – Minoans in the Atlantic? – The birth of a tradition – The edge of the world – Celtic Otherworlds and Norse monsters

Wherever there's a time-worn ancient landmark, there'll usually be at least one legend, often more, to explain why it's there. The Tower of Hercules lighthouse at the Galician port of A Coruña has two. Standing on the low, windswept headland of Punta Eiras, its light has been guiding ships into the shelter of A Coruña's harbour for the last 1,900 years or so: it is probably the world's oldest continuously functioning lighthouse. The 55-metre-high tower is known, from a fragmentary inscription, to have been built around AD 100 by a Lusitanian-Roman architect called Gaius Sevius Lupus. Gaius built structures to last and, though the tower's external appearance was much altered by a sympathetic neoclassical restoration in 1788–92, most of his original work still survives under the modern masonry veneer. The reason for the light's longevity isn't hard to find: just 40 kilometres to the west is the ominously named Costa da Morte – a notorious wrecking coast – which extends south around Cape Finisterre, the westernmost of Europe's three 'land's ends', beyond which there was once believed to be only the ocean and the edge of the world. Coruña has always needed its lighthouse.

When it was first built, and for a few hundred years afterwards, the tower was known prosaically as the *Farum Brigantium*, 'the lighthouse of Brigantium', the Roman name for A Coruña. The tower's modern name derives from a tradition that developed in the Middle Ages that the mythological hero Hercules, the Roman name for the Greek Heracles, ordered its construction to commemorate his victory over a three-headed Iberian giant called Geryon. A visitor might, then, reasonably expect that the modern granite statue of a bearded warrior which now guards the footpath to the tower would be Heracles, but they'd be wrong – it's another legendary hero with a rival claim to be its builder. This is Breoghan, in Irish myth the forefather of the Gaels. This displacement of the Greek superhero by a proto-Irishman is down to modern identity politics: Galicians are rediscovering ancient Celtic roots as they reassert their non-Castilian Spanish identity after the repression of the Franco era. Associations with Classical heroes just don't have the same resonance now that they did during the Middle Ages, when European nations competed with one another to dream up prestigious connections back to the ancient Greek and Roman world. While Breoghan is just as mythical as Heracles, the prehistoric Atlantic connections his story celebrates aren't. In prehistory, Galicia and Ireland alike were part of a wider Atlantic culture zone, extending from the Strait of Gibraltar north to the Shetland Islands, that was connected, rather than separated, by the sea.

Lebor Gabála Érenn

Breoghan is a key character in the *Lebor Gabála Érenn* ('The Book of the Taking of Ireland'), a legendary history of the settlement of Ireland; in English it is usually known as *The Book of Invasions.* The story is an imaginative synthesis of a wide range of Biblical, Classical and pagan Irish sources that was compiled by anonymous eleventh-century monks, together with material of their own invention. Confusingly, the *Lebor* exists in a number of versions, so there is no single canonical story. The monks didn't craft the story just to entertain; they had a serious purpose: they wanted to reconcile Ireland's pagan past and its Christian present to create for the Irish people a heroic origin story that would put them on a par with the greatest of the ancient peoples, the Romans and the Israelites. Migrations were central to their origin myths, so to match them the monks created their own tale of successive waves of maritime migration to Ireland.

The *Lebor Gabála* opens in exactly 2958 BC, with the arrival in Ireland of a band of refugees from the east led by Cessair, a granddaughter of the Biblical Noah. There was no room in Noah's Ark for Cessair (she was obviously not his favourite grandchild), so he advised her to flee with her followers to Ireland, the westernmost part of the world, to escape the coming Great Flood. Ireland was uninhabited, Noah told her, so God would spare it from the Flood, because, if there were no people, then there would be no sin there to punish. Cessair set out with three ships, but hers was the only one to survive the long voyage to the west. Aside from herself, the survivors were fifty women and just three men (even celibate monks are allowed their fantasies), Ladhra, Bith and Fintan. The men shared the women out between themselves, seventeen each to Bith and Fintan, who took Cessair, and sixteen to Ladhra. In the most spiced-up version of the tale, Ladhra and Bith, though willing, were not really up to the challenge of satisfying so many wives and they soon died of exhaustion. The frustrated widows set off in pursuit of Fintan, who, fearing the same fate, turned himself into a salmon and escaped into a river.

The widows were not left to suffer from sexual frustration for very long: the immigrants had brought their sins with them to Ireland, so it was inundated by the Flood along with the rest of the world. Luckily, having turned himself into a fish, which, in the medieval world view, could not suffer from the sin of carnal lust because they were cold-blooded, Fintan was the sole survivor. Fintan later turned himself back into a human and lived for another 5,500 years, witnessing all of the subsequent invasions of Ireland.

After the Flood, Noah's sons, Shem, Ham and Japheth, repopulated the world. Irish monks believed that the peoples of Europe were all descendants of Japheth and they invented a legion of sons for him who they claimed were ancestors to all the main European peoples, thus there was Grecus, Romanus, Francus and so on. The ancestors of the peoples of Britain and Ireland were Britus, forefather of the Britons (meaning, in those days, the Welsh), Saxus, forefather of the Saxons (English), and the Gaels (Irish) themselves were descended from Gáedel Glas, whose mother was an Egyptian princess called Scota who (predictably) gave her name to the Scots. Medieval monks loved this sort of etymological word play which could be invoked to explain how almost everything got its name.

The human recolonization of Ireland after the Flood began on 17 May 2680 BC (the authors of the *Lebor* used precise dates like this to lend authority to their story), when Partholón, a descendant of Gáedel Glas, and his followers arrived, having sailed from Sicily via Spain. Unlike Cessair, Partholón was a thoroughly well-organized settler, bringing with him to Ireland such useful things as cattle, the plough, houses, gold and, especially, beer. Unfortunately, Partholón found that he'd been beaten to it by a magical but malevolent fairy race called the Fomorians who, in some versions of the story, are said to have sailed to Ireland all the way from Asia. Conflict followed, but some 300 years after arriving, Partholón's people were completely wiped out by a plague, leaving Ireland to the Fomorians. Thirty years later, a third colonization began under Nemed, who had sailed to Ireland, presumably with some difficulty, from the landlocked Caspian Sea. The Fomorians outlasted these settlers too. After years of warfare, Nemed's surviving descendants gave up and left Ireland, scattering across the world in a precursor to the historical Irish diaspora of the modern age. One group of Nemed's descendants, the Tuatha Dé Danann ('the god people of Danu'), headed to the northern islands of the world, where they learned the skills of magic and Druidism. Another group of Nemed's descendants, the Fir Bolg, migrated to Greece, where they were enslaved and, like the Biblical Israelites in Egypt, put to work as labourers. Led by five quarrelsome kings, 5,000 of the Fir Bolg escaped from their Greek masters and fled back to Ireland, where they took control. Thirty-seven years later, the Tuatha Dé Danann also returned to Ireland in a fleet of 300 ships. After defeating the Fir Bolg at the battle of Mag Tuired (or Moytura), they turned on the Fomorians and defeated them too in a second battle at Mag Tuired, driving the survivors into the ocean to drown. This struggle between two magical races has obvious parallels with other mythologies, such as the overthrow of the Titans by the Olympians in Greek mythology and the war between the Æsir and the Vanir families of gods in Norse mythology: all may have their origin in the replacement of one pantheon of gods by another in religious belief.

In the *Lebor*'s narrative, the final settlers of Ireland were the Milesians, the direct ancestors of the Irish people of historical times. These were descendants of Gáedel Glas who had spent centuries wandering the world looking for a home before eventually conquering Spain. Their leader, Breoghan, founded the city of Brigantium, commemorating the event by building a monumental tower, the Tower of Hercules. One of Breoghan's sons, Íth, climbed the tower and, from the top, saw Ireland in the far distance. Even in the fabulous world of the *Lebor Gabála*, it might seem like stretching the readers' credulity too far to expect them to believe that Ireland could ever be seen from Spain under any circumstances, but it reflects the erroneous early medieval belief that the two places were much closer than they really are. Íth at once set out for Ireland with 150 warriors but was murdered by the Tuatha Dé Danann soon after his arrival. This led the eight sons of his brother Míl Espáine ('Warrior of Spain'), known as the Milesians, to invade Ireland to seek revenge against the Tuatha Dé Danann. After fighting many indecisive battles, the two sides agreed to share Ireland between them, with the Gaels taking the world above and the Tuatha Dé Danann becoming rulers of the Otherworld, the world below. Incorporating the old pagan gods into the national history as humans gave the *Lebor*'s Christian authors the freedom to discuss paganism without running the risk of being accused of heresy.

While no historian has regarded the *Lebor Gabála* as serious history for about 200 years, archaeology and, increasingly, genetics tells us that the post-glacial prehistory of Atlantic Europe really was one of successive waves of migrations, population replacements and cultural connectedness along the seaways. So could the *Lebor* really embody a mythologized folk memory of these movements? Or is it simply a coincidence that the monkish tales sometimes align with the archaeological evidence? Did the monks believe that the Gaels originally came from Spain for no better reason than the similarity between the names Iberia and Hibernia, the ancient name for Ireland? Such an etymological explanation would certainly have appealed to them. These are all questions that can probably never be answered conclusively because there is no way reliably to sift any truth from the fiction. It is simply not sound historical method to accept the parts of the tale that seem to fit the evidence as being genuine folk memory and dismiss the bits that don't as monkish invention: it might all be one or the other. However, to paraphrase Mark Twain,* it might be said of the *Lebor* that it may not be history but it does rhyme with history.

* Twain is reputed to have said that 'history doesn't repeat itself, but it does rhyme'.

Megaliths and migrants

By around 5000 BC, the shifting post-glacial sea levels had stabilized, and Europe's Atlantic coast would have looked much as it does today to any modern seafarer who was miraculously taken back in time to sail along it. However, any sense of familiarity would have ended a few metres beyond the high tide mark, where their eyes would have met a wall of oak forest stretching inland into the far distance. The only visible sign of a human presence in the landscape might have been a plume of smoke from a Mesolithic hunter's campfire. Over the next fifteen hundred years or so, this wild landscape was to change dramatically, as the Mesolithic hunting, fishing and gathering way of life gave way to the Neolithic ('New Stone Age') farming way of life. Only in the north of Norway, where the sub-Arctic environment was unsuited to farming, would that age-old way of life be continued into historical times by the ancestors of the modern Sámi people. The means by which agriculture was adopted across Europe was long contested, but the revolution in aDNA analysis of the last thirty years has settled the matter; it was spread by migrating farming peoples from Anatolia, who crossed the Bosphorus and settled in the Balkans around 6500 BC, and whose descendants subsequently expanded from this bridgehead across most of Europe.

Because their Middle Eastern crops and technologies were well suited to local conditions, the farmers advanced most rapidly across Mediterranean Europe, reaching the Atlantic in Spain and southwest France about 5500 BC. There followed a centuries-long hiatus until new strains of staple crops like wheat and barley emerged that were suited to the cooler and wetter climates found in northwestern Europe. Re-equipped, the farmers' advance resumed, on to Brittany around 4500 BC, Britain and Ireland around 4100 BC and southern Norway, via Denmark, by 3500 BC. The farmers' three-millennia-long advance through Europe was more of a slow-moving steamroller than a blitzkrieg. Farming can support much denser populations than hunting and gathering, so the migrants always enjoyed a substantial numerical advantage over the Mesolithic populations. As areas along the farming frontier became overpopulated, landless farmers encroached remorselessly on the territory still occupied by hunter-gatherers, pushing the farming frontier on, generation after generation. In historical times, hunter-gatherer peoples always vigorously defended their hunting and foraging territories, so there is no reason to think that it was any different in prehistory, but they always would have been outnumbered by the farmers, so much so that the spread of agriculture resulted in an at least partial, and in many areas, a near total, population replacement. Farming completely transformed the genetic map of Europe.

Across much of southern and central Europe, the Mesolithic population was, if perhaps not literally exterminated, genetically swamped out of existence by the immigrant farmers. In some areas, like peninsular Italy, they have left no genetic trace whatsoever, and in most places the modern indigenous populations have inherited less than 10 per cent of their genes from the hunter-gatherers. The main exception to this is Europe's Atlantic fringe. Because of the region's rich maritime resources, the Atlantic coast's Mesolithic population was already numerous and relatively sedentary, enabling it to adapt to the farming way of life quickly and so avoid the complete genetic swamping that occurred elsewhere. Modern Basques have inherited about 19 per cent of their DNA from Mesolithic hunter-gatherers, the English 14 per cent, Scots 23 per cent and Orcadians (from the Orkney Islands) 25 per cent. On the far northern limits of where farming was possible, the Finns and Estonians have inherited about 37 per cent of their genes from the Mesolithic population.

The advent of farming marked a sharp break with the Mesolithic way of life. People began to live all year around in permanent villages in substantial houses. New technologies of pottery and polished stone tools were introduced along with domesticated animals and plants, and landscapes and ecosystems were transformed as Europe's forests were felled to create fields. The human imprint on the land started to become very obvious. Even in many coastal areas, the break with the past was total. The first farmers to settle on the small Breton island of Hoëdic, for example, looked at the sea all around them and obviously ignored it completely as a source of food because evidence for the consumption of marine foods is entirely absent from their kitchen middens, and their bones, excavated from burials, lack the chemical markers associated with a diet of seafood. The likely explanation for this is that the farmers were all incomers from inland areas with no traditions of eating marine foods who preferred to stick to the grains, dairy products and meat they had always eaten. Perhaps there were even taboos about the consumption of 'inferior' hunter-gatherer foods. In the Orkney Islands, however, where there was greater genetic continuity with the Mesolithic population, the farmers at the early Neolithic village at Knap of Howar continued to eat significant amounts of marine food to judge by the contents of their kitchen middens.

While the newly arrived farmers might not have had much appetite for seafood, they took to seafaring very quickly. Artefacts from Spain turn up in early Neolithic burials in Brittany, suggesting that there were contacts – trade or gift exchange, possibly even migrations – by sea directly across the stormy Bay of Biscay. What was mostly traded in Neolithic Europe was probably perishable foodstuffs and hides and fleeces, but there was also a trade in flint for toolmaking and in high-quality polished stone axes. There was status to be had by owning an axe made of an exotic imported stone even if it functioned no better than a locally made one. Greenstone axes made in England's Lake District found their way to Italy, and jadeite axes made at Monte Beigua near Genoa found their way to England, but there is nothing to choose between them in functionality. It is possible, perhaps even likely, that those who went on trading voyages had other motives that were just as important as the desire to acquire scarce commodities. Seafaring was dangerous, so successfully completing a trading voyage, and having an exotic axe to show for it, may have conferred on a man the same sort of status that can come from displaying courage and skill in battle. Trade may also have been accompanied by exchange of marriage partners. Analysis of the aDNA in human remains found in tombs, such as that at Hazleton North in the west of England, suggests that Neolithic societies were exogamous, that is that women did not marry into their birth communities and went to live in their husband's community, so there may have been a constant small-scale movement of people along the coast: we can imagine the excitement that would have greeted a boat arriving with a new bride and a dowry of exotic stone and other goods.

For landless continental farmers seeking new opportunities to settle in Britain and Ireland, migrating by sea was, obviously, unavoidable. The farmers arrived by two different routes. The east of Britain was settled by migrants who crossed the narrow (33-kilometre-wide) Strait of Dover. Breton pottery in Neolithic burials in the north of Ireland and Western Scotland points to a more challenging second migration route directly from Brittany, across the Channel at its widest point, to southwest England and then north through the Irish Sea to Ireland and Scotland's west coast. Cultural differences between these two groups, continental-facing in the east and Atlantic-facing in the west, show that they identified themselves as separate peoples, and they were slow to integrate. The migrants' insatiable land hunger drove them on to settle every significant island in the entire British and Irish archipelago within a few hundred years of their arrival. Even the dramatic and now uninhabited St Kilda archipelago, 64 kilometres out in the Atlantic, northwest of Scotland's Outer Hebrides, was colonized by farmers by around 3100 BC. These settlers did not arrive by the easiest route. Several distinctive Neolithic stone tools known as Skaill knives (probably butchery tools) have been found on the main island of Hirta. These knives have never been found in Neolithic settlements in the Outer Hebrides but are common finds in the Orkney and Shetland islands, over 250 kilometres' sailing from St Kilda. Landing on St Kilda can be difficult even today, so reaching the islands in Neolithic times must have been a real challenge, making it all the more remarkable that the first settlers sailed so far over some of the world's wildest seas to get there.

Neolithic seafarers

Neolithic migrants had a lot to take with them: seed corn, livestock (probably tightly bound to stop it moving and upsetting the boat), axes for clearing land and other tools, and food supplies to see them through to the first harvest. There is a tendency to dismiss the possibility that the simple logboats that we know they and their Mesolithic predecessors used on sheltered waters could have been either large enough or seaworthy enough for a seaborne migration, but we may simply be projecting our own twenty-first-century risk averseness onto Neolithic people. Even today, every year several thousands of refugees and economic migrants make dangerous cross-Channel voyages in good weather in boats that are, often, barely seaworthy. Some of them tragically drown, but this risk doesn't deter people who feel that they have no other options. Neolithic farmers probably thought the same way: in an age when farming was the only way to make a living, the future for landless people can only have been bleak. Early Neolithic seafarers still lacked the carpentry skills needed to make boats with planks, but they could have made their logboats more stable and seaworthy by pairing them to make catamarans or by adding outriggers, as is the practice in the Indo-Pacific region. A substantial prehistoric logboat (7 metres long) that was recovered from the seabed off Gormanston in County Meath, Ireland, had notches cut into its gunwales that may well have been fittings for outriggers. Most archaeologists, however, believe it is more likely that, for their migrations, Neolithic seafarers relied mainly on hide boats, similar to the Inuit umiak or the Irish curach, both of which are very seaworthy. Proving this, however, is a remote possibility, because such lightly built boats decay quickly once they are abandoned, leaving few traces.

There is no evidence that seafarers anywhere in the world used sails before about 3500 BC, when they came into use on rivers in the Middle East and Egypt. Oars did not come into use until even later, so Neolithic seafarers must have relied entirely on paddling for propulsion. The 200-kilometre direct crossing from Brittany to Cornwall could not have been completed in a day by paddling, so seafarers must have had some way to hold a course in the hours of darkness. Many Neolithic monuments, most famously Stonehenge, display sophisticated astronomical knowledge in their design, so seafarers may have used this also to navigate out of sight of land and at night. However, even pre-modern seafarers as accomplished as the Vikings chose not to sail out of sight of land if they didn't need to. Paddling is energy-intensive, so seafarers probably stuck close to the coast most of the time, proceeding in short stages, hauling ashore at night to eat and rest, and to sit out bad weather. Computer modelling, taking into account tidal flows and currents, has concluded that a voyage from Orkney to Brittany might have been accomplished in as little as seventeen days, which seems optimistic given the unpredictable weather along Britain's west coast. Even so, travel by sea would still have been faster than travel on foot by land, and it was the only way to transport substantial quantities of trade goods: Neolithic Europe had neither pack animals nor wheeled vehicles.

When people travel, their ideas and beliefs go with them. Around 4800 BC, when farmers in Brittany began building a new type of monumental tomb called a passage grave, the concept spread quickly along the Atlantic seaways, south to Spain and Portugal and north to Britain, Ireland, the Netherlands and Denmark. Nowhere are passage tombs found than about 200 kilometres inland; they were the first material expression of an Atlantic cultural identity. Usually built with megaliths (literally 'big stones'), passage graves were places for communal burial designed so that the dead could continue to participate in the life of the community. The burial chambers were accessible by passages so that the living could enter the world of the dead and perform rituals in the presence of their revered ancestors, or consult with them about important decisions. In some cases, the passages were aligned on significant astronomical events, such as the midwinter sunrise, as in Ireland's enormous Newgrange tomb, or the midwinter sunset, as in the tomb at Maeshowe in the Orkney Islands. Passage graves sometimes remained in use for many generations. One of the oldest, at Barnenez in western Brittany, was originally built with just a single passage and grave chamber, but over the millennium that it remained in use it was progressively extended to accommodate ever more residents, so that in its final form it contained no less than eleven chambers, each accessed by its own passage. Around 3800 BC in southern Spain, the passage tomb evolved into the gallery tomb, in which the burial chamber was entered directly from the entrance, rather than via a passage. Like its predecessor, this type of tomb spread along the Atlantic seaways too, north as far as Britain and Ireland.

There are considerable local variations in the burial practices associated with megalithic tombs. Some contain cremations, others inhumations. Some have whole skeletons; in others only selected bones were kept, often sorted by type: long bones together, skulls together. Some have evidence, in the form of broken pottery, for example, that they hosted communal feasting; most don't. It was clearly primarily the idea of the tomb that travelled; there weren't megalithic missionaries traversing the seaways promoting a common religion. The substantial resources that communities devoted to the dead in Atlantic Europe are thought to be a reaction to local circumstances. So long as there was a frontier of settlement, conflicts over land within and between groups could be defused by expanding into hunter-gatherer territory. Once the frontier reached the Atlantic coast, there was nowhere left to expand into, resulting in population stress. Communities from Iberia to Scotland all shared a heightened need to demonstrate their ownership of their land. A prominent resting place for generations of ancestors became a sacred title deed to the land shouting 'this is our land, given to us by our ancestors who are still here with us'.

The Orkney 'Pompeii'

In most of Europe, it is only the farmers' tombs, and other megalithic ritual monuments like menhirs and stone circles, that remain visible in the modern landscape: the farmsteads and villages where they lived their everyday lives are mostly invisible now. Across most of Europe, Neolithic farmers built wooden houses whose presence is revealed in excavations only by the traces of the post-holes that held the main structural timbers. Farmers in the Orkney Islands, in the far northwest of the Neolithic world, didn't have this option; trees don't flourish in its windswept environment and, even before the land was cleared for fields and pasture, it supported only low, scrubby birch and willow woodland, so there was little timber suitable for building. Good stone was plentiful, however. Orkney's Devonian flagstone bedrock splits naturally into neat rectangular blocks ideally suited for building, so the farmers used that, not only for their houses and their passage graves and chamber tombs, but for their furniture too. Thanks to this, Orkney has some of Europe's best-preserved Neolithic settlements, the most outstanding of which is the UNESCO World Heritage site of Skara Brae, by the Bay of Skaill on the west coast of Mainland island. This site was thought to be nothing more than a natural hummock among sand dunes close to the bay's shore until a severe Atlantic storm in 1850 stripped away the sand and exposed a tracery of ancient masonry walls. The local laird had antiquarian interests and conducted a number of amateur excavations, but it was not until 1927 that a full scientific excavation of the village confirmed that the walls belonged to a Neolithic village that was occupied from *c.*3180 BC until *c.*2500 BC, when it was abandoned and soon after became completely buried in blown sand. The sand that smothered the village also protected and preserved it so perfectly that it has been described, with pardonable exaggeration, as Orkney's Pompeii. The village consisted of seven stone-built round houses huddled closely together, most of which still survive to roof height. No evidence of their roof structures survive but they probably had frames of driftwood, or of long rib bones taken from beached whales, and were covered with turf – a thatched roof wouldn't have lasted long in the Atlantic gales which can strike at any time of year.

For extra protection from the wind, the houses were built into a large midden from an earlier settlement and the passages between them were roofed with stone slabs, and, probably, turf, so that the inhabitants could visit their neighbours without being exposed to the wild Atlantic weather. All the houses have neatly made stone dressers and shelving, a central stone-lined hearth, box beds, seats and storage boxes. The layout of a house wasn't an expression of its owner's personal taste; it had some symbolic meaning, because it is the same in all the houses. The dressers are always opposite the entrance door, and the largest bed is always to the right of the entry and the smaller to the left. One possible explanation for this is that this is connected with gender, the larger bed being the husband's and the smaller being the wife's. Was there a women's side of the house and a men's side, a kind of domestic segregation? Or was one side for the adults and the other for the children? The houses each have a small antechamber with access to a communal drain which carried waste water away from the settlement towards the Atlantic. These were probably indoor privies, quite a luxury still for most working-class people in Britain in the early twentieth century AD, and probably much appreciated on winter nights. The furnishings make it easy to imagine families living in the houses, telling stories huddled around the fire on stormy winter nights. In historic times, Orcadians relied on peat for fuel, but the islands' extensive peat bogs had yet to form in the Neolithic, so the people of Skara Brae used dried seaweed, animal dung and driftwood. The fires probably smouldered rather than blazed, but the houses were so well insulated by the midden that they would have been comfortably warm even in winter. Today, restored and carefully maintained, the houses look a little too tidy, almost like Stone Age show homes, but when complete and inhabited, they would have been smoky and dark, with the only daylight entering through a smoke-hole in the roof, if there was one. In good weather, at least, the people of Skara Brae lived and worked mostly outdoors, where they could breathe fresh air and see what they were doing. There was also a small, free-standing workshop building, where excavators found evidence for heat-treating stone to improve its qualities for manufacturing stone tools.

The middens of domestic waste which insulated the villagers' homes also preserved evidence that they enjoyed a varied diet by Neolithic standards. Wheat and barley were grown in fields nearby – despite its bleakness, Orkney has fertile soils – and the villagers bred cattle, pigs, goats and sheep, and hunted red deer. Being close to the sea gave the villagers access to resources denied to those who lived inland, such as shellfish, fish, seabirds and seals. Life on the edge of the Atlantic was not all work. The villagers made jewellery from shells and bone, played dice, and made paints and incised geometrical decorations on stone slabs around the settlement, which possibly had a symbolic meaning now lost to us.

All the houses in the village were roughly the same size, with about 40 square metres of floor space, so this must have been an egalitarian community without great differences in wealth and status. However, Skara Brae wasn't an isolated community. The villagers joined with other communities from across Mainland in building a monumental walled ritual centre with twelve stone temples at the Ness of Brodgar, 8 kilometres away, where they enjoyed feasting together. Some of these feasts could be gargantuan; one may have involved the slaughter of 600 cattle. Quite how this amazing social enterprise was organized remains mysterious, as there is no evidence for the existence of any kind of centralized power in Orkney at this time. Associated with the site are two stone circles, the Stones of Stenness, which was erected *c.*3100 BC, to the south and the much larger Ring of Brodgar, erected 600 years later, to the north. No one lived at the Ness, but at Barnhouse nearby there was a contemporary settlement of fifteen stone houses, all built in a similar way to those at Skara Brae. Were they the guardians of the ceremonial centre? Orkney was no remote backwater either; the islanders were well connected by sea to the rest of Britain. Polished stone axes and pitchstone were imported from as far away as the Isle of Arran, and the nearest source for the flint they used for everyday tools was the Isle of Skye. A style of decorated pottery called Grooved Ware, which originated in Orkney, became fashionable across Britain after spreading along the seaways.

Some archaeologists, impressed by the scale and sophistication of its Neolithic monuments, have seen Orkney as the ultimate source of much of Britain's megalithic culture, including the inspiration for Stonehenge, the most famous of all megalithic monuments. Whether this is really the case, or is simply an artefact of the intensive archaeological investigation of Orkney's Neolithic sites in recent years, awaits to be seen. However, even if they did not provide the inspiration, Neolithic Orcadians probably did participate directly in the construction of Stonehenge and make pilgrimages there. People came from all over Britain to participate in rituals and construction at Stonehenge: that may even have been its main purpose, to bring the people of the east and the Atlantic west together and unite them in a common experience. Pilgrims to Stonehenge stayed in a village at Durrington Walls, about 3 kilometres away, where they held communal feasts of beef stew and roast pork. Isotope analysis of some of the enormous numbers of cattle and pig bones excavated at the site show that only a minority of the animals eaten in these feasts were reared locally. The majority were brought to the site from across Britain, and some of the bones have concentrations of sulphur, oxygen and strontium that match the geology of northeast Scotland and Orkney. Whole skeletons are present at the site, so the animals were brought there alive, maybe as sacrificial offerings, not as prepared cuts of meat. Unlike sheep and cattle, pigs just aren't built to be herded long distances, so those that were brought to Durrington must have travelled by sea most of the way, again pointing to the strong maritime links between the far north and the rest of Britain. The pigs slaughtered at Durrington were all about nine months old. Sows farrow in the spring, so this fixes the time of the feasts at the midwinter solstice. That people would have travelled so far by sea in the dead of winter makes these gatherings all the more remarkable: Stonehenge had real power.

Technology and social change

Beginning around 2800 BC, Europe's Atlantic façade began to transition from the Stone Age to the age of metals. Prehistoric archaeologists conventionally divide the metal age into three periods: the Chalcolithic, when soft metals like copper and gold came into use; the Bronze Age, when bronze came into use; and the Iron Age, when iron supplanted bronze as the most important metal for tools and weapons. The exact dates vary in different regions, but in western Europe the Chalcolithic is generally reckoned to last from *c.*2800 BC to *c.*1800 BC; the Bronze Age from *c.*2200 BC to *c.*500 BC; and the Iron Age from *c.*800 BC up to the end of the prehistoric period, which for most of western Europe was between the third and first centuries BC but in Scandinavia came not until the beginning of the Viking Age, *c.*AD 793.

Metal tools and weapons were far superior to those made of stone and far more versatile, but their introduction meant much more than getting a shiny new toolkit; they also brought great social and economic changes in their wake. This became very apparent after the introduction of bronze technology. Copper could be smelted and cast relatively easily, but it was too soft to be a complete replacement for stone tools – not so bronze. Bronze, an alloy containing around 12.5 per cent tin and 87.5 per cent copper, is considerably harder and more durable than pure copper, and it is also easier to cast. The advantages of bronze tools were obvious, but they came at a price – the end of local self-sufficiency – that was as transformative as the tools themselves. While stone suitable for toolmaking is widespread, copper ores are not, and cassiterite, the main tin ore, is actually quite rare. It is uncommon, too, for both metals to be found in the same place, so what the introduction of bronze technology did was turn long-distance trade into an absolute necessity. In the Atlantic, this directly led to the intensification of the maritime links established during the Neolithic and, ultimately, it ended the relative isolation of the Atlantic by linking it through wider trade systems to the early civilizations of the eastern Mediterranean and the Middle East.

Bronze's exotic origins, and the specialized skills needed to smelt and cast it, allowed a small elite to control its manufacture, distribution and use, greatly enhancing their status and power and accelerating the development of more hierarchical forms of society. Across most of Europe, this was marked by the emergence of a warrior class. In the Neolithic, most weapons, such as throwing spears and the bow and arrow, were designed for hunting and were available to all. Bronze allowed the creation of weapons, like swords, halberds and daggers, that were specialized for hand-to-hand fighting, and protective armour and helmets, but they were expensive and only available to the elite, which was bad news for everyone else. Fortifications became common for the first time, as communities sought to protect themselves from aggressive neighbours. The necessity of trade encouraged the emergence of full-time merchants and seafarers, and stimulated improvements in shipbuilding. Bronze-working also required specialized, and often itinerant, craftsmen who could work the magic of turning dull stones into burnished tools.

The metal-rich west

Tourists heading to Europe's Atlantic coast aren't going primarily to lie on the beach and get a sun tan: the weather is too unreliable; they're going for the rugged and dramatic scenery, itself a legacy of the region's geology. From Ireland south to Portugal, Europe's Atlantic coast is flanked by worn-down ranges of 300-million-year-old fold mountains which were once as high as the Himalayas. What's left is built of hard, erosion-resistant, volcanic and metamorphic rocks, and shot through with granite intrusions and veins rich in the ores of copper, tin, gold, silver, lead and iron, as well as numerous other minerals. Geologists describe the Atlantic fringe as a 'metal-rich zone'. Copper was fairly widespread in the zone, but there were only three substantial sources of cassiterite, in Galicia, northern Brittany and Cornwall, all areas with large exposures of granite, the rock in which the ore is most commonly found. Cassiterite can be mined, but back in the Bronze Age the ore was panned, like gold, from alluvial workings where it had been deposited by rivers and streams after it had been eroded out of the bedrock by natural weathering. The ore was smelted locally and was traded as ingots of pure tin. Galicia-Brittany-Cornwall naturally became the main axis of the Atlantic Bronze Age's metal trading network, for not only tin but also gold, silver and copper. At first, the network fed regional demand, but by the thirteenth century BC at the very latest, Atlantic tin was being exported, through Mediterranean intermediaries, to the resource-hungry civilizations of Greece, Crete, the Levant and Mesopotamia. Though they knew only that tin came from somewhere in the far west, the commercially minded Phoenicians of modern-day Lebanon gave the land a name, 'Kassiterid', from which tin ore gets its name. In time, the Phoenicians would sail west to try to discover its source. Greeks and Romans would follow, drawn to the Atlantic by its metallic wealth.

The world's earliest centre of metallurgy was the Middle East, but the secrets of extracting metals from rock were discovered independently in many other places. In Europe, these places included the Balkans and, on the Atlantic, central Portugal, where copper smelting began around 2800 BC in fortified megalithic hilltop towns, known as *castros*, such as Zambujal and Vila Nova de São Pedro. The *castros* were well-connected places with access to Baltic amber, North African elephant ivory and ostrich eggshells, callaïs* from Brittany and Andalusian copper, most of which must have been transported along the Atlantic sea lanes. A cowrie shell from the Indian Ocean, found at Zambujal, hints at even wider connections. Gold panned from alluvial sands in the nearby Tagus River was probably what paid for these imports. Kilns used for copper smelting have been excavated at Zambujal and other nearby sites. The smelting methods differed from those used at the time in the eastern Mediterranean and the Middle East, so there is no doubt that the people here worked this out for themselves; they were not taught by outsiders. A wide range of copper artefacts was manufactured, including axes, saws, awls, daggers and leaf-shaped arrowheads, but, to judge from the quantities of leftover slag, production was on a small scale.

Beakers and metalworkers

The subsequent spread of copper-working technology along the Atlantic is closely linked to a new fashion in pottery, the bell beaker, which also originated in central Portugal. First manufactured around 2800 BC–2700 BC, the bell beaker was a vase-sized drinking vessel shaped like an inverted bell, hence the name. As well as having a distinctive shape, beakers were decorated with horizontal bands of incised comb decoration and fired to an attractive deep red-brown colour. Pollen residues found in some bell beakers show that they once contained a honey-based brew like mead, and others have evidence that they contained beer, so they may have been associated with a drinking cult.

Bell beakers were, initially, spread not by gradual diffusion

* A green-blue semi-precious stone used to make beads.

outwards in all directions but by great maritime leaps, south to Andalusia and Morocco, and north directly across the Bay of Biscay to Morbihan in southwest Brittany and then by another leap across the sea to southwest Ireland, where copper smelting using locally mined ores began around 2400 BC at Ross Island, a site where early beaker pottery has been found. Irish copper axes, halberds and daggers began to circulate widely not only in Ireland but in western Britain too. Soon after this, alluvial gold deposits in the Wicklow Mountains began to be exploited. Much of this gold was used to make collar-like necklaces known, from their crescent moon shape, as *lunulae*. The locals kept most of these spectacular prestige objects for themselves, but a few examples have been found in Cornwall, Normandy, Brittany and even as far from Ireland as Denmark.

Bell beakers were not spread as trade goods: analysis of inclusions in the pots themselves shows that the vast majority were made from clay that had been dug close to the places where they were found. The earliest places where bell beakers appeared are all ore-rich regions, so the style was probably spread by itinerant miners and metalworkers who were exploring the Atlantic coast prospecting for new sources of copper. For the locals who adopted the bell beaker style for their own pottery, the attraction was likely to have been its association with the prestigious new metalworking technology that the prospectors brought with them. However, in its next phase, the spread of bell beakers and metallurgy was the result of a second mass migration into western Europe.

Brittany was a node from which the beaker style spread inland along an old established axe and stone trading route which followed the Loire river eastwards into the heart of Europe. Around 2700–2600 BC, the bell beaker style was adopted in the Rhineland by pastoralist peoples who belonged to the important north European Corded Ware cultural complex.* The Corded

* The name comes from the way that the Corded Ware people pressed twisted cords into the outside of their pots to create decorative patterns before they were fired.

Ware people were the vanguard of a new wave of migrants, this time from the western Eurasian steppes, who were destined to transform the culture, genetics and languages of Europe for a second time. Their arrival brought an immediate break with Neolithic traditions. They buried their dead in individual graves, in timber or stone chambers, accompanied by ritual offerings for the afterlife: those of high-status individuals were marked with earth barrows to make them prominent in the landscape. The newcomers were mobile; they bred horses, used wheeled vehicles and brought with them a knowledge of copper smelting that their ancestors had acquired on the steppes. The most important legacy of the Corded Ware people was invisible; they spoke Indo-European languages which are directly ancestral to the majority of the modern European languages.

In the Rhineland, the bell beaker became part of a distinct cultural package which is associated with burial rites. The dead were typically buried with a suite of grave goods which commonly included archery gear, a copper dagger and a bell beaker. Higher-status people were often accompanied by ornaments of gold, amber or jet to help maintain their superior social status even in death. The bell beakers were originally filled with a ritual drink to keep the deceased happily inebriated on their way to the afterlife. Migrants from the Rhineland took these burial practices with them as they continued to expand west across France to the Iberian Peninsula, south into Italy and across the southern North Sea to Britain and Ireland.

Where the migrants settled, the communal megalithic tombs which were so emblematic of the Neolithic Atlantic were abandoned, and often purposefully sealed, perhaps to ensure that the spirits of the former owners of the land did not come out and make trouble for the newcomers. However, some of the ritual sites, notably Stonehenge, continued to be used, and even modified, for centuries afterwards. The migrants may not have had deep roots in the land but they recognized that such impressive structures were places of ancient power and wanted to associate themselves with them; people still do: that's why thousands gather at Stonehenge every year to watch the midsummer sunrise over the Heel Stone. One of the earliest of these 'beaker people' to arrive in Britain was a man, known as the 'Amesbury Archer', who was buried near Stonehenge around 2300 BC with bell beakers, archery gear, small copper knives, two gold hair ornaments and metalworking tools. Isotope analysis of the man's tooth enamel showed that he had grown up somewhere in the Alps. His is only one of several known beaker burials in the vicinity of Stonehenge.

The scale of the migrations involved in the bell beaker phenomenon varied considerably. In some parts of Europe there was a genetic replacement on a scale approaching that which marked the transition from the Mesolithic to the Neolithic. The early Bronze Age inhabitants of Germany and much of central Europe and southern Scandinavia inherited around 90 per cent of their DNA from steppe ancestors, but in France there was greater genetic continuity with the Neolithic population; the immigrants may have imposed their cultural identity on the indigenous population, but they did not completely replace them. In Iberia, immigration of people of steppe ancestry was very limited and confined mostly to the central plateau: aDNA studies of beaker-related burials indicate that most of the immigrants were male, perhaps members of conquering war bands who took local women as wives. For no clear reason, the greatest degree of genetic continuity with the Neolithic population is found in the Basque Country, the area on both sides of the Pyrenees in the southeast corner of the Bay of Biscay that is the homeland of the modern Basque people.

In Britain, the genetic replacement was as near complete as it was in Germany. About 90 per cent of people whose remains have been found associated with bell beaker burials have been found to have varying degrees of steppe ancestry. This proportion of steppe ancestry is much higher than that of the Iron Age inhabitants of Britain, which is seen as evidence for a third major maritime migration into the isles towards the end of the Bronze Age, this time involving a population from a part of Europe, most likely western France, where the steppe genetic inheritance was less marked. Though the genetic evidence is still limited, the migration of steppe-origin peoples to Ireland seems also to have been substantial. A Neolithic woman from a megalithic burial at Ballynahatty near Belfast (dated to *c.*3300 BC–3000 BC) possessed a genome of primarily Middle Eastern origin and was more closely related to the modern Basques and Sardinians than she was to the modern population of Ireland. In contrast, three males from an early Bronze Age burial on Rathlin Island (dated to *c.*2000 BC–1500 BC) had approaching 40 per cent steppe ancestry and were comparable to Bronze Age populations in central Europe. Europe's Neolithic population had a broadly Mediterranean appearance, but the new populations descended from the steppe peoples had the fair skin, blue eyes and blond or red hair associated with modern Nordic and Celtic populations. They are also responsible for the very high degree of lactose tolerance among north Europeans, an evolutionary legacy of a pastoralist diet rich in dairy products. Most of the languages spoken in modern Europe are also, ultimately, a legacy of the steppe migrants, descendants of their Indo-European languages. The most important exception is Euskara, the language of the Basques, a 'language isolate' related to no other known language, which linguists believe is the sole descendant of the languages spoken in Neolithic Europe. Language matches genetics in this case.

The Celts and the Atlantic

As the steppe-origin migrants fanned out across Europe, like the mythical sons of Japheth in the *Lebor*, they lost contact with one another, and the ancestral Indo-European language that they spoke began to diversify and evolve into the modern European language families: Germanic, Romance, Greek, Slavic, Baltic and Celtic. None of these is more closely associated with the Atlantic than Celtic. Today, Celtic languages survive precariously, under constant pressure from English and French, on Europe's Atlantic edge in western Brittany, western Ireland, Scotland's Hebridean Islands and in Wales. This linguistic refugium is sometimes styled the 'Celtic Fringe', quite intentionally to emphasize the marginality of both the languages and those who speak them. However, back in their Iron Age heyday, Celtic language speakers dominated Atlantic Europe from the Shetland Islands south to Portugal and far beyond to the east into central Europe and northern Italy. There was even an enclave of Celtic-speakers in Anatolia, the product of a late migration.

Linguists and archaeologists for the most part agree that the Celtic languages evolved from the language or dialect spoken by a group of Corded Ware people or their direct descendants, but that's where the consensus ends. The when and where of Celtic language origins and the issue of how and when Celtic-speakers arrived on the Atlantic coast are highly contested. What passes for the 'establishment' theory is that Celtic originated in central Europe in the late Bronze Age and was spread west to the Atlantic by migrations. A more recent rival theory is that Celtic evolved in the west of continental Europe as a *lingua franca* along the Atlantic seaways and then spread east. Even more recently, a third contender has entered the ring, arguing that Celtic originated neither in the west or the east but somewhere in between. This is dangerous territory for a non-linguist, and the argument is unlikely to be settled anytime soon. What really matters is that when Mediterranean seafarers began to explore the Atlantic for themselves in the first millennium BC, they found that the all-important metal-trading network was largely controlled by Celtic-speaking peoples, and it would be they who dominated the Atlantic seaways for the next 1,500 years or more.

Plague and depopulation

The fate of northern Europe's Neolithic people was a complete mystery until recently. How could they simply have disappeared?

Were the people from the steppes filled with an extreme genocidal bloodlust? Probably not. In 2014, DNA traces of *Yersinia pestis*, the plague bacillus, were discovered in teeth from a mass burial of seventy-eight people in a late Neolithic megalithic tomb at Frälsegården in western Sweden. Radiocarbon dating of the remains gave a date of 3100 BC to 2900 BC for the burials, roughly the same time that the steppe peoples began their expansion into Europe. Traces of the bacillus have since been identified in other human remains from the same period in other parts of Europe, including two burial sites in Cumbria and Gloucestershire, near Britain's west coast. It looks as if the steppe peoples were able to migrate into areas that had already been largely depopulated by a plague pandemic in much the same way that Europeans were able to colonize the Americas after the indigenous population had been decimated by epidemics of the Old World diseases that they had brought with them. Occasions like the annual midwinter festival at Stonehenge would have been very effective 'super-spreader' events with the potential to spread the plague quickly over large areas.

Cultural conformity

While knowledge of copper smelting had spread along the Atlantic from south to north, the secret of making tin-bronze spread from north to south. In what appears to have been another independent indigenous development, around 2100 BC, bronze, made with local copper ores and Cornish tin, was being smelted in Ireland and Britain. The technique spread south from there to Brittany and, finally, to Iberia by around 1800 BC, by which time the whole bell beaker package had gone out of fashion. The intensified trade links which the new bronze technology made necessary promoted a high degree of cultural uniformity along the Atlantic littoral, from Britain and Ireland in the north, and south to the Tagus region in Portugal. The elite members of Atlantic Bronze Age society displayed their status through feasting, which involved such items as bronze cauldrons, flesh hooks and roasting spits, through ownership of specialized war-gear such as swords and armour, and spectacular gold torcs and bracelets, and, in death, through richly furnished burials under prominent earthen barrows. Fortified settlements on hilltops or spectacular coastal locations, such as headlands and promontories, proliferated along with a preference for living in roundhouses, something which would remain characteristic of the Atlantic coast until the Viking Age. Bronze may have been seen as a gift of underworld deities because enormous quantities of bronze artefacts, especially axes and weapons, were gifted back to the earth in ritual deposits in liminal locations, essentially interface zones, such as bogs, springs and rivers, where the borders of this world and the Otherworld came into close contact. One of the largest known Bronze Age hoards, found at Isleham in Cambridgeshire, England, contained an incredible 6,500 bronze objects.

The Great Orme copper mine

The history of one of Bronze Age Europe's largest copper mines, at Great Orme's Head in Wales, illustrates the way regional trade links worked in practice. The earliest known copper mining in the British Isles started at Ross Island near Killarney in southwest Ireland around 2400 BC. About two hundred years later, prospectors had begun mining copper at half a dozen other sites in Ireland, Wales and England. Early smelting methods left plenty of impurities in copper, the ratios of which give it a definitive 'signature' which allows the metal's source to be traced back to the place where it was mined. It's clear from analysis of bronze tools that production from these mines was insufficient to meet demand in Britain and Ireland, so much copper and bronze was imported from the continent. Around 1700 BC, copper mining began at Great Orme, a 207-metre-high limestone headland overlooking what is now the genteel Victorian seaside resort of Llandudno on the Irish Sea. The relatively soft green malachite copper ore was easy to extract from the limestone bedrock and production expanded rapidly, soon putting all other copper mines in Britain and Ireland out of business. Output was more than sufficient to meet all demand for copper in Britain and Ireland: continental imports came to an end and Great Orme copper began to be exported, much of it in the form of bronze palstave axes. Hoards of these axes, manufactured using Great Orme copper, have been found as far apart as Tréboul in Brittany, Voorhut in the Netherlands and Hönö on Sweden's west coast. It is possible that, at the height of its production between 1600 BC and 1400 BC, the Great Orme mine was supplying most of northern Europe's copper.

Archaeologists estimate that around 2,000 tonnes of malachite ore was mined and smelted at Great Orme, enough to make a staggering 100 million tools and weapons. Around 8 kilometres of tunnels, descending 67 metres below the surface, have so far been discovered and explored. Many of them contained abandoned mining tools, such as hammer stones collected from local beaches and bone picks, and the sooty smudges left by the flames of the flickering animal-fat-fuelled lamps that the toiling miners used for lighting. Some of the tunnels are so narrow that they could only have been dug by children as young as five or six. Mining was a family enterprise, it would seem. Production on this scale implies that there was a full-time mining community at Great Orme, who traded metal for food and other essentials, probably under the control of a regional chiefdom centred somewhere in northeast Wales which, in turn, controlled its onward distribution. By 1400 BC, most of the accessible ore at Great Orme was exhausted and production collapsed: the mine was finally abandoned around 900 BC. This didn't spark a revival of copper mining at other sites in Britain, however; the maritime links filled the gap in supply with imported copper, much of which came ultimately from the Italian Alps.

One area that was always dependent on imports for all its bronze was Scandinavia. Norway and, especially, Sweden do have rich deposits of copper ores, but these had not yet been discovered in the Bronze Age. Nor were there any known deposits of tin ores, so Scandinavia lacked all the ingredients of bronze. Southern Scandinavia had been an integral part of the Atlantic megalithic culture, but in the Bronze Age it also became closely linked to central Europe and, ultimately, to Greece. Bronze was imported into Scandinavia in the form of artefacts like axes, or as scrap metal, both of which were melted down and recast into artefacts more agreeable to local tastes. Some of this bronze came from Britain and Ireland, including the Great Orme mine, but most came from the Ore Mountains in central Europe by overland routes. Gold was also imported, mostly from Ireland. Scandinavian metalsmiths became highly skilled, creating such masterpieces as the amazing 'sun chariot' found at Trundholm in Denmark, a model of a four-wheeled horse-drawn cart on which was mounted a gleaming gold-finished solar disc, obviously a very precious votive offering for a sun cult. Scandinavia never seemed to have been short of bronze, because the votive hoards that were sunk in bogs were just as extravagant as they were anywhere in Atlantic Europe.

The amber route

The most important product that the Scandinavians gave in exchange for their metals was amber, which they collected from beaches in the southern Baltic Sea and on Denmark's North Sea coast. This 80 million-year-old, translucent, fiery-coloured fossil resin was prized in the ancient world not only because of its beauty but because of its seemingly magical properties: it was a stone but it floated in salt water, it burned with a pleasant piney smell (it was used for incense), and, when rubbed, it showed strange, inexplicable, electrostatic properties. Called electrum ('sunbeam') by the ancient Greeks, amber has given us the word 'electricity'. Amber was the subject of colourful myths, the most widespread being that it was made of sunbeams that had congealed in the sea at sunset, or that it was created by the

Earth sweating under the sun's heat, although some, such as the Roman naturalist Pliny the Elder, guessed correctly that it was pine tree resin. Amber's geographical origins remained mysterious outside Scandinavia. The fifth-century BC Greek historian Herodotus accepted that amber, like tin and gold, came from 'the far edges of the world', but he refused to believe in the existence of either the Baltic Sea or the North Sea, because he had never met an eyewitness who had seen either of these bodies of water for themselves

During the Neolithic, people in the south of Scandinavia wore chunky amber necklaces, embroidered their clothes with amber beads and made lavish sacrifices of amber, often with stone axes, to their gods by sinking it into bogs and lakes. The largest such sacrifice found at Læsten in Jutland, Denmark, contained over 4,000 beads and weighed 8.5 kilograms. When, with the transition to the Bronze Age, this lavish use of amber abruptly ended, both humans and the gods had to get by without it. If amber is found in Scandinavian Bronze Age contexts it is usually only as single beads that were worn as pendants or set in religious talismans, where it probably represented a solar deity. Scandinavia hadn't run out of amber; ownership had somehow been monopolized by the social elite so that they could exchange it for the all-important bronze: far more amber has been found on Bronze Age sites outside Scandinavia than in it.

The distribution of Baltic amber finds a mirror in the sources of metals. Not surprisingly, the largest concentrations have been found in central Europe, the main source of Scandinavia's bronze. Some of the amber that found its way there did not stay, but was re-exported along the network of trans-Alpine trade routes known as the 'Amber Road' to the eastern Mediterranean, to the Mycenaean kingdoms in Greece, and to Syria and Egypt. Tutankhamen was just one of the pharaohs who were buried with amber jewellery. For Ancient Egyptians, amber's golden translucency linked it with the sun-god Ra, the god also of kingship. Significant quantities of amber have been found in Bronze Age sites in Ireland, the source of Scandinavia's gold; in tin-mining areas of Cornwall; in North Wales not so far from the Great Orme mine; and in Wessex in south-central England, where there was an advanced amber-carving industry. Wessex was not a metal-producing area, but it was able to obtain amber through its role as a hub for a cross-Channel trade in metals between Britain and the Continent. Great Orme copper was likely traded to the Continent through Wessex, as with the Baltic amber that has been found in metal-producing areas in Iberia. One of the largest amber finds from Bronze Age Wessex comes from the grave of the so-called 'boy with the amber necklace' at Boscombe Down, only a few kilometres from Stonehenge. The boy died in his teens sometime around 1550 BC and was interred wearing a necklace of ninety Baltic amber beads around his neck. The necklace did not conform to local British styles, hinting that the boy might not have been a local. This was confirmed by analysis of the ratio of strontium to oxygen isotypes in his tooth enamel, which pointed to an upbringing in the Mediterranean area. Did the boy come to Britain for religious reasons – Stonehenge was still a revered ritual centre at the time of his death – or was he part of a group of itinerant metalworkers or amber traders? Irrespective, the boy embodies the long-distance connections between the Atlantic, the Baltic and the Mediterranean in the Bronze Age.

Shipwrecks and trade

One of the most important sources of information about trade in any period of history is shipwrecks. Because they so often contain commodities from many different locations, they can give a more complete picture of trade links at a particular moment in time than can archaeological sites on land. Bronze Age shipwrecks are relatively common in the Mediterranean, but they are rare in the Atlantic. This may be evidence that fewer ships plied the Bronze Age Atlantic, which is likely simply because it lacked the cities, kingdoms and empires which had developed around the

Mediterranean Sea by this time. However, the picture is probably distorted to some degree, because the Atlantic, with its strong tides and violent winter storms, can break up a sunken ship and scatter its cargo much more quickly than would happen in the comparatively placid Mediterranean, where a shipwreck can lie undisturbed for centuries.

The few shipwrecks that have been discovered confirm the existence of a flourishing trade in metals along the Atlantic coast. Probably the oldest, discovered on a dangerous reef near Salcombe in southwest England, dates to around 1200–1000 BC. The ship was probably sailing from France to Britain when it foundered just 100 metres from the rocky coastline, so close that at least some of the crew might have reached safety ashore. Over a period of fifteen years, divers recovered more than 300 artefacts from the wreck site, including 255 bun-shaped copper ingots and 31 very pure tin ingots. The cargo also included bronze palstave axes, bronze spear points and swords, and gold jewelry of northern French origin, as well as one bronze object of Sicilian origin. Probably all the metal artefacts were intended to be melted down and recast when they reached their destination, which was probably intended to be Britain. The ingots have been subjected to metallurgical analysis to try to determine their origin. The analysis ruled out a Mediterranean or Middle Eastern origin for the tin ingots, so they were most likely produced somewhere in Atlantic Europe, Cornish tin being the closest match. Ingots from this unidentified source were widely traded because ingots of identical composition also have been found in Bronze Age shipwrecks off Haifa in Israel and Uluburun in Turkey. The copper ingots had either a British or Atlantic European origin. A second Bronze Age shipwreck in British waters, at Langdon Cliff near Dover's harbour, contained at least 189 continental-style broken bronze tools and weapons; like those from the Salcombe wreck, these were scrap metal being exported to Britain, where it would be melted down and recast in new styles to suit local tastes.

Ships of the Bronze Age metal traders

We know, both from shipwrecks and from iconographical sources, that by around 2000 BC, sophisticated and seaworthy sailing ships were in widespread use in the Mediterranean, but much less is known about the ships used for trading along the Atlantic coast. The ships that were wrecked at Salcombe and Langdon Cliff were quite obviously engaged in long-distance maritime trade, but few clues survived about their construction or about where they were built. Just enough of the Salcombe ship survived to determine that it was built of planks and that it was about 12 metres long and 2 metres broad, but no evidence of its means of propulsion or construction method survived. No part of the Langdon Bay ship survived, so nothing can be said about the way it was built.

One of the best-preserved Bronze Age boats so far discovered anywhere is Ferriby 1, named for its find site near the village of North Ferriby on the Humber estuary in Yorkshire, England. This boat wasn't a shipwreck; it had simply been abandoned at the end of its useful life in a quiet muddy creek, where it was buried in silt before its timbers had a chance to rot away. It was quite a large vessel, over 13 metres long and 1.67 metres broad. Radiocarbon dated to between 1880 BC and 1680 BC, the boat was built of oak planks that had been sewn together, edge to edge, with lashings made of yew fibres, a technique which was used in other Bronze Age boats found in Britain. 'Sewn boats' were common in many parts of the world – for example, in Scandinavia, Russia, Egypt, the Indian Ocean, Southeast Asia and the Pacific – before metal fastenings became both widespread and affordable, and the technique has still not died out completely. The Ferriby boat was large enough to have carried up to thirty people and three tonnes of cargo or, with fewer people on board, up to five tonnes of cargo. The boat was paddled, but it might also have had a sail. Some maritime archaeologists have interpreted projections on the boat's base as supports for a mast, and sea trials with a full-sized modern replica, fitted with a light mast and sail, were successful. This is, of course, not the same thing as proving that it actually was a sailing ship. Loaded, Ferriby 1 would have had a freeboard of only about 40 centimetres, so some maritime archaeologists are sceptical that it would have been sailed on the open sea. However, a very similar, if slightly larger, boat, dated to around 1550 BC, that was found buried in an ancient creek at Dover in 1992, must have been used for sailing in the Channel, because there was nowhere else it could have sailed from this location. Like Ferriby 1, this was paddled, and there was no evidence that it carried a mast and sail.

Minoans in the Atlantic?

Open-sea voyages must have been very arduous if paddling was the only means of propulsion, but there is at least some evidence that the sail was known in the Bronze Age Atlantic. In 2009, archaeologists excavating a Bronze Age settlement at St Agnes in Cornwall's Scilly Isles, a known centre for the tin trade in the Iron Age, discovered a potsherd inscribed with a graffito of a sailing ship with a single mast and a long, raking prow. Dated to around 1300 BC, this may be the oldest evidence of the use of sailing ships in the Atlantic Ocean. More evidence for the presence of sailing ships in the Bronze Age Atlantic comes from three engravings of ships on rocks at Auga dos Cebros in Galicia which have been dated on stylistic grounds to 1325 BC–1050 BC. The three ships are crudely drawn, but all are obviously sailing ships, each carrying a single mast and rectangular sail. One has a distinctive beaked profile rather like an early eastern Mediterranean galley, while the other two have curved profiles that have been compared to a Bronze Age cargo ship discovered at Uluburun in southern Turkey. Were these locally built ships? Or might they have belonged to explorers or traders from the eastern Mediterranean?

There are certainly no contemporary records of direct merchant voyages between the metal-hungry civilizations of the eastern Mediterranean and the Atlantic before the arrival of Phoenician explorers around 1000 BC. Though these civilizations did acquire copper and tin from Atlantic Europe, they could have done so through any number of middlemen and have had absolutely no idea where it came from originally. If these ships did belong to visitors from the eastern Mediterranean, the most likely candidates would be the Minoan people of Crete, history's earliest recorded sea power. The Minoan civilization, which flourished from *c.*2000 BC to 1300 BC, was named after the legendary King Minos, who the ancient Greeks believed had ruled Crete three generations before the Trojan War, which they believed had ended with the fall of Troy in 1184 BC. In Greek myths, Minos cuts a rather sinister figure thanks to his association with the mythological half human-half bull monster, the Minotaur, which he kept locked in the original Labyrinth at his palace at Knossos and fed on captive Athenian youths. Other traditions remembered Minos more kindly, as a ruler so wise and just that, after his death, Zeus appointed him as one of the judges of the dead in Hades. In another tradition, recorded by the Athenian historian Thucydides (*c.*460 BC–400 BC), 'Minos was the first ruler to organize a navy. He controlled the greater part of what is now called the Hellenic Sea [the Aegean]; he ruled over the Cyclades islands, in most of which he founded the first colonies, putting his sons in as governors.'

Crete had neither copper nor tin, so the Minoans needed to trade. That wasn't a problem, as Crete produced four valuable and easily stored commodities: wheat, olive oil, woollen cloth and wine, which they exported across the eastern Mediterranean. The Minoans even had their own trading enclave at Avaris in Egypt's Nile Delta. Ships were essential to Crete's prosperity, and they feature prominently in Minoan art, such as a frieze showing a fleet of sailing ships in the Minoan palace at Akrotiri on the volcanic island of Thera (Santorini). Described as the 'Aegean Pompeii', the palace was buried by ash falls during a catastrophic eruption which blew the island apart, and generated tsunamis across the eastern Mediterranean in *c.*1628 BC. As in Pompeii, the ash preserved as much as it destroyed, and the frescoes, discovered in 1967, are still vibrantly coloured and detailed. The ships portrayed have a single mast with a single rectangular sail. The hulls are long and shallow, sharply upturned at the stern and long and raking at the prows like the ship portrayed on the St Agnes potsherd. The ships had no fixed rudders, instead being steered by a long oar at the stern, and many are shown with furled sails being paddled by around twenty men to each side. No details of the hull construction can been seen on the frescoes and in the only known Minoan shipwreck, no timbers survived, so it is not known how they were built, whether with planks or by some other method. These are the ships with which King Minos, if he really did exist, would have maintained his kingdom's economic and political hegemony in the eastern Mediterranean, but might they have sailed further afield? It's a romantic idea, but a few scratches on rocks and potsherds don't add up to a strong case.

The birth of a tradition

Scandinavians became Europe's most skilful and daring seafarers in the Viking Age, but there is little evidence that they ever sailed far from their own home coastal waters in prehistoric times. If there were direct maritime communications with the Atlantic metal-trading network, they were probably quite limited. Amber going to Britain and Ireland and gold and bronze going the other way need not have been carried all the way by sea. Despite this, there must have been a lot of short-distance seafaring, because local trade and social contact among the Danish islands and Norwegian fjords would have been impossible without it. Large quantities of marine food remains found in Bronze Age kitchen middens make it plain that the sea was also intensively exploited for subsistence by those Scandinavians who lived in coastal locations, where a hybrid farmer-fisher way of life developed. The importance of seafaring found artistic expression in thousands of ship images that were carved onto rocks and etched onto bronze pots and tools such as razors. Nowhere else in Bronze Age Europe is seafaring imagery so pervasive. Seafaring helped shape ideas about the afterlife. High-status graves were often marked with stone settings laid out in the shape of a ship, a practice which continued into the Viking Age (by which time the elite were being buried in real ships). The ship settings are generally considered to have been symbolic vessels that carried the deceased to the afterlife.

The ships most commonly portrayed in art are large canoes, many of them shown with crews of thirty or more warriors brandishing spears and axes. The ships are always shown in profile and have distinctive double-beaked prows at both ends. Some of the most accessible can be seen at Tanumshede on Sweden's west coast, where several hundred are depicted on sites spread across 51 hectares, along with scenes of warfare, hunting and agriculture. On the face of it, it would seem that Bronze Age Scandinavians were enthusiastically launching Viking-style raids on one another. Such raids certainly took place, but these images are unlikely to be recording actual voyages and battles. The warriors are often depicted in a rather obvious state of sexual arousal, which you might not expect if they were in a real battle, while the ships are often shown carrying sun discs, similar to that carried by the famous Trundholm sun chariot, and people playing lurs (a visually impressive type of long bronze horn). What these carvings depict are, therefore, mostly ritual or mythological scenes associated with a sun cult, with the boat conceived of as the vehicle for the sun's daily journey across the heavens.

While the scenes portrayed in art may have been ritual, the boats themselves were real enough. In 1921, a near-complete canoe was discovered in a bog at Hjortspring on the Danish island of Als together with sacrificed animals and enough weapons to have equipped a small army of at least 138 warriors. The boat and the weapons were likely to have been war booty sunk in the bog as an offering to the gods after a victory in battle. The boat itself dates to the early Iron Age, around 400 BC–300 BC, but, with its distinctive double-beaked prows, its appearance matches exactly that of those shown in Bronze Age petroglyphs. The boat was 19 metres long by 2 metres broad and was built from just five lime-wood planks: a broad keel plank with two narrower overlapping planks on each side. This method of building a hull from overlapped planks, known variously as clinker, lapstrake or Nordic construction, marks the Hjortspring boat out as the earliest known ancestor of the ships that the Norse would one day use to make the first Atlantic crossings. The ends of the Hjortspring boat were closed, with two carved wooden blocks which served as stemposts. The function, if any, of the projecting beaks is unknown: they don't seem to have had any structural function. They may have been intended to ride up over the gunwales of an enemy boat and capsize it, or they may simply be a hangover from an earlier stage in the development of the Nordic boat-building tradition that was retained because they gave the boat a sleek and racy appearance. No metal was used in the boat's construction: the planks were sewn together and fastened to internal strengthening ribs with ropes made of lime tree bast. The boat was paddled by a crew of twenty – a useful number for a raiding party – who sat on thwarts set at the level of the gunwale. There was a steering oar at both ends, so the boat could be sailed in either direction. This would have been a great advantage for raiding, because the boat could run right up a beach and the crew wouldn't have to turn it around if they needed to make a quick getaway. Sea trials with a replica have shown that it was a fast, stable, relatively seaworthy vessel, well suited to travel and raiding in coastal waters. At the time it was built, the Hjortspring boat was rather primitive compared to the ships that were then being used in the Mediterranean, and no one would have imagined that ships that evolved from these beginnings would, one day, be the first to cross the Atlantic.

The edge of the world

It isn't possible to say with any certainty what the prehistoric peoples of Atlantic Europe believed about the restless ocean they lived alongside. They must have had myths to explain its origin and stories and legends about what they believed might lie in it, but these were not literate societies so they have been long forgotten. Nevertheless, the accurate alignments on significant astronomical events preserved in hundreds of Neolithic and Bronze Age tombs and stone circles are enough to prove that they must have had well-developed cosmological beliefs. Another expression of these is the remarkable Nebra Sky Disc found at a ritual site in central Germany in association with a hoard of bronze tools and weapons. On the basis of the types of bronze tools and weapons that the disc was found with, this unique object has been dated to around 1600 BC.* This would make it the oldest representation of the cosmos ever found anywhere, predating by over a century the next oldest, painted in an Egyptian tomb. The 30-centimetre-diameter disc is a thoroughly international artefact, illustrating the connectedness of the Bronze Age world, made with copper from Austria, tin from Cornwall and gold from Cornwall and the Carpathian Mountains. The disc shows, marked out in thin gold foil, the Sun, a crescent Moon and two arcs representing the east and west horizons for the rising and setting positions of the Sun at the summer and winter solstices, each of them taking up 82 degrees of the circumference of the disc, which exactly reproduces the angular distance between sunrise and sunset in the summer and winter solstices at the latitude where the disc was found (51° north). The disc also portrays the instantly recognizable star cluster of the Pleiades, whose rising in the evening sky signals the onset of winter. There is also a semicircular gold band that could be either a rainbow or, more likely, a 'sun boat' motif. The disc was deposited in the earth, a practice associated with chthonic deities, so, in this cosmos, there was an underworld through which the heavenly bodies passed at night. Most interpretations of the disc see it as a two-dimensional model of a flat earth under a hemispherical sky across which the Sun, Moon and

* It is only fair to say that the Bronze Age date is not universally accepted: some archaeologists believe that the disc dates to the Iron Age.

stars moved, and leaves little room to doubt that, when Bronze Age Europeans looked out to sea, they believed that somewhere beyond the horizon there lay an edge to the world.

Celtic Otherworlds and Norse monsters

The human imagination hates a void, so it might be expected that the prehistoric peoples who lived along the Atlantic coast would sooner or later have begun to speculate about what might lie at the edges of their world. There's no way to know for certain what the people of the Bronze Age thought lay over the horizon, but some of their beliefs may have fed into those mythological traditions of their Iron Age pagan Celtic and Norse descendants that survived long enough to be recorded during the early Christian period. The Iron Age Celts of Britain and Ireland believed that the souls of the dead travelled with the setting sun into the western ocean to spend their afterlives on paradisiacal Otherworldly islands such as Tír na nÓg, the 'Land of the Young', whose inhabitants suffered neither sickness, old age nor death; Emain Ablach ('Emain of the Apples'), home of the sea god Mannanán mac Lir, the 'son of the sea', who could cloak his home in a mist of invisibility; and Annwfn, the prototype for the Avalon of medieval Arthurian legend. For Irish pagans, the island of Tech Duinn (House of the Dark One), often identified with the Bull Rock off the Beara Peninsula, was the place where the underworld god Donn gathered the souls of the dead before their onward journeys to the afterlife. The living could travel to these Otherworldly islands, either at the invitation of an Otherworldly being or by voyaging. However, it was always easier for a living mortal to find the Otherworld than to leave it. The Otherworlds existed in their own spatial and temporal plane which only intersected with the world of mortals. Those who returned to the world of the living felt that they had remained in the blissful Otherworld for weeks or months only to find that when they got home, many years had passed. A character from one legendary tale, Nechtan, lingered in the Otherworld so long that he far exceeded his mortal life span and instantly dissolved into dust the moment he set foot in Ireland again. These Celtic Otherworldly islands haunted the imaginations of mariners long after the pagan beliefs that had spawned them died out.

The pagan Norse vision of the Atlantic was an altogether darker one than the Celts'. The late Iron Age Norse conceived of the cosmos as a series of stacked plates, all linked by a vast sacred ash tree called Yggdrasil. The gods dwelled in the celestial realm of Asgard and the realm of the dead was the dank and cheerless underworld of Niflheim. In between was Midgard, the realm of humans. Midgard was surrounded by an ocean, on the far side of which was Jotunheim, the realm of the Jotun, malevolent agents of chaos who the gods had banished to the edges of the world. In the depths of the ocean lurked a fearsome ally of the Jotun, the mighty Jormundgandr, a serpent so vast that it completely encircled Midgard and could bite its own tail. So long as Jormungandr held on to its tail, life would continue, but when it let go, Ragnarok, the end of the world in battle, fire and flood, would quickly follow. However, when the Norse set out to explore the Atlantic in earnest in the ninth century, they seem to have been completely undeterred by thoughts of what terrors might lie on its far shores or lurk within its depths. All they saw was opportunity.

3

Masters of the sea

1100 BC–400 BC

Merchants for many isles – City of Heracles – Far Tarshish – The deer king – A contested identity – The Purple Isles – Following the Phoenician Bear – The ships of Tarshish – Carthaginian explorers – The first of the phantom islands – The Guanche problem – Hanno the Navigator – Did the Phoenicians circumnavigate Africa? – A fate worse than death

When Yahweh called on him to travel to Nineveh, the capital of the fearsome Assyrian Empire, and pronounce his judgement on its sinful people, the Biblical prophet Jonah was horrified and decided to put as much distance between himself and his god as he possibly could. He fled to the Mediterranean port of Jaffa and took passage on a merchant ship heading to the farthest land he knew of, the land of Tarshish. Jonah wasn't allowed to get that far, of course. Yahweh whipped up an almighty storm that threatened to sink the ship; sensing that its fury was unnatural, the terrified sailors cast lots to determine who had brought this misfortune upon them and, finding that it was Jonah, they threw him overboard to be swallowed by a 'great fish' that regurgitated him back onto the shore to give him a second chance to do Yahweh's will. Chastened, Jonah got the message: nowhere was too far away to escape from Yahweh's power. He promptly hurried off to perform his mission in Nineveh. Tarshish, the land Jonah never got to, is the Biblical name for Tartessos, the first historical kingdom of the Atlantic world, which lay at the very edge of the Old Testament's known world, in a place where geography shaded into legend.

Merchants for many isles

If there is any truth in the story, the sailors who were taking Jonah to Tartessos would have been Phoenicians, the people the ancient Greeks called 'the masters of the sea'. Cousins of the Canaanites and the Hebrews, the Phoenicians had a narrowly confined homeland on the coast of modern-day Syria, Lebanon and northern Israel, squeezed between the Mediterranean Sea on one side and the 3,000-metre-high Lebanon Mountains on the other. Phoenicia was a crossroads where the spheres of influence of the Egyptian, Mesopotamian, Anatolian and Greek civilizations met, mixed and, all too often, violently conflicted. It wasn't an easy place to live, as the Phoenicians frequently had to pay tribute to their mightier neighbours, but this made them the natural middlemen in regional trade, a role this enterprising people seized with alacrity. Blessed with possession of the best natural harbours in the eastern Mediterranean, small ports began to develop here as early as the third millennium BC, trading cedar wood, wine, olive oil, copper, woollen cloth, ivory, glass and an eye-wateringly expensive dye known as Tyrian purple with Egypt and the emerging Mesopotamian empires of Assyria and Babylon. By around 1100 BC, the most successful of these ports, Sidon (Sayda), Byblos (Jubayl), Arvad (Arwad) and Tyre, had developed into independent city-states, each under its own king. Although geographically insignificant, contemporaries were impressed by Phoenicia's wide connections. Tyre, always the dominant Phoenician city, was described in the Old Testament as 'the entry of the sea' and 'a merchant for many isles' whose borders 'are in the midst of the sea' (Ezekiel 17:4). This was a different kind of power, one defined not by territory and martial conquest but by fleets and commerce – a thalassocracy.

Taking advantage of growing demand for metals and exotic prestige goods by the ruling elites of Assyria and Babylon, the Phoenicians wove a steadily expanding web of trade routes beyond the Levant and Egypt, first to Cyprus (a rich source of copper) and Greece and then to North Africa, Malta, Sicily, Sardinia and Iberia: they were probably the first people who really knew the Mediterranean Sea as a whole and not just their own corner of it. Along the way they founded dozens of colonies at strategically located anchorages, giving them control of the trade routes to the west. Phoenician expansion was not militaristic. Colonies were usually founded by agreement with local rulers, who welcomed the Phoenicians for the trade they brought. Through their trade, the Phoenicians began to link the Middle East, the Mediterranean and the Atlantic fringe into a single economic zone and, in doing so, they laid the foundations for the Mediterranean-centred civilization of Classical Greece and Rome. Even today, their influence persists visibly in everything we read. The Phoenicians wrote with the Canaanite alphabet, the ancestor of all modern alphabets,* and they took it with them on their voyages across the Mediterranean, to Greece, Italy, North Africa and, in Spain, even to the shores of the Atlantic Ocean and, in so doing, they began its recorded history.

By around 1000 BC, Phoenician explorers had reached the Strait of Gibraltar. Before them lay the Atlantic Ocean, behind them the familiar inland sea that had nurtured their seafaring skills. These pioneers might well have hesitated and taken a deep breath before sailing through. Even before they reached the strait, they would have noticed a change in the sea: a strong current flows constantly into the Mediterranean to replace the water lost to evaporation during its hot summers. Though they didn't know it, they were literally sailing uphill, the surface of the Mediterranean being lower than the Atlantic thanks to all

* Hangul, the Korean alphabet, invented in 1443, is a possible exception: academics disagree whether this was a completely independent invention or was inspired by the example of Western alphabets.

that evaporation. Once through the strait, nothing in their experience would have prepared them for the Atlantic's surging tides and powerful storms, but it would have been the knowledge that they were crossing a significant cosmic threshold that made them most apprehensive. Some felt the need to appease their gods before crossing, stopping at Gorham's Cave on the Rock of Gibraltar to make votive offerings, unaware, of course, that in the rubble under their feet lay the remains of those Neanderthals who had been among the first humans to have lived on the Atlantic, 140,000 years before. The Phoenicians shared a common cosmology with the Babylonians, Assyrians, Israelites and other peoples of the ancient Middle East. Old Testament authors described the Earth as a flat disc floating in a global ocean with the heavens above and the underworld below. Beyond the ocean was a ring of mountains, described in the Old Testament as 'the ends of the Earth', which supported the heavens. In this cosmology, it would be possible to sail to the edge of the world but not over it. This world view is the same as that depicted on the oldest known world map, made in Babylon in *c.*600 BC. The map, inscribed on a clay tablet, shows the Babylonian known world completely surrounded by a circular ocean of uncertain breadth fringed on its far side by the mountainous 'outer regions' which held up the heavens. The first Phoenicians who sailed on that ocean must have feared being blown helplessly out to sea to whatever lay at 'the ends of the Earth'. Just as bad was the fear of what might lie beneath the waves. The ocean was believed to be home to the *tanninim*, sea serpents who represented chaos and evil in Canaanite and Hebrew mythology, and the seven-headed serpentine monster Lotan, implacable adversary of the Canaanite storm god Baal Hadad and prototype for other mythological sea monsters such as the Biblical Leviathan. Farmers might be able to tame the land, but who could tame the ever-changing, unpredictable, sea? It was the natural refuge of the forces of cosmological chaos. The Phoenicians quickly discovered that their worst fears were unfounded, but that only encouraged them to circulate lurid tales of sea monsters and other dangers to discourage commercial rivals from following them and taking a share of the riches they had found. The Greeks were never too sure how seriously to take Phoenician sea stories, and the philosopher Plato compared 'Phoenician tales' to myths and lies. However, once seeded with sea monsters, the Atlantic would never be free of them again.

The Phoenician explorers knew what they were looking for, and that it was worth the risks. Somewhere in the Ocean was the land of Kassiterid, the source of tin and other desirable metals. Once through the strait, they followed the Atlantic coast north and west along the Iberian coast and tapped into the long-established Atlantic metals trade, founding colonies and *emporia* (trading posts) as they went. Though it's not impossible, claims that the Phoenicians sailed as far as the tin-mining districts in southwest Britain are probably just romantic speculation: there is certainly no hard evidence that they ever did so. Although some Phoenician artefacts have been discovered further north, at present, the northernmost archaeologically attested Phoenician trading post is at Santa Olaia, at the mouth of the Mondego river, about 150 kilometres north of Lisbon, where evidence of another Phoenician trading post has been found beneath the city's Romanesque cathedral. Trading posts or settlements, each roughly a day's sailing apart, are also known at Alcácer do Sal, Portimão, Tavira, Castro Marim, Huelva, Cádiz and Carteia on the Bay of Gibraltar. The northern limit of Phoenician trade was probably determined by politics rather than by distance and seafaring ability. The Phoenicians lacked the military muscle to hold on to their colonies and trading posts by force. For their trade to flourish they needed the security that only cooperative local rulers with stable polities could give. In the early first millennium BC, such polities did not yet exist much further north than Portugal, effectively limiting Phoenician commercial expansion.

City of Heracles

Cádiz, known to the Phoenicians as Gadir (meaning 'the compound'), became the most important of Phoenicia's Atlantic colonies. When the Phoenicians first arrived there, 3,000 years ago, the Bay of Cádiz was much wider than it is today, while the peninsula on which the city stands was then a chain of narrow islands. It was on the northernmost of these islands, known as Erytheia by the Greeks, that the Phoenicians founded their colony of Gadir: Phoenicians typically preferred such sites for their colonies, conveniently close to land for trading purposes but also easy to defend if relations with the locals turned sour. By around 800 BC, Gadir had grown into a flourishing city – the first city on the Atlantic – and was beginning to spread onto the neighbouring islands, which eventually were all linked together by a causeway. The city boasted three impressive temples, to the storm god Baal Hamon, to Astarte, a goddess of sexuality but also associated with the stars and navigation, and to Melqart, the patron god of Tyre, Gadir's parent city. Outside this temple, following Tyrian custom, stood two bronze or gold pillars, each 8 cubits (about 4 metres) tall, erected in honour of Melqart. The temple became a major cult centre, not only for Phoenicians and local Iberians but also for Greeks and Romans to whom Melqart was the Tyrian incarnation of the demi-god Heracles. Devotees of Melqart-Heracles who came to sacrifice at this temple included Hannibal and Julius Caesar, though much good did it do either of them in the end. Another famous visitor was the well-travelled Greek geographer Posidonius (135 BC–51 BC), who wrote that the pillars of Melqart had been erected by Heracles himself to mark the edge of the world. Later tradition held that the twin pillars were inscribed with the warning *non plus ultra*, 'nothing further beyond'.

At least to begin with, Gadir was subject to Tyre but, being three months' sailing away, it was never going to be under close parental control, and by the seventh century, it had become the independent hub of a trading network that extended for hundreds of kilometres out along the Atlantic coasts of Iberia and Morocco. Gadir's shallow tidal bay and its warm, sunny climate were ideal for making salt, the ancient world's most important preservative, by evaporating sea water. Combined with rich fisheries off shore, Gadir became a centre for exporting salted fish and for producing a pungent fermented fish sauce which rapidly became wildly popular across the Mediterranean. The Romans, who called it *garum*, loved it so much some of them even drank it. The downside for its fans, as the poet Martial ironically implied when he congratulated a friend for his determination in trying to seduce a girl who had eaten six portions of *garum* for dinner, was bad breath. Fish sauce was a sideline for Gadir, however; its prosperity mainly came from its key role as middleman in the metal trade between the Atlantic fringe and the eastern Mediterranean.

Far Tarshish

Just one day's sail further west from Gadir was the kingdom of Tartessos, the Bible's Tarshish, centred on the valleys of the Tinto and Guadalquivir rivers. Tartessos's control extended north along the Tinto river into the Sierra Morena, a 400-kilometre-long range of rolling granite mountains richly seamed with silver, lead, gold, copper and tin ores, which, by this time, had already been mined on a small scale since as early as 4000 BC. It was this mineral wealth that earned Tartessos its fabulous reputation in the Middle East, the source, according to the Book of Ezekiel, of 'a multitude of all kind of riches' (27:12). Early Greek poets sang of 'silver-rooted Tartessos'. Another admirer was the Israelite King Solomon (r. *c.*970 BC–931 BC), who secured access to the riches of 'far Tarshish' through an alliance with Hiram, the King of Tyre. The all-conquering Assyrian King Esarhaddon (r. 681 BC–669 BC) claimed that Tartessos paid tribute to him: 'all the kings from the lands surrounded by the sea – from the country of Cyprus and Libya, as far as Tartessos – bowed to my feet,' he boasted. In reality, the Assyrians were not really sure where Tartessos actually was, so Esarhaddon was simply hoping that, by claiming it as his own, some of the fabled kingdom's glamour would rub off on him.

The natural outlet for Tartessos's metallic wealth was the port of Huelva, located at the confluence of the Tinto and Odiel rivers, a few kilometres from the open Atlantic. A large settlement began to develop here around 1250 BC, but there is no archaeological evidence for direct contacts with the Phoenicians dating to before around 1000 BC, when for the first time artefacts from the eastern Mediterranean began to be imported. Wine, olive oil, jewellery and ivory seem to have been the products most in demand. From around 900 BC, large amounts of Phoenician pottery were imported into Huelva. It is likely that much of this pottery was intended for the domestic use of Phoenician merchants who were now living permanently at Huelva. The Tartessians did not allow the Phoenicians to monopolize the metals trade. Greeks from Samos and Phocaea traded with Huelva in the late seventh and early sixth centuries BC. The substantial quantities of Greek pottery found at Huelva suggest that Greek merchants did not only visit but were also permitted to live permanently at Huelva, no doubt to the annoyance of the Phoenicians, who can't have welcomed the competition. A sixth-century BC Corinthian helmet recovered from the Odiel also speaks of a Greek presence. Regular visitors included metal traders from as far north as the tin-mining districts in Britain and all points in between, making Huelva a very cosmopolitan port. Huelva's wide-ranging connections are evident in a bronze hoard which was recovered from the Odiel near Huelva in 1923. The hoard contained over 400 items, including 78 swords, at least one of which was from Sicily, 22 daggers, 88 spearheads, some of Irish manufacture, fibula brooches from Phoenicia and a helmet. Fragments of wood associated with the finds have been radiocarbon dated to around 950 BC. When first discovered, the hoard was believed to be from a shipwreck, but it is now, on the basis of its location, thought more likely to be a votive hoard. The hoard's find spot, in salt marshes at the mouth of a river, is a classic liminal location where the different elements of land, salt water, fresh water and air all met in close proximity. It was in such places, European people of the Bronze and Iron Ages believed, that the boundary between this world and the Otherworld became very thin, so offerings placed in them would be most easily received by their intended recipients.

The arrival of Mediterranean traders caused a boom in the local mining industry, aided by the introduction of new smelting techniques by craftsmen from Cyprus and Phoenicia who worked alongside Tartessians in the mining districts. Silver was the metal most in demand. In the Rio Tinto mining areas, an astonishing 15 million tonnes of slag from smelting silver ores had accumulated by 500 BC. Lead pollution from smelting at the Tinto mines has been detected in ice cores drilled from the Greenland ice cap: it was the first time anywhere that human industrial activity had reached a scale sufficient for it to leave a global footprint. The spike in demand for silver was caused by the Assyrian Empire adopting a silver standard which linked all values to standard weights of silver, not only for trade goods but also for its subjects' taxes and the tribute paid by its vassals (who sometimes included the Phoenicians themselves). As Assyria was the dominant power of the Middle East, everyone needed silver. Globalization is thought of as a modern phenomenon, but 3,000 years ago, an administrative decision in Iraq could have an environmental impact on the far side of the Atlantic. Huge quantities of silver, most of it from Tartessos, were accumulated across the eastern Mediterranean and the Middle East, making possible one of the most important economic innovations of all time, the introduction of coinage for commercial transactions. The ubiquity of silver as a means of exchange eventually led to the introduction of silver tokens of standardized weight and purity, otherwise known as coins. The Greeks believed that the first coinage was issued by King Alyattes of Lydia in western Anatolia *c.*600 BC, but within a century the use of coins, most of them containing Tartessian silver, was widespread in the Mediterranean and Middle East.

The deer king

Only two of Tartessos's kings are known by name. The earliest of them, Habis, is the kingdom's semi-legendary founder who reigned during the never-never land of proto-history. Habis's legend only survives thanks to a summary of a lost history by a Gallo-Roman historian called Pompeius Trogus (*fl. c.*50 BC) written by an otherwise anonymous Roman author called Justin in AD 391:

> The forests of the Tartessians, in which it is said that the Titans waged war against the gods, were inhabited by the Curetes [a mythical Greek tribe], whose most ancient king Gargaris was the first to collect honey. This ruler, having a grandson born to him, his illegitimate offspring by his own daughter, tried various means, through shame for her unchastity [obviously, it was her fault he'd seduced her], to have the child put to death.

The child was abandoned in the wilderness but, thanks to the protection of the gods, he survived and was nursed by a deer – he grew antlers as a result – until one day Habis was captured by peasants, whose food he had tried to steal, and taken to the king. Despite his antlers, Gargaris immediately recognized the feral child as his grandson and repented of his actions.

> From admiration at his escapes from so many mischances and perils, he was appointed by his grandfather to succeed him on the throne. The name given to him was Habis ['he who was lost']; and, as soon as he became king, he gave such proofs of greatness, that he seemed to have been deliberately rescued, through the power of the gods, from so many exposures to death. He united the barbarous people by laws; he was the first who taught them to break oxen for the plough, and to raise corn from tillage; and he obliged them, instead of eating food procured from the wilds, to adopt a better diet, perhaps through dislike of what he had eaten in his childhood. The adventures of this prince might

> seem fabulous, were not the founders of Rome said to have been suckled by a wolf, and Cyrus, king of the Persians, to have been brought up by a dog. He ordered that the people should not carry out servile duties, and he divided the population among seven cities. After Habis was dead, the sovereignty was retained for many generations by his successors.[5]

Tartessos was already ancient history by Trogus's time – the kingdom had broken up around 500 BC – so Roman writers must have learned about the myth from the Phoenicians or Greeks, who had been the kingdom's main trading partners, and therefore it's not unlikely that it has been given a Classical makeover in the retelling. Habis emerges from the myth as a typical 'culture-hero' figure like the Greek Prometheus, who gives the benefits of the civilized arts to his people, while Trogus himself acknowledged the parallels with the story of Romulus and Remus, the mythological founders of Rome, who were abandoned by their Vestal Virgin mother in order to avoid public shame.

The other Tartessian king whose name is known is Arganthonios, who, according to Herodotus, ruled for eighty years before dying around 550 BC aged 120. Arganthonios's name seems to be related to the Indo-European word for silver (as in Latin *argentum* or Gaelic *airgead*), so it might be that merchants had mistaken a title, perhaps meaning 'treasurer' or something like it, for a personal name; this could account for Arganthonios's improbably long reign: he was not one ruler but a succession of rulers holding the same office. Because of its close contacts with Phoenicia and Greece, culturally, Tartessos came to belong more to the eastern Mediterranean than to the Atlantic. The Phoenicians introduced to the Atlantic world the new technologies of iron smelting and the potter's wheel. Tartessians adopted the Phoenician practice of building with ashlar stone, Phoenician temple, palace and tomb styles, and burial practices. Tartessian pottery, jewellery and ivory carving (a craft introduced by the Phoenicians) all incorporated eastern Mediterranean decorative motifs, such as griffins and sphinxes, transplanted far from their native environments; but perhaps the most important borrowing was writing. It is not going too far to describe Tartessos at its peak as an Atlantic-Phoenician hybrid.

A contested identity

When the Tartessians adopted writing using the Phoenician alphabet around 825 BC, theirs became the first literate civilization of the Atlantic. Later Greek writers believed that the Tartessians kept verse records of their history and laws, but all that has survived is ninety-five short inscriptions on aristocratic grave markers. Translating these inscriptions is the key to identifying who the Tartessians were, but there is no agreement among linguists about whether this is possible. A minority group claim to have identified words and phrases in the surviving inscriptions that point to Tartessian being a Celtic language. If they are right, many of the established assumptions about the origins of the Celts will need to be revised, because Celtic languages are currently not thought to have been spoken in Iberia before the sixth century BC. However, a large majority of linguists strongly reject this view, arguing that Tartessian vowel forms and word order is incompatible with Celtic language and that any similarities are largely coincidental. Their view is that Tartessian is a 'language isolate', that is, it is a language which is unrelated to any other known language: Euskara, the Basque language, is one of the best-known examples of an isolate today. Translating an extinct language isolate is usually only possible with the help of a bilingual inscription, like the Rosetta Stone, which was the key to deciphering Ancient Egyptian hieroglyphs. A Tartessian-Phoenician or Tartessian-Greek inscription would resolve the issue if one was found, but how likely is that? Given the lack of consensus among linguists, it is likely that the identity of the Tartessians will continue to be disputed for the foreseeable future.

The Purple Isles

On the African shore of the Strait of Gibraltar, the Phoenicians founded their first settlement at Tangier, within sight of Carteia on the opposite shore. Further south, they found an open coast of surf-pounded sandy beaches with only a few good harbours. Here the main Phoenician settlement was at Lixus, near modern Larache at the mouth of the Loukkos river. Another day's sail south, they founded Chella, near Rabat, and beyond that, 400 kilometres distant, was the Phoenicians' most southerly settlement on the small barren island of Mogador, lying a few kilometres offshore in the harbour of the modern Moroccan port of Essaouira. The attraction of Lixus and the other North African settlements was to take advantage of the Berber-controlled trans-Saharan trade routes to obtain ivory and gold from tropical West Africa. The attractions of Mogador were quite different: it had the resources to make the precious Tyrian purple dye. The dye – 6,6'-dibromoindigo to chemists – is produced in the mucus glands of carnivorous murex sea snails. The snails are widespread on rocky shorelines but there are only a few places where they are abundant enough to make harvesting them for dye-making a commercially viable proposition. One is the coastline of the eastern Mediterranean, another is the coast of Tunisia (an area intensely settled by Phoenicians), and there was Mogador and its surrounding surf-lashed islets and reefs, the *Purpura Insulae* ('Purple Islands').

Tyrian purple was so closely associated with the Phoenicians that it gave them the name by which they have been known since Homer's time at least, from 'phoinix', the Ancient Greek word for red. Weight for weight, the dye was by far the most valuable of the commodities traded by the Phoenicians, costing more than its weight in gold. It was not simply its intense colour that made Tyrian purple so desirable, it was, unlike the plant-based dyes that were most commonly used in ancient times, extremely colour-fast. Exposure to sunlight only made it brighter. Affordable only to the very wealthy, cloth dyed with Tyrian purple was one of the ultimate status symbols of the ancient Mediterranean world. In the Roman Empire, sumptuary laws permitted only those of patrician rank or above to wear purple-dyed clothing, and 'to be born in the purple' came to mean 'to possess royal blood'.

The price of Tyrian purple was justified by its astonishingly labour-intensive production. As it took around 10,000 snails to produce just a single gram of dye, the murex needed to be harvested in their millions. Most of the gathering was done by freedivers (working without breathing apparatus), but traps baited with shellfish were also used: it was arduous and dangerous work anywhere, but it was especially so in the strong tides and currents around Mogador Island. Dye works had seawater tanks where live snails could be stored until sufficient had been collected to start production. The mucus glands were individually removed by hand from the larger snails, but the smaller ones were simply crushed en-masse, shell and all, to extract the dye. The snails produce the dye, which contains active organobromine sedatives, primarily to immobilize their prey, but they also expel it as a defence mechanism, and this was triggered by the crushing. In Phoenician legend, it was the god Melqart, or, more exactly, his dog, who discovered that dye could be extracted by snails this way. Walking with its master along the seashore, Melqart's dog picked up a murex in its mouth and, by trying to bite through its shell, caused the snail to expel the dye. Archaeological evidence suggests that the Phoenicians really learned the technique from the Minoans of Crete, who had discovered it around 2000 BC.

The exact process of turning the colourful slime into the brilliant purple dye was a closely guarded secret, lost since the fall of the Roman Empire, but according to Pliny the Elder, the Roman naturalist whose curiosity famously proved fatal when he went to investigate the eruption of Vesuvius in AD 79, the mucus was boiled with urine and salt for nine days in lead tanks. The smell of this unappetizing seafood soup was exquisitely nauseating; a mariner searching for a Phoenician port in poor visibility might have been able to smell it before he saw it. Dye works were always built downwind from settlements so that the stench was blown away from people's homes: Mogador, remote, in those days, from major settlements, was an ideal site in this respect. However, this remoteness may also have been a commercial disadvantage, because the island was abandoned at least twice before dye production ceased permanently in the late Roman period. Not much remains to be seen of the Phoenician enterprise, just a ruined fort and the equally ruinous watchtower, or *migdal*, from which Mogador's name is derived. In its later history, Mogador has been a hermitage for a Muslim holy man, a fortress, a prison and a quarantine station for pilgrims returning from the Hajj; it is now a protected nature reserve, so the murex can stalk their prey undisturbed.

Mogador was also a base for 'silent trade' expeditions further south along the African coast. Common in pre-colonial Africa, silent trade wasn't stealthy, it was a way for people to do business together where, because they did not share any common language, they could not communicate verbally. Herodotus described how the Phoenicians conducted their silent trade on the African coast, by first unloading their merchandise and laying it out on the shore. They then lit a fire to send smoke signals to the local inhabitants that there was an opportunity to trade, before withdrawing to their ships. The local traders came to the shore, inspected the merchandise, laid down an amount of gold and then withdrew. The Phoenicians returned to the shore, examined the amount of gold: if they thought it was fair payment for the goods offered, they would take the gold and sail away. If, on the other hand, they thought it insufficient, the Phoenicians returned to their ship and waited to see if the local traders offered more gold. The Phoenicians would not touch the gold until they were happy that it was adequate payment for their merchandise. Nor would the local traders touch the merchandise until the Phoenicians had taken the gold. Herodotus claims that neither party ever tried to cheat the other. It would certainly not have been in either party's interests to do so if they wanted the trade to continue. No doubt the Phoenicians traded in the same way along the European Atlantic coast, where they would have faced the same obstacle of mutually incomprehensible languages.

Following the Phoenician Bear

The Greeks, no mean navigators themselves, believed that the Phoenicians were the first seafarers regularly to sail out of sight of land. According to the poet Callimachus, they gained the confidence to do this after learning to use the constellation of the Little Bear (Ursa Minor) to find the direction of north. This wasn't quite as easy as it is today, because 3,000 years ago there was no prominent star marking the position of the celestial pole. Because the direction of the Earth's rotational axis moves in a 25,000-year cycle, a phenomenon called precession, the position of the celestial pole slowly drifts against the background stars: sometimes there is a Pole Star, sometimes there isn't. For the last 1,600 years, the celestial pole has lain conveniently close to Polaris, the star at the tip of the Little Bear's tail, making it easy to locate precisely, but in Phoenician times it lay in the black void between the two stars, Kochab and Pherkad, which form the bear's head, so its position could only be estimated. However, this was quite good enough for the enclosed waters of the Mediterranean. The Greeks called this constellation the Phoenician Bear to distinguish it from the Great Bear (Ursa Major), which was the constellation they relied on to find the direction of north. Stellar navigation enabled the Phoenicians to sail at night but, for the most part, they preferred to minimize risks, sailing mostly in daylight, close to the coast, navigating by landmarks on shore, and anchoring in the safety of a harbour overnight. The only navigational device available to the Phoenicians was the leadline, essentially just a weight on the end of a rope, which was to gauge the depth of water when sailing close to the shore. To avoid winter storms, the Phoenician sailing season was short, from March to October: seafaring could be dangerous even in summer, and there was no point in taking unnecessary risks. Not paying proper respect to the gods was another avoidable risk. Before setting out on any voyage, Phoenician seafarers poured libations of wine and burned incense as offerings to the storm gods Baal Shamem and Baal Saphon, in whose hands they believed their safety ultimately lay. Offering-cups, portable altars and incense burners have been found in Phoenician shipwrecks, so the initial offerings are likely to have been topped up regularly throughout a voyage. Phoenicians did not see any real distinction between such appeasement rituals and practical navigational skills such as being able to set a course by the Little Bear. The gods of the ancient world were very much forces of nature, and they needed to be taken into account just as much as the direction of the wind and the height of the waves. Another Phoenician innovation was the first written navigation manuals, known in Greek as *periploi*, and in Latin as *peripli.* Meaning 'a sailing-around', a periplus gave brief notes on distances between harbours and useful landmarks as well as more detailed accounts of voyages of exploration. Committing useful navigational information to writing allowed it to be shared more widely, and accurately, than by word of mouth alone.

The ships of Tarshish

Phoenicians invested heavily in their ships, for without them they were nothing. The Phoenician way of building ships was, to the modern mind, rather counterintuitive. Most modern wooden ships and boats are built frame first – that is the keel is laid, the frames are attached to the keel and the hull is built up by fastening the planks onto them. In complete contrast, Phoenician shipwrights began by laying the keel, which was often little more than an extra-thick plank, and then attaching the planks of the hull. The hull's planks were precisely shaped to fit almost seamlessly edge to edge and then fastened tightly together with pegged mortise-and-tenon joints. While the tenons were made of hardwoods, like cedar or holm oak, the planks were made of soft woods like pine, which would absorb water and swell, tightening the fit of the planks both to the tenons and to one another. No plans were used, the shaping of the hull being judged by eye as work progressed. Frames were added as secondary strengthening only after the hull was completed and then only if they were needed. This method of shipbuilding required advanced joinery skills, and was very time-consuming, but it resulted in an exceptionally strong, watertight hull: no metal fastenings were used and only a little caulking or tarring was necessary for waterproofing. Phoenician merchant ships looked quite tub-like; they're often described in ancient texts as 'round ships'. They were built broad in relation to their length – the ratio of length to beam was about 3:1 – with deep, rounded hulls for maximum cargo capacity. The ships carried a single square-rigged sail and were steered by two side rudders, one on either side of the ship at the stern. 'Round ships' did not have great windward sailing ability, so, most of the time, captains would have waited until the wind was blowing in the right direction before setting out on a voyage. Such ships could be rowed by six or seven oarsmen on each side, but it would have been hard work, very slow and not really worth the effort except under dire circumstances, such as the storm that nearly sank Jonah's ship. Phoenician merchant ships started out quite small by modern standards; one of the earliest so far discovered, at Uluburun off southern Turkey, built around 1400 BC, was only 16 metres long, with a cargo capacity of about 20 tonnes. However, this building technique was capable of considerable scaling up, and by the sixth century BC, Phoenician ships carried around 45 tonnes of cargo. This was still nowhere near the limit, and by Roman times ships built this way could reach 55 metres in length and carry up to 1,200 tonnes of cargo: such large ships would not be built again until the seventeenth century, at least not in the West. As well as sailing ships, the Phoenicians built sailing galleys, equipped with bronze rams to sink enemy ships, to defend their cities from seaborne assault and also for transporting armies and settlers to newly founded colonies.

In the Bible, Phoenician merchant ships are described as 'ships of Tarshish'. Despite their modest proportions, to contemporaries they were technological and aesthetic marvels. The prophet Ezekiel's description of the materials used to construct a ship of Tarshish reads like a gazetteer of the world as it was known to the Hebrews:

> They have made all thy ship boards of fir trees of Senir [Mount Hermon]: they have taken cedars from Lebanon to make masts for thee. Of the oaks of Bashan [an Amorite kingdom in Jordan] have they made thine oars; the company of the Ashurites [one of the Twelve Tribes of Israelites] have made thy benches of ivory, brought out of the isles of Chittim [Cyprus]. Fine linen with broidered work from Egypt was that which thou spreadest forth to be thy sail: blue and purple from the isles of Elishah [Greece or Sicily] was that which covered thee. (Ezekiel 27:5–7)

Ezekiel might have added that Phoenician ships sported carvings of horse's heads on their prows, though it's not certain what they symbolized, and that they had ever watchful eyes painted on their prows to frighten off sea monsters and evil spirits. A Phoenician merchant ship was for show as well as hard use.

Carthaginian explorers

In 573 BC, Tyre submitted to the Babylonian Empire after a thirteen-year siege. The result was an almost complete collapse of the Phoenician trading system and the abandonment of nearly half of their overseas bases, including the dye production facility at Mogador. Offerings of high-status eastern Mediterranean imports quickly disappeared from the graves of Tartessian aristocrats. The resulting maritime and commercial power vacuum in the western Mediterranean was filled by Tyre's most successful colony, Carthage, which became independent under the kings of the Magonid dynasty. From its foundation in the ninth century BC, Carthage benefitted from its location at a natural choke point, on the African side of the Sicilian Channel, where the Mediterranean is only 175 kilometres wide. This made the city the natural hub for trade between the eastern and western Mediterranean and between Europe and Africa. Carthage also benefitted from a fertile hinterland, famed for its grain production, which allowed it to support a large and growing population.

While Carthage maintained the commercial interests of its Phoenician founders, the city's rulers also had imperial ambitions, which it pursued using its formidable navy. Carthage quickly assumed leadership of the surviving Phoenician colonies in Sicily, Sardinia, Malta, the Balearic Islands, North Africa and Iberia: Gadir submitted to Carthaginian rule around 530 BC. The same fleet allowed the Carthaginians aggressively to exclude Greek traders and colonists from the western Mediterranean and the Atlantic Ocean. Certainly, the Greek presence at Huelva seems to have come to an end before 500 BC.

Carthage saw potential for expansion in the Atlantic, and in the sixth century BC it sent out at least two expeditions to explore the coasts beyond the limits already known to the Phoenicians. The leaders of these expeditions, Himilco and Hanno, are the first Atlantic explorers whose names are actually known. Most of what is known about Himilco's voyage comes from a long and rather pompous fourth-century Latin poem called *Ora Maritima* ('The Sea Coast'), which the author, Rufus Festus Avienus, 'cut and pasted' together using extracts from now lost *periploi.* Himilco's vaguely described mission was 'to explore the parts beyond Europe'. Setting out from Gadir, Himilco first followed the route used by the Tartessian merchants who sailed north along the Atlantic coast to Oestrymnis – meaning the 'Extreme West' – to obtain tin and other metals. Avienus describes Oestrymnis as a towering, windswept, rocky headland, which doesn't do much to narrow down the possibilities for its location, since there are plenty of them along Europe's Atlantic coast. Beyond the headland was the Oestrymnian Gulf which was scattered with islands, which Avienus says were rich with lodes of lead and tin. These unnamed islands are probably Kassiterid, the same islands that the Greeks knew as the Cassiterides, the 'Tin Isles'. The metal traders here sailed not in wooden ships, Avienus tells us, but in curved boats covered with animal hides which must have been much like Irish curachs. Two days' sailing further on lay the 'holy island' of Ierne and nearby the broad island of Albion, which are certainly Ireland and Britain. Given the sailing time, this would make Brittany the most likely location of Oestrymnis, the headland being Pointe du Raz at its western extremity. The identity of the islands in the Oestrymnic Gulf are harder to identify, since none of the islands off the Breton coast have any veins of lead or tin, nor do the other likely candidates, the Isles of Scilly off the Cornish coast. Rather than literally being sources of tin, perhaps these islands were simply places where tin was traded. Avienus does not say that Himilco sailed on to Ierne or Albion, but Oestrymnis was not the end of his voyage. Sailing on, Himilco entered a sluggish, fog-cloaked, windless sea, crowded with sea monsters and a 'clustering growth of weed' so dense that the sea itself was powerless to move it. These dire conditions reported by Himilco may simply be deliberate Carthaginian disinformation intended to frighten off potential rivals, because he would certainly not have found a windless sea had he sailed north from Brittany. Had Himilco sailed west, rather than north, however, he would, after four or five thousand kilometres, have found such conditions in the Sargasso Sea, where calm seas, light winds and floating rafts of seaweed are common. Avienus tells us that Himilco's voyage lasted four months, which doesn't seem nearly long enough to explore the Atlantic coast as far north as Brittany and then sail most of the way across the Atlantic and back again to Gadir.

The first of the phantom islands

While it's unlikely that Himilco discovered the Sargasso Sea, there is some reason to believe that the Carthaginians were sailing far out into the Atlantic, even if only by accident. The Greek historian Diodorus Siculus (90 BC–30 BC) recorded that, in the sixth century BC, Phoenicians sailing along the North African coast had been blown many days' sailing out into the Atlantic by strong winds and discovered a large mountainous island of 'surpassing beauty'. 'Through it flow navigable rivers,' Diodorus wrote,

> which are used for irrigation, and the island contains many parks planted with trees of every variety and gardens in great multitudes which are traversed by streams of sweet water; on it also are private villas of costly construction, and throughout the gardens banqueting houses have been constructed in a setting of flowers, and in them the inhabitants pass their time during the summer season, since the land supplies in abundance everything which contributes to enjoyment and luxury. The mountainous part of the island is covered with dense thickets of great extent and with fruit-trees of every variety, and, inviting men to life among the mountains, it has cozy glens and springs in great number. In a word, this island is well supplied with springs of sweet water which not only makes the use of it enjoyable for those who pass their life there but also contribute to the health and vigour of their bodies. There is also excellent hunting of every manner of beast and wild animal, and the inhabitants, being well supplied with this game at their feasts, lack of nothing which pertains to luxury and extravagance; for in fact the sea which washes the shore of the island contains a multitude of fish, since the character of the ocean is such that it abounds throughout its extent with fish of every variety. And, speaking generally, the climate of the island is so altogether mild that it produces in abundance the fruits of the trees and the other seasonal fruits for the larger part of the year, so that it would appear that the island, because of its exceptional felicity, were a dwelling-place of a race of gods and not of men.[6]

Diodorus concludes by telling us that when news of the discovery leaked out, the Etruscans wished to go and settle the island but were prevented from doing so by the Carthaginians, who did not want to see a potential competitor moving into the Atlantic. The Etruscans can hardly be blamed for wanting to settle this veritable earthly paradise, but was it a real island or a phantom?

The only large islands in the Atlantic that were both inhabited at that time and have navigable rivers are Ireland and Britain, but their climate would hardly be considered mild by the

Phoenicians, who, in any case, knew of Britain's and Ireland's existence even if they had not actually been there. Allowing for some poetic licence, Madeira, or the large Azorean island of São Miguel, would be a convincing fit for the island's mild and wet climate, and its mountainous landscape and lush vegetation, but both were uninhabited at this time and devoid of terrestrial mammals which could have been hunted. However, in 1749 a small hoard of nine Carthaginian and two Greek coins, dating to the third century BC, was found in a pot by the seashore on Corvo, the smallest and most remote island of the Azores archipelago, over 1,400 kilometres west of Portugal. The coins, whose present whereabouts are unknown, were believed to be genuine at the time of their discovery, but there is always the possibility that they were planted as part of a hoax: recent surveys have found no other traces of Phoenician presence in the Azores. For all that, the subsequent history of the Atlantic is full of stories of accidental discoveries made by storm-driven seafarers, so there may be a historical basis to Diodorus's story. Another group of islands that the Phoenicians likely knew about is the Canaries, but they're rather too arid and, at little more than a day's sail away, too close to the African mainland to be a good fit for Diodorus's phantom island.

The Guanche problem

The Canaries do have in their favour the possibility that they were inhabited at this time by the ancestors of the Guanche* people, who were living there when the islands were discovered by Europeans in the fourteenth century. The Guanches do, however, present historians with a big problem – how did they actually get to the Canary Islands in the first place? Archaeological evidence

* The term Guanche originally applied only to the indigenous inhabitants of Tenerife before expanding in modern usage to include all indigenous Canary Islanders.

suggest that they settled the islands between around 600 BC and 300 BC, perhaps in more than one wave. They obviously arrived by sea and were farming peoples, who brought with them their domestic animals and crops: sheep, goats, pigs and dogs, wheat, barley, figs and lentils. They made fine pottery, but if their ancestors also brought metalworking skills with them, the Guanches soon lost them. The islands have no metal ore deposits and the islanders' outside contacts were too infrequent for them to have a reliable supply of imported metal tools, so, at the time of the first regular contacts with Europeans in the fourteenth century, they had an entirely Neolithic technology. Another missing skill was spinning and weaving textiles, and this despite their keeping huge herds of sheep and goats. Such clothing as the Guanches wore, simple loincloths, skirts and cloaks, were made of hides or woven palm leaves. Elaborate and colourful body-painting took the place of dressing up for special events. An even more surprising deficiency is the Guanches' apparent lack of any kind of seafaring technology at the time of their first contact with Europeans. Hard-to-date engravings on rocks in the Barranco de Adonai on Tenerife show ships with single masts and sails, including one with the distinctive beaked profile of an ancient Mediterranean galley, but the earliest eyewitness report of Guanches using boats, in this case a dugout canoe with a sail made of palm matting, dates only to the late sixteenth century, long after European contact. Without boats, travel between the islands and to the mainland was impossible. The Guanches were able to exploit their rich coastal waters only by fishing from the shore with hook and line and by gathering limpets on rocky coasts, which they did in enormous numbers to judge from surviving shell middens.

The Guanches' language became extinct around AD 1600, but not before some records of its vocabulary had been made by Franciscan missionaries. These show that the Guanches' language had close affinities with the Berber languages, which always suggested that they had a North African origin. Other evidence of the Guanches' Berber ancestry is their use of petroglyphs, which seem to be based on the ancient Libyco-Berber alphabet, and their pottery styles, which have clear similarities to prehistoric Berber pottery. This has now been confirmed by analysis of aDNA recovered from Guanche mummies, which has proven their close genetic relationship with the Berbers. The Guanches' ancestors needed to cross little more than 100 kilometres of ocean to reach Fuerteventura and Lanzarote, the nearest of the Canary Islands to the mainland, but how did they do even that without boats? Drifting across on rafts was not an option, because the southerly Canary Current would have taken them away from the islands: they would have needed sailing vessels to take advantage of westerly winds. One hypothesis is that the Guanches' ancestors possessed seafaring skills that were subsequently lost, but this seems inherently unlikely. Seagoing boats have been built in many parts of the world using essentially Neolithic technology, the Canary Islands have plenty of suitable timber and the opportunities for fishing, inter-island trade and social contact would have given the Guanches a strong incentive to preserve and develop those skills had they possessed them when they arrived. A more plausible hypothesis is that the Guanches were not voluntary emigrants at all but enslaved peoples, with no knowledge of seafaring or boatbuilding, who were transported to the islands against their will, most likely by the Phoenicians or Carthaginians. The intention may have been that the Guanches would gather the orchil lichen, the source of a red dye, which flourishes in the Canaries, and murex sea snails from the shores, in return for which the Phoenicians would deliver provisions. If this was the case, the scant material traces of Phoenician or Carthaginian presence in the islands suggests that the Guanches were very soon abandoned to their own devices, occasionally to be rediscovered by adventurous seafarers before being lost again. Left to themselves, and unable to communicate with one another, the inhabitants of each island evolved their own unique social, religious and linguistic characteristics, like human equivalents of Darwin's Galapagos finches.

Hanno the Navigator

Carthage's most famous explorer was Hanno, a prince of the ruling Magonid family who lived in the early fifth century BC. This might be why Hanno's periplus was given the special honour of being inscribed on the walls of the temple of the storm god Baal Hamon in Carthage, where it was seen and translated by a visiting Greek merchant. The original text was lost when the Romans destroyed Carthage in 146 BC, but the translation has survived. According to the periplus, Hanno's mission was to sail through the Pillars of Heracles and found Carthaginian settlements, but it is perhaps more likely that he was refounding settlements and trading posts that had been abandoned after the fall of Tyre. The expedition as described was a massive undertaking, involving sixty penteconters. These were all-purpose sailing galleys, with deep hulls for cargo and crews of fifty oarsmen, that were built both for war and for transporting armies or settlers. In addition, the periplus claims that the fleet carried 30,000 men and women settlers, and all necessary supplies. The Carthaginians could certainly raise war fleets of this size but, typically, they did not remain at sea for long periods. It is difficult to imagine how so many people, and the supplies needed to feed them for several months, could possibly have been squeezed into only sixty relatively slender ships, and it's hard not to suspect that its size has been grossly exaggerated.

After passing through the Pillars of Heracles, Hanno's fleet sailed south for two days and founded a colony called Thymiaterium. Continuing southwest, Hanno rounded a wooded cape called Solois, where he set up an altar to the sea god Neptune (perhaps meaning Baal). Half a day's sail further on the fleet arrived at a reedy marshland inhabited by numerous elephants and other wildlife. Sailing on for another day from the marsh, Hanno began to found colonies: Caricus, Murus, Gytta, Acra, Melitta and Arambys; the periplus does not say how far apart they were. After founding Arambys, Hanno put in at the mouth of a 'great river' called the Lixus which rose in high mountains further inland. The area was inhabited by a friendly tribe of nomadic herders who provided Hanno with guides and translators for the next stage of his voyage. Now unburdened by settlers, Hanno's fleet sailed south along an uninhabited desert coast for twelve days before turning east for another day to arrive at a bay which contained a small island which he called Cerne. Hanno calculated that the distance from Cerne to the Pillars of Heracles was the same as that as from Carthage to the Pillars. From Cerne, the fleet sailed up a river to a large lake with three islands. At the head of the lake, a full day's sail further on, the Carthaginians came to a mountain range inhabited by 'savage men wearing the skins of wild animals', who bombarded them with stones, preventing them from leaving their ships. Retreating, the Carthaginians next explored another river teeming with crocodiles and hippopotami before returning to Cerne.

Leaving Cerne, the fleet sailed south along the coast for another twelve days until they reached a range of forested mountains where the air was fragrant with the scent of aromatic shrubs. The periplus describes the people living along the coast as Æthiopians, in the Classical world a catch-all term for all Black Africans, whose speech the Carthaginians' Lixitae guides did not understand at all. Two days' sailing further on, the expedition came to the mouth of a wide inlet from the ocean, where they took on fresh water supplies. Looking inland at night, they could see fire 'leaping up on every side at intervals, now greater, now less'. For the rest of the outward leg of their expedition, the Carthaginians followed this burning coast. For five more days they sailed on along the coast until they came to a wide bay that the Lixitae told them was called the Horn of the West. In the bay there was a large island, and within that island there was 'a lake of the sea' in which there was another island. The Carthaginians landed on this island and could see only dense forest. However, at night, they saw many fires and 'they heard the sound of pipes and cymbals, and the noise of drums and a great uproar of shouting. Then fear possessed us, and the soothsayers advised us to leave the island.'

Sailing quickly on, they 'passed by a burning country full

of fragrance, from which great torrents of fire flowed down to the sea'. The heat of the fires was so intense that no landing was possible. Despite now being constantly fear-stricken, the Carthaginians continued until after four days' sailing they saw the land at night covered with flames. And in the midst there was a lofty fire, greater than the rest, which seemed to touch the stars. By day, this was seen to be a very high mountain which they called Theon Ochema ('The Chariot of the Gods'). They sailed along the coast of this burning country, passing yet more torrents of fire, until they arrived at another bay called the Horn of the South:

> In the corner of this bay, there was an island like the former one, having a lake, in which there was another island, inhabited by savages with hairy bodies, whom our interpreters called 'gorillas'. When we pursued the men, we were unable to capture any of them because all of them escaped by climbing cliffs and defending themselves with stones; but we took three of the women, who bit and scratched their captors and would not come with us. So we killed them and flayed them, and brought their skins back with us to Carthage. For we did not voyage further, provisions failing us.[7]

With that, the narrative of the periplus ends; nothing at all is said about the return voyage.

Ever since Roman times, historians have attempted to work out where exactly Hanno's voyage took him. Much of the problem comes from the unit of distance used – a day's sailing. This would have been perfectly meaningful to a Carthaginian mariner, who would have a good idea of how far an average day's sailing would take him, much as we might talk about a day's driving. Unfortunately, they didn't think to record this distance for our benefit. Much would depend on whether Hanno's fleet sailed only in daylight hours and anchored at night, as his Phoenician predecessors did, or if they sailed both day and night. There is also no mention of the winds and currents they faced, both of which could greatly speed or impede progress. Analysis of Roman records of sailing times suggests that with a following wind, ancient Mediterranean sailing ships could reach speeds of between 4.5 and 6 knots (8.3–11 kph), but in adverse winds they could be as slow as 1.5 to 3 knots (2.7–5.5 kph).[8] So in the most favourable conditions, sailing 24 hours a day, a day's sail could have been over 260 kilometres, but, in the most adverse conditions, sailing only in daylight, it could be little over 30 kilometres. Penteconters had the advantage that they could be rowed if the wind failed, but, because their hulls were deeper than those of specialist war galleys, they were not fast, having a maximum speed of around 5 knots in calm conditions and much slower than that if rowed against a headwind or adverse current. Unlike sails, oarsmen get tired, so over long distances rowing was actually slower than sailing because of the need to break the journey to allow crews to recover. All the uncertainties have led to wildly varying estimates of the distance covered by Hanno's fleet after it put the Pillars of Heracles astern. The gorillas don't really help to fix the end point of Hanno's voyage either: the gorilla ape was named after Hanno's 'gorillas', which could have been a different species of ape or monkey or might even have been humans. Stories about Hanno's gorillas probably gave birth to a group of phantom Atlantic islands called by Greek geographers the Gorgades, which were inhabited by hairy women who could have children without being impregnated by men. The hairy women were not exotic enough for later Roman writers, who repopulated the islands with snake-haired Gorgons who could turn any mariner unwise enough to land there into stone with a single glance. The main island of the Gorgades, which were two days' sail from the African coast, was called Cerna, which can only be derived from Hanno's Cerne at the mouth of the Chretes.

Only three of the places mentioned in the periplus can be identified with any certainty: Carthage itself, the Pillars of Heracles and the Lixus river, which can only have been the Leukkos, about 75 kilometres south of Tangier. Because they had no trouble communicating with the Lixitae, this area must already have been visited frequently by Carthaginian or Phoenician traders. There is archaeological evidence that Phoenicians settled in the area in the 8th century BC: the Lixitae may have been their descendents. Cerne may be St Louis Island at the mouth of the Senegal river, which could be reached in thirteen full days' sailing from the Leukkos in favourable conditions: the Senegal river would therefore be Hanno's Chretes. How far beyond that Hanno might have sailed is unclear. The best candidates for the 'great gulf' where Hanno took on fresh water would be the wide mouth of the Gambia River or the Canal de Gêba in Guinea-Bissau. This region of Africa is prone to spectacular summer bush fires, making it a good fit for the 'burning land'. This would likely mean that Hanno ended his voyage somewhere along the hilly coasts of Guinea or Sierra Leone. A potential candidate for the burning mountain, Theon Ochema, is the distinctively shaped Mount Kakoulima in southern Guinea, though, at only 998 metres high, it could hardly be said almost to touch the stars. Some historians have argued that Theon Ochema was Mount Cameroon, a highly active volcano which looms a genuinely star-skimming 4,040 metres over the Gulf of Guinea. However, nothing described in the periplus remotely resembles the 2,000 kilometres, or more, of low, forested, often mangrove-fringed coasts of equatorial West Africa that he would have had to sail along to get there. Nor does it seem that Hanno spent enough time at sea to get there.

The most problematic part of Hanno's voyage is his return. How did he get back? The winds along North Africa's Atlantic coast blow persistently towards the southwest, out to sea, and the ocean currents flow in the same direction. These make it easy enough to sail southwest along the coast but very difficult to sail back the same way. If it was indeed the Phoenicians who took the Guanches to the Canary Islands, this may have been why they were so quickly abandoned. Whatever it was that drew them to the Canaries in the first place wasn't valuable enough to justify the risk of being unable to make it back home again. It was not until the fifteenth century, when the Portuguese discovered how to use the *volta do mar*, that European seafarers dared to begin exploring the West African coast, and there is absolutely no evidence that the Phoenicians ever knew of this. Hanno's penteconters could be rowed against the wind and current, and this could have made a critical difference, but progress must have been agonizingly slow. The nine days' sailing with the wind and current from the Lixus to the Chretes could have stretched out into weeks of hard rowing on the return voyage along the desert coast, with few safe anchorages where the crews could rest and replenish food and water supplies. It must have been touch and go whether Hanno's crews made it back alive.

Did the Phoenicians circumnavigate Africa?

Hanno may have had some knowledge of the conditions he would face along the African coast before he set out. In a discussion of the boundaries of the continents, Herodotus claims that the Egyptian pharaoh Necho II (r. 610 BC–595 BC) was the first to prove that Africa was entirely surrounded by the sea:

> [Necho] sent some Phoenicians off on ships with orders to sail around Libya [i.e. Africa] and back through the Pillars of Heracles into the Mediterranean Sea and to return by that route to Egypt. And so the Phoenicians set out from the Erythraean Sea [Red Sea] and sailed the Southern Sea. Whenever autumn came, they would put into shore at whatever region of Libya they happened to have reached in order to sow seeds. There they would wait for the harvest, and after reaping their crops, they would sail on again. This they did for two years, and in the third, they came around through the Pillars of Heracles and returned to Egypt. They mentioned something else which I do not find credible, though someone else may: that when they were sailing around Libya, the sun was on their right side as they went.[9]

Herodotus clearly found this last claim hard to swallow, but for modern historians the same claim has tended to add credibility to the whole story of the Phoenician circumnavigation of Africa. Sailors circumnavigating Africa in a clockwise direction would have found the sun on the right-hand side, that is in the north, when they were south of the Equator. Though this doesn't prove the story is true, it does imply that some seafarers from the Mediterranean world or the Middle East had found their way south of the Equator to have known about the phenomenon. The Phoenicians themselves had some direct knowledge of the East African coast because they sailed from the Israelite port of Ezion-Geber on the Gulf of Aqaba and down the Red Sea to the land of Ophir, which was probably Afar in the Horn of Africa, to obtain gold, gems, ivory, apes and peacocks. From Afar, they might easily have explored the coast further south looking for trade opportunities. Had people known that the world was spherical, this detail could have been intuited, but at the time of Herodotus most people still believed that the world was flat, so the only way anyone could have known that was if they had actually been there and seen it for themselves. Other aspects of the story do strain credulity, however. Could the Phoenicians really have provisioned themselves in the way described? And there is also the problem of how they overcame the adverse currents and winds on the west coast of Africa, not only at Cape Bojador but also around the Cape of Good Hope and Namibia's infamous Skeleton Coast, where relentless west winds have driven countless ships onto its inhospitable desert shore. Like Hanno, did they have galleys? We aren't told.

In 2008–10, Philip Beale, a British adventurer, did successfully circumnavigate Africa in an anti-clockwise direction in *Phoenicia*, a 20-metre-long single-masted sailing ship, built at Arwad (Phoenician Arvad) in Syria using traditional Mediterranean materials and the pegged mortise-and-tenon method. This certainly demonstrated that such ships might have been up to the task, but beyond being a great adventure for the team members, does it actually prove anything else? The expedition set out with the full benefit of modern sea charts and modern knowledge of ocean currents and wind systems, GPS navigation, radio and the option of flying home if, at any point, it proved necessary to abandon the expedition. The expedition took full advantage of this knowledge after rounding the Cape of Good Hope into the Atlantic. Instead of hugging the African coast, as we have to presume the Phoenicians would have done, *Phoenicia* sailed out into the mid-Atlantic to take advantage of the more favourable winds there, returning via St Helena, Ascension Island and the Azores. Ancient sailors, with none of this modern knowledge and technology, would have seen the task and its attendant risks in entirely different terms. This is the problem with all such historical reconstruction voyages. While it is possible to reproduce ancient technology, it isn't possible to reproduce the world view and mental outlook of the people who used it.

A fate worse than death

Hanno may not have been the last Phoenician to explore the west coast of Africa. Herodotus[10] tells the story of a Persian nobleman called Sataspes who was sentenced to death by King Xerxes I (r. 486 BC–465 BC) for a kidnapping and rape. However, in an attempt to save him, Sataspes's mother Atossa, a member of the royal family, tried to convince Xerxes that it would be a much harsher punishment if he sentenced him to sail around Africa instead. Xerxes indulged Atossa: Sataspes would probably never come back, which was fine because it would save the king the bother of executing him. Sataspes acquired a Phoenician ship and crew in Egypt and sailed west, across the Mediterranean, through the Pillars of Heracles, then south along the African coast for several months until he met adverse currents which prevented further progress. Sataspes, or, more likely, his crew, who had more to lose than he did, saw no alternative but to turn around and sail back the way he had come. If he was hoping for a sympathetic hearing, Sataspes was to be disappointed. When he presented himself to

Xerxes, Sataspes gave an account of his voyage, describing all the difficulties he had faced and his encounters with a pygmy herding people who wore clothes made of palm leaves. Xerxes didn't believe a word of it and, unimpressed by his lame excuses for giving up, ordered Sataspes to be executed after all. There are few clues in Herodotus's brief account to help determine how far the faint-hearted Sataspes got, but it gives no reason to suppose that he came close to emulating Hanno's achievement. It was over 300 years before another attempt to circumnavigate Africa was made, by which time the Mediterranean was under Roman control and the Carthaginian monopoly on access to the Atlantic was a thing of the past.

4

Fortunate Islands

800 BC–AD 500

Oceanus – The Garden of the Hesperides – Phocaean pioneers – The Cassiterides – The shield of Achilles – Atlantis – The destruction of Thera – Pytheas's voyage to the far north – Celtic ships – Albion – Ultima Thule – Pax Romana – Caius the fish eater – The Islands of Dogs – Exploring in style – Edge of empire – A sea foaming with the beat of hostile oars

Long before the ancient Greeks ever set eyes on the Atlantic Ocean for themselves, they had explored it in their imaginations and made it a place both of mythological exile for fallen gods and of easeful afterlives for heroes. Farmers and seafarers, most ancient Greeks lived close to nature, and their gods embodied natural forces or were personifications of numinous places. The ocean itself was one such numinous place, a divinity personified by the sea god Oceanus (the son of the sky god Uranus and the earth goddess Gaia), who, by his wife Tethys, fathered a dynasty of thousands of sea nymphs and river gods. The myth reflects the ancient Greeks' intuitive understanding of the global water cycle: all of the world's rivers and springs are in reality the offspring of the ocean. Oceanus belonged to the Titans, an ancient dynasty of nature gods, led by his younger brother Cronus. However, there was a younger generation of gods, the Olympians, led by Cronus's son Zeus, who were impatient for power. In the great war that followed, the Olympians overthrew the Titans and imprisoned them in the hellish underworld realm of Tartarus. Victorious Zeus castrated his father and banished him to a tower on an island far away at the western edge of the world, 'near to the place of the summer sunset'. Unlike the other Titans, Oceanus had sided with the younger generation against their elders, so grateful Zeus permitted him and his family to continue to flow free as they had always done.

The Garden of the Hesperides

Another Titan exiled to the west was Atlas, a grandson of Oceanus, condemned by Zeus to stand forever at the edge of the world and hold up the weight of the heavens with his shoulders. Atlas's three daughters, nymphs of the evening light called the Hesperides, also dwelled in the far west, appointed by Zeus's wife Hera to tend a beautiful otherworldly garden containing an orchard of trees on which golden apples grew. The Greeks originally imagined the Garden of the Hesperides to be located in Cyrenaica, but as their known world expanded, poets relocated it to the still mysterious lands beyond the Strait of Gibraltar on the shores of the Ocean, near Lixus in Morocco or in Tartessos on the island of Erytheia, thought by some to have been where the Phoenicians founded their colony of Gadir. It is to Atlas that we owe the name of the Atlantic, *Atlantis thalassos*, the 'Sea of Atlas'. At least that's what the Greeks believed, but there is a more prosaic explanation: it may be named after Morocco's Atlas Mountains. These probably have nothing to do with the exiled Titan; the name is a corruption of *ádrār*, a Berber word meaning 'mountain'. Either way, for the Greeks and Romans, the Atlantic was most definitely just a sea, that part of the global Ocean immediately beyond the Pillars of Heracles. It would take Columbus to turn it into an ocean in its own right.

To atone for killing his family during a fit of insanity, the gods ordered the demi-god Heracles to serve King Eurystheus of Attica for ten years. Eurystheus made the most of the opportunity and ordered Heracles to perform twelve near-impossible 'labours'. For his eleventh labour, Eurystheus tasked Heracles with stealing three of the golden apples from the Hesperides and return them to him. Judging that the Hesperides would be more likely to allow their father into the garden than him, Heracles offered to shoulder Atlas's burden if he would steal the apples on his behalf. When Atlas returned with the apples he generously offered to deliver them to Eurystheus himself. Quick-witted Heracles agreed, asking only that Atlas take back the heavens for a moment while he rearranged his cloak to make a shoulder pad. Atlas, obviously being none too bright, agreed. Heracles made good his escape and, since the heavens haven't fallen yet, Atlas must be there still. In one version of the myth, Heracles kindly built two mountains, the Pillars of Heracles, at the edge of the world to take some of the weight off Atlas's shoulders. These pillars are the Rock of Gibraltar on the European side of the strait and Jebel Musa on the African side. There is no such thing as a canonical myth, however, and a more widely shared tradition has it that he created the Pillars on a different adventure, a quest to steal the cattle of the giant Geryon from Erytheia. Reaching the western limit of the Mediterranean, Heracles found a mountain blocking his way. In too much of a hurry to climb over it, he simply smashed his way through to the ocean beyond, creating the Strait of Gibraltar. A tidy worker, Heracles thoughtfully dumped the left over rubble in two mountain-sized piles on either side of the strait. It isn't clear why the Strait of Gibraltar became associated with Heracles in the first place, but it is probably because it was already associated with Melqart, his Phoenician equivalent, through his cult centre at Gadir.

Much further out in the Ocean, 'closest to where the Sun sets', were the Fortunate Isles, also known as the Isles of the Blessed, home to the paradise-like Elysian Fields, where, according to Homer, 'life is easiest for men. No snow is there, nor heavy storm, nor ever rain, but ever does Ocean send up blasts of the shrill-blowing West Wind that they may give cooling to men.' Here, mortal heroes with divine ancestors and other virtuous mortals favoured by the gods spent their blissful afterlives. Homer's near contemporary, the poet Hesiod, envisaged Elysium as an island paradise where Zeus granted the heroes of the Trojan War 'life and home apart from men, and settled them at the ends of the earth. These dwell with carefree hearts on the Isles of the Blessed Ones beside deep-swirling Oceanus, fortunate heroes, for whom the grain-giving soil bears its sweet fruits three times a year.'[11] The Greeks were, of course, not the only people to imagine the far west as the location of paradise; the Celts had their own archipelago of blissful islands. Both peoples believed absolutely that these islands existed in the Atlantic and were there to be discovered by adventurous mortals.

Phocaean pioneers

The Greeks began to explore the Atlantic Ocean for themselves towards the end of the seventh century BC. Beginning around 800 BC, the Greek city-states started to build a network of colonies across the eastern Mediterranean, Italy and the Black Sea, partly for trade and partly as a way to provide opportunities for fast-growing populations who might agitate for social reform at home if not gainfully employed. The Greeks also aspired to found colonies in the western Mediterranean, but the Phoenicians had got there first and had already claimed most of the best harbours, so the opportunities were few. Around 600 BC, an expedition from the thriving Ionian port of Phocaea (now the Turkish city of Foça) spotted a prime location that the Phoenicians had somehow missed, a sheltered cove on France's south coast where they founded a colony they named Massalia: it is now known as Marseille, France's most important Mediterranean port. It was not only its good anchorage that drew the Phocaeans to Massalia; its proximity to the mouth of the river Rhône made it the ideal place to take advantage of several important long-distance trade routes controlled by the Celtic Gauls. The Rhône is navigable for most of its length and gave access, via short overland passages, to other navigable rivers such as the Loire, the Seine and the Rhine, along which Celtic merchants transported valuable products like British tin and Baltic amber, together with everyday essentials like grain and hides, from northern Europe to the Mediterranean. The Phocaeans could now monopolize that trade, in return introducing the Celtic elite to the delights of drinking expensive and status-enhancing imported wine.

The Phocaeans were known as the most adventurous Greek seafarers. They had been the first to send out fleets of penteconters to explore and colonize the far reaches of the Mediterranean and the Black Sea, so, inevitably, Massalia became a base for further Phocaean exploration in the west. After fighting off a belated Carthaginian attempt to expel them, the Phocaeans ventured out through the Pillars of Heracles into the Atlantic and began trading with the Tartessian port of Huelva. Tartessos's silver mountains were already the stuff of legends, but the Phocaeans were also excited about reports of a fabulously profitable voyage made around 630 BC by Colaeus of Samos, the first Greek known to have sailed the Atlantic. Colaeus claimed that he had arrived at Tartessos by accident after he was blown off course while sailing from Greece to Cyrene (in modern Libya), right across the Mediterranean and out through the Pillars of Heracles into the Atlantic. It is 2,500 kilometres from Cyrene to Huelva by the shortest possible route, and the idea that any ship could have made it all that way without anywhere being driven ashore or finding a safe harbour in an inland sea crowded with islands seems fanciful, so this must have been a cover story to mislead his competitors. When he returned home with his hold full of silver, Colaeus donated one tenth of his profits to the temple of the goddess Hera, Samos's patron deity, a wise move given her reputation for jealousy and vindictiveness. Herodotus believed that only one Greek merchant had ever made a bigger profit from a single voyage than Colaeus did from his trip to Tartessos. The Phocaeans in turn found a warm welcome at Huelva, and they soon established a close relationship with King Arganthonios. The king learned that the Phocaeans felt threatened by the rising power of Persia, so he generously offered to help, both by paying to build a stone defensive wall for their city and by inviting the Phocaeans to resettle in Tartessos if they ever needed to. The Phocaeans said thank you very much for the silver – there must have been a lot of it; the walls they built around their city were over 5 kilometres long – but politely declined Arganthonios's offer to settle; they didn't want to live among 'barbarians'. Sadly, Arganthonios's largesse did not save Phocaea, for it was conquered by the Persian King Cyrus the Great in 546 BC. Rather than live under Persian rule, many of its citizens fled to Massalia and other Greek colonies.

The Cassiterides

Just by hanging around the harbour at Huelva and listening to sailors' tales, the Greeks would have learned a lot about navigating the Atlantic coasts. They would certainly also have picked up much decidedly dubious information about the vaguely located lands that the Phoenicians were rumoured to have discovered further out in the ocean. Some Greeks sailed as far as the Cassiterides to trade for tin, the first to do so being a merchant called Midacritus, but quite where these fabled islands were has left historians guessing: they are probably to be identified with Himilco's Oestrymnian Isles, but then, we don't know where they were for sure either. The Massaliot captain Euthymenes set off in his penteconter to explore the west coast of Africa, but whether he preceded or followed Hanno of Carthage isn't known. Euthymenes wrote a long-lost periplus of his voyage in which he claimed that he had discovered the source of the Nile. Sailing south along the African coast, he came to the mouth of a great river, probably, like Hanno's Chretes, the Senegal, flowing so strongly that the seawater was fresh to the taste far out from land. Perhaps confused by the unfamiliar Atlantic tides, Euthymenes thought that this fresh water was flowing into the river rather than out of it. Euthymenes entered the river and found that it was inhabited by crocodiles, just like the Nile, so he concluded that the two must be connected, and that, therefore, he had discovered that the source of the Nile was the Atlantic. Quite rightly, no one believed him, but this one implausible claim condemned the rest of his account to obscurity. If not for a few brief and sceptical comments in the works of later writers, both Euthymenes and his pioneering voyage would have been completely forgotten: only in Marseille is he remembered as a hero today.

Greek ventures into the Atlantic didn't continue for long. Just a century after Colaeus's voyage, the Greeks were abruptly shut out of the Atlantic. In 539, the Carthaginians got their revenge over the Phocaeans when, in alliance with the Etruscans of Tuscany, they defeated the Massaliot fleet off Corsica. After the battle, the Etruscans stoned their share of the Greek captives to death, just for the fun of it; the Carthaginians, being more commercially minded and not wanting to lose any opportunity to make money, sold their only slightly more fortunate captives into slavery. Around the same time, Carthage turned Carteia, on the Bay of Gibraltar, into a naval base complete with large ship sheds for storing war galleys, so that they could close the strait to outsiders. Henceforward, the Massaliots decided to concentrate their efforts on trading with the Celtic north, and it was this that would eventually take them back to the Atlantic.

The shield of Achilles

The Greeks might have been shut out of the Atlantic, but that didn't stop them thinking about it and coming to some radical conclusions. The Greeks of Homer's age lived on much the same flat Earth as the Phoenicians. In the *Iliad*,[12] Homer described the spectacularly decorated shield that Achilles had made specially for him by the smith-god Hephaestus. The shield displayed a model of the cosmos as the Greeks then understood it: the Sun, the Moon and the constellations of the Pleiades, the Hyades, the cosmic huntsman Orion and the north-pointing Great Bear, and, beneath them, on a flat Earth encircled by the flowing river-like global Ocean, humans living out their lives in peace and war. Homer composed his epics in the eighth century BC, shortly before the Greeks began their colonial expansion across the Mediterranean, and his *oikouménē*, the 'known world', did not extend far beyond the eastern Mediterranean and the Black Sea. Moreover, there was no sense that there might be more to the world than what was already known. However, as the Greeks gradually learned more about the extent of the world, they began to question this inherited cosmology and replace it with a revolutionary cosmos of their own.

A major problem with the traditional model of the universe was that it could not explain why the Sun did not rise and set at the same time for everyone, everywhere, as it should do if the world was simply a flat plate. This got the inquisitive Greeks asking, was the Earth really flat? Couldn't observed phenomena like this be better explained if it was actually a sphere? The first to make this bold intellectual leap was probably the mathematician Pythagoras (*c.*570 BC–*c.*495 BC), followed in the fifth century by Parmenides and Empedocles. Unfortunately, none of them left any work explaining why they rejected the idea of the flat Earth. Their ideas must have become widely accepted very quickly. Although the historian Herodotus (*c.*484 BC–*c.*425 BC) was still a convinced flat-Earther, the Athenian philosopher Plato (*c.*428 BC–*c.*348 BC) taught that 'the Earth is a round body in the centre of the heavens', but he took this proposition so much for granted that he never bothered to justify his position with evidence either, presumably because he didn't expect that anyone was going to argue with it. Plato's star student, Aristotle (384 BC–322 BC), was the first who left a reasoned argument in favour of the spherical Earth. Key for him was that, as an observer travelled from north to south, new constellations came into view that had not been visible further north. This could only be possible if the Earth had a curved surface, Aristotle argued. Aristotle also cited as evidence that the shadow of the Earth on the Moon during a lunar eclipse was curved. To the obvious objection – why wouldn't everything fall off the 'bottom' of the Earth? – Aristotle offered his theory of 'natural place', a sort of rudimentary theory of gravity which sought to explain why heavy things fell towards the centre of the Earth. Seafarers must have noticed very early in history that land appeared to sink below the horizon as they sailed away from it and rise above it as they sailed towards it, but, surprisingly, it was not until the first century AD that the geographer Strabo argued that this phenomenon was yet more evidence of the curvature of the Earth.

In 240 BC, the astronomer Eratosthenes used observations of the different lengths of the shadows cast by the midday Sun in two locations along the same meridian at the summer solstice to calculate the circumference of the Earth. The figure he came to, 252,000 stadia, roughly equivalent to 39,425 kilometres, is within 1.5 per cent of the Earth's true circumference of 40,008 kilometres (when measured around the poles). This novel spherical world was not something anyone could sail to, or over, the edge of, but it was far vaster than the old flat Earth was ever conceived to be. The real revelation for the Greeks, however, was that they knew so little of it: the *oikouménē* was really no more than a fraction of what there was to be known. In the second century BC, the philosopher Krates of Miletos graphically demonstrated this by making the earliest known world globe: most of it was a blank space waiting to be filled in by enterprising explorers. The three known continents, Europe, Africa and Asia, now lay in a truly global ocean, but the Greeks intuited that there couldn't just be sea and more sea, there must be other continents out there too, somewhere. The *oikouménē* comprised no more than a quarter of the globe, and most of that quarter was known to be land. If that was all the land there was, then surely, they reasoned, the world would be out of balance and wobbling all over the place. For the world to be in balance there had to be an equal amount of land in the southern hemisphere as in the northern, and an equal amount in the western hemisphere as in the eastern. Geographers speculated that, out west in the global Ocean, between Europe and

Asia, there must be a continent they styled the Perioeci ('beside the *oikouménē*'), and in the southern hemisphere the Antipodes ('under the feet') and the Antoeci ('opposite the *oikouménē*'). The Greeks understood that, in theory, a ship that sailed west from the Pillars of Heracles would eventually reach Asia, but they also knew that, in practice, no ship yet built could possibly survive such a voyage. The Ocean wasn't literally the edge of the world anymore, but it was still an impassable frontier.

The Roman conquest of Greece in the second century BC served only to amplify the influence of its civilization. While they thought the Greeks rather effete, the Romans admired their intellectual traditions. The wealthy employed, or bought, well-educated Greek tutors for their children, and many, like the orator Cicero, even went to Greece to study. By the first century BC, the educated Roman elite had fully accepted Greek cosmology as their own. 'We all agree on the Earth's shape. For surely we always speak of the round ball of the Earth,' wrote the Roman natural philosopher Pliny the Elder around AD 77. The conversion of the empire to Christianity in the fourth century did not change this. Despite some oddballs, like the monk and former Indian Ocean merchant Cosmas Indicopleustes (*fl.* 550), who believed that the universe was modelled on the Tabernacle of Moses, the spherical Earth, around which the Sun, Moon and planets circled, was incorporated into the official doctrine of the Catholic Church and, as a result, became embedded into the medieval European world view. How quickly the concept of the spherical Earth was accepted outside educated circles is much harder to gauge. When, in *c.*90 BC, the well-travelled Greek scientist Posidonius of Rhodes (135 BC–51 BC) visited Cape St Vincent, then believed to be the westernmost point of Europe,* the local Oestrimini, the 'dwellers in the far west', assured him that at sunset the sun could be heard hissing and boiling as it sank into the sea at the edge of the world. Such beliefs must have persisted for many centuries among the inhabitants of the Atlantic coast.

* The true westernmost point of Europe is Cabo da Roca, northwest of Lisbon.

Atlantis

It is ironic that it was one of the greatest minds of the rationalist tradition of Ancient Greek thought that gave birth to the most enduring myth of the Atlantic Ocean, that of the lost continent of Atlantis. Atlantis was first described by the philosopher Plato in two books, *Timaeus* and *Critias*, which he wrote around 360 BC. Plato gave the story of Atlantis credibility and authority by attributing it to the revered statesman and lawgiver Solon (*c.*630 BC–560 BC), whose social reforms are often credited with having laid the foundations of Athenian democracy. It was well known in Athens that Solon had visited Egypt, met the pharaoh Amasis II and studied its already ancient civilization and religion. Solon seems to have enjoyed discussing philosophy with Egyptian priests and, according to Plato's account, it was during a visit to the temple of the creator goddess Neith at Sais in the Nile Delta that one of her priests told him the story of Atlantis. On his return to Athens, Solon supposedly wrote an account of the story and later gave the manuscript to his friend Critias, whose descendants still possessed it in Plato's time.

The priest's story was set in a distant past, some 9,000 years before Solon's birth. All records of that time had been lost in the rest of the world because of a catastrophic global deluge that, thanks to its dry climate, Egypt alone had escaped. Atlantis, he claimed, was a large island, larger than North Africa and Asia Minor combined, in the Ocean opposite the Pillars of Heracles. When the gods divided the world among themselves, the sea god Poseidon chose this island as his own. Poseidon fell in love with Cleito, a mortal woman, by whom he fathered five pairs of boy twins. Poseidon made the eldest of the boys, Atlas, king over the island and named it Atlantis in his honour.* Poseidon turned a mountain into a citadel for Cleito and her descendants, carving a luxurious palace for her from the living rock: it even had hot and cold running water supplied by springs. The citadel was fortified

* From *Atlantis nesos* (Ancient Greek Ἀτλαντὶς νῆσος), 'Atlas's Island'.

with walls lined with tin on the inside and on the outside with orichalc, a mythical precious metal found only on Atlantis which gleamed like fire. Within the citadel was a temple to Poseidon covered with silver and decorated with golden sculptures, and there was a golden shrine on the spot where Poseidon and Cleito conceived their children. To make it completely secure, Poseidon surrounded the citadel with three concentric rings of sea. The citadel and the two rings of land within the rings of sea were all linked together with bridges. A canal linked the outer sea ring to the ocean and it became the city's harbour, packed with merchant ships from far and wide, the ocean being easily navigable in those days. Covered tunnels allowed ships to access the two inner sea rings as well. Where Atlanteans lived was determined by rank, with those of the highest rank living in the citadel alongside royalty and those of the lowest rank living on the outer land ring. The Atlanteans enjoyed their leisure time relaxing in delightful gardens or exercising in the city's many sports stadiums, and even the poorest homes had hot and cold water, carried around the city in aqueducts from the springs in the citadel.

As with most of the Atlantic's imaginary islands, like the Fortunate Isles, the living on Atlantis was blissfully easy. The capital city lay at the edge of a fertile rectangular plain, about 300 kilometres long by 200 kilometres wide, which was sheltered by mountains from the cold north winds. Rivers flowing down from the mountains were channelled into a grid of canals that both supplied water for irrigation and allowed boats to transport crops and other products between the city and the countryside. Food was plentiful: there were two crops each year, one in winter, one in summer. The mountains were higher and more beautiful than any others, with crystal lakes and verdant alpine pastures, while there were plains, forests and wetlands teeming with game, including elephants. With such abundant resources, Atlantis's population was both large and prosperous, able to support an army of 10,000 charioteers, 20,000 armoured hoplite infantrymen, over 100,000 archers and skirmishers, as well as a huge fleet of 1,200 triremes. Atlantis was a thalassocratic superpower.

At first, the Atlanteans were a thoroughly virtuous people, as befitted their divine ancestry; justice reigned in the land, and they did not allow their prosperity to corrupt them. As generation succeeded generation, however, the proportion of divine blood in their veins was diluted and they began to fall prey to all the usual all too human vices. Drunk on its power, Atlantis declared war on all who lived within the Pillars of Heracles: its fleets and armies conquered all the lands in their path as far as Italy and Egypt, enslaving their inhabitants. But Zeus had tired of the arrogant Atlanteans and decided to destroy them. In a violent cataclysm of floods and earthquakes, the entire island was sunk beneath the ocean in the course of a single day and night, its armies and fleets completely swallowed up. The island's shattered remains, lying just below the surface of the ocean, remained as a constant hazard to ships sailing the Atlantic.

In the Classical world, opinion was divided about the truth of Plato's story. Aristotle believed that his old mentor had invented Atlantis for didactic purposes, to illustrate what happened when a virtuous state turned bad, and never intended that anyone believe literally in its existence. This is probably still the majority opinion among philosophers and historians today, who see Atlantis as a metaphor for Periclean Athens, a democratic thalassocracy brought down by its own imperial ambitions. However, Plato was a much-respected figure, so many later scholars, such as the geographer Posidonius, believed that Atlantis must have been a real place. One of Plato's later followers, Crantor (d. *c.*276 BC), claimed that Egyptian priests had verified the story and that there was a column in the temple of Neith on which it was recorded in hieroglyphs. Crantor did not claim that it was he who had verified the story, or that he had ever seen the column himself, however, so its existence is questionable.

Belief in the reality of Atlantis became even stronger during the Middle Ages. Although Plato had been a pagan, his essentially monotheist philosophical beliefs were easily assimilated into Christian thought, so he continued to be a respected and revered figure, surely not the sort of person who would make things up. The European discovery of the New World following Columbus's trans-Atlantic voyage in 1492 led to speculation that this might have been a part of Atlantis that was not sunk. Might not the Aztecs, Maya or Inca be descendants of the Atlanteans? Speculation continues: Plato's myth has inspired a host of fringe theories, many of them racist, others involving extraterrestrials, and most years see a new alternative history claiming finally to have solved the ancient mystery. However, modern oceanographic surveys and the science of plate tectonics rule out absolutely any possibility that there ever existed any large landmass such as Plato described in the Atlantic Ocean. Whether he believed in it or not, Plato's Atlantis could never have existed. It is, however, harder to rule out the possibility that there might be at least a kernel of truth in the story.

The destruction of Thera

Santorini, known in ancient times as Thera, is unique among the islands in the Aegean Sea. Shaped like a west-facing crescent, the island almost encloses a cliff-lined 10-kilometre-wide bay in the centre of which is a small, active volcano. The volcano last erupted in 1950, but this was a minor affair compared to the one that created the bay in first place. The bay is actually a flooded caldera created by the collapse of a magma chamber following a massive volcanic eruption in around 1628 BC. Some 100 cubic kilometres of rock and ash were blasted into the atmosphere, making it the fifth most violent eruption of historical times. This was the eruption that buried the Minoan city at Akrotiri in ash (see p. 73). Earthquakes, ash falls and a tsunami caused damage all around the eastern Mediterranean, but it was most severe on Crete, the main centre of the Minoan civilization. It is possible that the economic damage was severe enough to send the Minoan civilization into a decline, contributing to its conquest by the Mycenaean Greeks *c.*1450 BC. If the story of Atlantis does have any factual basis, this city-engulfing, island-destroying catastrophe is surely the most likely source.

If the Mycenaeans or Minoans did make any records of the eruption of Thera, it should be no surprise that they have not survived. The Mycenaeans destroyed most of the Minoan palace archives when they conquered Crete. Then, around 1200 BC, the Mycenaean civilization itself abruptly and violently collapsed for reasons still unknown, writing fell out of use and Greece entered a dark age. By the time Greece emerged, 400 years later, the Minoans and Mycenaeans were barely half-remembered and then only through legends, not historical records. Egypt, which would have been rocked by the eruption of Thera, suffered no such civilizational collapse, so records of the event might conceivably have survived into Plato's time. It has been claimed that a record of the eruption has actually been found. This is the so-called Tempest Stele, erected by the Pharaoh Ahmose I at Thebes in Upper Egypt, which describes how a supernaturally dark and roaring storm came out of the west and caused immense flooding and damage in Egypt. This might well be how the Thera eruption was experienced in Egypt, with dark clouds of electrostatically charged ash drifting over the land, causing violent thunderstorms. However, it is unlikely that the storms described on the stele really were caused by the eruption. Ahmose is generally believed to have reigned from *c.*1550 BC to 1525 BC, and though there is some margin for error, both about these regnal dates and the exact date of the eruption, no amount of wishful massaging can make the two events contemporary.

Irrespective of whether Plato made the whole story up from scratch – the first sci-fi novel, as some have called it – or if he built it around a distant memory of the Thera eruption, Atlantis clearly has nothing to do with the real history of the Atlantic, but it has embedded itself into its imagined history. Plato may not have set out to deceive anyone, but he needed to make his idealized state plausible enough for his students to suspend their disbelief for long enough to engage with his teaching. In Plato's time, the bounds of the Mediterranean were far too well known for it ever to have contained an island the size of Atlantis, so he did what the poets had already done with the Hesperides and the Elysian Fields and located his tale in the ocean. The Greeks even had a word for this literary device; they called it 'oceanization' (*exokeanismos*). Even if Plato didn't believe that it was possible to sail over the edge of the world, the Atlantic was still so vast that it remained a place where almost anything might exist, or might have existed. Oceanization, in modified form, continues today. When the world becomes too small for an imaginary place, it can conveniently be located in outer space or a parallel universe.

Pytheas's voyage to the far north

Long-distance trade in the Iron Age was conducted through a chain of intermediaries, with the goods getting more expensive every time they changed hands. Goods could travel very long distances like this; for example, the aristocratic Celts who lived in the hillfort at Heuneburg in Germany not only drank Greek wine, they also dressed in Chinese silk. Greek traders from Massalia carried their goods about 400 kilometres up the Rhône and Saône rivers to Bragny-sur-Saône. The large quantities of Massaliot wine amphorae and Mediterranean pottery and glass that have been found here suggest that this was the major centre for the onward distribution of Mediterranean imports. Some Greeks went further into the Celtic lands. The sophisticated defences at Heuneberg were very likely designed by a Greek architect, for instance, while the bronze krater (a luxury Greek wine vessel) discovered in an aristocratic burial at Vix, in eastern France, was so large – it stood 1.64 metres tall and weighed 208 kilograms – and fragile that it could only have been made nearby by a Greek craftsman.

By far the most ambitious of these itinerant Greeks was Pytheas, a native of Massalia, who made a long voyage in the North Atlantic in the years around 320 BC. Pytheas was an experienced seafarer who already knew his way around the

Mediterranean and the Black Sea, and had probably also visited Gadir, so already knew something of the Atlantic. Although he was not a man of high social rank, he was well educated, and after his return to Massalia, he wrote a book about his travels entitled *On the Oceans*. Although his book became widely known, no copy of it has survived, and it is only known today from extracts quoted in the works of later Greek and Roman geographers. These, however, are enough to show that, for a man of his time, Pytheas was a scientifically minded traveller who made regular estimates of the latitude of the places he visited on his journey by measuring the height of the sun at noon and by the length of the days at midsummer, which was the standard way to calculate latitude in the ancient world. Unfortunately, Pytheas's amazing achievements were not fully recognized in his own time. His careful observations were regarded with scepticism by his contemporaries, and some even thought he'd never left home and just made it all up. Pytheas was also the victim of snobbery: the aristocratic Greek historian Polybius sniffily declared that it was unbelievable that an ordinary citizen could possibly have led such an ambitious expedition. If Pytheas's expedition had official backing, and it must have been paid for somehow, its primary motives were probably commercial, to seek out new trading opportunities for Massalia in areas not monopolized by Carthage. However, Pytheas clearly was also out to satisfy his own curiosity; he was the first traveller to be captivated by the far north's magnetic aura of inaccessibility. Later explorers who shared Pytheas's passion went in search of the North Pole, but he probably hoped to find Hyperborea, a blessed land of eternal daylight that the Greeks believed lay beyond the home of Boreas, the deified personification of the North Wind.

Celtic ships

When he set out from Massalia, Pytheas bypassed hostile Carthaginian territory by travelling across Gaul, perhaps along the rivers Rhône and Loire to the Bay of Biscay, a journey that, because it was largely by riverboat, took only about seven days: sailing via the Pillars of Heracles would have taken weeks even if the Carthaginians had allowed it. Once he arrived at the Atlantic coast, Pytheas chartered a ship, crew and an experienced pilot from one of the local Celtic tribes to take him on to Britain. The Veneti of Armorica (Brittany) were particularly well known for building sturdy wooden sailing ships, with which they carried on a brisk trade in tin with Britain. The ships built by the continental Celts were the future of wooden shipbuilding. Celtic shipwrights laid the ship's keel, attached the ribs and then laid the planks of the hull side to side, using iron nails to fasten them to the ribs. Planks laid this way did not fit as tightly as those using the Mediterranean pegged mortice-and-tenon technique, so tar- or fat-soaked wool, rope or moss was hammered between the planks to make the hull watertight. High prows and sterns protected the ships against swamping in the rough Atlantic storms. The ships carried a single mast with a square-rigged leather or linen sail and were steered with a side rudder. Unlike Mediterranean ships, where the strength of the hull lay in the planks and their fastenings, the strength of Celtic ships lay in the keel and the frames, and, consequently, they tended to be rather heavily built. Julius Caesar, who fought a sea battle against the Veneti in Quiberon Bay in 57 BC, remarked that the hulls of the Celtic ships were so thick that the rams of the Roman galleys could make no impression on them. The tough Celtic ships easily outsailed Caesar's galleys on the open Atlantic, but their reliance on sails alone left them vulnerable when the wind failed. Caesar's galleys closed in like a wolf pack around the becalmed Celtic ships. First the Roman crews used scythes attached to long poles to cut the Celtic ships' rigging, so preventing them escaping if the wind picked up again. Then the galleys grappled with the disabled Celtic ships, and the legionaries stormed aboard and cleared their decks in hand-to-hand fighting, the sort of slaughterhouse work at which they excelled. Caesar's victory was total, but he owed much to the weather.

A great advantage of the Celtic frame-first method was its relative simplicity compared to the painstaking Mediterranean method: ships could be built more quickly and cheaply by less skilled carpenters. By the early centuries AD, the Celts' frame-first method had been adopted by their German neighbours as well as their Roman conquerors, and it eventually became nearly universal throughout Europe. It may have something to do with their modern romanticized Otherworldly image, but it is surprising that the Celts are not commonly recognized as the technological innovators they were. Another of their inventions was the wooden barrel, which completely replaced the pottery amphora as the standard container for shipping liquids and salted, pickled and dried foodstuffs by around the seventh century AD. The European seafarers of the Age of Exploration would have found it much harder to carry sufficient supplies for long oceanic voyages if they had still needed to rely on the smaller, heavier, more fragile and less capacious amphorae.

Albion

After a ten-day voyage, Pytheas made landfall at Belerion (Cornwall) and, after visiting a tin-mining area, travelled the length of Britain. Pytheas called the island Albion and the people who lived on it the Pretani. Because the Romans were not very good at pronouncing their p's, the Pretani later became known as the Britanni and their island as Britannia after them. Albion, which is the earliest recorded name for Britain, probably got its name from the White Cliffs of Dover, which, when seen on a sunny day from the Pas de Calais, show as a gleaming white rampart on the far side of the Channel (from Ancient Greek *albos*, meaning 'white'). Pytheas, like all ancient travellers from the tideless Mediterranean who witnessed them for the first time, was impressed by the surging Atlantic tides, making the somewhat exaggerated claim that they reached up 80 cubits (35 metres): even the world's highest tide, in the Bay of Fundy in

Nova Scotia, is only 16.3 metres. The highest tide Pytheas could possibly have experienced on his journey would have been in the Severn estuary between England and Wales, where tides of 15 metres are common. Pytheas was on stronger ground when he linked the ebb and flow of the tides to the movements of the Moon. Pytheas was ahead of his time in this: Plato believed that tides were caused by water ebbing and flowing in vast submarine caves, while Pytheas's contemporary Aristotle thought that they were caused by the winds.

Everything the Greeks knew about Britain up until then was based on second- or third-hand travellers' tales. For the first time, Pytheas provided some reliable facts. He described how tin ore was mined, smelted and worked into ingots the shape of cow's knucklebones. Ingots this shape, about 10 cm long, have been discovered in the Bronze Age shipwreck off Salcombe in Devon (see pp. 70–1), confirming the accuracy of Pytheas's observations. The ingots were carted from the mining areas to the island of Ictis, which was the centre for the export trade. As Pytheas noted that it was linked to the mainland by a causeway at low tide, Ictis was probably St Michael's Mount, not far from Land's End. Pytheas travelled extensively enough around Britain to make a remarkably accurate estimate of the length of its coastline: 40,000 stades (7,250 kilometres), a mere 300 kilometres short of its true length. If it was a guess, it was a very lucky one.

Ultima Thule

The next stage of Pytheas's journey took him far beyond the edge of what the Greeks considered to be the known world. Setting out from an unidentified island called Berrice off Britain's north coast, Pytheas sailed north for six days until he reached what he described as a large island called Thule. Pytheas's observation that the Sun was below the horizon for only two or three hours at midsummer fixes Thule's latitude at about 64° north. However, like other early navigators, Pytheas had no means of calculating longitude: there is no doubt that Thule was a land in the far north, but where exactly? The uncertainty of its location has made Thule into a metaphor for ultimate hyperborean remoteness, closer to myth than reality. To later Classical and medieval writers, it became another of the Atlantic's phantom islands, somewhere to fire the imagination of north-minded explorers, somewhere they would search for in vain – *Ultima Thule* ('Farthermost Thule'). Thule's presumed location was pushed ever further northwards as the frontier of geographical knowledge expanded: the Thule of today is an early twentieth-century settlement, named after Pytheas's Thule, in Greenland at latitude 76° 31' north.*

Iceland, Greenland, Norway, the Faeroe Islands and the Shetland Islands have all been proposed as possible locations for Pytheas's Thule, but, as this comment on Pytheas's account by the Greek geographer Strabo (*c.*63/4 BC–AD 24) makes clear, Thule was inhabited by farming peoples:

> [Pytheas] might possibly seem to have made adequate use of the facts as regards the people who live close to the frozen zone, when he says that, the people live on millet and other herbs, and on fruits and roots; and where there are grain and honey, the people get their beverage, also, from them. As for the grain, he says, since they have no pure sunshine, that they pound it out in large storehouses, after first gathering in the ears thither; for the threshing floors become useless because of this lack of sunshine and because of the rains.[13]

Greenland was inhabited only by pre-Inuit hunter-gatherers of the Dorset culture at this time, and Iceland and the Faeroes by no one at all, so none of them could have been Pytheas's Thule. The Shetland Islands, which were inhabited by farmers, are too far south, so this means that Pytheas's landfall must have been

* Not counting a couple of islands in the Antarctic and a feature on the dumbbell-shaped trans-Neptunian object Arrokoth.

somewhere around Trondheim Fjord on Norway's west coast. Despite its northerly latitude, the Norwegian coast has a relatively mild climate thanks to the influence of the warm Atlantic Gulf Stream current, which makes arable farming possible even north of the Arctic Circle. Mountains shelter Trondheim Fjord from the worst of the Atlantic storm systems, while its south and east shores have some of Norway's most fertile soils. Neolithic farmers began to settle in this area as early as 2800 BC. Pytheas sailed still further north, and his observations make it clear that he crossed the Arctic Circle. He also claimed that a day's sail north of Thule was a 'congealed sea' with a spongy consistency like a sort of 'sea lung' across which it was possible neither to walk nor sail.

This was one of Pytheas's claims that his contemporaries found most incredible. The Greeks believed that, because of the twenty-four-hour summer daylight, the polar regions would be pleasantly warm and ice-free. Greek science was always more theoretical than experimental and observational, so there was an inherent unwillingness to let an inconvenient fact undermine a beautiful theory. This particular misconception died very hard. Even in the sixteenth century, cartographers were producing world maps showing a Hyperborean island set in an ice-free Arctic Ocean, inspiring explorers to go and look for it. The Dutch explorer Willem Barentsz was convinced that, once through the inconvenient barrier of pack ice, it would be possible to sail this imaginary ice-free ocean right across the North Pole to China. He died trying in 1597, an unsuccessful Arctic Columbus. Some scepticism about Pytheas's claim is warranted, because it would take several days' sailing to reach the edge of the permanent sea ice in summer from Arctic Norway today (although it could have been done if Thule was, instead, Iceland). However, Pytheas's voyage took place during the Iron Age Cold Epoch (900 BC–300 BC), when global temperatures were as much as 2°C lower than they are today, so the edge of the permanent sea ice may then have been further south. If Pytheas was simply relying on the testimony of other seafarers, who might they have been? It is very doubtful that anyone in

Norway at that time possessed the skills to build a ship capable of sailing so far on the open sea.

The 'congealed sea' was an impassable obstacle to further progress north. Pytheas returned to Thule, headed south, and left the Atlantic to explore the Baltic Sea, which he must have reached via the Skagerrak, the Kattegat and one of the passages through the Danish islands: these are the 'belts' from which the name of the Baltic is derived. Pytheas visited an island called Abalus, from whose shores amber was collected, so becoming the first person from the literate civilizations to discover this strange and beautiful stone's true origins. Amber burns well, and Pytheas tells us that, before they realized its value to others, the islanders used it as fuel, which seems improbable given the antiquity of the amber trade. Abalus has been identified as the Danish islands of Sjælland or Bornholm, the Samland peninsula near Kaliningrad (the richest source of amber today) and the North Sea island of Heligoland. Heligoland seems unlikely, as Pytheas says that Abalus was a day's sail from the lands of the Goths, who at that time lived on the Baltic Sea coast.

Pytheas explored the Baltic at least as far east as the Vistula before returning to Massalia. The Greek historian Polybius says that Pytheas returned by way of the Greek colony of Tanais, at the mouth of the Don river on the Sea of Azov. Although he would easily have found a ship there to take him home, it would have involved a journey of more than 2,000 kilometres by land and river through eastern Europe for no very obvious purpose, when he could have taken the much shorter 'Amber Road', the overland trade route which linked the Baltic with the Adriatic Sea. Whatever route he took, Pytheas obviously got home safely from his pioneering voyage, but nothing is known about his later life. As for Pytheas's sponsors, they were probably disappointed with their investment. It was all very interesting knowing how the Britons smelted tin and how amber was gathered in the Baltic, but trade in these commodities was already flourishing and, as for Thule, there was clearly nothing there worth bothering with. At any rate, Pytheas found no imitators.

Pax Romana

Wars are always easier to start than to end, and small conflicts have an unpredictable habit of spiralling out of control. In 264 BC, a quarrel between two Greek cities in Sicily drew Carthage and the rising Italian city-state of Rome into a series of three bitter wars for the domination of the Mediterranean. In 146 BC, the Romans finally crushed Carthage and brought all its dominions into the Roman Empire. Triumphant, the Roman Empire began two and a half centuries of continuous expansion, which brought not only all of the Mediterranean under its control but also Europe's Atlantic coast from the Pillars of Heracles, north to the island of Britain. Fleets of warships demonstrated Roman power as far north as the Orkney Islands.

The *Pax Romana* encouraged the growth of long-distance trade both by land and sea. Piracy and banditry was suppressed and there were no political barriers to travel, the whole empire being a single vast free trade zone. Yet it seems that the impact of this on the Atlantic sea lanes was small. With the Carthaginian empire consigned to history, the Atlantic was open to all Mediterranean seafarers again, but there was no rush of explorers or of merchants either; it was a case of continuity rather than change. The reason is that most of the new trade stimulated by the *Pax Romana* was diverted to the safer, shorter river routes across now peaceful Roman-controlled Gaul. It was less than half the distance, for example, to travel from Rome to Britain via the Rhône, the Saône, the Rhine and the short sea crossing of the Channel, as it was to sail via the Atlantic. Why risk the ocean if you didn't need to? It's not surprising, then, that Greek Massalia continued to flourish under Roman rule.

Roman-period shipwrecks are rare in the Atlantic – only about nineteen are known, compared to nearly 1,800 in the Mediterranean – but this doesn't necessarily mean that there was little shipping. The Atlantic is a more violent environment, where wrecks are broken up much more quickly than in the quieter Mediterranean, so what survives may not be a representative sample. A well-preserved Greco-Roman lead anchor stock recovered from the Irish Sea near Porth Felen in North Wales proves that, despite the risks, Mediterranean ships sometimes did brave the Atlantic and sail all the way to Britain. Other shipwrecks, such as the ship carrying a cargo of Samian Ware pottery from Gaul that was wrecked on the Pudding Pan Bank off Whitstable in Kent, the ship wrecked off St Peter Port, Guernsey, carrying pitch, and a third wrecked off the Sept-Îles, Brittany, carrying British lead ingots, were all built in the local Celtic tradition. These wrecks tell us that the regular cabotage (port-to-port) trade along the Atlantic coast remained largely in the hands of local Celtic, Lusitanian and Iberian ship-owners, just as it had for centuries. Gades (Cádiz), as Gadir was now known, continued to prosper as the main Atlantic entrepôt, where Mediterranean merchants sold their cargoes for onward distribution by local shippers before retreating to calmer waters. The volume of shipping cannot have been negligible. Lighthouses were built to aid navigation along the empire's coasts; seven are known to have been built along the Atlantic coast, at Cádiz, Chipiona (Andalusia), Cabo Espichel (Portugal), the famous Tower of Hercules at A Coruña (Galicia), Gijón (Asturias), and at Boulogne and Dover on opposite sides of the Strait of Dover. These all represent a considerable investment of resources, and they are very likely not to have been the only ones.

Caius the fish eater

Despite the lighthouses, ships still went far astray. A second-century Roman cooking pot dredged up by a Welsh trawler from the 200-metre-deep Porcupine Bank, some 200 kilometres west of Ireland, must have come from one such ship that was blown off course and foundered in bad weather. The pot had the name C. Pisce Fagi engraved on its base, together with a sketchy drawing of a quadrupedal animal with a long tail. Was this the name of the pot's owner, Caius Piscus Fagus, the first named seafarer to have drowned in the North Atlantic? Or was it the name of the equally unfortunate ship's cat, Caius Pisce Fagi, a Latin-Greek joke meaning 'Caius the fish eater'? Luckier were the sailors from Gades who, in 80 BC, told the Roman general Sertorius that they had been driven some 10,000 stades (approximately 1,850 kilometres*) west from the African coast to a group of two islands separated by a narrow channel, which they believed were the Fortunate Islands. 'Rains fall there seldom,' they told Sertorius,

> and these are moderate, but for the most part they enjoy gentle breezes carrying dew, and so the islands not only provide soil rich for plowing and planting, but also bear fruit that grows on its own, abundant and sweet, to feed the inhabitants who enjoy leisure without toil or trouble. With temperate seasons that change only moderately, the islands possess a pleasant climate. The north and east winds blowing out from that region over the long distance dissipate in the open space and lose their force, while the south and west winds passing over the ocean bring occasional gentle showers from the sea, but often bring cool to the moist, clear weather and gently nourish the soil.[14]

Sertorius 'was seized with a wondrous desire to settle these islands and live there in peace, freed from tyranny and unending war', but he chose instead to pursue his political ambitions which, ultimately, ended with his murder by rivals. The distance from Africa to the two islands corresponds almost exactly with the position of the Azores, but the geography fits Madeira and its smaller neighbour Porto Santo better – although neither group of islands was inhabited at the time. The islands' blissful environment is comparable to that of those discovered by the stray Phoenician seafarers in the sixth century so may well be the same. This is a repeating story, because sailors had no way to fix their longitude, newly discovered islands could not be precisely located and were repeatedly discovered, lost, rediscovered and, to

* A Roman *stadia* was 625 Roman feet or approximately 185 metres.

confuse things still more, sometimes given new names. Sertorius's biographer, Plutarch, however, was not convinced that the sailors had really visited the islands, seeing their story, instead, as evidence that 'even among the barbarians a firm belief prevails that here [in the Atlantic] are the Elysian Fields and the abode of the blessed, of which Homer sang'.

The Islands of Dogs

The only really significant Atlantic voyage of the Roman imperial period was the first recorded discovery of the Canary Islands by an expedition led by Juba II (r. 25 BC–AD 23), the Romans' vassal king of Mauretania (present-day Morocco and Algeria, not the modern country of the same name). Although Juba was a Berber, he was brought up and educated in Rome, where he had learned to speak and write Latin and Greek fluently. Juba earned a reputation as a polymath, with interests ranging from art and theatre to archaeology, history and geography. He is known to have written a book about the voyage of Hanno of Carthage and it was this interest that motivated Juba to lead his own expedition south along the African coast. At Mogador, Juba re-established the Tyrian purple dye works and sailed on to explore the Canary Islands, apparently visiting six of the seven main islands, where he found houses, livestock and a multitude of snarling dogs but no people. Juba may have thought he was visiting the mythical Fortunate Isles, but, unfavourably impressed by the number of yapping dogs, he gave the islands another name, *Canariae Insulae*, meaning 'the Islands of Dogs' (from *canis*, Latin for dog). The two names were used interchangeably to identify the islands for the next 1,500 years, with some geographers believing that the Canary Islands and the Fortunate Isles were the same and others, in a case of oceanization, believing that the Fortunate Isles must be sought in some other, more inaccessible place. Finds of Roman artefacts, such as amphorae and glass, on archaeological sites, and at least one shipwreck, are evidence that, after Juba's visit, Roman merchants became at least occasional visitors to the Canaries. Not surprisingly, analysis of the style of the amphorae suggests that most of these traders came from southern Spain or North Africa. These contacts had ceased by the late fourth century, but an awareness of the islands as the western edge of the known world persisted into the Middle Ages, even if some of the things that were written about them were more appropriate to phantom islands than real ones.

Exploring in style

Despite his enthusiasm for Hanno, Juba did not attempt to emulate him by voyaging any further south than the Canaries. His reluctance may have had something to do with the fate of Eudoxus of Cyzicus, the ancient world's most flamboyant explorer. In 118 BC, Eudoxus, a Greek merchant in the service of Pharaoh Ptolemy VIII, discovered how to use the Indian Ocean's annual monsoon winds to sail directly to southern India and back to Egypt in the same year, a voyage which had formerly taken two years of painfully slow coast-hugging. Returning from a subsequent voyage to India, Eudoxus was blown off course down the East African coast. According to the Greek geographer Strabo, there 'he found the end of a wooden prow that had come from a wrecked ship and had a horse carved on it'. When he was told by local people that the wreckage came from a ship that was voyaging from the west, Eudoxus decided to take it with him back to Egypt. Shipmasters there told him that the figurehead must have belonged to a type of small fishing boat called, from their horse-head-shaped prows, a *hippoi*, from Gades. Many fishing boats were lost at sea and they speculated that this one had sailed too far down the African coast and been unable to return against the wind and currents. The crew, they told Eudoxus, must have made a desperate attempt to get home by sailing around Africa, into the Indian Ocean, and had come close to succeeding before being shipwrecked. That at least was what Eudoxus believed. Fired by ambition to add to his laurels as a pioneering navigator, Eudoxus mounted his own lavishly equipped expedition – he even took dancing girls in his crew to keep him entertained – to sail around Africa from Gades and create another new route to India. After working his way south down the West African coast, losing a ship along the way, Eudoxus arrived at a land inhabited by 'Æthiopians', where he turned back, discovering an uninhabited but well-watered forested island on the way. 'Æthiopian' was the usual term used to describe Black Africans, but these are described as neighbours of the North African Berber kingdom of Mauretania, so he cannot have got far beyond Morocco. Undeterred, a year later, Eudoxus launched a second, equally well-equipped expedition from Gades and was never heard from again.[15] Was there music and dancing on the deck of his penteconter as he sailed off into oblivion? The Phoenicians and Carthaginians had always worked hard to create and reinforce the perception of the Atlantic as a frightful place, and they had succeeded rather well. Eudoxus's disappearance probably only reinforced that message. Outsiders would not pluck up the courage again and return to explore the shadowy 'Æthiopian Sea', as the South Atlantic was known, for all of 1,400 years.

Edge of empire

The Romans saw the 'monster-filled' Atlantic as the *maris exterior*, the 'outer sea', in contrast to the enclosed *mare internum* of the Mediterranean. Like any other imperial frontier, the ocean was an unwelcome reminder to the Romans that their power had limits. It was different only in that when they looked across this frontier they saw neither the opportunity for conquest nor the threat of invasion. 'Where Ocean with its waves surrounds the world no land will meet you with opposing arms,' wrote the poet Tibullus in 27 BC, except, that was, in Britain, whose conquest he thought was just a matter of time. Julius Caesar had already led punitive expeditions to Britain in 55 BC and 54 BC, but it was not until AD 43 that the Romans invaded Britain with the intention of conquering the entire island. The plan didn't work out. Roman armies advanced as far north as the Moray Firth in the northeast of Scotland, but the British tribes of the wild Highlands could not be subdued, at least not at a price the Romans thought was worth paying. By 105, the Romans had withdrawn to the 110-kilometre-wide isthmus between the Solway Firth on the Irish Sea and the Tyne river on the North Sea. This was where the expansion of the Roman Empire ran out of steam. The emperor Hadrian ordered the isthmus to be fortified with a stone wall in 122, and it was there that the frontier in Britain remained, a couple of short periods excepted, until the end of Roman rule in Britain in 410. Although there is plenty of evidence for trade contacts, after their failure to complete the conquest of Britain, the Romans wisely decided against attempting the conquest of Ireland: it would have been just as difficult and unprofitable to subdue as the Highlands.

Hadrian's Wall proved effective at protecting Roman territory from overland raids by the northern British tribes, who by this time had taken to calling themselves Picts, but they could still outflank it by sea at both ends. The coasts of Roman Britain were also exposed to raids by an Irish people called the Scotti from the west and, in the east, by Germanic tribes from the islands and wetlands around the Rhine estuary and the Waddensee, the shallow sea that lies between the Frisian Islands and the mainland along the North Sea coast of the Netherlands, Germany and Denmark. The Roman naturalist Pliny the Elder, writing around AD 77, noted that the Germanic tribes had recently begun fitting sails, woven from flax, to their ships, a practice they'd adopted from their Celtic neighbours in Gaul. With their newfound mobility, Germanic pirates began raiding around the North Sea, on occasions even attacking Brittany and entering the Bay of Biscay. Piracy escalated out of control in the third century with the emergence of the Saxons, a powerful new coalition of Germanic tribes who lived between the Ems River and the neck of the Jutland peninsula. Saxon raiders ranged almost as widely as the Vikings would later do, plundering in the Orkney Islands and Ireland, both shores of the Channel, Brittany and into the Bay of Biscay as far as the Loire and the Garonne. Shipping grain across the Channel from Britain to the garrisons defending the embattled Rhine frontier became all but impossible at times. The Romans created a dedicated naval command to defend the 'Saxon Shore', backed up by coastal watchtowers and fortified fleet bases on the east coast of Britain and on the Channel coast of Gaul. Forty-oared galleys, painted sea-green for camouflage, patrolled the British seas, but the Roman historian Ammianus Marcellinus complained that, despite these defences, the Saxons' raids were still difficult to counter because 'they could go wherever the wind took them', meaning that they could choose their moment to strike: the tactical initiative was always going to be with them, as it would be later with the Vikings. The Gallo-Roman bishop Sidonius Apollinaris even claimed that the Saxons were so confident of their seafaring skills that they deliberately waited for bad weather before setting out on a raid to increase their chances of achieving surprise. The good bishop was also horrified by the Saxon practice of sacrificing a number of their captives to their gods in the hope that they would, in return, send a favourable wind for their voyage home. It's clear from Roman sources that Saxon seafarers used sails, but nothing else is known about their ships. It is usually assumed that the Saxons built ships in the Nordic tradition, as their neighbours in southern Jutland, the Angles, are known to have done from archaeological sites at Nydam in Jutland and Sutton Hoo in England, but that can't be taken for granted. There is no conclusive evidence that the Angles had yet adopted sail technology, so it may be as likely that the Saxons actually built ships in the tradition of their Celtic neighbours to the west.

The most prominent leader among the raiders from Ireland was Niall of the Nine Hostages, a proto-historical king of the Uí Néill dynasty, who was active in the later part of the fourth century or early fifth century. Niall is said to have led seven raids on Britain and across the Channel in Brittany: one tradition holds that he was eventually killed in battle with a rival pirate leader on the Loire river in France. Irish raiders were mainly after captives for the slave trade: Niall's most famous victim, at least according to tradition, was a sixteen-year-old British Christian boy named Patrick, who was destined to play an important part in Ireland's history. The Irish raided in hide boats called curachs, but they also built wooden ships from pine and oak which they usually described as 'long-ships': both types of ship could be sailed and rowed. A gold hoard found in 1896 by two ploughman near Broighter in Northern Ireland contained an 18-centimetre-long model ship, equipped with nine pairs of oars, a loosely attached steering oar at the stern and a single mast with a spar for a square sail. It is easy to imagine Niall and other Irish pirates setting out in ships like this for their slave raids. Seaworthy, lightweight and with a shallow draught, curachs made excellent assault boats. There would not have been room for many captives in such ships, but there were a lot of them. An Old Irish text called the *Senchus Fer nAlban* ('The History of the Men of Scotland') describes how, in the seventh century, the Irish clans of Dálriada could raise a fleet of 177 ships, each with 14 oarsmen – nearly 2,500 warriors in total – a truly formidable raiding party.

A sea foaming with the beat of hostile oars

As the Roman Empire's woes multiplied, it seemed to the poet Claudian that the seas off its western coasts literally 'foamed with the beat of hostile oars'. The Scots, Picts and Saxons secretly formed an alliance and, in June 367, their predatory fleets fell upon the British coasts from all sides at once, overwhelming the Roman defences. The pirates plundered the Roman province from end to end, and one group, called the Attacotti, were even accused of feasting on their British captives. However, the raiders were not, yet, bent on conquest, and the Romans regained control after two years of hard fighting. Though the defences were restored, an inescapable air of decay and insecurity now hung over Roman Britain; towns shrank and many country villas were abandoned.

By this time, the empire was under attack by Germanic tribes along its entire European frontier, from the Black Sea to the North Sea. Troops were frequently withdrawn from Britain to shore up defences elsewhere or to fight in civil wars. By 410, the Britons had had enough, so they expelled the Roman administration and declared independence. British unity was short-lived, however, as old tribal conflicts, long suppressed by Roman rule, re-emerged. Sensing opportunity, the Saxons came to stay. This time, according to later historical traditions, they were joined by the Angles and smaller groups of Jutes (also from Jutland). Archaeological evidence suggests that there were probably also Frisians and Franks among the settlers. Once they had established small tribal kingdoms in their east coast bridgehead, the Germanic settlers, now known collectively as the Anglo-Saxons, began to extend their control steadily westwards to the Irish Sea and the Atlantic.

The exact nature of the Anglo-Saxon settlement has been much debated. The earliest account, written by the British monk Gildas around 540, described what he called the *adventus Saxonum* ('the coming of the Saxons') in apocalyptic terms. Hordes of pagan invaders massacred the, by now, Christian Britons and drove the survivors into exile overseas or forced them to take refuge in the mountainous west of Britain. Later monastic historians, such as the Anglo-Saxon monk Bede, incorporated Gildas's work into their own influential accounts of the Anglo-Saxon settlement of what soon became known, after the Angles, as England. It wasn't until the later twentieth century that these early histories were critically reassessed. As is so often the case with historical revisionism, many of the revisionists rushed to the opposite extreme and denied the possibility of large-scale migrations across the North Sea, seeing such claims as monkish hyperbole. The cultural and linguistic changes that marked early medieval Britain could, they argued, be accounted for by small bands of aristocratic Germanic warriors displacing the native elite and imposing their rule on the British population, which then adopted the prestigious identity, culture and language of their new rulers. A decade or more of intensive research into the aDNA of human remains in early medieval cemeteries across eastern England may finally have settled the issue. Gildas was right that there was a large-scale maritime migration of people of Continental North European (CNE)* descent into Britain from the other side of the North Sea following the end of Roman rule: it was in fact the largest migration into the British Isles since the Bronze Age. On the other hand, the research also shows that Gildas's genocidal massacres and ethnic cleansing probably never happened: the genetic evidence also points to a high degree of continuity with the Romano-British population. Large numbers of Britons clearly continued to live among, and intermarry with, the Germanic newcomers, gradually assimilating their identity, culture and Old English language.

On the other side of the Irish Sea, the Scots too seized the opportunity presented by Britain's post-Roman power vacuum and founded a small kingdom across the North Channel in Argyll. The Scots called their kingdom Dálriada, but as it grew, eventually, to incorporate all the territory of the Picts, it acquired a new name, Alba, from Albion, the ancient name for Britain. Latin writers, however, called it Scotia, meaning, confusingly, 'Land of the Irish' or, in English, 'Scotland'. The fate of the Picts was similar to that of the Britons who lived under the Anglo-Saxons: they were completely assimilated to the Scots' identity and Gaelic language. Other Irish groups settled in parts of west Wales, although here it was they who were assimilated into the native population. Meanwhile, Britons from Cornwall and Devon began their own maritime migration and founded new kingdoms across the Channel in Brittany. The scale of British

* Researchers into aDNA avoid using modern ethnic identifications like Anglo-Saxon, Germanic or Celtic, because of the well-founded concern that their work might be misused for political purposes.

emigration is uncertain, but there were clearly enough of them to give Brittany its name, from the Latin *Britannia Minor*, meaning 'Little Britain'. Other groups of Britons followed the Atlantic seaways south and settled in Galicia, founding the relatively short-lived colony of Britonia in the area between A Coruña and Lugo. By 476, the Western Roman Empire was all but gone and, with it, went the *Pax Romana*. In its place was a mosaic of mutually hostile kingdoms founded by migrating coalitions of Germanic peoples, Visigoths, Ostrogoths, Vandals, Sueves, Burgundians, Alamanni and Franks, as well as the Saxons and Angles. The continental routes between the Mediterranean and the Atlantic and the North Sea were no longer secure, and that led to a revival of the old Atlantic sea lanes.

5

Promised lands

AD 400–1500

Exiles for Christ – Brittany – The green martyrdom – Rowing about – St Brendan's search for the Promised Land of the Saints – Journey's end – Putting St Brendan on the map – Return to Thule – Peat, barley and sheep – Navigating a curach – Did the Irish discover America? – The red martyrdom – The sea road to Santiago – The pilgrim's complaint – The Great Isle of the Solstice

In 1233, Earl Richard of Cornwall built a castle on the breathtakingly exposed headland of Tintagel on north Cornwall's wild Atlantic coast. The headland, now almost severed from the mainland by centuries of coastal erosion, is a natural stronghold, but Earl Richard's castle was built in a deliberately old-fashioned style that betrays that its true purpose was not defensive. The castle was built to look older than it really was so that the earl could associate himself with Tintagel's ancient connections with King Arthur, the legendary ruler who led the Britons in their fight against the invading Saxons. Having served its political purpose, the castle was abandoned by Richard's successors, and within a century of its completion the roofs had fallen in and it was well on the way to becoming the romantically picturesque ruin it is today.

Because of its Arthurian connections, Tintagel has been one of Cornwall's major tourist attractions since the nineteenth century, but it was already well known in Earl Richard's day thanks to Geoffrey of Monmouth's (1095–1155) medieval best-seller *The History of the Kings of Britain*, in which he identified it as Arthur's birthplace. Long before that, even, Tintagel was associated in local folk history with the kings of Dumnonia, a British kingdom comprising Cornwall and Devon, that flourished from the fifth century until its conquest by the Anglo-Saxons around 825. Excavations conducted at Tintagel since the 1930s haven't found any evidence for the existence of King Arthur, but they did prove that there was substance to the local traditions. The headland was indeed a high-status site in that period and one whose inhabitants were remarkably well connected, feasting on oysters and pork with fine tableware imported from Gaul, Anatolia and Tunisia and enjoying eastern Mediterranean wine in Spanish glass goblets. Olive oil was also consumed on the site, some of it, to judge from the type of amphorae that it was imported in, originating in Syria. Graffiti on an inscribed slate window ledge, dated to the seventh century, shows that residents or visitors to Tintagel were literate in Latin and Greek as well as the native Celtic language. While the amount of imported pottery found at Tintagel is exceptional – it was perhaps a distribution centre for imports – evidence for trade with the Mediterranean has been found at over a dozen other contemporary high-status sites from the west coast of Britain and from Ireland. Significantly, no such evidence has been found in the Anglo-Saxon-occupied areas in eastern Britain, clear evidence that these Mediterranean imports were reaching Britain not via the Roman-period continental river routes but by sea: the old Atlantic sea lanes were reasserting themselves.

While some of these imports may have reached Britain and Ireland directly in ships from the eastern Mediterranean, most probably came via intermediaries in the Iberian Peninsula. Greek merchants took on cargoes in the eastern Mediterranean and sailed west, picking up additional cargo in Carthage before sailing through the Strait of Gibraltar into the Atlantic. Although there is a record that the bishop St Martin of Braga was able to find a ship to take him directly from the Holy Land to Galicia in *c.*550, most Greek merchants probably sailed no further than ports around the mouths of the Tagus and Mondego rivers in Portugal. Concentrations of imported pottery imply that these ports were entrepôts where eastern Mediterranean products were unloaded and sold on to Gaulish, British and Irish merchants who took them the rest of the way. In the seventh century, Irish merchants are known to have visited the tidal island of Noirmoutier in the Bay of Biscay with a large cargo of leather goods and woollens. These are the kinds of products Britain exported in Roman times, along with tin and lead, so demand for them may have continued undiminished despite the fall of the empire.

Exiles for Christ

The activities of early medieval merchants along the Atlantic coast may be largely undocumented, but that isn't the case for another class of seafarer: Christian monks and missionaries. Christianity first spread through the Roman Empire as a religion of the urban poor, but the people of the countryside, the *pagani*, were much slower adopters, so it was not until the religion began to be promoted by the emperors in the fourth century that it became firmly established in the largely rural west. No sooner was it Christianized than the Western Roman Empire was over-run by migrating Germanic tribes. Many of these tribes, such as the Visigoths, who occupied Iberia, and the Ostrogoths, who occupied Italy, were already Christian but belonged to the Arian church, which Orthodox Catholics regarded as heretical. Others, like the Franks, who conquered northern Gaul, and the Anglo-Saxons were still pagans. Between them, the pagans and the Arians came close to cutting off the now independent Celtic Christian communities in Britain and western Gaul from the main centres of Orthodox Christianity in the Mediterranean and, in particular, Rome, whose authoritarian bishops, the popes, claimed doctrinal supremacy over all Christians. Because both sides of the narrow Dover Strait were controlled by pagans, all contacts between the Celtic churches had by necessity to be via the Atlantic seaways. While it never formally rejected papal authority, this relative isolation gave the Celtic church space to develop its own distinctive spiritual practices, one of which was an ascetic form of monasticism, inspired by the eremitical early Christian Desert Fathers, that valued contemplative solitude over communal prayer. Celtic monasticism also did not require a monk to stay in the same monastery his whole life, as the dominant Benedictine form of monasticism did: a Celtic monk could wander and embark on a *peregrinatio*, a journey for the love of God. Between them, the two practices created a unique tradition of monastic seafaring.

One of the first to describe a missionary voyage as a *peregrinatio* was St Patrick, Ireland's patron saint. Born around 385, Patrick was one of thousands of Britons captured and taken to Ireland as slaves in the dying days of Roman rule in Britain. This must have been a particularly degrading experience for Patrick, because, by his own account, his family were people of rank in the Roman administration. He described his father, Calpurnius, as a decurion (a city governor) and a deacon in the church, while his grandfather was a priest in an unidentified town he calls *Bannavem Taberniae*, which he states was close to Britain's Irish Sea coast. One possible candidate is Ravenglass (Roman *Glannoventa*), a small and exposed port on the Cumbrian coast, but Patrick has plenty of other claimants, and certainty is impossible. Patrick, then still in his teens, was put to work by his captors as a shepherd, and in this humble occupation he found God. When, after six years in captivity, he escaped back to Britain on a merchant ship, Patrick decided to train as a priest. Ignoring his family's pleas to stay safe at home, he sailed to Gaul to study under St Germanus, the bishop of Auxerre, who had close links with the British church. During one of his visits to Britain, he is said to have led the Britons to a bloodless victory in battle against a Pictish-Saxon alliance, his war cry of 'alleluia' being sufficient to scare the pagans off. Patrick's *peregrinatio* began around 435, when he returned as a missionary to Ireland, where he remained until his death around 461. Although he is known as 'the Apostle of Ireland', Patrick was certainly not the first missionary to preach the Gospel there. The first missions were sent by the church in Gaul in the late fourth or early fifth century, and by 431 there were already enough converts to justify Pope Celestine I appointing Palladius of Auxerre as the first bishop of the Irish. Other continental missionaries active in Ireland around this time included St Auxillius, St Iserninus and St Secundinus. This Gaulish-led mission concentrated on the south of Ireland, while Patrick's achievement was the conversion of the still completely pagan north of Ireland. Ireland had escaped occupation by the Roman Empire and, despite trade links, it had remained defiantly un-Romanized, clinging to its own distinctive version of the late Iron Age La Tène culture. However, these seafaring missionaries brought with them more than a religion. Medieval Christianity was a cultural package that included the Latin alphabet and language and, with them, all the literature of the Classical world. Ireland's cultural horizons perceptibly widened as Christianity became established and Irish monks became learned not only in Christian theology but in the Classics too.

Brittany

There were close links by sea too between the churches in Wales, Devon and Cornwall with the British colonies in Brittany. Indeed, it is very likely that the church was actively involved in the British settlement there. Early medieval monastic writers, such as the gloom-laden Welsh monk Gildas and the Anglo-Saxon historian Bede, characterized the Britons who emigrated to Brittany during the fifth century as terrified and demoralized refugees fleeing the triumphant Anglo-Saxon invaders. However, most of the emigrants came from areas in the west of Britain that had seen little of the invaders, so it is likely that the settlement was a more opportunistic affair to take advantage of land left vacant as a result of the population decline, resulting from plague, war and other factors, which afflicted many areas of the late Roman Empire. Certainly, pollen samples from peat bogs point to a widespread decline and abandonment of farmland and a corresponding advance of woodland in late Roman Brittany: there clearly was land there going spare.

The main wave of British immigration came in the hundred years or so between the mid-fifth century and mid-sixth century, but our sources of information are so sparse that we don't even know if the British settlers were resisted or welcomed by the local population. There seem to have been two waves of migration. The first took place in the late 460s under the leadership of a king called Riothamus. This may have taken place with the agreement of the Romans, as Riothamus was an ally of the Roman Emperor Anthemius against the Visigoths, who had occupied southwest Gaul. A second and more sustained migration took place in the first half of the sixth century. Later traditions recorded in the *vitae* (religious biographies) of early Breton saints suggest that this migration was organized by aristocrats with close links to the royal family of Dumnonia. By the later sixth century, three main regional powers had emerged: the names of two of them, Cornouaille in the west and Domnonée in the north, betray their links to Cornwall and Devon. The third, Broërech, in the south-east, is named for its founder, Waroc. The most obvious evidence of the British settlement today comes from place names. The similarities between Breton and Cornish and Welsh place names are immediately obvious, even to a non-linguist. Common Breton place-name elements of British origin include Plou (Welsh *plwyf*, 'people'), Lan (Welsh *llan*, 'church'), tré (Welsh *tref*, a subdivision of a parish), ker (Welsh *caer*, 'town'), coët (Welsh *coed*, wood) and lis or lez (Welsh *llys*, a hall, i.e. the residence of a notable person). These British-influenced place-name elements are concentrated in northern and western Brittany and probably give a good idea of where the main British settlements were. The British settlement is evidenced not only in place names, of course, but also in the Breton language itself, which is closely related to modern Welsh and Cornish.

The cross-Channel migration was accompanied by a major movement of British clergy, who introduced the practices of the Celtic church. A majority of the leading clergy seem to have been from Wales: of the 'Seven Founding Saints' of the Breton church, five were certainly Welsh. These clergy were probably an integral part of the leadership of the colonies because, according to their *vitae*, most of them had some genealogical connections to British or early Breton royal houses: they were people with political as well as spiritual status. The *vitae* tell how priests and monks, such as the Welshman St Paul Aurelian (St Pol), founded churches and monasteries among the ruins of abandoned villas and deserted Roman towns inhabited only by wild animals. Others, like St Budoc, who spent part of his life on the island of Bréhat, followed the tradition of the *peregrini* and sought out offshore islands for their monasteries. The ecclesiastical traffic was not one-way. The Breton-born St Magloire (d. 575) was sent as a child to Wales to study under St Illtud, who was later claimed to have been a cousin of the legendary King Arthur, before returning to Brittany, where he became bishop of Dol. Many of the miracles attributed to Magloire have a maritime setting, for example, saving a group of children swept out to sea in a storm and seeing off a Saxon pirate attack on the Channel Island of Sark. Another Breton saint, Gwenhael, made missionary journeys to Britain and Ireland, introducing the cult of his spiritual mentor St Winwaloe (Breton Gwenole), the founder of the important Breton abbey of Landévennec. Churches dedicated to Winwaloe in Wales, Cornwall and Brittany are lasting testament to the cross-Channel nature of his cult, and there were many others.

The green martyrdom

While the concept of *peregrinatio* originated in Britain, it was the Irish who took it, and themselves, furthest. Most Irish monks who became *peregrini* headed south to continental Europe, where their high reputation for learning made them much in demand as teachers at monastic schools. For these monks, going to sea was merely an incidental necessity – Ireland is an island, after all. For others, the hardships and dangers of seafaring were embraced as an act of submission to the will of God. Irish monasticism was inspired by the ascetic traditions of the Desert Fathers, devout Christian hermits who had formed loose communities for mutual support in the Egyptian desert in the early fourth century. Living an austerely simple life in the desert was not only about finding solitude for contemplation and prayer, it was a substitute for the ultimate sacrifice for faith of martyrdom, a kind of death in life. Ireland is short of deserts, but it had many ideal alternatives in the storm-battered islands off its rugged Atlantic coast. In fact, Irish monks called this kind of life the 'green martyrdom', in contrast to the 'white martyrdom' of the Desert Fathers and the 'red martyrdom' of those who had been killed for their faith. 'This is our denial of ourselves,' an early Irish homily declared, 'if we do not indulge our desires and if we abjure our sins. This is our taking-up of our cross upon us if we receive loss and martyrdom and suffering for Christ's sake.' Adopting this life was not for the faint-hearted. Early medieval Ireland was a warlike society and monks, most of whom came from the warrior aristocracy, saw themselves as spiritual warriors battling the Devil with prayer and meditation on behalf of all Christians. The monks considered their battles to be more important than the warrior's. Human bodies were ephemeral things, after all; they would perish soon enough, with or without help from swords and spears, while the physical suffering of the ascetic life was but a thing of the moment. The soul, however, was immortal and, should the Devil claim it, it faced an eternity of unimaginable suffering in Hell.

Surely the most spectacular of these island monasteries was Skellig Michael, a jagged twin-peaked splinter of rock rising over 200 metres above the Atlantic off the coast of County Kerry. Landing on Skellig Michael is difficult at the best of times, and in winter the community would have been cut off from the outside world for weeks on end. The monastery, reached from the landing place by a steep and exposed stone stairway, was situated on the lower of the island's two summits, fully exposed to the elements. Here the monks lived in individual domed beehive-shaped huts built of unmortared stone called clocháns, coming together only for communal prayer in the two corbel-roofed oratories. Late in the monastery's history, a church was built of mortared sandstone brought from Valentia Island, some 30 kilometres away. Every stone had to be laboriously carried up the steep stairway from the sea, a penance in itself. Perched on a tiny ledge a couple hundred metres away, just below the higher, needle-sharp south peak, was another oratory and a hermitage. The 'path' to this is a steep rock climb that made it accessible only to monks blessed with either a very good head for heights or an unshakable faith that the angels would catch them if they fell: there would have been nothing else between them and eternity. Life on this windswept rock was hard but not impossible. Rainwater was the monks' only drink, but the blustery Atlantic weather systems provided plenty of it. The monks' cells were unheated but, thanks to the Gulf Stream, winter temperatures rarely fall below a mild 5°C, not comfortable but survivable with warm clothing. There was enough soil on ledges here and there to grow vegetables and a little barley and oats, there were fish all year and, in spring and summer, plentiful seabird eggs for those willing to brave the cliffs, and the oily and strongly flavoured flesh of the seabirds themselves, which could be eaten fresh or dried for winter. All in all, Skellig Michael was rich in the kind of virtuous discomforts necessary for the green martyrdom.

Some monks enjoyed the isolation of such places, finding the play of the ocean and the clamour of seabirds exhilarating. 'Delightful I think it is,' wrote one anonymous hermit about somewhere that sounds very much like Skellig Michael, 'to be in the bosom of an island, on the peak of a rock that I might often see there the calm of the sea. That I might see its splendid flocks of birds over the full-watered ocean; that I might see its mighty whales, greatest of wonders.'[16] Others, however, for all their faith, found this an unremittingly hard life, like the hermit who lamented of his life, 'alone in my little hut without a human being in my company'. His bed was cold, the loneliness made him anxious, and his starvation diet of bread and water had left him with sunken cheeks and dry leathery skin, but this, he thought, was 'a pure, holy blemish'. 'Dear has been the pilgrimage before going to meet death', but this was the price of avoiding all worldly temptation, and he was glad to pay it.

In the sixth century, with their work of Christianizing Ireland complete, Irish monks headed to Britain to convert the still pagan Picts and Anglo-Saxons. The most influential centre of Irish evangelism in Britain was on the small Hebridean island of Iona, off the coast of Mull, founded in 563 by St Columba (Irish Gaelic Colm Cille). Reputed to be a great-great-grandson of the pirate king Niall of the Nine Hostages, Columba was born in Donegal in 521 to an aristocratic family with close links to the ruling Uí Néill dynasty. Little is known about the first forty years of Columba's life, but it seems that his family committed him to the church at an early age. A defining moment in Columba's life came in 561, when he was involved in the bloody battle of Cúl Dreihme between the Uí Néill and Diarmit, the king of Tara, in which over 3,000 men are said to have been killed. The true causes of the battle are unknown, but, in legend, it all began with a quarrel between Columba and Abbot Finnian of Movilla over who had the right to copy a book. Whatever the reason, monks were not supposed to get involved in battles, so Columba was excommunicated and exiled. Filled with remorse, Columba swore never to return to Ireland until he had saved as many souls as had been lost in the battle.

With a small group of followers, Columba sailed for Scotland, where he was welcomed by his kinsman Conall mac Comgaill, King of Dálriada, who gave him Iona to settle on. Although dozens of other Scottish islands became homes for small groups of monks seeking the green martyrdom, this wasn't part of either Columba's or Conall's plans. Politics and religion were always bedfellows in medieval Europe. Conall hoped that allowing

Columba to found a monastery would create a centre of literacy, education and administrative expertise which would benefit him directly in governing his kingdom. He would also have seen giving support to Columba's missionary work among the Picts as a means to project Scots' influence into Pictland. Columba's mission was as political as it was religious.

Iona may be a small island (it's a little over 8 square kilometres in area), but it is no Skellig Michael. While its exposed west coast is an unpromising mixture of windswept rock, heather and bog, Iona's sheltered east coast has a long fringe of fertile *machair*,* which allowed the monastery to be comfortably self-sufficient in food; the monks did not depend on dried seabirds, and there were safe harbours by its gleaming white shell-sand beaches. The harbours were an important part of the island's attractions, because Columba's monastery was never intended to be a retreat from the secular world. Iona may be remote in modern terms, but in the early Middle Ages, when travel was faster and easier by sea, it was an ideal communications hub for an evangelizing mission, close to everywhere that mattered. Ireland lies only 110 kilometres away to the south, a day's sail in fair weather; the main royal power centre of Dálriada, at Dunadd, was only 50 kilometres away across the Firth of Lorn; and Iona also had easy access by sea to the Great Glen, the main west–east overland route across the northern Highlands, leading directly to the main power centres of the still pagan northern Picts. Although his mission was completely dependent on sea communications, seafaring held no terrors for Columba: according to his hagiographers, a short prayer from him was always sufficient to calm the worst storm or turn the wind to a favourable direction. Although heavily mythologized – among his many miraculous adventures, Columba is said to have encountered, and vanquished, an early incarnation of the Loch Ness monster during one of his journeys – his missionary work among the Picts was successful

* Grassland on light alkine soils rich in wind-blown shell sand found on many Hebridean islands.

from both religious and political points of view, beginning their Christianization and paving the way for their eventual takeover by the Scots.

Columba was a worldly monk, but for those of his compatriots who were seeking solitude, the west coast of Scotland offered a wide choice of remote, uninhabited islands. None, not even the St Kilda archipelago, were more remote than the neighbouring islands of North Rona and Sula Sgeir, some 70 kilometres north of the Isle of Lewis, both of which were home to anchorites in the early Middle Ages. North Rona, at 1 square kilometre in area the larger of the two islands, was home to St Ronan, though exactly which St Ronan is anyone's guess – twelve Irish saints go by the same name. A small, well-preserved dry-stone oratory, much like those built by the monks on Skellig Michael, survives on the island, as does a crude stone cross carved with a strangely explicit figure of a naked man which seems more pagan than Christian.* Legend has it that Ronan was tormented by the vicious gossip of the women of Lewis. After praying to God for deliverance, he was directed in a dream to go to a nearby beach, where he found a friendly whale which ferried him over to North Rona. However, Ronan's difficulties were not over. Satan tried to oppose the holy man's landing with a pack of monstrous hounds, whose eyes glowed like hot coals, and, when that failed, he tried unsuccessfully to blow Ronan clean off the island with a great storm.

The only land Ronan would have been able to see from North Rona was tiny Sula Sgeir, 18 kilometres to the west. Again according to legend, this was home to Ronan's sister Brenhilda, who had been exiled there for some unspecified sin – gossiping with the ladies of Lewis, perhaps? Traces of a monk's cell, known as the Taigh Beannaichte ('Blessed House'), still survive, suggesting that, even if Brenhilda is a fictional character, the island was used as a sanctuary from time to time. Life would have been tough for Brenhilda: Sula Sgeir is barely one tenth the size of Rona and, in winter, storm waves break right over the whole

* The cross is now displayed in Ness Museum on Lewis.

island. While North Rona can, at least, support a small flock of sheep, Brenhilda's only source of food would have been the gannets which give the island its name (from Old Norse *súla sker*, meaning 'gannet skerry') and their eggs. Brenhilda spent her days gazing over the restless sea to North Rona while pining away for her saintly brother. She received few visitors and must have been dead for some time before her remains were discovered, with a cormorant nesting in her ribcage.

Other Irish monks sought solitude not on islands but in the 'pathless sea' itself. Under its entry for the year 891, the *Anglo-Saxon Chronicle* records that

> three Irishmen came to king Alfred in a boat without any oars from Ireland, whence they had stolen away because they wished to go on pilgrimage for the love of God, they cared not where. The boat in which they travelled was made of two and a half hides; and they took with them only enough food for seven days. And after seven days, they came to land in Cornwall, and then went immediately to king Alfred. Their names were Dubslaine, Macbethath and Maelinmuin.[17]

These brave, or very foolish, monks had embarked on the most extreme form of *peregrinatio*. By setting sail in a boat that they could not steer, the monks had placed their fate entirely in the hands of God. Irish *peregrini* were not by any means the first seafarers to sail out of sight of land, but they were perhaps the first who not only accepted the risk that it might happen but actually saw it as desirable. Many *peregrini*, like Dubslaine and his two friends, made safe landfalls in known and, sometimes, unknown lands and returned home to tell the tale. How many others didn't and, perhaps feeling abandoned by their God, simply vanished into the open ocean, never to be heard of again? Their sacrifice has no name, but the 'blue martyrdom' would be apt.

While Ronan may have sailed by whale, and Piran, the patron saint of Cornwall, supposedly crossed the Irish Sea on a millstone, most Irish monks preferred to use curachs for their voyages. The

Irish monastic tradition prized self-sufficiency, so monks were more than capable of building their own boats and ships. One Irish text describes how monks

> made a curach using iron tools. The ribs and frame were of wood, as is the custom in those parts, and the covering was tanned ox-hide stretched over oak bark. They greased all the seams on the outer surface of the skin with fat and stored forty days' supplies, fat for waterproofing the skins, tools and utensils. A mast, a sail and various pieces of equipment for steering the vessel were fitted into the curach.[18]

Curachs may seem like flimsy vessels for ocean voyaging, but they had a reputation for being almost unsinkable when handled by an experienced crew, their light and flexible construction allowing them to ride comfortably over waves that would swamp a more rigid wooden boat of the same size. Thanks to their virtues, the art of building curachs remains alive on Ireland's Atlantic coast today, though canvas, rather than hide, is now used to cover their hulls.

Rowing about

Seafaring Irish monks left no factual accounts of their voyages comparable to the ancient world's *periploi*, but the stories they told inspired two genres of travel tales, the *echtrae* and the *immrama. Echtrae*, meaning 'adventures', were straightforward stories about travels to distant and exciting places that, even if they were sometimes imaginary, were at least conceived of as existing within the inhabited world of humanity. *Immrama*, meaning 'rowings about', were about miraculous sea voyages to remote and Otherworldly islands that lay well beyond the known world. The *immrama* include convincing details of seafaring in the North Atlantic, which must be drawn from the practical experiences of *peregrini*, but they also include a multitude of Christian and pagan mythological elements drawn from a wide variety of sources, chiefly the Bible and the *vitae* of early Irish saints, pagan Celtic tales of voyages to the Otherworld, such as *The Voyage of Bran*, and Classical literature, especially Homer's *Odyssey* and mythological tales of the Hesperides and the Fortunate Isles. The result is that any truth in the tales is deeply buried among imaginative fiction and religious symbolism. This is, of course, very frustrating for modern historians hoping to learn what the Irish really knew about the Atlantic, but accurately describing geographical discoveries was never the point of *immrama*. For the monks who read these tales, the Atlantic wasn't important as a physical ocean so much as a metaphor for the search for spiritual enlightenment, while the dangers encountered symbolized the temptations of the world which could damn the unwary soul. The voyaging monks were seeking salvation, not new lands, so *immrama* are not really about journeys of the body, they're about journeys of the soul, with a good measure of entertaining fantasy thrown in to sweeten the didactic pill. Physical geography very much takes a back seat. It isn't just the ocean that is symbolic in these tales: the ships themselves are metaphors for the church, which is steered by Christ as it carries its cargo of souls through the temptations of life to salvation.

Far and away the most famous and colourful of the *immrama* is the *Navigatio sancti Brendani abbatis* ('The Voyage of St Brendan the Abbot'), which recounts a legendary voyage made by St Brendan in search of a paradise-like 'Promised Land of the Saints' (*terra repromissionis sanctorum*). Written in the late eighth century, the *Navigatio* became one of the most copied books of medieval Europe, surviving in over 100 copies, as well as versions in vernacular languages including French, English, German, Flemish, Welsh, Breton and Gaelic. There is no doubt about Brendan's historicity, but hard facts about his life and personality are in short supply. It is fairly certain that he was born in Tralee on the coast of County Kerry in southwest Ireland around 484 and was ordained as a priest at the age of twenty-six. Soon afterwards, he became a *peregrinus* for twenty years, sailing to Scotland, Wales and Brittany, preaching and founding monasteries as he went, before returning to Ireland and founding monasteries at Clonfert, Ardferth and Shanakeel, at the foot of 934-metre-high Mount Brandon on the Dingle Peninsula. Even after this long expedition, Brendan did not turn his back on the sea, and later voyages took him back to Scotland and Wales before he settled at Annaghdown in County Galway, where he died in 577. There's no reliable evidence that Brendan ever did lead an expedition to find the Promised Land of the Saints, but his well-earned reputation as a traveller made him the ideal spiritual action hero for an *immram*.

St Brendan's search for the Promised Land of the Saints

The story of the *Navigatio* begins with a meeting between Brendan and another monk called Barrind. Barrind tells Brendan about a visit he has made to his godson Mernóc, who was abbot of a monastery on the Island of Delights, three days' sail west from Ireland. Walking together at night, Mernóc took Barrind to the island's western shore, where they set sail further into the west in a small curach. They were immediately enveloped in a fog so dark and thick that they could see neither the prow nor the stern of their boat. After sailing for only an hour or two, they emerged from the darkness of the fog into bright daylight on the shore of a beautiful green land full of flowers, fruit trees and precious stones.

The two monks set out to walk across the island and, after fifteen days, they came to a great river where an angel suddenly appeared in front of them. The angel explained that God had shown them this island, his Promised Land of the Saints, but they could go no further and must return where they came from. The monks believed that they had been on the island for fifteen days, but the angel revealed that a whole year had passed since their arrival. In all that time they had never once felt the need to

. Cape St Blaize, Mossel Bay. Coastal caves like this in the Western Cape, South Africa, provide the earliest evidence of modern human behaviour.

2. A Yaghan bark canoe. The Yaghan were the last people on the Atlantic to follow the prehistoric hunter-fisher-gatherer way of life.

3. The Neolithic village of Skara Brae in Scotland's Orkney Islands is the best preserved of the early farming settlements on Europe's Atlantic coast.

4. At its peak of production between 1600 BC and 1400 BC, the Great Orme mine in North Wales was northern Europe's most important source of copper.

5. The Tower at A Coruña, built *c.*AD 100, is associated with several Atlantic legends, including of Breoghan (foreground), in medieval Irish tradition, the forefather of the Gaels.

. Typical artefacts of the early Atlantic Bronze Age, including a bell beaker, archery gear, copper knives and gold ornaments, from the grave of the 'Amesbury archer', buried near Stonehenge *c.*2300 BC.

. The murex sea snail was the source of the xpensive Tyrian purple dye, made by the hoenicians on the island of Mogador off Morocco's Atlantic coast.

8. A coin from the Phoenician port of Sidon shows a galley on one side and the god Melqart on the other. Galleys were the Phoenicians' preferred ships for exploration.

9. *Hercules and Atlas* (*c*.1536), by Lucas Cranach the Elder, depicts Hercules relieving Atlas of the task of carrying the heavens. Behind are the two pillars he erected at the Straits of Gibraltar to mark the edge of the world.

10. The thirteenth-century castle at Tintagel was built by Earl Richard of Cornwall to associate himself with the site's legendary reputation as the birthplace of King Arthur.

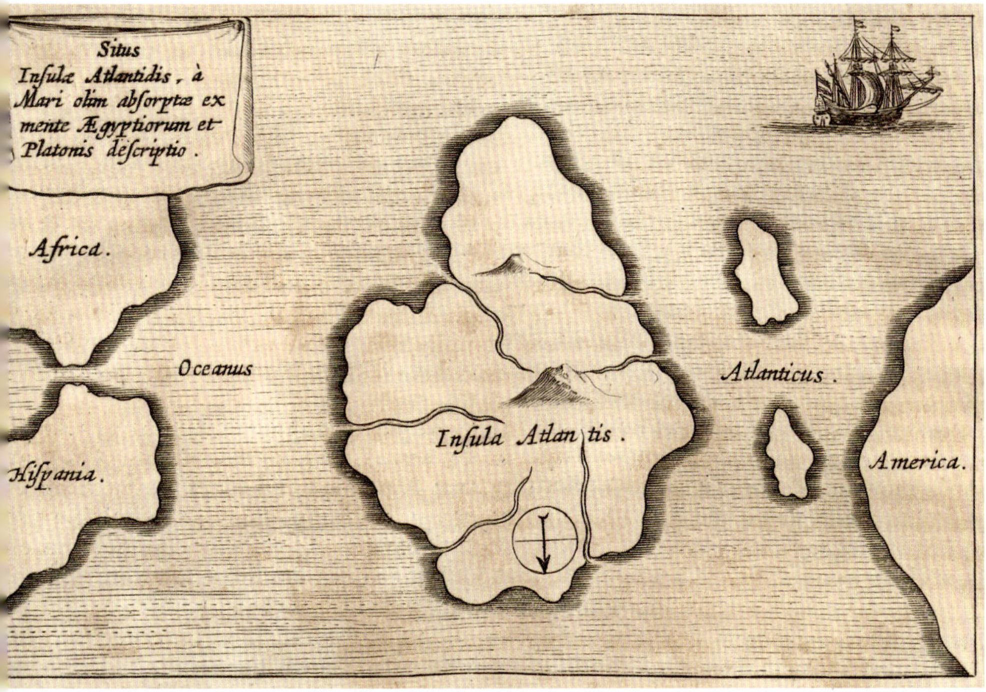

11. The legendary lost island of Atlantis, envisioned as a mid-Atlantic continent by the seventeenth-century Jesuit scholar Athanasius Kircher. North is at the bottom of the map.

12. A seventeenth-century Irish currach under sail and, beneath it, the construction of the boat's wicker frame prior to it being covered in waterproofed hides.

13. Early medieval monks' beehive huts on the summi the spectacular island of Sk Michael off the southweste coast of Ireland. Irish monk sought out such isolated sites in search of a closer communion with God.

14. Modern reconstruction of a Norse chieftain's longhouse at Borg in the Lofoten Islands in Arctic Norway. The Norse took this style of dwelling with them wherever they settled around the North Atlantic.

15. 'St Brendan and the Whale', from a manuscript (*c.*1460) of the *Navigatio sancti Brendani abbatis*, a popular tale of the Irish monk's adventures voyaging in the North Atlantic.

16. Jarlshof in the Shetland Islands. A substantial fortified sixteenth-century manor house stands above the foundations of Bronze and Iron Age roundhouses. The foundations of several Norese longhouses can be found a little further inland.

17. *Vidfamne* (Widefathom), a modern replica of a Norse *knarr* found near Göteborg, Sweden. Built for long-distance trade, *knarrs* were also used for the Norse voyages of settlement in the North Atlantic.

18. Thingvellir was the meeting place of the Icelandic parliament, the Althing, from *c.*930 to 1798. The site lies at the western edge of a lava plain lying over the Mid-Atlantic Rift.

19. The ruins of Brattahlið (Qassiarsuk), Erik the Red's settlement on the sheltered Tunulliarfik Fjord in Greenland. The fields now grow hay for Inuit sheep farmers.

eat, drink or sleep, for it had been daylight all the time, the Lord Jesus Christ being the light, they were told. The angel escorted the monks back to their boat and they sailed through the barrier of fog back to the Island of Delights, from where Barrind made his way home to Ireland.

Excited by Barrind's story, Brendan immediately begins preparations for his own voyage in search of this promised land. With a group of fourteen followers, Brendan observes a succession of three-day fasts over a forty-day period, after which they sail to the island of St Enda to receive his blessing. Returning to the mainland, the monks camp on a mountain called Brendan's Seat while they build a curach and load it with supplies for forty days. Just as Brendan is about to set sail on the evening of the summer solstice (21 June), a significant date in Celtic paganism, three monks run down to the beach and beg to be allowed to take part. Brendan allows them to board but warns them that none of them will complete the voyage. The adventures of the seven-year voyage that followed, some of them borrowed from other *immrama*, are essentially a series of tests which he and his disciples must pass if they are to be deemed spiritually worthy of being allowed to visit the Promised Land. As they crossed and re-crossed the ocean, the monks visited, and sometimes revisited, numerous islands, some of which were already inhabited by holy monks and hermits; on others they encountered demons and monsters, who tried to hinder their progress, and angelic beings, who helped to guide them on their way.

The monks sail with the wind for fifteen days, and when the wind fails they row until they are exhausted. Brendan tells his monks that they should not despair, but from now on put themselves wholly into the hands of God and allow him to fill the sail as he wishes. After forty days at sea, they make their first landfall. Although they have run out of provisions and are hungry, tired and thirsty, their search for a landing place takes a further three days. The monks find a deserted hall on the island, with tables laid out with food and drink for them. Brendan warns his monks against giving in to temptation by taking anything from the unattended hall. After three days of this mysterious hospitality, the monks prepare to leave, but one of the three late-comers confesses to having stolen a necklace. Brendan exorcises a demon which has possessed the monk for seven years and, after receiving holy communion, the repentant monk dies and his soul is carried to Heaven by angels. Before the monks set sail, a divine messenger comes to the beach and gives them provisions to last until their next landfall, which, he tells them, will not be until Easter, more than six months away. In the narrative, the monks never want for provisions, as they are always resupplied in a timely way by a variety of divine messengers.

The monks make their predicted landfall, right on schedule, on Maundy Thursday, on a lush and grassy island with rivers full of fish and grazed by flocks of pure white sheep, all as large as cattle. As the next day is Good Friday, the day of Christ's crucifixion, Brendan makes one of the spotless animals a sacrifice to God, just as God sacrificed his sinless son for the salvation of humankind. On Easter Saturday, a divine messenger arrives and directs them to sail a short distance to a second island. God wants them to celebrate Christ's resurrection on Easter Sunday there, he tells them, after which they will sail on to a third island that the messenger tells them is called the Paradise of Birds. Except for Brendan, who remains in the ship, the monks spend the Saturday night on the second island, which is strangely bare and smooth and has no beach, before celebrating mass on Sunday morning. After the service, the monks light a fire to cook a celebratory meal of meat and fish. As soon as the fire gets going, the island begins to heave and the terrified monks flee back to their boat, leaving their meal behind them. As the monks watch the island disappearing into the distance, Brendan explains to them what he, with a certain saintly smugness, had known all along but not told them for fear of frightening them, that they had spent the night on the back of a giant whale called Jasconius. Such tales of seafarers mistaking whales for islands were very popular in medieval Europe, so you have to wonder why the monks weren't more suspicious about Brendan's reluctance to leave the curach.

Celebrating their narrow escape, the monks sail on to the Paradise of Birds, which they find is inhabited by a huge flock of white birds which loudly sing the praises of God. One of the birds tells the monks that they are fallen angels who God in his mercy has spared from Hell but who are banished from Heaven and must roam the world forever. The monks remain on the island until Pentecost (the seventh Sunday after Easter Sunday), by which time they have spent ten months on their voyage. Before they set sail again, one of the birds tells them that they will return to the Island of Sheep, Jasconius and the Paradise of Birds to celebrate Easter six more times before their journey's end.

After sailing for another eight months, the monks arrive at the Island of the Monastery of St Ailbe, where they spend Christmas. Sailing on after Epiphany, the monks have a narrow escape from an island whose waters send them into an unnatural sleep and they then spend time becalmed in a 'coagulated sea' before returning, or, perhaps, more accurately, they are returned by God, to the Island of Sheep, Jasconius and the Paradise of Birds for Easter as predicted. Forty days' sailing after leaving the Paradise of Birds again, they are attacked by an enormous sea monster, but God answers their prayers for deliverance by sending a fire-breathing monster to rend it into three parts, one of which, the tail, they later find washed up on an island and eat cooked with herbs. Later, they arrive at a flat island barely higher than the waves, where they are greeted by three choirs singing psalms. Here, the second of the late-coming monks leaves the party to join the island community. Honeyed, watermelon-sized fruits called *caltae* sustain Brendan and his crew for the next twelve days' sailing, after which he orders a fast for three days. At the end of the fast, a bird, obviously a divine messenger, flies over the curach and drops a branch hung with a bunch of enormous red grapes the size of apples, which sustain the monks for another twelve days. They fast again for three days, at the end of which they come to an island covered with trees bearing the same miraculous fruits. The fragrance of pomegranates pervades the whole island. The monks camp on the island for forty easeful days, resting and feasting on fruits and herbs. Shortly after setting sail again, the party is attacked by a ferocious gryphon. The monks fear being eaten, but the same bird that delivered the giant grapes appears and first blinds and then kills the gryphon, whose lifeless carcass falls into the sea near the curach. A few days later, they alight on St Ailbe's island again, spending another Christmas there.

Now into the third year of their voyage, the monks settle into a routine, spending Easter at the Island of Sheep, Jasconius and the Paradise of Birds, and Christmas at Ailbe. The rest of the time, they are alone on the open sea, but the monotony is relieved by occasional fantastic encounters. One day, the monks come across an immense pillar of pure crystal surrounded by a wide-meshed net floating on the sea. The pillar is so tall that the monks can scarcely see its summit. Brendan sails around the pillar and finds that its four sides are all exactly the same length, 1,400 cubits long (about 700 metres). After four days exploring the pillar, Brendan finds a chalice made of the same substance as the net with a paten (a liturgical plate) made of the same substance as the pillar. Believing them to be miraculous, Brendan takes the vessels with him when they leave. They next encounter the barren Island of Smiths, dotted with slag heaps and blazing forges. Avalanches of burning stones tumble into the sea, making it boil like a cauldron of stew. Deafened by the sounds of hammers on anvils, the monks row away as fast as they can when they are spotted by demons, who hurl burning coals at them. A day later, the monks see a high mountain to the north, belching smoke and flames. Here, the third of the late-comers is seized by demons and carried off to Hell, although the exact nature of his mortal sin is not revealed. They later encounter Judas Iscariot, whose punishment for betraying Jesus is to be chained to a rock in the ocean while being tormented by demons and, on another island, a 140-year-old hermit who is fed fish by otters.

Journey's end

After seven years of wandering the ocean, Brendan and his companions are finally deemed spiritually worthy to be allowed to see the Promised Land. On leaving the Paradise of Birds for the last time, a divine messenger pilots the monks across the ocean for forty days until their ship is engulfed in a dense and dark fog. As they emerge from the fog, they see the same brilliantly lit, beautiful, fruitful land that Barrind had described to Brendan. Joyously, Brendan and his monks explore the island for forty days, until they reach the great river, where they are met by an angelic youth. The youth kisses the monks, calling them all by name, and tells them that they have, at last, reached the land they have been seeking for so many years, but that now they must return home. The monks returned to their ship and, after passing through the fog again, arrived at the Island of Delights, from where they returned to Ireland, to tell the amazing story of their adventures.

It would be impossible to draw a map of St Brendan's legendary wanderings. Sailing directions are rarely given, and all distances are given in terms of the number of days' sailing. It would be pointless to try to speculate how far a curach might reasonably be expected to sail in a day, because, in most cases, each leg of the voyage corresponds to a symbolic number, most commonly forty days and three days, forty days being the time that Christ spent in the Judaean wilderness being tempted by Satan following his baptism, and three being the number of days between Christ's crucifixion and his resurrection, as well as representing the Trinity. The three islands to which the monks return every year at Easter share the same symbolism. The length of the voyage, seven years, is also symbolic. In the Old Testament, seven represents completeness, and it is prominent in the symbolism of the New Testament Book of Revelation – for example, the seventh angel sounds the last trumpet to herald the end of the world and the Last Judgement. Brendan's choice of fourteen companions for his voyage is a reference to the Gospel of

St Matthew, which states that there were fourteen generations from the prophet Abraham to King David, fourteen from David to the Babylonian Exile, and fourteen from the exile to Jesus Christ. The three late-comers disrupt this holy number, but they all fall by the wayside, so that the all-important sacred arithmetic is restored by the end of the voyage.

Other aspects of the *Navigatio* have a ring of truth about them, and it is hard to dismiss them merely as products of a fertile imagination. In the days before whales were driven to the brink of extinction by modern industrial whaling, encounters between seafarers and whales must have been common and frightening, especially for those sailing in small boats like an Irish curach. However, the main purpose of the whales in this story is symbolic. In medieval beast-lore, whales, because they live in the depths of the ocean, and can drag unwary mariners down with them, are associated with Hell: celebrating the Resurrection on a whale's back is a powerful symbol of Christ's triumph over death. The 'coagulated sea' is comparable to Pytheas's 'congealed sea', and may be inspired by an encounter with the edge of the permanent sea ice in the Arctic Ocean. Likewise, the crystal pillar must surely be based on an encounter with one of the large icebergs that calve from Greenland's glaciers and drift south into the Atlantic. The pillar's dimensions, though, are purely symbolic, corresponding to the New Jerusalem described in the *Book of Revelation*. Only two of the places mentioned in the *Navigatio* can be identified with certainty. The mountain it calls Brendan's Seat is obviously Mount Brandon, while St Enda's island would be Inishmore in Galway Bay, where he is known to have founded a monastery. Mernóc and Ailbe are real people, but their islands are probably fictitious. According to another legend, Ailbe was a *peregrinus* who vanished into the Atlantic, and it seems that the author of the *Navigatio* has provided him with a safe landfall. The Island of Sheep has often been identified with the Faeroe Islands, whose name means 'sheep islands' (*faer øyar*) in the Old Norse language of its later Viking Age settlers, while the Paradise of Birds could easily have been inspired by one of the North

Atlantic's many clamorous seabird colonies. The Island of Smiths and the burning mountain to its north are clearly volcanoes, but the Atlantic has many possible candidates. If one of the volcanic Vestmannaeyjar off Iceland's south coast was the Island of Smiths, then the burning mountain could have been the Mount Hekla volcano on the Icelandic mainland, but there are also active volcanoes in the Azores and the Canary Islands.

However, nowhere in the North Atlantic remotely matches the *Navigatio*'s description of the Promised Land of the Saints. This is obviously not based on any real place; it is a Christianized version of the pagan Celtic Otherworld, which was envisaged as an island paradise in the far west, which too was hidden behind barriers of mist and had a time-bending quality, where mortal visitors returned home from what they imagined to be brief visits only to find that years had passed in their own world. The author of the *Navigatio* probably never conceived of the Promised Land of the Saints as having any geographical location at all. Barrind and Mernóc reach the Promised Land after only a couple of hours' sailing from the Island of Delights, but that doesn't mean they were thought to be geographically close together. The fog which surrounds the Promised Land isn't a physical barrier through which anyone can pass if they are daring enough, it is a cosmic threshold, or a portal, between parallel worlds or dimensions which can only be crossed by those whom God has judged to be spiritually worthy. No matter how long he had voyaged, or how far, Brendan could never have found the Promised Land of the Saints unless he had been directed to it by God. No explorer can stumble upon it because it doesn't exist in our reality, and that should warn us against drawing too many conclusions from the geography of the *Navigatio*; it is a spiritual, not a physical, geography.

Putting St Brendan on the map

The *Navigatio* tells a good adventure story and, with time, its spiritual message got sidelined and it was read not as an allegory of the journey of the soul but literally as an exciting travel narrative. Instead of being thought of as a symbolic Otherworldly place, 'St Brendan's Island' was believed to be a real place, and we shouldn't be too surprised at this. In an age of faith, stories about saints, no matter how far-fetched their adventures and miracles, tended to be taken literally. And if St Brendan's Island was real, then it belonged on a map. The island makes its earliest known appearance on a map on the Ebstorf *mappa mundi*, made in Germany around 1234, where it is shown as a rectangular box off the African coast, roughly where the Canary Islands should be, labelled as 'the lost island discovered by St Brendan, which nobody has seen since he sailed away'. The cartographer, thought to have been the English monk Gervase of Tilbury, was probably taking his lead from Classical cartographers and equated St Brendan's Island with the equally mythical Fortunate Islands or the Isles of the Blessed, which were often located in roughly the same place on Roman and medieval maps. This identification is made explicit on the Hereford *mappa mundi*, made around 1275, where St Brendan's Island is shown in the same location as part of an archipelago labelled 'the Isles of the Blessed and the Island of St Brendan'. *Mappa mundi* were purely schematic maps that were never intended to chart the world accurately. In the fourteenth century, far more accurate navigational maps, known as Portolan charts, began to be produced in Europe. These showed known island groups, like the Canaries, Madeira and the Azores, in their true positions for the first time. It no longer seemed possible that these could be locations for St Brendan's Island, so it was relocated to vague mid-Atlantic positions between Madeira and Ireland. As the Atlantic became increasingly well charted in the sixteenth century, the island retreated back into the remaining blank spaces on the map, but belief in its existence died hard and sightings were still being reported well into the eighteenth century. In 1721, Juan de Mur y Aguerre, the military governor of the Canary Islands, ordered captain Gaspar Dominguez to make a thorough investigation of the sightings, but he found nothing and, after this, reported sightings of the island declined. The last refuge of St Brendan's Island was in Newfoundland's Bonavista Bay, but, in 1884, it was renamed Cottel Island. Of course, if the author of the *Navigatio* is right, the island still exists in its Otherworldly realm and the lack of recent sightings is simply a sad reflection of the spiritual state of the modern world.

Return to Thule

Rather like elite universities today, the well-funded palace schools of the Frankish emperors Charlemagne (r. 768–814) and his son Louis the Pious (r. 814–40) exercised a magnetic pull on foreign scholars, drawing them in from across the Christian world. One Irish *peregrinus* who found a welcome there as a teacher of Latin grammar was Dicuil. Born around 760, Dicuil spent his early life travelling between monasteries around the coasts of Britain and Ireland before heading to the Frankish kingdom sometime before 810. By the standards of his age, Dicuil was getting to be an old man by this time, and he was grateful to settle into a comfortable life teaching Latin to the children of the Frankish aristocracy. Dicuil showed his appreciation by writing praise poems to Louis the Pious, but the emperor found them pompous and boring and stopped listening when he was reciting them: those few modern scholars who have bothered to study them tend to sympathize with the emperor. If these were all Dicuil had ever written, he would be justifiably forgotten about today, but he was also interested in astronomy and geography, which were perhaps a legacy of his seafaring days.

Dicuil wrote his most important work, *De Mensura Orbis Terrae* ('The Book of the Measurement of the Earth'), sometime around 825. In his book, Dicuil recalled that about thirty years earlier, Irish *peregrini* had told him about a distant uninhabited island, where they lived from February until the beginning of August. 'There,' they told him,

> not only at the summer solstice, but in the days around it, the sun setting in the evening hides itself as though behind a small hill in such a way that there was no darkness in that very small space of time, and a man could do as he wished as though the sun were there, even remove lice from his shirt.[19]

Cleanliness was obviously not next to Godliness, as far as Irish monks were concerned. With the exaggerated respect for Classical authors that was typical of the Middle Ages, the monks had assumed that the remote island they had discovered must have been Pytheas's Thule. In support, Dicuil quoted Pliny the Elder, who 'informs us in his fourth book that Pytheas of Massalia states that Thule lies six days' sail to the north of Britain' and the encyclopaedist Isidore of Seville, who states that 'Thule is the farthest island of the ocean'. Dicuil goes on to say that, though ancient authors had stated that Thule was ice-bound and shrouded in perpetual darkness during the winter, the monks had been able to reach this island 'in the natural period for great cold', and that even at that time there was still the normal succession of night and day. Some monks had sailed for two days north of Thule and found that the sea was frozen, he wrote. However, the monks' summer refuge could not have been Pytheas's Thule: Norway at that time was in the early throes of the Viking Age, so they would have found only slavery there. If Dicuil's Thule wasn't Norway, it could only have been Iceland.

Dicuil goes on to say that

> there are many other islands in the ocean to the north of Britain which can be reached from the northern islands of Britain in a direct voyage of two days and nights with sails filled with continuously favourable wind. A devout priest told me that in two summer days and the intervening night he sailed in a two-benched boat and entered one of them. There is another group of small islands, nearly separated by narrow stretches of water; in these for nearly a hundred years hermits sailing from our country, Ireland, have lived. But just as they were always

> deserted from the beginning of the world, so now because of the Northmen they are emptied of anchorites, and are filled with countless sheep and very many diverse kinds of seabirds. I have never found these islands mentioned in the [Classical] authorities.[20]

Historians have long assumed that the group of small islands that Dicuil describes were the Faeroe Islands, but for a long time, the only independent evidence to support this conclusion was limited to place names. The Norse often encountered Irish monks during their voyages in the ninth and tenth centuries, and place names derived from *papar*, as the Norse called them, are common in the Hebrides, Orkney and Shetland. The largest group of *papar* place names are islands. Five Hebridean islands are called Pabbay, from *papar* and *ø*, meaning 'island of the papar'. The Faeroe Islands also have a few *papar* place names, including Papurshílsur near Saksun, and Paparøkur ('papar ledges'), near Vestmanna on the largest island of Streymoy. Vestmanna, in fact, is short for *Vestmannahøvn*, meaning the 'harbour of the Westmen', Westmen being the name the Norse gave to the Irish in general. These all offer circumstantial evidence that Irish monks were already present in the Faeroes when the Norse arrived.

Peat, barley and sheep

Archaeological evidence that humans were present in the Faeroes before the Viking Age finally came in 2013. Ash from peat fires containing charred barley grains, found in windblown sand deposits at Á Sondum on Sandoy in the southern Faeroes, was radiocarbon dated to between the fourth and sixth centuries AD. A second, more recent, layer of ash, deposited in the eighth century, was also found on the site, suggesting that it may have been visited repeatedly over a long period. Although no trace of buildings has yet been found, the ash probably came from domestic hearths and had been thrown out onto the sand to help control erosion, which was a common practice at the time. Because peat was not used as a fuel in Scandinavia at this time but was widely used in Britain and Ireland, this evidence suggests that someone, at least, had discovered and settled for a time in the Faeroes not long after Ireland's conversion to Christianity, some three hundred years before the Norse arrived. More recently, further signs of human activity have been identified in sediment cores drilled from the bed of a lake near the village of Eiði on the island of Eysturoy, which provide evidence for the introduction of large numbers of sheep, most probably between 492 and 512: it would seem that the Norse name for the islands really was justified. So far, no structures that can be associated with Irish monks have been found, but there are only so many attractive sites for settlement in the mountainous Faeroes, so, if there were any monasteries, they may now lie underneath later Norse farms. The Faeroese coastline has also suffered considerable erosion since the early Middle Ages, so some early settlement sites might have been lost to the sea.

Early Icelandic histories record that early Norse settlers found that Irish monks were already living in Iceland when they arrived in the ninth century. The monks, wisely, didn't hang around; they immediately fled to avoid living alongside heathens, leaving croziers and other ecclesiastical artefacts behind to be found by the settlers. There are also a few *papar* place names dating back to the settlement period, such as the islands of Papós and Papey, in the east of Iceland, which elsewhere are associated with the presence of Irish monks. There seems no good reason to doubt the literary evidence, but so far, no really conclusive archaeological evidence has been found to confirm the presence of Irish monks in Iceland before the Norse settlement. If the monks really did leave ecclesiastical artefacts behind to be found by the Norse, they are now long lost, and none have been found since. Many of the early Norse settlers funded themselves by going on Viking raids first, so it is, perhaps, just as likely that any such items arrived in Iceland as loot. A similar caveat applies to crosses that are carved on the walls of caves at Kverkarhellir and Seljalandshellar, in the Seljaland region on Iceland's south coast, which, it has been claimed, were carved by Irish monks. Over a hundred simple crosses, and twenty-four more elaborately carved or sculpted examples, have been found in these caves, and all of them resemble similar early medieval crosses found in the Hebrides and other west coast districts of Scotland and Ireland. However, such simple carvings are hard to date precisely, and, in the later ninth century, thousands of Christian Irish slaves were taken to Iceland by early Norse settlers. It can't be ruled out that these crosses were carved by some of them: slaves were not closely supervised in Viking Age Iceland. Perhaps more promising is a cluster of circular structures or enclosures which was identified by aerial photography on the Seltjarnarnes peninsula near Reykjavik in the 1980s. Circular buildings were characteristic of Irish ecclesiastical architecture until around the twelfth century, but until the site is scientifically excavated the claims that have been made that it is an Irish monastic settlement will necessarily remain speculative. Archaeology is currently rewriting the accepted history of the Norse settlement of Iceland (see Chapter 7), so it may yet provide unambiguous evidence to back up the plausible literary evidence of an earlier Irish presence.

Unless they helped God decide where to send them by waiting until the wind was blowing in a particular direction, *peregrini* setting out from Ireland without a steering oar were probably as likely to be blown southwest as northwest. There are fewer potential landfalls in this direction, but there is a real possibility that Irish monks discovered the Azores archipelago and used it as a retreat in the same way as Iceland and the Faeroes. It had long been believed that the Azores had always been uninhabited before the arrival of Portuguese settlers in the fifteenth century, the only evidence of previous human visitors being the dubious pot of Carthaginian coins found on Corvo in the eighteenth century (see p. 102): this is certainly what the Portuguese themselves believed. New evidence from the analysis of lake sediments has turned this assumption on its head, however. As part of a wider environmental study, core samples were drilled from sediments in five lakes on the islands of São Miguel, Pico, Flores, Corvo, and Terceira in 2015 and sent to laboratories to be tested for evidence of human activity. The sediment taken from the lakes on São Miguel and Pico contained evidence that, around 700–850, there was an increase in organic compounds that serve as bio-indicators for the presence of faeces from livestock and humans. Declines in tree pollen and increases in charcoal particles, and other chemical compounds produced when wood is burned, dating to the same period, are potential evidence of land being cleared for grazing.

As no other archaeological evidence of a human presence has been found, there are no clues to the identity of these visitors. The dating alone makes it unlikely that they were Norse, however; it's just too early. The Norse also took pride in their adventurousness, but there is nothing in their saga tradition to suggest that they made any settlements in that part of the Atlantic. That leaves the Irish as the most likely candidates for the honour of being the first settlers of the Azores. The monks, all being celibate males, did not found any permanent self-sustaining communities on any of the islands they visited, which could explain the fleeting nature of the human presence. Once the tradition of *peregrinatio* came to an end, and the last monks left, the Azores became once again uninhabited.

Navigating a curach

Because of their essentially religious purpose, the *immrama* are short on details about navigation – it is, after all, God who really decides where the voyaging monks will end up. Dicuil says that Irish monks sailed to Thule in February, a time of year when Norse ships were still tucked away for the winter in boat sheds and also well before the traditional Mediterranean sailing season. A later Faeroese tradition, which says that the Irish chose to sail so early in the year in order to avoid the fogs and light nights of late spring and summer, implies that they relied on celestial navigation to find their way: in high latitudes the stars are not visible between May and August. Knowledge of the marine environment, wildlife movements and key landmarks on shore must also have been shared by the monks, but this must have been a purely oral tradition, because no written records of their navigational knowledge are known.

Did the Irish discover America?

It seems safe to say that the Irish probably knew more of the northeastern Atlantic Ocean than any previous seafarers: how much further might they have gone? Claims that St Brendan beat Leif Eriksson and Columbus to America go back a long way, but there is no evidence at all that he, or any other Irish monk, ever reached the American continent. In 1976, the British adventurer Tim Severin set out to prove that it was at least a technical possibility, by sailing a traditionally built curach across the Atlantic. Severin made the crossing in stages, spread out over a year (May 1976–June 1977), island hopping from the Dingle Peninsula to the Hebrides, then the Faeroe Islands and Iceland and, from there, a single, demanding stage to Newfoundland. This route is similar to that used by the Norse for their Atlantic crossing, and it is much more realistic to imagine that any pre-Norse Atlantic crossing went this way than directly across the Atlantic in the way Columbus did. Of course, Severin had the advantage of knowing that the Atlantic could be crossed this way, and that there was something on the other side, which the Irish didn't. Against that, it might be argued that many *peregrini* didn't actually care where they were going, as that was God's choice, so couldn't some have been blown all the way to America? The curach proved its seaworthiness, surviving some terrible conditions, including force nine gales, but, without the modern waterproof survival gear Severin's crew wore, could Irish monks really have survived such conditions, inured to hardships though they were? Almost certainly not. Ultimately, proof that a certain type of historical boat or ship was capable of making any particular journey is not evidence that they actually did.

The red martyrdom

By the time Dubslaine, Macbethath and Maelinmuin turned up at King Alfred's court, the tradition of *peregrinatio* was in decline. As both Dicuil and the early Icelandic histories imply, the main factor in this was the Vikings, whose raids on western Europe had started around 793 with an attack on the Northumbrian island monastery of Lindisfarne. St Columba's monastery on Iona shared its fate two years later. Monasteries were specially targeted by Viking raiders because they were wealthy and undefended – early medieval Christians over-optimistically trusted in the protection of the saints. No monastery in Ireland, Britain, Germany or France that could be reached by sea or navigable river was safe. Even Skellig Michael, on its inaccessible island peak, was sacked, and its abbot killed, in 824, and it was raided a second time in 833. The Vikings were not only after objects made of precious metals like communion vessels and reliquaries – the communities of monks themselves were a marketable commodity. Over the next 200 years, many thousands of monks must have found themselves making involuntary voyages in longships which were destined to end at slave markets in Constantinople and Baghdad. Men who constantly fought the Devil with prayer were not easily intimidated by mere human evil, and many bravely refused to flee from their monasteries in the full knowledge that they were likely to face real, blood-red martyrdom at the hands of raiders. One of those was Blathmacc, the prior of Iona, who positively welcomed the opportunity, because, as he put it, he 'wished to endure Christ's wounds'. When, in 825, he received warning that a Viking fleet was nearing the abbey, he gave permission for those monks who did not think they could endure martyrdom to flee, while he remained behind with a hardcore of willing martyrs. When the Vikings burst into the church, they immediately slew Blathmacc's companions: Blathmacc himself was tortured to death for refusing to reveal the hiding place of the precious reliquary containing St Columba's holy remains.

As the Viking fury abated in the tenth and eleventh centuries, western Europe's monasteries were gradually rebuilt, but there was no revival of the Celtic tradition of *peregrinatio*. The restoration was led by monks trained in the Benedictine tradition of monasticism favoured by the papacy. Monks now had to take vows of 'stability' that committed them to stay in their chosen monastery for the rest of their lives, leaving only with the permission of the abbot. There was no place any more for the spiritual individualism of the Celtic church, but that didn't mean the end of religiously motivated seafaring in the Atlantic.

The sea road to Santiago

The seventh century saw the emergence of a new religion and a new empire. In the early seventh century, the prophet Muhammad converted the Arabs to the Islamic religion and imposed a fragile unity on them through diplomacy and war. After Muhammad's death in 632, his successors, the caliphs, attempted to preserve Arab unity by raiding the neighbouring Persian and Byzantine empires and met with astonishing success. By the end of the century, the Arabs had conquered a vast empire, the largest in history up to that time, that stretched from the Indus River in the east, across the Middle East and North Africa to the Atlantic Ocean in the west. An immediate consequence of the Arab conquests was disruption to established trade routes, which broke the links between Atlantic Europe and the eastern Mediterranean. Then, in 711, the Arabs, reinforced by the newly converted Moors (Berbers) of North Africa, crossed the Strait of Gibraltar and invaded Spain. The traditional landing place of the Arab army, the Rock of Gibraltar, known in the Roman world as

Mons Calpe, was renamed in honour of the Arab commander, Tariq ibn Ziyad, Jebel al-Tariq ('Mount Tariq'). The Germanic Visigoths who ruled Spain had never been fully accepted by their Iberian subjects, and their kingdom collapsed. Within a year, the only part of Spain that remained under Christian rule was a thin strip of mountainous territory in Asturias and Galicia along the northern coast. This area was a natural stronghold, and the Christians successfully fought off Muslim attempts to complete their conquest of the peninsula and, by the end of the century, had even regained some territory. In Spanish historical tradition, this was the beginning of the *Reconquista*, the long series of conflicts between Christian and Muslim kingdoms that culminated in 1492 with the fall of Granada, the last Muslim stronghold in Iberia. However, it was centuries before that outcome began to look at all likely, and the Christian kingdoms of the north desperately needed some rallying point to inspire and unite them in their struggle against the Moors.

The means was provided by a very political miracle. According to legend, in 812, a hermit called Pelagius told the Galician bishop Theodomir that he had many times seen strange lights, like a shower of stars, in woods near the village of Compostela ('Field of Stars'). After going and seeing the lights for himself, the bishop ordered that the site be excavated and found there the remains of an ancient church which contained a marble tomb. The bishop declared that an inscription on the tomb identified it as the resting place of the apostle and martyr St James the Great (Santiago), the son of Zebedee. There is no scriptural evidence that St James ever left Palestine, but by the fifth century a tradition had developed that James had visited Spain and preached the Gospel at the nearby port of Padrón. Thanks to this, the tomb was readily accepted as authentic, but there was a problem: James was known to have been beheaded in Jerusalem on the orders of King Herod in AD 44, so how had his remains finished up in Spain? Obviously, by some miraculous means. James's followers had taken his body to Jaffa, the port that Jonah had long ago set out for Tartessos from, where they found a rudderless, crew-less ship all ready to sail. After they boarded with James's remains, the ship miraculously sailed itself all the way to Padrón in just seven days. After they had disembarked, James's followers placed his body on a great stone that was hollowed out like a tomb and the rock immediately closed over it. Later, James's tomb was taken to Compostela, where it was rediscovered centuries later by bishop Theodomir. The tomb on which the legend is based may have been real; excavations in the cathedral in the twentieth century showed that it was built on the site of a Roman cemetery. Theodomir persuaded King Alfonso II of Asturias to found a church on the site of James's supposed grave, and it quickly became a popular pilgrimage centre of growing international importance. Compostela was important enough for the great Moorish general Almanzor to make a point of sacking it in 997, during the course of what, with the benefit of hindsight, turned out to be the last concerted attempt by the Moors to destroy the Christian kingdoms.

Pilgrimage to the shrines of the saints was one of the most important expressions of popular piety in medieval Europe. Not only was it a way for people, lay as well as clerics, to show their devotion to saints, the difficulties and dangers that they might face on their way made the journey as significant as the destination. Becoming a pilgrim was a way to serve penance for sins, earn spiritual merit or express gratitude for answered prayers, and they also provided opportunities to satisfy a desire for travel and adventure – in effect, spiritual tourism. Naturally, the church did not approve of people who went on pilgrimage for such frivolous reasons. Jerusalem and Rome were the ultimate pilgrim destinations but, following the birth of the crusading movement in the late eleventh century, St James's shrine gained huge prestige thanks to Spain's long history as the frontline of the Christian struggle against Islam, and the pilgrims began to pour in. Many crusaders travelling to the Holy Land by sea broke their journeys to visit Compostela; the first who is known to have done so was King Sigurd, 'the Jerusalem-Farer', of Norway, in 1108. Compostela was especially popular with northern Europeans, because its relative accessibility made it a more achievable objective than Rome or distant, perpetually troubled Jerusalem. French and German pilgrims could make the whole of their journeys to Compostela overland: a prosperous industry grew up to provide the pilgrims with food, lodgings, entertainments and souvenirs along the most popular routes. For most pilgrims, this was a once-in-a-lifetime experience, and they liked to take advantage of their freedom from the restrictions of their everyday lives. They could even allow themselves a little licence; after all, the spiritual merit earned by completing the pilgrimage would more than cover any little venial sins they committed along the way.

Pilgrims from Ireland, Britain and northern Europe were able to make a large part of their journeys to Compostela by sea, with sea sickness and fear of shipwreck providing the spiritually meritorious hardships instead of blistered feet and weary limbs. Ports like Dublin, Pembroke, Bristol, Plymouth and Southampton, as well as Hamburg and Ribe, on Denmark's east coast, had strong links with Gascony and Spain thanks to a flourishing wine trade. Pilgrims could sail to Bordeaux and from there join one of the overland routes crossing the Pyrenees, or they could sail direct to A Coruña or Ferrol, leaving them less than 100 kilometres to walk or ride. This route is known as the *Camino Inglés* (the 'English Way'), and the certifying authority at the cathedral of Santiago no longer considers it difficult enough to qualify as a proper pilgrimage unless pilgrims also complete another short pilgrimage in their home country first: flying or sailing to Spain just doesn't involve sufficient hardships to earn any spiritual merit these days. At first, pilgrims sailed as passengers on merchant ships, but by the fourteenth century, there were dedicated pilgrim ships with cabins carrying up to 400 passengers direct to A Coruña. In 1434, 3,120 pilgrims are known to have sailed from Plymouth alone. Sailings were dependent on the weather as well as availability, so pilgrims turning up in a port needed lodgings. So they wouldn't be exploited by greedy landlords, the bishop of Dublin founded a pilgrim hospice on the banks of the Liffey in 1216. To ensure that merchants and other travellers were not using pilgrimage as a cover for illicit commercial activities, pilgrims were required to swear on the Eucharist that they would not take more money with them than was strictly necessary to pay for their journey. This busy traffic came to a sudden end in the sixteenth century, when England, Scotland and the Scandinavian kingdoms converted to Protestantism and banned their subjects from going on pilgrimages.

The pilgrim's complaint

Walking to Compostela could take months, but, in good conditions, and in the right ship, sailing direct from England or Ireland took just three to five days. Despite this, most pilgrims had never been to sea before, and they did not feel that they were getting an easy ride. In *The Pilgrim's Sea Voyage*, one anonymous fourteenth-century English pilgrim described his harrowing voyage from England to Compostela in verse. He begins with a riposte to those who think that going on pilgrimage is just a good excuse for a holiday. 'Men may think it's all a game to sail to St James! But many a man finds it dreadful when they begin to sail. For, once they have set out to sea, from Sandwich, Winchelsea, at Brystow, or wherever that it be, their hearts begin to fail.' The crew all talk in incomprehensible seafaring jargon as they clear the decks in the expectation that before the day is out the pilgrims will be running out on deck to 'cough and groan' with seasickness. The captain swaggers about like a lord, ordering everyone about. As they're tossed up and down, the pilgrim feels not at all reassured when the sailors tell him how well their 'good ship' sails in a storm. The food is just beer, bread and salt, but that doesn't really matter, because all the pilgrims feel too sick to eat anyway; even roast meat wouldn't tempt them, he says. With only flimsy partitions between the cabins, there's no privacy. The pilgrims fervently read their prayer books or lie groaning on straw mattresses, keeping their bowls close by them in case they need to throw up before they can get up on deck. It is all perfectly awful; he thinks he'd rather be sleeping out in a forest without food and drink than be on a ship. Worst of all, his bed is next to the ship's pump, and the smell of the bilge water is overpowering, 'a man were good to be dead as smell thereof the stink!' An Irish *peregrinus* of the early Middle Ages, inured to the hardships of sailing in an open curach, might have thought this voyage quite luxurious, but the risks were real enough. Annals record the loss of many pilgrim ships at sea, including one from Iceland in 1354, and infectious diseases spread quickly in the crowded, unhygienic conditions onboard. Pirates were also a threat. In 1473, 400 Irish pilgrims sailing on the ship *Mary of London* were captured by pirates while returning home from A Coruña: after terms were agreed, the ship was released and landed the pilgrims safely at Youghal in County Cork. After that, it would have taken a very ungenerous person to complain that their experience had been too comfortable to count as a 'real' pilgrimage.

Once they had visited the shrine of St James at Compostela, many pilgrims hiked another seventy kilometres to Cape Finisterre to collect a scallop shell from the ocean as a token to prove that they had completed their pilgrimage. By the twelfth century, the scallop shell had become the recognized symbol of St James, and pilgrims no longer had to walk to Finisterre to acquire one, they could buy one instead from the stalls that had been set up outside the cathedral. Those who wanted something a bit more elaborate could buy a lead badge or pendant that they could wear on their clothing or around their neck, in a medieval version of virtue signalling, to show others when they got home that they had completed the pilgrimage to St James. Some pilgrims took their souvenirs to their graves – they're not uncommon finds in medieval burials across Europe – presumably to make extra sure that their virtue would be remembered at their resurrection on the Day of Judgement. The affluent were not just concerned that God should remember their pilgrimages; they had scallop shells carved on their tombs so their virtue wouldn't be forgotten in this world either.

The Great Isle of the Solstice

Like the pilgrims in Geoffrey Chaucer's *Canterbury Tales*, the pilgrims on route to Compostela must have told each other tales to help pass the time. With their rich heritage of Celtic myth and the popular *immrama* to draw on, Irish pilgrims would have found appreciative audiences wherever they went. One anonymous eleventh-century Galician author was inspired by the *immrama* to write his own tale of a mystical journey to an Otherworldly island he called the Great Isle of the Solstice (*Magna Insula Solstitialis*). In the tale, an eighth-century monk called Trezenzonio, a refugee from the Moorish invaders, climbed the Tower of Hercules at A Coruña and saw, with the aid of a magic mirror, a large island on the far western horizon brilliantly lit by the rays of the rising sun. Trezenzonio built himself a boat and, after entrusting himself to the protection of God, set sail one morning and miraculously arrived at this distant island in mid-afternoon, a sure sign that this was an Otherworldly journey. Disembarking, Trezenzonio followed a narrow trail for eight days until he came to a magnificent church dedicated to the early Christian martyr St Thecla. The church was decorated with jewels, and choirs of angels sang God's praises. The weather on the island was always fine, the season always springtime, the air was fragrant with blossoms, food was left for him by angels, and he felt neither fear, pain nor hunger, or harboured impure thoughts of any kind. Trezenzonio spent seven blissful years on the island until an angel appeared to him and ordered him to return home. Understandably reluctant to leave this earthly paradise, Trezenzonio lingered. Losing patience, the angel afflicted him with leprosy and blindness until he prayed to God to heal him. At last, ready to leave, an angel took him to a boat on the shore and he was guided by God's hand, back over the ocean to A Coruña. The moment his boat touched the shore, the meat and fish he had brought with him rotted away; just as with the Celtic Otherworld, it was not permitted for mortal visitors to take anything away with them. Trezenzonio sought out his old teacher,

Bishop Adelfio, but who would believe such a fantastic tale? The island was never seen again.

Another paradisiacal phantom island which probably emerged from the same tradition was Antillia, the Island of the Seven Cities. The origins of the name are uncertain, but it most likely derives from Portuguese *ante*, meaning opposite, and *ilha*, meaning island, so 'the island opposite Portugal'. The legend emerged in the same period that the Irish *peregrini* were active, and also of that short-lived human presence in the Azores, which might provide a context. Like the *immrama*, it is a tale of holy men putting their fate into the hands of God on the high seas. In the oldest version of the legend, an archbishop of Porto, with six of his fellow bishops, decided to flee as soon as the Moors invaded in 711. Taking as many of their flocks with them as they could, they set sail out into the Atlantic and, guided by God, they discovered an island where each bishop founded a new city. Seven cities founded by seven bishops represents the same kind of sacred numerology found in the *immrama*, so it's no wonder God was so helpful. The legend kept a low profile until 1414, when the crew of a Spanish ship claimed that they had actually sighted Antillia, and soon after it appeared on a map for the first time. Once it was on the map, Antillia temporarily lost its phantom status and became a real island, one that explorers would set out hoping to discover for themselves: Columbus was one of them.

6

Of mice and Northmen

793–1468

The Earl's House – A violent and competitive society – The longships – The first ships to cross the Atlantic – Widening connections – The raids – Viking mice discover Madeira – The first stepping stone – Norse DNA – An unpaid dowry

During a brief lull in the Napoleonic Wars, in the summer of 1814, the superstar Scottish novelist Walter Scott accepted an invitation from his friend, the master lighthouse-builder Robert Stevenson, to join him on a six-week cruise along the coast of Scotland. Stevenson's employer, the Commission of Northern Lighthouses, had despatched him to identify suitable sites for new lights as part of its mission to make navigating the rugged Scottish coast safer. Scott was planning a new romantic novel, *The Pirate*, and seized the chance to search out suitably dramatic locations for the action. While Stevenson was surveying Sumburgh Head, the 100-metre-tall headland that marks the southernmost point of the Shetland Islands, for the lighthouse which stands there still, Scott went looking for locations. By the sandy Atlantic-facing bay of West Voe, he spotted the ruins of a substantial fortified house, half smothered in sand blown in from the beach. This house had been built by the local laird in the sixteenth century but had been abandoned at the end of the seventeenth century for a slightly more sheltered site a little further inland.

The Earl's House

Romanticizing the ruin for his novel, Scott imagined that it had been the hall of a Viking chieftain, or even of one of the Norse *jarls* ('earls') who had ruled the Shetland and Orkney islands until the fifteenth century.* The locals knew the ruin simply as the Laird's House, but Scott dreamed up a much more romantic name that evoked the Norse past he had imagined for it, Jarlshof, the 'Earl's House'. Though *The Pirate* was not one of Scott's most successful novels, it created a romantic aura around Shetland's Norse past that brought tourists flocking to the islands, and they all, of course, wanted to visit not the ruined Laird's House but Jarlshof. Tourism triumphed over local tradition, and Jarlshof it became. Scott's melodramatic novels don't find much favour with modern readers, and Jarlshof is about the only thing *The Pirate* is remembered for today. But the author's new name for the house turned out to be strangely prescient. Nearly a century after his visit, one of Shetland's frequent Atlantic storms bit deeply into the shoreline, exposing a jumble of stones from older buildings lying beneath the old laird's house. Subsequent archaeological excavations unearthed the first Norse longhouse ever to be identified in the British Isles.

Excavations from 1925 onwards gradually revealed that Jarlshof was a complex, multi-period site which had already been occupied almost continuously since the Bronze Age by the time the Norse arrived. West Voe is exposed to Atlantic gales, but those same winds have blown shell sand inland from the beach, creating a large area of light, fertile *machair*, making it an attractive place to settle. The Norse arrived in the early ninth century and would eventually build seven longhouses on the site, though no more than two of them were ever occupied at the same time. The

* 'Viking' and 'Norseman' are often used interchangeably to describe medieval Scandinavians (the Danes, Norwegians and Swedes). However, strictly speaking, only those Norse who went *í víking*, that is on plundering raids, should be described as Vikings, so in this book, the term is used only in a warlike context.

longhouse is the characteristic Norse farmhouse, a long rectangular building, narrowing slightly towards each end, with family accommodation at one end and a byre for their livestock at the other. The plan is a complete break with the circular dwellings, typical of the Atlantic Celts, that preceded it on the site. The longhouses were built like those in western Norway, where the settlers probably came from, with walls built mainly from stone and turf and timber used only to line the inside walls and for the structural timbers which supported the turf-covered roof. This became the signature building style for the Norse in the North Atlantic: it was the discovery of the remains of a longhouse at L'Anse aux Meadows in Newfoundland that proved that the Norse had crossed the Atlantic hundreds of years before Columbus. The way of life at Jarlshof was also transplanted from the west of Norway. Sheep, cattle, pigs and ponies were bred, and barley was grown, but, because of the cool, damp climate, it needed to be dried in a grain-drying kiln before it could be stored. The people at Jarlshof were also fishermen, catching cod, saithe and ling, together with an occasional seal or beached whale. The settlement was very self-sufficient. Local bog iron ore was dug and smelted in a smithy to produce essential everyday tools, from fish hooks to knives, shears and sickles. Pottery was not used at Jarlshof; cooking pots and storage vessels carved from soft, locally quarried soapstone were preferred. Numerous spindle whorls and loom weights found at the settlement show that the spinning and weaving of woollen cloth was an important occupation. Timber was Jarlshof's main deficiency. Shetland once supported low, scrubby woodland of birch, hazel and willow, but this had mostly been cleared long before the Norse arrived, so timber for houses or boats had to be imported. Driftwood was a valued resource for building, but peat, cut on Shetland's boggy moorlands, was probably the main source of fuel.

The arrival of Norse settlers at Jarlshof marked the beginning of a new age of Atlantic exploration, one which would see them complete, in a leisurely 200 years, the first trans-Atlantic crossing in history. These were difficult and dangerous seas, so it doesn't diminish their achievement to say that their task was made much easier thanks to the North Atlantic's numerous islands, none of them more than around 600 kilometres apart, that the Norse were able to use as 'stepping stones' to the New World. In any other part of the Atlantic, a crossing involves a minimum 3,000 kilometres of open-sea sailing, something that would have been practically impossible for the small, open-decked ships used by the Norse. While Columbus, benefitting from revolutionary advances in European shipbuilding, would spend thirty-three days out of sight of land on his trans-Atlantic crossing, from the Canary Islands to the Bahamas, the Norse were able to cross in stages, in favourable weather, of just three to seven days. The Norse were also fortunate in their timing because the global climate was on a warming trend, culminating in a period known as the Medieval Climatic Optimum (*c.*950–1250), when average temperatures in the North Atlantic reached as much as 1°C above twentieth-century average temperatures.

A violent and competitive society

The Norse exploration of the North Atlantic was only a small part of what has come to be known as the Viking Age (*c.*793–*c.*1100), Scandinavia's age of state formation and overseas expansion. While it's the overseas expansion that gets most of the attention, the dynamic which drove it was provided by state formation. In the century or so before the beginning of the Viking Age, Scandinavia was a land of chiefdoms and small kingdoms. Most of the kingdoms were no larger than a single island or mountain valley, but three had become regional powers. These were located in southern Jutland in Denmark, around Lake Mälaren in central Sweden and in Vestfold in southern Norway. In the course of the Viking Age, these three centres of power would swallow up their smaller neighbours to become, by the eleventh century, recognizably the national kingdoms of Denmark, Norway and Sweden. Power is rarely centralized peacefully – no one who exercises independent power wants to give it up if they can help it – but it was a particularly bloody process in Scandinavia. Norse kingship was elective, and there was no presumption in favour of a king's eldest son. All that was necessary to be eligible to become a king was to have inherited royal blood from one parent; even illegitimacy was no bar. This custom created a relatively large class of men who could aspire to rule but for whom the opportunities to do so were steadily diminishing. Competition for power became intense, and succession disputes were frequent and bloody. The losers in these disputes – if they survived – were usually forced into exile, but all was not lost. Norse custom held that any man possessed of royal blood who could raise enough men to crew a longship was entitled to be called a king. Such landless kings were called 'sea kings': the lack of a physical kingdom wasn't a problem, because Norse kings were, first and foremost, rulers of men rather than territory. By going *í víking* (plundering) to build up their wealth and reputation, sea kings could hope to win a loyal following of warriors who would support a bid for power at home. The Norse practice of partible inheritance left many men with insufficient land to make a good living, so there was no shortage of men willing to follow even a landless king on a Viking raid, gambling that, if successful, their shares of the plunder would set them up for life. No part of Europe's Atlantic coast would escape these raids.

In this violently competitive society, status symbols became all-important, encouraging Norse merchants to roam ever further to acquire silver, silks, furs, glassware, weapons and other luxuries for the ambitious social climber to use to create an image of power and success for themselves and to hand out as gifts to valued followers to confirm their loyalty: a king was expected to be generous to his followers. These goods were often paid for with plunder, captives or the tribute paid by the victims of Viking raids; slave trading was probably their most profitable business. The dynamics of state formation also encouraged a wave of emigration and settlement overseas. Exiled kings might win a rich kingdom by conquering territory in Britain, Ireland or

France, while the newly discovered islands in the Atlantic proved attractive to members of the local chieftain class, who found that the growing power of kings was encroaching more and more on their traditional autonomy. Social and economic dynamics, however, were not enough by themselves. Since Scandinavia is almost entirely surrounded by water, the Norse could not have gone anywhere without good ships.

The longships

Despite having a shipbuilding tradition stretching back to before the Bronze Age, the development of true seagoing ships came surprisingly late to Scandinavia. While their Celtic, German and Roman neighbours and trading partners were using well-developed sailing ships and galleys, the Norse were still happily paddling around in boats much like the Hjortspring boat (see Chapter 2) until they made the switch to more energy-efficient rowing around AD 100. Even though it is impossible that the Norse were unaware of them, sails seem to have come into use even later. The earliest iconographic evidence of sailing ships in the north dates only to the sixth century, and the oldest archaeological remains of a Norse sailing ship discovered so far, a ship found in a burial at Salme on the Estonian island of Saaremaa, is estimated to have been built between 650 and 700. However, sailing ships were probably used by the fifth century, when the first Norse overseas forays are recorded. The Angles from southern Jutland migrated to Britain at this time alongside their Saxon neighbours, who certainly used sailing ships, while another Jutland tribe, the Heruls, launched successful pirate raids as far away as the Bay of Biscay and northern Spain; it is hard to believe that they achieved this in rowing boats.

'Longship' has become a catch-all name, commonly applied indiscriminately to describe any Viking Age Norse ship, but in reality there was never a standard, all-purpose ship: different types of ship were built for different tasks and environments. Whatever their purpose, however, all Norse ships shared a strong family likeness. Their hulls were always built of overlapping planks (a technique known as 'clinker' or 'lapstrake' building) that were fastened together with iron rivets; they had double-ended hulls, with the bow and stern both built in the same way; they were steered by a single side rudder, which was always fitted onto the right-hand side of the ship (the *steorbord* side, hence starboard), because most people are right-handed; and they carried a single mast and a single square-rigged sail. 'Square' hasn't got anything to do with the shape of the sail (which was always rectangular); instead it means that the sail was carried on a horizontal spar that was rigged on the mast so that it was square to the ship's keel – that is, at an angle of 90°.

The iconic longships were specialist ships, built for war, though much more for transporting armies and raiding parties than for fighting sea battles, which were actually quite rare. It would have been no consolation to someone at the wrong end of a Viking axe, but longships have an undeniable grace and glamour, a perfect fusion of form and function. Poets waxed lyrical about them, and chieftains and kings were buried in them. Longships were sailing galleys, built to be rowed as well as sailed. A merchant could afford to wait for a favourable wind, but a raider couldn't; when sailing up rivers or fighting a sea battle, it was essential to be able to manoeuvre independently of the wind. The commonest type of longship was the *snekkja*, built to carry a crew of around twenty-four to forty oarsmen, which was also about the minimum useful size for an independent raiding party. As the name suggests, longships were long in relation to their width. *Snekkjas* typically had a length-to-breadth ratio of around 7:1; most would have been around 17–20 metres long and about 2.5 metres wide. *Snekkjas* also had a very shallow draft, sometimes less than half a metre. Sea trials with a replica of a small Danish *snekkja*, known as Skuldelev 5, have shown it to have been swift, able to reach 9 knots under sails and 5 knots when rowed, while its shallow draft would have made it ideal for raiding in the shallow waters of the Baltic or southern North

Sea, as well as for penetrating far inland along rivers. The downside was that the ship was not very seaworthy; because of its low freeboard, it would have been easily swamped in a rough sea. In the later Viking Age, a type of 'super-longship', called a *drakkar* ('dragon'), came into use. These ships had a length of 30 metres or more, and sixty to seventy oarsmen. Drakkars were built with sea fighting very much in mind, with high prows and sides to allow their crews to shoot down into smaller enemy ships and to make boarding more difficult. While a local chieftain could afford to own a *snekkja*, ships the size of a *drakkar* were so expensive that they were the exclusive preserve of the Viking Age super-rich, the jarls and the kings. The higher freeboard also made them more seaworthy than a *snekkja*, and it is clear that at least some of them made long voyages. Analysis of the timbers of a wrecked *drakkar* found in Skuldelev Fjord in Denmark showed that the ship had been built in Ireland, probably at Dublin.

The first ships to cross the Atlantic

Trade ships were shorter and broader than warships, with deeper and heavier hulls for maximum cargo-carrying capacity. Apart from carrying a few oars for manoeuvring into and out of harbour, trade ships relied entirely on their single sail for propulsion, and their masts were permanently fixed. The indispensable workhorse of Viking long-distance trade was the *knarr*, a sturdy, broad and deep-hulled sailing ship which could be sailed by a crew of six to eight. Sea trials with modern replicas have shown that *knarrs* were exceptionally seaworthy. *Saga Siglar*, a replica of a 15.25-metre-long *knarr*, known as Skuldelev 1, found in Roskilde Fjord in Denmark, successfully circumnavigated the world in 1984–6 (though it later sank off the Spanish coast, in 1992). Skuldelev 1 probably carried around 20 tonnes of cargo, but the largest known *knarr*, a wreck discovered in the harbour at the Viking Age town of Hedeby, near Schleswig, which was 25 metres long, 5.7 metres broad and 2.5 metres deep, had a cargo capacity of 38 tonnes. As well as its use for trade, the *knarr*'s seaworthiness made it the preferred ship for voyages of settlement and exploration in the North Atlantic.

The ships known as *karves*, which were intermediate between longships and trade ships, were probably built as the private travelling vessels of chieftains and their households. The late ninth-century ship from Gokstad, now displayed in the Viking ship museum in Oslo, is thought to be an example of a *karve*. Though these ships had full crews of oarsmen, their proportions are closer to Norse trading ships than longships. As a result, they would have been able to carry a large retinue plus all the tents, portable furniture and supplies, and commercial cargo, which would have accompanied a trader-chieftain travelling in style. The deeper, wider hull and higher freeboard made *karves* more seaworthy than longships, and they may have been the kind of ships used for raiding in the deeper, stormier waters around Scotland and Ireland.

Unlike modern wooden ships and boats, where the hull is built by laying planks onto a pre-erected skeleton of frames, Viking ships were built hull first, and the frames were added later. Viking shipbuilders started by laying the keel and adding the bow and stern posts. The hull was built up gradually using planks which were carefully shaped by eye to produce a hull with the desired lines. Viking Age Scandinavian shipbuilders used only unseasoned wood; oak was preferred, as it was easier to work. Planks were split radially from logs, never sawed, and finished with a woodworking axe. Because they never cut across the grain of the wood, radially split planking utilized its natural strength and flexibility to its best advantage, creating a ship that was both strong and flexible: in a high sea it might bend but it wouldn't break. The hull was made watertight by pressing caulking of wool, cattle hair, cloth or plant fibres and moss into the spaces between the planks and then by tarring. Internal strengthening frames were fitted in stages as the hull was completed. The single mast was fitted in a mast-step, a long, heavy timber designed to spread the load of the mast and sail over a large area of the keel and hull. Decking, side rudder, rigging and sail completed the ship's fitting out. The sail was one of the costliest parts of the ship, and probably the only one made by women. Even the sail of a small longship would require the wool of fifty sheep or more, which had to be spun, woven into strips, sewn together and greased to make it waterproof, a task which would have kept two people fully employed for a year. For a chieftain's or a king's longship, the expense didn't end there. The hull would be painted, carved figureheads fitted to the stems and, perhaps, as a finishing touch, a gilded weather vane added to top the mast or prow. Show was always as important as functionality for the status-conscious elite, and there was no greater status symbol than a longship; it embodied leadership, military prowess and wealth.

No matter how expensive they were, Norse ships were all basically just open boats that offered precious little in the way of creature comforts. There were no cabins, so crew and passengers had little protection from the weather and sea spray, so sailing in bad weather must have been miserable at best and life-threatening, from hypothermia, at worst. In harbour, an awning or a tent could be put up on the deck, but this was probably rarely done at sea, because they could catch side winds and drive a ship off course. In coastal sailing, a ship could anchor at night, allowing its crew to get a hot meal and a good night's sleep under shelter, but cooking was impossible at sea, so the crew would subsist for the duration of the voyage on water or ale and dried fish. Sleeping was also difficult at sea, especially in longships with their large crews. Finding enough space just to lie down among the clutter of sea chests, provisions, ropes and all the other sailing gear would not have been easy. Modern re-enactors, sailing in replica longships, have found that crews tire quickly on multi-day voyages. In his poem *The Seafarer*, composed around 700, an anonymous Anglo-Saxon poet perfectly expressed what must have been the sheer unadulterated misery of sailing the northern seas in hard weather:

> I can tell the true riddle of my own self, and speak of my experiences – how I have often suffered times of hardship

> and days of toil, how I have endured cruel anxiety at heart and experienced many anxious lodging-places afloat, and the terrible surging of the waves. There the hazardous night-watch has often found me at the ship's prow when it is jostling along the cliffs. My feet were pinched by the cold, shackled by the frost in cold chains, while anxieties sighed hot around my heart. Hunger tore from within at the mind of one wearied by the ocean.[21]

Sailing was a deadly serious business. No one went to sea for fun.

Widening connections

The warm-up stages of Scandinavia's political and social upheavals took place beyond the horizon of the literate Christian world. In early medieval Europe, few people outside the church could read and write, and churchmen were much more interested in the Bible, the Church Fathers and the inherited literary culture of the Roman world than they were in writing about the goings-on in distant pagan countries. As a consequence, there are few recorded contacts between Scandinavia and the rest of Europe before Viking raids on churches and monasteries finally grabbed the horrified attention of ecclesiastical writers. There is, however, plentiful archaeological evidence for close trade links with the south, especially Frisia, the Rhineland and England, where the Norse were certainly not strangers. This shouldn't come as a surprise. The Anglian half of the Anglo-Saxons actually originated in the far south of Scandinavia – the neck of the Jutland peninsula – and they didn't abandon their links with the north when they migrated to Britain. The elaborately decorated helmet excavated from the early seventh-century royal ship burial at Sutton Hoo in Suffolk was, for example, a Swedish import. This richly furnished burial probably belonged to the East Anglian King Rædwald, whose family even traced its ancestry back to

Sweden. This wasn't the only dynastic link between England and Scandinavia. Isotope analysis of the bones of a young, high-status woman who was buried *c.*550 in the Bowl Hole cemetery at Bamburgh Castle, the stronghold of the kings of Northumbria, showed that she had been born in Norway. The most likely explanation for her presence in England was that she had been sent as a bride to cement an alliance between Northumbria and an early Norwegian kingdom. Four men and a young child who were buried in the same cemetery also had Scandinavian origins. A little over a century later, an anonymous Anglo-Saxon poet composed the epic *Beowulf*, set in Denmark, which was full of allusions to now lost tales of early Norse heroes which the poet clearly took for granted that the tale's audience would be familiar with. In the eighth century, the Norse were so familiar to the English that, the cleric Alcuin of York complained, they even adopted their hairstyles.

Scandinavia had been linked in to trade routes extending as far as the Middle East and Egypt since the days of the Bronze Age amber trade. In the centuries immediately before the Viking Age, that long-distance trade began to increase. Thanks to the rise of the powerful kingdom of the Franks, Europe was enjoying a degree of peace and political security not seen since the collapse of the Roman Empire, and prosperity was on the rise for everyone. The effects were felt even at the far edges of the Norse world. The chieftain of a huge 83-metre-long longhouse at Borg in the Lofoten Islands in Arctic Norway impressed his guests at feasts by serving them mead poured from high-quality Rhenish pottery jugs into fine drinking glasses from England and the Low Countries. The flickering torchlight of a midwinter feast would have lent the exotic glassware a jewel-like quality. Excavations of the longhouse have provided evidence of other fine imports from the south, including jewellery, gold and silver objects, and fine riding gear.

Despite being 200 kilometres north of the Arctic Circle, the Lofoten Islands had been settled by Norse livestock farmers as early as 250 BC, but it wasn't Borg's herds of sheep and cattle that provided the wealth to pay for imported luxuries. Nor was it Lofoten's rich cod fisheries which became the region's economic staple later in the Middle Ages; they were as yet only exploited for local consumption. The Borg chieftain was engaged in the luxury trade himself, sending furs, sealskins and walrus ivory south to support his high-status lifestyle. Around 890, one such chieftain-trader from Arctic Norway, Ottar, paid a visit to the court of the English King Alfred the Great, making him a diplomatic gift of ivory walrus tusks. Elephant ivory, used for ornamental carvings, had been hard to come by in Europe since the Islamic Arab conquest of North Africa in the seventh century, so this would have been a welcome gift even for a king. Alfred listened attentively to Ottar's description of his trade and travels, while one of the royal scribes took notes. Ottar claimed that he 'lived furthest north of all the Northmen, beside the West Sea (the Atlantic)', and that further north only nomadic Sámi fishermen and reindeer hunters lived. Ottar told the king that he had a farm with a little ploughland, a few dozen sheep, cattle and pigs, and 600 domesticated reindeer, valuable mainly for their hides and antlers, which were a favoured material for making combs in medieval Europe. However, Ottar claimed that his main wealth came from tribute paid to him by the Sámi in eider down, furs, walrus tusks and tough, waterproof ships' ropes made from walrus hide and sealskin. Ottar had also made a fifteen-day voyage far to the north, into the White Sea, where his men killed sixty walrus* for their tusks and hides. All these goods Ottar traded at the ports of Kaupang in southern Norway and Hedeby in Denmark, both over a month's sail to the south, as well as in England.

Another site that demonstrates how connected Scandinavia already was on the eve of the Viking Age is Helgö, a seasonal trading place near Stockholm that was occupied from the fifth to the eighth century. Large quantities of late Roman coins found at the site indicate that, at first, Helgö's trade links were

* Walrus were hunted to extinction in the White Sea by the eighteenth century.

mainly with the Western Roman Empire and its successor states to the south, but by the seventh century some very exotic objects were turning up from very distant places indeed. These include a gilt-bronze crozier of Irish manufacture, silver Coptic baptismal spoons from Egypt and a small bronze Buddha figurine from northern India. These objects aren't evidence that Norse merchants were actually going to Egypt and India in person; they probably found their way to Sweden through many intermediaries, making the final part of their journeys to Sweden along the trade routes that linked the Baltic with the Black Sea and the Caspian Sea via the great rivers of eastern Europe, such as the Dnipro and the Volga. Early in the Viking Age, Swedish Vikings, called Rus by the Slavs of eastern Europe, took control of these routes and established direct trade with the Abbasid Caliphate and the Byzantine Empire.

The raids

The first securely dated Viking raid took place on 7 June 793, when Vikings from Hordaland in west Norway plundered the wealthy monastery on the island of Lindisfarne off England's North Sea coast. After Iona, Lindisfarne was probably the most influential monastery in Britain, so the attack got international attention. It's certain, though, that this 'spectacular' was not nearly the first Viking raid, not even on Britain. Already, a year earlier, the Anglo-Saxon King Offa had ordered the preparation of coast defences in Kent, and in *c.*789 a royal official called Beaduheard was killed in a clash with Norwegians at Portland on the south coast. Unlucky Beaduheard had assumed that the Norwegians were merchants, and it was probably only with hindsight that this was recognized as a Viking raid and not an argument over tolls that turned violent. Only a few years before, a dispute between Frisian merchants and locals had left bodies in the streets of York.

Vikings had been raiding and plundering closer to home for a long time already. Raids are a common feature in Scandinavia's semi-legendary proto-historical traditions. While these can't be considered to be reliable sources, they are backed up by the Salme ship burial. This burial, which actually included two ships, the sailing ship and a second, smaller ship which was too poorly preserved to determine its means of propulsion, contained the skeletal remains of forty-two men, most of whom were aged between twenty and forty, who had been killed in battle. Isotope analysis of teeth, together with the style of the weapons and other artefacts that were buried with the men, showed that they came from central Sweden. Analysis of their aDNA has shown, too, that several of them were close relatives: raiding was a family business.

Viking raiding on western Europe unfolded in three stages. In the first, from the 790s to the 830s, most raids were of the kind that the Vikings called *strandhögg*, 'hit and run' attacks on undefended coastal targets such as monasteries like Lindisfarne and Iona, involving small numbers of ships. This was very much a seasonal activity, fitted in between the demands of the farming year. The *Orkneyinga Saga* described how one Viking chief, Svein Asleifarson, used to live:

> Winter he would spend at home on Gairsay, where he entertained some eighty men at his own expense. His drinking hall was so big, there was nothing in Orkney to compare with it. In the spring he had more than enough to occupy him, with a great deal of seed to sow, which he saw to carefully himself. Then, when the job was done, he would go off plundering in the Hebrides and Ireland on what he called his 'spring-trip', then back home just after midsummer, where he stayed until the cornfields had been reaped and the grain was safely in. After that he would go off raiding again, and never came back until the first month of winter was ended. This he called his 'autumn-trip'.[22]

There was a marked intensification of Viking activity from the 830s through to the 850s. Irish, Anglo-Saxon and Frankish annalists recorded a steady increase in the size of raiding fleets from twenty to thirty-five ships in the 830s until, by the 850s, fleets hundreds of ships strong had become commonplace. Strength in numbers made the Vikings bolder, and they now began to sail up navigable rivers, the Shannon in Ireland, the Severn, Trent and Thames in England, the Rhine, Seine, Loire and Garonne in Francia, the Guadalquivir in Spain, to attack river ports far inland. Dorestad, the Frankish Empire's richest port, 80 kilometres inland on the Rhine, was sacked in 834 and again in 835, 836 and 837. Nantes was sacked in 843, Lisbon, Cádiz and Seville in 844, Paris in 845, London in 851. By the 880s, few western European towns accessible by ship had not been sacked by Vikings at least once. In the first decades of raiding, the Vikings had at least gone home in the autumn, and their victims could expect that winter storms would give them a respite until spring was well advanced. Now, the Vikings began to make fortified winter camps at strategic locations so they could continue raiding later in the year and make an earlier start in the spring. Two of the earliest were on the island of Noirmoutier in the Bay of Biscay, conveniently close to the mouth of the Loire river and its rich rural hinterland, and Dublin, on Ireland's east coast, from which raiders could strike at the whole Irish Sea area. The Vikings moved on from Noirmoutier after a few years, but at Dublin they stayed, developing it into an important slave trade port.

In 859, two Viking leaders, Björn Ironsides and Hastein, set out from their base on the Loire with a fleet of sixty-two ships on what was probably the most audacious of all Viking raids. The fleet sailed south across the Bay of Biscay to raid along the coast of Galicia and Asturias in the Christian-controlled north of Iberia. Finding local resistance uncomfortably vigorous, the Vikings moved on to pillage Iberia's Atlantic coast, most of which was controlled by the wealthy and powerful Moorish Emirate of Córdoba. Here, they enjoyed greater success, but they faced stiff resistance when they attacked Lisbon, and the fleet was repulsed when it landed at Niebla near Huelva. The fleet next put into the mouth of the Guadalquivir, probably with the intention of sacking Seville, but it was confronted by the emirate's fleet. The Vikings had no defence against its incendiary weapons, and they fled after several longships were burned. The Viking tactic was always to move on if resistance proved too strong in one place, knowing that sooner or later they would catch somebody unprepared. Finally, at Algeciras, near Gibraltar, they achieved complete surprise, taking and sacking the town and burning its main mosque.

Björn and Hastein took their fleet through the Strait of Gibraltar into the Mediterranean. The Vikings landed first at Melilla on the North African coast. The local forces fled after only token resistance, allowing the Vikings to plunder freely for a week, taking hundreds of captives for the slave trade, including the harem of a local ruler, which was later ransomed by the emir of Córdoba. From Melilla, Björn and Hastein returned to Iberia, plundering the coast of Murcia and then the Balearic Islands. Returning to the mainland, the Vikings continued north along the Mediterranean coast, sacking Narbonne and then setting up a winter camp on an island in the Camargue, the marshy delta of the river Rhône. In the spring, Björn and Hastein sailed over 160 kilometres up the Rhône, sacking Nîmes, Arles and Valence before returning to the open sea and sailing east along the Côte d'Azur to Italy, where they plundered the Ligurian town of Luni, which they are, improbably, said to have mistaken for Rome. Moving on, the Vikings next sacked Pisa and sailed up the Arno river to sack the hill town of Fiesole near Florence. With wine aplenty, endless sunshine, calm seas and little opposition, life probably didn't get much better for a Viking. After this, the Viking fleet disappears from sight for a year. Late Arabic and Spanish sources claim that at some unspecified time Vikings raided Greece and Alexandria; if they did it was probably Björn's and Hastein's fleet that did it.

The fleet reappears in contemporary records in 861, when it

passed through the Strait of Gibraltar back into the Atlantic, on its way home. The strait is only 13 kilometres wide, and the Moorish fleet was ready and waiting for them. Of Björn's and Hastein's remaining sixty ships, only twenty escaped the ambush the Moors had prepared for them. Undiscouraged, Björn and Hastein continued to raid as they followed the coast north. Just before they left Iberian waters, they raided into the small Christian kingdom of Navarre, sacked Pamplona, its capital, and pretty much hit the jackpot. In a spectacular coup, they captured its king, Garcia I, and ransomed him for the incredible sum of 70,000 gold dinars (approximately 308 kilograms of gold, worth around $20 million today but substantially more then). The survivors of the expedition returned to the Loire in 862 very rich men. After the expedition, Björn and Hastein split up. Björn headed back to Denmark but never made it: he died in Frisia after losing everything in a shipwreck. Hastein went on to enjoy a long and profitable career raiding in England and Francia and died sometime after 895, probably of old age, a remarkable achievement for a Viking chief.

Viking mice discover Madeira

Most Vikings who raided Iberia were not as lucky as Björn and Hastein. Faced with determined and well-organized resistance wherever they landed, Viking raiding became a once-in-a-generation event. The lure of the emirate's wealth would draw a raiding fleet south only for it to retire hurt. The memory of defeat would deter further attacks until a new generation of Vikings came along and tried its luck: the last recorded raid was the 1030s. At least one Viking ship, sailing to or from Iberia, was blown off course out into the Atlantic to Madeira, unless, that is, mice are much better swimmers than we realize. In 2014, researchers studying the genome of Madeiran mice found, to their surprise, that they were most closely related to Norwegian mice and not, as they expected, to mice on the Portuguese mainland. The analysis also revealed that the Madeiran mice had been separated from their ancestral population in Norway for about 1,000 years – that is, they arrived there during the Viking Age. The most obvious explanation for this is that the mice arrived in Madeira as stowaways in Norse ships which had been driven out into the Atlantic during trading or raiding voyages to Spain. More recently, genome studies have shown that mice in the Azores also have Norwegian ancestry: these too may have arrived as stowaways on another stray Norse ship, but it is also possible that they were carried in a Portuguese ship sailing between Madeira and the Azores in the fifteenth century. More than most peoples, the Norse were fixated about memorializing their achievements, on runestones, in poetry and in sagas, yet none of these sources preserve any traditions about discoveries in this part of the Atlantic. This rather suggests that the Norse visitors did not actually get to leave again and tell anyone about what they'd found. There are not many good harbours in either Madeira or the Azores, so the most likely scenario is that the mice were survivors of shipwrecks: any that made it ashore alive would have found an environment devoid of terrestrial predators and flourished. Human survivors would, however, have found less to sustain them. Had the Norse actually gone equipped to settle the Azores, they would probably have flourished like the mice and still been there when the Portuguese arrived in the fifteenth century. The Norse were primarily pastoralists, and these volcanic islands, with their warm, wet climate, fertile soils and lush vegetation, would have been ideal for rearing livestock: dairying is still a major activity in the Azores islands today.

The arrival in England in 865 of a 'great heathen army' marked another step change in Viking activity. This army's aim was not simply to plunder but to conquer land for its leaders to rule and their followers to settle. In the next ten years, this mainly Danish army conquered a great swathe of eastern England, which for centuries afterwards was known as the Danelaw: their main centre was the city of York. Other settlements were made on conquered lands in Ireland, northwest England, Wales, Scotland's Hebridean archipelago, the Northern Isles, Brittany and Normandy. Once they had settled down on their conquered lands, the Vikings lost their main military advantage, their mobility, and their independence was short-lived. The Norse settlers were in most places a minority among the native population and, usually, within about three generations they had been assimilated through conversion to Christianity and intermarriage. On the wider scale, the Scandinavian kingdoms were themselves assimilated into Christian Europe by conversion in the late tenth and early eleventh centuries. This was a very top-down process, imposed by kings who saw the church, and its literate personnel, as allies who could help them administer their kingdoms more efficiently. As Denmark, Norway and Sweden emerged as stable kingdoms in the course of the eleventh century, the Viking impulse gradually fizzled out.

The first stepping stone

The area where the transition from raiding to settlement started first was the Northern Isles – the Orkney and Shetland islands off the northern coast of Scotland. Although Shetland is only 220 kilometres west of Norway, there is no evidence of any contacts between Scandinavia and the Northern Isles before the Viking Age, but the Norse must have known of their existence by 795, when Viking raiders sailed through the Hebrides and sacked St Columba's monastery on Iona.* The Shetland Islands must have

* A long-standing theory that there had been pre-Viking Age contacts was based on the belief that combs found in high-status Pictish settlements, such as the Brough of Birsay in Orkney, were made of reindeer antler imported from Scandinavia: they have recently been proven, by mass spectrometry, to be made of Scottish red deer antler.

looked immediately attractive to Norwegians. With its deeply indented coastline and rough hills, the look of the land is similar to western Norway's. Like most of Norway, the Shetland Islands are predominantly built of ancient crystalline rocks which weather slowly to create infertile, acid soils. As a result, the islands are largely covered with peat moors and rough pasture: most of the areas suitable for arable farming, a mere 5 per cent of the islands' land, are close to the sea, where wind-blown shell sand has created pockets of light fertile soils, as it has at Jarlshof. The climate too is scarcely different from western Norway's. This was obviously a place where Norse settlers could easily transplant their traditional pastoral-farming way of life and barely feel that they had left home. Like Shetland, the Orkney Islands are also windswept and treeless, but this is deceptive. These islands are built of sedimentary rocks – sandstones and marls – which have weathered to create large areas of fertile arable land. The islands look much more like northeastern Scotland than they do the Shetland Islands, not that that this would have put the Norse off, since land as good as this was in short supply in Norway. The islands also had the advantages of good communications, not too far from the support of family back home and also providing good bases for Viking raids further south along both the east and west coast of Britain.

The only obstacle was that the islands were already inhabited: they formed a small Pictish kingdom. There are no records at all of the Norse occupation of the isles, but it is unlikely that the Picts could have held out for long under the Viking onslaught. How could a kingdom whose population was scattered across dozens of islands have concentrated its forces to fight off attacks by such a mobile enemy as the Vikings? Gather the warriors in Orkney and leave Shetland undefended? Or gather them in Shetland and leave Orkney defenceless? Violence there must have been, however, as shown by a major hoard of eighth-century silver jewellery, sword fittings and drinking bowls found buried near a Pictish monastery on St Ninian's Isle in Shetland. The date of this hoard makes it likely that it was buried to hide it from

Viking raiders, and the fact that such a valuable hoard was not recovered suggests that its owner came to a bad end.

Norse DNA

The process of Norse settlement was probably already underway in the first decades of the ninth century, and it was a very intensive process. In all areas that the Norse settled in this period that already had an indigenous population, the fate of the settlers was, ultimately, to be assimilated into the local population. This is what happened in England and Normandy. However, the Northern Isles became an enduring extension of the Scandinavian world, becoming completely Norse in culture and language. Until recently, it was thought that this was because the Vikings had actually slaughtered or expelled most of the Pictish population. The Norse settlement certainly marks a clear break in the islands' history. No Pictish place names survive anywhere in the islands, and no Pictish settlements show evidence of continuing occupation after *c.*800, though some, as at the Brough of Birsay, were later built over by Norse settlements. Few Pictish artefacts have ever been found in Norse settlements, indicating that there was little interaction between settlers and locals. On the face of it, it appears that the Picts disappeared without trace. Thanks to the new science of DNA profiling, the genes of the modern population of the Northern Isles tell a subtler story. Analysis of the male population's Y chromosomes, which are passed only through the male line from father to son, showed that 44 per cent of men in Shetland and 33 per cent of men in Orkney carry a distinctive genetic marker called the M17 haplotype, which is also carried by a majority of Norwegian and Swedish (but not Danish) men. Factoring out post-medieval immigration, this indicates that more than half the male population of the isles in the Viking Age was of Scandinavian origin. Studies of mitochondrial DNA, possessed by both sexes but passed on only through the female line, found that the same proportions of women in

Shetland and Orkney have Scandinavian ancestry. This indicates that the settlers came as family groups, a sign that they felt secure and unthreatened by native resistance. So what happened to the Picts? The process of conquest must have thinned their numbers in various ways; some were killed in battle, others perhaps took to their boats and fled to the mainland, and many more would have been rounded up for the slave trade and sold off the islands. The outnumbered survivors, reduced to a servile condition, were soon completely assimilated to Norse culture and language.

By the late ninth century, the Pictish kingdom had been replaced by a Norse earldom. Historical traditions recorded in the thirteenth-century *Orkneyinga Saga* say that the islands were being used as bases by Viking pirates for raids on Norway, which in itself is not unlikely. Vikings were not nationalists, and they were as happy to plunder their fellow Norse as anyone else. This prompted the Norwegian King Harald Fairhair to take a fleet across the North Sea and give the islands a good ravaging to teach the pirates a lesson. Harald offered to appoint his loyal supporter Jarl Rognvald of Møre to govern the islands as compensation for the death of his son during the campaign. Rognvald wasn't interested and offered the job instead to his brother Sigurd, who Harald duly installed as the first Jarl of Orkney and Shetland. Harald's reign could have been anytime between around 870 and 930, so this doesn't really shed much light on the origins of the jarldom, and the story may be a later invention, to justify Norwegian claims to sovereignty over the islands. Whatever its theoretical status, the jarls of Orkney enjoyed effective independence until the end of the twelfth century, by which time the Norwegian crown was strong enough to make its claims to sovereignty real.

Thanks to its extensive arable land, Orkney was relatively self-sufficient: bleaker and boggier, Shetland was not. After the settlement period, Shetlanders turned increasingly to the sea for a living, selling salt cod (*klippfisk*) and herrings to merchants from the German-dominated Hanseatic League in exchange for cash, salt, beer, grain and fishing gear. Orkney later had its moment in Atlantic economic history as an important base for the whaling industry, but in the Middle Ages, at least, most fishing was for local consumption: Orkney was a land of farmers who fished, while Shetland was a land of fishers who farmed.

An unpaid dowry

In 1380, Norway and its possessions came under the Danish crown. The kings of Denmark treated Orkney and Shetland with casual indifference. In 1468, King Christian I pledged the islands as security for a dowry for his daughter Margaret, who was to marry King James III of Scotland. However, the hard-up monarch couldn't find the cash to redeem the islands, and in 1472 they passed officially to the Scottish crown. As a concession, the islanders continued to live under Norwegian laws and customs until 1611, when Scottish law was introduced, and the local Norse dialect, known as Norn, gradually died out, to be replaced by a local dialect of English around 1700, which, however, includes many hundreds of words of Norse origin.

There was no resistance to the Scottish annexation. Scottish influence in the isles had been growing for a long time, and the fact that the title to the jarldom had been inherited by the Scottish Sinclair family nearly a century before perhaps gave a sense of inevitability to the final annexation when it came. While the islanders accepted Scottish rule, perhaps a little grudgingly in Shetland at times, they would never completely buy into the Scottish national identity. They continued to see themselves not as Norse living under foreign rule but as Orcadians and Shetlanders. That strong sense of Norse identity which is increasingly in evidence in the islands today is really a product of the nineteenth-century romanticization of the Vikings by historians, artists, composers and novelists, like Scott, who led the islanders to rediscover their Viking past.

7

Land-takings

825–1262

The settlement of the Faeroe Islands – Iceland's foundation myth – The foster-brothers' tale – Dating the settlement – Freedom-loving exiles – Celtic connections – Taking the land – Iceland's environment – Founding the Althing – Thingvellir – Conversion to Christianity – Loss of independence

Not long after they had settled the Shetland Islands, the Norse took their second step out across the Atlantic by settling the Faeroe islands, some two days' sailing to the northwest. It is not known how the Norse came to discover the Faeroes, but the most likely answer is that they learned about the islands from the unfortunate Irish monks they captured in their Viking raids on monasteries on the coasts of Britain and Ireland. Once the monks had described the islands to them, the Norse would not have needed any more encouragement to go and take a look for themselves. The Faeroes may be mountainous, windswept and treeless, but they have a mild climate for their latitude of around 62° north and have good pastures and plenty of rough grazing on the mountains. This would have made them immediately attractive to settlers from western Norway, where pastoralism was much more important than arable farming. The Norse would have been encouraged too by descriptions of the islands' huge seabird colonies, which offered a rich seasonal source of eggs and meat. Perhaps the monks told them too that pods of pilot whales were frequent visitors to the fjords, where they could be easily hunted.

The settlement of the Faeroe Islands

Surprisingly, the Norse themselves had little to say about their settlement of the Faeroes: perhaps, compared to their later discoveries in the North Atlantic, it just didn't seem exciting enough to be worth writing about. The few early traditions about the Norse settlement were compiled together in the *Færeyingar Saga* in the thirteenth century, a good four hundred years after the events it describes. According to the saga, the first Norse settler of the Faeroes was Grímur Kamban, who it claims settled at Funningur, on Eysturoy, the second largest of the Faeroe Islands, after he fled the rule of the famously tyrannical Norwegian King Harald Fairhair. While the exact dates of Harald's rule are not known, this would place the beginning of the Norse settlement no earlier than the late ninth century. This is contradicted by the Irish monk Dicuil who, writing around 825, complained that the Norse had recently arrived in the Faeroes and driven off his fellow monks who were using the islands as a retreat. As Dicuil was a contemporary of the events he describes, his testament is more likely to be accurate than the much later saga tradition. It is also unlikely that Grímur, if he was the first settler, emigrated directly from Norway. Grímur's second name is of Gaelic origin (from *cambán*, meaning 'crooked one'), so he had probably spent some time living in the Hebrides before emigrating to the Faeroes. A more plausible scenario for his decision to emigrate is that he was part of the first wave of Norse settlers in the Hebrides but he had found the local Gaels somewhat unwelcoming and thought that he'd find a quieter life in the unpopulated Faeroes. The early settlers were pleased to find the islands well stocked with sheep, which had probably been introduced by the Irish monks as a ready source of food.

So far, archaeology has shed no additional light on the date of the Norse settlement. Norse settlements, artefacts or burials that can be securely dated earlier than the tenth century have simply not been found. This doesn't mean that they don't exist. Archaeological evidence of the Norse settlement has proved elusive probably for the same reasons that evidence of the earlier Irish presence has been hard to find: there has been considerable coastal erosion since the Viking Age, and there are a limited number of attractive sites for settlements, most of which are still occupied by working farms. Dicuil's account, therefore, remains our best evidence for the date of the Norse settlement.

The Norse settlement of the Faeroe Islands really deserves more attention than it gets; it was, after all, the first truly oceanic migration, not only out of Europe, but in the Atlantic Ocean. Every Atlantic island that had been permanently settled up to this time* had been intervisible with another land mass that was already inhabited; no one had needed to sail out of sight of land to reach any of them. A nervous seafarer could even sail from Norway to the Shetland Islands without sailing the open sea if they were prepared to go the long way around, hugging the coast of the North Sea. There was no long way around to the Faeroes; sailors had to commit to an open-sea voyage out of sight of land. The Norse themselves were certainly aware that they had crossed some sort of threshold by settling the Faeroes. It was possible to sail a longship to Shetland, but not so the Faeroes. 'Longships cannot get there,' says the *Færeyingar Saga*, 'on account of the gales and tidal streams, which are often found to be so strong that even a merchant ship can scarcely bear up against them.' The open Atlantic was the realm of the *knarr*.

* Irish monks don't count as permanent settlers because they did not found sustainable communities; they were only visitors to the lands they discovered.

Iceland's foundation myth

In contrast to the settlement of the Faeroes, the next Norse movement out into the Atlantic – their settlement of Iceland – is one of the best documented events of the Viking Age. Medieval Icelanders were fascinated by genealogy, not only because, like many emigrant communities, they wanted to know where their families had originally come from, but because this knowledge was essential when it came to establishing property rights. That fascination continues to the present day, and a majority of modern Icelanders can trace their ancestry back to the settlement period. In a small community like Iceland (its population in 2021 was only 368,000), a good knowledge of family history also helps people avoid marrying partners who are too closely related to them.

At first, family traditions about the settlement period must have been passed down orally from one generation to the next, but in the early twelfth century they were committed to writing in the two earliest written records of Icelandic history, *Landnámabók* and *Íslendingabók*, both of which were written in the Old Norse language. *Íslendingabók* ('The Book of the Icelanders') is a short chronicle of Icelandic history from the discovery of Iceland to 1118, written between 1122 and 1132 by Ari Thorgilsson. Ari belonged to one of Iceland's most influential landowning families, but he went into the church and became a priest at Staðarstaður on the spectacular Snæfellsnes Peninsula in western Iceland. As a churchman, Ari had received a classical education in Latin but was also steeped in Icelandic oral storytelling traditions, and he chose to write in his own language. Ari relied on oral traditions of family history and, for more recent events, on eyewitnesses. Ari added authority to his work by naming his sources. Unlike most Christian authors of his day, who were quick to see the hand of God guiding historical events, Ari avoided supernatural explanations of events, which has also added to his credibility in the eyes of modern historians. Though it's not proven, it is generally thought, on the basis of similarities of style and method, that Ari was also one of the contributors to *Landnámabók* ('The Book of the Settlements'), if he was not actually the sole author. This book recounts the Norse discovery of Iceland in more detail than *Íslendingabók* and records the names, genealogies, geographical origins and land claims of hundreds of Iceland's original Norse settlers. The original text of *Landnámabók* is long lost, but it survives in five later copies which differ from one another in some important details. These two foundational works read as if they are both objective and impartial and, until recently, their reliability has never been seriously challenged. However, recent archaeological and genetic research increasingly shows that they offer a distinctly selective and idealized, and to a degree even fabricated, version of the Norse settlement of Iceland. Rather than being works of objective history, *Íslendingabók* and *Landnámabók* embody Iceland's national foundation myth.

Different versions of *Landnámabók* disagree about who actually discovered Iceland. The version preserved in the *Hauksbók** gives the credit for the discovery to a Swede called Gardar Svavarson. Gardar had set out on a voyage from Denmark, where he had made his home, to the Norse settlements in the Hebrides, to claim some land that his wife had inherited. While passing through the Pentland Firth, the turbulent strait that separates the Orkney Islands from the Scottish mainland, Gardar's ship was caught in a storm and blown far out into the Atlantic. Gardar eventually sighted the mountainous coast of an unknown land: it was the rugged Eastern Horn on Iceland's forbidding south-east coast, guarded by high cliffs with huge unstable scree slopes tumbling chaotically into the sea. Gardar found a landing place east of the Horn and decided that the land looked worth exploring. Gardar began following the coastline westwards. At first, the views inland would have been dominated by vast ice cap of

* A fourteenth-century compilation of Icelandic texts including as well as *Landnámabók*, several sagas and other texts. It is named after its probable owner, the lawspeaker Haukr Erlendsson.

the Vatnajökull and the huge glaciers which snake down from it towards the sea. It was not an inviting prospect. Undiscouraged, Gardar continued to follow the coast, eventually circumnavigating Iceland, establishing that this newfound land was in fact a large island and that there were many areas favourable to settlement. Gardar spent nearly a year in his exploration, spending the winter in a hut he built at Husavik, a favourite resort of humpback whales, on Iceland's north coast. When he set sail in the spring, Gardar left behind a crewman called Nattfari, together with a male slave and a bondswoman, when the small rowing boat in which they were returning from the shore accidentally (or, perhaps, intentionally) drifted away from the ship. These three survived and were still at Husavik when the first wave of settlers began to turn up a few years later, inadvertently becoming Iceland's first permanent inhabitants. *Landnámabók* gives them no credit for this, probably because of their low birth or the suspicion that they were really fugitives. Gardar modestly named his discovery Gardarsholm (Gardar's island) after himself before sailing east to Norway, where he began to sing its praises. While Gardar never returned to Iceland, his son Uni later settled there.

An alternative tradition, preserved in the *Sturlubók*,* claims that Iceland was discovered by Naddod the Viking: he was sailing from Norway to the Faeroe Islands when, like Gardar, he too was blown off course and made a landfall in Iceland's Eastern Fjords. No longer actively volcanic, the landscape of this part of Iceland would have looked quite familiar to anyone like Naddod who was already acquainted with the Faeroe Islands. Naddod lacked Gardar's sense of curiosity; after all, he hadn't planned to go exploring. He climbed a mountain to look for signs of anything worth plundering and, seeing that the land was uninhabited, left without more ado. Because it was snowing heavily when he set sail, he decided to call his discovery Snæland (Snowland), although he was generous with his praise for the

* A late thirteenth-century copy of *Landnámabók* named after its creator, Sturla Þórðarson.

land when he got home. No specific date is given in any source for either of these explorations, but circumstantial details given in *Landnámabók* show that its authors believed that they could not have happened long before *c.*870.

Inspired by Gardar's reports, Floki Vilgerdarson set out from his home in Rogaland in southwest Norway with the intention of settling in the newly discovered land. Floki had won a reputation as a great Viking warrior, but he was also a skillful navigator. *Landnámabók* describes how Floki sailed to Iceland in stages, first from Norway to the Shetland Islands and then on to the Faeroe Islands. Before setting out on the final leg of his voyage, Floki took on board three caged ravens to help him find land. A few days into his voyage, Floki released one of the ravens and it immediately flew off back in the direction of the Faeroes. Later in the voyage, Floki released a second raven. The raven flew up and circled around for a while before returning to the ship. It was clear to Floki, therefore, that no land was near: ravens don't like being caged, but they like drowning even less. When Floki finally released the third raven and watched it fly off to the northwest, he knew that he was not far from his destination and land was soon sighted. This is a great tale but it is suspiciously similar to the story of Noah in the Biblical book of Genesis, in which, after the Ark grounds on top of Mount Ararat, Noah sends first a raven and then a dove out to try to discover if any dry land has yet emerged from the Deluge.[23] This makes it likely that this element of Floki's story is mythical, perhaps invented to appeal to a Christian audience by making him a sort of Viking Noah.

Floki may have been a great navigator, but he turned out to be a clueless settler. He spent the summer at Vatnsfjörður on Breiðarfjörður in northwest Iceland, hunting seals, no doubt for their valuable skins, but he neglected to make any hay, with the result that all the livestock he had brought with him starved to death over the winter. This doomed his attempt at settlement, but he was unable to return home in the spring, as he wished, because the fjord was choked with ice floes. By the time the pack ice finally broke up it was too late in the year to risk trying to return to Norway, so Floki was forced to stay another winter, this time at Borgarfjörður further to the south. The discovery of a beached whale there helped them survive the winter. Thoroughly disillusioned by his experiences, Floki decided to rename the island 'Iceland' when he finally got home to Norway. Floki's new name was the one that stuck, even though two of his men, Herjolf and Thorolf, praised the island's suitability for settlement; the most enthusiastic of the two, Thorolf, swore that it was so lush that butter dripped from every blade of grass. For his enthusiasm, he was known ever afterwards as Thorolf Butter. Both Herjolf and Thorolf would go back to Iceland to settle, and so eventually would Floki.

Thorolf's enthusiasm for Iceland did not strike much of a chord with the Danes and Swedes (they were arable farmers), but for farmers from Norway's mild and wet west coast, butter was just what they were looking for. Iceland didn't sound like it was so very different from places like the Hebrides, and the Orkney, Shetland and Faeroe islands that Norwegians had already settled in some numbers: it was clearly the kind of place they could settle and continue their familiar way of life with a minimum of adaptation.

The foster-brothers' tale

The first to act on the reports from Floki's voyage were two Norwegian foster-brothers, Ingolf Arnarson and Hjorleif Hrodmarsson. The foster-brothers had lost their estates paying compensation to Jarl Atli of Gaular for killing his sons, so they had little to lose and much to gain by seeking land overseas, well out of the jarl's reach. The foster-brothers first made a reconnaissance trip to the Eastern Fjords to assess the prospects for settlements. Liking what they saw, they made preparations to emigrate. Ingolf already had the resources to fund his expedition, but Hjorleif did not, so he set out on a *víking* trip to Ireland, where he plundered a hoard of treasure and captured ten Irish slaves to take with him to Iceland to do the heavy work. Before setting out, Ingolf sacrificed to the gods and gained favourable auguries. Hjorleif didn't bother: he never sacrificed. *Landnámabók* gives the date of their departure as the year that 'Harald Fairhair had been King of Norway for twelve years: there had passed since the creation of the world 6,073 winters, and from the Incarnation of Our Lord 874 years'. The foster-brothers sailed in company until they made landfall at the place now known as Ingolfshöfði ('Ingolf's Headland'), on the southeast coast at the foot of Iceland's highest mountain, Öræfajökull. Here they went their separate ways. The more impatient of the two, Hjorleif, sailed another 100 kilometres west along the coast before settling at the place now called Hjörleifshöfði. Ingolf, still piously seeking the guidance of the gods, cast the carved pillars of his high-seat overboard, vowing to settle wherever they were washed ashore. Finding the pillars would take Ingolf nearly three years.

After spending the first winter at Hjörleifshöfði, Hjorleif was ready to sow crops. He had only brought one ox, so he ordered his slaves to draw the plough. It wasn't long before the slaves had had enough of this: they murdered Hjorleif and the other men in his party in an ambush, and fled with his possessions and the women to a group of offshore islands about 50 kilometres to the west. These became known after them as the Vestmannaeyjar ('Isles of the Irish'). Shortly after the killing, two of Ingolf's slaves, who were following the coast looking for his high-seat pillars, came to Hjörleifshöfði and found Hjorleif's body. Ingolf was upset by the killing, 'but so it goes,' he said, 'with those who are not prepared to offer up sacrifice'. Seeing that Hjorleif's ship had gone, Ingolf guessed that the Irish had fled to the Vestmannaeyjar and went after them. Surprising the Irish while they were eating a meal, Ingolf slew some of them. The others died leaping off a cliff in their panic to escape. After spending a third winter in Iceland, Ingolf's slaves finally found his high-seat pillars washed up on the southern shores of the great bay of Faxaflói, nearly 400 kilometres west of Ingolfshöfði. Ingolf named the place Reykjavik, the 'bay of smoke', after the many steaming hot springs in the area. It is now Iceland's capital. Ingolf took into his possession the whole of the Reykjanes Peninsula west of the Öxará river as his estate and settled his followers and slaves on it as his dependants.

The story of Ingolf and Hjorleif is really a pagan morality tale – the brother who respected the gods was rewarded, the one who didn't came to an appropriately grisly end – and this makes it hard to believe that it is literally true. *Landnámabók* claims that Ingolf's high-seat pillars were still there in the house that he built at Reykjavik, but the story still sounds improbable. However, the ocean current along Iceland's south coast does flow from east to west, so, had he thrown them into the sea at Ingolfshöfði, the pillars certainly would have drifted in the right direction, but what would the chances have been, even with slaves to do the searching, of finding two relatively small lengths of carved timber among all the Siberian driftwood that washes up on Iceland's often rocky shores? Similar stories are told of the settlers who followed Ingolf, but it seems unlikely that the settlement really proceeded in such a haphazard way; the pitfalls are obvious – what if your high-seat pillars were washed up somewhere uninhabitable, or on land already claimed by someone else, or were not washed up at all? – so these stories are probably best interpreted as being about establishing the legitimacy of land claims. The settlers were attempting to do something which no Europeans since distant prehistory had done, colonize a completely uninhabited land with no pre-existing framework for establishing land ownership. Under such circumstances, it would not be surprising if the settlers recruited the gods to legitimize their land claims.

Ingolf's arrival in Iceland is considered to mark what is known, after *Landnámabók*, as the *Landnám* or settlement period. This continued until *c.*930, by which time, according to *Landnámabók*, all the best land had been claimed, after which, it tells us, few new immigrants came to Iceland. *Landnámabók* gives us the names of 400 leading settlers, or *lándnámsmenn* ('land-takers'), and over 3,000 other settlers, most of them men, who migrated to Iceland in the *Landnám* period. Most of the named settlers are said to have come from western Norway, but there were also a few Swedes and Danes, as well as a significant number who came from the Norse colonies in the Hebrides, which were under constant pressure from the native Gaels. This group included the only female chieftain to be mentioned in *Landnámabók*, Aud the Deep-Minded.

Dating the settlement

Iceland's volcanoes have provided archaeologists with the means to test the reliability of the chronology of the settlement recorded in the traditional written sources. As well as lava and toxic gases, volcanic eruptions can produce large quantities of fine, glassy, volcanic ash known as tephra, which can be blasted high into the atmosphere. Spread by the wind, sometimes for hundreds or even thousands of miles, the tephra gradually settles over the surrounding landscape. Major historic falls of tephra can be identified in archaeological excavations because they form lighter layers within the accumulations of darker organic-rich soils. These layers can be dated quite precisely by radiometric dating of organic materials buried immediately below the tephra or from tephra layers in ice cores drilled from glaciers. Because the chemical fingerprint of tephra is unique to a particular eruption, it is possible to identify the same tephra layer over a wide area. It is this that makes it so useful for archaeologists as a tool for establishing chronologies.

The most important tephra for Icelandic archaeology is known as the *Landnám* or settlement layer. This layer, which was spread over about 80 per cent of Iceland, originated from an eruption of the Vatnaöldur volcanic system in central Iceland which took place in AD 871±2. Plentiful archaeological evidence of human occupation has been found above this layer but, until very recently, none was found below it, apparently confirming that the year 874 given in *Landnámabók* as the start of the Norse settlement was more or less accurate. From time to time, claims were made for sites that supposedly pre-dated the *Landnám* layer but none stood up to examination until the discovery of a *Landnám*-period longhouse during excavations for the foundations of a new hotel on Aðalstræti in downtown Reykjavik in 2001. The longhouse itself was built around 930, but north of this were the remains of a low turf wall that had been covered by the *Landnám* tephra: there had, after all, been people living in Iceland before the eruption of 871. The site was deemed so important that it has been preserved in a special basement under the hotel as the main exhibit in the Settlement Exhibition Reykjavik 871±2 museum.

This discovery* by itself did not present much of a challenge to the traditional chronology of the settlement, as a few years here or there don't really make that much difference. However, since 2001, two more sites have been discovered that apparently predate the *Landnám* tephra not by a few years but by decades. These sites, at Stöð, on Stöðvarfjörður in the East Fjords, and at Vogur, near Hafnir on the western tip of the Reykjanes Peninsula, are both longhouses, but in neither case is there any evidence that their inhabitants were engaged in farming. Longhouses are the typical Norse dwelling, ruling out any possibility that they were built by Irish monks, as they built circular 'beehive' huts as dwellings.

The site at Vogur comprised the remains of a small dwelling house and storage sheds. Radiocarbon dating of organic remains from the site suggest that it was built around 840, although a date as early as 770 has been claimed. Stöð is a larger and more complex site, excavated in 2017, comprising two longhouses, one built completely inside the footprint of the other which, at 40 metres long, is one of the largest yet discovered in Iceland. Dating these houses precisely is difficult because the *Landnám* tephra did not fall in this part of Iceland. Charcoal from hearths in the larger longhouse has been radiocarbon dated to between 777 and

* Two other sites in southeast Iceland, at Húshólmi and Hrísbrú, may also have been occupied just before the eruption of 871±2.

883, while tephra found on the tops of the turf blocks that were used to build its walls came from an eruption of the Grímsvötn volcano that occurred around 800. As the tephra was lying on top of the turf blocks, it could not have been lying long on the ground before they were cut. On the basis of this evidence, the excavators estimate that the longhouse was built not long after 800, around seventy years before the traditional date for the first Norse settlements. Cattle bones found in association with the smaller longhouse are evidence that this was part of a conventional farming settlement. Radiocarbon dating of charcoal from its hearths suggest that it was built early in the *Landnám* period. Glass beads, coins and other objects of silver, and a fragment of gold excavated from the house mean it could only have belonged to a wealthy chieftain.

The discovery of these very early sites requires a rewriting of the history of the Norse discovery and settlement of Iceland. *Landnámabók* is clearly not far wrong in claiming that the permanent Norse *farming* settlement began in 874. However, the story of the discovery and early exploration of Iceland is plainly fabricated. If Gardar and Nadodd ever really did visit Iceland, it was not under the circumstances described. The stories of 'Raven' Floki and Ingolf may equally be partly or wholly fictional, dreamed up in the long tradition of mythologizing the Atlantic Ocean. The Norse had clearly known about Iceland for a long time before the *Landnám* period and had been visiting it and staying long enough for them to think it was worthwhile to build some substantial houses for themselves. So what were these pioneers doing? Most likely these early settlements were bases for commercial seal hunters, men like Ottar from Hålogaland, perhaps, or the anonymous trader-chieftain from Borg in the Lofoten Islands (see pp. 200–1), who returned seasonally or even stayed several years at a time. Sealskins were the Viking Age equivalent of Goretex and were in great demand for waterproof clothing, boots and bags. They may also have scoured the shores searching for beached sperm whales whose teeth were in demand in Europe for ivory carving. At this time, there were colonies of walrus on the coast of northwestern Iceland and they too might have been hunted for their ivory tusks; they were certainly later hunted to extinction. There is no way of knowing for certain how these hunters discovered Iceland. The most likely scenario is that, like the Faeroes, they learned about it from Irish monks captured in the course of early Viking raids on Scotland and Ireland. This begs the question, why is there no mention at all of this commercially motivated activity in the Icelandic sources when it must have been common knowledge among the *Landnám*-period settlers even before they left Norway? The builder of the smaller longhouse at Stöð could hardly have failed to notice that he was building his house within the walls of an older building, but no settlement is recorded there until the arrival of Thorhadd the Old in the *Landnám* period.

Freedom-loving exiles

According to the traditions recorded in *Landnámabók*, *Íslendingabók* and the later Icelandic family sagas, the settlers of Iceland were independent-minded, self-reliant chieftains fleeing the tyrannical rule that King Harald Fairhair is supposed to have imposed after he defeated his rivals at the battle of Hafrsfjord in 872 and united Norway into a single kingdom. This story is undoubtedly a rationalization of the migration. Because he is not mentioned in any remotely contemporary sources, the date of Harald's reign is not known for certain and neither is the extent of his power. Harald probably died *c.*930 and, as Viking Age kings tended not to die in bed of old age, it is very unlikely that his reign could have begun as early as the 870s. Nor is there any evidence at all that Norway was a single kingdom until the later tenth century, so Harald was probably no more than a regional king, one among many. The saga traditions associate him with the fertile Vestfold region around Oslofjord, far from the west coast districts most of the settlers are said to have come from, so he couldn't have tyrannized them. There are historians who would go so far as to dismiss Harald as an entirely fictional character dreamed up solely to provide Iceland with its origin myth. However, while they cannot be literally true, the Icelandic traditions do contain a deeper truth. The leaders of the settlement were all members of the district chieftain class who made up the lower ranks of the Norse aristocracy: there were no jarls or kings among the settlers. The eighth and ninth centuries were a time of growing royal power in Scandinavia, and this was steadily undermining the local autonomy of the chieftains, turning them into agents of the crown. For men of this class, the opportunity to emigrate to a land that was beyond the reach of kings must have been an attractive one. Those settlers who came from the Hebrides may have found Iceland attractive also because it was unpopulated and so they would be able to hold their land in greater security than in the isles, where they were always exposed to attack by the Gaels.

There is also reason to doubt the authenticity of the genealogies recorded in *Landnámabók* and family sagas. Many clearly contain fictive elements because they go back to characters, like the famous Viking Ragnar Lodbrok, who historians now regard as legendary figures like Robin Hood, but who were believed by medieval Icelanders to be real historical figures. It is also clear that *Landnámabók* was compiled not so much as a work of objective historical record but to secure the proprietary rights of the leading families of the day over their land. This alone must place a question mark over its reliability, because these families would have had every interest in curating self-serving traditions about the settlement period.

Celtic connections

The developing science of DNA profiling has now revealed the real origins of Iceland's first settlers. Analysis of the Y chromosomes* of modern Icelandic men indicate that 75 per cent have

* Y chromosomes, the male sex-determining chromosome, are passed on only through the direct male line, from father to son.

Scandinavian ancestry, while 25 per cent have British or Irish ancestry. Strikingly, analysis of mitochondrial DNA (mtDNA)* of modern Icelandic women shows that the majority – 65 per cent – have Irish or British ancestry, with only 35 per cent having Scandinavian ancestry. The best way of accounting for the sexual imbalance is that most of the Norse settlers were single men, who had been unable to marry at home, most likely because they were of low social rank and had no access to land. While the leading settlers may have had political motives, most settlers emigrated simply because this wild, untamed island offered their best chance of getting a farm and having a family life, even if that meant marrying a slave woman. Genetic analysis of the modern Faeroese population tells a similar story. Analysis of the Y chromosomes of modern Faeroese men indicates that 87 per cent of them have Scandinavian ancestry, while analysis of modern Faeroese women's mitochondrial DNA indicates that 84 per cent of them have British or Irish origins. As it was in Iceland, the majority of Norse settlers in the Faeroes must have been unmarried low-status men who acquired wives en route.

The traditional sources record that many settlers brought Irish or Scottish slaves with them, but the DNA evidence shows that there actually must have been almost as many slaves as free settlers. Not all of the Irish DNA would necessarily have come from slaves, however, because some of the Norse settlers who arrived from the Hebrides, like Helgi the Lean and Dufthakr (an Irish name), had already intermarried with Gaelic families. It would seem that, like modern family historians, medieval Icelanders brought preconceived beliefs and aspirations to their search for their ancestors. Few family historians are delighted to discover, after months of painstaking research, that all their ancestors were anonymous peasants with not even a tenuous link to someone famous or infamous, aristocratic or royal. Medieval Icelanders were no different. It was real or fictive links back to the leading

* Although men inherit mitochondrial DNA from their mothers, they cannot pass it on to their children, male or female.

settlers that they chose to remember, while their enslaved ancestors were deliberately forgotten. The descendants of Helgi and Dufthakr were probably proud to remember their Irish ancestry only because it led back to a king, Cerball mac Dúnlainge (r. 842–88). Modern Icelanders seem to have readily assimilated these genetic revelations into their identity, but it has probably helped that the Celts, like the Vikings, are surrounded with a distinctly romantic aura, making them desirable ancestors. Although only a bare majority of the settlers were Scandinavian, their social, political and cultural dominance was total. This is seen most clearly in the Icelandic language, which, apart from some personal names, shows only insignificant Celtic influences.

Another new source of information about Iceland's settlers comes from isotopic* analysis of human remains, which can give insights into diet and the environments they grew up and lived in. The exact ratios of chemical isotopes incorporated by organic tissues vary according to the local climate, geology and diet. Bone tissue is continually replaced throughout the human lifetime, so the isotope ratios found in it reflect an individual's diet and environment in the later stages of their lifetime. The dentine in teeth is never replaced (if it was, dentists would have less work to do), and therefore its isotopic ratios reflect the environment the individual grew up in. It is these contrasting properties of teeth and bone that make isotopic analysis a powerful tool for studying the origins of migrant communities. These techniques have been applied to the remains of one of Iceland's early inhabitants, the so-called 'Lady in Blue'. Bone does not survive well in Iceland's acid soils, so little could be learned from her very fragmentary remains when they were accidentally discovered by road workers at Ketilsstaðir in the Eastfjords in 1938: even her sex had to be inferred from the typically female grave goods she was interred with, so little bone remained. Subjected to isotopic analysis, even

* Isotopes are atoms of the same chemical element that, while having the same chemical properties, have different numbers of neutrons in the nucleus. Oxygen, for example, has three isotopes: 16O, 17O and 18O.

the small amount of surviving bone has revealed a lot about her life. The lady was buried wearing a blue dress, from which she gets her name, made from wool which was sourced locally. The grave goods, including two gilded alloy oval brooches, a necklace of glass, amber and jet beads, an alloy trefoil brooch, a bone-handled knife, a whetstone and a spindle whorl, mark the lady as a reasonably prosperous pagan Norse woman, respectable but not wealthy. However, the lady was born in neither Iceland nor Scandinavia. Her teeth indicated that she was born and spent her early years in western or northern Britain and had a very land-based diet. The lady's bones indicate that she had a period of poor nutrition later in her childhood and a change of diet to one which included more seafood. Radiometric dating of the lady's tooth collagen suggests she was probably born between 878 and 882, not long after the settlement of Iceland began. The lady was probably not very old when she died, perhaps still in her mid-twenties, a dangerous age for a woman in pre-industrial societies because of the perils of childbirth. Based on the evidence, a credible life story for the lady is that she was born a Scottish or Anglo-Saxon Christian and was kidnapped by Viking slavers during a raid and taken to Iceland. While she may not have been treated well at first, she caught the eye of a single Norse immigrant and was taken in marriage. In the process, the lady became assimilated to Norse culture and identity. When she died, perhaps in childbirth, her husband cared for her enough to give her a respectable burial for a freewoman, her slave origins forgotten, at least in death.

Taking the land

Most of the leading settlers, or *lándnámsmenn* ('land-takers'), arrived in their own ships. These were not the longships used for raiding but the sturdy *knarrs*. The direct voyage to Iceland from the west coast of Norway took about seven days in good weather, but some emigrants took longer, breaking the journey in the Shetland and Faeroe islands. Some would-be settlers likely never made it; in one bad year (1118), all but eight of thirty-five ships setting out from Norway for Iceland were wrecked.

In the early years of the settlement, the leading settlers, the *lándnámsmenn*, found plenty of land to go around, and they needed no formal legal institutions for establishing ownership. Possession was what mattered. The *lándnámsmenn* claimed as much land as they thought they needed to support themselves and their free and servile dependants, but they usually chose clear boundaries for their claims, such as rivers and watersheds. The 400 leading settlers, and over 3,000 other settlers named in *Landnámabók*, would have brought with them wives, children, dependants and slaves, so it is likely that around 20,000 people migrated to Iceland in the *Landnám* period. There was little fresh immigration after *c.*930 because, by this time, all the best grazing land had been claimed. Late-comers struggled to find viable farms. Except in the southwest, which became the most densely populated part of Iceland, most of the settlements were close to the sea: the interior was, as it remains, uninhabited.

Iceland's environment

Hard up against the Arctic Circle, Iceland would not be a place that was even slightly smeared with butter if it were not for the influence of the North Atlantic Current, the northern extension of the Gulf Stream, which moves warm water from the Caribbean north and west across the Atlantic. This current exercises a moderating influence on the climate of the whole northeast Atlantic region, keeping winter temperatures much milder than equivalent latitudes on the western side of the Atlantic. At around 0.7°C, the mean January temperature in southwest Iceland is about the same as that experienced in New York City, more than 2,600 kilometres further south. Despite the large glaciers and ice caps, Iceland is mostly free of the permafrost which holds most places at this latitude in deep freeze. Icelandic summers are decidedly cool, with July temperatures averaging only around 12°C, even with near twenty-four-hour daylight. While summer temperatures like that can't support much in the way of arable farming, Iceland's thin volcanic soils are fertile and can support lush grazing.

Iceland's landscapes are epic in scale, but they also can be forbiddingly austere, dominated more by volcanism than the ice from which it gets its name. Almost completely treeless, less than a quarter of the island supports any vegetation today. Ice caps and glaciers cover about 14 per cent of the country; of the rest, around 60 per cent is barren ash desert, volcanic cones and chaotic lava fields covered with pale grey-green lichens. In bad weather, which is common enough, this makes for a dark and brooding landscape. However, this is not the landscape that would have been seen by Gardar and the other pioneers. Before the Norse settlement, around 40 per cent of Iceland was covered with low, scrubby birch and willow woodland, and there were extensive lush upland pastures, so the landscape would have looked far greener than it does today after centuries of deforestation and over-grazing. Also, by the end of the ninth century, the world was entering what climatologists call the Medieval Warm Period, making Iceland somewhat less icy than it is now: summers were a little warmer and less of the country was covered in permanent ice. Even so, Iceland turned out to be a distinctly marginal environment for European settlement, and the settlers would find that they were very vulnerable to the everyday vagaries of the weather, climate change and volcanic eruptions. Iceland's climate might be mild for its latitude, but it's still a tough place to make a living from the land.

The Icelandic economy depended mainly on animal husbandry, primarily cattle, for meat, milk and hides, and sheep for meat, milk and wool. Pigs were a high-status luxury animal. Cattle needed to be kept indoors during the long winters and needed good fodder if they were to continue to provide milk. For this reason, as Floki Vilgerdarson had discovered to his cost, the hay crop was of crucial importance. The settlers bred horses for both transport and meat. Small but hardy, Icelandic horses have a unique gait that makes for a more comfortable ride over rough ground. Recent genetic studies indicate that the original breeding stock probably originated in England rather than Scandinavia: it was not only slaves that the Norse took with them from Britain. Barley could be grown on a small scale in sheltered areas near the south coast, but grain and flour were mostly imported luxuries. Icelandic farming provided a diet that was rich in meat and dairy products but short on carbohydrates and fresh vegetables. Fishing, hunting of seals, seabirds and waterfowl, gathering seabird's eggs, berries and shellfish added welcome variety to the Icelanders' diet. Occasional beached whales provided a bounty of meat and blubber for entire communities. Despite early Icelanders having what today would be considered an unbalanced diet, studies of the skeletal remains show that the population was well nourished and healthy. Wood was the main building material in Scandinavia, but, from the outset, good timber was in short supply in Iceland. Driftwood, mostly originating in Siberia, was a valuable resource and formed an important part of property rights. The settlers adapted, building the walls of their longhouses from blocks of turf laid on stone foundations, so that wood was only needed for the roofs (which were covered with turf) and to line the interior walls. The turf was durable and gave excellent insulation against wind and cold. Easily extracted bog iron ore was plentiful in Iceland's many bogs, so the settlements were self-sufficient in iron. However, iron production declined owing to fuel shortages as Iceland's sparse woodland was felled and had ended by the close of the Middle Ages.

For all its importance in the initial stages of the Norse settlement, slavery did not survive long as an institution in Iceland. Most slaves were eventually freed and allowed to become tenant farmers on their former owners' land. This might have been partly due to security concerns – Hjorleif was not the only settler who was killed by malcontent slaves – but the motives were mainly economic. For obvious reasons, slaves don't make highly motivated workers, so they need to be closely supervised. However,

Iceland's cool climate is unsuitable for intensive agriculture, and the land was most economically used as pasture with widely dispersed farmsteads and seasonal shielings in the uplands. Slaves could not be closely supervised under these circumstances – if they were unhappy with their rations they could start eating the livestock and later plausibly claim that the missing animals had died in falls or from bad weather – so it made more sense to free them and make them rent-paying tenants instead.

Founding the Althing

As Iceland began to fill up with settlers, it became increasingly lawless, as disputes over land turned violent and escalated into protracted blood feuds. Local leadership was assumed by the *goðar*, a small group of wealthy chieftains who could offer advocacy and protection to smaller landowners in return for their political and military support. *Goði* literally means 'priest', which probably derives from the chieftains' religious duties because, in pagan times, it was they who performed the rituals at the key seasonal festivals on behalf of their communities. Without the support of a *goði* it was all but impossible for an ordinary freeman to hold on to his land, but this did not mean that the *goðar* could take the loyalty of their followers for granted. As freemen they could, and did, transfer their allegiance to another *goði* if their opinions were not taken into account or if their interests were neglected.

The only governmental institution in Viking Age Scandinavia apart from monarchy was the *thing*, an assembly of freemen at which local disputes and criminal offences were judged and at which new laws were made. The Norse always took this institution with them wherever they emigrated and the *goðar* were quick to set up district things to settle local disputes following the initial settlement. However, by the early tenth century it had become clear that there was a need for a higher authority to deal with wider disputes that the district things could not resolve. Appealing to the king of Norway was ruled out because that would have limited Iceland's independence, defeating the whole point of emigration for many of the settlers. Around 930, the *goðar* agreed to set up an all-Iceland assembly, the Althing (Alþingi). However, before the Althing could meet, Iceland needed a national law code, so it was decided to send a man called Úlfljótr to Norway for three years to adapt the Gulaþing laws of western Norway to Icelandic conditions. This was not simply a matter of picking up a law book – there weren't any. Although the Norse used the runic alphabet for writing spells and memorials, Viking Age Scandinavia was not a truly literate society. Úlfljótr would have needed a 'lawman' to recite the laws to him so that he could memorize them.

Thingvellir

It was while Úlfljótr was learning about Norwegian law that his half-brother Grímur Goatbeard decided the Althing would meet at Bláskógar, known ever since as Thingvellir ('thing plain'), a dramatic place of waterfalls and ravines in southwest Iceland's Öxará river valley. Grímur had spent a year travelling the country in search of a suitable location before making his decision. Thingvellir was in the most densely populated part of Iceland, so it had the advantage that most people would not have to travel too far to attend the Althing; it also had the, possibly even greater, attraction that its owner had recently been outlawed for murder, so the land could be seized without paying any compensation. Thingvellir is a fractured lava plain lying right over the Mid-Atlantic Rift, the place where tectonic forces are tearing the Eurasian and North American tectonic plates apart. As these forces have stretched the lava plain, its surface has cracked, forming numerous chasms and ravines, and it was in the shelter of the deepest of these, Almannagjá, at the plain's western edge, that the Althing was held. The stretching is an ongoing process; a new fissure opened by the path that leads down into Almannagjá in 2011, so access is now by a footbridge.

The Althing met annually for two weeks during June, when travelling was easiest and there was almost twenty-four-hour daylight. Meetings were always held in the open air. People attending the Althing lived in temporary booths, the turf foundations of some of which can still be seen, or in tents. The main business of the Althing was conducted from two different locations, the Lögberg ('Law Rock'), a natural platform for making speeches, and Neðri-Vellir, a level place on the west bank of the Öxará, where the legislative council, the *Lögretta* ('Law Council'), met. The Icelandic republic (also described as a free state or commonwealth) had only one public office, that of the Lawspeaker (*Lögsögumaðr*). The *goðar* elected the Lawspeaker on the first day of the Althing for a three-year renewable term immediately after the outgoing Lawspeaker had opened proceedings. The Lawspeaker's main task was to recite the law from the Law Rock, one third of the code in each year of his tenure. Unsurprisingly, Úlfljótr was elected the first Lawspeaker; after all, he was the only person in Iceland who knew what the law was. Not everyone who attended the Althing had legal business: it became just as much a social event as a legal one. The meeting brought the widely dispersed people of Iceland together, allowing people to meet their relatives, renew friendships, share news, strike business deals and arrange marriages. Merchants, tradesmen and entertainers flocked to Thingvellir to tend to the visitors' every need, giving the meetings a festive atmosphere.

It is often claimed that Iceland is the oldest democracy in the world: this is part of the national myth, but the reality is unique enough. Though all freemen had the right to attend and speak, the Althing was really an aristocratic oligarchy, a 'republic of farmer chieftains', not a democracy. All judicial and legislative power was in the hands of the thirty-six *goðar*, who alone had the right to vote in the *Lögretta*. Iceland did not actually become a democracy until the twentieth century. Although the Althing was ultimately controlled by the *goðar*, decision-making tended to be consensual, as they needed to consider the opinions of their 'thingmen' (followers). Failure to do this might lead them to transfer their allegiance to another *goði*. The *goðar* were also expected to help enforce judgements on behalf of their followers, as the Icelandic state had no law enforcement officers. In return for their advocacy and protection, the *goðar* could call upon the armed support of their followers in their feuds with other *goðar*. And those *goðar* with the largest numbers of followers to back them up naturally enjoyed more influence at the Althing.

Conversion to Christianity

The Althing was highly successful at conflict resolution: perhaps the greatest of its achievements was ensuring a peaceful transition from paganism to Christianity. Icelandic traditions hold that this took place in 1000, but it is likely that the conversion actually happened a year earlier and that the date was subsequently 'improved' to the more memorable and significant millennium. In 995, Olaf Tryggvason became king of Norway. Only a year before, Olaf had converted to Christianity while on a Viking expedition to France, and now that he was king he began a gratuitously violent campaign to convert his new subjects to Christianity. Encouraged by the church, Olaf, like other medieval Christian rulers, saw resistance to conversion as a useful pretext for invading and annexing pagan territory. In 995, Olaf intervened in Orkney to impose Christianity on the Norse settlers there, and it was clear that he would do the same in the Faeroes and Iceland as soon as the opportunity arose. The Icelanders feared that Olaf's intervention would not end with forced conversion; he would also demand political allegiance, ending Iceland's independence. And wasn't it to get away from overbearing kings that their ancestors had come to Iceland in the first place?

There had been Christians among the first settlers, not only among slaves taken from Christian countries but also among the Hebridean Norse. Others, like Helgi the Lean, who worshipped Christ on land and Thor at sea, were partly Christianized.

However, the religion did not take root in Iceland, and it died out with the first generation of settlers. Missions to convert the Icelanders began in the 980s and, though they made many converts, their progress was too slow to satisfy King Olaf. In 999, Olaf turned to economic sanctions and hostage taking. He closed Norwegian ports to Icelanders – a severe blow, because Norway was Iceland's main trading partner – and imprisoned all the Icelanders then in Norway. Olaf threatened to maim or kill his prisoners unless Iceland accepted Christianity.

Under this severe pressure, the Icelanders divided into pro- and anti-Christian camps. The Christians refused to be judged by pagans and threatened to set up their own parallel system of things and courts, driving the country to the brink of civil war. Matters came to a head at the Althing, but violence was averted when the *goðar* agreed to treat the issue like a bloodfeud that needed settling and submitting it to arbitration. Mediators chose the Lawspeaker, Thorgeir Thorkelsson, to adjudicate. Thorgeir was a sincere pagan, but he counted many leading Christians among his close friends, so both sides accepted him as an impartial judge. Thorgeir spent a day and a night huddled under a cloak while he deliberated on his decision. After receiving assurances from both sides that they would abide by his ruling, Thorgeir announced 'that all people should become Christian and that those who here in the land were yet unbaptized should be baptized'. People would still be allowed to sacrifice to the old gods in private, but if they did it publicly they would be outlawed. Although most Icelanders were still pagan, Thorgeir's compromise was accepted peacefully; no one wanted to give King Olaf the pretext, which a civil war might have offered, to assert any kind of sovereignty over their country. When Thorgeir returned to his home in the north of Iceland, he demonstrated his own commitment to the decision by demolishing his pagan shrine and throwing its idols into a waterfall, known since as Goðafoss ('falls of the gods').

The wisdom of the Icelanders' decision was soon made apparent. In 1000, Olaf commissioned Sigmundur Brestisson, a Faeroese exile in Norway, to convert the Faeroe Islanders to Christianity and to bring them under the Norwegian crown. The leader of the pagan party was Tróndur of Gøtu, who publicly cursed Christianity by Thor's hammer. Sigmundur and his men broke into Tróndur's home one night and offered him the choice of conversion or having his head cut off. Confronted with such a persuasive theological argument, Tróndur chose Christianity, and the rest of the islanders quickly decided that they were persuaded too and followed suit. Sigmundur became a hated figure and he was murdered in 1005, but the Faeroes never regained their independence.

Loss of independence

Royal power did eventually catch up with Iceland. The country's oligarchic system of government worked well enough while all the *goðar* were of roughly equal wealth, power and status, but it was unable to cope with the emergence, in the early thirteenth century, of six paramount chieftains, known as the *stórgoðar* ('great chieftains'). Through inheritance and political marriages, these chieftains had built regional lordships, taking over the chieftaincies of lesser *goðar*, together with their rights to vote at the Althing. Competition for power among the *stórgoðar* became steadily more violent the more it intensified, and the country was constantly riven by destabilizing bloodfeuds. The expansionist Norwegian King Hákon IV (r. 1217–63) ruthlessly exploited these rivalries in a classic strategy of divide and rule, offering his support first to one *stórgoðar* and then to another, steadily increasing his influence. Finally, faced with the prospect of outright civil war, the Icelanders accepted Hákon's overlordship in 1262 as the only way to restore peace. The leaders of the settlement of Iceland had been chieftains who had wanted to rule their followers independently of kings. Four hundred years later, the forces of political centralization that they had fled finally caught up with their descendants: Iceland would not regain its independence for nearly 700 years.

8

The walrus and the unicorn

900–1261

Gunnbjorn discovers Greenland – Erik the Red founds the Greenland colony – Brattahlið – Unicorn horns – Hunting in the Norðsetr – How to get to Greenland – Northern Lights

Thorvald Asvaldsson was a man with anger management problems. These had led to 'some killings' that had got him outlawed from his home in Norway. Medieval outlaws were literally outside the protection of the law; they had no rights and could be killed with impunity. An outlaw's best chance of survival was to flee the country and go into exile. Taking his wife and his young son Erik with him, Thorvald decided to go to Iceland. The 960s were not a good time to be emigrating there, as all the good land had been claimed decades before, but Thorvald didn't have many options; the days when a man who was handy with weapons might join a Viking band and seize some land in England or Normandy were over. Thorvald was probably pleased enough to settle on a poor farm at Drangar in the bleak Hornstrandir peninsula in the West Fjords, about as far from his enemies in Norway as he could get.

Thorvald kept out of trouble in Iceland and died peacefully on his farm. It isn't clear exactly when this happened, but by the time his father died, Erik had grown to manhood and already sported the flaming-red beard and red hair which gave him the nickname, by which he is usually known today, Erik the Red. Thoroughly dissatisfied with his inheritance of stones and bog, Erik moved further south with his new wife Thjodhild and cleared some land for a farm in the fertile Haukadal by Breiðafjörður. Haukadal's existing families saw Erik as an interloper and, as he shared his father's temperament, he was soon involved in a violent feud with his neighbours. After a number of killings, Erik was sentenced to three years' outlawry and, for the second time in his life, went into exile. Protected by his friends while he readied his ship, Erik set out to explore a land sighted in the west some eighty years before by Gunnbjorn Ulf-Krakuson. Erik's expedition would make him the leader of Europe's first colony in the Americas.

Gunnbjorn discovers Greenland

Once the Norse had begun sailing regularly to Iceland, it was really only a matter of time before some seafarer overshot his intended destination and finished up in Greenland. This is what happened to Gunnbjorn. Sometime around 900, Gunnbjorn set out from Norway to join family members who had already emigrated to Iceland. On the way, he was caught in a storm and blown past Iceland, far to the west. When the storm abated, Gunnbjorn sighted a scatter of islands which became known as the Gunnbjorn Skerries. This is generally believed to be the first European sighting of Greenland and, therefore, because the island lies on the North American continental shelf, of any part of the Americas.* Gunnbjorn's Skerries have not been identified

* It is not likely, as is sometimes claimed, that the Icelanders could already have sighted Greenland from the mountains of western Iceland. The shortest distance between Iceland and Greenland is about 300 kilometres, and neither the mountains of western Iceland nor those in eastern Greenland are high enough to be intervisible across that distance. Reported sightings of Greenland from Iceland are probably superior mirages (*hafgerðingar* in the Icelandic language) resulting from temperature inversions, which are common in high latitudes.

for certain, and sixteenth- and seventeenth-century cartographers have only added to the confusion by imaginative guesses as to their location. Ivar Bardarson, a Norwegian priest who visited Greenland in the fourteenth century, located the skerries two days' sail due west of Snæfellsnes on Iceland's west coast. He is likely to have known what he was talking about, so the skerries were probably the group of ice-free islands between the Ammassalik and Sermiligaaq fjords, east of Tasiilaq, on Greenland's inhospitable and generally heavily glaciated east coast.

Gunnbjorn did not attempt to land but reported his sighting when he finally reached Iceland. With good land still to be claimed, Gunnbjorn's discovery did not excite much interest at first, but it was not forgotten. As the population of Iceland grew, both natives and late-comers were forced onto more and more marginal land: Erik the Red's father was one of them. The summer of 975–6 was a cold one. Grass didn't grow well enough for many farmers to make enough hay to feed their livestock through the following winter. Animals starved to death and soon so too did people. Interest in the skerries revived, and in 978, Snæbjorn Galti set out with twenty-four followers to explore them. Snæbjorn's expedition was famous enough for him to have had his own saga which, unfortunately, has not survived: what we know about it comes from a brief account in *Landnámabók*. No specific purpose is given for Snæbjorn's venture, but, given what we now know about the earliest Norse settlements in Iceland, it is likely that they were looking for seals and walrus to hunt, rather than lands to farm. Having found the skerries, the group built themselves a hall but disagreements about what to do next broke out in the party almost at once. Because the skerries are at roughly the same latitude as Iceland, Snæbjorn may have expected the climate to be the same too. If so, the severity of the winter would have come as a shock. The house was completely buried under snow, and it was early March before the party was able to dig itself out, by which time they were suffering from a bad case of cabin fever. The disagreements within the group turned violent and, after

Snæbjorn was murdered, the would-be colonists left, returning to Iceland via Norway.

Erik the Red founds the Greenland colony

Erik's friends escorted his ship for the first part of his voyage down Breiðafjörður in case he should be ambushed by his enemies. On reaching the open sea at Snæfellsnes, Erik said his goodbyes and set sail west, making landfall in Greenland at a prominent glacier later known to the Norse as Blåserk ('blue shirt'). The polar explorer Fridtjof Nansen proposed that this was the Rigny Bjerg glacier, some 300 kilometres north of the Arctic Circle, but this does not seem like an obvious first landfall if leaving Iceland for Greenland from Snæfellsnes. In any case, Greenland's east coast is not short of impressive glaciers, so which one it was is really anyone's guess. Erik would have been well aware of the failure of Snæbjorn Galti's attempt to settle the Gunnbjorn Skerries, and it seems that he did not linger on the east coast. Heading south, he rounded Cape Farewell, at Greenland's southern tip, and discovered that the coast turned northwest. Following the coast, Erik began to explore Greenland's western fjords, sailing at least as far north as present-day Nuuk, the capital of Greenland. In these deep and sheltered fjords, he found much good grazing land and scrubby woodlands of dwarf willow and birch similar to those that had covered Iceland before the Norse arrived. He surely also must have weighed up the prospects for commercial hunting of caribou (the North American sub-species of reindeer), seal and walrus, which were plentiful in Greenland. Erik spent three summers exploring the fjords, long enough to learn that, though the winters were considerably colder and snowier than Iceland's, the summers, at least in the inner fjords, were sunnier and drier, even if they were plagued by clouds of insatiably hungry mosquitoes on still days.

Though Erik found the fjords completely uninhabited, scatters of stone tools and broken wooden boat parts along the shorelines told him that this had not always been the case. The people who had left these relics belonged to the Dorset culture,* which flourished across the eastern Arctic and as far south as Newfoundland from around 500 BC to AD 1300. The Dorset people had left this part of Greenland around a century before Erik's arrival, driven out by the same warming climate that was facilitating the Norse colonization of the North Atlantic. The Dorset peoples' way of life was based on seal hunting, which was most easily done in late winter and spring, when the seals were exposed on sea ice. Because of the warmer conditions, the southwestern fjords had become ice-free nearly all year around, so the Dorset retreated to the Baffin Bay area further north, where the hunting was better. A few Norse artefacts have been discovered on Dorset sites, evidence that there were at least occasional encounters between the two peoples. Although Norse sources have nothing to say about the Dorset, it is possible that some accounts of their customs did make it back to Europe. The Arab geographer Muhammad al-Idrisi, writing in Sicily around 1150, praised the North Atlantic for its rich fisheries and went on to state that 'there are also sea animals of such enormous size that the inhabitants of the inner islands use their bones and vertebrae in place of wood in constructing houses. They also use them for making clubs, darts, lances, knives, seats, ladders and, in general, all things which elsewhere are made from wood.' If the enormous sea animals al-Idrisi refers to are whales, and that seems a reasonable assumption, the only people living on the North Atlantic at this time who would fit that description were the Dorset.

On his return to Iceland, Erik began recruiting followers to join him in founding a colony in Greenland. For Erik, this was an opportunity to increase his status dramatically. In Iceland, he had always been an outsider; now he had the chance to become a *lándnámsmann*, a chief in a new unsettled land. A natural real-estate salesman, Erik decided to call his new land Greenland

* Named for an archaeological site at Cape Dorset (now known as Kinngait) in Nunavut, Canada, where evidence of their culture was first found in 1925.

'because,' he said, 'men would be drawn to go there if it had an attractive name'. Thanks to the recent famine, many families were interested, and when Erik returned to Greenland the next summer, twenty-five ships sailed with him. According to *Íslendingabók*, this happened fourteen or fifteen years before the Icelanders converted to Christianity, which would make it around 985–6. Icebergs and turbulent seas make the crossing from Iceland to Greenland hazardous, and of the twenty-five ships that set out with Erik, only fourteen made it safely to the western fjords: the rest either turned back or were lost at sea. For the survivors, the risks were worth it for the chance to have first pick of the best sites for settlement.

Erik and the other early arrivers claimed lands in the southwest, in the fjords around modern Qaqortok, which had Greenland's largest area of fertile land. This became known as the Eastern Settlement. It is not known how many settlers there were in the first wave. Thorbjorn Vifilsson, a friend of Erik's who migrated to Greenland some years after the initial settlement, brought thirty followers with him in his ship, only half of whom survived the difficult passage. If this was typical, the Greenland colony would have started with no more than 400 people. Later arrivals were directed about 450 kilometres further northwest to the deep fjords inland of modern Nuuk, at the northernmost limit of Erik's initial exploration. This area, which became known as the Western Settlement, might initially have been seen as second best, but it came to play an important role in the commercial development of the colony, because it was more favourably situated for hunting expeditions. Later, a smaller settlement, the Middle Settlement, was founded about halfway between the two main settlements. The names of the settlements have caused confusion in the past. Early historians of Greenland spent years fruitlessly searching Greenland's east coast for the Eastern Settlement before it was realized that both were on the west coast.

Brattahlið

Erik's own estate was at Brattahlið, named after his childhood home in Norway – he must have been a sentimental man at heart – about 85 kilometres from the open sea on an isthmus between the head of Tunulliarfik Fjord (which, in Erik's time, was known, after him, as Eiriksfjord) and Nordre Sermilik Fjord. Brattahlið is sheltered from the north wind by low hills and has a long strip of west-facing, well-drained grassland stretching alongside the fjord for around 2 kilometres. Another attraction was a good harbour, with water deep enough for ships to dock at a landing stage. This remained home for Erik's descendants until the fifteenth century. Excavations at Brattahlið have uncovered the stone foundations of three longhouses and their associated cowsheds, barns and stores, a probable smithy and the foundations of a stone church. These stone buildings all date from the thirteenth and fourteenth centuries, and they have likely obliterated all traces of Erik's original longhouse, which, like contemporary buildings in Iceland, would have been built entirely of turf. About a kilometre from the farm, archaeologists have identified the meeting place of the Greenland Althing. Erik was probably the colony's first Lawspeaker, and the office may have remained hereditary in his family.

The stone church had an associated graveyard containing around 144 burials. A few of these had gravestones, including one which bore a short runic inscription reading simply 'Ingibjørg's grave'. There was also a mass burial of thirteen people, some of whose skeletons bore the signs of injuries caused by sharp bladed weapons, making it likely that all were victims of a single act of violence. Obviously, not everything was peace and harmony in the colony. In the graveyard, archaeologists also found the remains of a very small turf church with external dimensions of 4 metres broad by 5 metres long. However, the walls were so thick that the interior was a cramped 2 metres broad by 3.5 metres long. Despite its tiny dimensions, the interior was divided by a wooden partition into a sanctuary, where the altar was, and a nave, where the obviously very small congregation stood during services. This church can be directly associated with Erik's wife Thjodhild. According to a story told in the *Greenlanders' Saga*, Erik's son Leif converted to Christianity while visiting King Olaf's court in Norway in *c.*1000. When Leif was ready to return home, King Olaf asked him to preach Christianity in Greenland and provided him with a priest to instruct and baptize the people. Erik, a loyal pagan, stubbornly refused to convert, but Thjodihild embraced Christianity immediately and built a small church near the farm, where she and other new converts prayed. Erik paid a high personal price for sticking with the old religion; after her conversion, Thjodhild refused to sleep with him anymore, because he was an ignorant pagan.

The new Greenland colony prospered, and by around 1100, its population had grown to between 2,000 and 2,500 people. The dominant Eastern Settlement had 190 farms, twelve parish churches, an Augustinian monastery, a Benedictine nunnery and a modest cathedral at Garðar (now Igaliku). Greenland's first bishop was appointed in 1124, and the cathedral was begun two years later: its dedication to St Nicholas, the patron saint of sailors, was a pragmatic choice given how much the colony depended on its maritime communications. The Western Settlement had ninety farms and four churches, while the Middle Settlement had twenty farms. Sheep and goat rearing, for milk, meat, wool and hides, was the main occupation of most farmers, but the chieftains and church kept substantial numbers of cattle on their farms – the bishop's farm at Garðar had around 160 – and small numbers of pigs and horses were also bred. The settlers maximized their grazing resources by taking livestock to upland shielings for the summer. Wandering polar bears were an occasional risk for livestock but, given the choice, they preferred to hunt seals which, having more fat on them, offered better food value. Most of the fields around the farms were used for growing hay for winter fodder, but it was possible to grow a little barley in some sheltered areas in the Eastern Settlement. Farming is a very minor part of the modern Greenland economy, but it is telling that all of the thirty or so farms in the country today are on the site of former Norse farms. Brattahlið, now known as Qassiarsuk, is one of them, a sheep farm since 1924. With most of the fertile area again growing hay for winter feed, Brattahlið probably looks now much as it did in Erik's time, especially as there are reconstructions of a longhouse and Thjodhild's church not far from their historical locations.

Farming in the Norse colony was probably at least as important for cultural reasons as for its economic significance in that it helped maintain a northern European lifestyle for the colonists, with familiar foods like milk, butter and cheese, and wool for European clothes: it certainly did not provide the colony with self-sufficiency. Timber for houses and ships, iron tools and weapons, tar for waterproofing ships and house timbers, salt, linen and wax – all needed to be imported from Iceland or Norway. Wheat was so expensive that only chieftains got to eat bread regularly. Malt for brewing beer was another European staple that was hard to get in Greenland. Serving beer to their guests at Yuletide feasts was an important way for chieftains to show their status. A story in Erik the Red's saga tells how Erik became increasingly depressed as Yule approached, because he had house guests and feared that after they left they would tell everyone what miserable hospitality he shown them because he had nothing to brew beer with. Happily, Yule was saved when it turned out that one of his guests had plenty of malt in his ship's cargo, which he invited Erik to help himself to.

Fortunately, the Greenlanders were well able to pay for their essential imports, and it is likely that Erik's colonizing venture was always as much a search for commercial opportunities as it was for new lands to farm. Agricultural exports were limited to cow and calf hides, sheepskins and wadmal (homespun woolen cloth), but these alone would not have gone far towards paying the colony's way. It was Greenland's wildlife that did this. Probably the most important export by value was walrus ivory, which was in demand in Europe because better-quality elephant ivory had become more difficult to obtain following the Islamic conquest of North Africa. The famous Lewis chessmen were carved from Greenland walrus ivory, probably in a workshop in Trondheim. Walrus hides were also in demand for making waterproof ships' ropes. These were reputedly so strong that even sixty men were not strong enough to break them. Sealskins were another staple, used for waterproof boots, cloaks and bags. The rest of the seals were not wasted; their strongly flavoured meat was an important part of the diet, especially for the poorer Greenlanders, and the blubber was rendered to produce oil for lighting and heating. Caribou hides and antlers, used for comb making, were also exported. Greenland additionally had some very exotic luxuries, such as the pure-white furs of Arctic foxes and polar bears. Polar bear cubs were also trapped and exported live to make exotic, and, when they were fully grown, rather dangerous, high-status pets for European rulers, such as the Holy Roman Emperor Henry III, who was gifted one by an early bishop of Greenland. Greenland became famous for its gyrfalcons, the most expensive of all birds of prey used in the elite medieval sport of falconry. In the Islamic world, a gyrfalcon cost around 1,000 gold dinars. Translating that into a modern cash equivalent (that amount of gold would be worth nearly $200,000 today) understates the birds' real price, because gold had four or five times greater purchasing power in the Middle Ages. These were million-dollar birds.

Unicorn horns

Another almost literally mythical Greenland luxury were the slender, spiralling narwhal tusks which medieval Europeans credulously believed were unicorn horns. Look at any medieval depiction of a unicorn, for example in the Royal Arms of Scotland, and they all sport narwhal tusks on their heads. There was good money to be made from the deception. Powdered unicorn horn was believed to be a universal antidote to poisons, so paranoid rulers were willing to pay extravagant sums to acquire them. England's Queen Elizabeth I, who knew that plenty of people wished her dead, owned one valued at £10,000, the equivalent of over £2 million ($2.5 million) today. Although the true source of these unicorn horns was certainly known by some in Norway by the thirteenth century, it did not become widely known until the deception was exposed by the Danish scientist Ole Worm in 1638. Even then, as late as 1672 King Frederick III of Denmark ordered a coronation throne made of 'unicorn' horn. Although it is no longer used for coronations, the throne can still be seen in Rosenborg palace in Copenhagen. It is, of course, made with narwhal tusks. If anyone knew the truth about Queen Elizabeth's unicorn horn, they probably thought it wiser to keep it to themselves: she was notoriously short-tempered, and it would have taken someone quite brave to tell her she'd been conned out of the price of a couple of galleons.*

Stockfish, air-dried cod, was an important part of the diet of medieval Icelanders and Norwegians and also one of their most lucrative exports to the rest of Europe (see Chapter 13), where there was high demand for fish because of the church's prohibition of eating meat on Fridays and other holy days. The Greenland settlements were within the range of Atlantic cod, so it is surprising that there is very little evidence that the Norse Greenlanders ever caught cod, either for their own consumption or to produce stockfish for export. Fishbones are common finds in medieval Icelandic and Norwegian domestic middens, but they are almost completely absent from domestic middens in the settlements, despite excellent conditions for the preservation of organic remains. Distance from markets cannot be the reason for this, because stockfish is easily transported and, so long as it is kept dry, remains edible for years. The explanation may be that producing stockfish is a winter activity, and sea ice would have prevented the Greenlanders from fishing.

* *Ark Royal*, the brand-new fifty-five-gun flagship of the English fleet that defeated the Spanish Armada in 1588, cost just £5,000.

Hunting in the Norðsetr

While there were seals to be had in the waters around the settlements and in the 'unsettled wilds' of the east coast, most of Greenland's high-value exports were acquired on annual hunting expeditions to the Norðsetr, the uninhabited area around Disko Bay about 400 kilometres north of the Arctic Circle. This was where the Western Settlement came into its own, as it was only fifteen days' sailing from the hunting grounds: the journey took an extra twelve days from the Eastern Settlement. The hunting expeditions were controlled by the wealthier farmers, who owned and equipped the ships, while the hunters were probably recruited from the ranks of their tenant farmers. Small but manoeuvrable six-oared sailing boats were most commonly used for hunting trips. These were good at navigating through drifting ice but could carry only small hunting parties and had only a limited cargo capacity. During their expeditions, the hunters based themselves at summer camps or shielings, with storage and drying sheds. At least one of these, known as the Bear Trap, has been identified with certainty on the Nuussuaq Peninsula at over 70° north. This was a well-built stone structure with a narrow entrance and very thick walls, probably both to keep the interior cool and to keep out scavenging polar bears in search of an easy meal. As well as hunting, the men were kept busy rendering seal and walrus blubber, pouring the melted fat into skin bags, which were then hung up in well-ventilated sheds to be cured by the wind. The settlements were always short of timber, so gathering driftwood to take home was a worthwhile sideline.

The hunting season was a short one, restricted to the late summer and early autumn, when sea ice was at its minimum. Hunters probably aimed to return before the end of August so they could participate in the critical hay harvest. This made expeditions a race against time. The hunters worked quickly, skinning seals and hacking the tusks out of walrus' mouths. The rest of the carcasses were simply abandoned, because there was neither time to process them nor cargo space to carry them. Winter in

Greenland was reckoned to start around 16 October, and hunters who were still out after that risked being frozen in for a long and difficult winter of extreme cold at constant risk of malnutrition, scurvy and attack by hungry polar bears. When hunters failed to return by the onset of winter they were generally given up for dead but some certainly survived despite the hardships. In 1824, an Inuit hunter called Pelimut discovered a runic inscription on a small flat stone on a cairn on the small rocky island of Kingigtorssuaq, a little over 72° north: 'Erlingur the son of Sigvaths and Baarne Thordars son and Enriði son, Washingday [Saturday] before Rogation Day (25 April) raised this mound and rode' it reads. Rode where? The inscription ends with six unique runes which are presumed to be a secret code. Perhaps they had discovered a new walrus colony and did not want to take a chance on rival hunters discovering the location? It is not possible that the three men could have sailed so far north in April (the sea ice would not have started to break up for another two months), so they must have spent the winter somewhere in the vicinity. With the worst of the winter behind them, and seal hunting at its best, the three would have had a good chance of surviving until the ice broke up and allowed them to return home.

In their search for hunting grounds, it is likely that the Norse eventually explored the whole of Greenland's east coast, penetrating far into the high Arctic. In 1875, a British oceanographic expedition led by George Nares discovered two ancient cairns on a prominent rocky headland on Washington Irving Island off Greenland's north coast at 79° 34' north. The British dismantled the cairns to see if earlier explorers had left any messages inside, a common practice at the time, but found none. Nares knew of only one, American, expedition that had sailed so far north before, and that was in 1855. Nares observed that 'lichens which had spread from stone to stone proved that they were of great age', far too old to have been raised so recently. The British therefore concluded that the cairns must have been built by Norse explorers. If the British were right, this may have been the place where the Norse trans-Atlantic expansion finally ran out steam,

1,200 kilometres from the North Pole. Modern researchers who have examined what was left of the cairns agree that they are unlikely to have been built by the Inuit. Large numbers of Norse artefacts have been discovered on nearby medieval Inuit sites, strengthening the case that these cairns were of Norse origin but, in the absence of other datable evidence, the identity of the builders is likely to remain a mystery.

How to get to Greenland

Greenland's trade with the rest of the world was mostly conducted through Norwegian merchants based at the west coast port of Bergen, but there was also direct trade with Iceland and the Norse-ruled Orkney Islands. In what was the first trans-Atlantic trade route, the Norwegian merchants sailed their *knarrs* direct to Greenland. *Landnámabók* gives detailed directions for the route. Leaving Bergen, ships would sail through the coastal archipelagos north to the island of Hernar. From there, 'one must sail a direct course west to Hvarf (Cape Farewell) in Greenland, in which case you must sail north of Shetland so that you only sight land in clear weather only, then south of the Faeroes so that the sea looks halfway up the mountainsides, then south of Iceland so that one gets sight of birds and whales from there'.[24] In favourable weather, the voyage could take less than two weeks, but it was always hazardous. A thirteenth-century Norwegian handbook on rulership, *The King's Mirror*, advised seafarers against making landfalls on Greenland's wild east coast because of the dangers of being wrecked or trapped by sea ice, which was much more prevalent than on the west coast. One such group was discovered by the Greenlander Sigurd Njalsson on a hunting trip to the east coast. The party's catch had been a poor one, and the summer was almost over. 'What would you rather do,' he asked his men, 'turn back or go on?' Sigurd's men (there were fifteen in his party) were all for turning back; sailing the fjords under glaciers was a dangerous business, they contended. Sigurd, however, persuaded his men to continue the trip a little longer. Sailing up a fjord, Sigurd spotted a large, grounded *knarr*, a smaller ship drawn up onshore, and a tent and wooden hall. Approaching warily, the hunters found two emaciated corpses lying outside the hall. Now having a good idea what they would find inside, the hunters broke into the hall and found more bodies. Sigurd recognized the ship as belonging to a party of Norwegians who had gone missing the previous year: they must have lost their way, got frozen in for the winter and died of starvation. The Norwegians had brought cauldrons with them to trade. Sigurd now used them to boil their remains to clean their bones, which he took with him to the Eastern Settlement to give them a Christian burial. Sigurd also removed all the nails from the *knarr* before he left: iron was expensive in Greenland. In desperate attempts to avoid a similar fate, some shipwrecked travellers attempted to cross the inland ice to reach the Eastern Settlement only for their frozen remains to be discovered years later.

Only slightly more fortunate was another party shipwrecked on the east coast under Torgils Orrabeinfostre. Using his ship's boat, Torgils, his wife and about thirty followers and slaves began to make their way slowly south, hoping to reach the Eastern Settlement, struggling constantly with sea ice and bad weather and surviving by hunting seals. On their way, the starving Norse saw two 'witches' butchering a seal that they had speared through a hole in the ice. After the Norse attacked them, the witches fled, leaving behind a welcome meal for the group. Later, the Norse lost their boat only to have it returned to them by another two witches. It is likely that these 'witches' were actually part of an isolated band of Dorset people, still making a living on Greenland's east coast. Disease and hunger steadily took its toll on the party. During their first winter on the east coast, Torgil's wife gave birth to a son, but she was later murdered by some of the slaves, who stole the boat and the party's provisions and sailed off, never to be heard of again. Torgils and the few survivors who had stayed loyal built themselves a new boat from driftwood and sealskins and pressed on. Finally, four years after his shipwreck,

Torgils, his son and two other survivors made it to safety in the Norse settlements. Some part of this hostile coast, or perhaps Jan Mayen Island, may have been the 'Svalbard' (meaning 'cold rim') discovered by Icelandic seafarers six days' sail north of Iceland in 1194: it certainly wasn't the modern Svalbard (or Spitsbergen) archipelago; ships of that period could not have reached it from Iceland so quickly.

The natural first landfall for ships after rounding Cape Farewell was Herjolfsnes, the most southerly of all the Norse settlements and one of the very few that were on the open coast. The settlement here was founded by Erik's friend and fellow *lándnámsmann* Herjolf Bardarson, who must have immediately spotted its commercial possibilities: the growing season on the open coast is several weeks shorter than it is in the sheltered inner fjords, so it is not likely Herjolf chose it for its farming potential. Known as Sand to North Atlantic seafarers, Herjolfsnes became the main transit station for Greenland's overseas trade, where Norwegian and Icelandic merchants could exchange their goods for the products of the settlement's farms and hunting grounds. Herjolfsnes's prosperity was displayed in its large feasting hall. In addition, there was a variety of farm buildings and warehouses close to the landing place, and a substantial stone church. The churchyard was used for burials not only of locals but also for seafarers who died on voyages to Greenland. It was the custom to give those who were lost or buried at sea a symbolic burial by placing a commemorative rune stick in the churchyard. One, buried in an empty coffin, reads 'this woman, who was called Gudveig, was laid overboard in the Greenland Sea'. Medieval Christians believed in the bodily, as well as spiritual, resurrection of the dead on the Day of Judgement. Poor Gudveig's body could not be interred because it had been eaten by fishes, so this symbolic burial in consecrated ground was an act of kindness by her companions to ensure her resurrection and entry into eternal life.

The dangers of sailing to Greenland were such that it prompted the anonymous author of *The King's Mirror* to ask, rhetorically (the book is written as a dialogue about statecraft between a Norwegian king and his son), why 'men should be so eager to fare thither, where there are such great perils to beware of?' His answer:

> One motive is fame and rivalry, for it is in the nature of man to seek places where great dangers may be met, and thus to win fame. A second motive is curiosity, for it is also in man's nature to wish to see and experience things that he has heard about, and thus to learn whether the facts are as told or not. The third is the desire for gain: for men seek wealth wherever it is to be gotten, though, on the other hand, there may be great dangers too.[25]

So long as there was money to be made in Greenland trade, the colony was secure.

Northern Lights

The author of *The King's Mirror* was well educated in both theology and statecraft, so he was probably a churchman who had served for some time as part of the Norwegian royal court. His writing also reveals a deep knowledge of seafaring and international trade, and his observations about the geography of Greenland and Iceland are clearly based on eyewitness testimony, so it is likely that he had sailed the Atlantic, on church or royal business, and visited Iceland and Greenland and seen them for himself. His description of displays of the Northern Lights (i.e. the Aurora Borealis) is so vivid and accurate that he must have been writing from personal experience:

> These northern lights have this peculiar nature, that the darker the night is, the brighter they seem; and they always appear at night but never by day, most frequently in the densest darkness and rarely by moonlight. In appearance they resemble a vast

> flame of fire viewed from a great distance. It also looks as if sharp points were shot from this flame up into the sky; these are of uneven height and in constant motion, now one, now another darting highest; and the light appears to blaze like a living flame. While these rays are at their highest and brightest, they give forth so much light that people out of doors can easily find their way about and can even go hunting, if need be.[26]

The author considered different explanations for the phenomenon but thought it most plausible that they were emanations of the inland ice cap, where 'the frost and the glaciers have become so powerful there that they are able to radiate forth these flames'.

The king and the king's son who are the mouthpieces for the *King's Mirror*'s dialogue are not named, but it was probably written for the education of Hákon IV's son Magnus Lawmender (r. 1263–80). Hákon (r. 1217–63) was the most expansionist of Norway's medieval kings, and he dedicated his reign to asserting his authority over all the Norse colonies in the North Atlantic. While Hákon had manipulated the rivalries between the *stórgoðar* to gain control in Iceland in 1262, in Greenland his chosen instruments were the bishops of Garðar who controlled much of the economy. The Greenland colony does not seem to have been a conflicted society like Iceland, so it may have been fear of commercial isolation that led the Greenlanders to accept Norwegian rule in 1261: part of the deal was a guarantee of just one supply ship a year from Norway, the so-called 'Greenland *knarr*'. The Greenland colony had problems, and they were soon going to get a lot worse.

9

The Vinland saga

1000–1121

The Greenlanders' saga – Erik the Red's saga – A disaster at sea – The Norse settlement at L'Anse aux Meadows – Where was Vinland? – Land of the White Men – Norse and Skrælings – Vinland and the medieval world view – The last voyages – Link-up

Who is the most famous Viking Age Norseman? Almost certainly, it is Leif Eriksson, hailed as the first European to set foot on the North American continent, the man who beat Columbus to it by nearly 500 years. As the first to complete a trans-Atlantic crossing, Leif fully deserves his fame, but, unlike Columbus, he did not take a leap into the dark; almost all of his route had already been pioneered by others in the course of the Norse settlement of the North Atlantic. Every step the Norse took increased the chances of more discoveries and brought them closer to completing the first crossing of the Atlantic Ocean. The Eastern Settlement in Greenland was less than 1,000 kilometres from Labrador on the North American continental mainland, while the Western Settlement was only 500 kilometres from Baffin Island in the Canadian Arctic, distances that were well within the capacity of Norse sailing ships.

The story of the Norse discovery of America is told in two Icelandic sagas, the *Grænlendinga saga* ('The Saga of the Greenlanders'), written *c.*1200, and *Eiríks saga rauða* ('Erik the

Red's saga'), written *c.*1265, known collectively as the Vinland sagas after the name Leif gave to his newfound land. Erik's saga, which does not actually have much to say at all about Erik the Red, tells such a different story to the Greenlanders' saga that it is impossible completely to reconcile the two accounts. Both sagas also contain fantastical elements, a revenant and a phantom island in the Greenlanders' saga and a mythical monster in Erik's saga, which throw their reliability into doubt. Archaeology has proven beyond doubt that there is substance to the sagas but, despite that, neither can be read as attempts to write objective history: the Vinland sagas should really be considered as exciting works of historical fiction based loosely on real people and events. As it's impossible to disentangle fact and fiction, or to reconcile the accounts, it seems only fair to tell both stories of the discovery of Vinland.

The Greenlanders' saga

According to the account in *Grænlendinga saga*, the first sighting of land west of Greenland was made by a wealthy Icelandic merchant called Bjarni Herjolfsson (the son of Erik the Red's friend Herjolf Bardarsson). Bjarni returned home from a successful trading trip to Norway in 986 and was taken aback to learn that his father had sold up and emigrated to Greenland with Erik the Red. Determined to spend the winter with his father, as he always did, Bjarni refused to unload his ship and set out at once for Greenland. Neither Bjarni nor any of his crew had ever been there, of course, so he knew little about it other than that it was a mountainous land with glaciers, no trees and good pastures along sheltered fjords. Bjarni told his crew that people would think he was being foolhardy, but they agreed to sail with him anyway. Three days into the voyage, the weather turned bad; fog and a north wind set in, and for many days he was unable to get his bearings. When at last the weather cleared, he found himself off the coast of a densely forested, hilly land. This obviously could not be Greenland, so Bjarni turned his ship north and after two days made another landfall, this time off a flat, forested land. Bjarni's crew wanted to land but he cautiously refused; he was a merchant, not an explorer, he said. He continued to the northeast and after three days encountered a rocky, mountainous and heavily glaciated land. This land seemed to Bjarni to be too barren to be Greenland, and once again he refused to land, telling his by now disgruntled crew that the land was obviously worthless and not worth exploring. Putting it astern, Bjarni sailed west for four days and finally reached the Eastern Settlement and his father's farm at Herjolfsnes.

Bjarni got no credit for his cautious refusal to investigate the unknown lands he had sighted. There was much excited talk in Greenland about exploring these new lands, but it was not until about fifteen years later that Erik the Red's son Leif decided to mount a follow-up expedition. Leif bought Bjarni's ship, engaged a crew of thirty-five men and set out to retrace Bjarni's route. Leif sailed northwest to the last of the lands Bjarni had sighted. Unlike Bjarni, Leif and his men landed to explore but, seeing little other than bare rock and glaciers, concluded that this land was indeed worthless. Satisfied that he had gone one better than Bjarni, Leif named this land Helluland ('rock slab land') and set sail south. Sometime later, they sighted a low forested land with white sand beaches. After going ashore to explore, Leif named this land Markland ('forest land'). Sailing south for another two days, Leif came to a third land, where the rivers teemed with salmon and grapes grew wild. Leif decided to name this land Vinland ('wine land'). It must have been late summer by this time, because they decided to spend the winter there, building some substantial houses for themselves at a place afterwards called Leifsbuðir ('Leif's booths'). The winter was mild and frost free, and the days were longer than they were in Greenland at that time of year. The men spent their time cutting timber, which was in short supply in Greenland, and gathering and drying the wild grapes, which they took home with them in the spring. After Erik died the following winter (*c.*1002), Leif succeeded him as chieftain and gave up seafaring.

Grænlendinga saga goes on to describe four more expeditions to Vinland. The saga mentions that the leaders of these expeditions needed Leif's permission to use Leifsbuðir, implying that he directed them in the same way that Greenland chieftains later directed hunting expeditions to the Norðsetr even if he didn't actually go on them himself. The first follow-up expedition was led by Leif's brother Thorvald. After arriving at Leifsbuðir, Thorvald and his men spent the winter fishing. The next summer, they explored the coast to the west, finding no trace of human habitation apart from a ruined shack on a small island. After another quiet winter, Thorvald continued his explorations, this time to the east. Entering a fjord, Thorvald for the first time encountered native peoples, who the sagas call Skrælings. Spotting three upside-down hide-covered canoes, the Norse went to investigate and found three men sleeping underneath each of them. The Norse immediately attacked them, capturing and killing eight of them: the saga gives no explanation or justification for what looks, on the face of it, to be pointless unprovoked slaughter. Unfortunately for the Norse, the ninth escaped in one of the canoes and fled to a nearby village with the news that distinctly unfriendly strangers had arrived in the fjord. Tired out by their exertions, the Norse chose this moment to relax and have an afternoon nap, waking up just in time to see a hoard of angry locals furiously paddling their canoes down the fjord towards them. Taking refuge in their ship, the outnumbered Norse beat off the Skrælings' attack but Thorvald was struck by an arrow and bled to death. The dying Thorvald made a prediction: 'we have won a fine and fruitful country, but will hardly be allowed to enjoy it'. His crew gave Thorvald a Christian burial, the first in North America, before returning to Leifsbuðir for the winter and returning to Greenland the next spring.

The second follow-up expedition failed even to get to Vinland. Another of Leif's brothers, Thorstein, wanted to recover Thorvald's body and bring it home to Brattahlið, but his expedition was dogged by bad weather from the start. Accurate navigation was impossible, and Thorstein never knew where he was or where he was going. Finally, at the beginning of October, he arrived at Lysufjord in the Western Settlement. Too late in the year to risk sailing on to his home in the Eastern Settlement, Thorstein was forced to spend the winter there but died in an epidemic, along with many of his crew.

The summer after Thorstein's death, an Icelandic merchant called Thorfinn Karlsefni arrived at Brattahlið. During the winter, Thorfinn married Thorstein's widow Gudrid, who persuaded him to mount his own expedition to Vinland. The couple took with them a crew of sixty men, five women and a variety of livestock. Their first winter at Leifsbuðir was uneventful, except that Gudrid gave birth to a boy, Snorri, the first European to be born in continental America. During the summer, the party had a peaceful encounter with Skrælings, trading milk for furs. Karlsefni now ordered their settlement to be fortified with a wooden stockade as a precaution. Early the next winter, the Skrælings returned to trade, but this time a fight broke out when one of them tried to steal some weapons and several were killed. Fearing retaliation, Karlsefni's party left for Greenland as soon as they could in the spring.

The final expedition to Vinland was led by Erik the Red's daughter Freydis and her husband Thorvard. Freydis invited two Icelandic brothers called Helgi and Finnbogi to join them in partnership: it seems that the main purpose of the expedition was to cut timber. The parties agreed to take thirty men and five women each in their ships, but Freydis secretly took five extra men with her. The saga portrays Freydis as a domineering and uncompromising woman who was intent on causing conflict with the brothers from the start, refusing to allow them to use the buildings at Leifsbuðir. Ill feeling between the two parties grew over the winter and in the spring Freydis sent her men to kill the brothers and their followers following a contrived argument over a ship. When her men refused to kill the five women in the group, Freydis grabbed an axe and killed them herself. When she returned to Greenland without the Icelanders, she claimed that they had stayed behind in Vinland, but others from the party exposed her crimes. Though Leif did not punish Freydis, she and her husband were shunned from then on.

Erik the Red's saga

The story told in Erik's saga is a very different one. Leif Eriksson is relegated to the role of accidental discoverer and only two other expeditions to Vinland are described, those of his brother Thorstein and of Thorfinn Karlsefni, who, rather than Leif or his father, is the dominant character of the saga. It is thought that the author of the saga deliberately rewrote the story of the discovery of Vinland in this way in order to flatter Karlsefni's politically powerful Icelandic descendants. Freydis too appears, but as a brave member of Karlsefni's expedition rather than as the scheming Lady Macbeth character she is in the Greenlanders' saga. Erik's saga is also much richer in geographical details than the Greenlanders' saga.

According to Erik's saga, Leif was returning to Greenland from Norway when he was blown off course to an unknown land where wheat and vines grew wild and there were maple trees large enough for house building. The saga identifies this land as Vinland. After landing and taking samples of these things, Leif left and successfully found his way back to Greenland. Thorstein subsequently set out to explore the new land his brother had discovered, but the weather turned bad and he was blown off course almost all the way across the Atlantic to Ireland, eventually returning exhausted to Brattahlið at the beginning of winter only to die soon afterwards.

Some years later, Thorfinn Karlsefni arrived in the Eastern Settlement and married Thorstein's widow while spending the winter at Brattahlið. In the spring, Karlsefni and his new wife led a major expedition to explore Vinland, comprising altogether three ships, 160 people and livestock. There were several women in the crew, including Leif's sister Freydis. The small fleet set out by sailing north from Brattahlið to the Western

Settlement and then on to the 'Bear Islands'. From there, they sailed the open sea for two days until they reached a land of bare rock slabs, which they called Helluland. Two days' sail further south they reached a forested land, rich in game, which they called Markland. They then sailed to an island which they called Bjarney ('bear island'), because they found bears there. As the fleet continued south, they sailed past a long coast of white sand beaches which they called Firðustrandir ('wonder beaches'). Two Irish slaves who were sent ashore to explore returned after three days with grapes and wild wheat: they were now in Vinland. The expedition soon came upon a fjord with a very strong current. Naming it Straumfjord ('strong-current fjord'), they decided to set up a winter camp near its entrance: the country was beautiful and mountainous with lush grasslands. The Norse had spent so long exploring that they did not have time to gather provisions for the winter. The weather was severe and the hunting was poor, but they were saved from starvation by a beached whale.

In the spring, the expedition split up. A professional hunter called Thorhall left in a boat with nine men intending to hunt further north: he ended up being blown off course right across the Atlantic to Ireland, where he and his men were taken captive and enslaved. Karlsefni left most of his men at the Straumfjord camp and sailed south with forty men for a long time until they came to a river that flowed out of mountains into a tidal lagoon and then into the sea. There were sand bars across the river mouth so their ships could only enter the lagoon at high tide. They decided to call this place Hóp ('tidal lagoon'). The natural resources of the area were abundant, with wild wheat and vines, plenty of game and rivers full of fish. They built fish traps in the lagoon, catching halibut and other fish. Two weeks after their arrival, a group of Skrælings approached them in canoes. The two groups simply stared at each other until the Skrælings paddled off. The party stayed the winter at Hóp. There was no snow and the livestock they had brought with them had no shortage of grass to eat.

In the spring, the Skrælings returned carrying bundles of furs, which they traded with the Norse for red cloth, although they were really more interested in acquiring iron weapons. Karlsefni, however, refused to trade them. Three weeks later, the Skrælings returned in greater strength, waving their weapons aggressively. A fight broke out and four natives and two Norsemen were killed. The Norse were in danger of being routed, but Freydis, who was pregnant, saved the day. Snatching up the sword of a fallen Norseman to defend herself, she bared one of her breasts and slapped it vigorously with the flat of the sword. The sight of this dauntless woman terrified the Skrælings so much that they immediately fled. The attack convinced Karlsefni that, 'though the quality of the land was admirable, there would always be fear and strife dogging them on account of those who already inhabited it', so he abandoned the settlement and returned to Straumfjord for the winter. Unaware of his fate, Karlsefni and a small party searched fruitlessly for Thorhall. Supposedly, in the course of their search, the group encountered a uniped, a mythical humanoid monster, which hops around on a single leg with a giant foot. Karlsefni returned to Straumfjord and spent another winter there before departing for Greenland in the spring. On their way, they captured two Skræling boys on the coast of Markland, who they taught to speak Norse and had baptized. The boys told the Norse about a fourth country west of Greenland 'where the people went about in white clothing and uttered loud cries and carried poles with patches of cloth attached'. This land the Norse thought was Hvítramannaland ('White Man's Land').

A disaster at sea

Karlsefni returned safely to Greenland with Gudrid and his American-born son Snorri, but not everyone in the expedition made it home. One ship, captained by an Icelander called Bjarni Grimolfsson, was blown far off course into warmer waters. The ship's hull became infested with driftwood-eating worms and began to leak. The ship's boat was only large enough to take half the crew. Bjarni decreed that lots would be drawn to decide who would go in the boat, and who remain behind in the ship. Bjarni was one of those who drew a place in the boat. As Bjarni prepared to depart with the boat, a young Icelander asked, 'Are you going to leave me here, Bjarni?'

'That is how it has to be,' replied Bjarni.

The Icelander said, 'But that is not what you promised when I left my father's farm in Iceland to go with you.'

'I see no other way,' said Bjarni. 'What do you suggest?'

'I suggest we change places. You come up here and I shall go down there.'

'So be it,' said Bjarni. 'I can see that you would spare no effort to live and are afraid to die.'[27]

With that, Bjarni climbed back into the sinking ship and the young Icelander took his place in the boat. Those in the ship's boat reached safety in Ireland; Bjarni and everyone left with him in the ship were never seen again.

This is more than a tale of disaster at sea (which are common enough in Icelandic sagas); it is a social drama which the saga's original audience would have understood without needing to have things spelled out for them. Bjarni was within his rights to refuse to change places with the Icelander, but could not have done so without also appearing to be afraid of death. The young Icelander had deliberately put him in a difficult situation. Bjarni could save his life or his honour, but not both. For a proud man like Bjarni, it was not a difficult dilemma to resolve. By giving up his place in the boat, Bjarni saved his honour, secured his posthumous reputation and was remembered as a brave man by future generations. The young Icelander, however, had been publicly accused of cowardice and had not defended his honour; he therefore became a *niðing*, literally 'nothing', and would have lived the rest of his life as a social outcast, unwelcome even back at his father's farm. No one remembers his name. This was the Norse's own brutally effective 'cancel culture' in action.

The Norse settlement at L'Anse aux Meadows

Because of the Vinland sagas' contradictions and fictive elements, historians were for a long time divided about how seriously to take them as evidence that the Norse really had crossed the Atlantic Ocean hundreds of years before Columbus. Everything changed in 1961, when the Norwegian explorer Helge Ingstad discovered possible Norse longhouses at L'Anse aux Meadows at the tip of Newfoundland's Great Northern Peninsula. Excavations led by Ingstad's archaeologist wife Anne Stine Ingstad in 1963–8 uncovered a wealth of typical Norse artefacts, confirming that this was indeed a Norse settlement and proving beyond further argument that the Vinland sagas really were based on historical events.

L'Anse aux Meadows is a rather exposed cove with a stony beach and several offshore reefs and rocky islets. Although the surrounding landscape is a mix of open grassland and dense crowberry bushes, the name actually has nothing to do with meadows; it is probably an English corruption of the name given by early French settlers, Anse à la Médée, meaning 'Medea's Bay'.* Although L'Anse aux Meadows was uninhabited when the Norse arrived, they were not the first to live there; there had been several phases of occupation by early Inuit seal hunters spread over 5,000 years. The Norse settlement is not actually by the bay from which it takes its name; it is half a kilometre away by the neighbouring Epaves Bay, which offers a slightly more sheltered anchorage and has the fresh water source of Black Duck Brook flowing into it.

It is pretty clear, on visiting the site, that the Norse did not choose it primarily for its anchorage, because there are several more sheltered bays and inlets within a few kilometres. Nor is

* The alternative interpretation, first proposed by the Canadian environmentalist Farley Mowat, that L'Anse aux Meadows is a corruption of L'Anse à la Méduses, meaning 'Jellyfish Bay', has been widely repeated by historians, including myself, but there seems to be no hard evidence to support this. Anse à la Médée is the earliest recorded name for the bay (1862).

this boggy and windswept place an obvious choice for a farming settlement; it is far less hospitable than the sunny, sheltered inner fjords of the Eastern Settlement. What the site does have, however, is a commanding position at the northern entrance to the Strait of Belle Isle and a clear view to the west across it to the hills of Labrador less than 50 kilometres away. This made L'Anse aux Meadows an ideal gateway site that could be located easily by seafarers approaching from the north. The remains of the settlement are not in themselves spectacular, just low, grassy humps in the ground; it's what they stand for that really grabs the imagination: a tiny Norse toehold on the edge of an unknown continent that was far vaster, richer and more challenging than anything its adventurous inhabitants could possibly have realized.

The settlement consisted of eight buildings, all of them built of turf and lined with timber. Three of the buildings were longhouses, and the others were probably workshops or stores. The longhouses had thick walls for insulation in cold weather and large central hearths and would have made comfortable winter accommodation. It is likely that each of the longhouses was home to one ship's crew, with the largest of the three belonging to the leader of the expedition and his crew. The leader had his own private room in this house. Altogether, the three houses could have accommodated up to about ninety people, many times more than would have lived on even the wealthiest farms in Greenland and Iceland. Splinters of a flinty rock called jasper, which the Norse used to strike sparks for fire lighting, were found in all of the houses. The jasper found in the larger longhouse was sourced in Greenland, and that found in the smaller two longhouses came from Iceland. This would suggest that, while the leader of the expedition was a Greenlander, the majority of the participants were Icelanders. According to the sagas, many of the participants in the expeditions were, like Thorhall the hunter, hired hands recruited because of their special skills, while others were slaves taken along to do the heavy work. Radiocarbon dating of organic materials indicates that the houses were occupied *c.*980–1020, which accords well with the saga traditions. In 2021, dendrochronology* determined that three timbers found on the site had been cut by an iron axe in exactly 1021. The middens associated with the houses are very small, and there are no signs that any of the houses were ever repaired or rebuilt. These are clear signs that L'Anse aux Meadows was not occupied for very long, perhaps for a few years only and no longer than a decade.

Even though the Vinland sagas say that the Norse took livestock with them, the excavations at L'Anse aux Meadows have provided no evidence at all for farming or the presence of European domesticated animals. The settlers were, however, active hunters. The bones of caribou, wolf, fox, bear, lynx, marten, seal, whale and walrus, and of many species of fish and wildfowl, have been found on the site. When expeditions returned to Greenland, they would have taken with them a rich haul of valuable furs, hides and ivory. Though there is no archaeological evidence for this, the sagas also claim that cutting timber for building was an important activity: there would certainly have been a ready market for it in Greenland. A spindle whorl, loom weights, needles and a pair of scissors are indications of textile production at the site. They also confirm the saga accounts that women went on the Vinland voyages, because, in Norse society, spinning and weaving were exclusively female activities.

The most important activity on the site was probably ship repair, as there is evidence of both carpentry and iron smelting and blacksmithing to make ships' nails. The availability of bog iron ore in the local bogs may have been one of the attractions of L'Anse aux Meadows. Bog iron, a soft, low-grade ore that accumulates in bogs from iron leached by groundwater, was the main form of iron ore exploited in Viking Age Scandinavia. The ore is common in bogs in Scandinavia and Iceland, and it is easily extracted with hand tools: it was, however, so rare in Greenland that the settlers sometimes had to resort to sewing the planks of their ships together with sinews instead of using nails. The ore was smelted in a hut by the brook using charcoal that was

* Dating by counting tree growth rings.

manufactured on site from the stunted pine trees growing in the bay's hinterland. Bog iron is very impure, and it takes about 8 kilograms of ore to make a kilogram of workable iron. The amount of waste slag indicates that only about 3–5 kilograms of iron was produced, enough for about 200 nails – no more, perhaps, than were needed to repair a single ship.

L'Anse aux Meadows most likely served as a depot, repair shop and winter quarters for expeditions that were heading further south. That such expeditions, like Karlsefni's, took place is proven by the presence of butternuts among food remains on the site. An American species of walnut, butternuts grow no further north than New Brunswick and the lower Gulf of St Lawrence, more than 800 kilometres south of L'Anse aux Meadows. Such a base was a necessity for expeditions sailing so far south. The shortest distance between L'Anse aux Meadows and the Eastern Settlement is 1,200 kilometres, but it is more than likely that the Norse sailed a longer indirect but safer course, making the shorter open-sea crossing of the Labrador Sea to the coast of Labrador, which, if followed south, would lead them unerringly to the Strait of Belle Isle. The sailing season in the north is a short one. Expeditions could not leave Greenland until June, and Norse seafarers liked to be home by the autumn equinox (21 September) and, of this brief window, two months would need to be allowed for the outward and return voyages, leaving only four or five weeks for exploration and hunting. There is no way they could have made a return journey from Greenland to the Gulf of St Lawrence in a single sailing season. Instead, expeditions were probably made over at least three years, sailing from Greenland to L'Anse aux Meadows in the first summer and spending the winter there. Then, come the spring, parties would head out to hunt and explore before returning to L'Anse aux Meadows in the autumn, to spend another winter there before sailing back to Greenland with their hides, furs and timber the next spring.

Where was Vinland?

The unavoidable question is, was L'Anse aux Meadows Vinland? While identifying the places named in the Vinland sagas with absolute certainty is impossible, we can make some informed guesses. Barren, rocky Helluland is probably Baffin Island and forested Markland almost certainly is Labrador, but there is nowhere on the east coast of North America that exactly fits the Greenlanders' saga descriptions of Vinland. The Hudson River is the southern limit of Atlantic salmon, while the St Lawrence is the northern limit of wild grapes, which would place Vinland in New England or the Canadian Maritimes. However, winters in these areas are certainly not frost-free today and probably were not even in the milder conditions of the early Medieval Warm Period, although snow-free winters might have been possible. According to the Greenlanders' saga, Leif observed that on the shortest day the sun rose before 9 a.m. and did not set until after 3 p.m., but these are not clock times, because the Norse did not have clocks, so they cannot help us determine Vinland's latitude: we would need to know the altitude of the sun at noon on a specific date to do this. There is also the possibility that the Norse misidentified some other sort of berry as wild grapes, as they might never have seen vines for themselves. However, the Greenlanders' saga says that the grapes were identified by a German slave called Tyrkir the Southerner, who had been brought up in a vine-growing area and so would have known what he was looking at (unless this detail was invented to add authenticity to the claim).

The Straumfjord of Erik the Red's saga is a good fit for the Strait of Belle Isle, and the settlement there was used as a depot and winter quarters in exactly the way the archaeological evidence indicates that the settlement at L'Anse aux Meadows was used. So if L'Anse aux Meadows is the Straumfjord settlement, was it also Leifsbuðir? If we accept that the delights of Vinland may have been somewhat exaggerated in the sagas for literary effect, the answer is most probably yes. It is quite something to be able to say that the private room in the chieftain's longhouse might well have been Leif Eriksson's bedroom: it is rare that archaeology can be quite so personal. That leaves Hóp. This was an area with mountains, tidal lagoons separated from the sea by sand bars, rich game, salmon-filled rivers, wild grapes and self-sown wheat and, unlike Straumfjord/Leifsbuðir, it was inhabited by native peoples. The only place on the east coast where all these conditions are met is the Kouchibouguac and Miramachi Bay area on the northeast coast of New Brunswick. This is also an area where butternut trees grow (and the self-sown wheat of the sagas would likely have been wild rye, which flourishes locally). The native peoples in this area also covered their canoes with deer or moose hide, instead of the birch bark more common elsewhere in northeastern North America. For archaeologists looking for a second Norse settlement in North America, this would be the place to look. However, a summer shieling, which is what Hóp would have been, would have had less substantial buildings than those at L'Anse aux Meadows, and they may have left little more trace on the landscape than a few post-holes in the ground.

The Norse probably saw the Gulf of St Lawrence as an inland sea, like the Baltic perhaps, which was connected to the ocean through Straumfjord. Vinland was not a single location but all the land around the shores of this inland sea. Both Hóp and Leifsbuðir were in Vinland. It seems unlikely that the Norse ever found the Cabot Strait between Newfoundland and Cape Breton or knew that Newfoundland was an island: if they had known, Straumfjord would probably have been called Straumsund ('strong current sound'), because 'sund' (sound) is the name used in the Scandinavian languages to describe a channel that separates an island from the mainland. This alone would make it most unlikely that the Norse ever sailed further south to explore Nova Scotia or New England. Logistically, it is even more unlikely that the Norse sailed further south than New Brunswick. We know from the way L'Anse aux Meadows functioned that a round trip from Greenland to Hóp took three sailing seasons. To have reached New England and returned would have taken another three sailing seasons: the first season to Leifsbuðir, a second to

Hóp, a third to New England with the need to spend a winter there, a fourth season back to Hóp, a fifth to Leifsbuðir again for a final winter, and a sixth back to Greenland. The Norse were in Vinland for little more than a decade, they simply didn't have time to go further; what they did achieve with the resources they had was remarkable enough.

Despite the best efforts of fraudsters and practical jokers to supply archaeological evidence that the Norse really did explore the present-day USA, only one authentic Norse artefact has ever been discovered anywhere in the United States. This is a worn silver penny minted during the reign of the Norwegian King Olaf Kyrre (r. 1067–93) that was found during excavations of a large Native American village at Goddard Point on the coast of Maine. The exact circumstances in which the coin was found are undocumented, and the possibility that it was planted on the site has never been ruled out. Even if this was not the case, the coin is not evidence that Norse seafarers visited Maine. The Goddard site provided abundant evidence that it was at the centre of an extensive trade network which extended as far as Arctic Canada and the Great Lakes. As the Greenland Norse continued to visit Labrador until the fourteenth century, the coin, which was pierced so that it could be worn on a necklace, could originally have been acquired as an exotic curio by an Inuit and have found its way to Maine along the native trade routes, probably changing hands many times along the way. As the evidence stands at the moment, there is no reason to believe that Leif Eriksson, or any other Northman or woman, ever set foot in the present-day USA.

Land of the White Men

The fourth of the lands west of Greenland that appear in the Vinland sagas is Hvítramannaland. This country is mentioned in a number of Norse sources, including *Landnámabók*, which states that it was discovered by Ari Marsson six days' sailing west of Ireland sometime around 983. The story is attributed to a seafarer called Hrafn the Limerick-Farer, who traded with the Norse-Irish city of Limerick. Unlike Vinland, Markland and Helluland, Hvítramannaland is one of the Atlantic's many phantom islands. While the Canadian environmentalist Farley Mowat, among others, has claimed that it was a lost colony of Irish monks, Hvítramannaland is most probably derived from Tír na bhFear bhFionn ('Land of the White Men') or one of the other incarnations of the Celtic Otherworld which Hrafn must have been told about during one of his visits to Ireland. In other sources, Hvítramannaland is also called Great Ireland or Albania, which also means 'White Man's Land'. Just like the Celtic Otherworld, once someone strayed there, it was very difficult to escape, and Ari was said still to be there. Another who failed to get away was Bjorn the Breidavik-Champion. Sometime around 1029, Gudleif Gudlaugsson, an Icelandic merchant, was supposedly blown off course to the west while sailing from Dublin to Iceland. Days later, his crew sighted land. Although they had no idea where they were, they needed a safe harbour and decided to land. Local people soon began to gather at the harbour. The Icelanders:

> didn't know who the inhabitants were but they seemed to be talking Irish. Soon a great crowd gathered there, hundreds of them. They attacked the crew, took them all prisoner, shackled them, and marched them some distance inland, where they were taken to a court to be tried and sentenced. Gudleif and his men realised that that some of the people wanted to put them to death, but that others proposed to share them out as slaves.[28]

They were saved by the intervention of a Norse-speaking chief, who questioned them closely about affairs in Iceland before giving them leave to depart. The chief refused to identify himself, because, he said, he did not want his Icelandic kinsmen to come looking for him and get stuck there like him. From what he had told them, Gudleif realized that the chief must be Bjorn the Breidavik-Champion, who had been exiled from Iceland thirty years before.

Norse and Skrælings

The Vinland voyages resulted in the first contacts between Europeans and Native Americans: they did not go well. The two peoples, as might be expected, regarded each other with mutual suspicion, but in the saga accounts it was the Norse who resorted to violence first. Some of these attacks were entirely unprovoked, while others were the result, probably, of cultural misunderstandings, since neither side could understand the other's language. This was very likely the case on the occasion, described in the Greenlander's saga, when a Norseman killed a Native American for trying to steal an iron weapon: the Native American, however, probably did not see his action as theft so much as asking a fair price for his furs. The sagas imply that the Native Americans' desire for iron weapons signalled hostile intent, but this was not necessarily the case. Exchange was an important way for the peoples of the North American Northeast to maintain and extend their social, cultural and spiritual horizons, and they may have desired the iron tools because their unfamiliarity lent them supernatural power in the same way that the exotic shells and crystals they exchanged over long distances to secure their spiritual well-being in this world and the next did.

The Norse indiscriminately described all the native peoples they met on the Vinland voyages as Skrælings. The origins of the word have been endlessly debated, but it was certainly meant to be pejorative in the same way that later European explorers would refer to the indigenous peoples they encountered as savages. One theory is that the word is related to Old Norse *skrækja*, which means something like 'screamers', probably from their incomprehensible language. A parallel to this would be 'barbarian', a word that the ancient Greeks originally used to describe peoples who could not speak Greek but could only make, to their ears, incomprehensible 'bar-bar' noises. In modern Icelandic usage, *skrælingi* means 'barbarian'. Another possibility is that skræling is related to Old Norse *skrá*, meaning dried skin, possibly a reference to clothing made from hides. Exactly who the Skrælings were depends on where the encounters took place. No encounters are mentioned at Leifsbuðir, so this would rule out the now extinct Dorset people, who lived in Newfoundland at this time, or the Native American Beothuk people, whose ancestors arrived in Newfoundland only after the Norse had left. Most of the encounters took place at or near Hóp. If Hóp was in New Brunswick, as seems likely, the natives probably belonged to the Mi'kmaq nation, one of the Algonquian peoples of northern New England and the Canadian Maritimes. The Skræling boys captured by Karlsefni in Markland, the first Native Americans to be able to communicate with the Norse, would probably either have been from the Innu, who still live in Labrador and Quebec, or the Dorset people, who also lived in Labrador at that time.

Unlike post-Columbian contact between Europeans and Native Americans, the consequences of this first contact were, beyond the immediate casualties of violence, almost zero. No waves of European settlers followed the Norse discovery. Iron weapons alone could not make up for their lack of numbers and neither were their ships suitable for sustaining a colonizing effort so far from home. The Greenland colony was still not fully established, and its small population, of only a few hundred people, lacked the resources to support a new colonizing venture. Nor did it have the numbers to sustain the casualties from conflict with the natives and from shipwreck, even with reinforcements from Iceland. Vinland also lacked any commercial commodities which could not mostly be obtained in the Norðsetr, much closer to home and, at that time, with no risk of violent encounters with native peoples. The small groups of Norse explorers were effectively quarantined by the long journey times, so the native peoples escaped the deadly epidemics of unintentionally introduced European diseases that killed countless millions in the wake of Columbus's voyages. The Native Americans soon forgot their fleeting encounters with the aggressive fair-skinned foreigners, with their iron weapons and wooden ships, and, as far as they were concerned, the Vinland voyages might as well never have happened.

Vinland and the medieval world view

News of the discovery of Vinland soon found its way back to Europe. The earliest written record of Vinland is found in a work by the German cleric Adam of Bremen, written in *c.*1075, predating the Vinland sagas by about 150 years, but knowledge of the discovery had no impact at all on the European world view. There were believed to be only three continents, Europe, Asia and Africa, so Vinland had somehow to belong to one of them, either as a sort of peninsula or as an associated island. Medieval geographers were simply not open to the idea that Vinland could be part of an unknown fourth continent. Adam of Bremen assumed that both Vinland and Greenland were, like Iceland, European islands in the great world-encircling ocean. A more common belief, which persisted until the late seventeenth century, was that Greenland was a peninsula of the north European mainland. On some early world maps, like the Fra Mauro map of 1490, it can be seen stretching like a scythe from Russia across the north of Iceland. Vinland never made it onto any genuine medieval world maps,* but the anonymous author of a fourteenth-century Icelandic geographical treatise thought it was actually part of Africa:

> to the north of Norway lies Finnmark; from where the land sweeps north-east to Bjarmaland [Perm in northern Russia] … From Bjarmaland there is uninhabited land stretching all the way to the north until Greenland begins. To the south of Greenland lies Helluland and then Markland; and from there it is not far to Vinland, which some people think extends from Africa.[29]

* The so-called 'Vinland Map' is a twentieth-century forgery.

To this author, the Atlantic was not part of the global ocean at all, it was a closed sea almost encircled by two long peninsulas stretching far out from Africa and Europe.

The belief that Vinland was part of Africa explains the seemingly bizarre encounter with a uniped in Erik's saga. Medieval Europeans believed unipeds lived in Africa, so the saga's author probably thought that he was adding authenticity to his account by including one in his story. Unfortunately, it had exactly the opposite effect to the one intended when read by sceptical post-Enlightenment scholars, encouraging them to dismiss the whole story of the Norse discovery of Vinland as fiction.

The last voyages

In 1121, almost exactly a century after L'Anse aux Meadows was abandoned, Erik Gnupsson, the bishop of Greenland, set off on a new expedition to Vinland, but its fate is not recorded. As a new bishop was sent to Greenland in 1124, Erik may not have returned and been given up for dead. Or perhaps he finished up in Hvítramannaland and, like its other Norse visitors, was unable to leave. After this interest in Vinland faded and by the time the Vinland sagas were written, it had largely been forgotten outside Iceland and Greenland. There is no evidence, for example, that Columbus knew of Vinland's existence when he set off on his voyage across the Atlantic in 1492 in search of a route to the Indies, only to find the Americas blocking the way.

Voyages from Greenland to Markland, however, continued at least until the fourteenth century. The only recorded expedition was in 1347, when a small ship with seventeen Greenlanders was blown off course to Iceland while returning from cutting timber in Markland, but archaeological evidence from a chieftain's farm at Sandnes in the Western Settlement points to other journeys. Hair fibres from bison skins and black or brown bear furs found there could only have come from continental North America, since none of these animals is native to Greenland, and there were reused ship's timbers made of larch, which is common in Labrador but did not grow in Greenland, Iceland or Norway at that time. Voyages to Markland were not without risk, because the Norse would have been trespassing on Native American territory: a chert arrowhead of a type used in Labrador *c.*1000–1500 that was found in the cemetery at Sandnes was likely brought to Greenland in the body of a Norseman. Markland's timber would have made such risks worthwhile. The driftwood logs from Siberia that washed up on Greenland's shores were fine for roof timbers and fuel, but saturation in sea water turns wood hard and inflexible, making it useless for shipbuilding. Norse shipbuilders preferred to use unseasoned timber because it is more flexible, so once it was cut it could be used immediately. An experienced crew could build a ship in a few months, so the Greenlanders could easily have built a ship over the summer and sailed it home in the autumn. While the Greenland Norse had valuable products to trade, they could rely on Norwegian and Icelandic merchants to sail to Greenland, but they still needed ships of their own to reach the hunting grounds which supplied them. Without ships, the colony was simply not viable. Norse ships had a useful life of only about twenty years, so regular supplies of shipbuilding timber were essential. Markland was a lot nearer to Greenland than Norway, the closest alternative source of good timber, and there were no middlemen to pay. It is also possible that the Norse continued to visit Helluland (Baffin Island) too. A fourteenth-century site at Tanfield Valley near the southern tip of Baffin Island was identified as a Norse walrus-hunting site in 2012 after excavations uncovered what was claimed to be evidence of the use of metal tools and woven textiles, neither of which the Inuit possessed. However, the claim remains controversial, in part because of the lingering doubts over the dating of the site.

Link-up

If the Norse discovery of North America was not the transformative event in world history that Columbus's later discovery was, it was still a symbolically significant moment. Some 70,000 years ago, anatomically modern humans, *Homo sapiens sapiens*, left their ancestral homeland in Africa and began a long diaspora across the globe that lasted for hundreds of generations. That fatal encounter in Vinland between the Norse and Native Americans was the first time that descendants of one branch of humanity who had left Africa and migrated west met the descendants of another branch of humanity who, after leaving Africa, had migrated east. Their violent meeting completed the human circumnavigation of the world.

10

A change in the weather

1300–1500

Iceland lives up to its name – Plagues and seaways – Greenland in trouble – Fashion victims – Enter the Inuit – Skræling Island – The Western Settlement is abandoned – A wedding and then darkness – 'Blonde Eskimos'

By the time Iceland and Greenland submitted to Norwegian rule, those mild climatic conditions that had been so favourable to Norse expansion in the North Atlantic were starting to change for the worse. The change was imperceptible at first, just an occasional unusually cold, long winter, or a damper, cooler summer that led to a disappointing harvest, but little more than a century later, these conditions had become the norm rather than the exception in the North Atlantic: the Earth had entered a period of global cooling which has been called the Little Ice Age (approximately 1400–1800). The exact causes of the cooling are uncertain, but its onset coincided with an extended period of low solar activity and three huge eruptions by the Samalas volcano in Indonesia, El Chichón in Mexico and Quilotoa in Ecuador, which blasted vast amounts of sulphate aerosols into the stratosphere, where they reflected the diminished sunlight back into space, cooling the lower atmosphere. In the North Atlantic region, average temperatures fell by around 1°C. This was nowhere near enough to trigger a real Ice Age, but in the Alps, Norway, Iceland and Greenland, new mountain glaciers formed and the old ones advanced lower down the slopes into the valleys below. Arctic sea ice spread further south in the winter and broke up more slowly in the summer, hindering shipping. On occasions, Iceland's coasts became completely ice-bound in winter, the Thames froze so solidly in London that 'Frost Fairs' were held on its surface, Venetians skated on the Lagoon and, once, the Bosphorus froze over, making it possible to walk from Europe to Asia. These severe winters had a lasting impact on the European imagination, indelibly imprinting the idea that Christmases ought to be white. Though less spectacular than the freezing winters, it was really the cooler summers, and shorter growing season, that had the worst impact, causing an increase in crop failures and frequent famines across Europe. A weakened population fell easy prey to the Black Death which ravaged Europe in 1347–51, and remained endemic for three centuries thereafter, causing catastrophic demographic decline.

Iceland lives up to its name

As it is with climate change today, the impact of the Little Ice Age fell disproportionately in areas where settlement was already marginal, like Iceland and Greenland. Icelandic farmers were already having problems even before the climate turned for the worse. Already, by the end of the Landnám period (*c.*930), most of Iceland's woodland had been felled for fuel and building materials, while overgrazing by cattle and sheep prevented any regeneration. Iceland's soils are fertile but thin, and the loss of tree cover accelerated soil erosion, turning much of the interior into a cold, barren desert. Volcanic eruptions exacerbated the situation by smothering grazing land in ash and by *jökulhlaups* ('glacier bursts'), sudden destructive floods caused when an eruption melted the glaciers that capped so many volcanoes. One of the worst incidents was in 1362, when an eruption under the huge Vatnajökul ice cap triggered massive floods that swept away two entire parishes and buried hundreds of square kilometres of farmland under knee-deep ash. Countless farms on marginal lands were abandoned as Icelanders increasingly turned to the sea to make a living in the stockfish (dried cod) trade or fishing for the Greenland shark, whose liver was the source of valuable, clean-burning lamp oil. The flesh of the half-tonne Greenland shark is toxic to humans, but it must have pained the undernourished Icelanders to throw so much protein-rich meat away, and they found a way to render it edible, if not exactly appetizing, by burying it in the ground for two or three months to ferment and press the toxins out. The result, *hákarl*, smells strongly of ammonia and is eaten today in small pieces as a 'delicacy' washed down with aquavit. Traditionally, though, no one ate *hákarl* this way; it was added as a protein supplement to broths and stews with other ingredients to disguise the pungent flavour. This was very much the cuisine of poverty: life for Icelanders was very hard in the late Middle Ages and early modern period.

Another Icelandic product that there was a growing demand for in the late Middle Ages was sulphur, mined from volcanic vents, an essential ingredient of the gunpowder that was just then coming into use in European warfare. Unfortunately for the Icelanders, they were not in a position to set the terms of trade for these valuable exports. Right from the beginning, Iceland lacked timber suitable for shipbuilding, so when the settlers' ships began to rot they could only be replaced by buying abroad, which was expensive. This gave an advantage to foreign merchants, initially mainly Norwegians, allowing them to take control of much of Iceland's trade. The Icelanders were dependent on imports, especially for timber, iron, salt and grain, and, if the foreign merchants didn't come, or profiteered, there would be hardship. One of the promises King Hákon IV made to the Icelanders when they submitted to Norwegian sovereignty in 1262 was that, 'unless lawfully hindered', six trade ships laden with 'useful articles' would be sent to Iceland every summer, two to the south, two to the north and one each to the east and west. This, perhaps predictably, only opened the door to the imposition of royal tolls, licensing and monopolies. By the beginning of the fourteenth century, most of the ships trading with Iceland belonged either to the Norwegian crown or to the Archbishopric of Nidarós (Trondheim). And, sometimes, the promised ships did not even turn up. The situation deteriorated still further after 1379, when Norway and its dependencies were united to the Danish crown. This shifted Norway's political and economic centre of gravity to Oslo, in the southeast, because it had better communications with Denmark, causing Bergen to go into decline as a trading port. Danish indifference allowed the trade of Norway and Iceland to fall increasingly under the control of the Germans and the English.

Plagues and seaways

Iceland's isolation at least protected it from the Black Death, the worst disaster ever to strike medieval Europe. Mortality from the Black Death was simply enormous; most estimates are in the range of 50–60 per cent of the European population dying in less than four years. The Black Death was caused by the plague bacillus *Yersinia pestis*, but the germ theory of disease was still centuries in the future and medieval Europeans had absolutely no idea what was killing them or how it was spread, nor did they have any way of treating it. God was obviously angry about something, and the only remedy was prayer. The radical and rapid depopulation caused economic and social upheavals that took decades to work through and its terrifying psychological impact darkened Europeans' outlook for a century.

The pandemic originated in northern Kyrgyzstan sometime around 1338. The plague was then spread to Europe, North Africa and the Middle East along the main overland and maritime trade routes: the better connected a place was, the more vulnerable it was, while a few lucky areas, remote from major trade routes, escaped the plague completely. The plague was carried west to Europe along one of the branches of the Silk Road in the ranks of the Mongol army of the Golden Horde which laid siege, unsuccessfully, to the Genoese merchant-colony at Kaffa on the Black Sea in 1345–6. Before retreating, the plague-ravaged besiegers are said to have catapulted the bodies of plague victims into the city as a gruesome leaving present. From Kaffa, Genoese ships carried the plague along the Mediterranean maritime trade routes, via Constantinople and Greece, as far west as Sicily, Genoa and Marseille by the summer of 1347. From Marseille, the plague spread overland to the thriving and well-connected wine-trade port of Bordeaux, an ideal entry point for Atlantic Europe. A ship full of pilgrims bound for Compostela carried the plague from Bordeaux to Coruña in June 1348 and, from there, merchant ships carried it quickly on to Lisbon. At the same time, the infected crew of a wine-ship carried the plague north to Weymouth on England's Channel coast, where the first outbreak was recorded on 24 June. Other ships sailing from Bordeaux introduced the plague to Bristol and Southampton only a little time later. Plague outbreaks were recorded in the Irish ports of Dublin and Drogheda in July, taken there either from Bristol or direct from Bordeaux. London recorded its first outbreaks in September, and it is thought that a ship from there introduced the plague to Oslo in southern Norway in the autumn. From Oslo, the plague was carried along the trade routes to Denmark, Sweden and the Baltic. The plague opened a second front in Norway in August 1349, when a ship carrying wool from King's Lynn in Norfolk arrived in Bergen. According to the Icelandic *Lawman's Annal*, the ship

> pulled into the bay of Bergen, and some of its cargo was unloaded. Then, all the people on the ship died. As soon as the goods from this ship were brought into the town, the townsmen began to die. Thereafter, the pestilence swept all over Norway and wrought such havoc that not one-third of the people survived. The English ship sank with its cargo and the dead men and was not unloaded. More ships, cargo vessels, and many other ships, sank or drifted widely around. And the same

> pestilence visited the Shetland Islands, the Orkney Islands, the Hebrides, and the Faeroe Islands …[30]

But not to Iceland or Greenland. It was said that a ship was about to sail for Iceland from Bergen, but when one of the crew fell ill with the plague, the captain called the voyage off. No ship landed in Iceland until after the plague had burned itself out in 1351. Rumours of the plague spread faster than the disease, so the Icelanders and Greenlanders may have known that something grim and terrifying was overwhelming Europe and heading their way. The sudden end to communications must have made them fear that they were last people left on Earth. When the first ship arrived in 1352, was it greeted with fear that it was bringing the plague or with relief that the world had not ended? The Greenlanders had to live with the uncertainty even longer, as it was not until 1355 that another ship sailed there.

Iceland wasn't quite far enough away from Europe to be protected forever. In the autumn of 1402, Hval-Einar Jónsson brought his ship home from Norway to Hvalfjörður on Iceland's southwest coast. Some of his crew were infected with the plague, which spread slowly but steadily through Iceland's scattered population. By the time it ended in the spring of 1404, between a quarter and a half of the island's population had died, a much lower proportion of the population than died in Norway, one of Europe's worst-affected countries. The plague is endemic in rats and other rodents and in the fleas that feed on their blood. The disease can be spread to humans when they are in close proximity to infected rats and their fleas which, abandoning a dying host, jump onto the nearest warm body. The bacillus is introduced to the body through an infected flea bite and attacks the lymphatic system, causing huge, painful, black swellings (hence the Black Death) called bubos, in the groin and armpits. In this bubonic form, the plague has a mortality rate of around 60 per cent, but if it progresses to infect the bloodstream, as septicaemic plague, or the lungs, as pneumonic plague, mortality is close to 100 per cent. The pneumonic form was the most contagious, because it was spread in the air by the breath of infected people, as well as by bites from infected rat and human fleas. Maritime trade was the perfect vector for the plague, because the holds of most merchant ships were infested with rats which could, in such confined spaces, very easily spread their fleas to the passengers and crew. Because of its extreme lethality, the plague runs out of human hosts in a year or two and dies out, but it remains endemic among the rat population and periodically re-infects humans, beginning a new epidemic: it hasn't gone away, either; the most recent epidemic was in Madagascar in 2017. Medieval Iceland was fortunate in not having any rats. Once the plague had run its course in the human population it became extinct: without rats to harbour it, it could not become endemic. While most European countries suffered repeated plague outbreaks into the eighteenth century, Iceland had only one more outbreak, in 1494–6.

The Norse Greenland colony escaped the plague entirely. The plague needs a large host population to remain active for any length of time: in a small group of people, such as the crew of a single ship, it would run out of hosts and die out in a matter of days. The plague has an incubation period of only two to three days, and once symptoms show, it runs its course in about forty-eight hours, by which time the victim is either dead (in most cases) or recovering and no longer infectious. For this reason, the plague could not very easily cross an ocean – if a ship set sail with an infected crew member on a voyage that was more than a week long, the rest of the crew would likely have become infected too and have died before they reached their destination: there are many stories from the period of ships being found drifting at sea, their crews all dead of the plague, so this probably did happen many times. At about a week's sail away from Norway and the British Isles, Iceland was at the extreme limit of the plague's reach. Even more distant than Iceland, the Greenland colony was very effectively quarantined by the Atlantic Ocean, which was just as well: the colony was already in trouble, its population in decline, and an outbreak of plague might well have finished it off altogether. As it turned out, it was only a stay of execution. Within a century, the colony had become extinct.

Greenland in trouble

The Greenland colony's troubles are usually blamed on the Little Ice Age. The argument is that Greenland was a marginal environment for a north European farming economy even in the relatively balmy Early Medieval Warm Period. As the climate deteriorated in the fourteenth century, the farming economy began to collapse, and the conservative Norse failed to adapt. Unwilling to give up their European cultural identity and learn from native peoples who were better adapted to life in the Arctic, the Norse struggled on on their failing farms as the glaciers came ever closer to the fields until they either starved to death or found some way to leave.* It is certainly true that the Greenlanders' farming economy did fail because of the deteriorating climate, and there is good evidence that at least some people did starve to death in hard winters, but the conventional view misses the point that the Greenland colony was never really about farming, which was a sideline; it was about trade. The colony was never self-sufficient, even at the beginning, when the climate was at its most favourable, as it relied on trade for iron, grain, malt, salt, timber and many other essentials. So long as there were customers for Greenland products, the colony should have been able to survive the decline of its farming economy. Clearly, the decline of the colony wasn't just about farming.

* The case is most persuasively argued by Jared Diamond in his 2005 bestseller *Collapse: How Societies Choose to Fail or Survive*.

Fashion victims

The worst thing that can happen to a trading colony is that its trade goods go out of fashion. The mainstay of Greenland's trade was walrus ivory, but demand in Europe fluctuated depending on the supply of superior elephant ivory from Africa and Asia. Christian Europe could only obtain elephant ivory through Muslim middlemen in the Middle East and North Africa, so supplies were often interrupted when hostilities broke out, especially during the period of the Crusades (1095–1291). With the conquest of the last Crusader outposts in the Holy Land in the second half of the thirteenth century, European imports of elephant ivory increased rapidly. This was a commercial disaster for the Greenlanders. Demand for walrus ivory fell and with it the price. The Greenlanders had paid their 'Peter's Pence', a tithe to the papacy, in walrus tusks and sealskins, but in 1282, Pope Martin IV asked for payment in gold instead: Greenland products were getting hard to sell at reasonable prices. The last recorded shipment of walrus ivory to Norway was in 1327, but the trade probably did continue after that, unrecorded. Analysis of preserved walrus ivory carvings in European collections has shown that the size of the walrus being hunted by the Greenlanders began to decrease in the thirteenth century. The best explanation for this is that they were trying to compensate for the lower prices they were paid by intensifying their hunting to increase supply. DNA analysis of waste walrus bone from ivory workshops shows that, by 1300, the Norse had begun hunting a genetically different walrus population that was native not to the traditional hunting grounds in the Norðsetr but to Baffin Bay, much further north. This is a sign of desperation. The further north the Greenlanders sailed to hunt, the shorter the hunting season and the greater the risk of getting trapped by sea ice in the autumn. The only plausible reason for this is that the Greenlanders had hunted the walrus to commercial extinction in the Norðsetr. Worse was to come (although walrus and elephants probably wouldn't have agreed, had they known). Around the end of the fourteenth century, ivory carving went out of fashion in Europe, and demand for ivory of all kinds collapsed.

And if this wasn't problem enough, the Greenlanders were now being out-competed in the fur trade by the Russians and Germans. The centre of the Russian fur trade was the city of Novgorod, founded by the Rus (Swedish Vikings) around 930 as a trading post along the long river route which linked the Baltic Sea with Constantinople via Kyiv and the Black Sea. From the start, Novgorod was a centre where Finnish and Karelian fur trappers from the taiga (boreal forest) to the north could exchange their wares for iron tools, textiles, grain and other commodities. Most in demand by wealthy consumers were the silver-grey winter coats of foxes and the pure-white winter coats of squirrels (known as miniver) and stoats (ermine), and the black fur of the pine marten (sable). In the twelfth century, Novgorod became an independent principality and extended its territory north through Karelia to the White Sea and the Arctic Ocean and east to the Urals, bringing a vast area of the taiga under its control. The Karelians, Sámi, Komi, Nenets and other indigenous Finno-Ugrian hunter-gatherers and reindeer herders who became Novgorod's subjects were forced to pay tribute in furs: their value was so great that they became known as Russia's 'white gold'. The flow of Russian furs to western Europe rapidly increased in the thirteenth century, after the German-dominated Hanseatic League of merchant cities was allowed to establish a *kontor* (colony) in Novgorod. The cost of shipping furs from Novgorod across the Baltic to western European markets through the Hanse's efficient distribution system was much lower than bringing them across the Atlantic, so the German merchants had no difficulty undercutting the Greenlanders.

As the value of Greenland's exports fell, thanks to the changing climate, the costs and risks of shipping them to Europe greatly increased, making them still less attractive. Ívar Bárdsson, a Norwegian priest who had been sent to Greenland to become the steward of the cathedral at Garðar in 1341, wrote after his return to Norway in 1364 that the traditional sea route to the colony, via the

Gunnbjorn Skerries, could no longer be sailed without 'extreme peril', because there was too much drift ice even in the summer. Ships now had to take a longer course, clearing Cape Farewell well to the south before turning north to the settlements. After the Black Death pandemic, regular communications between Norway and Greenland began to break down. After the long-serving bishop Arni of Garðar died in 1348, his appointed successor Jón Skalli Eiríksson delayed taking up his post until he managed to get himself transferred to the slightly more comfortable see of Holar in Iceland instead. Another successor, Álfur, was not appointed until 1364, and he did not actually arrive in Greenland until 1368. In that year, the royal Greenland *knarr* was lost at sea and never replaced. Bishop Álfur died in 1377 or 1378, but the news did not reach Norway until an Icelandic ship sailed from Greenland to Bergen in 1383. A new bishop of Garðar, Henricus, was appointed, but neither he nor any of his twelve successors ever felt any inclination to brave the ocean and go to Greenland to take up their see in person: they left its management to stewards and, at some point, even stewards weren't sent anymore. When the last bishop, Vincenz Kampe, died in 1537, the fate of the Greenland colony had already been a mystery for decades.

The end of official sailings from Norway did not mean that the Greenland settlements were completely cut off from the rest of the world; unofficial sailings continued long after. The captain of *Ólafssúdinn*, the ship that brought news of bishop Álfur's death to Norway, was accused of trading with Greenland without a royal licence, but the charge was withdrawn when he argued, in his defence, that he had really meant to go to Iceland but had 'drifted off' to Greenland by accident in bad weather. Two of the crew swore blind that the Greenlanders had forced them to trade with them, and that as they depended on them for shelter and sustenance during their accidental stay, they had no choice but to comply. Six years later, another Icelander, the wealthy ship owner Björn Einarsson the 'Jerusalem-Farer', got away with the same excuse despite having taken four ships to trade with the Greenlanders: he was simply ordered to pay the standard import taxes and the matter of the licence was overlooked. Sailing the North Atlantic was known to be fraught with danger, so it was impossible for the authorities to disprove such justifications for what they were no doubt convinced was blatant illegal trading intended to evade royal and ecclesiastical tolls and taxes.

Enter the Inuit

In line with the archaeological evidence, the Icelandic annals recorded that, in 1266, the Greenlanders sailed further north to hunt than usual to an area where they found traces of recent human occupation. Another thirteenth-century Norwegian chronicle states that 'farther to the north, hunters have encountered small people whom they call Skrælings; when they are hit their wounds turn white and they do not bleed, but when they die there is no end to their bleeding. They possess no iron, but use walrus tusk for missiles and sharpened stones instead of knives.' These particular Skrælings, the catch-all Norse term for all Native American peoples, were the Thule,* the direct ancestors of the modern Inuit peoples, who were newly arrived in Greenland from the western Arctic.

The Thule culture developed a long way from Greenland, on St Lawrence and Diomede Islands in the Bering Strait and on neighbouring areas of Siberia's Chukchi Peninsula, in the period 200 BC–AD 800 among groups of highly specialized marine mammal hunters. The Thule particularly targeted the slow-swimming bowhead whales and seals, which they hunted at sea from kayaks and umiaks using toggling harpoons. Unlike earlier harpoons used by Arctic hunters, which were made in one piece, the head of a toggling harpoon was detachable. When the harpoon was thrust into the prey, the head was designed to

* The name is derived from an archaeological site near the town of Thule (now called Qaanaaq) in north Greenland, where the culture was first identified in 1916.

detach and twist so that it lodged sideways in the muscle under the skin and blubber and could not be shaken loose. The harpoon's head was attached by a rope to an inflated seal bladder, which created drag, slowing and exhausting the wounded animal as it tried to escape and preventing it from submerging or, when it died, sinking, so hard-won catches were not lost. The Inuit delighted in eating the whale's blubber raw, but they had little regard for the meat, most of which they fed to their dogs. In winter, the Thule used dog-sleds, which could carry far more gear than a hunter on foot, to hunt seals on the frozen sea ice. These and other innovations provided the Thule with reliable year-round richly nutritious food and a strong competitive advantage over other Arctic hunter-gatherers: no previous hunter-gatherers had been so well adapted to the Arctic environment. Beginning around AD 1000, the Thule began to expand their range eastwards, at first to Alaska and then through the Canadian Arctic archipelagos to reach northern Greenland around AD 1200, completely displacing the Dorset people from their hunting grounds. In later Inuit legend, the Dorset, who they called the Tuniit, were remembered as a timid, if immensely strong, people who would run away when approached. Research into the DNA of the Dorset and Thule peoples has shown that the two groups were genetically distinct, therefore not closely related, nor is there any evidence of intermarriage between them or, indeed, of cultural interaction. The Dorset were probably forced into ever more marginal hunting grounds, eventually becoming extinct: their last holdout was in Quebec's Ungava Peninsula, where they survived until around 1500. Despite their sophisticated technology, the onset of climatic deterioration began to make life harder in the high Arctic, encouraging the Thule to migrate south along both the east and west coasts of Greenland until they met Norse hunters moving north.

Skræling Island

At best, it's likely that the first meetings between the Thule and the Norse would have been cautious and full of mutual suspicion; at worst, they would have been violent like the first encounter between the Norse and 'Skrælings' in Vinland or Torgils Orrabeinfostre's meeting with the two 'witches' on Greenland's east coast. Fights over hunting territories were the commonest cause of violent death among men in traditional hunter-gatherer societies, so it's equally likely that violence could have been initiated by the Thule. Norse artefacts have been found on many Inuit archaeological sites in the Canadian Arctic and northern Greenland, and these have usually been interpreted as evidence that a cooperative trading relationship quickly developed: there are, however, other explanations for their presence which are less benign. The Inuit site which has so far produced the greatest number of Norse artefacts is Skræling Island, a small island off Ellesmere Island nearly 78° north, which was occupied repeatedly by indigenous Arctic peoples over a period of more than 5,000 years. The big attraction of the island was its proximity to the North Water Polynya, a large, permanently ice-free area in northern Baffin Bay (between Ellesmere Island and Greenland), which attracts large numbers of seals and whales in winter. The Thule arrived on Skræling Island in the thirteeenth century and built a cluster of winter houses from stones, turf and whalebones.

The Norse artefacts from Skræling Island include pieces of woven woollen cloth, iron ship rivets, knife and spear blades, a carpenter's plane (with its blade missing), an awl, iron wedges (for splitting wood), pieces of mail armour, and fragments of boxes and barrels. Thule artefacts included harpoon heads, pieces of meteoritic iron blades and a small wood carving of a face with non-Inuit features. Similar carvings, known as *kavdlunaits* from the Inuit word for foreigner ('white strangers'), have been found at other Thule sites. Some are depicted wearing European-style hoods and cloaks and are thought to be Inuit portrayals of the Norse. One, found near Aasiaat in Greenland, of a female *kavdlunait* figure, is evidence that the Inuit had met Norse women in the far north and so they must have taken part in hunting expeditions with the men. Radiocarbon dates for some of the Norse artefacts from Skræling Island cluster around the middle of the thirteenth century. A similar range of Norse artefacts found at an Inuit site on Ruin Island, about 60 miles away on the Greenland side of the Nares Strait, have been dated to the same period.

The Inuit did have the furs, seal skins and ivory that the Norse needed to maintain their trade links with Europe, but what could the Norse offer them in return? Wood was a precious commodity this far north, but the Greenland Norse were always short of timber too. Iron tools might have been traded, but these were also always in short supply in the Norse settlements and, at least in Vinland, they had previously been reluctant to trade these valuable, hard-to-replace objects with indigenous peoples. The Inuit had access to meteoritic iron from northern Greenland, which they worked into blades by cold hammering. Norse wrought iron was better quality but would also have been harder to work without the additional technology of a forge. Rather than indicating a regular trade, an alternative, minimalist explanation for the presence of these artefacts is that they all come from a single Norse expedition to the far north, perhaps the same one that built the cairns on Washington Irving Island (see p. 252). The ship rivets were not new when they came into Inuit hands; they look as if they have been salvaged from ship planks. The Norse would hardly have traded away the planks of their own ship, so it is much more likely that they were salvaged from a shipwreck along with the other artefacts. Or perhaps the Inuit fought the Norse interlopers and captured and looted the ship. Back in the settlements, this was just another expedition that set out on the dangerous Arctic seas bound for the Norðsetr and was never heard of again. An Icelandic chronicle for 1379 which recorded a Skræling attack on the Greenlanders in which eighteen men were killed and two boys and a bondwoman were captured may refer to a hunting party like this that was ambushed by the Thule.

This is, however, the only Norse source that refers to hostilities between Greenlanders and the Thule. Inuit folk tales, collected by Danish missionaries to Greenland in the nineteenth century, about the people they called the Kavdlunait, held that their first meetings, in the vicinity of the Western Settlement, had been friendly, but that later there had been vicious blood feuds and killings on both sides. One folk tale tells how an Inuit chief called Kaisape avenged himself against a Norse chief called Ungortok, who had killed his brother in an attack on one of their villages. Using white skins to camouflage their kayaks among the icebergs, the Inuit approached Ungortok's farm undetected. When everyone had retired inside the house for the night, the Inuit packed bundles of juniper branches around it and set them on fire. Those Norse who tried to escape were shot down with arrows as they emerged from the house, while the rest perished in the flames. Only Ungortok escaped, but Kaisape eventually hunted him down and killed him with a magic arrow.

The Thule very likely played a part in the demise of the Dorset people by pushing them out of their hunting grounds, but did they also play a part in the decline of the Norse Greenland colony? Violent encounters between the Thule and the Norse would not have been one-sided affairs. The Norse Greenlanders' iron weapons and mail armour, which at least some of them owned, would have given them an advantage in close-quarters fighting, but the Thule possessed powerful sinew-backed compound bows whose bone-tipped arrows were quite capable of penetrating between the links in a mail shirt. However, no archaeological evidence, such as the remains of burned longhouses, has ever been found to back up the stories of violence between the Norse and the Thule, so it is hard to quantify how frequent it really was and whether casualties were sufficient to have a demographic impact on the settlements. However, even if the presence of the Thule did nothing more than deter Norse hunting expeditions, the commercial viability of the settlements would have been affected.

The Greenlanders may also have faced attacks from overseas.

An Inuit folk tale tells how they agreed to help the Norse drive off pirates who had raided the settlements. When the pirates returned, the Inuit rescued five women and two children. When the Inuit discovered that the pirates had carried off the rest of the Norse as captives, the survivors were adopted into their community. English, German and Moorish pirates certainly raided Iceland in the fifteenth century, seizing people to sell as slaves on the Barbary Coast, and there is one record in a papal letter dated to 1448 of a rumoured pirate raid on the Eastern Settlement some thirty years earlier, so the tale has the ring of truth about it. The impact of a methodical slave raid on the small Norse community could have been much more devastating than any skirmishes with the Inuit. Accidental losses at sea, on trade voyages or hunting expeditions, could also have been keenly felt in a declining community which, even at its peak, had never numbered more than about 3,000 people.

The Western Settlement is abandoned

The colder conditions of the Little Ice Age certainly did impact the lives of the Norse Greenlanders, but they adapted to the new circumstances. When they arrived in Greenland, the settlers built the same sort of longhouses they had lived in in Iceland. These became too difficult to keep warm in winter, and they were abandoned in favour of smaller dwellings with much thicker, better insulated walls. Byres and stores were built directly adjacent to the dwelling house and were accessed by covered passages so that the inhabitants didn't have to expose themselves to the bitter cold outside. The climatic deterioration adversely affected the Greenlanders' farming economy, but it wasn't just the colder summer temperatures and shorter growing season – the climate became drier too, making it much harder to produce enough hay to feed livestock through the longer, harder winters. Farmers intensified the fertilization of their fields and, as Erik the Red's descendants did at his old farm at Brattahlið, built dams in the hills to trap spring meltwater and networks of ditches to distribute the water to the hayfields to help the grass grow better. Everything depended on the hay harvest. The longer winters meant that livestock had to be kept in the byres for longer, so the Greenlanders' dependence on hay was increasing even as their ability to provide it was declining. By spring, animals were so weak that their owners actually had to carry them out of their winter byres and into the fields to graze. Expensive to feed, cattle gradually became a rarity, a luxury food source for chieftains; pigs disappeared completely, but hardier sheep continued to be bred, for their essential wool as much as for meat. Farming was on the very edge of viability. One bad summer, one failed hay crop and the livestock would starve to death before spring came, but if their livestock starved, does it follow that the Norse would too?

At some point during his twenty-year stay in Greenland, Ívar Bárdsson sailed north to collect the tolls and taxes due to the church from the Western Settlement. What he found was spookily deserted farms and the only signs of life a few sheep, cattle and horses running wild. Ívar's men rounded up as much of the livestock as they could, slaughtered it, and set off back to Garðar and the Eastern Settlement. Ívar thought that the inhabitants had been abducted or killed by the Skrælings. Most historians down the years have taken Ívar's account to mean that the Western Settlement had been abandoned. Others have thought that if this was the case, why was there livestock running free? Sheep might have survived a Greenland winter outdoors, but cattle and horses could not have done so. Perhaps the inhabitants had seen Ívar coming and, guessing what he was after, had all rushed off to hide until he departed. This would have required the inhabitants to be remarkably prescient – why would they assume a ship turning up was full of tax collectors and not merchants or hunters on their way to the Norðsetr? – and the loss of their livestock must have hurt just as much as paying their taxes. Ívar's account would suggest a sudden and complete abandonment of the Western Settlement, a flight almost, but the archaeological evidence points to a slow death spread over a few decades, with the last farms not being abandoned until the end of the fourteenth century. Many of the farms were abandoned in an orderly way: the people who lived there packed up all their possessions and even took the valuable roof timbers with them when they moved out. This was not always the case, however. At Sandnes, archaeological evidence suggests that the entire parish may have starved to death in a hard winter in the mid-fourteenth century. At the chieftain's farm, the skeletons of nine hunting dogs were found on a stable floor: they had been butchered. This was an act of desperation indeed: the inhabitants had already eaten their livestock, including a newborn calf and a lamb. Even if its owners survived the winter, the farm had no future, it was finished. When the houses of the parish were abandoned, many artefacts were left behind, as were the roof timbers. With wood in such short supply in Greenland, this is unlikely to have happened had there been many survivors.

While it is clear that the climatic deterioration killed off the Western Settlement, it is far from clear that it played a decisive role in the end of the Eastern Settlement. Farming declined there too, but there is little evidence that people went hungry. Human remains excavated from the late Norse cemetery at Herjolfsnes show that the people of the Eastern Settlement were still physically robust and basically well nourished. Isotope analysis of their skeletal remains indicates that, by the fifteenth century, Greenlanders relied on seal meat for 80 per cent of their nutrition. Animal bones from middens also show an increasing dependence on wild caribou and seals for food. It would seem that, far from refusing to adapt, the Norse were eating pretty much the same diet as the Thule. Despite their increasing reliance on seals, the Norse did not adopt any of the Thule's hunting technology, not even the toggling harpoon. This has been taken to be evidence of a fatal cultural conservatism, as if adopting the ways of the pagan Thule would threaten their European Christian identity. However, the lack of obvious signs of general malnutrition would suggest that the Norse didn't adopt the technology because they didn't need to: they were catching enough seals the way they always had, by using nets strung between boats to drive them down fjords into killing zones from which they could not escape.

A wedding and then darkness

Early in the fifteenth century, the chieftain at Herjolfsnes built a new feasting hall: it's not an investment anyone would be likely to make if they were anticipating the imminent demise of their community, but the chieftain's confidence in the future was misplaced. The last recorded ship to visit the Greenland settlement arrived in 1406, after it was, or perhaps wasn't really, blown off course on a return voyage from Norway back to Iceland. Pack ice in the fjords prevented it from setting sail again for four years. When one of the crew, Snorri Torfason, finally got home he found that his wife had given him up for dead and remarried. The ship's captain, Thorstein Olafsson, on the other hand, took a bride home with him. Thorstein's wife, Sigrid Björnsdottir, had been born in Iceland but had been living in Greenland for ten years: she had probably been sent there to marry the son of a chieftain but was, by 1406, a widow. Thorstein brought Sigrid the devastating news that her whole family had died in the plague epidemic of 1402–4. As sole heiress to her father's extensive estates in Iceland, she was now a wealthy landowner, and a very attractive match for an ambitious ship owner. The couple married in the small stone church at Hvalsey, in the Eastern Settlement: remarkably, though roofless, it still stands, the most impressive and evocative Norse ruin in Greenland. Many guests attended the ceremony which was held on 16 September 1408 and enjoyed a feast of seal meat afterwards in the local chief's new feasting hall next door to the church. The banns had been read publicly on three Sundays before the wedding and afterwards the priest Paul Hallvardsson gave the happy couple a marriage certificate, which was later deposited in the archives of the cathedral at Nidarós: it is the only document written in the Norse Greenland colony which has survived. Everything about the wedding was done by the book, so it would seem that, at that time, all was still well with the Eastern Settlement. It was a fully functioning medieval European community in which the church enforced conformity to Christian values. Only a year before the wedding, a man called Kollgrim had been burned alive after being found guilty of using black arts to seduce another man's wife.

There are no recorded contacts with Greenland after Thorstein and his wife left in 1410 to start their new life together in Iceland. It is as if the last guest to leave their wedding party turned the lights off and no one turned them on again. It would take a person of very stunted imagination to be able to stand among the ruins at Hvalsey and not wonder about that last leave-taking. Thorstein probably felt only relief that the sea ice had cleared enough for him to escape, but did Sigrid feel any regret about leaving the people she had lived with for so long? Or did she just think 'no more seal meat for me, thank God'? And what of those left behind watching from the shore as the ship gradually receded from sight among the ice floes? Did they see Sigrid's departure as another nail in the coffin of a dying community? Or feel optimistic that in Thorstein they would now have a promising new business contact in Iceland? If it was the latter, they may have been bitterly disappointed.

When he finally returned to Iceland, Thorstein seems to have given up on seafaring – he was an important landowner now – and, if he sent anyone else to trade with Greenland on his behalf, it went unrecorded. The Danish cartographer Claudius Clavus 'Svart' created a map of Greenland and the North Atlantic in 1424–7, which some historians have taken as evidence that he had recently visited the Norse colony and travelled as far north as the Norðsetr, but this is far from certain; there are other sources he could have gathered his information from. In 1426, a Greenlander called Peder was in Norway, but it is not known when he had arrived or if he ever went home. There must have been some outside contacts after that time, because King Erik complained of English merchants trading illegally in Greenland in 1431.

Clothing preserved in graves from the cemetery at Herjolfsnes in the Eastern Settlement shows that the Greenlanders were still managing to keep up to date with European fashions until around 1450 at the latest, but there is no archaeological evidence for contacts after that time. By the end of the fifteenth century, the Norse Greenland colony had become a distant memory and even its exact location had been forgotten. No sea captains who knew the way to Greenland could be found at Bergen in 1484. In 1492, Pope Alexander VI wrote about Greenland as a lost land:

> The people there have no bread, wine or oil but live on dried fish and milk. Very few sailings because of the ice on the sea and these only in the month of August, when the ice has melted. It is thought that no ship has sailed there for eighty years and that no bishop or priest has lived there during this period. Because there are no priests, many of the people there who were formerly Catholics, have renounced the sacrament of baptism and have nothing else to remind of the Christian faith than a sacred altar cloth which is exhibited once a year, which was used by the last priest to say mass a hundred years ago.[31]

It is ironic that Alexander was writing in the same year that Christopher Columbus made his first trans-Atlantic voyage. Europeans now possessed the technology to achieve what had been beyond the resources of the Greenlanders' Viking ancestors: the colonization of the Americas.

The fate of the last Norse Greenlanders may never be known for certain, but it is likely that, by the time Pope Alexander was writing, their settlements were already deserted and abandoned. Certainly, seafarers who visited Greenland in the sixteenth century met only Inuit. It is impossible to identify a single decisive factor in the colony's demise. If all the Greenland Norse aspired to in life was bare subsistence, it seems that they could have held on in the Eastern Settlement into the sixteenth century to be 'rediscovered' by a new generation of mainly English explorers searching for the Northwest Passage to the Pacific Ocean. However, the

Greenland Norse wanted the same kinds of lives that other Christian Europeans enjoyed, and this must have become harder and harder to achieve. Exclusion from hunting grounds by the Thule, and the collapse of the farming economy because of the Little Ice Age, were, in the end, probably less important than the increasing economic and social isolation caused by the decline of their overseas trade. Among fifteenth-century burials in the settlements there is a marked lack of women of child-bearing age. Death from the complications associated with childbirth was sadly very common in medieval Europe, so this absence must be significant. Faced with few options in the settlement beyond seal hunting, it is likely that the younger people drifted off to seek better opportunities elsewhere. This is part of a pattern of rural depopulation the world over. Perhaps Sigrid wasn't the only person to leave Greenland for good on Thorstein's ship. In the end, only those who felt too old to start a new life would have remained and, with the young people gone, the extinction of the colony was just a matter of time. It was probably old age that killed the last outpost of the Viking world, not a climate change catastrophe.

'Blonde Eskimos'

If the Norse Greenlanders didn't die of starvation, or weren't all massacred by the Thule, where did they go? In a history of Greenland that he wrote in *c.*1637, Gísli Oddson, the bishop of Skálholt, speculated (that is, he did not provide any supporting evidence for his claim) that the missing settlers might have 'joined the people of America'. Not long afterwards, Nicholas Tunes, the captain of a Dutch whaler, claimed he had encountered tall, fair-skinned Inuit in Baffin Island. In 1721, the Norwegian missionary Hans Egede claimed to have discovered a tribe of white-skinned Inuit in Greenland. More claims of encounters with 'white' or 'blonde Eskimos' followed in the nineteenth century. In 1910, the Canadian explorer and ethnologist Vilhjalmar Stefansson made the sensational claim that he had discovered thirteen tribes of white Eskimos living in the neighbourhood of Coronation Gulf and Victoria Island in the Canadian Arctic. Stefansson said he believed the 'white Eskimos were descendants of the colony which set out from Norway to Greenland sometime after the discovery of that island. Ethnologically, the white Eskimos bear not a single trace of the Mongolian type, differing in the shape of the skull and general features, colour of eyes, and texture of hair, which in many cases is red. They spoke Eskimo', though he thought he 'detected some Norse words. They probably numbered two thousand. Many of them had perfectly blue eyes and blonde eyebrows.' After the First World War, anthropological expeditions set out to look for the 'white Eskimos', but none were found. They never have been because they never existed. Extensive genetic studies carried out in the early 2000s have found no evidence of European genetic inheritance among modern Inuit before the nineteenth century. The Norse Greenlanders did not join 'the people of the Americas'. The destination of the missing Greenlanders is probably the obvious one. The original settlers were Icelanders, and Sigrid Björnsdottir's presence in Greenland in 1406 shows that the Greenlanders maintained their family, social and economic ties to Iceland throughout the colony's existence. When the Norse Greenlanders gave up on the colony, they most likely went home to Iceland.

11

Guiding stars

800–1500

Hafvilla – Fair weather seafarers – Waiting for the wind – The Ship Star – Star Oddi's Dream – Bird watching – Thor's hammers and Ægir's ale – Modern myths – The mariner's compass – The first sea charts – The mariner's astrolabe – The decline of traditional pilotage

Hafvilla is an Old Norse word meaning 'sea confusion'. It encapsulated the state of mind of a seafarer who had completely lost his bearings after sailing for days in conditions of such poor visibility that he had had sightings of neither the sun nor the stars and had no idea which direction his ship had been heading – north, south, east or west, every direction looked the same. Although they didn't all know it by that name, *hafvilla* was something all seafarers, everywhere in the world, were vulnerable to before the invention of the mariner's compass began the age of instrument-led navigation. *Hafvilla* was what Bjarni Herjolfsson was suffering from when he became the first European to sight the mainland of North America. Yet despite finding himself in seas no European had ever sailed before and having no idea where he was, in a masterly feat of navigation, Bjarni calmly recovered the situation and brought his ship and crew safely to his intended destination in Greenland, a place he had also never visited before. It is striking that when he finally arrived in Greenland, no one seemed to think that Bjarni had done anything exceptional; quite the opposite in fact: he was thought to have been rather timid because of his failure to explore properly the new lands he had sighted.

In their day, the Norse were without doubt the most accomplished seafarers ever to sail the Atlantic. While they may have learned much from the Irish, both the scale of Norse traffic and the range of their exploration far exceeded anything the *peregrini* had achieved. Once they had found their way to Greenland, the Norse were so confident of their abilities that they regularly sailed there directly from Norway, without using any of the 'stepping stones' along the way, a distance of over 2,750 kilometres. At that time, only the Malays in the Indian Ocean and the Polynesians in the Pacific were making longer open-sea voyages, and that was in warmer and less stormy seas. For all their ambition, however, the Norse still relied on tried and tested methods of navigation which had been handed down orally by generations of seafarers.

Fair weather seafarers

The instinct of Norse seafarers, like other early seafarers, was to try to minimize risks whenever possible. Going to sea was dangerous enough in summer, so, except in emergency, the Norse avoided sailing in winter. The rule of thumb was to try to be home by the autumn equinox. The ship would then be stripped of its sailing gear, the mast, sail and rigging would be taken down and stored, and the hull would be hauled into a naust (a boatshed or, often, just a sheltered hollow) for the winter. Through the winter, any necessary repairs would be carried out and fresh tar applied to the timbers so that the ship was ready to go to sea as soon as the new sailing season began at the spring equinox. This caution also applied to selecting a route. The Norse, where possible, preferred to sail within sight of land, navigating from landmarks on shore. They did this even if it was not the shortest route. The Viking kingdom of York in northern England was less than 500 kilometres due west of Denmark, but, rather than sail there direct, Danish captains preferred to sail south and west along the coasts of Germany and the Low Countries to the Dover Strait and then follow the English coast north to their destination, even though that made their voyage over 50 per cent longer. The advantages of being able to make a hot meal and get a good night's sleep in a safe harbour and find shelter if the weather began to turn bad outweighed the time-saving of a direct route. Coastal navigation also made sense for raiding fleets: with the land to one side always marking the way, it was easier to keep the fleet together and to designate rendezvous points where stragglers could catch up. There were also the same benefits of being able to rest overnight and find shelter in bad weather and, no doubt, the chance for an opportunistic *strandhögg* along the way. For the Danes, who were mainly active in the North Sea and around the coasts of France, and the Swedes, who dominated the Baltic Sea, it was never necessary to sail out of sight of land for very long. Not so for the Norwegians, who had no choice but to become expert at navigating the open sea to maintain contact and trade with their far-flung Atlantic colonies.

Waiting for the wind

Norse ships had quite good windward sailing performance, and they could even make progress into the wind by tacking back and forth, but this was rarely done in practice because it was so slow and put so much strain on both the crew and the ship that it was barely worth the effort. Norse sailing rig was most efficient when the wind was directly astern and, for this reason, it was more usual for ships to wait until the wind was blowing in the direction of the intended destination. Norse shipping operated to no timetables, so if this meant waiting for weeks so be it: patience was a necessary virtue. An extreme example of this was William the Conqueror's invasion of England in 1066. England's King Harold Godwinson was challenged for the throne not only by William, the duke of Normandy, but by King Harald Hardrada of Norway too. Harold had no idea who would strike first; in the end it was the wind that decided. William had his fleet of longships ready by May, but the wind blew persistently from the north, keeping him in port for month after month, which used up his supplies. Those same winds carried Harald Hardrada and his fleet across the North Sea from Norway to England, only for him to be defeated and killed by Harold at the battle of Stamford Bridge, near York, on 24 September. King Harold Godwinson had no time to enjoy his victory. A few days later, the wind finally turned and, after over four months of waiting, William finally set sail and landed in England on 28 September. Harold hurried south with his exhausted army to defeat and death at the battle of Hastings on 14 October. Had the north wind held for another week or two, William would have been forced to disband his army for the winter, and English history might have followed a very different course.

Longships could be rowed, of course, but no one set out on an overseas raid by rowing into the wind, as it was far too exhausting and inefficient. This was explicitly recognized in the law code of the Swedish island of Gotland. The islanders were required to supply and crew longships for the royal fleet. However, if, when they were summoned to join the fleet, the wind was unfavourable, they were exempted from their obligation because it was 'not possible to cross the sea by rowing, only under sail'. There was no point in the men joining the fleet if they were too tired to fight even before the campaign started. Rowing was usually only resorted to in battle, when entering or leaving harbour and on inland waterways.

The Ship Star

Navigation was a very specialized occupation, and the *leiðsagnarmaðr* (pilot) might be the only professional seaman on a ship. This did not mean he was the captain: the ship's owner was always the captain, even if he was not a professional sailor, but, generally, if he had a strong survival instinct, he would leave the day-to-day sailing of the ship in the hands of the pilot. To get their bearings, Norse navigators relied mostly on the position of the Sun at noon, for due south, and, at night, on Polaris, the Pole Star, for due north. Unlike other stars, the position and altitude of the Pole Star is constant throughout the year for any given latitude. This makes the Pole Star a reliable guide not only to the direction of north but also for latitude. The altitude of the Sun at noon can be used for the same purpose but is less reliable because it changes throughout the year with the length of the day. The Norse did not have a modern concept of latitude; until as late as the thirteenth century, they still believed, as their pagan ancestors had, that the Earth was a flat disc, but they knew that observations of the altitude of the Sun and Pole Star could be used to hold a true course east or west in a technique now known as latitude sailing. If the Sun was being used as the reference in latitude sailing, a lower altitude at noon than expected meant that the ship had drifted north of its intended course; if the Sun was higher, the ship had drifted south, and the navigator could adjust his course accordingly. If the Pole Star was the reference, things worked the other way around: a higher altitude indicated a drift to the north, lower altitude a drift to the south. The importance of the Pole Star for navigation is apparent in its name. For the Norse it was the *Leiðarstjarna*, the 'Guide Star', or, for the English, the 'Ship Star'. English sea captains liked to set sail at nightfall so they could start their voyage with an accurate bearing from observations of the Pole Star. A limitation with stellar navigation, which was mainly a problem for the Norse, is that in high latitudes in summer there is too much light in the northern sky to see the Pole Star. At these times, the Norse used the bright star Vega, the *Suðrstjarna*, the 'South Star', which is prominently high in the southern sky in summer as an alternative but more approximate guide.

Star-Oddi's Dream

Towards the end of the Viking Age, an Icelander, Oddi Helgason (*c.*1070/80–1130/40), produced what may be the earliest written manual of astronomical information for navigators. Only a couple of pages of Oddi's observations have survived. These give the altitude of the Sun at noon at the main ports in Iceland for every week of the year and the directions of the Sun at sunrise and sunset at the winter and summer solstices. Oddi was a farm labourer, but his employer sent him off on fishing trips, giving him the opportunity to travel around Iceland to make his observations. Oddi's manuals earned him the nickname Star-Oddi and he was remembered with his own short saga, *Star-Oddi's Dream*, in which he makes a fantastical dream-journey to Gotland. According to the saga, Oddi frequently 'mused about the stars, since he had always been in the habit of observing during the night when the stars could be seen' and 'was so skilled in calendar calculation that, in his day, no one in Iceland was a match for him'.

While latitude was something that could be determined easily in clear weather, determining longitude accurately at sea was a problem that was not solved until the invention of the marine chronometer in the eighteenth century. When it came to estimating how far east or west of their point of departure they had sailed, Norse captains had to rely on the inexact process of dead reckoning based on their own experience of how far their particular ship would likely be able to sail under the prevailing weather and sea conditions and how long such journeys had taken in the past. As well as having a good feel for the ship's speed and heading, a navigator also needed to be able to judge leeway, the degree to which the ship was drifting sideways due to wind or current, and be able to compensate for this to keep on course. A merchant *knarr*, the type of ship the Norse used in the North Atlantic, could comfortably sail around 140 kilometres a day, but in practice this would have varied considerably, and the Norse had no way to measure the ship's speed accurately. In the twelfth century, a voyage from Stad in Norway to Hofn in Iceland (almost exactly 1,000 kilometres) in fair weather was reckoned to take on average seven days, but a voyage of roughly the same distance from Ireland to Iceland might take only five days in the same ship, because the prevailing winds were usually more favourable in that part of the Atlantic. These were all factors a captain would need to take into account in trying to estimate where exactly in his voyage he was.

Bird watching

Knowledge of the marine environment was of great importance to all early seafarers. Whales and seabirds have favoured feeding grounds which, if known, could help a seafarer establish his position more accurately. Such information was incorporated into *Landnámabók*'s sailing directions for Greenland, for example (see p. 257). During the breeding season, which was almost the same as the Norse sailing season, seabirds feed at sea but must return regularly to their nests to feed their chicks and to roost at night. Different species of bird range further than others. Kittiwakes, a species of gull, may fly over 150 kilometres out to sea to feed, but smaller seabirds, like puffins and guillemots, rarely fly more than 10. A seafarer who found his ship suddenly surrounded by puffins in a fog would immediately start listening out for the sound of surf on rocks, knowing that puffins live in burrows on top of sea cliffs. Observing the direction of flight of the longer-ranging seabirds at dawn and dusk is an accurate guide to the direction of land. Clouds build up over land, especially in the afternoon, giving further clues to the possible location of land beyond the horizon. Although they didn't have a word to describe it, Norse sailors also knew how to interpret iceblink, a white light reflected into the sky off ice sheets beyond the horizon. According to the *Historia Norvegicus*, Iceland 'contains countless mountains covered with uninterrupted sheets of ice and by their sheen mariners at sea and far from land customarily set their course for the haven best suited to them'. They might well have looked out for Greenland the same way. The colour and clarity of seawater varies for several reasons. Major rivers discharge huge quantities of silt into the sea, clouding the water for miles offshore, for example. Every pilot probably had his own personal stock of such pointers: survival was the best evidence of their usefulness.

Compasses or lodestones were unknown to the Norse, but they did use other simple navigation aids. One of these was the sounding lead, which the Norse are thought to have adopted from the English late in the Viking Age. This was simply a rope with a weight tied on to one end that was lowered from the ship into the sea to measure its depth. It was especially useful in the shallow shoally waters of the Baltic or southern North Sea. English navigators liked to keep about 10 fathoms (60 feet) of water under their keels when coasting, but the Norse had their own formula which did not depend on soundings: it was to sail just so far offshore 'that the sea [i.e. the horizon] came halfway up the mountains'. If forced to coast at night, navigators tried to sense the reflection of the waves off the land against the ship's hull. The second device was just as simple. It was the weather vane, used to determine the wind direction. Several elaborately decorated 'luxury' weathervanes made of gilt bronze have survived: perforations along the edges show that they carried streamers to increase their effectiveness and, no doubt, their showiness. Iconographic sources suggest that these devices could be fitted on the high prows of longships as well as on mastheads. Most merchant seafarers probably made do with flags, much cheaper and just as effective.

Thor's hammers and Ægir's ale

Despite their skills, Norse seafarers were under no illusions about the dangers of seafaring. Early medieval chronicles and Icelandic sagas are full of stories of shipwrecks, some of which were catastrophic in scale. In one of the worst incidents, in 876, an entire Danish Viking fleet, numbering around 120 ships, was wrecked by a storm on the south coast of England, which might have been bad news for the Danes but was obviously good news for the English, who escaped a nasty ravaging. For the crew of a ship that foundered on the open sea, there was little or no chance of survival, but there was hope for those sailing close to a coast. When shipwreck became inevitable, crews could resort to the desperate expedient of hoisting full sail and deliberately running their ship ashore head-on as fast as possible. On a sandy shore, there was a surprisingly good chance that the ship might be carried high enough up the beach for the crew to scramble to safety through the breakers. This is what the Icelander Egil Skallagrímsson did when he was wrecked on the Yorkshire coast around 948. Though their ship was broken beyond repair, he and all his crew survived, and they were even able to recover their cargo. If the coast turned out to be rocky, however, the crew, cargo and ship alike would be smashed by the power of the waves.

Popular lore was useful for predicting weather for a couple of days ahead, but on a longer voyage there was no way to tell how long fair weather would last. Seafarers sought to control the weather in the only way they knew how, by propitiating the right gods. The Norse believed that the weather was controlled by the high-god Odin and that storms at sea were caused by the sea god Njord, so it was wise to make sacrifices to both before starting a voyage. These gods, however, were feared rather than loved, and it seems that the sailor's god of choice was the hammer-wielding thunder god Thor. Because he protected humans from the malicious *jötnar*, the enemies of the gods, Thor was thought to be well disposed towards humans and was regarded with genuine affection. Even Christians like Helgi the Lean (see p. 237) trusted to Thor's protection at sea. It is likely that most seafarers regarded a protective silver Thor's hammer amulet as an essential part of their sea gear: they are such common finds on Viking Age archaeological sites that they must have been mass-produced by craftsmen. Should Thor's protection fail, a drowning sailor would be swept up by the goddess Rán in her fishing net and taken to spend his afterlife with her husband, the sea god Ægir in his hall at Hlésey, which was a sort of soggy Valhalla for seafarers. There, the drowned sailors could enjoy Ægir's ale, reputedly the finest brewed by any of the gods, and the company of his many lovely daughters, the waves. Would any of them really have regretted missing out on the opportunity to spend their afterlives hacking one another to pieces as the warriors who went to Valhalla were destined to do? Following the conversion to Christianity, Norse sailors shifted their allegiance to St Nicholas, the patron saint of seafarers, whose cult was already popular among sailors across the Christian world. Another favourite was Norway's royal saint, St Olaf, who, in popular devotion, became a thinly disguised substitute for Odin, absorbing many of his characteristics, including his control over the weather.

Modern myths

There is no evidence from contemporary Norse literature that Norse seafarers ever used any kind of navigational instrument other than the sounding lead and the weather vane. Despite this, it is often claimed that they may have used two other navigation aids, the so-called sun stone and a sun compass. The sun stone is mentioned in a couple of thirteenth-century sagas and is supposed to have been a crystal which was used to locate the position of the Sun on overcast days. 'The Story of Rauð and his Sons' describes the use of a sun stone on land:

> The weather was thick and snowy as Sigurd had predicted. Then king Olaf summoned Sigurd and Dagur to him. The king made people look out and nowhere could they see a clear sky. Then he asked Sigurd to tell where the sun was at that time. He gave a clear assertion. Then the king made them bring the sun stone and held it up and saw where light radiated from the stone and thus directly verified Sigurd's prediction.[32]

The sun stone is thought to have been the transparent

crystalline form of calcium carbonate called, because it is common there, Iceland spar, which is known for its polarizing qualities. However, modern experiments indicate that the polarizing effect is not strong enough to locate the Sun's position under a heavy overcast and works only under a clear sky or light overcast when the Sun's position can be seen with the naked eye anyway. In this respect, it is significant that, in *The Story of Rauð*, the sun stone was used only to confirm a naked-eye sighting of the Sun through cloud. Modern experimenters have fitted sun stones into various devices to try to improve their polarizing performance, but none of them are based on any kind of historical evidence. No sun stone has ever been found in a Viking Age context, either, but one has been recovered from an Elizabethan shipwreck off the Channel Island of Alderney. This does not prove that it was being used for navigation, however: Iceland spar is attractive, so it might just have been a sailor's souvenir.

The existence of the sun compass rests on even more slender evidence than the sun stone. In 1948, excavations of a thirteenth-century Benedictine convent on Uunartoq Fjord in Greenland uncovered half of a small wooden disc, around 7 centimetres in diameter, with a hole in the centre and approximately equidistant notches cut around the edges. When complete, there were probably 32 notches, similar to a compass rose. The surface of the disc is incised with lines, some of which are roughly parabolic. It is these parabolic lines that have led to the disc being interpreted as part of a sun compass. If the disc had at its centre a gnomon, then, it is claimed, these parabolic lines might represent the course of the sun's shadow through the day. These devices are easy to make and, as well as indicating the direction of north, they would have been a useful aid to latitude sailing. If the course of the Sun's shadow was plotted onto the disc at the port of departure, a ship's latitude relative to the starting place could easily be determined by measuring the length of the Sun's shadow daily at noon. If the shadow falls short of the line, the shorter shadow shows that the Sun is higher in the sky, meaning that the ship has sailed south relative to its starting point. If the shadow crosses the line, the longer shadow shows that the Sun is lower in the sky, meaning that the ship has sailed north relative to its starting point. So goes the theory, but it isn't as simple as that. Because the altitude of the Sun varies with the time of year as well as with latitude, the device would have been absolutely accurate only on the day it was made, and it would have become increasingly unreliable the longer a voyage was, limiting its usefulness, especially in high latitudes, where such changes are most rapid. Another limitation is that the compass has to be held absolutely level while a reading is being taken – no easy thing in a small ship on a choppy sea. Floating the compass in a bucket of water might have solved this problem, but only if some way could be found to stop it spinning. Ultimately, it has to be said, no amount of modern experimentation, no matter how successful, can prove that such devices were ever used by the Norse. The author's own experiments with making and using a sun compass suggest that the Uunartoq disc is far too small for it to have made a practicable sun compass. No contemporary medieval document mentions the use of such devices, so the disc may simply have been part of a child's toy or was, more likely, given that it was found in a religious setting, a 'confession disc', similar to those used by Icelandic priests to count the number of people taking confession or holy communion. Another navigational device which it has been claimed the Norse might have used is the 'sun board', a simpler version of a sun compass which could be used to determine latitude from the length of the Sun's shadow at noon. Like the sun stone and the sun compass, there is no evidence that any such device was ever used by the Viking Age Norse.

The belief that the Norse must have had some technological aids to help them navigate on their extraordinary voyages probably says more about us than it does about them or, indeed, any of the other highly accomplished pre-modern navigators, like the Polynesians, who confidently sailed the oceans without charts or navigation instruments. Ever-improving navigational technology has steadily de-skilled modern humans when it comes to finding their way around the world. The intimate environmental knowledge and keen observational skills employed by pre-modern seafarers are long gone and, thanks to the instant availability of satellite navigation on cellphones, even the ability to read maps is in decline. When we look out at the open sea, we just see an undifferentiated expanse, but to the Norse, and other pre-modern seafarers, it was full of clues and signposts for those who knew how to read them; the sea was just another kind of 'terrain', much more challenging to navigate than the land but a terrain nevertheless. It's our own lack of natural route-finding ability that makes us so willing to give so much credence to hypothetical navigational devices for which there is actually no evidence at all: it's a case of projecting our own helpless technological dependence onto the past. For all that, we should also recognize that the Norse pushed their natural route-finding abilities to the limit of what was possible in their voyages: to truly master the Atlantic Ocean, Europeans were going to need new technology.

The mariner's compass

Looking back on a turbulent century of European global exploration and conquest from the perspective of 1605, the English philosopher Francis Bacon (1561–1626) wrote that the Americas 'had not been discovered, if the use of the mariner's needle, had not been first discovered'. The mariner's compass was, he thought, one of the three inventions that had led to the birth of his modern world, the others being gunpowder and printing. All three were Chinese inventions, but it was Europeans who exploited their full potential and transformed the world with them. Many cultures around the world independently discovered that lodestones, naturally occurring magnets composed of iron-rich magnetite ore, could attract iron objects to them, but this was commonly treated simply as a natural oddity with no practical uses. It was the Chinese who, sometime before AD 100, recognized that a lodestone could be used to determine the direction of south, an auspicious direction in Chinese geomancy. The first Chinese compasses, which were used in feng shui and for fortune-telling, did not look anything like a modern compass: they were made from a single piece of lodestone carved into the shape of a spoon, so finely balanced that, when placed on a flat surface, it could rotate freely, allowing its handle always to turn towards the south. It wasn't until the eleventh century that the compass's potential as an aid for navigation was recognized and used for navigation at sea. Chinese navigational compasses were not the works of art that the south-pointing spoons were: they consisted simply of an iron needle that had been magnetized by stroking it with a lodestone and then floated on a small piece of wood or a reed in a bowl of water so that it could rotate, or 'swim', freely to point in the direction of south. Later, the Chinese also invented a 'dry compass', which used a needle balanced on a pivot pin.

The magnetic compass probably came into use in Europe around the middle of the twelfth century. The usual way in which Chinese technology was transferred to Europe in the Middle Ages was via the Islamic world. Medieval Arab seafarers made direct trading voyages to China from the Persian Gulf and the Red Sea, so we might expect that knowledge of the magnetic compass spread first to Persia and Egypt, and from there to the Mediterranean. The timing of this technological transfer is very uncertain, because the earliest documented use of the magnetic compass in the Islamic world post-dates its documented use in Europe. Later tradition credited seamen from the Italian port of Amalfi as the first European adopters of the new technology, but the earliest documented use of the magnetic compass in Europe actually comes from England. Returning home from a cross-Channel study trip to France in *c.*1190, the English monk Alexander Neckham described how sailors used the compass: 'as they sail over the sea, when in cloudy weather they can no longer profit by the light of the sun, or when the world is wrapped up in the darkness of the shades of night, and they are ignorant to what point of the compass their ship's course is directed, they touch the magnet with a needle, which (the needle) is whirled round in a circle until, when its motion ceases, its point looks direct to the north'. Neckham says that, among the stores of a ship, there must be 'a needle mounted on a pivot, which will oscillate and turn until the point looks to the north, and the sailors will thus know how to direct their course when the polar star is concealed through the troubled state of the atmosphere'.[33] It is clear from Neckham's matter-of-fact account that seamen didn't regard the compass as a novelty: it was already established as a perfectly normal, even essential, part of a ship's equipment.

These simple compasses allowed navigators to orientate themselves in relation to north, but they weren't yet true mariner's compasses that enabled a ship to sail a true course on a bearing. In the thirteenth century, in the Mediterranean, the compass was refined by mounting a pivoted needle over a card marked with a wind rose, which named and showed the directions of the eight main Mediterranean winds: Tramontane (north), Gregale (northeast), Levante (east), Scirroco (southeast), Ostro (south), Libeccio (southwest), Ponente (west), and Maestro (northwest). In Atlantic Europe, the names of the Mediterranean winds were rather irrelevant, so the practice there was to mark and name the eight primary directions, north, northeast, east and so on, and this eventually became standard practice everywhere. The rose evolved to show sixteen directions and, by 1391, thirty-two, the number on a modern compass rose. The final stage in the development of the mariner's compass came in the early fifteenth century, when compass makers in Antwerp began mounting the compass card on top of the pivoted needle. When placed in a box mounted in line with the ship's keel, the mounted card would turn as the ship changed course, so it always indicated which direction it was sailing. This allowed the ship to maintain a steady course from compass readings alone.

When it came to explaining how a compass works, it was at first believed that the compass needle pointed north because it was attracted in some way to the Pole Star. As the compass became more refined, it became increasingly obvious that the compass needle pointed not actually exactly to the Pole Star but slightly to the west of it; probably the first to notice this deviation was the English philosopher Roger Bacon (1219–1292). Some other explanation was clearly needed. In the fourteenth century, the anonymous author of a now lost account of an English friar's travels in the North Atlantic called *Inventio Fortunata* ('Fortunate Discovery') claimed that compass needles were attracted to the *Rupes Nigra*, the 'Black Rock', a magnetic phantom island, supposedly 33 French miles wide, surrounded by a giant whirlpool in the Arctic Ocean. It is quite possible that the journey described in the *Inventio* is entirely fictional, but medieval readers tended to be quite uncritical of travelogues, no matter how fantastical – they expected the world to be full of wonders – so it was taken seriously and, for want of a better explanation, the *Rupes Nigra* became a fixture on European world maps until the seventeenth century.

It was Elizabeth I's physician, William Gilbert (1544–1603), who finally provided a scientific explanation for magnetic variation, when he demonstrated that the Earth was itself a giant magnet. The compass needle was attracted to the Earth's north magnetic pole, which just happened not to be in the same place as the geographical pole: it was later discovered that the magnetic pole was not a fixed point like the geographical pole; it drifted constantly. Despite not yet understanding its cause, late medieval compass makers attempted to compensate for magnetic variation by offsetting the needle under the card a few degrees east, so the card itself would point to true north. The navigators who actually used the compasses soon found that this was no solution at all, because the degree of deviation from true north was not the same everywhere; for example, it was approximately twice as great in northern Europe as it was in the Mediterranean. The answer was to measure the variation against astronomical observations of true north regularly during a voyage, daily if possible, and compensate for this when calculating a magnetic bearing. Despite the compass, sailors still heaved a sigh of relief when the night sky was clear.

Because of its limitations, the compass did not result in an immediate revolution in seafaring. In its basic form as a north-pointing needle, the compass was useful mainly as a supplement to traditional methods of pilotage, but the more it was refined, the more navigators came to rely on it. By the end of the fourteenth century, Mediterranean sailors were confident about sailing all year around. In the Atlantic too, wintertime sailing became more common, because sailors felt more comfortable about going to sea in conditions of poor visibility. The ships carrying wine and pilgrims between Iberia and the British Isles cut their journey times by sailing direct across the Bay of Biscay instead of hugging the coast. And, after 1300, the word *hafvilla* fell out of use in the Norse languages, no doubt because, thanks to the compass, seafarers always had at least some idea which direction they were sailing in.

The first sea charts

Running in parallel with the development of the mariner's compass was the development of the first true sea charts. Most medieval land maps were made to represent a spiritual world view, so, although they could be very detailed, they didn't need to be geographically accurate, because no one was going to use them to try to find their way from A to B. The most common European world map was the 'T and O' map. These always had east, the direction of Jerusalem, and, it was believed, Paradise, at the top. The three known continents were shown as roughly circular, with Asia at the top, taking up about half the land mass, and Europe, to the bottom left, and Africa, to the bottom right, amounting to about a quarter each. The Mediterranean, which divided the three continents, was the 'T', while the Ocean which surrounded them all was the 'O'. They're reminiscent of a map of the world in the age of Pangea. In contrast to these maps, even the earliest sea charts look strikingly modern, showing coastlines that are realistic and immediately recognizable. Sea charts were developed from mariner's handbooks of sailing directions and distances known as *portolani* ('port books'), which began to be produced in the major Italian ports, such as Amalfi, Genoa and Venice, in the thirteenth century. Though similar in principle to the *periploi* of ancient mariners, the *portolani* differed in one important respect: they expressed directions as compass rose points. By the end of that century, the directions in *portolani* were being used to create sea charts of the Mediterranean and Black seas, known as portolan charts. These were the first maps to be drawn to scale and, because they were designed to be used in conjunction with a magnetic compass for navigation at sea, they have north at the top. This is where the most striking feature of the portolans comes in: they are criss-crossed by intersecting straight lines radiating out of wind roses. As with the wind rose cards used for compasses, sixteen, later thirty-two, of these lines, known as rhumb lines, radiate from each rose. By 1375, the wind roses had been replaced as radiants for the rhumb lines by compass roses. The rhumb lines served as references that allowed a navigator to calculate an accurate compass bearing from one port to another. Portolan charts were also the first to have scale bars so that the navigator could calculate the distance to be sailed as well as the direction. These were very much maps of the sea. Coasts were shown in great detail and ports and coastal features were named, but, apart from navigable rivers, inland areas were shown sketchily or not at all, as with modern sea charts.

Early portolan charts represented the Mediterranean and Black Seas with great accuracy – after all, their bounds had been well known for centuries – but the coasts of Atlantic Europe were still very sketchy. Navigators had an interest in accurate maps and gave map makers constant feedback which led to rapid improvements, especially after portolan charts started to be made in Spain and Portugal in the fourteenth century. By 1485, the Portuguese had begun producing charts which marked latitudes in degrees. As Europeans discovered more and more of the world in the fifteenth and sixteenth centuries, it became apparent that portolan charts weren't able to take into account the curvature of the Earth, and they were eventually replaced with charts of the Mercator projection, the basis of all modern sea charts, which allowed a true compass bearing to be drawn between any two places anywhere on the map. As well as the compass, portolan charts could be used with tables called *toleta* which enabled more accurate course corrections to be calculated, and there was an improvement to the accuracy of dead reckoning with the introduction of the Dutchman's log. In its simplest form, this was a float which was thrown overboard at the bows. Its passage towards the stern was then timed with a sand glass to estimate the ship's speed. As an aid for dead reckoning, many ships carried hourglasses as part of their navigational equipment. The earliest record of such is a receipt for a total of sixteen 'glass horologes' for King Edward III's ship *La George* dated to 1345.

The mariner's astrolabe

In the fifteenth century, the magnetic compass was joined by two new instruments, the quadrant and the mariner's astrolabe, both of them simplified versions of the astrolabe (from Greek 'star seeker'), the most important astronomical instrument of the pre-telescope age. First made in Greece in the second century BC, astrolabes were two-dimensional representations of the universe engraved on a metal plate with attached rotatable cut-out discs and pointers which allowed the user to carry out a wide range of tasks, perhaps the most important of which was to measure accurately the altitude and azimuth of stars. The mariner's astrolabe was a much simplified version which was made solely for this purpose. The earliest recorded use of the mariner's astrolabe was in a treatise by Majorcan navigators in 1295. By the fifteenth century, mariner's astrolabes were in widespread use: the Portuguese sea captain Diogo de Azambuja took one with him on a voyage to West Africa in 1481, and Bartholomeu Dias,

Columbus and Vasco da Gama all took them on their voyages too. Early mariner's astrolabes were made of wood, but late in the fifteenth century more accurate instruments made of brass were developed. The oldest surviving example, found in the wreck of the Portuguese ship *Sodré*, which sank off the coast of Oman in 1502, was manufactured around 1496–1501. On mariner's astrolabes, degrees were only marked at 5° intervals, rather than 1° as on normal astrolabes. This was probably no more than a practical recognition of the difficulty of making accurate measurements on the heaving deck of a ship at sea. An astrolabe could determine a ship's latitude with great accuracy but only if the observations could be taken from nearby land. This limited their usefulness on the open sea. To try to improve their accuracy, wooden astrolabes were ballasted to stop them blowing about in the wind, but the best answer to this particular problem came in the early sixteenth century when brass astrolabes made in the form of an open ring came into use. These were much heavier than wooden astrolabes and offered less wind resistance, making it easier to get an accurate observation.

The invention of the quadrant, so called because it was just a quarter of a disc (they looked rather like a protractor broken in half), came soon after the invention of the astrolabe itself and, like the mariner's astrolabe, they were optimized for measuring the altitude and azimuth of stars. The first quadrants were built large, for accuracy, and needed fixed mountings, but in the Middle Ages, small, portable versions were made: they were first used by land surveyors when calculating the height of hills and buildings. The first recorded use of the quadrant at sea for determining the altitude of the Pole Star was by the Portuguese sea captain Diogo Gomes during a voyage to West Africa in 1461. This enabled Gomes to make accurate calculations of the distance he had travelled south of his home port of Lisbon. The scale on early navigational quadrants was often marked with the names of places where the latitude had been established rather than in degrees. Once tables of the Sun's declination became available – the first appeared in 1484 in the *Regimento do astrolabio e do quadrante*, a navigation manual produced on the orders of Portugal's King João II – the arc of the quadrant was graduated in degrees and minutes so that altitudes could be read in angles. By the early sixteenth century, the quadrant had been universally adopted by European seafarers, and it remained in wide use until it was superseded by the more accurate sextant in the eighteenth century.

A third astronomical instrument which was just coming into use for navigation at sea at the end of the fifteenth century was the Jacob's staff or cross staff, which was used for measuring the altitudes of the Sun, Moon and stars. First described in the early fourteenth century by the French-Jewish mathematician Levi ben Gerson, these consisted of a wooden staff 1.5 metres long and about 2.5 centimetres wide, marked with graduations and a cross piece or transom, used for sighting, which slid along the staff. To make a measurement, the transom was moved along the staff until the lower edge was aligned with the horizon and the upper edge was aligned on the Sun or star whose altitude was being measured. The altitude could then be calculated from the position of the transom on the graduated scale on the staff. The first experiments with using the cross staff for navigation at sea were carried out by the German mathematician and cartographer Martin Behaim (1459–1507), who, in the service of the Portuguese king, sailed to West Africa in 1485 (he also made the first brass mariner's astrolabe for the voyage). The cross staff was difficult to use on a moving ship and observations of the Sun required the navigator to look directly into the Sun's glare. Often, a piece of smoked glass was fixed to the upper edge of the transom to reduce the glare. Like the quadrant, the cross staff was eventually superseded by the sextant.

The decline of traditional pilotage

The growing use of technology, charts and astronomical tables for navigation marked an upheaval in traditional pilotage. Pilots had always controlled their traditional knowledge of coastal outlines, tides, currents and wind patterns. It took long apprenticeships, trained memories and years of sea time for pilots to acquire their skills, and it was up to them who they shared them with. Traditional pilotage, based on intimate knowledge of the environment, still has an important place in seafaring, even in the age of satellite navigation, but the increasing use of instruments, charts and tables steadily undermined the pilots' exclusive custodianship of navigational knowledge by allowing the wider and easier dissemination and acquisition of these skills. It did not take years to learn how to plot a course from a chart, take a compass bearing or make accurate astronomical observations with an astrolabe or quadrant. The Italian navigator Amerigo Vespucci made their declining status painfully clear to the traditional pilots who sailed with him on an early voyage to Brazil in 1501. In mid-Atlantic, he said,

> we were wandering and uncertain in our course, and only the instruments for taking the altitudes of the heavenly bodies showed us our true course precisely; and these were the quadrant and the astrolabe, which all men have come to know. For this reason, they subsequently made me the object of great honour; for I showed them that though a man without practical experience, yet through the teaching of the marine chart for navigators I was more skilled than all the ship-masters of the whole world. For these have no knowledge except of those waters to which they have often sailed.[34]

As the great age of European exploration began, European seafarers were already the world's most scientific navigators, able to chart a course across the widest oceans by instruments alone.

12

Sea of Darkness

700–1492

The Encircling Ocean – Triangulating the world – Islam and the Atlantic – The first Atlantic slave trade – Reintegration – Muslim explorers – The Seduced Ones in the Sea of Darkness – The 27,000 phantom islands – Between legend and geography – Pre-colonial West Africa and the Atlantic – On great white wings – To discover the furthest limit of the ocean

Abu Rayhan al-Biruni discovered America 400 years before Columbus without ever seeing the Atlantic Ocean with his own eyes. Born to a Persian-speaking family in Uzbekistan in 973, he spent most his life at Ghazni in Afghanistan, and the only sea he ever saw was the landlocked and tideless Caspian Sea. This didn't stop from al-Biruni thinking about what the Muslim world knew as *Al-Bahr al-Muhit*, 'the Encircling Ocean', or, more poetically, *Bahr as-Zulamat*, 'the Sea of Darkness'. Al-Biruni's discovery of America was an exercise in reductive logic based on a pioneering approach to geologic processes.

A mathematician, astronomer and geographer, al-Biruni was a brilliant product of the most brilliant period of Islamic civilization, the Abbasid period (750–1258). The Islamic world was, with the Christian world, an equal heir to the culture of Greco-Roman antiquity. In the early medieval Catholic west, it was the literary heritage of the ancient world that was most valued, but in the Islamic world, it was its science, mathematics and philosophy that excited most interest: the Orthodox Christian east had little time for either; it was all pagan learning best forgotten. Under the Abbasid dynasty, Muslim scholars first assimilated Classical learning and then began to build on it. Baghdad, the capital of the Abbasid caliphs, became the world's most vibrant centre of learning, the home of vast libraries of Arabic translations of Ancient Greek, Roman and Persian works, most of which have not survived in their original languages. When the spirit of intellectual inquiry began to revive in western Europe in the twelfth century, it was through Arabic translations that scholars rediscovered the works of Classical scientists, mathematicians and philosophers and began to lay the foundations of the scientific revolution of the early modern period. By this time, however, Islamic science itself was in terminal decline, killed off in part by the catastrophic cultural destruction wrought by the Mongol invasions of the thirteenth and fourteenth centuries and in part by the opposition of fundamentalist clerics who feared that rational enquiry would undermine religious faith.

Eager to emulate the glittering Abbasid court, rival Muslim rulers also became patrons of learning, creating unrivalled opportunities for Muslim scholars across the Islamic world, from Córdoba in the west to Ghazni in the east. Few Muslim scholars spent their whole lives studying at the same centre of learning, and al-Biruni was no exception. Al-Biruni was a complete polymath, studying theology, law, mathematics, astronomy, geography, cartography, grammar, medicine and physics at his home city of Kath, before moving to Bukhara in 995 and then, a few years later, to Qabus and then Rey in Iran. In 1017, Rey was captured by the Ghaznavid sultan Mahmud and, along with all the city's scholars, al-Biruni was taken as a sort of high-value, and rather pampered, cultural war trophy to become the sultan's court astrologer at Ghazni, where he died around 1050. Along the way, al-Biruni added engineering, history, geology, geodesy and anthropology to his already eclectic portfolio of disciplines: he was a Renaissance Man before the Renaissance. He found time also to write almost 150 books, including the *Codex Masudi*, completed in 1037, in which he deduced the existence of an unknown continent between Europe and Asia.

Triangulating the world

Geography was a subject Muslims took seriously for religious as well as intellectual reasons. While early medieval Christians were content with the schematic representation of the world epitomized by the 'T and O' map, Muslims needed to know exactly where they were in relation to Mecca to determine the *qiblah*, the correct direction for Islamic prayer. Astronomy, geodesy and cartography were their chosen tools. The Qur'an says that God has made 'the earth as a bed' (Surah 20, verse 53), which might suggest that the Arabs of Muhammad's time still adhered to an essentially Babylonian flat-Earth cosmography. However, the passage has rarely been interpreted literally, and it did not stand in the way of Muslims, or at least the educated elite, adopting the Ptolemaic model once they became acquainted with Greek astronomy. 'There is unanimity among men of learning that the Earth with all its territorial and oceanic parts is a sphere, like a ball,' wrote the geographer Ahmad ibn 'Umar ibn Rustah in 890.

One of al-Biruni's most important contributions to Islamic geographical knowledge came from his pioneering use of triangulation to measure distances accurately. Aided by an astrolabe, he used this technique to calculate the size of the Earth from a mountaintop fortress in what is now Pakistan. Despite incorrectly assuming that the Earth is a perfect sphere – it's actually slightly flattened towards the poles – al-Biruni's calculation that the radius of the Earth was 3,928.77 Islamic miles, around 6,339.6 kilometres, gives a circumference of 39,832.9 kilometres, which is within a fraction of the true figure of 40,008 kilometres, an accuracy that was not achieved in Europe until the sixteenth century. From these calculations, al-Biruni estimated that the known east–west expanse of Eurasia would amount to only about two fifths of the circumference of the Earth. Could it really be true that most of the Earth was covered with nothing but water? The ancient Greeks had not thought so, and al-Biruni was probably familiar with their belief that other continents must exist if the Earth was to remain properly balanced in space (see p. 122). However, he did not, as was so common in the Middle Ages, appeal to ancient authority to support his argument. In his writings, al-Biruni had recorded pioneering observations of geomorphological processes in action, such as the erosion of mountains and the transportation and laying down of sediments by rivers. The movement and redistribution of materials by water, al-Biruni argued, would constantly alter the centre of gravity of the world. This would raise up some places, while other places would subside and become flooded, so 'with the passing of time, the sea becomes dry land, and dry land the sea'. Fossils of marine creatures found in rocks on land, he said, supported his theory. Surely, he reasoned, these same processes must be at work everywhere, so, logically, there must be another great western landmass waiting to be discovered in the unknown three fifths of the world, most likely somewhere in the ocean between Europe and Asia. Having established, at least to his own satisfaction, that this western continent must exist, he asked if it would be inhabited. Muslim geographers had inherited from the Greeks the idea that the world was divided into climate zones, with uninhabitable frigid zones at each pole and two temperate zones, one in each hemisphere, separated by a torrid zone around the Equator. The torrid zone was thought to be an impenetrable barrier, so the Greeks believed that even if there were continents in the southern hemisphere, they would be uninhabited. Although he did not know how far south Africa extended, it certainly spanned the torrid zone, and it was all inhabited. The same processes which created land in the northern hemisphere were obviously also active in the southern hemisphere, so there was no reason to believe that his hypothetical western continent would not also span the Equator. The Eurasian-African landmass was habitable, so it followed that the hypothetical western continent would be too, and if it was habitable it would be inhabited, because everywhere in the known world that was habitable was inhabited. He concluded that 'there is nothing to prohibit the existence of inhabited lands in the Eastern and Western parts. Neither extreme heat nor extreme cold stand in the way … it is, therefore, necessary that some supposed regions do exist beyond the [known] remaining regions of the world surrounded by water on all the sides.'

Al-Biruni got the right answers to his questions – there really was an inhabited western continent exactly where he said it would be – but the premises of his argument were, as we now know, false. Our modern understanding of plate tectonics tells us that there is no geological reason why all the world's landmass should not be concentrated in one place, as it was some 300 million years ago in the age of the supercontinent Pangea. Al-Biruni 'discovered' America only by accident, much as Columbus was going to do, more literally, 400 years later.

Islam and the Atlantic

Despite their sophisticated understanding of cosmology, medieval Muslim writings about the Atlantic struggle to shake off the lingering influence of the flat-Earth belief that it was the literal edge of the world. That maybe shouldn't be a surprise, because the centre of the Muslim world was the Middle East and the Indian Ocean, and from that perspective, the Atlantic was really very peripheral. The well-travelled Moorish geographer Muhammad al-Idrisi (1100–1165) summed up what was probably most Muslims' attitude to the Atlantic:

> Beyond this ocean of fogs it is not known what exists there. Nobody has sure knowledge of it, because it is very difficult to traverse it. Its atmosphere is foggy, its waves are very strong, its dangers are perilous, its beasts are terrible, and its winds are full of tempests. There are many islands, some of which are

inhabited, others are submerged. No navigator traverses them but bypasses them remaining near their coast.[35]

The Atlantic was home to *tinnin*, descendants of the Canaanite *tanninim*, terrifying dragons that lived in the depths of the ocean and whipped up storms: such awful creatures were unknown in the Indian Ocean. This was a more threatening sea than the friendly Mediterranean or the familiar Indian Ocean; it was a hostile sea, a sea to turn your back on. Some Muslim scholars apparently even believed that it was impossible for a ship to pass through the Strait of Gibraltar from the Mediterranean into the Atlantic because the magical influence of a giant bronze statue at Cádiz, said to be over 100 Arabic cubits tall (approximately 54 metres), created adverse winds and currents. This strange legend may perhaps have attached itself to a statue on the Roman lighthouse which stood at Cádiz into the Islamic era. The statue's imagined malign influence was ended in 1145 by the Almoravid emir Abd al-Mumin, who melted it down to make coins. That a fantastic, and easily debunked, tale like this could be taken seriously and circulate widely among educated Muslims as late as the twelfth century speaks volumes.

Muslims had many names for the Atlantic. As well as the 'Encircling Ocean' and the 'Sea of Darkness', Arabic had many other names for the Atlantic, some of them not very inviting. It was *Al-Bahr al-Aswad*, the 'Black Sea', or *Al-Bahr al-Adar*, the 'Green Sea', both in contrast to *Al-Bahr al-Abyad al-Mutawassit*, the 'White Mediterranean Sea'. Or *Al-Bahr al-Kabir*, the 'Great Sea'; the *Al-Bahr al-Garbi*, the 'Western Sea'; and simply *Al-Muhit al-Atlasi*, the 'Sea of the Atlas Mountains', and *Uqiyanus*, the 'Ocean' from Greek *Okeanos*. The lack of knowledge of the Atlantic is obvious when it comes to Arabic sea names. Arabic has names for over a dozen subsidiary seas within the Mediterranean Sea, and three dozen or more in the Indian Ocean, which Arab seafarers knew intimately: Arabic has no sea names at all for the Atlantic Ocean beyond the *Bahr az-Zuqaq*, the 'Sea of the Strait [of Gibraltar]', which suggests that Muslim seafarers did not have much direct knowledge of the Atlantic beyond the coasts they actually controlled. Medieval Islamic cartographers, however, must have had access to reliable sources of geographical information, because their maps show the coasts of northern Europe with at least as much accuracy as contemporary Christian maps.

While the wider Islamic world was indifferent to the Atlantic, it remained central to the lives of those who lived on its shores. The long-established seafaring traditions of the Maghreb and al-Andalus, as Iberia was known in the Muslim world, continued unbroken by the Arab conquests. The Islamic conquests did not involve population replacements or even forcible conversions. Life went on. Fishermen still set out from Lisbon, the Algarve and Cádiz to catch tuna, even if many of them had converted to Islam. The ancient seafaring lore continued to be passed on from one generation to the next. The region's largely Mediterranean shipbuilding traditions continued too.

Where trade was concerned, however, Al-Andalus and the Maghreb really did turn their backs on the Atlantic as they became integrated into the world's wealthiest maritime network, one that extended east across the Mediterranean, through the Indian Ocean, and ultimately as far as China. This marginalized Atlantic ports like Cádiz and Lisbon in favour of Mediterranean ports like Málaga, Almería, Cartagena and Valencia with better links to North Africa and the Middle East. It didn't help that trade along the Atlantic coast with northern Europe was interrupted by the mutual hostility of the Islamic and Christian worlds, which effectively closed the Strait of Gibraltar to Christian shipping. Trade with northern Europe did continue, but it was often conducted by 'neutral' Jewish middlemen, known to the Arabs as al-Radhaniya, and it went mostly either by land through the Christian kingdoms of northern Spain or via the Mediterranean ports in Italian ships from Amalfi, Genoa and Pisa, rather than the Atlantic. Olive oil aside, Al-Andalus's exports to Christian Europe were mostly luxuries like silk cloth, glazed pottery and tiles, silver and gold coins (treated as bullion by their recipients), and African elephant ivory which reached al-Andulus via the Saharan caravan routes and the Maghreb. What they received in return from northern Europe was slaves and furs.

One group that was in direct maritime contact with the Moors in al-Andalus and the Maghrib was the still pagan Vikings, although the Moors might have preferred that they weren't, because it was the wrong kind of contact. Viking raids, however, were for the emirate a nuisance rather than an existential threat. The emirate had a well-equipped professional standing army which could react quickly to any incursions from the sea as well as a professional navy equipped with large sailing galleys called *dromons*. These were crewed by fifty to a hundred oarsmen and as many soldiers, far more than any Viking ship of the time, and had two masts carrying lateen sails, giving them a superior windward sailing ability compared to the square-rigged Viking longships. The *dromons* also carried catapults that could fire incendiary bombs filled with naphtha, something that Vikings had no defence against. From its main Atlantic naval base at Algeciras, the Moorish fleet controlled navigation through the Strait of Gibraltar. Björn Ironside's and Hastein's fleet was the only one to make it through the strait, but it didn't get out again unscathed. Additional naval bases at Silves, on the Algarve, and at Alcácer do Sal, near the mouth of the Tagus river, gave the emirate's Atlantic coast a high degree of security and were used to send fleets north to harass the coasts of the Christian kingdoms in Galicia and Asturias.

The first Atlantic slave trade

Taking captives for the slave trade was always one of the main objectives of Viking raids. In eastern Europe, it was the Slavs who they particularly targeted, and in the west it was the Irish, but the Vikings weren't fussy. From the 840s, the Norse established fortified bases on the Irish coast, chief among them Dublin, from which they launched their plundering and slaving raids on the

Irish, systematically milking Ireland of its surplus population for the next 200 years. It is impossible to quantify the scale of this trade, as no one kept statistics in those days, but if one raid on the Welsh island of Anglesey, which took 2,000 captives for the Dublin slave markets, was at all typical, the total number of victims trafficked by the Norse must have been at the very least in the hundreds of thousands. Among the many captives taken by Hastein and Björn Ironsides were some Black Africans, who they described as *blámenn* ('blue men') on account of their dark skins, and who had been brought across the Sahara to North Africa by Berber slave traders. The Vikings found a ready market for these exotic slaves in Ireland: they may well have been the first Black Africans to have been trafficked by sea on the Atlantic.

Dublin was one of Europe's premier slave markets, and it is very likely that it was frequented by continental slave traders looking for fair-skinned slaves to traffic to al-Andalus, which had the reputation as being the main supplier of eunuchs to the Islamic world. Following an unsuccessful attack on Seville in 844, the Vikings sought peace with the emir, Abd ar-Rahman II, who sent an embassy under the diplomat al-Ghazal to visit the king of the Majus ('fire worshippers'), as the Moors usually called the Norse on account of their paganism. According to the historian Ibn Dihyah (d. 1235), Al-Ghazal sailed north in his own ship but in company with a Norse longship, which acted as his guide. Al-Ghazal described the land of the Majus as a large and lush island, three days' journey from the continent. There were other islands in the vicinity which the king claimed that he ruled too. Before his audience, al-Ghazal insisted that he should not be asked to kneel before the king. The Majus readily agreed, but when he arrived at the king's hall he found that the entrance had been lowered so that he would be forced to enter on his knees. Thinking quickly, al-Ghazal preserved as much of his dignity as he could by lying on his back and pushing himself through the entrance feet first. The king's wife Noud apparently took a fancy to the exotic visitor and seduced him, assuring him that the Majus did not suffer from sexual jealousy. This was certainly not true:

had al-Ghazal been caught in the act, Noud's husband would have had the right to kill him on the spot. If this incident really happened, then al-Ghazal had probably only been introduced to a concubine rather than the king's wife. Unfortunately, neither the king nor the island are named in the surviving account, but the description most closely fits Ireland, which would have been the obvious place to go if the purpose of al-Ghazal's mission was to secure a regular supply of slaves. Al-Ghazal's mission was probably unsuccessful. The one thing the Norse most wanted from the Islamic world was the high-quality silver coins called dirhams. However, no coins from al-Andalus or North Africa have ever been found in Viking Age hoards in Ireland. Those Islamic coins that have been found in hoards, and they number only in the dozens, all come from Iraq, Armenia, Persia and central Asia, so most likely reached Ireland from Scandinavia via the river routes of eastern Europe. Irish slaves bound for Moorish markets were probably trafficked by continental middlemen, like the Radhaniya, rather than by direct maritime trade.

Reintegration

The Atlantic trade routes began to revive in the twelfth century as the Christian *Reconquista* gathered pace in the wake of a civil war which fragmented al-Andalus into over twenty petty kingdoms or *taifas*. The newly founded kingdom of Portugal began slowly chipping away at Moorish control of the Iberian coast, a landmark being the capture of Lisbon in 1147 with the support of a fleet of English and Flemish crusaders who stopped off to strike an early blow against the infidel on their way to the Holy Land. Following their catastrophic defeat by a grand alliance of Castile, Navarre and Aragon at the battle of Las Navas de Tolosa in 1212, the Moors' hold on Iberia began to collapse. By 1250, Moorish rule was restricted to the Emirate of Granada, which held out in the south behind the barrier of the 3,000-metre-high Sierra Nevada mountains. The capture of

Cádiz in 1262 and the fall of Tarifa, at the western entrance to the Strait of Gibraltar, in 1292 established Christian control of the whole of Iberia's Atlantic coast. Gibraltar itself fell in 1462. At the same time, the fleets of Aragon, Castile, Genoa and Venice won control of the Mediterranean, so the Moors could no longer prevent Christian shipping once again passing through the Strait of Gibraltar. In 1277, a Genoese merchant galley sailed direct to England for the first time, and by the early 1300s, both they and the Venetians were delivering alum (a dye fixative), cotton, wine, spices, silk and other Mediterranean and Asian products directly to England and Flanders. The butt of Malmsey wine that the future King Richard III's brother, George, Duke of Clarence, was reputedly drowned in in 1478 would have been delivered directly to London from Crete in a Venetian ship. On their return voyages, the Italians took such staples as wool, cloth, grain and fish. Because of this Christian dominance of the sea lanes, what was left of Moorish Spain had already been reintegrated into the Atlantic economy long before the 'Catholic Monarchs', Ferdinand and Isabella, completed the *Reconquista* with the surrender of Granada in 1492.

While the war fleets of al-Andalus did not survive the civil wars of the eleventh century, ports along what Europeans called the Barbary Coast (from Berber) of Morocco and Algeria continued to be used as bases for attacks on Christian shipping and *razzias* (slave raids), both in the Mediterranean and the Atlantic, some of them ranging as far north as Iceland. By the time they were finally suppressed in the early nineteenth century, it is estimated that around one and a quarter million Europeans had been enslaved by the Barbary pirates. The *razzias* didn't just go one way, of course: taking captives for the slave trade was considered to be a legitimate and profitable part of war by both sides. The Castilians, for example, enslaved over 3,000 people in a single raid on the notorious pirate port of Salé on Morocco's Atlantic coast in 1260. The ultimate remedy for the problem of Moorish piracy was, however, conquest. In 1415, the Portuguese, fired by crusading spirit, secured a foothold on the Moroccan side of the strait when they captured Ceuta (see Chapter 16, p. 429), but there would be no Christian *Reconquista* of North Africa. The Portuguese exploited their naval power to seize more ports, taking Ksar es-Seghir in 1458, and Tangier and Asilah in 1471. By 1505, Portugal held a chain of a dozen fortress-ports as far south along Morocco's Atlantic coast as Agadir: this the Portuguese liked to call the 'Berber Algarve'. However, all attempts to expand beyond these coastal enclaves were costly failures, and simply holding on to them was a constant drain on Portugal's resources. By the end of the seventeenth century, the Berber Algarve belonged to the Berbers again.

Muslim explorers

Our knowledge of Moorish seafaring is circumscribed to some extent by a lack of surviving sources. Al-Andalus's early Umayyad dynasty rulers fostered learning and built up well-stocked libraries in cities like Seville and Córdoba. Civil wars in the tenth century saw many of these libraries broken up, and then the invasion of the fundamentalist Almoravid dynasty of Morocco saw the deliberate destruction of manuscripts deemed un-Islamic. The final blow was struck by the Inquisition following the completion of the *Reconquista* in 1492, which ordered the burning of more than a million Arabic manuscripts in 1499.

Despite this, there are a few records of Moorish exploration in the Atlantic. The earliest was by a Moorish naval commander, Khashkhash ibn Sa'id ibn Aswad, who had led the fleet that had fought against Hastein and Björn on their way home from their great Mediterranean raid in 861. In his encyclopaedic world history *Meadows of Gold*, the Arab historian al-Masudi (896–956) wrote briefly about the expedition, which he believed took place around 869:

> In the ocean of fogs there are many curiosities which we have mentioned in detail in our Akhbar az-Zaman [News of our Era], on the basis of what we saw there, adventurers who

> penetrated it on the risk of their life, some returning safely, others perishing in the attempt. Thus a certain inhabitant of Cordoba, Khashkhash by name, assembled a group of young men, his co-citizens, and went on a voyage on this ocean.[36]

Khashkhash sailed from Palos de la Frontera, the port that Columbus would sail from in 1492, but al-Masudi gives no other details of his voyage other than that he visited an unknown land and that 'after a long time he returned with booty'. Al-Masudi added, helpfully, that 'their story is well known among the people of al-Andalus', so he obviously saw no point in writing it down again. Unfortunately, al-Masudi's *Akhbar as-Zaman* has not survived, but his casual reference here to other adventurers suggests that voyages of exploration were not that unusual.

The Seduced Ones in the Sea of Darkness

A more detailed and colourful account of a Muslim voyage of exploration in the Atlantic was written by the well-travelled Moorish geographer Muhammad al-Idrisi (1100–1165) in his *Kitab nuzhat al-mushtaq fi'khtiraq al-'afaq* ('The Book of Pleasant Journeys into Faraway Lands'), a compendious medieval equivalent of a coffee-table book for armchair travellers. Al-Idrisi describes the explorers as the Mugharrirun, which literally means the 'Seduced Ones' but is presumably a metaphor for having a sense of adventure rather than anything supernatural or sexual. The Mugharrirun, eighty in number, set out from Lisbon 'to sail the Sea of Darkness in order to discover what was in it and where it ended'. On a large, new, ship, provisioned for several months at sea,

> they set sail with the first gentle easterly and sailed for about eleven days, until they came to a sea with heavy waves, evil-smelling, ridden with reefs and with very little light. They were sure they were about to perish, so they changed course to the south and sailed for twelve days, until they came to Sheep

> Island. There were so many sheep it was impossible to count them, and they ranged freely, with no one to watch them. They landed and found a spring of flowing water and a wild fig tree beside it. They caught some of the sheep and slaughtered them, but the flesh was so bitter they could not eat it. They took some sheepskins and sailed on to the south for another twelve days until they sighted an island. They could see it was inhabited and under cultivation. They headed toward it in order to explore and when they were not far offshore, they suddenly found themselves surrounded by boats, which forced their ship to land beside a city on the shore. They saw the men who lived there; they were light-complexioned, with very little facial hair. The hair on their heads was lank. They were tall, and their womenfolk were very beautiful.

The adventurers were imprisoned for three days until an Arabic-speaking interpreter arrived and interrogated them about their origins and their expedition. Apparently satisfied by their answers, the interpreter assured them of his king's goodwill and told them not to worry. The next day, the adventurers were given an audience with the island's king, who asked them the same questions they'd been asked the day before by the interpreter:

> They told him what they had told the interpreter, of how they had embarked upon the ocean in order to find out about it and see the wonders it contained, and how they had come to this place. When the king heard this, he laughed and told the interpreter to tell them the following: 'My father ordered some of his slaves to sail this sea and they sailed across it for a month until there was no more light; they came back having found nothing of any use at all.' Then the king ordered the interpreter to treat them well so they would have a good impression of the kingdom, and he did so. They were then taken back to their place of confinement until the west wind began to blow. A boat was prepared for them, their eyes were bound, and they were at sea for some time. They said: 'We were at sea about

20. Part of a hoard of ninety-three walrus ivory chess pieces discovered on the Hebridean island of Lewis in 1831. Dating to the twelfth century, the pieces were probably carved in Norway.

21. The foundations of the chieftain's longhouse at the short-lived Norse settlement at L'Anse aux Meadows, Newfoundland, the only proven evidence of pre-Columbian contact with America.

22. The ruins of Hvalsey church in the Norse Eastern Settlement in Greenland. A wedding held here in 1408 is the last documented event in the history of the Norse Greenland settlement.

23. This seal from the Baltic Hanseatic port of Stralsund, dated 1329, shows a cog, the sturdy, slow, capacious cargo ship that helped the Hanseatic League achieve commercial domination in Northern Europe.

24. The Hereford Mappa Mundi (*c.*1300) is a typical medieval T and O world map, with Jerusalem at the centre and east at the top. The T is the Mediterranean and the Nile separating the three known continents of Asia, Africa and Europe.

25. A stockfish drying rack in the Lofoten Islands. Stockfish (air-dried cod) was Norway's most important export in the Middle Ages.

26. A portolan chart made in 1439 by the Majorcan cartographer Gabriel de Vallseca. The chart shows the latest Portuguese discoveries along the African coast and the Madeira and Azores archipelagos.

27. A Portuguese caravel from a sixteenth-century manuscript. The caravel's lateen sails allowed it to sail closer to the wind than a square-rigged ship, making it well suited to exploring unknown coasts.

28. A sixteenth-century mariner's compass housed in a turned ivory case. The widespread adoption of the mariner's compass in late medieval Europe began the age of instrument-led navigation.

29. A mariner's astrolabe from *c.*1600. Introduced in the late fifteenth century, the mariner's astrolabe enabled seafarers to take accurate measurements of the altitude of stars and the sun.

30. Seal of the French Basque Country po of Biarritz (1351) showing a whale-huntin scene. The Basques were the first Europear to hunt whales on the open sea.

31. A well-preserved Basque *txalupa* whale boat) recovered from the sixteenth-century Basque whaling station at Red Bay, Labrador.

32. The *Matthew*, a modern replica of a fifteenth-century carrack, a type of ship used by many explorers including Columbus, Cabot, da Gama and Magellan.

33. The conquistador Alonso Fernández de Lugo accepts the submission of the Guanche kings of Tenerife in 1496, as depicted in a painting in the *ayuntamiento* building of San Cristóbal de La Laguna.

34. Plan of San Cristóbal de La Laguna, founded in 1496 as the first Spanish capital of Tenerife and, later, the Canary Islands. The city's grid plan became the template for Spanish colonial cities in the Americas.

35. The Infante Dom Henrique, commonly known as Prince Henry the Navigator, portrayed on the São Vicente de Fora altarpiece. Dom Henrique was the prime instigator of the Portuguese age of exploration.

36. Posthumous portrait of the Genoese explorer Christopher Columbus by the Italian artist Sebastiano del Piombo (1519 Columbus' voyage in 1492 began the modern age.

37. The oldest extant European building in sub-Saharan Africa, Elmina Castle, in present-day Ghana, built by the Portuguese in 1482 as a base from which they hoped to monopolise the West African gold trade.

38. A replica of the *padrão* erected at Cape Cross in Namibia erected by Diogo Cão in 1485. The Portuguese used *padrãos* to mark their progress and act as landmarks for the seafarers who came after them.

39. The frontispiece for Francis Bacon's *Novum Organum* (1620), showing a galleon sailing between the Pillars of Hercules, celebrates the geographical and scientific discoveries of his age.

> three days and nights. Then we came to the mainland and they put us ashore. They tied us up and left us there. When dawn broke and the sun rose, we found we were in great pain because we had been so tightly bound. Then we heard noises and the sound of people and we all cried out. Some people approached and, seeing our difficulty, released us. They asked us what had happened and we told them the whole story. They were Berbers. One of them asked us: 'Do you know how far you are from your country?' 'No,' we answered. 'Two months' journey!' he replied. Our leader said, 'Wa asafi!' (Woe is me!') and to this day the place is known as Asfi (Safi, Morocco).[37]

Apart from the first and last places in the account, it is impossible to identify any of the places the adventurers visited with certainty, although the sailing directions and times would fit reasonably well with a voyage from Lisbon to the Azores, where we know that someone had introduced livestock in the early Middle Ages (see Chapter 6), on to the Canary Islands, where they had an encounter with the Guanche, and a return to Morocco. Elsewhere, al-Idrisi says that near Sheep Island there is another island called Raqa. Large, fig-like fruits which grow there are an antidote to all known poisons, he says. The island is also home to a large red bird like an eagle which catches fish with its claws. It may be no more than a coincidence, but the Azores are named after a species of goshawk, called an açor in Portuguese, which lived in the islands at the time of their discovery. At some time in the past, al-Idrisi says, the king of the Franks had sent an expedition to the island to bring back some of the figs and the birds but that it never returned. Al-Idrisi does not give a date for the expedition, but his account follows a brief mention of an abortive expedition to the Canary Islands ordered by Ali ibn Yusuf ibn Tashfin (r. 1061–1106), the Almoravid emir of Morocco. Ibn Tashfin wanted to investigate distant sightings of smoke, probably from an erupting Canarian volcano, west of the Moroccan coast, but he died before his fleet was ready to sail. This would mean that the voyage of the Mugharrirun took place in the first half of the twelfth century, between the death of ibn Tashfin in 1106 and the fall of Lisbon to the Portuguese in 1147.

The 27,000 phantom islands

All the familiar terrors of the Classical Atlantic are there in al-Idrisi's account, while the miraculous fruits and the Mugharrirun's mysterious blindfold journey home has distinct echoes of Irish *immrama*. As well as being aware of Classical accounts of the Atlantic, it seems likely that the Moors had also heard tales of Otherworldly Atlantic islands from Irish slaves or the Norse. There are Otherworldly echoes, too, in another of al-Idrisi's works, the *Tabula Rogeriana*, the famous world atlas that he compiled for his Christian patron King Roger II of Sicily. A note in this atlas says that one day's sail west of Iceland is *Irlandah-al-Kabirah*, 'Great Ireland'. While this may refer to Greenland, in Irish myth, Great Ireland is an Otherworldly island, the same island as the Hvítramannaland of the Vinland sagas (see Chapter 9, p. 273). Certainly, al-Idrisi's work reveals that the Islamic Atlantic was not short of phantom islands – there were 27,000 of them altogether, he says. Thankfully, Al-Idrisi spares his readers from information overload and only names those that he says are close to Africa. Some of them have meaningful names, while others can't be translated. These islands included Sawa, which was inhabited by hostile natives who pelted Alexander the Great with stones when he landed on the island during his campaigns. The Island of Demons (al-Suali) was populated by ferocious demonic asexual humans with protruding canine teeth, who fought sea monsters and wore clothing made of leaves. Hasran was high and mountainous and inhabited by short brown-skinned people with big ears who ate grass. Al-Ghawr was a long, broad, well-watered island, lush with vegetation, inhabited by donkeys and long-horned cattle but apparently no people. Qalhan's inhabitants were animal-headed people who swam in the sea to catch fish.

Seals, perhaps? Not far from the Moroccan coast was the Island of the Two Brothers. These were Shirham and Shiram, whom God had turned to stone to punish them for piracy. Laqa was an island known for its scented aloe trees. Merchants visited this island to harvest their deep-black wood, which they sold to kings in the far west, al-Idrisi says. The island used to be inhabited, but its cities had fallen into ruin and now no one could land there because of an infestation of serpents. It has been suggested that Laqa was Madeira, but Madeira is snake-free and aloes are not native to any of the Atlantic islands. Perhaps the strangest of these phantom islands is the Isle of Lamentations (al-Mustashkin), a large, fertile and mountainous island with rivers, orchards, cultivated fields and a town with high walls, whose inhabitants were terrorized by a dragon, which they duly appeased with sacrifices of bulls, donkeys and even humans. The townsfolk appealed for help to Alexander the Great when he visited the island. Alexander fed the dragon an explosive mixture and blew it to pieces. It's a surprise to find Alexander the Great exploring the Atlantic when in life he never went anywhere near it. However, in Islamic tradition, Alexander had been transformed into a legendary superhero figure who often replaced Heracles and other Classical mythological figures in fantastic travel tales. The ultimate source of this dragon-slaying story might be Heracles' mythological quest to steal the Golden Apples of the Hesperides, in one version of which he killed a dragon called Ladon.

Between legend and geography

The Guanches were deadly accurate stone-throwers, so Sawa may have been one of the Canary Islands – so too the Isle of Lamentations, as well as the nameless island visited by the Mugharrirun. After the end of Roman rule in the west, awareness of the Canaries had faded again, so that for Muslim geographers they existed in the twilight zone between legend and reality.

The Arabic name for the islands, 'The Eternal Isles' (*Jaza'ir al-Khalidat*), suggests that they were equated with the Fortunate Isles, in line with the Classical geographers whose works they had inherited. Some Arabic writers clearly still regarded the islands as existing on the darker side of the twilight. Many repeated a story that on each of the islands there was a mysterious pillar, like those at Cádiz, inscribed with a message warning seafarers to go no further. Al-Idrisi too begins his account of the islands with legends. Alexander the Great visited them, he tells us, and on one of them lies the marble and polychrome glass tomb of an ancient king, but he also possessed some real geographical knowledge. Two of the Eternal Isles are named as Masfahan and Laghus on his world map: Masfahan has a high, round mountain at its centre, so is probably Tenerife, with its 3,600-metre-high volcano, Pico de Teide. Laghus may be Gran Canaria. Unlike the names of many of his phantom islands, these names are not Arabic, nor are they corruptions of Greek or Latin names. They may, therefore, be authentic, either the names used by Berber seafarers, who, al-Idrisi says, occasionally visited the islands to buy 'amber',* or by the Guanches who lived there. Andalusian merchants are known to have sailed regularly down the Moroccan coast as far as Massa, a small port at the end of one of the trans-Saharan caravan routes about 60 kilometres south of Agadir. Might they have sailed further and visited the Canary Islands? An eighteenth-century Spanish history of the islands claims that an Andalusian merchant called ibn Farrukh visited the islands in 999, while the fifteenth-century Castilian chronicler Alvar García de Santa María claimed that the great Moorish general Almanzor had even conquered them. However, neither of these stories, though often repeated, are based on any known Arabic sources. They feel more like political legends, invented to justify Spanish claims to the islands as a continuation of the *Reconquista*, than authentic traditions. At least the

* Probably the red resin, used as a pigment, known as dragon's blood, obtained from the Canary Islands dragon tree, *Dracaena draco*.

emir Yusuf ibn Tashfin regarded the islands as real places that could be conquered, but perhaps the fact that his planned expedition was abandoned the moment he was dead suggests that, for many Moors, they retained a lingering Otherworldly aura as a place best left well alone.

Apart from a dubious folk tale about a seafarer called ibn Fatima who was supposedly shipwrecked on the Ras Nouadhibou peninsula in Mauretania *c.*1200, there is no evidence at all that Arab or Berber seafarers ever ventured south of the Canary Islands. It's fair to ask, why not? The adverse winds and currents are certainly part of the answer. The Arabs regarded the cape they called Abu Khatar, the 'Father of Danger', as the point of no return for coastal navigation. In Spanish, Abu Khatar became Boxador and in Portuguese, Bojador, the name by which it is most widely known today. Cape Bojador (26° 08' north), on the coast of Moroccan-occupied Western Sahara, is where the southwest-trending coast of North Africa takes a sharp turn to the south-southwest. For something that inspired so much fear, the cape is nothing much to look at; before a lighthouse was built on the cape in 1903 it was hard to spot from the sea because it lies low on a uniformly low-lying coast. That was part of its dangers. Offshore from the cape, the sea is shallow, with dangerous reefs and sandbanks extending as much as 5 kilometres out. However, shipwrecks weren't what made the cape notorious. South of the cape, the Trade Winds blow relentlessly to the west, out to sea, and the ocean currents too are against a seafarer trying to sail north along the African coast. A ship which rounded the cape from the north, it was believed, would never make it back. The cape was seen as a point of no return, the southern edge of the known world, for centuries, making it a psychological as much as a physical barrier for Muslim and Christian seafarers alike.

The fearsome cape probably wasn't the only factor. In ancient times, the only easy overland trade route between tropical Africa and the Mediterranean was along the Nile valley to Egypt. The long distances between oases made travel across the Sahara Desert arduous and hazardous, limiting direct contacts between the

Mediterranean and tropical West Africa. The introduction of camels to the desert around 100 BC changed that in a big way. Tropical West Africa had much to offer that was in demand in the Mediterranean world, chief among them gold dust, ivory, ebony wood, gum, melegueta pepper and slaves. Very quickly, trans-Saharan caravan routes developed, carrying West African products north to the Maghrib and returning with glass beads, pottery, textiles, copper, exotic seashells (used as currency), horses, salt and foodstuffs. Portuguese explorers of the fifteenth century were surprised to discover that the caravaneers used the stars and the magnetic compass to navigate the desert, just as if they had been at sea. Berber and Tuareg nomads, thanks to their intimate knowledge of the desert, were the natural middlemen in this trade, and, for as long as no one would sail around Cape Bojador, the Moorish emirates of the Maghreb had a monopoly on the onward distribution of West African products to Mediterranean and European markets. There was no incentive to challenge this status quo, so why take risks? Indeed, like the Phoenicians before them, it was very much in their interests that terrifying stories about the Atlantic continued to circulate. Some of the wilder stories of what lay beyond Cape Bojador probably originated with the Berbers. The sea beyond the cape literally boiled in the scorching wind blowing from the Sahara. Even more lurid was the rumour that the ocean was made of blood. This story, at least, had some foundation: sandstorms blowing from the desert sometimes dump iron-rich dust into the Atlantic, turning it a reddish colour. On account of these stories, coupled with the very real and well-known problems of the adverse winds and currents, Muslim seafarers gave the cape a wide berth, regarding Ras Barsig (29° 16' north), 600 kilometres northeast, in Morocco, as the safe limit for navigation: the Portuguese knew it as Cabo do Não, 'Cape No'.

Muslim navigators from the Indian Ocean showed the same lack of interest in pushing the bounds of navigation along the East African coast. For medieval Muslims, the starting point of geographical knowledge was Ptolemy's world map, which showed Africa extending so far south that it closed off the Atlantic from direct sea communication with the Indian Ocean. If this was true, there would be no point in trying to sail around Africa from the east. However, Ptolemy's geography was not unchallenged. Al-Biruni, for one, believed that the Indian and the Atlantic oceans joined south of Africa, 'for traces of such a junction have been discovered, even though no one has actually seen it'. By the fifteenth century, at the latest, there were Indian Ocean navigators who believed that they had actually seen such a junction. In the notes to his world map of 1450, the Venetian cartographer Fra Mauro (*c.*1400–1464), who believed that the two oceans were connected, mentions two stories he had heard from travellers in the east to support his opinion:

> Around 1420 a *çoncho* [junk] from India crossed the Sea of India towards the Island of Men and the Island of Women, off Cape Diab [Madagascar], between the Green Islands and the shadows. It sailed for forty days in a south-westerly direction without ever finding anything other than wind and water. According to these people themselves, the ship went some 2,000 *miglia* [Italian miles*] ahead until, once favourable conditions came to an end, it turned around and sailed back to Cape Diab in seventy days …

'What is more,' Fra Mauro added,

> I have spoken with a person worthy of trust, who says that he sailed in an Indian ship caught in the fury of a tempest for forty days out in the Sea of India, beyond the Cape of Sofala and the Green Islands towards west-southwest; and according to the astrologers who act as their guides, they had advanced almost 2,000 *miglia*. Thus one can believe and confirm what is said by both these and those, and that they had therefore sailed 4,000 *miglia* …[38]

* An Italian mile was about two thirds of an English statute mile.

So far west that they must have sailed into the Atlantic.

But if Indian Ocean seafarers believed that Africa could be circumnavigated, why didn't they try? The reasons are probably much the same as those that explain why seafarers from Muslim North Africa didn't try to round Cape Bojador. If the Atlantic was the edge of the world, the Indian Ocean was its centre, its merchants and seafarers the world's middlemen. The Mediterranean was separated from the Red Sea only by a 160-kilometre caravan route, so what possible use would a new trade route around Africa be to them? The main maritime trade route along the East African coast terminated at Sofala, the main port of trade with the gold-rich inland kingdoms of Great Zimbabwe and Mwenemutapa. Another 200 kilometres south from Sofala there was the Indian Ocean's equivalent of Cape Bojador to contend with, Cape Correntes on Mozambique's Inhambane peninsula. Like Cape Bojador, Cape Correntes looks quite innocuous: its dangers are a consequence of a convergence of strong winds, which stir up unpredictable sea conditions, and the south-flowing Mozambique current, which was so strong that sailing ships found it difficult to make headway against it. The fears were not unfounded; in the sixteenth century, the Portuguese regarded the cape as the most dangerous coast in the Indian Ocean, and many galleons were wrecked there. The far south of Africa was known to be inhabited only by Stone Age Khoisan herders and hunter-gatherers, so there were no trading opportunities there that would repay the risks of sailing further south, so Cape Correntes became the Indian Ocean's point of no return, somewhere to be passed only by accident.

Pre-colonial West Africa and the Atlantic

Between the two points of no return, it was only on the tropical West African coast between the Senegal river and the Volta river in modern Ghana that there were any seafaring traditions before the arrival of Europeans in the fifteenth century. It is easy to see why seafaring was so limited from a quick glance at a map of Africa. The eye traces the outline of the west coast quickly: there is a profound shortage of the deep bays, inlets, navigable estuaries, inland seas and offshore archipelagos that in other parts of the world encouraged the early development of seafaring traditions. On long stretches of the coast, access to the open sea is made difficult by mangrove swamps. Others are pounded by persistent heavy surf, further discouraging seafaring. Fishermen set out from the few favourable coasts to exploit the rich inshore fisheries, but they were careful always to stay within sight of land. The few islands that could be seen from the mainland, such as Guinea-Bissau's Bijagós archipelago or the large volcanic island of Bioko, 30 kilometres off the coast of Cameroon, were all settled in prehistory. Those African islands that lay hidden beyond the horizon – the Cape Verde Islands, São Tomé, Príncipe and Annobón – all remained unknown, unvisited and uninhabited until the arrival of the Portuguese in the late fifteenth century. The empty ocean promised only death by drowning or thirst. It was a different story on inland waterways, however. Dense forest made overland travel arduous, and all loads had to be carried by human porters: draught animals such as cattle and horses could not survive for long in the region because of the prevalence of the tsetse fly, which carried fatal trypanosomiasis ('sleeping sickness'). Under these circumstances, the only practical way to transport large loads, and for large groups to travel, was by boat on rivers and coastal lagoons.

Early European visitors to tropical West Africa described the boats they encountered there as 'pirogues', in other words dugout canoes. This hardly does them justice: some very large trees grew in the coastal rainforest, and they were used to make impressively large canoes. In the Niger river delta and on the Senegal river, canoes of over 20 metres in length, capable of carrying as many as 120 people, were not unusual. Some of those used by royalty had cabins and, after the Portuguese introduced gunpowder weapons, even mounted small cannon. The small canoes that were commonly used for fishing on sheltered coastal lagoons and rivers were simple vessels that did not require specialized skills to build. However, building the larger canoes that were used for transport, for war parties and for fishing on the open sea was a job for professionals. The main part of the hull was roughed out in the forest, wherever the tree was felled. Construction began by hollowing out the tree trunk using adzes and fire until the bottom of the boat was about two finger breadths thick and the sides about one finger breadth thick. The hull was then floated downriver to the coast for fitting out. There, the freeboard was increased by fitting extra planks to the sides of the hull. Internal ribs were added to strengthen the hull and thwarts were fitted for the crew to sit or stand on while they paddled the boat. Boats intended for use at sea were built with higher prows and sterns so they could ride through the heavy coastal surf without getting swamped. These surf boats, superbly well designed for this purpose, became essential tenders for transporting trade goods and slaves between the shore and European merchant ships anchored off the coast well into the twentieth century.

On great white wings

Before the arrival of Europeans, the only reason for going on the open sea was to fish. Sea fishing was a daytime activity that took advantage of the reliable daily shifts in wind direction. It made sense for the boats to head out in the early morning, when the crew had the land breeze behind them, and then return to shore in the early evening with the sea breeze. The fishermen never ventured more than about 15 kilometres out to sea, well within sight of land. Fishermen who found themselves out at sea at night used rudimentary stellar navigation to get their bearings. The Pole Star is too low in the sky in the equatorial regions to be a useful guide, so fishermen used their own choice of seasonally prominent stars. There was a limited amount of short-distance trade along the coast, most of it taking advantage of the sheltered lagoons which run parallel to the open sea in many areas.

The main limiting factor for open-sea sailing was the lack of sails. The Venetian explorer and merchant Alvise da Cadamosto (also known as Alvise da Cà da Mosto), sailing in the service of the Portuguese crown in 1455, reported that when their ships were first sighted along the coast of Mauretania, the inhabitants thought they were seeing 'great white wings' or ghosts: they had never seen anything like a sailing ship before. Had there been direct maritime contacts with the Moorish kingdoms in North Africa, they most certainly would already have been familiar with sailing ships. Further south at Cayor in Senegal, Cadamosto wrote that the people 'were struck with admiration by the construction of our ship, and by her equipment – masts, sails, rigging and anchors', all of which they were unfamiliar with. In Gambia in the following year, Cadamosto reported that a local man who came onboard his ship marvelled 'at the method of navigating by means of sails, for they knew of no method except rowing their canoes with paddles and considered no other way possible … all their navigation is by means of paddles'. At the Geba river in Guinea, he found, again, that people were mystified by his ship's mast and yards: 'they did not know what they were, nor their use'. West Africans were equally mystified by the ability of the Portuguese to navigate out of sight of land, initially regarding it as a form of witchcraft. West African boat-builders and seamen soon took to the new technology and began to rig masts and sails, made of cloth or rush matting, to their seagoing canoes. Fishermen were able to sail three times further offshore to fish and still return to shore by nightfall, and longer coastal trading trips became possible. West African seamen learned about the Atlantic coast while serving as crewmen on European ships and later exploited this knowledge to embark on their own trading voyages in seagoing canoes. Traders from Ghana sometimes travelled as far as Angola, a distance of around 2,500 kilometres. Such voyages took weeks and had to be carefully prepared for. The Ghanaians took as their staple food hard baked biscuits, like the hardtack carried on European ships, that would keep for up to four months if necessary.

Sandwiched between the Atlantic to the south and the Sahara Desert to the north, the peoples of tropical West Africa had little awareness of the wider world before the arrival of Europeans in the fifteenth century. The new knowledge they brought about other populated lands that existed beyond the ocean challenged West African cosmological beliefs. Before European contact, West Africans generally believed in a flat Earth in which the land lay within an encircling ocean. The Yoruba of modern Nigeria, for example, believed that the ocean had once covered the whole world until the ancestral creator god Oduduwa came down from Heaven and created dry land in the middle of the water. This was a closed world, conceived of as the inside of a hollowed-out calabash (bottle gourd), the upper half being the sky and the lower half the sea, with the land floating in between. The horizon was the place where the ocean and the sky met: there was nothing beyond. Most West African peoples had gods or goddesses, such as the Yoruba goddess Yemoja, who were associated with watery places in general, but deities linked exclusively with the sea seem to have been rare, a sign of its relative lack of importance in their lives. The Atlantic began to loom much larger in West Africans' religious beliefs as they evolved in response to their contacts with the Europeans: in a cosmological sense, they were discovering the Atlantic for the first time, as it was vaster and mightier than they had ever imagined. The ocean became central to the economy of the whole region. It carried great wealth to West Africa, but it also carried people away through the growing slave trade. To the Kongo people, who believed that water separated the land of the dead from the land of the living, the slave trade represented a kind of witchcraft which transported living people prematurely to a land of the dead beyond the Atlantic, which was not really so far from the truth. The white people who took them there were initially believed to be the returning spirits of previously deceased Africans. In several West African societies, the sea itself was deified and became closely associated with the wealth that trade brought. The sea wasn't seen simply as a passive medium that the Europeans sailed over; it had agency in bringing them to Africa. A rough sea now meant more than a halt to fishing. In Benin and Yorubaland, the god Olokun, 'the owner of the sea', was believed to have rich storehouses in his palace beneath its waters. He was appeased with sacrifices so that rough seas would not disrupt the profitable trade with the Europeans. Such customs were widespread, and in Dahomey, the sea was even offered human sacrifices. There was always some ambiguity to the Atlantic: there was opportunity there, and danger.

The tropical coast's flat-Earth world view was not shared throughout West Africa. In the eighth century, Berber merchants from the Maghreb introduced the Islamic religion to the caravan cities on the Sahel, the dry and dusty savannah region that lay between the forested tropical coast and the Sahara Desert. Some of these cities, like Timbuktu in Mali, became noted centres of Islamic learning that drew scholars from the wider Islamic world. Along with the religious texts came works of Islamic astronomy, mathematics, philosophy, medicine and geography, some of which were even translated into local languages such as Songhay and Wolof. Ironically, in the heart of the Sahel, far from the sea, the educated elite, at least, shared the same understanding of the Atlantic Ocean as the rest of the Islamic and Christian worlds and could conceive that it had bounds and that there might be other, inhabited lands within it or beyond it.

To discover the furthest limit of the ocean

In 1325, the Arab historian Ibn Fadlallah al-Umari met the *Mansa* ('emperor') Kankan Musa (r. 1312–37) of Mali in Cairo when he was returning from a pilgrimage to Mecca. Mali controlled the trans-Saharan gold trade, and Musa was so fabulously rich that he was said to use a boulder of solid gold as a hitching post for his horse. When he passed through Cairo on his outward journey to Mecca, he gave away so much gold as alms to the poor that it devalued the local currency and sparked an inflation crisis. During their meeting, Musa told al-Umari many stories, including a tale of Atlantic exploration. 'The king who was my predecessor [Muhammad ibn Qu] believed that it was possible to discover the furthest limit of the ocean and wished vehemently to do so,' Musa told al-Umari,

> so he equipped 200 ships filled with men and the same number equipped with gold, water, and provisions enough to last them for many years, and said to the man deputed to lead them: 'Do not return until you reach the end of it or your provisions and water give out.' They departed and a long time passed before anyone came back. Then one ship returned and we asked the captain what news they brought. He said: 'Yes, O Sultan, we traveled for a long time until there appeared in the open sea as it were a river with a powerful current. Mine was the last of those ships. The other ships went on ahead but when they reached that place they did not return and no more was seen of them and we do not know what became of them. As for me, I went about at once and did not enter that river.' But the sultan disbelieved him. Then that sultan got ready two thousand ships, one thousand for himself and the men whom he took with him and one thousand for water and provisions. He left me to deputize for him and embarked on the ocean with his men. That was the last we saw of him and all those who were with him, and so I became king in my own right.[39]

The story is obviously an audacious and imaginative justification of a successful usurpation of power, but it has inevitably attracted claims of a pre-Columbian African discovery of America. This is about as credible as Musa's claim that his predecessor conveniently disappeared at sea: the Mali Empire lacked the technology necessary for oceanic voyaging.

13

The Fish Event Horizon

1000–1500

The cure for lust – Hjeller and skrei – The Norwegian stockfish trade – The Hanseatic League – The Baltic herring trade – The ordeal of Pietro Querini – Cogs and cargoes – Bigger and better: the carrack – Pirate brotherhoods – The legend of Willem Beuckelszoon – The first factory ships – England's first oceanic trade route – Cod wars

Garbage, kitchen middens, shell mounds – the ancient leftovers of people's meals have featured frequently in this book so far. Archaeologists are not joking when they describe their discipline as 'the science of rubbish'. Revealing details about a population's diet, health, technology and trade links, the contents of an ancient midden or latrine can reveal a lot more about the human past than any number of Indiana Jones-style crystal skulls and the like, eye-catching though they might be. It was by patiently sifting the leftovers of Norse and Anglo-Saxon meals that archaeologists discovered the 'Fish Event Horizon', a sudden increase in the amount of marine foods eaten by medieval Europeans. This new appetite, fed by stockfish (air-dried cod) and salted herrings, sent more ships than ever before out into the North Atlantic, driving the advances in shipbuilding, geographical knowledge and navigational skills that were needed for successful oceanic exploration.

The cure for lust

The rising demand for fish in medieval Europe is usually explained by the papal ban on Christians eating meat on holy days, of which there were certainly rather a lot, at around 166 a year. The theological rationale for this was that the flesh of warm-blooded terrestrial mammals was considered to be a 'hot' food which might, therefore, turn a person's thoughts to sex when they should really be thinking about God. Because they lived their lives in water, fish were considered to be 'cold' foods, passion-killers, which could safely be eaten on holy days without the risk that it would excite inappropriate lustful thoughts. This idea of fish as a cure for lust became part of popular culture. In Germany, it was jokingly said that the best way to ensure that an amorous young woman kept her virginity until she was married was to salt her down like a preserved herring.

The religious ban on meat-eating doubtless does have a lot to do with the demand for fish, but it can't be the whole story, because abstinence on holy days had been part of Christian practice since the earliest days of the church. Most people in medieval Europe were peasant subsistence farmers who couldn't afford to eat much meat anyway, and if they couldn't afford meat they couldn't afford fish either, because it was even more expensive. The most important factor is probably rising prosperity in western Europe. In the eleventh century, Europe turned a corner, finally putting the instability and economic stagnation of the post-Roman years behind it. In the four or five centuries that followed, Europeans laid the economic, technological and cultural foundations of the global dominance they would achieve in the modern period. Key to this were agricultural improvements, such as the three-field system of crop rotation and the heavy plough, which increased food production and supported a fast-growing urban population. Townspeople – merchants, craftsmen, shopkeepers and innkeepers – were the nearest thing medieval Europe had to a middle class, between the hard-up peasant majority and the wealthy landowners. These were aspirational people with a bit of money to spare, to wear professionally woven cloth rather than homespun, and to eat a more varied and high-status diet than the peasant staples of bread and pottage. And if you could eat fish on a holy day, all the better – you could be conspicuously virtuous and still have a good dinner. It wasn't just fish that was increasingly in demand. Prosperous urbanites also fuelled a boom in the cloth trade and a boom in demand for other luxury foods such as exotic spices from Asia, while all classes of townsfolk needed everyday staples such as grain, which had to be imported from increasingly far away, as the growing towns outpaced the surrounding countryside's ability to feed them. Trade links multiplied like new synapses in a growing neural net, creating an international network which, by the end of the fifteenth century, would outgrow Europe and spread across the entire planet. Humble codfish bones in urban middens mark when it all started.

Hjeller and *skrei*

Stockfish was first produced in Arctic Norway's rugged Lofoten Islands archipelago. Though the trade is not what it was before the invention of refrigerated transport made fresh fish widely available, the large, tent-shaped timber frames which are used to dry the cod can still be seen around the outskirts of the islands' fishing villages. These frames are called *hjeller* or, in English, stocks or fish flakes. It's these that have given stockfish its name, 'stick fish'. In the brief Arctic summer, the frames are usually bare and their purpose isn't immediately obvious, but in the late winter they are crowded with codfish hanging by their tails to dry in the wind. The cod are caught in winter and early spring when they migrate a thousand kilometres south from their summer feeding grounds in the Barents Sea to spawning grounds in the North Atlantic off the islands' coasts, close enough to the shore that they can be caught from small inshore fishing boats using hooked lines and landed onshore for processing on the same day.

Cod caught at this time of year, known in Norway as *skrei*, is ideal for drying: because the fish don't feed on their migration, their flesh is almost fat-free; they're just protein and water (oily fish like herrings are unsuitable for drying).

Once landed, the fish are headed and gutted and split along the backbone as far as the tail before being hung on the *hjeller* to dry. This method of preparation helps archaeologists studying cod bones from ancient middens to determine whether they most likely come from locally caught fresh fish or imported stockfish. In the Middle Ages, fresh fish were sold whole, so the presence of head bones in the assemblage likely indicates that the bone came from a locally caught fish, whereas if head bones are absent, it's likely to be stockfish. Winter conditions in the Lofoten Islands are ideal for drying cod. The humidity of the cold winter air is lower than it is in summer, and the temperature on the coast, very mild for the latitude, critically, hovers mostly around freezing point. The fish repeatedly freeze at night and thaw slightly during the day, allowing them to dry slowly without starting to rot or lose their nutritional value. Once drying is complete, the stockfish is as hard as board, almost odourless, and, so long as it is kept dry, can be stored for several years. The process is extremely economical; in warmer climates, most fish preservation methods require the use of substantial amounts of salt, an expensive commodity in the Middle Ages. However, any stockfish that are not thoroughly dried by the end of April will be spoiled because, as soon as the weather grows warmer, they begin to decay and can become infested by insects. Raw stockfish was a staple food for Viking Age seafarers on long open-sea voyages, when cooking was impossible for days on end: it is chewy, like a kind of fish jerky, and not strongly flavoured. Preparing a cooked meal with stockfish requires advance planning, because it must first be rehydrated by soaking in cold, fresh water. For a large fish, this can take a few days, so it's not exactly convenience food. According to some medieval recipes, battering the stockfish with a hammer for an hour or so before soaking speeded up the rehydration process. Once cooked, the rehydrated stockfish has a firmer texture and a slightly stronger flavour than fresh cod. Because of the lack of refrigeration, fresh fish had a very short shelf-life in medieval Europe, and the only people who got to eat it either lived near the sea or owned a private fish pond. Easily transported and easily stored, stockfish made fish available to the masses.

The Norwegian stockfish trade

The stockfish trade began during the Viking Age, perhaps initially as a sideline for merchants from Arctic Norway who would be carrying the stuff with them on their ships anyway as provisions. The earliest archaeological evidence that stockfish was being traded outside Arctic Norway comes from the important Viking Age port of Hedeby, at the neck of the Jutland peninsula near Schleswig. Hedeby is now in Germany but was then part of the kingdom of the Danes. Cod bones are plentiful in the town's ninth- to eleventh-century middens. To learn whether the fish these bones came from were being caught locally in the Baltic or the North Sea, researchers extracted aDNA from them and compared it to the DNA of modern cod populations in the Barents Sea, the North Atlantic around Iceland, the North Sea and the Baltic Sea. The aDNA most closely matched that of the Barents Sea cod, proving that the fish were not caught locally and, therefore, must have been imported as stockfish.

The thirteenth-century *Egil's Saga* describes how Thorolf Kveldulfsson, a Norwegian chieftain from Hålogaland, sent merchant ships to England with cargoes of stockfish around 875, but this might be an anachronism. By the time the saga was written, stockfish was north Norway's main export, and this might well have influenced the author's idea of what a Viking Age Norwegian merchant ship would be carrying on a voyage to England. Ottar, the merchant from Arctic Norway who visited King Alfred around 890, gave his host a long list of the commodities he traded in, and stockfish wasn't one of them. The earliest hard evidence that stockfish was being exported to England comes from middens, again, this time in the south-coast port of Southampton. Archaeologists discovered that there was a change in the species of fish eaten in the town around 1030. Before that date, the townspeople were eating locally caught fish such as eels, and after that it was cod. A generation earlier, the English didn't even have a word for cod (probably derived from *gadus*, the Latin word for cod). Londoners enjoyed a similar change of diet around the same time, and by 1225, Norwegian stockfish had almost completely squeezed locally caught fish out of the market. While it's clear that marine foods never became a major part of the medieval English diet, the increase in consumption was marked enough to be detectable through isotope analysis of human bones from several cemeteries in Yorkshire. This change of diet happened not only in England; it was mirrored across western Europe, and there too, much of the demand was met by Norwegian stockfish.

Stockfish was exported through the port of Bergen, from the twelfth century, Norway's leading royal and commercial centre. To modern eyes, Bergen's position out on the west coast looks isolated, but medieval Norway was a land linked by the sheltered coastal sea routes through its barrier of offshore archipelagos and skerries, the 'North Way' from which the country gets its name, not by overland travel, which was impossible for much of the year. This west-coast location made Bergen an extraordinarily well-connected and accessible place, a good base for mercantile voyages west across the North Atlantic to the Norse colonies in the Faeroes, Iceland and Greenland, north to the Arctic and southwest to Scotland, England, Ireland and Germany. The Norwegian kings built their main residence, the Bergenhus castle, where it could dominate Bergen's harbour: tolls and taxes on the trade made an important contribution to the growth of royal government.

The English were the most prominent foreign merchants trading at Bergen for much of the twelfth century, but by the end of that century, increasing numbers of Germans were turning up. The English brought cloth and grain to trade for stockfish, and the Germans brought wine. The wine went down well – too well, in a population used to drinking ale and, inevitably, Bergen suffered frequent outbreaks of drunken violence. After a number of people were killed in 1186, King Sverre decided to give both the locals and the foreign merchants a good talking to and ordered them to attend the thing. According to his biography, *Sverris Saga*, Sverre began his address by thanking

> all Englishmen who have arrived here, bringing with them wheat and honey, flour or cloth. We also want to thank all those men who have brought here linen or flax, wax or cauldrons. We would also like to mention those who have come from Orkney, Shetland, the Faeroe Islands and Iceland and all those who have brought to this country such things as it can hardly do without and are for the best of the country. But as to the Germans – who have arrived here in large numbers and with large ships, and intend to take away butter and cod to the detriment of the country, and bring in return wine that people go in for buying, both my men and the townsmen or merchants – their trade has brought much evil and nothing good.[40]

The Germans were impervious to royal disapproval, however, and they steadily elbowed out the competition, both the foreigners and the natives, to achieve a virtual monopoly of Norwegian stockfish exports by the end of the thirteenth century.

The Hanseatic League

It wasn't just in Norway that German merchants were achieving commercial dominance in the thirteenth century. It was happening in Denmark, Sweden, England, Flanders, Poland, Livonia and even far-away Novgorod. This remarkable German takeover of northern Europe's trade was a result of the foundation of the Hanseatic League. In the twelfth and thirteenth centuries, many German cities were reaching free trade agreements with one another, to promote their own commerce and to exclude competitors. It was from one of these agreements, between the Baltic port of Lübeck and the North Sea port of Hamburg in 1241, that the Hanseatic League* grew. As alliances go, this one had immense potential, because, between them, the two cities commanded the shortest, fastest and safest route between the North Sea and the Baltic Sea, an overland crossing of just 58 kilometres, compared to the nearly 1,000-kilometre sea passage through the Skaggerak and the shoal-ridden Kattegat. By the time the league was formalized in the 1360s, around 170 German and Baltic cities had joined, but only about twenty of them really counted and regularly attended the league's occasional meetings of the *Hansetag* (council). The smaller cities delegated their voting rights to the larger cities, a bit like private shareholders in a major company today. Lübeck, known as 'the Queen of the Baltic', was the acknowledged leader; other major players included Hamburg, Bremen, Cologne, Wismar, Rostock, Stralsund, Stettin (Szczecin), Danzig (Gdansk), Visby, Königsberg (Kaliningrad), Riga and Reval (Tallinn).

Though it's often compared to a medieval precursor of the European Union, there's nothing really quite like the Hanseatic League in the modern world. The Hanse never aimed for territorial domination and had no institutions other than the *Hansetag*: more than anything, it operated as an international commercial cartel. None of the member cities were, strictly speaking, independent, but the leaders all enjoyed considerable autonomy as free imperial cities within the Holy Roman Empire. The league could not have existed except for the weak nature of royal governments in the Middle Ages. Medieval rulers depended on the landed aristocracy to supply their armies, but if they couldn't enforce their obedience, they were left impotent. Rulers were, therefore, desperate to find alternative sources of income which could free them from this uncomfortable dependence. Tolls and taxes on trade were one source, and rulers found that city

* The name comes from German *hansa*, meaning 'guild'.

governments were often willing to pay for grants of privileges, such as monopoly rights on particular trade goods. A big trading alliance like the Hanseatic League, therefore, had plenty of leverage to negotiate very favourable deals for itself.

The Baltic herring trade

Lübeck's pre-eminence came in large part from its control of the trade of medieval Europe's other favourite fish, Baltic salted herrings. Europe's most important herring fishing ground at that time was in the southern Baltic close to the coast of the Falsterbo peninsula in Skåne (then part of Denmark, now Sweden), where they gathered to spawn in August through to October. The herrings were so densely packed that it was said, perhaps with some exaggeration, that they could be scooped up by hand (we know that the fishermen actually used nets). The herrings were landed at the ports of Falsterbo, Skanör, Ystad, Dragør, Køge and Malmö, where they were gutted by 'gill women', salted to preserve them and packed into airtight barrels. In a medieval version of the 'best before date', the barrels were branded with the date of the catch: the herrings had a shelf-life of about a year. At the height of the season, the Danes held a herring-selling fair, the Skåne Market, which attracted merchants from Germany, Flanders, England, Scotland and Normandy. Tolls on the fishing boats and taxes on the herring market were a major money-spinner for the Danish crown, providing a third of its annual revenue, and was a big source of resentment for German fishermen, who thought it was all very unfair, because 'the Danes got the herrings from God for free'. The weak link in the Danish business model was the salt supply. The process required one part salt to three parts herring, and, as the catch ran to many millions of herrings, a lot of salt was needed. The cool climate and the low salinity of the Baltic meant it was impractical to make sea salt in the Baltic region, so this essential product had to be imported. The only salt mines in the region at that time were at Lüneburg, in territory controlled by Lübeck's ally Hamburg. Without salt, the Danes might as well have left the herrings in the sea. By 1260, simply by monopolizing the region's salt supply, Lübeck had won exemption from the hated tolls, a massive competitive advantage over other foreign merchants, which, effectively, handed it control of the Skåne herring market. When the Danish King Valdemar Atterdag sent a fleet to force the Germans out of the herring fishery by force, the Hanseatic League organized a fleet and in retaliation burned Copenhagen in 1368. The conflict ended two years later, when Valdemar agreed the humiliating Treaty of Stralsund, which gave the league an effective monopoly over all of Denmark's trade.

The Hanse also had its eye on Norway's stockfish exports. Norway wasn't self-sufficient in grain, and it became reliant on imports of rye and wheat from Prussia and Poland – one of medieval Europe's most important grain-producing regions – which was supplied by Lübeck, Rostock and other Baltic Hanseatic towns. The dependency became even greater after King Håkon IV agreed a free trade treaty with Lübeck. Their unrivalled access to the Baltic grain lands allowed the Hanseatic towns to outcompete Norwegian and other foreign traders alike: Norway was steadily losing control of its overseas trade. The availability of cheap Baltic grain also had the effect of reducing Norway's own grain production even further, as, unable to compete, farmers in coastal areas increasingly turned to fishing to supply the more lucrative stockfish trade. When Eirik II attempted to restrict the activities of German merchants in 1284, he was met by an economic blockade which cut off Norway's grain supply. With famine threatening, Eirik was forced to climb down in 1294 and grant the Hanseatics a wide range of legal privileges in Bergen. Bergen became the staple port for the export of stockfish and the Hanseatics won the right to free trade with all ports in the south of Norway. Trade north of Bergen, and with the dependencies of the Faeroe Islands, Iceland and Greenland, was to be a Norwegian monopoly, however. This arrangement cemented Bergen's place as Norway's leading port. Norwegian merchants delivered stockfish and other North Atlantic products to Bergen for sale and took products like rye and wheat, beer and cloth, bought from Hanseatic merchants, back on their return voyages. Norwegian and foreign merchants were not banned from Bergen but, such was their competitive advantage, the Hanseatics completely dominated the export of stockfish. The Germans consolidated their dominance of Bergen in the fourteenth century, and by around 1360 they had their own autonomous enclave or *kontor*, one of four, the others being at London (for wool), Bruges (for cloth) and Novgorod (for furs), where the merchants could live and trade by their own laws. While the Hanse's dominance was resented by the Norwegian merchant class, it benefitted the stockfish industry by providing it with a reliable and efficient distribution network: there was no point in catching the fish if they couldn't be sold, and the Hanse found ever-widening markets beyond northern Europe, to Spain, Portugal and, in the fifteenth century, to Italy.

The ordeal of Pietro Querini

The plot of Norwegian composer Henning Sommerro's opera *Querini* is one of a kind; it's about the beginning of the Italian market for stockfish (in Italian *stoccafisso*). Though it sounds like it should be incredibly dull, it's inspired by a gritty tale about a desperate struggle for survival in the North Atlantic. In April 1431, Pietro Querini, a wealthy Venetian merchant-ship captain, set sail from Heraklion in Crete in his ship, the *Gemma Querina*, with a cargo of Malvasia wine, cotton and spices bound for Bruges. He and his crew of sixty-eight sailors never made it. The ship made slow progress: it was late summer before it entered the Atlantic and the weather was already turning bad. They were repeatedly battered by storms, and Querini tried to keep close to the coast, but in late September, off Cape Finisterre, they were blown out into the Atlantic. Weeks later, off the west coast of Ireland, the ship's mast and rudder were broken beyond repair in yet another storm. Querini's ship now drifted helplessly north on the Gulf Stream. Shortly before Christmas, Querini decided to abandon the ship and make a desperate attempt to reach land in the ship's two boats. Querini soon lost contact with the smaller boat, which was never seen again. Querini's boat, with forty-seven men on board, drifted at sea for three weeks, his crew dying one by one of cold, thirst and hunger, before it was wrecked on skerries off the Lofoten Islands in early January 1432. It was mid-winter in the Arctic dark time. The survivors fashioned a hut with their wrecked boat and, luckily, found a beached whale carcass, which became their only source of food for twenty-nine days, until they were rescued in February by cod fishermen from the tiny Lofoten island of Røst. Of Querini's crew, only ten were still alive. The Venetians were kindly treated by the islanders, who fed them meals of stockfish cooked with butter and herbs until they recovered their strength. They liked the stockfish very much, as they did the islanders' easy-going attitude to extramarital sex, but they found their habit of socializing naked, men and women together, in a communal sauna every Thursday rather disconcerting. However, after joining in a few times, Querini recalled, 'it became as natural to us as it was to them'. The Venetians were immensely grateful to the islanders. Querini described his enforced stay as 'one hundred days in paradise' and Røst itself as 'salvation's island', even if it was at 'the arse-end of the world' (*in culo mundi*). In May, Querini and his men said their farewells to their kind hosts and sailed south on the ship that was taking that season's stockfish to market. Querini took sixty stockfish with him and, when he finally made it home, via London, he set himself up as Italy's first importer. Italy became, and remains, Norway's biggest customer for stockfish. Querini's role in getting the trade started is still celebrated at Røst, and this was where Sommerro's opera premiered in 2012: the music critic of the London *Financial Times* wrote, perhaps slightly tongue in cheek, that it was 'the most moving work of musical theatre ever to be written about dried fish'.[41] Admittedly, there isn't much competition.

Cogs and cargoes

The Hanse's success wasn't just down to leverage; they also had a new type of ship, the cog, which made transporting relatively low-value bulk cargoes much more economical than at any time since the Roman Empire. Cogs were sturdy, broad-beamed (with a length-to-beam ratio of *c.*2.7:1), fully decked cargo ships, with a single mast and square-rigged sail. They were distinctly sluggish ships, managing only about 4 knots at best, compared to a Norse *knarr*'s 8 knots, but they were tough and, thanks to their high freeboard, very seaworthy. The earliest cogs of the eleventh and twelfth centuries could carry 50 tonnes of cargo, more than the largest *knarrs*, and could be managed by a crew of the same size, around five or six, making them more economical to operate too. Moreover, the basic cog design was capable of a lot more scaling up than the *knarr*. A well-preserved fourteenth-century cog recovered from the Weser river at Bremen could have carried around 140 tonnes of cargo, and some were built that could carry over 200 tonnes. Not since Roman times had the Atlantic seen ships that could carry that weight of cargo. Cogs were not just cheaper to operate than *knarrs*, they were also cheaper and quicker to build than a *knarr* because they used sawn planks, which were less labour-intensive to make, and wasted less wood than the radially split planks preferred by Norse shipbuilders. These weren't as strong as the planks used for *knarrs* (see Chapter 6), but shipbuilders compensated with heavier framing. One of the cog's innovations was that its rudder was fixed to the sternpost by a socket-like pintle and gudgeon hinge. This kind of rudder is now more or less universal, so it looks more 'modern' than the side rudders used on Norse and ancient Mediterranean ships, but it was adopted not because it was more effective (it isn't), but because it was stronger. Side rudders were much more liable to get torn off in bad weather or damaged by collisions in harbour.

With its many advantages, the cog had largely replaced the *knarr* as the main merchant ship in the Baltic, the North Sea and the Atlantic by around 1300. More surprisingly, in view of its leisurely sailing performance, it also took over from the sleek longships as the main ship for war. No way was a cog ever going to outsail a fully crewed longship. An anonymous fourteenth-century Danish artist had fun with this idea when he painted a scene on the ceiling of Skamdrup church in Jutland showing the Norwegian King St Olaf, sailing in a cog, winning a race with his brother Harald, who is sailing in a longship. It *would* take a miracle for a cog to sail faster than a longship. So what made the cog a good warship? The answer lies in the nature of medieval naval warfare. Sea battles were rare events and usually took place in confined waters, where speed and manoeuvrability counted for little. Before cannon were mounted on ships in the fifteenth century, the aim was to capture rather than sink the enemy ships. A captain had to get his ship alongside the enemy ship, board it and clear its decks in hand-to-hand fighting. Just as height counted in a battle on land, it counted too in a sea battle. In that respect, thanks to their ship's high freeboard, the crew of a cog had a clear advantage over the crew of a longship. Cogs could be made even more effective in battle by adding fortified fore- and aftcastles at the bows and stern as raised fighting platforms. A fleet's main wartime function, however, was not fighting but transporting armies, and cogs won out there too because of their greater carrying capacity.

Bigger and better: the carrack

As cogs became ever larger, they evolved into a three- or four-masted sailing ship known as a carrack, also known in Spain as a *nao* (Portugues *nau*), meaning, simply, a ship, from Latin *navis*. This evolution began in Genoa and Venice. In 1304, large cogs from the Basque Country began sailing into the Mediterranean with cargoes of wool. Cogs required smaller crews than typical Mediterranean ships of the time, so Genoese and Venetian shipwrights began to copy the design, but they didn't do so slavishly. Cogs were clinker-built ships, in the north European tradition (see Chapter 6). The Genoese and Venetians built their *cocha*, as they called them, frame-first and with smooth-finished hulls of planks laid edge to edge in the Mediterranean tradition, an approach that was much more suited to building large ships. By the 1350s, they had also added an extra mast, aft, which carried a typically Mediterranean triangular lateen sail. Lateen sails were nowhere near as efficient as a square-rigged sail with a following wind, but they had much better performance when sailing against the wind. By adding an extra mast to their *cocha*, the Genoese and Venetians combined both types of sail – square sail on the foremast, lateen on the mizzenmast (the aft mast) – to create a new type of ship with greatly improved sailing performance called the *carraca* or, in English, carrack. In the fifteenth century, third and even fourth masts were added, hugely increasing the area of sail carried. These large Genoese and Venetian carracks sailed regularly to England and Flanders, but it was well into the fifteenth century before north-European shipwrights acquired the skills to build them too: some of the largest were built in Hanseatic shipyards, including one of Henry VIII's favourite warships, the *Jesus of Lübeck*. Carracks were built broad in relation to their length to maximize their cargo capacity: some fifteenth-century carracks could carry over 600 tonnes of cargo and, by the sixteenth century, more than 900 tonnes. Apart from the multiple masts, a distinctive feature of carracks was their high fore- and aftcastles, which made them look dangerously top-heavy. These, however, made good fighting platforms, while the carrack's large size made it easy to adapt them to carrying the cannon that were now becoming important in European warfare. With their capacious holds and excellent sailing performance, carracks were as well suited to exploration as they were to long-distance trade and war. It would be in carracks, like Columbus's *Santa Maria*, John Cabot's *Matthew*, Vasco Da Gama's flagship *São Gabriel* and Ferdinand Magellan's *Victoria*, the first ship to circumnavigate the world, that Europeans would make the world's oceans their own.

Pirate brotherhoods

As a mercantile power, the Hanseatic League recognized that its success depended on safe sea lanes. Securing these was partly a matter of providing charts and building lighthouses and coastal landmarks to act as navigational aids and partly a matter of providing armed cogs, known as 'peace ships', to protect convoys of merchant ships against pirates. The end of the Viking Age hadn't brought peace and security at sea; piracy continued to be a threat right through the Middle Ages: the buccaneers of the Caribbean didn't have to reinvent piracy, as it had never gone away. Pirates have always favoured shipping bottlenecks. Today, it's the Malacca Strait and the approaches to the Red Sea; in medieval Europe it was the English Channel, the southern North Sea, the ways in and out of the Baltic Sea, and the Strait of Gibraltar. Wartime, which was quite a lot of the time in the Middle Ages, was particularly dangerous, because pirates could sign up as privateers in royal service with a licence to capture enemy shipping. Trouble was, what was an unemployed privateer to do when the war was over? Most went back to piracy. This was the case with medieval Europe's most notorious pirates, the 2,000-strong Vitalienbrüder ('Victual Brothers'), who styled themselves 'God's friend and all the world's foe'. The king of Sweden, Albert of Mecklenburg, raised the Vitalienbrüder in Wismar and Rostock in 1371 to run supplies to Stockholm, which was besieged by the Danes, and to attack Danish shipping. Instead of wages, Albert offered 'all who wished to harm the realms of Denmark and Norway "letters-of-marque", official permission to commit acts of piracy, which gave them leave freely to share out, exchange and sell the plundered goods'. The recruits were opportunistic sea captains and unemployed seamen, runaway peasants, criminals, poor townsfolk and not a few hard-up aristocrats.

Albert won his war but, rather than disband, the ruthless pirate brotherhood he had created simply changed its name to the Likedeelers ('equal sharers') and carried on plundering. Now, it was not only Danish and Norwegian ships the

Likedeelers plundered but Swedish and Hanseatic ships too, strangling commerce in the Baltic for years to come, all the while enjoying protection of the city authorities at Rostock, which profited from dealing in their stolen goods. This was despite their city's membership of the Hanseatic League. In 1393, the brothers extended their raids into the North Sea and sacked Bergen, where 'they took many valuables of gold and silver and costly garments, household goods and even fish. With this great treasure they sailed back unhindered to Rostock and sold it among the citizenry.' The brothers were finally expelled from the Baltic in 1398, but they continued to attack shipping in the North Sea and the English Channel until a Hanseatic fleet captured their leader, who went by the *nom de guerre* Klaus Störtebeker, in a sea battle off their base on the island of Heligoland. Störtebeker, whose name means 'drain the mug in one gulp' (which comes from his supposed ability to drain a gallon (four-litre) mug of ale in one go), cultivated a Robin Hood-style image as someone who robbed greedy merchants to give alms to poor widows and the church. Doubtless, he was paying hush money to the local fishermen, farmers and village priests who lived around the creeks where he hid his ships. With around seventy of his men, Störtebeker was taken to Hamburg for execution by beheading. Störtebeker asked his executioner to grant him, as a last request, that he would free every man who he could touch after he had had his head cut off. Feeling sure that no harm could possibly come of this, the executioner readily agreed before he proceeded to strike the pirate's head off. Then, to everyone's quite understandable astonishment, Störtebeker stood up and ran, touching eleven of his men, before someone threw a plank of wood between his legs and tripped him up. The executioner immediately went back on his word and executed the eleven men Störtebeker had touched, along with all the rest. According to legend, of course. A skull said to be that of Störtebeker has been displayed at Hamburg's history museum since 1922, but efforts to authenticate it have so far been inconclusive.

The legend of Willem Beuckelszoon

In the course of the fifteenth century, the Hanseatic League entered a long and slow decline which ended in its dissolution in the seventeenth century. It was the Dutch who made the first successful challenge to the Hanse's commercial dominance, by breaking its monopoly over the herring trade. The traditional story is that, around 1386, a Dutch fisherman called Willem Beuckelszoon discovered a new way of processing herrings known as gibbing or sousing. Instead of packing them in salt in the time-honoured way, Beuckelszoon tried pickling the herrings in brine and found that it worked just as well and cost less too. Another of his refinements was leaving the liver in the fish. While the fish was pickling (unknown to him, of course), the liver released trypsin enzyme, which gave it a mellow flavour and, because far less salt had been used in its preservation, it did not need to be steeped in fresh water before it could be eaten: it was altogether a superior product to Baltic salt herring, tastier and more convenient. Sousing wasn't revolutionary just because of this though; it could also be done at sea. The lack of refrigeration was always a problem for medieval fishermen: the catch had to be landed quickly for processing while it was still fresh. This kept fishermen close to the land. Sousing on board ship freed fishermen to sail much further out to sea and for longer, bringing within reach the vast unexploited herring shoals that swam above that long-submerged mammoth steppe that was now the North Sea's Dogger Bank. Soon, the Dutch were making serious inroads into the international herring trade, outcompeting the Hanseatic merchants as even consumers in the Baltic preferred their herrings. It's a classic case of a plucky underdog taking on a monopolistic corporate giant and winning: if only the story was about something more glamorous than salt fish, it would make a good movie.

Modern research has, alas, exposed the story of Willem Beuckelszoon, the game-changing innovator, as a seventeenth-century patriotic myth. It hasn't even proved possible to identify who Beuckelszoon was: there were quite a lot of Willem Beuckelszoons in the Netherlands during the fourteenth century. The Danes, it seems, were already sousing their herrings in the early fourteenth century. A limited number of Dutch fishermen were licensed to take part in the Baltic herring fishery, so it was most likely from the Danes that they learned about sousing and introduced the technique back home. Was a Willem Beuckelszoon one of them? Who knows? As for the bit about leaving the liver in the fish, that was probably accidental. With millions of fish to process, gibbers worked fast, each gutting an incredible 2,000 herrings an hour, so it's likely that they weren't always that thorough and often left some gibblety bits behind. The real reason for the rise of the Dutch herring trade was more mundane but no less damaging for the Hanse: between 1390 and 1420, the Baltic herring shoals simply disappeared from the coasts of Skåne. The Danish and German fishermen headed out into the Baltic during the spawning season, as they had always done, but the herrings never came. No one is quite sure what happened. At the time, it was thought that the fish had migrated to the North Sea, but modern marine biologists generally discount that possibility. Given the well-documented tendency of modern fishermen to fish their prey to the edge of extinction, or even beyond, it's tempting to blame over-exploitation but, with the technology available at the time, that doesn't seem very likely either. It has been proposed that changes in water temperature, salinity or sea currents may have led the herrings to spawn elsewhere, but where? Whatever the cause, it was the collapse of the Baltic herring fishery that gave the Dutch their big opportunity.

The first factory ships

There is a part of the Beuckelszoon story that is true. The Dutch probably were the first to start salting their fish at sea, they just needed to have a fishing boat that was large enough and seaworthy enough to make it economically viable. As it happened, they did – it was called a herring buss. The first records of herring busses date to 1415, so it looks like their development may have been a direct response to the new opportunities created by the collapse of the Baltic herring fishery. A typical buss had two or three masts, each with a single sail, was about 20 metres in length and 4 metres in the beam, and displaced between 60 and 100 tonnes. For comparison, this was around twice the displacement of what was the most common type of North Sea fishing boat at the time, the one- or two-masted dogger (which were so ubiquitous that the Dogger Bank is named for them). The large deck area provided plenty of space for landing and processing the catch. The crews, usually about thirteen strong, included not just fishermen but professional gibbers and coopers, whose job it was to assemble barrels for packing the fish and ensuring that they were airtight. A buss could stay at sea for up to two months, allowing fishermen to follow the herring shoals in their summer migrations. The season began around 14 June off the Shetland Islands and the fishing fleets followed the herrings as they migrated south to the Dogger Bank, where they spawned in August and September. After spawning, the exhausted fish were considered 'spent' and not worth catching until they had fully recovered next summer. The fishery became increasingly industrialized in the sixteenth and seventeenth centuries. Fleets of 500 busses headed out into the North Sea for the whole season, fishing with drift nets twenty-four hours a day. From the fifteenth century, laws specified minimum mesh sizes to avoid catching young fish. Regular supply ships, called *ventjagers*, sailed out from Holland carrying salt, barrel staves, fresh food, water and beer to the fleet and, after paying the fishing captains in hard cash, carried the filled barrels back to land for the market. This system enabled a single buss to catch up to 200 tonnes of herrings (around 2.5 million fish) in a season, several times more than its cargo capacity. New deep-sea herring grounds in the Atlantic, off the Norwegian coast and Iceland, also came within range for exploitation. At the time that the Beuckelszoon myth was dreamed up, Dutch herrings really were considered to be a premium product, but this was after many years of refining their quality. When the trade started, herrings soused at sea were actually thought to be inferior to those soused on land, but it wasn't like consumers could buy their herrings from anyone else, so the Dutch quickly took over the market. By 1450, the Hanseatic towns were importing most of their herrings from the Dutch.

The success of the Dutch deep-sea herring fishery wasn't just about new ships and new ways of processing fish; it also required a revolution in the way the fishing industry was financed. Inshore fishing, like the Baltic herring fishery, using open boats on day trips, did not need much investment. Most fishermen owned and operated their own boats, with a crew of family members or a few hired hands. In contrast, building and fitting out a herring buss, effectively a medieval factory ship, was expensive and well beyond the means of most inshore fishermen. Operating costs – provisions and wages for the crew for two months, salt, barrels and fishing nets – were also high. Consequently, there were few owner-operators in the deep-sea fishery; most fishing boats were owned and financed by consortiums of merchant investors who had the capital to pay the up-front operating costs, much as modern deep-sea fishing boats are. With profits for a season sometimes exceeding 100 per cent per ship, the investors grew very rich. Amsterdam, it was said, was built on herring bones. Well-financed merchants and seamen with long experience of spending months at sea later placed the Netherlands in a strong position to take advantage of the new sea routes opened by the Portuguese and Spanish in the sixteenth century.

England's first oceanic trade route

Faced with Hanseatic control of the stockfish market and Dutch dominance of the North Sea herring fishery, English fishermen from east-coast ports literally cast their nets wider and searched for new fishing grounds. They found them in the Atlantic south of Iceland. The great Elizabethan chronicler of English maritime prowess, Richard Hakluyt, claimed that fishermen from the east-coast port of Blakeney began sailing to Iceland in search of cod as early as the reign of Edward III (1327–77). However, according to the eighteenth-century antiquarian Francis Blomefield, Robert Bacon of Cromer, another east-coast fishing port, was the first to sail to Iceland, sometime during the reign of Henry IV (1399–1413). Whether or not Bacon really was the first, this fits rather well with English Parliamentary records, which give the date of the first voyages as spring in 1408 or 1409, and with Icelandic annals, which mention the presence of English fishermen for the first time in 1412. Just one boat was recorded that time, but the next year thirty came, and with them came an English merchant ship to trade butter, flour, wine, beeswax, honey, cloth, shirts, shoes and hardware like pots and kettles and horseshoes for stockfish and fish oil. The six annual trade ships promised them by the Norwegian crown back in 1262 rarely materialized, and things had only got worse after Norway entered a dynastic union with Denmark in 1379. Not surprisingly, the Icelanders welcomed the English merchants and not just for the much-needed goods they brought; they also paid 50 per cent more for their stockfish than the Norwegians and the Hanse. A few merchants obtained licences from either the Danish or English crowns, but most of this trade was illegal. In 1414, five English merchant ships arrived to trade at the Vestmannaeyjar. One of the ship's captains presented a letter from King Henry V, addressed 'to the commons and all the best men in the land', requesting his subjects be allowed to trade. Paying lip service to the law, the islanders told the English, insincerely, that they must go to Bergen if they wanted to trade. When the English refused, they settled down to do business with them happily enough, as they did when six English merchant ships arrived the next year. Arnfinn Thorsteinsson, the governor of Iceland, hardly set a good example for his subjects. Come the autumn, he sailed to England in one of these ships, taking with him silver and a cargo of stockfish, to do a bit of trading on his own behalf.

In a striking turnaround from the days of King Sverre, who

had praised the good behaviour of English merchants, the Danish King Erik of Pomerania wrote an ill-tempered letter to Henry V, reminding him that foreigners were forbidden to trade with Iceland and other possessions of the Danish crown. With a war with France on his hands, Henry didn't need another one with Denmark, so he ordered that a proclamation, forbidding any of his subjects to sail to Iceland, to fish or to trade, be read at what reads like a gazetteer of English east-coast ports, from Berwick on the Scottish border south to Essex on the Thames estuary. The ban caused protests in Parliament, and it was generally ignored by the English and Icelanders alike. The Icelanders felt justified in ignoring the law, reminding their king that it had been agreed 'that six ships should come here from Norway every year, which has not happened for a long time, a cause from which our country has suffered most grievous harm'. The English were soon back. In 1419, governor Arnfinn licensed the master of the English ship *Christopher* to trade and fish wherever he liked around Iceland. That same year, dozens of English boats were once again fishing off Iceland: at least twenty-five of them were wrecked in a terrible snowstorm on Maundy Thursday, with all hands lost, leaving some rich pickings for beachcombers. This put nobody off, as such occasional disasters were priced in by fishermen, and they kept coming, as many as 100 fishing boats every year. The rapid build-up of English voyaging to Iceland is remarkable. Up to this time, the English had mainly been coast huggers, and these were their first regular open-ocean voyages anywhere and not in the friendliest of seas, either. Many English fishermen sailed for Iceland as early in the year as February to catch the cod at their best. English confidence came, at least in part, from their widespread adoption of the magnetic compass – every fishing boat captain seems to have had one.

In 1429, King Erik issued another decree banning the English from visiting Iceland on pain of death or forfeiture of property. The English government made a show of trying to enforce the ban but to little effect. In 1431, King Erik complained that for the last twenty years the English had also been trading illegally in Greenland and in the stockfish-producing region of Finnmark in Arctic Norway. No English voyages to Greenland, either to fish or to trade, are recorded in this period, but the fishermen and merchants alike would have had an incentive to keep quiet about it because of its illegality. The dispute came to a head in 1467, when English merchants murdered the governor of Iceland, Björn Thorleifsson, at Ríf on the west coast. The governor's outraged widow, Ólöf, was instrumental in persuading King Christian I to declare war on England in alliance with the Hanse, which had its own issues with English privateers preying on their ships. The war, fought mainly by privateers, did serious long-term damage to English trade with Iceland and the Baltic. During the war, the Danish crown licensed Hanseatic ships to trade in Iceland and, after peace was agreed in 1474, the Germans vigorously defended their privileges when the English attempted to make a comeback. The English merchants weren't for giving ground to the Germans either, so violent clashes were common: the worst, in 1532, a dispute over a purchase of stockfish, left forty English, and an unknown number of German, sailors dead. It seems that the Germans thought they'd sealed a deal for the stockfish, but the English offered to pay more and secured the cargo. If this wasn't bad enough, the English then started taunting the Germans, which was just too much for them to take.

Cod wars

It was the Danish crown and the Hanse that opposed the English traders in Iceland, but, as far as the Icelanders were concerned, it was the English fishermen who were the real problem. Icelandic fishermen complained that the English were taking so many fish on the open sea that there were none left for them to catch in inshore waters. That probably wasn't true, but it may have felt like it was, because it was extremely difficult for the Icelanders, with only small inshore fishing boats, to compete with the much larger English fishing boats, which could stay at sea for weeks or months. Like Dutch deep-sea fishermen, the English also had the backing of wealthy merchant consortiums in their home ports; there were no such companies in Iceland. Nor was there any prospect of the locals being able to compete by building bigger fishing boats for themselves, because Iceland had no shipbuilding timber and Icelanders lacked the capital to buy them from abroad. Worse than this, even, was that the English fishermen were violent and predatory right from the start. On only their second known expedition to Iceland, in 1413, English fishermen landed on the island of Papey, off the southeast coast, and stole all the cattle. From around 1420, English fishermen from Hull and other east-coast ports began wintering illegally in the Vestmannaeyjar, probably so they could dry their own stockfish. Iceland's new governor, Hannes Pálsson, complained to the Danish king that the English used the islands as if they owned them, even building houses and growing their own crops. The English beat up any local fishermen who tried to stop them, smashed their boats and prevented them selling their own stockfish until they had all that they wanted, he continued. They cheated the king of his revenues, took people captive and carried them back to England, plundered and robbed and even burned churches. The English fishermen had no respect for authority at all and had even sacked the governor's residence at Bessastaðir (near Reykjavik) and killed one of his officials. Even allowing for some righteous hyperbole here, it's clear that the English often crossed the line between illegal fishing and outright piracy. The fishermen also provided cover for illegal trading. Most of the cod caught by the English was salted and packed in barrels, but many of them also took cargoes of cloth, flour and other goods along on their voyages, which they'd trade with the Icelanders for stockfish – that is, if they didn't decide to steal it instead. Unlike governor Arnfinn, Hannes took his responsibilities to the king seriously. In 1425, along with another official called Balthasar van Dammin, he set out in two ships intending to arrest the English fishermen who had taken over the Vestmannaeyjar, and to confiscate their boats. That would teach them a lesson. The governor had completely underestimated his enemy. The English beat off the governor's attack and burned his ships. Unable to escape, Hannes and van Dammin soon found themselves on their way to England as the fishermen's prisoners, later to be ransomed. English fishermen didn't have it all their own way. Although the Germans did not fish in Icelandic waters, English fishermen ran the risk of capture by hostile Hanseatic ships and, on their outward and homeward voyages along Britain's northeast coast, the threat of attacks by the Scots was so serious that Richard III ordered all fishing boats to gather in the Humber and sail to and from Iceland in convoy for mutual protection. This was a trade that really mattered to England; should the fleet be intercepted, Thomas Howard, the duke of Surrey, declared, 'the coasts of Norfolk and Suffolk will be undone, and all England would be destitute of fish'.

As there was no getting rid of the English, King Hans of Denmark decided in 1491 that he might as well get some benefit from them and introduced seven-year licences which gave them the right to trade and fish in Icelandic waters. When the legislation came up before the Althing, the Icelanders immediately struck out the clauses granting the English fishing rights and substituted clauses permitting them to fish only if they also imported goods which they needed and exchanged them for stockfish. Obviously, the Icelanders still wanted an alternative to trading exclusively with the monopolistic Hanseatic merchants, but the laws could not be enforced. In 1500, the Althing complained that the large English fishing boats were still standing offshore and taking all the fish from the local inshore fishermen. English fishermen would continue to do this for the next 450 years, until the Icelanders, independent at last from Denmark, took back control of their fisheries in the three so-called Cod Wars, 'fought' between 1958 and 1976, destroying the British deep-sea fishing industry, and the economies of the ports dependent on it, in the process. Hull, whose fishermen had caused Hannes Pálsson so much trouble back in the fifteenth century, was one of the ports most seriously afflicted.

14

Uncontaminated gentiles

1300–1496

The River of Gold – The Vivaldi brothers – The Canary Islands rediscovered – Noble savages or brute beasts? – The turn of the sea – The birth year of European imperialism – The Treaty of Alcáçovas – The conquest of Tenerife – 'A country strongly fortified by nature' – Extinction – Remaking the Canary Islands

For more than a millennium after Eudoxus and his crew of dancing girls disappeared into the Atlantic in 118 BC, Cape Bojador's sinister reputation as the point of no return deterred navigators, Christian and Muslim alike, from exploring Africa's west coast. The Muslims didn't need to, and the Christians knew of nothing south of the cape that was worth the risk of disappearing without trace. At least not until the thirteenth century, that was, when rumours began to reach Europe about a fabulous 'River of Gold' somewhere in West Africa. 'River of Gold' was the name that the Berbers and Tuaregs who guided the caravans back and forth across the Sahara Desert gave to the 'Western Nile', a conflation of the Senegal and Niger rivers which were thought until the nineteenth century to be a single river flowing through the heart of West Africa's alluvial gold fields into the Atlantic. Some geographers thought that it might even be connected to the headwaters of the Nile in East Africa. This was something to capture the imagination of gold-hungry Europeans. The first rumours about the river were vague and fantastical. In its earliest known appearance on a European map, on the Hereford *Mappa Mundi*, made *c.*1300, the river is shown running through territory densely populated by giant gold-mining ants and other monsters. After Mansa Musa's famously gold-laden visit to Cairo in 1325 (see Chapter 12, p. 359), more reliable geographical knowledge of West Africa began to circulate in Europe. The position of the mouth of the Senegal river was mapped accurately on portolan charts, even if its course inland was shown speculatively and always embellished with pictures of African kings wearing golden crowns, sitting on golden thrones, clutching golden orbs and sceptres, all highlighted with expensive gold-leaf, as if to emphasize the point that 'River of Gold' was not just a poetic metaphor. Even the caravan routes which carried the sacks of gold dust to North Africa were known. European knowledge about the river might have been entirely second-hand, but they did know that between them and all that gold were some formidable obstacles, namely the hostile Moors, the Sahara Desert and Cape Bojador.

The Vivaldi brothers

There wasn't much that could be done about the Moors and the Sahara Desert, so maybe it was time to question the long-held assumptions about Cape Bojador. The first to do so were not, as might be expected, the Spanish, Portuguese, Basques or English, who actually lived on the Atlantic, but two Genoese brothers, Vandino and Ugolino Vivaldi, who had a bold plan to sail to India. Genoese and Venetian merchants had been quick to establish direct trade with northern Europe following the reopening of the Strait of Gibraltar to Christian shipping in the mid-thirteenth century. At the same time, other Genoese and Venetian merchants began trading along Morocco's Atlantic coast, gradually feeling their way further and further south and becoming increasingly familiar with its harbours, sea conditions and wind patterns as they did so. The Genoese had a special interest in exploring the African coast. Genoese sea captains and pilots had already gained considerable knowledge of the Indian Ocean trade routes, and their commercial opportunities, by sailing in the service of the Mongol Ilkhan rulers of Persia and Iraq, and they knew there was potentially an even bigger prize than the River of Gold to be had by exploring the African coast: a direct sea route to India. The profits would be enormous. Thanks to Italy's advanced systems of banking and marine insurance, adventurous Italian navigators, like the Vivaldis, with an exciting proposal could win the support of well-financed venture capitalists who would invest in speculative voyages of exploration in return for guaranteed monopolies should they deliver new commercial opportunities: the prominence of Italian navigators in opening up the Atlantic really does have a lot to with where the money was in Renaissance Europe.

The main record of the Vivaldis' expedition appears under the year 1291 in the Genoese chronicle of Jacopo Doria, whose wealthy merchant family were its chief financial backers:

> Tedisio Doria [Jacopo's nephew], Ugolino Vivaldi and a brother of the latter [Vandino], together with a few other citizens of Genoa, initiated an expedition which no one up to that time had ever attempted. They fitted out two galleys in splendid fashion. Having stocked them with provisions, water and other necessities, they sent them on their way, in the month of May, toward the Strait of Gibraltar in order that the galleys might sail through the ocean sea to India and return with useful merchandise. The two above-mentioned brothers sailed on the vessels in person, and also two Franciscan friars; all of which truly astonished those who witnessed them as well as those who heard of them. After the travellers passed a place called Gozora [Ras Barsig, i.e. 'Cape No'] there was no further news of them. May God watch over them and bring them back safely.[42]

After the Vivaldis left Cape No behind, where did they go? One school of thought is that they were precursors of Columbus who attempted to reach India by sailing directly across the Atlantic. However, it's clear from all the speculation that followed their disappearance that their contemporaries believed they had been shipwrecked while trying to circumnavigate Africa.

The Canary Islands rediscovered

The Vivaldis' disappearance confirmed the ancient fears and legends about Cape Bojador, but they weren't quite the deterrent they had been. Where they had gone, others soon followed. One who suffered the same fate was the Majorcan seafarer Jaume Ferrer, who sailed his galley south of Cape Bojador in 1346 hoping to find the River of Gold and also vanished without trace. Another Genoese hopeful, Lancelotto Malocello, who set out to search for the Vivaldis in 1312, was luckier: he got no further than the Canary Islands, but at least he survived to tell the tale. The circumstances of Malocello's discovery are unknown, but he ended up spending twenty years on the arid easternmost of the Canary Islands, which became known after him as Lanzarote. One possibility is that Malocello was shipwrecked, and another is that he and his crew investigated the island as they sailed south and saw an opportunity to make themselves lords over its Guanche inhabitants. Either way, the Guanches eventually had enough of him and kicked him out. Malocello's temporary residence ended the islands' shadowy status as the mythical Fortunate Isles for good, and just a few years after his return to Europe, the *Insula de Lanzarotus Malocelus*, marked with a Genoese flag, appeared on a portolan chart made by the Italian cartographer Angelino Dulcert. The Canaries had been discovered several times before and then been lost again, but that wouldn't happen this time.

In 1341, another Genoese sea captain, Nicoloso da Recco, sailed from Lisbon with a small fleet and a commission from the Portuguese King Afonso IV to follow up on Malocello's discovery and claim the islands for Portugal. Recco and his multinational crew of Italians, Portuguese, Castilians and Catalans set out for the Canaries expecting that the Guanches would be much like the Moors and took along all the heavy weapons they'd need to assault castles and fortified towns. Instead, the explorers encountered what the sixteenth-century Spanish Franciscan missionary Alonso de Espinosa would call 'uncontaminated gentiles' – that is, indigenous peoples who had lived in relative isolation from the rest of the world and had no knowledge at all of Christianity, Judaism or Islam. There would be many more such encounters during the age of European exploration and colonialism that followed Columbus's voyage to the New World, and they were invariably catastrophically destructive for the indigenous peoples.

On the first island they landed on, Recco's crew saw men and women walking around naked, or as good as naked in prudish Christian eyes. The explorers sailed on to a larger island, which they named *Canaria* (now Gran Canaria). Curious islanders crowded the shore to watch as the strange ships approached. Once again, the men and women were 'naked', but some wore decorative cloaks that seemed to the explorers to be signs of status. Having no boats, some of the islanders swam out to the ships, but neither party understood the other's language. When da Recco sent a party of twenty-five armed sailors ashore, the natives' curiosity immediately evaporated and they fled in terror. The sailors broke into a few houses and stole some dried figs and wheat, noting how tidy and clean they were, at least until they kicked the doors down and ransacked them. They also looted a statue from what they believed was a simple, unadorned temple. Later, the explorers learned that the inhabitants practised agriculture, kept herds, had marriage customs and were ruled by chieftains.

The explorers circumnavigated Gran Canaria and then spent five months surveying all of the main Canary Islands before returning to Lisbon with four young men from Gran Canaria who had apparently gone along willingly enough out of curiosity. As their languages were mutually incomprehensible, the Europeans and the Guanches communicated by sign language.

The young men were good-natured and trusting; they shared their food equally with one another and could sing and dance well. When offered European food, they accepted the bread but refused wine, preferring water. Most of the European artefacts the explorers showed them were complete novelties to the Guanches. The Europeans were especially disappointed that the young men failed to recognize gold and silver coins and jewelry; they were hoping that they might have known something about the location of the River of Gold. The islands appeared to contain little of value, and the goatskins and orchil dye that they took home barely defrayed the costs of the expedition. It isn't known if the four young Guanches ever made it back to Gran Canaria: it is not unlikely that their trust was rewarded with a lifetime of slavery, the same fate that awaited thousands of their compatriots.

Noble savages or brute beasts?

The reactions of contemporary Europeans to reports of Recco's encounters with the Guanches set the tone for all future encounters between Europeans and indigenous peoples in Africa, the Americas and Australasia. Medieval European cartographers, like the maker of the Hereford *Mappa Mundi*, liked to populate the unknown reaches of the world with humanoid monsters, like the dog-headed Cynoscephalae, the headless Blemmyes and the one-legged Unipeds, so the discovery that the inhabitants of the Canary Islands were, at least physically, perfectly normal humans was a revelation in itself. The Florentine poet Giovanni Boccaccio, who was steeped in Renaissance Humanism, saw the Guanches through the lens of Roman pastoral poets like Virgil and Horace, as living an idyllic Arcadian existence in a state of nature as 'noble savages' uncorrupted by civilization. Their ignorance of gold and silver was a sign of their lack of materialism: their nakedness, so shameful for Christians, was evidence not of lustfulness but of their innocence, like Adam and Eve before the Fall and their expulsion from Paradise. For Boccaccio, the Guanches' paganism was a positive thing, but for most Christians this presented an obvious theological problem. If it was only the baptized who could be saved from eternal damnation, why had God allowed the Guanches to live in isolation for so many centuries without the possibility of conversion? For Alonso de Espinosa, the answer was that such indigenous peoples lived in a state of semi-grace as pre-Christians rather than as non-Christians. This semi-grace ended, of course, the moment the missionaries turned up and started preaching. The views of Boccaccio's humanist friend Francesco Petrarca (Petrarch), who saw little to admire in the Guanches, were probably more representative. To him, in their solitary, isolated existence, they were 'so little unlike brute beasts that their action is more the outcome of natural instinct than of rational choice'. Five hundred years later, Darwin would write in exactly the same terms about the Yaghan after his first encounter with them in Tierra del Fuego (see p. 33). Such attitudes left indigenous peoples like the Guanches desperately vulnerable to forced conversion (for their own good, naturally), deculturization, economic exploitation, enslavement and genocide.

In the wake of Recco's expedition, traffic to the Canary Islands steadily grew. Seeing the Guanches as easy victims, Majorcan, Castilian, Catalan and Portuguese slavers began cruising the islands to seize captives for the slave markets in Lisbon and Seville. The Atlantic slave trade did not begin with enslaved Black Africans. Lanzarote and Fuerteventura, the two islands closest to Africa, were the most seriously impacted by these raids. There was also some legitimate trade for the orchil and dragon's blood dyes, which could be obtained cheaply from the Guanches in exchange for iron tools, cooking pots and fish hooks. After the slavers, missionaries were the most numerous visitors. Franciscan friars from Majorca began visiting the islands in 1352, but the malign activities of the slavers made all Europeans suspect in the eyes of the islanders, making the work of conversion slow and dangerous. On at least two occasions, in 1354 and 1391, the inhabitants of Gran Canaria turned on the friars and massacred them. Despite these incidents, most missionaries continued to believe in the essential virtue of the Guanches and persevered in their work despite the risks. A less hazardous approach to evangelization was to convert enslaved Guanches in Spain and then return them to their home islands as 'influencers'. As these converts had been taught to speak Spanish, they proved useful to European missionaries and conquerors alike as interpreters and negotiators, frequently helping persuade their fellow islanders of the futility of resistance to the invaders and their powerful god. All contacts with Europeans, whether they were well meaning or not, threatened the Guanches' survival by exposure to common European diseases to which, thanks to their long isolation, they had little natural immunity. One of the worst was an epidemic of plague, introduced to Gran Canaria by slavers in the 1390s, which killed around two thirds of the population. While the slavers raided and the missionaries preached, the Portuguese, Castilians, Majorcans and Aragonese pursued rival claims to the islands, but the few small-scale attempts at colonization that actually got off the ground were all repulsed by the Guanches.

The turn of the sea

The problem with the Canary Islands wasn't that they were hard to reach, it was that they were hard to get home from. The prevailing northeast Trade Winds and the southwest-flowing coastal Canary current swept sailing ships almost effortlessly from Iberia down the Moroccan coast towards the islands. Getting there was the easy bit: getting back again, sailing northeast against the wind and current, was a lot harder, especially in a square-rigged ship. This was why the islands had been discovered and lost so many times in the past: seafarers who had visited the islands and painfully clawed their way back home against the wind really didn't feel like going back again in case, next time, they didn't make it back at all. Fourteenth-century mariners, however, were a lot more confident in their ships and their abilities to navigate on the open sea than their coast-hugging forebears. At some point, possibly during Recco's voyage or very soon after it, Portuguese mariners learned that, counterintuitively, it was best to set a course across the prevailing wind, northwest, away from the coast, out into the Atlantic where they would eventually pick up a westerly wind which would reliably return them to Europe. What the Portuguese had discovered, although they certainly did not fully understand it until they began sailing south of the Equator in the fifteenth century, was that the global winds circulate in bands. Between 30° and 60° latitude, both north and south of the Equator, the prevailing winds are westerlies, and between the Equator and 30° latitude, they are easterlies: these are the so-called Trade Winds (and around the Equator itself, between the two zones of easterlies, is the relatively windless zone known as the Doldrums). The Portuguese called this phenomenon, which was probably discovered simply by trial and error, rather than by any flash of theoretical insight, the *volta do mar*, meaning the 'turn of the sea' or, perhaps, originally, the 'return from the sea'.

If Cape Bojador was a locked door keeping Europeans out of the world's oceans, knowledge of the *volta do mar* was the key that would soon open it: it would be exploited both by Columbus during his voyage to the New World in 1492 and, in the southern hemisphere, by Vasco da Gama during his direct voyage to India in 1497. The immediate consequence of the new knowledge was the definitive discovery of the long-extinct volcanic Madeira archipelago. A sixteenth-century tradition, which seems to have originated in Portugal, credits a Bristol-based English merchant, Robert Machim, with discovering the islands around 1344, after his ship was blown off course from the coast of France, but it seems just as likely that the islands were discovered by Portuguese, Majorcan or Genoese slave traders taking advantage of the *volta* to return home. No contemporary document or chronicle records any sightings of the islands, but sightings there must have been, because they start to appear on Italian and Catalan portolan charts from 1351 onwards. In the Venetian *Corbitis Atlas*, made between 1384 and 1410, Madeira,

Porto Santo and the three barren neighbouring Desertas islands are not only mapped, they even have their modern names. Maps from this period also show a north–south chain of eight islands in the Atlantic opposite Portugal which might be the Azores archipelago. However, with two exceptions, the names given to these islands bear no relation to their modern names, so they may actually be phantom islands, which are only coincidentally in roughly the right place to be the Azores.

The birth year of European imperialism

The year 1402, when the European conquest of the Canary Islands began in earnest, has been described as 'the birth year of modern European imperialism'.[43] The French adventurer Jean de Béthencourt landed on Lanzarote in July with a small band of Norman soldiers, two priests and two Guanche converts to act as interpreters. While Béthencourt's expedition had the approval of France's King Charles VI, he had to fund his expedition himself by mortgaging his French estates. Béthencourt's motives were those of the sixteenth-century conquistadors, God and gold. God provided the legitimacy: Pope Benedict XIII awarded him the status of a crusader for bringing pagan peoples under Christian rule. Pope Benedict was quite clear-sighted about the geopolitical benefits of establishing a Christian colony off the coast of Muslim North Africa. Gold was the Christian warrior's just reward in this life, and Heaven in the next. Béthencourt didn't expect to find gold in the Canary Islands themselves; he wanted the islands as a base to support exploration of the African coast to find that rumoured golden river and become fabulously rich. Most of Lanzarote's indigenous population had already been captured by slavers by the time Béthencourt arrived, leaving just a few hundred Guanche behind. When Béthencourt presented himself to the survivors as a protector against the feared slavers, they gratefully allowed him to build a fort. It was a decision they soon regretted. The French were secretly in league with the slavers; when the islanders found out, they rebelled. From their fort, the French raided across the island, killing, captive-taking and driving away the islanders' livestock so that they starved. The islanders resisted but, with only wooden spears and stones to fight back against the armoured French, it was a one-sided battle. The surrender and baptism of the island's chief early in 1404 ended the islanders' resistance.

It quickly became clear to Béthencourt that his small French force was wholly insufficient to conquer the whole archipelago, so he took a ship to Cádiz to recruit reinforcements. When he returned, it was bearing the title king of the Canary Islands, but to get his reinforcements he had also paid homage to the Castilian King Enrique III and would hold his conquests only as a vassal of Castile; the future of the islands would be Spanish, not French. For King Enrique, it was a cost-free way to establish a *de facto* claim to sovereignty over the islands ahead of the Portuguese, who considered the islands to be theirs by right of prior discovery. By the end of 1405, Béthencourt had added Fuerteventura and El Hierro to his kingdom using the same mixture of violence, starvation, negotiation and bad faith he had used on Lanzarote. Within a few years, much of the Guanche population of Béthencourt's kingdom had been sold into slavery off the islands and replaced with peasant farmers and artisans recruited in Castile, Galicia and Normandy, who struggled to adapt to the arid climate. At this point, Béthencourt's campaign of conquest stalled. The open landscapes of Lanzarote and Fuerteventura provided few natural refuges for the inhabitants, while all three islands had already lost much of their populations to slave raiders. They were the low-hanging fruit. The remaining islands, La Gomera, Tenerife, Las Palmas and Gran Canaria, were beyond his reach. All had larger populations and rugged, forested landscapes that the lightly armed Guanches used skillfully to defy Béthencourt's attempts at conquest. It probably did not help him that he was abandoned by his most able lieutenant, Gadifer de la Salle, following a quarrel over his submission to Castile: Gadifer seems to have been much the better soldier of the two. The petty three-island kingdom he was left with would never provide the resources to support his ambition to explore the African coast, and in 1412 Béthencourt, thoroughly disillusioned, returned to Normandy, leaving his nephew, Maciot, in command.

The Treaty of Alcáçovas

In 1418, Maciot sold his rights to conquer the remaining islands to a Castilian count, Enrique Pérez de Guzmán. The next sixty years of Canarian history were marked by frequent changes of lordship, Guanche rebellions, the conquest of La Gomera by the Castilian nobleman Hernán Peraza in 1450 and several unsuccessful attempts by the Portuguese to make good their own claim to the islands. This last dispute was finally settled in Castile's favour in 1479 by the Treaty of Alcáçovas as part of a wider agreement about spheres of influence in the Atlantic. The downside of the treaty for Castile was that it gave Portugal the exclusive right to explore the West African coast. Considering that the original motive for conquering the Canary Islands had been to use them as a base to find the River of Gold, this was a considerable disappointment for the Castilians, but there was still the prospect that the islands would be a profitable colony in their own right. The year of the treaty also marked the birth of modern Spain, with the kingdoms of Castile and Aragon entering a dynastic union when Queen Isabella of Castile's husband Ferdinand became king of Aragon. The couple, both of them equally determined to build the power of the new Spanish kingdom, began to take a more direct interest in the conquest of the remaining three independent Canary Islands, La Palma, Gran Canaria and Tenerife. The priority of the Catholic Monarchs, as Isabella and Ferdinand styled themselves, was, however, completing the conquest of Granada, the last Moorish state in Iberia, and they had few resources to spare, so the final stages of the islands' conquest were largely funded by commercial interests in Seville and Genoa, by which they hoped to recoup their investments through trading privileges, sugar plantations and slaves.

The conquest of Gran Canaria began on 24 June 1478 and took nearly five years. The Spanish later considered that it cost more in blood to conquer the island and convert its people to Christianity than any other of the Canaries. A well-equipped 600-strong force, armed with horses, firearms and cannon, led by the Aragonese nobleman Juan Rejón, landed in the north of the island and built a stockade in a palm grove that became the nucleus around which the city of Las Palmas developed. Four days after the Spanish landing, a 2,000-strong Guanche army tried to storm the stockade, but it was defeated with heavy losses by a cavalry charge. The Canarians retreated to the mountainous interior and turned to guerilla warfare under a charismatic warrior called Doramas, a commoner appointed as war-leader by the island's ruler, Tenesor Semidán. A long stalemate followed, with raids and counter-raids, which was finally broken by a new commander, Pedro da Vera, who brought in reinforcements from La Gomera. These included a large contingent of Gomeran Guanches. Because of their long isolation from one another, the Guanches had no sense of common identity, so the people of one island did not see it as collaboration with a common enemy to fight for the Castilians against the people of another island, any more than the Tlaxcalans would later do when they allied with the Spanish against their long-time enemies the Aztecs. To try to break Guanche resistance, de Vera hunted Doramas down and succeeded in killing him, supposedly in chivalrous single combat, at the battle of Arucas in August 1481. Doramas's head was triumphantly displayed at Las Palmas, but the war continued. De Vera resorted increasingly to scorched earth and terror, driving off livestock and burning captives alive in retaliation for the deaths of Spanish soldiers. Despite these atrocities, it was only with the capture of Tenesor Semidán in February the next year that Guanche resistance finally began to crack. Tenesor was taken to Spain for baptism: he returned as Fernando Guanarteme and, thereafter, remained a loyal supporter of the Catholic Monarchs, encouraging his people to convert and fighting with the Spanish during the conquest of Tenerife. One last chief, Betejuí, continued to hold out in the mountain fortress of La Fortaleza with Tenesor's daughter Guayarmina, who he may actually have kidnapped for her symbolic importance as a member of the ruling class. Through Tenesor Semidán's mediation, Guayarmina surrendered the fortress on 29 April 1483, but, rather than submit, Betejuí committed an operatic suicide by leaping from a high cliff shouting '*Atis Tirma*' (for my land): many of his followers did the same sooner than face slavery. Baptized as Margarita Fernández Guanarteme, Guayarmina was then married to the hidalgo Miguel de Trejo Carvajo, just one of several diplomatic marriages made during the conquest between high-ranking indigenous women and conquistadors, a practice that continued in the New World.

In September 1492, the conquistador Alonso Fernández de Lugo, one of de Vera's subordinates in the conquest of Gran Canaria, invaded La Palma with orders to conquer the island within twelve months: it took him just seven. One of the smaller Canary islands, La Palma, with a population estimated to have been no more than 4,000, could raise only a few hundred warriors to oppose the Spanish. Most of the island's chiefs immediately submitted to the Spanish, but one chief, Tanausú, held out in the Caldera de Taburiente, a spectacular natural fortress in the centre of the island, a roughly circular valley surrounded by 2,000-metre-high cliffs, created by volcanic activity and erosion some 2 million years ago. The caldera can be entered only through two narrow defiles, and it proved to be impregnable to direct assault. After a seven-month standoff, on 3 May 1493, de Lugo enticed Tanausú out of the safety of the caldera by offering a truce and gifts through the intermediary of a Christian convert. The offer was made in bad faith; Tanausú was captured in an ambush and sold into slavery off the islands: he reputedly starved himself to death soon afterwards.

Flushed with his easy victory on La Palma, de Lugo petitioned Queen Isabella to give him command of the conquest of Tenerife, the last unconquered Canary Island. She agreed, but at a price: de Lugo had to surrender to the crown his rights to the revenues of La Palma to which he was entitled as conqueror, and he had to self-fund the expedition, which he did by selling his sugar plantations on Gran Canaria. It was a good deal for the crown and a big risk for de Lugo. Over the preceding 150 years, the Guanches of Tenerife had earned a reputation for fierceness. Slave raiders had usually beaten a hasty retreat to their boats under a hail of stones and javelins, and two previous attempts at conquest, in 1434, by the Portuguese, and in 1464 and 1492, by the Spanish, had already been defeated. However, de Lugo still had reasons to be hopeful.

The conquest of Tenerife

De Lugo landed near present-day Santa Cruz, on Tenerife's southeast coast, in April 1494 with 2,000 Spanish infantry and 200 cavalry, together with Guanche auxiliaries recruited from Gran Canaria and La Gomera. He had chosen his landing place with great care to exploit divisions on the island. Tenerife was divided into nine chiefdoms or *menceyatos* under chiefs called *menceys*, who were far from united about how to react to the Spanish. The patient work of missionaries over the previous century had built a small Christian congregation on the island's southeast coast: it even had its own cult in the Virgin of Candelaria. According to legend, around 1392, two goatherds found on the seashore a miraculous statue of a woman carrying a child in one hand and a green candle in the other (hence Candelaria). The Guanches associated the statue with their goddess Chaxiraxi, the Sun Mother, but around fifty years later it was recognized as the Virgin Mary by Antón Guanche, a former slave who had been converted to Christianity on Lanzarote and returned to the island. The original statue was destroyed by a tsunami in 1826, but it is known to have been carved with a meaningless inscription in the Latin alphabet, which suggests that it was made by someone who was familiar with writing but was not actually literate, most likely a Guanche convert. Since its earliest days, the Catholic Church was adept at appropriating and assimilating pagan cults and festivals to make Christianity more acceptable to converts. That this was the case here is all the more likely because the feast of the Virgin is celebrated on 14–15 August, the same time as the Guanches' Beñesmer harvest festival. The *menceys* of this semi-Christianized part of Tenerife formed a 'peace party' who favoured negotiations with the Spanish rather than war. Añaterve, the *mencey* of Güímar, even provided auxiliaries for de Lugo.

After building a fortified camp, de Lugo began to advance into the island's mountainous interior. He tried to negotiate with Bencomo, the powerful *mencey* of the anti-Spanish faction, who rejected his peace terms. Perhaps through overconfidence or poor scouting, at the end of May, de Lugo led his army into the narrow Barranco de San Antonio in Acentejo, where it was ambushed by Bencomo's 3,000-strong Guanche army. The lightly armed Guanches moved quickly and freely across the craggy terrain, raining stones and spears down on the Spanish, who had no space to manoeuvre or deploy their cavalry effectively. De Lugo narrowly escaped the debacle disguised as a common soldier, but he left over 900 of his troops behind, dead on the battlefield. Also left behind were most of his teeth; they were knocked out by a rock thrown by a Guanche warrior. With his couple of hundred survivors, de Lugo retreated to Gran Canaria to rebuild his army, raising the funds from Italian business interests and the sale of the last of his property. After his departure, a demoralizing epidemic, called by the Guanche 'the great drowsiness', thought to have been smallpox or typhus, ripped through the island. Christians saw the hand of God at work, and, very likely, so too did the pagan Guanches, whose own gods were obviously powerless to protect them. One friar, Abreu de Galindo, believed that the epidemic killed two thirds of the 15,000 Guanches on the island. While this is probably an exaggeration, Friar Espinosa wrote that, 'had it not been for the pestilence, the conquest would have taken much longer, the people being warlike, stubborn and wary'.

De Lugo returned to Tenerife in November. This new army was about the same size as the first, but it included many veterans of the conquest of Granada and was well equipped with crossbows, arquebuses and cannon. This time, de Lugo's scouts did their job well and it was Bencomo who was caught unawares at Aguere and forced to fight on open ground that favoured the Spanish. Bencomo was killed in the battle, along with his brother Tinguaro and as many as 2,000 of their warriors. A year's guerilla warfare followed before Guanche forces, now led by Bencomo's grandson Bentor, were brought to battle again and defeated at Acentejo on Christmas Day 1495. After such catastrophic losses, Guanche resistance collapsed and Bentor, like Betejuí before him, committed suicide by leaping from a cliff, in February 1496. With Guanche resistance crushed, de Lugo moved quickly to establish administrative control of the island, founding the new city of San Cristóbal de La Laguna as his capital on the land of a pro-Spanish *mencey* in the north of the island. The first settlers were the soldiers of de Lugo's army, and they built their homes haphazardly wherever they liked. In 1502, the city was refounded on a tidy rectangular grid plan, with wide streets and public plazas, inspired by Leonardo da Vinci's plan for the Italian city of Imola. The plan subsequently became the model for Spanish colonial towns across the New World, for which reason the city was recognized as a UNESCO World Heritage Site in 1999. Since the Spanish felt confident that no resistance was now to be expected from the Guanche, San Cristóbal was planned from the start to be completely unfortified. De Lugo's reward for his efforts was the title *adelantado* (military governor) of the Canary Islands with vice-regal authority over the distribution of land and water rights.

'A country strongly fortified by nature'

It had taken the Spanish almost a century to conquer at most 80,000 Stone Age herders. Why had it taken so long? The answer is only partly to do with the brave and determined Guanche resistance. The conquest proceeded in a distinctly haphazard way, without central direction or any colonial masterplan: the conquest of each island was the result of an individual initiative by an opportunistic conquistador who had to fund his expedition by mortgaging property or by offering commercial opportunities to merchant investors. The Castilian crown offered legitimacy for the expeditions but little in the way of cash, ships or troops. Except on Lanzarote and Fuerteventura, the Guanches had the advantages of terrain that they knew intimately and was easy to defend. George Glas, a Scottish merchant resident in the Canary Islands in the 1760s, wondered how the Spanish had ever managed to conquer them, because they 'are so full of deep narrow valleys, or gullies, high rugged mountains, and narrow difficult passes that a body of men cannot march into any of them the distance of a league from the shore, before they come to places where a hundred men may easily baffle the efforts of a thousand. This being the case, where could shipping enough be found to transport a sufficient number of troops to subdue such a people and in a country so strongly fortified by nature?' In such terrain, iron swords and pikes, and their slow-firing early firearms, were only decisive advantages for the Spanish on the rare occasions when the Guanches could be brought to battle on open ground. A more important advantage for the Spanish was their horses, which terrified the Guanches every bit as much as they would later terrify the Aztecs and Incas. A cavalry charge by a few dozen Spanish horsemen was usually enough to disperse thousands of Guanche warriors.

Difficult terrain and courage could not in the end overcome all the advantages the Spanish possessed. First among these was the lack of unity of the Guanches themselves. They did not see themselves as a single people, and how could they have? Before the Europeans arrived, they may not even have known that the other Canary Islands were inhabited. Even if the Guanches could have seen the Spanish as a common enemy, their lack of seafaring technology would have prevented the people of one island helping those of another. This gave the Spanish the luxury of being able to conquer one island at a time and recruit Guanches of one island to fight against those of another. When the Spanish did suffer serious defeats, they simply retreated to the safety of their ships and regrouped on one of the previously pacified islands, secure in the knowledge that their enemy could not pursue them. The Guanches' lack of outside support also left them vulnerable to Spanish scorched earth tactics. Even if they could not defeat the Guanches in battle, the Spanish could still burn crops and drive off livestock to starve them into submission. This kind of attritional warfare was devastatingly effective, because the Guanches had no means of bringing in food supplies from the outside. Although it was not their specific objective, the activities of missionaries also helped undermine Guanche resistance. By creating small Christian congregations on unconquered islands, they helped foster internal divisions, with the converts forming a pro-Spanish faction, which favoured negotiations, and the pagans an anti-Spanish faction, which favoured war. Although their impact is hard to quantify, epidemics of European diseases, to which the isolated Guanches were vulnerable, also took their toll, as they would do later in the Americas and Australasia.

Extinction

The extinction of the Guanches came quickly after the completion of the conquest. At the time of their first European contacts, around 80,000 Guanches lived on the Canary Islands: by the end of the conquest, barely 20,000 still survived. The male Guanche population declined more quickly than the female. Thousands of Guanche men had been killed fighting the Spanish, while thousands more who had been captured in these battles were sold into slavery off the islands. Defeated rebels were punished in the same way. After a rebellion in 1488, 260 Gomeran warriors were enslaved and sold off the island to forestall future rebellions. Even those who cooperated with the Spanish were not protected from enslavement. After his defeat on Tenerife in 1494, de Lugo sold 350 of his Gomeran allies into slavery to help recoup his financial losses. The completion of the conquest did not end enslavement: de Lugo was a harsh governor, and he treated all Guanches as the spoils of war. Slave traders put the highest value on able-bodied men who were capable of hard labour, so women were less likely to find buyers. Even those not enslaved lost their lands and flocks. Only about fifty of the Guanche chiefs who had allied with the Spanish were granted lands and then not on their home islands and not on good lands either.

Faced with economic marginalization and social discrimination, even after converting to Christianity, many Guanche men left the islands voluntarily, signing on as crew on ships or fighting as mercenaries in Spain's wars in North Africa. Others emigrated to the new Spanish colonies in the Caribbean. Early post-conquest visitors to the Canaries were struck by the small numbers of Guanche men they saw compared to women. The Guanches were replaced by settlers from Castile, Catalonia, the Basque Country, Portugal and Italy seeking farming and trade opportunities. Like many frontier societies, there were fewer women than men, so many Guanche women, willingly or not, were able to integrate into colonial society by marriage to settlers. The sexual imbalance is reflected in the DNA of the modern Canary Islanders, around 33–43 per cent of whom have inherited Guanche DNA through the female line, while just 7–8 per cent have inherited Guanche DNA though the male line. The Guanche were probably effectively extinct as a people by the middle of the sixteenth century. The Italian merchant Girolamo Benzoni, who visited La Palma on his way to the New World in 1541, met only one Guanche man, an octogenarian who chose to remain drunk all the time rather than witness the extinction of his people: the Guanches 'were nearly all at an end', Benzoni thought. Fifty years later, the missionary friar Espinosa observed that only a few Guanches still survived and they were all 'mixed-bloods'. The extinction of the Guanches has been described as 'Europe's first overseas settler genocide'.[44] Of course, the Spanish did not actually set out to exterminate the Guanches, but enslavement, deportation, cultural repression and economic marginalization can be just as effective as violent genocide. The Guanches were just the first of many indigenous peoples driven to extinction during the centuries of European colonial expansion: the story would stay the same, it was just the names and locations that changed. It is likely, too, that the prehistoric extinctions of Europe's Mesolithic hunter-gatherers and Neolithic farmers as a result of their encounters with technologically superior immigrants followed similar trajectories, and similar examples can be found on other continents too. It seems to be a recurrent theme in world history that doesn't reflect too well on the human race.

Remaking the Canary Islands

Even before the conquest was completed, the settlers had begun remaking the Canary Islands in their image, transforming the landscape with crops and livestock introduced from the Mediterranean. Cattle, camels, donkeys, rabbits, chickens, pigeons, partridges, ducks, honeybees, grapevines, melons and, most important of all, sugar cane. The two islands that had been conquered first, Lanzarote and Fuerteventura, were arid to begin with, and overgrazing by camels and feral donkeys turned large areas into semi-desert in the sixteenth century. The two islands enjoyed some economic importance as suppliers of grain to the other islands, but they made no one rich. The western islands of Tenerife, Gran Canaria, La Gomera and La Palma, however, proved very suitable for growing sugar cane. One of the pioneers of sugar production was Pedro da Vera, who set up a sugar mill on Gran Canaria in 1484 to compete with the Portuguese, who had been growing sugar cane on Madeira since around 1450. The settlers began clearing the islands' forests for building timber and to fuel the furnaces that were used to reduce the cane juice in the islands' sugar mills, while introduced livestock prevented regeneration and left land vulnerable to erosion from flash floods. Deforestation quickly impacted the islands' fresh water supplies, much of which came from condensation dripping off the leaves of the trees in the highland cloud forests. When Columbus visited the islands in 1492, he observed that the deforestation had caused many watercourses to dry up. The Canary Islands' sugar boom was over by 1600, out-competed by slave-worked plantations in the New World. By this time, however, the Canary Islands had achieved a new strategic importance. As Columbus had realized in 1492, the mid-Atlantic wind patterns made the islands the ideal departure point for voyages to the New World.

15

Keeping the lights burning

670–1495

Survivors – Celtic connections – The 'royal fish' – Blood in the water – The first modern whalers – Inventing the whaleboat – Did the Basques beat Columbus to America? – In search of phantoms – Plans and rumours – The search for Brasil – Avalon in the Atlantic – 'Exterior parts'

A coat of arms is always a statement about identity and heritage. Not surprisingly, the coat of arms of the upmarket French Basque Country seaside resort of Biarritz has a distinctly maritime look about it, a guiding star, two scallop shells, symbolizing long voyages to distant lands, and an improbably cheerful-looking whale being pursued by a whaleboat. Further south and west along the Bay of Biscay from Biarritz, the whale and whaleboat motif is repeated on the arms of the ports of Hendaye, Getaria, Hondarribia, Ondarroa and Lekeito, and others. In every case, they commemorate the historical importance of whaling to the regional economy in the medieval and early modern periods. Shipbuilding, trade and fishing first led the Basques to the sea, but it was their unique skills as whalers that made them famous. When the English decided to get into the Arctic whaling business at the beginning of the seventeenth century, they went straight to the acknowledged masters, the Basques, to show them how it was done. Twenty-four Basques joined the first English commercial whaling expedition to Svalbard in 1611 to harpoon the whales and direct the flensing and boiling of the blubber. Two years later, a Dutch whaling expedition took twelve Basques with them to Svalbard to do the same jobs and the Danes followed suit in 1617, recruiting eighteen Basques for a whaling expedition to Svalbard: the Basques taught their fellow Europeans how to become commercial whalers. With whales now a conservation icon, that might not seem like a recommendation, but for centuries whale oil kept Europe's lights burning and lubricated its machinery. The skills developed by medieval Basque whalers quite literally helped oil the wheels of the Industrial Revolution.

Survivors

The Basques are Europe's great survivors, a last relict of its Neolithic population which, somehow, held its ground during the early Bronze Age population replacement. Despite periods of persecution, they have succeeded in preserving their unique identity and language in their homeland in the southeastern corner of the great bay that is named after them, Biscay, for 4,000 years without ever being politically united or having a national state of their own. The Basque Country straddles the Pyrenees, and for most of the Middle Ages it was shared between the small Iberian kingdom of Navarre and the French duchy of Aquitaine, which was a possession of the English crown from 1154 to 1453. The Basques' homeland is mountainous, and its main resources were timber and wool from large flocks of sheep kept on upland pastures. It was this lack of resources that encouraged the Basques to turn to the sea, but it wasn't as simple as going fishing. The richest fishing grounds are always found in the shallow, fertile waters of the continental shelves, but the Basque Country's coast doesn't have one; it descends steeply down into the dark and cold of the abyss. It was as merchant seamen, not as fishers or whalers, that the Basques first learned their seafaring skills.

Like the Phoenicians in the ancient Mediterranean, the

Basques capitalized on their geographical position on the Bay of Biscay, which made them natural middlemen for the exchange of goods between the central Spanish kingdom of Castile and northern Europe. Sailing in ships that they built with local timber in their own shipyards, Basque merchants became frequent visitors to Flanders, England and Ireland, trading Iberian wine, wool, olive oil, raisins, dried figs, saffron, iron and mercury for fine cloth and fish. Skills learned on voyages back and forth across Biscay's notoriously stormy waters opened up new opportunities for the Basques to exploit the distant, but rich, English and Irish fisheries, and for pioneering whale hunting on the open seas. Thanks to their experience as open-sea navigators, Basque seafarers were in great demand as pilots and crew on the early trans-Atlantic expeditions to the New World. At least eighteen of the eighty-seven crew of Columbus's expedition in 1492 were Basques, and his flagship, the *Santa Maria*, was Basque-built, as was the first ship ever to circumnavigate the world, Magellan's *Victoria*: the man who sailed it home after Magellan's death in the Philippines, Juan Sebastián Elcano, was himself a Basque.

Celtic connections

Basque fishermen first began crossing the Bay of Biscay to catch herrings, pilchards and hake off the coast of Cornwall as early as 1202, but they had to buy licences from the English crown to salt or dry their catch onshore. Once the practice of processing fish at sea became established in the fifteenth century, it became much harder for the English crown to regulate their activities and also allowed the Basques to extend their activities further out to Ireland's Atlantic coast, where they found the local Gaelic chieftains very welcoming. Herrings and pilchards could be salted at sea, but hake, a member of the cod family, the Basques still needed to process on land. Ireland is too mild and humid to produce stockfish, so the hake was heavily salted to help dehydrate and preserve it before it was laid out on bare rock surfaces to finish drying: this salted and dried hake might actually have been the original *bacalao* (*bacalhau* in Portugal), the salted and dried cod which is still one of the staples of Iberian cuisine. Such large numbers of fishing boats from the Basque Country and other parts of Spain (possibly as many as 600 every year) were operating off Ireland's Atlantic coast in the fifteenth century that the English crown, which nominally ruled Ireland, became seriously worried about lost revenue from what it regarded as illegal fish exports. However, effective English power did not extend far beyond the merchant towns of Ireland's east coast, so there was very little they could do about it. In 1465, the English crown introduced licences for foreign boats to fish in Irish waters, but they could only enforce this in the Irish Sea, leaving the chieftains of the Atlantic west free to operate their own rival licensing systems. The O'Driscolls of Baltimore in County Cork charged fishing boats nineteen shillings, a fairly hefty sum at the time, plus a barrel each of flour and salt, a hogshead of beer (around 300 litres) and a dish of fish three times a week in return for the use of the local fishing grounds and anchorages. If the crew wanted to land and 'dry their catch on a rock' they had to pay an extra eight shillings and six pence. The fishermen were allowed to buy provisions on shore at prices fixed by the chieftains: a cow would cost them eight pence and a sheep or a pig, a penny. Like the English fishermen in Iceland, the Basques and other foreign fishermen liked to do a bit of trade on the side, and the chieftains, of course, expected their cut. The O'Driscolls claimed the right to 4 gallons from every butt* of wine landed and any goods that were imported had first to be offered to the chieftain at a preferential rate. The chieftains enforced the rules using their galley fleet and tried violators in a weekly court in Baltimore. The O'Donnells of Donegal were so deeply involved in the fishing trade that they became known as 'the Lords of the Fish' on the continent. For the chieftains, the importance of the Basque fishing fleet went beyond commercial opportunism. Licensing

* A medieval butt contained 106 English gallons or 126 US gallons or 482 litres.

was an assertion of sovereignty and the revenues helped finance the chieftains' ongoing struggle to maintain their independence from the English crown. It was only after the final suppression of the Gaelic lordships at the beginning of the seventeenth century that the English government was able to end the illegal Basque fishery, but by this time they were heading even further afield, to fish and hunt whales off Newfoundland and Labrador.

The 'royal fish'

Medieval Europeans would have been puzzled by the modern distinction between fishing and whaling. Despite being well aware that they breathe air, they thought of whales simply as being very big fish: fish live in water, whales look like fish and live in water, therefore, the reasoning went, whales must be fish too. Theologically this mattered, because whale meat counted as a 'cold' food which could safely be eaten on holy days, creating a ready market for it. Whales were 'royal fish' and their meat was considered a high-status food fit for a king, or a queen, for that matter: Elizabeth I of England was just one of those monarchs known to have enjoyed feasting on porpoise meat. In most of the kingdoms that possessed an Atlantic coastline, the crown imposed tolls and levies on the whales that were either washed up on their shores or caught in their waters. The kings of Castile claimed one in fifteen whales caught off its coast, the Danish kings a more modest one in thirty. Whale meat is lean and easily preserved by salting or by cutting it up into strips and air-drying it to make jerky. Modern Europeans generally pale at the thought of eating the whitish rubbery blubber, but their medieval ancestors enjoyed it, as the Inuit still do. The tongue was considered the tastiest part of the whale, but the hunters rarely got to eat it themselves: if the crown didn't claim it as a toll, the local port or ecclesiastical authorities did.

As whaling became more commercialized in the later Middle Ages, the meat became less important than the blubber, which was rendered to produce a golden-coloured lamp oil. Whale oil might have smelled slightly fishy, but its flame burned brighter and with less smoke than tallow and vegetable oil lamps and it was less expensive than beeswax candles, which were the gold-standard of medieval lighting. Demand was especially strong from the church, and the earliest record of Basques trading in whale products was the sale of forty 220-litre casks of whale oil to the French abbey of Jumièges by the French Basque Country port of Bayonne in 670. Another whale product that was traded internationally was 'whalebone', which is not strictly a bone at all but baleen, the keratin feeding filters from a baleen whale's mouth. This was valued where lightness, strength and flexibility was at a premium, for example for belts and riding gear, in lightweight body armour, such as jerkins and helmets (think of it as medieval kevlar), and for stiffening women's bodices. These precursors of the whalebone corset became a must-have fashion item around 1450 after Agnès Sorel, the notoriously exhibitionist mistress of France's King Charles VII, made it acceptable for a woman to display her cleavage to the world. Over the next few centuries, an awful lot of whales were going to die in the cause of forcing women's bodies to conform to a preconceived ideal of feminine beauty.

Beached whales were being scavenged in the Basque Country in the Palaeolithic period, and this ancient practice was still an important, if unreliable, source of whale products in the Middle Ages all along the Atlantic coast. The whale oil Bayonne shipped to Jumièges was most likely from a single beached whale. Beached whales and drift whales (dead or dying animals found floating at sea) were eagerly scavenged, and in the hard winters of the Little Ice Age even a single carcass could be enough to save a famine-struck Icelandic or Faeroese community from starvation. Grateful communities were inclined to see such lucky finds as evidence of God's providential nature. A whale carcass was so valuable that disputes between the finders and the owners of the shore on which they were beached were common. The thirteenth-century *Grettir's Saga* describes how one such dispute in Iceland turned violent. The carcass of a large baleen whale was found by a farmer called Thorstein on a beach in Reykjanes whose ownership was disputed by two chieftains, Flosi and Thorgrim. Icelandic law required whale finders to notify the landowner about the stranding. Thorstein chose to notify his friend Flosi. By the time Thorgrim and his followers arrived, having heard rumours of the discovery, Flosi's men were already butchering the carcass and loading meat and blubber into their boats. Both parties had come prepared with axes and knives to butcher the whale and neither side was willing to back down. In the ensuing fight over possession, at least three men were killed, one of whom was battered to death with one of the whale's rib bones, one lost a leg and many others were injured. Flosi was one of those injured and, to make things worse for him, he was held responsible for the killings when the dispute came before the Althing and he was outlawed. The Norwegian Gulaþing law code of *c.*1250 provided clear guidelines to try to prevent this sort of violent ownership dispute. Shares were apportioned depending on the circumstances in which the whale was found, but, no matter whose land the whale had been washed up on, the finder was always entitled to as much of the blubber as would safely fill a boat nine ells long (about 4 metres). The law was designed to discourage greed: if the finder overloaded his boat so much that it sank, he lost his entitlement to any share of the whale.

Blood in the water

While they must have been going on since prehistoric times, the earliest recorded Atlantic whale hunts date to the Viking Age. Ottar, the Norwegian merchant who visited King Alfred in *c.*890, boasted of his whaling exploits along the coast of Arctic Norway, and whale hunts are recorded from around the same time in the Faeroe Islands, Ireland and Normandy, all of them areas with Norse settlements. Norse whaling was small-scale and largely for subsistence rather than as part of a commercial enterprise. Whales were hunted only in sheltered inshore waters, never on the open sea. The usual tactic was to use fleets of small fishing boats to trap schools of small whales, like pilot whales, dolphins and porpoises, when they swam into confined fjords and bays. The larger whales were usually avoided, because of both the physical dangers and their satanic associations. News of a sighting was spread by bonfires and flags. Local fishermen would scramble for their boats to cut the whales off from the open sea, then they used shouting, beating drums and oars slapped on the water to frighten the animals into a stampede, and nets to herd them into shallow water by the shore, where they could be killed easily with spears, harpoons and large *grindaknívur* ('whale knives').

Lucas Debes, a Faeroese minister, described one such hunt in the seventeenth century. The hunters, he wrote,

> drive the whales with great crying, noise and casting of stones, driving them as fast as they can upon the sands. In the meantime some of the people lie in ambush on the land, till the whales are come on ground, and wade to them as deep as they can, and then kill them chiefly with their weapons, with such fury on both sides, that the water becometh as red as blood, whereby the whale is also blinded, so that it cannot see to run away, it is a strange thing to see that these strong creatures make no resistance, but only plunge as well as they can before the boats, and people, till death cometh upon them, and then they strike terribly with their tails, so that they beat sometimes boats to pieces, and the men come in danger.[45]

A festival atmosphere prevailed after a successful hunt, and there would be feasting and dancing late into the night. The traditional Faeroese *grindadráp* is still conducted in much the same way, and with the same excitement, today as it has been for the last thousand years. In 1298, King Håkon V legislated in the so-called 'Sheep Letter' for the equal distribution of meat and blubber from such kills between the hunters, the church and the crown, but today the *grindadráp* is a non-commercial enterprise and the custom now is to share the meat free with everyone in the local community, even if they have not been actively involved in the hunt. It is this rare opportunity to bring the whole community together in a shared enterprise that makes the *grindadráp* such a valued tradition for the Faeroese, even though they no longer depend on it for subsistence. At its present levels, the hunt is widely acknowledged to be sustainable and the barrage of criticism they receive from foreign animal rights activists is unlikely to persuade the Faeroese to abandon something they regard as central to their national identity.

The first modern whalers

What makes the Basques so important is that they took whaling to the next level, turning it from an opportunist subsistence activity into a fully commercial enterprise that sustained a shore-based processing industry and exported whale products far beyond the local area. The Bay of Biscay had plenty of whales, but the coastline of the Basque Country has few deep bays and inlets into which they could conveniently be herded and trapped. If the Basques were going to catch whales in any numbers, they were going to have to go out and look for them on the open sea. Chasing small, fast, agile whales like dolphins, porpoises and pilot whales on open water was not a practical proposition, but fortunately for the Basques there was slower, and much larger, prey to be had. Every October, pods of North Atlantic right whales (*Eubalena glacialis*) migrated south from their summer feeding grounds in the Arctic Ocean to calve in the warmer waters of the bay and would remain there until March. Twenty metres long and weighing around 90 tonnes when adult, right whales are among the larger baleen whales (for comparison, a blue whale, the largest of all whales, weighs on average 100 tonnes). Around 40 per cent of the whale's body weight is blubber, enough to produce on average around 7,000 litres of oil after rendering, which would be worth around $320,000 at modern prices. The blubber makes right whales buoyant and, very conveniently for whalers, keeps them afloat after they have been killed, making it easy to recover the carcass. Another attraction for whalers is that right whales are slow swimmers by whale standards, managing only around 6 kilometres per hour, much less than a good crew of strong oarsmen can manage. Slow doesn't mean docile, however; right whales fight back hard when attacked, by lobtailing, slapping their enormous tail flukes down hard upon the sea, and they can easily capsize or smash a small boat. Right whales, famously, are supposed to have got their name because they were the 'right whales' to catch. It makes perfect sense given their characteristics, but it's a case of modern folk etymology based on a linguistic misunderstanding. When the name was first recorded in the early eighteenth century, 'right' was used in the sense of 'true' or 'typical', so, in modern usage, 'right whale' meant something like 'the regular whale'. Right whales were the regular whales in the sense that they were the ones that whalers were most likely to encounter, because they spent most of their lives in coastal waters where they could be spotted from the land.

The main Basque whaling ports were Bayonne, Saint-Jean-de-Luz, Getaria and Biarritz in the French Basque Country, Lekeitio, Bermeo, Santander, Mutriku, San Sebastián, Ondarroa and Hondarribia in the Spanish Basque Country, and Castro Urdiales in Cantabria, but dozens of smaller ports also took part. Commercial whaling must, however, have been established by 1059, when King Sancho IV of Navarre legislated to regulate the market for whale meat at Bayonne. From this time on, the whaling business was systematically regulated and taxed by the kings of Navarre and, north of the Pyrenees, by the English crown. When, in 1237, King Ferdinand III of Navarre granted the port of Zarautz a town charter, he ordered that 'in accordance with custom', the crown was to receive a slice of every whale, cut from the head to the tail. In nearby Getaria, the tax was the whole of the first whale landed each year, though the custom was that the king graciously returned half the value to the town. In the fourteenth century, England's King Edward III levied a tax of £6 on every whale landed at Biarritz, the equivalent of about £40,000 ($48,000) today: whales were valuable. City authorities also took their cut from the trade. The *cabildo* (council) of San Sebastián charged a toll of two silver *dineros* on cargoes of whalebone warehoused in the town, while in Lekeitio the *cabildo* divided all the whalebone that was landed in the port in 1381 into three parts, two of which were used to pay for essential harbour maintenance, and the third for rebuilding the parish church. One of the heaviest tolls was imposed by the *cabildo* of Getaria in 1478, when it decreed that half the value of every whale landed be used to pay for repairs to the harbour and the church, and that was on top of the king's share.

Inventing the whaleboat

During the whaling season, the Basques manned *vigilias*, lookout towers, on high ground above their fishing villages to watch for whales spouting close to the coast. On sighting a whale, the watchers alerted the village by lighting a beacon, raising a flag or ringing a bell, triggering a rush to the shore, where the hunters' whaleboats, called *txalupas*, were kept ready for immediate launching. The Basque *txalupa* (Spanish *chalupa*, English 'shallop') was the first boat to be built specifically for hunting whales; it was the direct ancestor of the famous Nantucket whaleboats. Although in the modern period they would be fitted with small sails, the medieval *txalupa* was a rowing boat, built long and narrow for speed, around 8 to 9 metres long, and 2 metres broad. *Txalupas* had crews of four or six oarsmen, a steersman, who sat at the stern with a steering oar, and a harpooner, who stood at the prow. The boats were double-ended and clinker-built above the waterline, like a Viking ship, but smooth hulled below the waterline. The partial clinker construction is thought to be evidence of a Norse influence on Basque shipbuilding, which might well have come from maritime contacts with Normandy.

The whaleboats worked in groups to get within harpoon-throwing range of a whale as quickly but, at the same time, as stealthily as possible. Oars were often wrapped in rags to muffle their sound as they dipped into the water. It was essential not to alarm the whale and cause it to flee before the harpooner was ready to strike. The moment of throwing the harpoon was accompanied by a prayer to God to allow the crew to kill the whale quickly without it capsizing the boat or dragging it, and them, into the depths of the ocean. A single harpoon strike was never sufficient to kill a whale, the whalers knew that. The Basques used a type of toggling harpoon that lodged itself in the whale's body in the same way as those used by the Thule Inuit on the other side of the Atlantic (see p. 292). The first harpoon was attached to a large, hollowed-out gourd that was thrown into the water both to act as a drogue, to create drag, and as a buoy to help the whalers keep sight of the whale as, hurt and frightened, it attempted to flee. When the pursuing whalers could approach close enough, they struck more harpoons home: these were attached to wooden drogues, which created more drag to slow the whale down and gradually tire it out. The chase often continued for five or six hours. Only when the whale was completely exhausted did the whalers close in for the kill, now using long lances to penetrate the blubber and strike at its heart. This might take several blows and was the most dangerous part of the hunt because the whale's last desperate struggles for life could be very violent. A thrashing tail could capsize or smash a whaleboat, drowning, injuring or killing the whalers: whaling took courage as well as skill. Once the whale was dead, the whalers attached ropes to its tail so that they could tow their prize back to port for processing. Larger boats, with more oarsmen, which shadowed the hunt, helped the tired whalers with the towing.

Back in port, the whale was winched above the high tide level for butchering. Almost every part of the animal found some use. The thick layer of blubber under the skin was the most important part of the whale as far as the Basques were concerned. This was stripped from the carcass using specialized flensing knives, cut up into small pieces, taken to the tryworks and boiled in large cauldrons called trypots to extract the valuable oil, which was stored in barrels for export. The smell produced by the boiling blubber was, apparently, nauseating, so most tryworks were banished to the outskirts of the community, much as the garum manufacturers of the ancient world had been. The 200 or so strips of baleen were removed from the whale's mouth, and washed and dried prior to sale. The whale's rib bones were used for fencing and even the whale's brightly coloured faeces were processed to make a red dye for fabrics (the colour comes from the iron-rich crustaceans which form the basis of a baleen whale's diet). The whale's skin was used to make leather for boots and ropes and the meat was sold on the local markets, except for the tongue, which, as a delicacy, was reserved for the town's governors.

There are no reliable estimates of the total number of whales taken by medieval Basque whalers. Records of whale catches for the two boats operated by the Spanish Basque Country port of Lekeitio show that, between 1517 and 1662, the average annual catch was two and a half whales. The greatest number killed in a single year was six, recorded in 1536 and 1538. If the catches of the other major ports were comparable, the annual catch may have been from several dozens up to around 100 whales. While this doesn't sound like a lot, right whales are slow breeders, and the species had been hunted to commercial extinction in the Bay of Biscay by the seventeenth century. The last sighting of a right whale in the bay was in 1977. In their hunts, the Basques often targeted calves first. When the mother swam to protect her injured calf, she was also killed, providing two whales for the effort of chasing one. While this was obviously an efficient hunting strategy, it only exacerbated the long-term unsustainability of the hunt. Not that the whalers understood this. Medieval Christians believed that all creatures, from the lowest to the highest all the way up to God himself, were linked in a hierarchy known as the Great Chain of Being. This concept did not allow for the possibility of extinction, because this would break the divinely ordained chain of creation, and God, of course, would not allow this. If the whales had disappeared from Basque waters, it had to be because they had gone somewhere else. All the whalers had to do was look further afield to find them.

In order to meet the growing demand for whale oil, in the thirteenth century, the Basques extended their hunts west to the coasts of Cantabria and Galicia, where they rented seasonal shore stations to process their catches. A century later, whalers from San Sebastián were operating off the south coast of Ireland alongside the hake and pilchard fishermen. Using larger sailing ships as a mother-ship for the *txalupas* allowed whalers to make more extended trips away from the coast. Thanks to their buoyancy, whales could be flensed at sea and the blubber chopped up and stored in barrels until it could be landed onshore for rendering. It's likely that, before the end of the fifteenth century, Basque whalers had begun operating in the Atlantic off Ireland's west coast, in the North Sea and possibly also in Icelandic waters. And then, in 1492, Basques sailed with Columbus to the New World – but might they already have been there? The sixteenth-century Breton historian Bertrand d'Argentré certainly thought they had.

Did the Basques beat Columbus to America?

The Basques and their Breton neighbours from across the Bay of Biscay were certainly very quick to exploit the rich cod-fishing grounds off Newfoundland after their discovery by John Cabot in 1497. The Bretons were there to fish by 1504 and the Basques, to fish and whale, not long after, but, in his *Histoire de Bretaigne*, published in 1588, d'Argentré claimed that both the Basques and the Bretons had actually been secretly fishing off Newfoundland long before this, having discovered 'the New World before any other people'. Nearly a century later, the French historian Étienne de Clairac, who used d'Argentré's book as a source, went further and claimed the Basques had discovered the New World a century before Columbus while pursuing whales across the Atlantic. Moreover, Columbus hadn't discovered the New World for himself, a Basque pilot had shown him the way. By the time the Belgian cetologist Pierre-Joseph Van Beneden wrote on the subject in 1889, this claimed discovery had acquired a firm date, 1372, a full 120 years before Columbus's voyage. However, no documentary or archaeological evidence has ever been found to support claims of a pre-Columbian Basque or Breton presence anywhere in the New World. It has been argued that the Basques and Bretons kept their discoveries shrouded in secrecy to exclude competitors. While it's true that absence of evidence isn't evidence of absence, it isn't evidence of presence either. The truth is probably that, like many subsequent pre-Columbian contact theories, both d'Argentré's original claim, and de Clairac's later elaboration of it, were motivated by reasons of ethnic prestige and nationalism at a time when there were good political reasons for making dubious claims to the prior discovery of a continent Spain claimed as exclusively its own: the needs of the moment probably trumped sound historical method.

In search of phantoms

If the Basques and Bretons did not get to the New World before Columbus, might anyone else have done? By the early 1400s, more ships than ever – Dutch, English, Hanseatic, Basque, Portuguese – were sailing the cold waters of the North Atlantic, trading or chasing fish and whales, and their crews were reporting many sightings of unknown lands, glimpsed through teasingly short breaks in fog and rain. This made the late Middle Ages a particularly fertile period for the discovery of phantom islands. There was Mayda, out in the Atlantic west of Brittany, that first appeared on a sea chart in 1367. Then there was mist-shrouded Brasil, west of Ireland, that first made it onto a map in 1325. In 1424, Antillia, the Island of the Seven Cities, appeared on a map for the first time, on a portolan chart by the Venetian cartographer Zuane Pizzigano, along with the ominously named Satanazes ('the island of devils') and its neighbours, Royllo and Tanmar, three 'newly discovered' legendary islands, all still searching for legends to explain their origins. Somewhere, too, there was Terra do Bacalhau, the 'Land of Cod', claimed by some to be evidence of a pre-Columbian discovery of Newfoundland. There was no shortage, either, of sightings of lands which were given no names. A Madeiran sugar merchant called Antonio Leme claimed to have seen three islands in the west when he was blown off course on a voyage to Africa. The Spanish pilot Pedro de Velasco believed that during a storm he had sailed into the sheltered lee of an island to the west of Ireland. Sure, he couldn't see the island for the rain and fog, but his seaman's instincts told him that it must be there, because the sea had become calm even though the wind was as fierce as ever. There were countless similar, unconfirmed sightings that may just have been another cloud bank or a mirage enhanced by wishful thinking.

Plans and rumours

Irrespective of the truth about these phantom islands, it's hard not to conclude that there was a 'buzz' in the northern ports, an infectious excitement about these sightings, a feeling, a conviction even, that all those Otherworldly islands of legend might actually be real places, slippery and elusive maybe, but places that could be discovered and plotted on a sea chart. The Portuguese discoveries further south, which finally pinned down the locations of the Canary Islands, Madeira and the Azores, must have had something to do with this. These gave substance to those ancient legends about the Fortunate Isles and the Hesperides, and if they had a basis in truth, then what about the other phantom islands, were they real too? In 1462, King Afonso V of Portugal offered a reward to anyone who discovered any of the rumoured islands in the western Atlantic. Plans were laid, but most of them came to nothing.

In 1472, Afonso wrote to the Danish King Christian I, urging him to send out an expedition to look for new lands and islands in the North Atlantic. King Christian certainly got as far as commissioning two German ex-pirates, Didrik Pining and Hans Pothorst, to sail to Iceland and the 'neighbouring regions' (*regiones finitimae*), a vague term which historians have interpreted variously as Newfoundland, a search for the Northwest Passage or an attempt to re-establish contact with the Norse colonies in Greenland. A letter from Carsten Griep, the mayor of Kiel, to Christian I's grandson, Christian III, written in 1551, claims that the expedition landed on the east coast of Greenland at a mountain called *Hvitserk* ('white shirt'), probably 3,694-metre-high Gunnbjørn Fjeld, around 270 kilometres north of the Arctic Circle, where they encountered 'pygmies', by which he probably meant Inuit. Writing just a few years later, the Swedish bishop Olaus Magnus described how the pair had erected some kind of giant compass on a hill there. Conscious of their past, the bishop thought this was somehow intended to guide them on renewed piratical adventures – they did both return to piracy – but it might simply have been a landmark to affirm Denmark's claim to Greenland. There is no evidence, however, that the expedition went any further than this, not even as far as the old Norse settlements, which may, in any case, have been deserted by this time. Uncertainty also surrounds a proposed voyage of exploration by the Portuguese knight Fernão Teles in 1475. King Afonso granted Teles 'the Island of Seven Cities [Antillia] and any other populated islands' that he might find in the Atlantic Ocean, but he most likely never set sail, because he was fighting in Spain in 1476 and got himself killed in a drunken street brawl the year after. Afonso's successor, João II, also commissioned a voyage, this one to be led jointly by Ferdinand van Olmen (Fernão Dulmo), a Flemish settler from the Azores, and João Afonso do Estreito, to discover 'the Island of the Seven Cities' or any 'great islands or the coast of a mainland'. The mainland of what is a fair question; was the voyage intended to follow up on an earlier discovery? The expedition sailed on 1 March 1487, but van Olmen and Estreito were never heard of again. The Azores lie squarely in the middle of the zone of Atlantic westerlies, against which the two explorers would have battled in vain. Their most likely fate was that they ran out of supplies before they got anywhere near the New World.

The search for Brasil

There is less doubt, but still enormous speculation, about the voyages made from the English West Country port of Bristol in search of the phantom island of Brasil in the 1480s. Today, Brasil is usually thought of as part of that extensive archipelago of Celtic Otherworldly islands that was believed to lie a few days' sail west of Ireland. It's true that on maps Brasil was often conflated with phantom islands from that imaginary archipelago, such as St Brendan's Island, but it does not feature in any ancient Celtic myths or in medieval Irish folklore traditions. Brasil's adoption into the Otherworld seems to date only from the eighteenth century, and then on the basis of little more than a conviction that any magical place in the Atlantic must have a Celtic connection. If Brasil isn't Celtic, where else might it come from? The name offers a clue. In the fifteenth century, Brasil was believed to be the source of brazilwood, a tropical Asian hardwood that was used to make a valuable red dye.* This was why the Bristolians wanted to go there, to make money from the dye. In the Genoese dialect, the word *brasil*, literally meaning the glowing embers of a fire, was used loosely in the fifteenth century to describe red dyes, not only that obtained from brazilwood but also the orchil dye that was harvested in the Canary Islands and the Azores: the Azorean island of Terceira was at first even thought to be Brasil, although it was soon decided that it was not, after all, the phantom island. Given how active Genoese mariners were in the Atlantic in the

* Brazilwood also gave its name to the modern country of Brazil, where a related species was found to grow.

fourteenth and fifteenth centuries, a Genoese origin for the legend seems more likely than a Celtic one.

In the fifteenth century, Bristol was England's second port after London, and it remained so until it was overtaken by Liverpool in the eighteenth century. Bristol took advantage of its west-coast position to dominate the lucrative wine trade with Bordeaux and Lisbon, the capital of England's ally, Portugal. With Chester, further north, Bristol was also closely involved in trade with Ireland, and by the 1430s, its merchants were also sailing to Iceland to trade for stockfish, sometimes legitimately and just as often not. Although the Iceland trade was nowhere nearly as important to Bristol as it was to east-coast ports like Hull, the new Atlantic trade route was a good fit with the city's primary trade with Bordeaux and Lisbon. Ships set out for Iceland mostly in the spring and early summer, to arrive when the previous winter's stockfish had finished drying and when the unpredictable North Atlantic weather was at its most settled. In contrast, the voyages to Bordeaux and Portugal mainly took place in the autumn and early winter, when the summer season's new wine, olive oil and dried fruit became available. The Bristol merchants could work their ships hard, making two trading voyages a year, while the city's sea captains became adept at year-round oceanic navigation. Thanks to its close links with Lisbon, Bristol's merchants and sea captains were well informed, too, about Portuguese exploration of the African coast and of their discovery and colonization of Madeira and the Azores. These profitable discoveries probably had a lot to do with the Bristolians' fascination with Brasil. Exploration could lead to new trading opportunities, and Bristol was definitely in need of those: the fall of Bordeaux to the French in 1453 had disrupted the wine trade, while the Hanseatic League's harassment of English merchants was making trading with Iceland increasingly difficult. Likely just as important, however, was that they believed that a Bristol sea captain had already visited Brasil and come back with a valuable cargo.

Avalon in the Atlantic

Like most medieval people, the Basque chronicler Lope García de Salazar firmly believed King Arthur to have been a real historical person. Writing about the history of Britain sometime between 1471 and his death in 1476, Salazar identified Brasil with the legendary Isle of Avalon, which was widely believed to be Arthur's burial place. With the uncritical respect for authority that was so common among medieval writers, Salazar justified his belief in Brasil on the grounds that it had been shown on maps for years – why would it be on a map if it didn't exist? – and because the English claimed to have been there. Salazar wrote that the English claimed 'a vessel from Bristol found it [Brasil] one dawn and, not knowing that it was it, took on there much wood for firewood, which was all of brazil, took it to their owner and, recognising it, he became very rich. He and others went in search of it, and they could not find it. And sometimes ships saw it but due a storm could not reach it. And it is round and small and flat.'[46] The island, he said, was only about 25 leagues (75 nautical miles/140 kilometres) from an unidentified Irish cape Salazar called Langnaes, which should have made it easy enough to find. Eager to acquire another cargo of brazilwood, the merchant sent a return expedition, but it was unable to find the island again. Salazar's informant helpfully explained that Brasil could be found only if the ship spotted the island before the island spotted the ship. Salazar might have heard the story directly from an English sailor, but it is more likely that his informant was one of the many Basque sea captains who were trading with Bristol around this time.

'Exterior parts'

It would be easy to dismiss Salazar's as just another apocryphal story about phantom islands, but a mysterious voyage by a Bristol-based Welsh shipmaster called Thomas or John Lloyd suggests that the search for Brasil was underway as early as the 1460s. Surviving customs records show that Lloyd sailed to many European ports, but the voyage he set out on in 1466 was unusual because he did not state his destination, describing it only as 'exterior parts'. This might simply have been cover for illegal trading, but such vagueness would have been bound to excite the interest of suspicious-minded customs officers, wondering what toll-dodging scam he was planning: it is much more likely that this was a voyage of exploration. It was Lloyd, 'the most expert shipmaster of all England', too who led an expedition which sailed from Bristol on 15 July 1480 to search for Brasil. Lloyd's unnamed ship, owned by a merchant called John Jay, who probably funded the expedition, weighed about 80 tonnes, not large even by the standards of the day but still perfectly able to make long ocean voyages: Magellan's *Victoria* was probably no larger. Word finally reached Bristol on 18 September that the ship had 'covered the seas for about nine weeks, and did not find the island, but were driven back by storms to the port in Ireland for the restoration of the ship and the men'.

Another expedition to search for Brasil sailed from Bristol on 6 July the next year, involving two large merchant ships, the *Trinity* and the *George*, but this did not report any discoveries either. The ships had set sail with 40 bushels (about a tonne) of salt each. The local customs officer thought this a suspiciously large quantity, and Thomas Croft, one of the owners of the ships, was accused of illegal trading. Croft was acquitted because the salt was for 'the reparacion and sustentacion of the said ships or Balingers* and not by cause of marchandise but to thentent to serch and fynde a certain isle called the Isle of Brasile'. Why so much salt? It was much more than would be needed for even a long trading voyage. It is possible that the salt was to preserve cod caught on the Grand Banks off Newfoundland, which ships from Bristol had discovered on an earlier, unrecorded voyage. A fair objection to this theory, however, is that the amount of salt

* A small, fast transport ship that could be rowed as well as sailed.

carried was small as a proportion of the cargo capacity of the two ships, 300 tonnes for the *Trinity* and perhaps 150 for the *George*. If the intention was to return with full cargoes of salt cod, the ships would have needed to carry around sixty times as much. One argument is that this was a 'proof of concept' mission, following up on the discovery of the Grand Banks by an earlier expedition, equipped with enough salt for a trial fishery. However, Bristol was not a fishing port, and, while it might trade in fish, it never before or after this time showed any interest in actually catching them. A more likely scenario is that an unusually large quantity of salt was carried because this was a voyage of exploration of uncertain length and the crew might need to preserve fish or game taken on some newly discovered land as provisions for a long journey home.

These two were certainly not the last expeditions sent from Bristol to search for Brasil. Writing just after the return of the Italian navigator John Cabot from his successful voyage from Bristol to Newfoundland in 1497, the Spanish ambassador in London, Pedro de Ayala, reported to King Ferdinand and Queen Isabella that 'for the last seven years the people of Bristol have equipped two, three, four caravels to go in search of the island of Brasil and the Seven Cities'. Did these expeditions make any discoveries? It was certainly widely believed at the time that they had. In December 1497, a Bristol merchant called John Day wrote to a Spanish admiral, probably Christopher Columbus, about Cabot's discoveries, claiming that 'it is considered certain that the cape of the said land was found and discovered in the past by men from Bristol who found "Brasil" as your Lordship well knows. It was called the Island of Brasil and it is assumed and believed to be the mainland that the men from Bristol discovered.' Where was this 'mainland'? Could one of the Bristol ships ploughing the stormy North Atlantic in search of Brasil have sighted the coast of North America? If anyone did cross the Atlantic between the Norse and Columbus, this is surely where they would have done it; the Newfoundland route is the shortest possible crossing and, of course, it had been done before.

If even Columbus believed that Bristol seafarers had discovered an unknown mainland in the North Atlantic, why is there no firmer evidence than this that they did so? Bristol launched at least nine expeditions to search for Brasil, and it's hard to believe that the city's merchants would have continued to invest so much time, effort and money in the enterprise had they not found something that convinced them that it was worthwhile. However, if Bristol seamen had sighted or even landed on some part of North America in the last decades of the fifteenth century, would they have realized how significant their discovery was? They were looking for an island, not a new continent, which the medieval world view had no place for anyway. But, while it might seem at least plausible that Bristol seamen unknowingly sighted America a decade or more before Columbus, the case in favour is entirely circumstantial and it falls a long way short of proving that they did. The Norse remain the only Europeans who we can be certain visited America before Columbus. The Bristol voyages still matter, however. For the first time, ships had set out on regular expeditions to crisscross the open ocean simply to discover if there was anything there. This was quite unlike Columbus thinking he was taking a shortcut to somewhere everyone already knew existed, or the Portuguese following a coastline to see where it led. The Bristolians had such faith in their ships and navigation skills that they could sail for weeks or months far from any known coast and still feel confident that they would find their way home again. It was this adventurous spirit and willingness to venture into the unknown that attracted John Cabot to come to the city in 1495 looking for investors to support a proposal of his own, one which led to the rediscovery of North America.

16

Going beyond pain

1434–88

Europe on the rise – Henry the Navigator – Ships of the discoverers – The failed crusader – A plague of rabbits – Sugar and slaves – The Azores – Crossing the barrier of fear – The Portuguese and slavery – Discovering the Guinea coast – The doctrine of discovery – A chance encounter – New stars in the sky – End of an era – Europe's first colonial war – Spheres of influence – The Atlantic Machiavelli – Watch the waves – Push for the Cape – Bartolomeu Dias

In 1434, the Portuguese navigator Gil Eanes successfully sailed past Cape Bojador and returned safely to tell the tale. It was one of the most important events in world history that most people have never heard of. For 2,000 years, the cape had been like a locked door, keeping European seafarers bottled up in the northeast Atlantic. Rounding the cape suddenly opened up the world's seas to European exploration and exploitation. Exactly 500 years later, the Portuguese poet Fernando Pessoa wrote of the price in lives his nation had paid for those voyages in his epic historical poem *Mensagem* ('Message'). Capturing the symbolic importance of rounding Cape Bojador, Pessoa wrote: 'Who wants to go beyond Bojador / Must also go beyond pain.'[47] But before they could go beyond the pain, they first had to go beyond fear, the fear of the unknown, of the boiling ocean, and of the adverse winds and currents that would stop them ever returning home.

Europe on the rise

Europe at the dawn of the fifteenth century was no longer the culturally and economically backward region it had become in the centuries after the fall of Rome. Imported technologies, such as gunpowder weapons, the magnetic compass and papermaking were being steadily refined and improved, printing, using woodblocks, was coming into use, while the home-grown technologies of clock-making and glass were the most advanced in the world. Water and wind power were widely employed in agriculture and industry. Increasingly efficient farming fed growing urban populations that were slowly beginning to recover from the ravages of the Black Death, and there had been a revolution in shipbuilding. As recently as the thirteenth century, most western European ships had been large open boats with just a single mast and sail and a cargo capacity of only a few tens of tonnes. Now, Europeans were building two- or three-masted ships, with multiple decks and cargo capacities of hundreds of tonnes, that could stay at sea for weeks or months in almost any weather. There were less visible economic developments too, in banking and insurance, for example, which laid the foundations of modern capitalism. Western Europe was getting rich, Italy especially so: by per capita GDP, it was probably the richest place in the world. All that Renaissance art didn't come cheap.

One thing that hadn't changed, however, was geography: Europe was still the end of the road where world trade was concerned. Asia was the source of silk, spices and other luxuries, but they were all carried to Europe along the Central Asian Silk Road or the Indian Ocean 'Spice Route', and they were both Muslim-controlled. Having to buy their luxuries from Muslims irked Christian Europeans, and it wasn't simply religious prejudice; it felt like they were helping to pay for their enemies' armies and navies. Islam might be on the brink of extinction in Iberia, but Christian Europeans still felt anything but secure: Islam had a new and mighty champion in the Ottoman Turkish empire, which was now steadily making inroads from its Anatolian heartlands into the Balkans. Finding a way to cut out the Muslim middlemen was good politics as well as good business. The question was, could it be done? Fear of what lay beyond Cape Bojador was deep-rooted, but, even if it could be safely passed, no one knew how far south Africa extended. If, as the respected Greek astronomer Claudius Ptolemy had believed, the Indian Ocean was a closed sea to the west, then there could be no direct sea route to India. The fate of the Vivaldis wasn't encouraging.

Henry the Navigator

The successful rounding of Cape Bojador is inextricably entwined with the ambitions of the Infante Dom Henrique de Avis (1394–1460), commonly known in the English-speaking world as Prince Henry 'the Navigator'. Despite his nickname, which is rarely used in his homeland, Portugal, Henrique wasn't an explorer, and he seldom went to sea: his importance was as a sponsor of voyages of exploration. Henrique supplied the money and the ships, while others supplied the skills and the courage to go beyond fear. Because the voyages he sponsored ushered in the modern world, Henrique is widely lauded as a forward-looking visionary, but he was actually a completely medieval man and so was his vision. Henrique was born at a time of growing Portuguese national self-confidence. In 1385, King João I (r. 1385–1433), with a little help from his English allies, defeated an attempt by neighbouring Castile to annex his country at the battle of Aljubarrota. Two years later, the alliance with England was cemented when King João married Philippa of Lancaster, the granddaughter of King Edward III. Prince Henrique was King João's third surviving son by Philippa; his elder brother Duarte would become king in 1433 after the death of their father. Henrique grew up steeped in the chivalric culture of the Portuguese court and in the uniquely Iberian spirit of militant Christianity that had been forged in the long wars of the *Reconquista* against the Moors. This upbringing gave Henrique a lifelong commitment to the crusading movement, which continued despite the loss of the Holy Land in 1291, and the voyages he sponsored served that cause, not the cause of geographical discovery: he was looking for new opportunities to attack the infidel.

Henrique got his first chance to fight the infidel in 1415, when he took part in his father's conquest of the Moroccan port of Ceuta, which guards the eastern entrance to the Strait of Gibraltar. Ceuta became the first possession of the Portuguese maritime empire but only just. Fearing that the cost of defending the city would be prohibitive, King João considered torching it and going home with his loot, but Henrique persuaded him to keep it as a bridgehead for more Christian conquests in Muslim North Africa. Henrique also persuaded the king to give him overall responsibility for the governance of Ceuta, a position he exploited to pursue his wider ambitions by making constant demands on the kingdom's revenues to pay for the city's defence only to divert much of it to fund voyages of exploration. In 1419, King João appointed Henrique governor of the Algarve, bringing him further revenues, including a monopoly of the tuna-fishing industry. A year later, the pope appointed the prince Grand Master of the crusading Order of Christ, giving him control of its extensive Portuguese estates and revenues too. Not even this, however, was enough to support his ambitions; he actively courted investment in exploration from the wealthy Italian maritime cities and his own country's Jewish merchants, and he borrowed widely.

Henrique saw crusading in North Africa as a natural extension of the *Reconquista*, but war was expensive and Portugal was neither wealthy nor populous. As part of a grand strategy against the Moors, Henrique sent expeditions to explore Africa's west coast in search of gold and Christian allies. Finding the source of Africa's gold and diverting the trade away from the Saharan caravan routes would strengthen Portugal and weaken the Muslims at the same time. Henrique had a particular ally in mind, the legendary Christian King Prester John. Rumours were circulating that Prester John ruled an empire so vast that he was served by seventy-two vassal kings; he could field a million-strong army of soldiers who fought in crocodile-skin armour; he was wealthier even than Mansa Musa, and in the lands he ruled gold was so super-abundant that his subjects roofed their houses with gold tiles and lined their rooms with gold sheets. It seems incredible today that Henrique could take these stories seriously, but he was far from alone, and few idealistic people are completely immune to wishful thinking. When the legend first surfaced in the twelfth century, Prester John was said to be a king of the 'Indies', a vague term which at that time could mean almost anywhere around the Indian Ocean from the East Indies to India and East Africa. By Prince Henrique's time, however, the fabulous ruler had become specifically associated with the isolated and little-known Christian empire of Ethiopia in the Horn of Africa.

Henrique took a pragmatic interest in navigation and cartography, commissioning the leading cartographer of his day, the Majorcan Jew Jehudà Cresques, to produce portolan charts, and he offered patronage and employment to experienced seafarers, merchants and adventurous young nobles out to make names for themselves. This made Henrique's court a centre for the exchange of information and expertise, but the school of navigation he is often said to have founded near his residence at Cape Sagres in the Algarve never existed. Nor is there any evidence that he ever thirsted for geographical and scientific knowledge for its own sake: from what we know of the contents of his library, Henrique's favourite reading was theology. If he ever owned any portolans, navigation handbooks or travel literature, the prince must have gifted them to other individuals or institutions before he died, because none are listed in the inventory of his possessions that was compiled after his death.

Ships of the discoverers

One of Lisbon's best-known landmarks is the gleaming limestone *Monument of the Discoveries* which dominates the waterfront at

Belém. This romanticized tribute to Portugal's maritime pioneers takes the shape of a highly stylized three-masted ship. Standing at its prow, leading a cavalcade of reverent Portuguese explorers, conquerors, missionaries and kings into a heroic future, is Prince Henrique, gazing like a visionary far out to sea. In his hands, the prince clutches a model of another three-masted sailing ship, in much the same way that medieval saints were depicted clutching the symbols of their sainthood. Both ships are caravels, a type of ship which has become almost as closely identified with the beginnings of Portuguese maritime expansion as Prince Henrique himself: he has even been credited with inventing it, although that is most unlikely.

For such an important ship, very little is known about the caravel's origins. No archaeological remains of a caravel have ever been found, and, as ships were still built by eye in the fifteenth century, no plans have survived either. If it wasn't for the delight medieval cartographers took in ornamenting their sea charts with neat little pictures of ships, we would have very little idea of what they even looked like. The name suggests that the caravel may be a development of the Moorish *caravo* or *qarib*, a small ship with a single mast that was used for fishing and coastal trade around the coasts of Iberia and North Africa in the thirteenth century: it is likely to have been the type of ship used by the *Mugharrirun* of Lisbon for their Atlantic adventure (see pp. 339–43). More immediate precursors may have been the *barinel* and the *barca*, both of them small, fast cargo ships that were used for some of the earliest Portuguese voyages to the Atlantic islands and North Africa: it was in a *barca* that Gil Eanes rounded Cape Bojador. *Barinels* mounted two masts, the foremast carrying a single square sail and the mizzen mast a lateen sail, while the *barca* had three masts, all carrying lateen sails; both could also be rowed if the wind failed.

The caravel of the early fifteenth century was a small but seaworthy cargo ship, with two or three masts, each carrying a single triangular lateen sail, with a cargo capacity of around 60–80 tonnes. Unlike *barcas* and *barinels*, they relied entirely on their sails for propulsion, greatly reducing the size of crew needed:

some could be sailed by as few as seven sailors, a great advantage for a kingdom that was always short of manpower. Caravels were built frame-first, with the planks laid edge to edge and fastened directly to the frames to create a smoothly finished hull. There was nothing revolutionary about this technique (it had been around since Celtic times), but in northern Europe, where clinker building was still the norm, it became so closely identified with the caravel that in English it is known as 'carvel building'. In an age when most cargo ships were built broad and tubby to maximize cargo space, caravels looked distinctly racy, with a low superstructure, a forward-raking foremast, and relatively long and slender hulls, making them fast under sail with a top speed of around 8 knots, about twice the speed of a Hanseatic cog. Although their distinctive lateen sails had been used throughout the Mediterranean since Roman times, they were still a bit of novelty in the Atlantic. Most Atlantic ships still relied on tried and tested square-rigged sails. Lateen sails are less efficient in a following wind than square-rigged sails, but they enable a ship to sail much closer to the wind. By way of comparison, a square-rigged cog, the standard cargo carrier in the Atlantic, could sail at best about 72° off the wind, but a caravel could manage 56° or closer, giving them substantially more room for manoeuvre. It was this superior sailing performance that made caravels especially valuable when faced with the adverse prevailing winds along the West African coast. As the Portuguese explored further and further along the African coast, the limitations of the caravel's reliance on the lateen sail started to become apparent. This led to the development of the three-masted *caravela redonda*, or 'round caravel'. This might sound like it was a caravel with a broader beam, but it's actually to do with the rig: the lateen sail on the foremast was replaced with one or two square-rigged sails to take better advantage of following winds. The name comes from the round appearance of these sails when they were billowing full of wind. Later in the fifteenth century, caravels sprouted a fourth mast. These had lateen sails on the two aft masts and square rig on the two forward masts.

The failed crusader

In 1418, Pope Martin V issued a papal bull (decree) granting King João the right to the possession of any lands he conquered in Africa. Those lands never came in his lifetime, nor that of his successor Duarte (r. 1433–8), and almost not in Prince Henrique's long life either. Ceuta never became the bridgehead that Henrique had dreamed it would be, nor did he prove to be the great crusader he aspired to be. His greatest expedition, an attempt to capture the major Moroccan port of Tangier in 1437, was a humiliating disaster, and his only conquest, the capture of the tiny port of Ksar es-Seghir, about 25 kilometres west of Ceuta, in 1458, was hardly the great blow against the infidel he had spent his life yearning to strike. Henrique failed, too, in several attempts to seize the Canary Islands from the Castilians, despite enjoying the political support of the papacy. These failures damaged Prince Henrique's reputation in his own lifetime and, had his voyages of exploration been as unsuccessful as his crusades, he would probably now largely be forgotten even in Portugal. Fortunately for his posthumous reputation, they were not.

The first achievements of Henrique's voyages were almost incidental to his wider ambitions: the discovery and settlement of the Madeira and Azores archipelagos. In 1419, Henrique sent two of his household squires, João Gonçalves Zarco and Tristão Vaz Teixeira, off on a *razzia* (slave raid) to Morocco's Atlantic coast. On their return voyage, a storm swept them far out into the Atlantic, and they made an unexpected landfall on an island they named Porto Santo ('holy harbour') out of gratitude for avoiding shipwreck. They reported to Henrique that they'd discovered an island that looked suitable for colonization, and the following year, the prince sent the pair back, with another of his retainers, Bartolomeu Perestrello, to claim it formally for Portugal. Investigating a dark mass of cloud some 45 kilometres southwest of Porto Santo, the explorers this time also discovered the much larger, mountainous island of Madeira towering out of the sea. At least that is the official version, but it can't be entirely true.

Zarco and Teixeira may not have intended to sail so far out into the Atlantic but, while they may have been the first to realize Madeira's potential for settlement, they were certainly not the first to visit; the islands had already been shown on portolans for decades by this time (see Chapter 14, p. 389).

A plague of rabbits

Settlement of the archipelago was well underway by 1425, when King João declared it a province of Portugal and gifted it to Henrique's Order of Christ. Most of the early settlers were minor nobles and poor farmers from the Algarve and the mountainous north of Portugal attracted by the islands' fertile volcanic soils and sub-tropical climate. The untouched natural environment that greeted the settlers would be swept away within twenty years of their arrival. On Porto Santo, the smaller and lower of the two main islands, the results were nothing short of disastrous. Dry and semi-arid, Porto Santo offered its settlers a poor living right from the start. The island's main natural resource was dragon's blood trees, but, in their greed to harvest their valuable resin, the settlers quickly bled every last tree to death. Things got a great deal worse in 1445, when Perestrello, now the island's governor, released a family of rabbits. With no predators, they did what rabbits do best and quickly overran the island, stripping it of its native vegetation, devouring the settlers' crops the moment they began to grow and exposing the light, dry soils to erosion. After they failed to eradicate the rabbits by hunting them, the settlers gave up the struggle and abandoned the island for several years. Settlers returned in 1455 and found a way to live with the rabbits – they became a major part of Porto Santo's cuisine – but the island's environment has never recovered. This was only the first of countless ecological disasters that would result from similarly ill-conceived European introductions of alien plants and animals into new environments where they had no competitors or predators.

Human intervention is even more obvious in Madeira's landscape, spectacularly so, but its consequences were less disastrous than on Porto Santo, thanks largely to its higher rainfall. Warm, humid ocean air rising up Madeira's 1,800-metre-high peaks generates abundant year-round rainfall that once supported lush virgin evergreen laurel forest over the entire island, from the seashore to the mountaintops. It was this forest that gave Madeira its name, which simply means 'wood' in Portuguese, but most of it would be gone within a decade as the settlers cleared the land for farming. Fire was the main agent of deforestation: it was said that the forest burned continuously for seven years after the settlement began. After that, the rooting and grazing of pigs and cattle inhibited natural regeneration, but the endemic laurel forest still covers about 19 per cent of Madeira today. Madeira's mountains fall precipitously to the sea and there are no coastal plains worth mentioning, so fields had to be created by cutting terraces on the steep mountain slopes. Water courses flowing down from the mountains have cut deep and narrow ravines, making water difficult to access. Channels, called *levadas*, were built to carry water from the ravines to irrigate the terraced fields. These amazing feats of hydraulic engineering tunnel through mountains, follow narrow ridges and traverse vertical cliffs; most of them are still functioning today. The bulk of the hard labour for this often dangerous work of landscape transformation was performed not by the Portuguese settlers themselves but by thousands of enslaved Guanches transported from the Canary Islands. By the end of the fifteenth century, African slaves began to join the Guanches, and together they made up about one-third of Madeira's population of 20,000.

Sugar and slaves

Wheat and vines were soon found to grow well in Madeira, but the colony only prospered after the introduction of sugar cane around 1450. Sugar cane was indigenous to tropical Southeast

Asia, but it remained unknown in the west until it was introduced to the Levant and Egypt by the Arabs in the ninth century. By the thirteenth century, sugar cane cultivation had spread to Cyprus, Sicily, Moorish Spain and Morocco. Today, high sugar consumption is widely associated with poverty, but 'honey made without bees' was such a luxury in medieval Europe that it was treated as a spice, like cloves, nutmeg and pepper. Because honey, the only other sweetener available, was also expensive, having a mouthful of rotting teeth was quite the status symbol, so much so that the less well-off sometimes artificially blackened their healthy teeth. It was not enough for the wealthy just to flavour their food with sugar, they wanted to be seen to be eating sugar so everyone would know how wealthy and privileged they were. To make a proper spectacle of it, they commissioned elaborate sugar sculptures of ships, castles and cathedrals, flowering plants, fabulous beasts and legendary heroes. These they served at feasts, first to be admired by their guests as art and then greedily devoured.

Sugar cane flourished in Madeira's warm, humid climate and, with enormous unmet demand in Europe, production boomed. In 1452, the crown licensed the first water-powered sugar mill on the island, and by 1455 annual production reached 6,000 arrobas (72,000 kg). To judge from the numbers of recipes that include sugar in surviving fifteenth-century cookbooks, the English had a particularly sweet tooth, and, in 1456, ships from Bristol began regular sailings to Madeira to take on cargoes of sugar. By 1472, production had increased 150 per cent, and, by 1500, Madeira was the world's largest sugar producer, with exports totaling 140,000 arrobas (1,680,000 kg) going to England, Flanders, France, Italy and the Ottoman Empire. The boom was not to last. On his second voyage to the New World in 1493, Columbus took sugar cane with him to establish plantations in the new colony he intended to found, and in the sixteenth century, the Madeiran model of the slave-worked sugar plantation was transplanted wholesale to the Caribbean and Brazil. Even with slave labour, Madeiran growers could not compete with New World producers on price, and production collapsed as cane fields were turned over to vines to produce the wines for which the island is now famous. Slavery declined as rapidly as sugar production, and by the mid-seventeenth century the only slaves left in Madeira were in domestic servitude.

The Azores

The definitive discovery of the Azores archipelago came in 1427, when the Portuguese navigator Diogo de Silves first sighted the islands, most likely while returning to Portugal from Africa using the *volta*. An archipelago of nine volcanic islands sitting astride the Mid-Atlantic Rift, the Azores are lush, fertile and mountainous like Madeira, but their milder climate made them unsuitable for sugar cane. Lacking the 'get rich quick' appeal of Madeira, the settlement of the Azores took longer and did not involve the import of large numbers of slaves. One crop that did grow well in the Azores was woad, the source of a popular blue dye. This was responsible for the surprising interest Flemings showed in the islands: Flanders was home to medieval Europe's most important textile industry, and it had an insatiable demand for dyestuffs. Columbus would stop in the Azores for fresh supplies on his journey home from the New World in 1493, and it was in this role, as a waystation on the sea routes to and from the New World and Asia, that the colony really began to flourish, supplying scurvy-addled sailors with their first fresh fruit and vegetables after months at sea. Something like 2 million European seafarers would die of scurvy between 1500 and 1800, far more than would die in sea battles, accidents and shipwrecks put together: stopovers in the Azores saved many lives.

Crossing the barrier of fear

Madeira and the Azores provided welcome new sources of income for Prince Henrique, but his real obsession remained Africa. In

1424, he sent the first of a dozen expeditions to attempt to round Cape Bojador. All of them turned back before they got anywhere near the dreaded cape after their captains lost their nerve. The choice between what they feared would be certain death in the Boiling Sea and a royal dressing down was an easy one. 'Why,' his captains are supposed to have asked, 'should we attempt to pass the limits which our forefathers set up, and what profit can result for the prince by the loss of our bodies and souls?'

In 1433, Henrique appointed Gil Eanes, a minor nobleman from the Algarve port of Lagos, to lead yet another expedition to round the cape. Eanes got as far as the Canary Islands, where, just like all his predecessors, he too lost his nerve and sailed home. By now, Henrique had invested a lot of money for nothing, and he was losing patience. Eanes came home to a verbal roasting. Why, asked the prince, was he listening to all this superstitious nonsense peddled by mariners who 'knew nothing of either chart or needle for navigation' and had never even seen the cape? Was the prince's certainty anything more than royal arrogance? Henrique may have interviewed Moorish or Berber traders who had told him the truth, that the sea did not really boil south of Cape Bojador, but it's more likely that he had been taken in by a popular, but largely fictitious, travel book, *The Book of Knowledge of All the Kingdoms*, written around 1384, whose anonymous author claimed that he'd already sailed south of Cape Bojador in a Moorish ship and returned safely.

Henrique ordered Eanes to try again the next year, leaving him in no doubt that if he didn't succeed this time his career was over. Seeing no alternative, Eanes put his fate into the hands of God and rounded the cape, anchoring in a bay just to its south. The prince's confidence had been justified, the sea conditions were in no way different than they were north of the cape: the winds and currents were the same, it did not boil and it was not made of blood. Eanes went ashore in the ship's boat but saw no signs of people or any habitations. On his return to Portugal, Eanes told the prince, 'I thought that I ought to bring some token of the land since I was on it, I gathered these herbs which I here present to your grace; the which we in this country call Roses of Saint Mary.' Henrique would probably have preferred slaves or gold to a bouquet of flowers, but he was pleased enough with them to knight Eanes for his achievement. Eanes's voyage seems timid, no more than a very cautious toe in the water, but it was enough to shatter what had become a purely psychological barrier. Those who had sailed past Cape Bojador before Eanes had disappeared because they did not know how to use the *volta do mar* to return against the wind and the current: Eanes, or, maybe more to the point, his pilot, did, and it made all the difference. The barrier of fear was passed and, thanks to Eanes, the South Atlantic now lay open to European exploration.

For the next few years, follow-up expeditions cautiously explored the desert coast south of Bojador. Early landmarks were the first crossing by a European ship of the Tropic of Cancer (23° 26' north) in 1436 and the first use of a caravel for exploration in 1441. Apart from sealskins and a few unwary Sanhaja Berber fishermen and herders who were kidnapped along the way, the explorers brought back little of value until 1442, when Antão Gonçalves returned with ten captive Berbers, some gold dust and, strangely, some ostrich eggs and an oxhide shield. Henrique was delighted with the results; the captives could be converted to Christianity (and sold, of course), the gold gave hope that they were getting close to the eponymous river and even the ostrich eggs, when they were served up at the prince's table, were 'as fresh and as good as though they had been the eggs of any other domestic fowls'. God, mammon and epicureanism were all served at the same time. It's not known what the prince did with the shield. In the same year, Henrique's brother Peter, acting as regent for their grand-nephew, the eight-year-old King Afonso V (r. 1438–81), granted him a monopoly on voyages beyond Cape Bojador, together with a fifth share of any profits to reimburse him for the costs of his expeditions and encourage further exploration.

The Portuguese and slavery

In 1443, the veteran explorer Nuno Tristão discovered the small and arid Arguin Island, off the coast of Mauretania, where he and his men captured twenty-nine fishermen, as many captives as his caravel could carry, before sailing for home. Tristão learned from his captives that this otherwise barren island possessed one of the few permanent fresh-water springs on the Sahara's Atlantic coast. The prospect of easy slaving drew a fleet of six caravels back to Arguin on a grand *razzia* the following year. They returned with 235 captives. The chronicler Gomes Eannes de Azurara, an eyewitness, describes the scene when the captives were taken ashore at Lagos in the Algarve. This was the first major delivery of enslaved Africans to Portugal, and a large and noisy crowd of excited townspeople and country folk gathered to watch the novel spectacle.

Prince Henrique, overseeing the proceedings on horseback, ordered that the captives, many of whom were sick, and all of whom were anxious and fearful, be gathered in a field outside the city walls and divided into five parts. Azurara thought the captives were a marvellous but pitiful sight, for

> what heart could be so hard as not to be pierced with piteous feeling to see that company? For some kept their heads low and their faces bathed in tears, looking one upon another; others stood groaning very dolorously, looking up to the height of heaven, fixing their eyes upon it, crying out loudly, as if asking help of the Father of Nature; others struck their faces with the palms of their hands, throwing themselves at full length upon the ground; others made their lamentations in the manner of a dirge, after the custom of their country … But to increase their sufferings still more, there now arrived those who had charge of the division of the captives, and who began to separate one from another, in order to make an equal partition of the fifths; and then was it needful to part fathers from sons, husbands from wives, brothers from brothers. No respect was shown either to friends or relations, but each fell where his lot took him.[48]

Azurara's heart might have been 'pierced with piteous feeling' for the plight of the captives, but he did not question the legitimacy of their enslavement. Medieval Europeans believed that the social hierarchy was divinely ordained, so it was quite possible, as Azurara did, to sympathize with the people whose place was at the bottom without feeling that there was anything unjust about this. It was just, Azurara wrote, the turning of Fortune's wheel. By turning people into commodities, slavery dehumanized them, so such sympathy as the enslaved might receive did not last long. In medieval Europe, it was religion that determined who could be enslaved. The Catholic Church taught that slavery was sinful under most circumstances and, for this reason, it had died out across most of Europe by Azurara's time (although it was often replaced by other forms of bondage, such as serfdom). However, there was a loophole: the church still endorsed the enslavement of non-Christians. This kept both slavery and slave trading very much alive at the conflicted interface between the Christian and Islamic worlds, in Portugal, Castile, Aragon and Italy, because there was a reliable supply of non-Christian war captives who could legitimately be enslaved. By extension, the Muslim Berbers, pagan Guanches and Black Africans the Portuguese encountered during their expeditions could also be legitimately enslaved. In religious terms, enslavement of non-Christians was a good thing because of the opportunity it gave for them to be converted to Christianity, and it was surely better to be a Christian slave than a free but damned infidel. Azurara would have us believe that the perpetually impecunious prince cared little about the price he would get for the forty-six slaves that were his share 'for his chief riches lay in his purpose; for he reflected with great pleasure upon the salvation of those souls that before were lost'. Racial ideology played no role in legitimizing slavery; that came later, in the early modern period, as a way to justify the ubiquity of African slavery in Europe's New World colonies. Medieval Europeans did not believe that differences in skin colour represented fundamental differences in human nature, as they were caused by different levels of exposure to sunlight. The peoples of the sunless far north had fairer skin than those who lived in the sunny Mediterranean who were in turn fairer than those who lived close to the Equator under the hot tropical sun. This belief did not long survive the discovery of the New World, however. Writing around 1506, the Portuguese explorer Duarte Pacheco Pereira noted that 'the people of Guinea are very black, whereas the people who live beyond the Ocean Sea to the west (who have an equal amount of sun with the blacks of Guinea) are brown and some almost white'. Pereira concluded that 'we can say that the sun does not affect one more than the others. Now it only remains to find out if they are both descended from Adam.' How convenient it would be for slave traders if they weren't.

Discovering the Guinea coast

In 1444, Tristão reached the mouth of the Senegal river. The desert was finally left behind, but it wasn't only the environment that changed: the river was the border between the Muslim Berber peoples of the Sahara and the still mostly pagan Black African peoples to its south, a region the Portuguese called *Guiné* or Guinea. The origins of the name, which was used to describe the whole of the African coast south and east of the Senegal river as far as the Equator, was probably derived from the Berber name for the region, *Akal n-Iguinawen*, meaning the 'land of the blacks'. Following Tristão later in the same year, Dinis Dias, an elderly noble who had taken up exploring to stop himself going soft in his old age, pushed even further south and discovered a wooded cape surmounted by two low hills, both of them long extinct volcanic cones. Dias had sailed past a lot of parched land to get there, so it's perhaps not surprising that he called it Cape Verde (now Cap-Vert in Senegal). Although Dias did not know it, he had discovered the westernmost point of Africa's continental mainland.

Along the Saharan coast, the Portuguese had faced little resistance from the small fishing villages they'd preyed on. If they thought that was going to continue on the Guinea coast, they were sadly mistaken. In 1446, Tristão anchored his caravel in an unidentified river mouth south of Cape Verde and, with twenty-two of his crew, confidently set off in the ship's boat in search of a village to raid. Unfortunately for him and his crew, the reputation of the Portuguese had gone before them, and they were ambushed and showered with poisoned arrows by around eighty warriors in a fleet of canoes. Only two of the party made it back to the ship, and Tristão wasn't one of them. Two years later, Álvaro Fernandes beat a hasty retreat in the face of swift and effective retaliation after he kidnapped some fishermen in Senegal, and a Dane called Vallarte was killed while on a mission to gather intelligence about the location of Prester John's kingdom. These hard lessons brought an abrupt change of policy, from slave raiding to engagement with tropical Africa's indigenous slave trade. In 1449, the Portuguese returned to Arguin and established a *feitoria* (a fortified trading post) in the hopes of diverting Berber gold traders away from the Saharan caravan routes. Arguin was not particularly successful – Berber slave traders seized the opportunity to avoid the arduous desert trek which claimed many slaves' lives before they could be got to a market, but the gold traders stayed away – but it became the template for future Portuguese commercial expansion in Africa and Asia and, when adopted also by the English, Dutch, French and others, an important instrument of European colonialism.

The doctrine of discovery

To protect their developing African trade from foreign competition, King Afonso appealed to the papacy, the ultimate source of legitimacy in medieval Europe, to grant Portugal monopoly rights. In 1452, Pope Nicholas V obligingly issued the bull *Dum diversas* which authorized King Afonso to 'attack, conquer, and subjugate Muslims, pagans and other enemies of Christ wherever they may be found, as well as their kingdoms, duchies, counties, principalities, and other property … and to reduce their persons into perpetual servitude'. These privileges were confirmed and extended by two more papal bulls, *Romanus pontifex* in 1455 and *Inter caetera* in 1456, which awarded Portugal the exclusive right to trade everywhere between Morocco and the Indies, including the right to conquer, enslave and convert the inhabitants. The pope concluded the last with the pious hope that 'those peoples will be converted to the faith or at least the souls of many of them will be gained for Christ'. The papacy saw these bulls as part of a wider effort to organize crusades to halt the steadily expanding power of the Ottoman Turkish Empire in the Balkans and North Africa, and it did not at first appreciate the wider meaning that the bulls would acquire in the context of European colonial expansion in the wider non-Christian world. Together, they formed the basis of what came to be known as the 'doctrine of discovery', the right of any Christian power to claim sovereignty over any non-Christian territory if it had not already been claimed by another Christian power.

A chance encounter

In summer 1454, three Venetian merchant galleys on route to Flanders took shelter from a storm in the lee of Cape Sagres. One of the passengers was the twenty-two-year-old merchant Alvise da Cadamosto (*c.*1432–88). Cadamosto was down on his luck; his wealthy merchant father Giovanni da Mosto had lost the family's property, having been convicted of corruption and exiled. When a couple of Prince Henrique's retainers visited Cadamosto's ship and gave a glowing account of the Portuguese discoveries and the potential profits to be had by trading in Guinea, he was immediately 'inflamed with the desire to visit these newly discovered regions'. Cadamosto was granted an audience with the prince and was offered a contract to sail on an expedition to Guinea. Henrique would fit out a caravel for him, and provide an experienced captain, all in return for 50 per cent of the expedition's profits. This was the break Cadamosto needed, and he readily agreed.

Cadamosto's caravel sailed for Guinea in 1455 via Madeira, the Canary Islands and Arguin, and then to the Senegal river. Cadamosto first tried to establish trade relations with a Wolof king he calls Zuchalin, but he thought the king's authority was too weak to guarantee the safety of foreign merchants. Further south, Cadamosto made contact with King Budomel, ruler of the powerful Wolof kingdom of Cayor, who he found to be a much more impressive ruler than Zuchalin. Cadamosto had learned that horses were prized status symbols in Guinea and so had taken seven along with him on his voyage. These he exchanged with Budomel for 100 slaves. Leaving Cayor, Cadamosto continued to sail south along the coast. At Cape Verde, he met another Portuguese caravel, this one captained by another hard-up Italian, Antoniotto Usodimare, a Genoese merchant who had entered Prince Henrique's service around the same time that he had. Together, they reached the wide, mangrove-fringed mouth of the Gambia river and cautiously began to sail upstream, only to be attacked by a large fleet of canoes and showered with the now dreaded poison arrows. Four cannon shots failed to scare off their attackers, who withdrew only after several had been killed by crossbow fire. Cadamosto's Wolof interpreters were able to speak to some of the attackers, who told them that they believed the Portuguese were cannibals, out to buy black people to eat. Faced with such hostility, the two captains decided to retreat back to the open sea and set course home to Portugal.

New stars in the sky

As his ship left the Gambia river, Cadamosto made the significant observation that the Pole Star was now so low in the sky that it almost touched the horizon and was, therefore, no longer useful for navigation. Although they were leaving their familiar stars behind, Cadamosto also noted that, at this latitude, around 13°

north, a new and distinctive constellation had become visible in the southern sky. He called it the *Carro dell'Ostro*, the 'southern chariot': we know it today as the Southern Cross or, to astronomers, as Crux. The cross wasn't a perfect substitute for Polaris, but its axis conveniently points in the direction of the south celestial pole, the southern hemisphere's own pole star, Sigma Octantis, being so faint that it is useless for navigation. As they explored further south, the Portuguese felt that the stars sparkled less brightly and, perhaps because of the absence of the familiar constellations and their mythological associations, the skies seemed emptier and, somehow, unpopulated.

The following year, Prince Henrique sent Cadamosto and Usodimare back to Guinea, in company with a third, unknown captain, with orders to sail directly to the Gambia river. Sailing in fleets of three or four ships now became the norm for Portuguese expeditions; there was safety in numbers, and the loss of one or even two ships would not threaten the success of the expedition as a whole. The small fleet got as far as Cape Verde when a storm struck and forced them to sail due west for two days and three nights, some 570 kilometres, until they ran into a low, uninhabited desert island which, being relieved to make a landfall, they named Boa Vista ('Good View'). This was the easternmost of the so far undiscovered Cape Verde Islands, a horseshoe-shaped archipelago of ten volcanic islands. Cadamosto and his companions spent a little time exploring and discovered another three arid, uninhabited islands, including the largest of the Cape Verdes, Santiago. The islands being too arid for sugar cane, the Portuguese would import African slaves there to grow cotton for export to Guinea. Later, slaves would be trained to weave cotton textiles designed specifically to appeal to the markets in Guinea, greatly increasing the profitably of the plantation system.

After their brief exploration, Cadamosto and Usodimare continued their voyage to the Gambia. After their previous hostile reception, the Portuguese were wary, but this time they faced no opposition when they sailed upstream. Cadamosto was able to establish friendly relations and do a little trade with several of the local Mandinka kings. All seemed to be going well, but after eleven days in the area, the Portuguese started falling ill with malarial fevers and hurriedly retreated to the open sea. The Portuguese soon discovered that this was an inescapable, and all too often fatal, hazard of trading in Guinea. It was by the distribution of pathogens that the fates of continents were decided. Native Americans fell before Europe's pathogens and Europeans fell before Africa's: no significant European colonial population would ever be established in tropical Africa. Back at sea, the Portuguese recovered their health and Cadamosto was able to continue his exploration of the coast south as far as the Bijagós archipelago off the coast of the modern Republic of Guinea before returning to Portugal and Venice to concentrate on restoring his family's reputation and fortunes.

To publicize his considerable achievements, Cadamosto wrote an account of his voyages, the *Navigazioni*, which provides the first eyewitness descriptions of life and customs in pre-colonial West Africa. During his visit to Cayor in 1455, Cadamosto had enjoyed King Budomel's hospitality for four weeks and witnessed African kingship in action. Like many European visitors after him, Cadamosto found that the kingdoms of Guinea did not fit his Eurocentric preconceptions of what a kingdom should look like. They did not cover large territories, they did not possess wealth in money or treasure, nor did they have cities, palaces or castles, only villages of grass huts. For all that, Cadamosto was deeply impressed by the authority of Guinean kings. 'Such men,' he said, 'were not lords by virtue of treasure or money, for they possess neither … but on account of ceremonies and the following of people they may truly be called lords.' No matter 'how considerable he who seeks an audience may be, or however high born, on entering the door of Budomel's courtyard, he throws himself down on his knees, bows his head to the ground, and with both hands scatters sand upon his naked shoulders and head. This is their manner of greeting their lord,' he wrote,

> no man would be bold enough to come before him to parley unless he stripped himself naked save for the girdle of leather they wear. The client remains in this posture for a good while, scattering sand over himself; then, without rising but groveling on hands and knees he draws nearer. When within two paces, he begins to relate his business, without ceasing to scatter sand, and with head bowed as a sign of greatest humility. The lord scarcely deigns to take notice of him, continuing to speak to others: then, when his vassal has done, he replies arrogantly in few words: thus by this act he shows much haughtiness and reserve.[49]

Such ceremonies convinced Cadamosto that kings like Budomel were absolute monarchs who possessed the power of life and death over their subjects. Faced with such strong rulers, the doctrine of discovery was irrelevant. The combination of a hostile environment and well-organized native armies meant that conquest was not an option. The Portuguese could exercise direct military power no further inland than the few hundred metres their primitive cannon could fire. The Portuguese pragmatically accepted the need to recognize the sovereignty of Guinean rulers and deal with them as diplomatic equals: there would have been no trade in slaves, or any other commodity, without their cooperation. As they advanced further along the African coast, the Portuguese actively sought out strong rulers like Budomel, 'a notable and upright ruler, in whom one could trust', with whom they could agree treaties and trade securely.

Slavery as practised in pre-colonial Guinea took many different forms and fulfilled many different social and economic functions, but for Cadamosto it was all about royal power. Kings, he claimed, used the threat of enslavement to 'exact obedience and fear from the people' and they waged war 'continuously' to take captives for the slave trade. People, he says, rarely left their home territory because 'they are not safe from one district to the next from being taken by the Blacks and sold into slavery'. In this way, Cadamosto presented slavery as entirely a product of the greed and despotism of the Guinean rulers, so absolving himself of any responsibility. The slaves he bought had already been enslaved legitimately according to the laws and customs of their land; he hadn't enslaved them. For the duration of the Atlantic slave trade, variations on this self-serving reasoning continued to be the main way European slave traders and slave owners denied their own personal responsibility for slavery, ignoring the reality that the slaves they bought had been enslaved for no other reason than to supply European demand.

End of an era

In November 1460, Prince Henrique fell ill and died at his favourite residence near Cape Sagres: he was aged sixty-six. Despite the vast incomes he had enjoyed from his estates and trade monopolies, he was deep in debt. Without the prince's strong direction and money, the pace of Portuguese exploration briefly faltered. While he'd always been sympathetic to his uncle's projects, King Afonso was not prepared to continue pouring vast sums of the crown's money into promoting exploration of the Guinea coast. He was, however, quite willing to allow others to do so, for a price, of course. In 1469, Afonso granted Fernão Gomes a trading monopoly in Guinea in return for 200,000 *reais* annual rent and, for another 100,000 a year, a monopoly in melegueta pepper, a popular substitute for black pepper that was also known as 'Grains of Paradise'. To keep his immensely valuable monopoly, Gomes was also required to explore 100 leagues (around 555 kilometres) of the African coast every year for five years. It was a price worth paying.

The Guinea coast was not easy to navigate. Sailing close to the coast during the hot summer months meant getting a buffeting from monsoon winds and violent thunderstorms, but a ship that tried to avoid them by holding a course further out to sea risked being becalmed in the scorching heat of the doldrums. In the cooler winter months, the danger was from the violent and unpredictable northeasterly Harmattan winds blowing into the Gulf of Guinea from the Sahara Desert. On top of that, there were countless uncharted reefs and shoals to negotiate, river estuaries choked with mangroves, heavy surf, precious few safe landing places and tropical diseases to contend with. Despite all these difficulties, the team of captains Gomes recruited exceeded his target, exploring the coast for more than 3,000 kilometres east to the head of the Gulf of Guinea and crossing the Equator into the southern hemisphere by 1474. The coasts they explored became known for the resources they found there: the Grain or Pepper Coast of modern Liberia; the Ivory Coast, now Côte d'Ivoire: the Gold Coast of modern Ghana, the source of about two thirds of Africa's gold; and the Slave Coast along the coasts of present-day Togo, Benin and Nigeria. In 1472, Fernão do Pó discovered the volcanic island at the eastern end of the Gulf of Guinea which in the colonial period was named after him but which is now called Bioko. Bioko, within sight of the mainland, was found to be inhabited by Bantu-speaking peoples, but in 1474, beyond the horizon, Lopo Gonçalves and Rui de Sequeira discovered three more, uninhabited, volcanic islands, São Tomé, Príncipe and Annobón, the last almost two degrees south of the Equator. Within a few years, these islands were turned into new Madeiras, with sugar cane plantations worked by African slaves imported from the mainland.

Europe's first colonial war

Portuguese exploration came to a standstill in 1475, when King Afonso intervened in a disputed succession to the throne of Castile in favour of the claims of his Castilian wife, Joanna of Trastamara. Afonso was really not a great soldier, and by the end of 1476 Joanna's supporters had been defeated by those of her rival, Isabella of Castile, and her husband Ferdinand, heir to the throne of Aragon. However, the succession wasn't the only point at issue between Portugal and Castile. Both powers claimed sovereignty over the Canary Islands by right of prior discovery, and the Portuguese resented what they considered to be illegal Castilian trading in Guinea, so the war continued, developing into what can fairly be called the first colonial war between European powers.

After the outbreak of war, Isabella made a counter-claim to Guinea on the basis that her Visigothic ancestors had briefly ruled a small part of Morocco around Ceuta. It wasn't a terribly convincing claim to possession of an entire continent, but it was enough to encourage Castilian merchants to sail south in large numbers to trade in Guinea. More aggressive Castilian interventions followed. In 1476, a fleet of twelve Castilian ships plundered the Portuguese settlements on Santiago in the Cape Verde Islands and captured its governor, António de Noli. Two years later, the Portuguese received the news that a Castilian fleet of around thirty-five ships had sailed from Seville to attack Portuguese traders in Guinea and establish trade relations with local rulers. A Portuguese fleet of eleven ships set out in pursuit, finally catching up with the Castilians on the Gold Coast, where they had already been happily trading for gold dust and launching slave raids for two months. Though outnumbered, the Portuguese had the advantage of surprise, attacking at dawn, when most of the Castilians were still asleep. The drowsy Castilians put up little resistance and their entire fleet was captured, along with the large quantity of gold they had acquired. The victory decisively ended the Castilian challenge in Guinea.

Spheres of influence

The war was finally ended in 1479 with the Treaty of Alcáçovas, the terms of which were more favourable to Portugal than Castile. King Afonso's marriage to Joanna was annulled on the grounds of consanguinity (they were cousins) and both had to renounce any claims to the Castilian throne. Afonso also had to accept Castilian sovereignty over the Canary Islands, but in return Castile paid an indemnity and recognized Portugal's right to 'all lands discovered and to be discovered, found and to be found ... and all the islands already discovered and to be discovered, and any other island which might be found and conquered from the Canary Islands beyond toward Guinea'. Assuming the Portuguese could maintain it, the whole South Atlantic was to be legally a *mare clausam* ('closed sea') and no one else, not just the Castilians, had a right to enter without their permission; it would be Portugal's private ocean. Add the exclusive right to conquer the kingdom of Morocco, and the treaty effectively gave Portugal the whole West African coastline to do with what it would, or could.

The treaty was a landmark in the history of European colonialism, the first formal assertion of the ideological principle that the European powers were entitled to divide the rest of the world into national spheres of influence, and found colonies and settlements, without the need to obtain the consent of the indigenous peoples who already lived there. In 1481, Pope Sixtus IV issued the bull *Aeterni regis* confirming the treaty and giving it the full moral authority of the papacy. As God's vice-regents on earth, the popes harboured no doubts that the world was theirs to bind and loose as they saw fit. As such, the Treaty of Alcáçovas was the precursor of all later colonial carve-ups, from the Treaty of Tordesillas in 1494 to the Berlin Conference of 1885, which began the 'Scramble for Africa', and the Sykes–Picot Agreement of 1916, by which Great Britain and France divided the Middle East between themselves. Such thinking might have been thought to have become extinct following decolonization, but the emergence of neo-imperialist regimes in Russia and China in the twenty-first century unfortunately would suggest otherwise.

The Atlantic Machiavelli

In 1481, King Afonso died and was succeeded by his more energetic, and more ruthless, son João II (r. 1481–95). João inherited an over-mighty nobility and an empty treasury, which he dealt with in that order, beginning his reign with a bloody crackdown on the nobility, which involved him personally murdering his own brother-in-law, the poisoning of an inconvenient bishop and dozens of summary executions. The Machiavellian way he reasserted the authority of the monarchy earned him the posthumous epithet, 'the Perfect Prince'.[50] African gold was the obvious way to solve his financial problems, and João abandoned his father's hands-off approach. He not only threw the full weight of the crown behind the exploration of the African coast but, for the first time, made discovering a direct route from Portugal to the Indies an explicit goal. João had also inherited his family's commitment to carrying the *Reconquista* to the Moors in North Africa, and he intensified the search for Prester John, both by sea and, secretly, by land. Unlike his great-uncle, whose interests were mainly religious, João may also have had an interest in discovery for its own sake, being described by the contemporary chronicler Rui de Pina as 'a man of an inquiring spirit, desirous of investigating the secrets of nature'.

The Portuguese had started their exploration of the African coast to search for gold, but it was not until the discovery of the Gold Coast in 1471 that they really found what they were looking for. The steadily increasing flow of gold to Portugal persuaded João not to renew Gomes's contract to explore and instead establish a royal monopoly over the Guinea trade. João appointed Diogo de Azambuja, an experienced soldier, to lead a fleet of eleven ships to establish a *feitoria* on the Gold Coast. A great deal of thought had been put into the enterprise. To ensure that the work was completed quickly, much of the fort, including its stone foundations, was prefabricated in Portugal. A work force of 100 stonemasons, 500 other workers and soldiers, and trained African interpreters went along with the fleet, together with provisions, trade goods and diplomatic gifts of brass tableware, manillas (brass bracelets which were used as currency or were melted down for recasting) and fine textiles to smooth negotiations with local rulers: the Portuguese hoped to be able to found their trading post by consent rather than force. The planned fortifications were as much, if not more, about defending their prime retail space against the Castilians, and other potential European competitors such as the French and the English, as they were about protection from local rulers if relations turned hostile.

Watch the waves

In January 1482, Azambuja found what he thought was the perfect site, a low hill on a narrow peninsula overlooking the sheltered mouth of the small Benya river. There was a safe anchorage; the site could be easily defended; there was stone for building; and there was a large village nearby whose inhabitants could supply the garrison with fresh food and drinking water. Thanks to its slight elevation, the site was also exposed to sea breezes which kept it relatively mosquito-free. While the Portuguese did not understand the role of mosquitos in spreading diseases like malaria – they thought it was the result of bad air (hence mal-aria) – they did recognize that the closer to the sea breezes they stayed, the longer they were likely to live. Most of the European trading posts founded along the Guinea coast in the following centuries would be in similar locations, on peninsulas or offshore islands, for the same reasons. On landing, Azambuja opened negotiations with the local Akan king, Kwamena Ansa, for permission to build the *feitoria*. Both sides put on a show. The Portuguese wore their best brocades and silks, but they were completely upstaged by Kwamena Ansa, who arrived naked except for an awesome mass of gold jewelry – what are fine clothes compared to pure gold? – and attended by a colourful retinue of musicians, armed warriors and naked servant boys. Kwamena Ansa was wary of allowing the *feitoria* on his territory, telling Azambuja that he should 'watch the waves'. Just as they came to the shore, reached the shore and retreated, so too should he continue to come to trade then return home to Portugal; as the king argued, 'friends who met from time to time treated each other with greater affection than if they were neighbours'. Azambuja offered gifts and compensation for the land, but what finally persuaded the king to give his permission was the threat that the Portuguese would open negotiations with his rivals instead. Work began the next day, before the gifts and compensation had been paid, and trouble broke out almost at once when the stonemasons began quarrying away a rock formation that was held to be sacred to the local river god. The outraged locals took arms and killed a number of the Portuguese, who retaliated by burning their village. Gifts and compensation from the Portuguese smoothed things over, but it was not a propitious start. Despite the local opposition, and many deaths from malaria, the Portuguese craftsmen completed the foundations of the walls, a tower and most of the warehouses in just twenty days, thanks to the prefabrication. Azambuja formally named the new trading post Castello São Jorge da Mina, but it became better known simply, and for good reason, as Elmina, 'the Mine'.

The foundation of Elmina marked the beginning of the permanent European involvement in sub-Saharan Africa. For the Portuguese, Elmina was nothing short of transformational. While they never achieved the complete monopoly they desired, Elmina succeeded, where Arguin had failed, in diverting enormous quantities of gold away from the Muslim-controlled trans-Saharan trade routes. Nothing was allowed to distract from building up the gold trade, and by 1500, Elmina was exporting nearly 24,000 ounces (680 kilograms) of gold annually, amounting to about one tenth of the total world supply. This was ten times the value of the slave and pepper trades combined. On the back of it, the Portuguese crown began minting the *português*, containing 35 grams of gold; it was the most valuable and prestigious coin of the early sixteenth century. Portugal was becoming a rich country, one with the means to finance global voyages of exploration. The royal monopoly was vigorously maintained. At Elmina, all transactions had to be conducted within the walls of the *feitoria*, not in the African town. Ships were required to sail from Lisbon only, directly to Elmina. The loading of the crew's rations for the month-long voyage was closely supervised to ensure that no one loaded any private cargoes they could sell on the side. An extra precaution was that a pilot boat accompanied ships until they cleared the Tagus to prevent rendezvous with boats carrying contraband. On return voyages, the chests of gold were sealed and the sailors' own sea chests were searched for contraband gold. The Portuguese paid for their gold with cotton and linen textiles, brassware, manillas, weapons, glass beads, cowrie shells and slaves, who they sourced from other parts of Africa: many of these slaves were put to work by African rulers in the gold mining districts to increase production.

Elmina grew rapidly, as African merchants and craftsmen migrated there and settled outside the *feitoria* to take advantage of the Portuguese trade. Archaeological excavations at Elmina have shown that many of the settlers built houses with European-style ground plans and adopted much European material culture but also that they retained their traditional religious beliefs and cultural practices. This is perhaps not so surprising, because there were never more than sixty Portuguese resident at Elmina at any one time, while the African population numbered in the thousands. The Portuguese rarely intervened in the running of the African settlement: if there were disputes, the Africans could, and did, exercise the ultimate sanction of abandoning the town *en masse*, making normal trade impossible. While the Portuguese could not exercise much direct power beyond the coast, they could still enforce their commercial monopoly in the region through divide and rule tactics, punishing chiefs or kings who traded with anyone else by forming alliances with their rivals. This, combined with the disruption of traditional inland trade routes, inevitably destabilized existing power structures and intensified conflict in the region by increasing the incentives for slave raiding. This was just the beginning: the effect would be multiplied many times over as the number of European trading posts on the Guinea coast grew over the next three centuries.

Push for the Cape

Within months of the foundation of Elmina, João restored momentum to the exploration of the African coast by commissioning a new expedition under Diogo Cão, an experienced seafarer, to explore the coast south of the Equator. On their early voyages, Portuguese explorers had erected large wooden crosses, known as *padrãos*, or 'mariners' milestones', at prominent coastal features such as headlands and river mouths to mark their progress and act as landmarks for those who would come after them. Being perishable, these did not last very long under tropical conditions, so João supplied Cão with durable stone *padrãos* to erect on his voyages. These were pillars carved with the arms of Portugal and surmounted by a cross: there was also space for an inscription recording the date, the name of the king who had ordered the voyage and its commander. They were not just landmarks, of course, but also territorial claims. They were thought to be so important that their locations were marked on maps. What did the local inhabitants think about these monuments that laid claim to their land? Most likely, they were not recognized for what they were, because a surprising number have survived, either in fragments or even intact.

Cão set out on his voyage in early summer 1482, stopped briefly to replenish his supplies at Elmina, before continuing to follow the coast east and south, past the furthest point reached by Gomes's seamen and into as yet unexplored territory. By August, Cão had discovered the mouth of the Congo river. Cão couldn't have known that the Congo is, by volume of discharge, the world's third largest river after the Amazon and the Ganges, but he certainly realized that this must be a truly vast river, because the water was discoloured with silt several hundred kilometres out to sea and was still perfectly fresh 5 leagues (28 kilometres) from land. On the southern side of the river's mouth, at Shark Point, Cão erected the first of his *padrãos*, one of those which have survived to the present day, albeit in fragments, the result of vandalism by the Dutch in 1642. Cão sailed a little way upriver, probably to the town of Mpinda, where he made the first diplomatic contacts with the powerful kingdom of Kongo (from which the river gets its name), which ruled much of modern-day Angola. Leaving behind four Black Christian converts with gifts for the manikongo (king), Nzinga-a-Nkuwu (r. 1470–1509), Cão continued his voyage south as far as the barren Cabo de Santa Maria, just over 13° degrees of latitude south of the Equator. Here, he erected the second of his *padrãos*, now in a museum in Porto, before returning to the Congo river to recover his messengers. Finding, to his annoyance, that the king had not released the messengers, Cão took four local men hostage, one of them a chief called 'Caçuto', telling their friends that they would be returned in fifteen months' time and exchanged for his messengers.

Cão returned to Lisbon early in 1484, and in April a grateful King João ennobled him, granting him a coat of arms which features the two *padrãos* he had erected on the African coast. Later that year, Portugal's ambassador to the papal court boasted that Portuguese ships had reached the edge of the 'Gulf of Arabia', meaning the Indian Ocean. They hadn't, but it was a sign of a growing conviction that Africa could be circumnavigated. The king sent Cão back to Africa in 1485 with instructions to press even further south: he took with him his hostages, who had been held in a monastery during their involuntary stay, baptized and taught to speak Portuguese so that they could help as interlocutors and influencers in negotiations with the king of Kongo. On this voyage, Cão sailed as far south as Cape Cross on Namibia's infamously dangerous Skeleton Coast, where he and his crew probably became the first Europeans ever to see penguins. The *padrão* he set up here was found fallen but still intact by the commander of a German warship, the SMS *Falke*, in 1893. Namibia was at that time a German colony, so the cross was removed and taken to Berlin as a trophy, eventually to be returned in 2019. From Cape Cross, Cão sailed back to the Congo river to disembark his African passengers. Diplomatic relations were established with Nzinga-a-Nkuwu, who sent Caçuto back to the Portuguese court as his ambassador. Caçuto returned in 1491 with Portuguese missionaries who baptized Nzinga-a-Nkuwu, giving him the Christian name João in honour of the Portuguese king. While this established the Roman Catholic church in sub-Saharan Africa, Nzinga-a-Nkuwu did not convert out of religious conviction; it was part of a diplomatic deal that gave him the support of Portuguese troops and firearms to expand his territory at the expense of his neighbours. Many of the captives taken and enslaved during these wars were sold to the Portuguese. Kongo subsequently became an important partner for Portugal in the Atlantic slave trade. To end his already highly successful expedition, Cão set out to sail up the Congo river in the belief that it would take him to Prester John's kingdom. However, Cão got only as far as the Falls of Yellala, an impenetrable barrier of rapids about 130 kilometres upstream from the sea. On a rock here, he left this inscription: 'To this place came the ships of the illustrious João II, King of Portugal – Diogo Cão, Pero Annes, Pero da Costa' and, nearby, another recording the deaths of two crew members from disease. They probably weren't the only ones: Cão never made it back to Portugal, so he too may have died at the falls.

Around the time that Cão began his second voyage, his pilot from his first voyage, João Afonso de Aveiro, was given his own ship to trade with the Edo kingdom of Benin in modern Nigeria. De Aveiro returned with a cargo of melegueta pepper and also intelligence about a Christian king called Ogané who he had been told ruled in the interior some twenty moons' march east of Benin. Convinced that Ogané must be the elusive Prester John, João commissioned two new expeditions to find him. The first to set out, in May 1487, was a secretive reconnaissance mission by two diplomats, both of them fluent Arabic speakers, Pêro de Covilhã, who was also a spy, and Afonso de Paiva, to gather intelligence about the Indian Ocean spice trade and to contact Prester John. Disguised as Arab merchants, the pair travelled together, via Crete and Cairo, as far as Aden, where they split up, de Paiva crossing the Red Sea to Ethiopia and Covilhã catching a trading dhow across the Indian Ocean to Calicut, the main hub of the spice trade, and Goa. Crossing the Indian Ocean again, Covilhã hitched rides on dhows along the coast of East Africa as far south as Sofala, in Mozambique, where he met mariners who convinced him that it was possible to sail between the Indian and the Atlantic oceans around the southern tip of Africa. In 1491, Covilhã returned to Cairo, where he learned that de Paiva had died before reaching Prester John's kingdom. Covilhã sent a detailed report of his travels back to King João before setting out again to complete de Paiva's mission himself. In 1493, Covilhã finally became the first Portuguese to set eyes on 'Prester John', the negus (emperor) Eskender of Ethiopia, whose power and wealth fell far short of the legend. Covilhã found a number of Italians who, like him, had come expecting to find a rich and mighty emperor and, having discovered the truth, had been prevented from leaving and held in comfortable captivity. Though treated generously by the negus, Covilhã would not be allowed to leave either. When a Portuguese embassy arrived in Ethiopia in 1520, Covilhã was still alive, wealthy and married to an Ethiopian noblewoman, but he still wept for joy at meeting some of his fellow countrymen again. The intelligence about the spice trade provided by Covilhã's reports proved invaluable in planning Vasco da Gama's pioneering direct voyage from Portugal to India in 1497, but, in one important respect, it was out of date even before he even sent it: King João already knew that it was possible to circumnavigate Africa.

Bartolomeu Dias

King João's second expedition of 1487 set sail in July under Bartolomeu Dias, an experienced veteran seafarer with two or three successful trading voyages to Guinea behind him. Dias's instructions were explicit: he was to find a route around Africa to the Indian Ocean and make contact with Prester John. Dias had two caravels, the *St Christopher* and the *St Pantaleon*, and a small square-rigged supply ship, which would be abandoned once its stores were used up. Dias had with him pilots who had sailed on Cão's voyages and his younger brother Diogo. Like Cão before him, Dias carried a set of stone *padrãos* to mark his progress.

Instead of hugging the African coast all the way, as previous explorers had done, Dias swept southeast around the bulge of West Africa and across the Gulf of Guinea direct to the Congo river, so avoiding the worst of the doldrums. From here, Dias followed the increasingly desolate coast south: progress was slow, because the small fleet was sailing against both the strong north-flowing Benguela Current and the southeasterly trade winds. In early December, Dias passed Cape Cross, Cão's 'furthest south', and on 8 December, he dropped anchor in the broad natural harbour at Walvis Bay in what is now Namibia, 150 kilometres further south. By Christmas Day, Dias had reached Lüderitz Bay, another good natural harbour, where he erected the first of his *padrãos*. It was here that Dias decided to leave the supply ship and nine men behind to await his return. Progress continued to be slow and, having spent a futile five days trying to round Cape Voltas, just south of the mouth of the Orange river, Dias changed course and headed southwest out to sea. It's not clear if Dias's ships were blown away from the coast by a storm or if he was acting on a hunch that the wind patterns of the northern hemisphere would be repeated in the southern hemisphere. Whichever it was, Dias discovered the southern hemisphere's own *volta do mar* when, after several stormy days' sailing southwest, at around 40° latitude, he entered the zone of the powerful southern westerlies. Dias changed course to run before the westerlies, expecting to make a landfall on the African coast. When he didn't, he changed course again to the north and, finally, after thirty days at sea, made landfall at Mossel Bay on 3 February 1488. When the Portuguese landed to collect fresh water, local Khoekhoe cattle herders pelted them with stones before fleeing with their livestock when one of them was killed by a crossbow bolt. The Portuguese were scathing about the herders and hunter-gatherers they encountered in southern Africa: they had nothing to trade, and, as for the land, it 'produced nothing to gladden a man's heart'.

Dias did not yet know it, but he had sailed around 200 kilometres past Cape Aghulas, at 34° 49' south, the southernmost point of Africa, and was now in the Indian Ocean. Seeing that the coast trended eastwards, Dias pressed on, excited now by the possibility that he might have achieved his goal. Once again, progress was painfully slow due to adverse currents and winds, and it took Dias nearly two months to cover the 350 kilometres to the broad Algoa Bay, the site of modern-day Gqeberha (Port Elizabeth). Dias crossed the bay, landing on some of its many bird islands as he went, passed the low, sandy headland now called Cape Padrone and, a few kilometres further east, landed by the low promontory of Kwaaihoek, close to the mouth of the Boesmans river, where he erected his second *padrão*. Broken fragments of the *padrão* were found buried in sand there in 1938. The date of Dias's landing is uncertain, as Dias's logs were all lost in the devastating 1755 Lisbon earthquake, but it was probably in mid-March 1488. From Kwaaihoek, it could be seen that the coast turned sharply to the northeast, putting to rest any doubts Dias might still have had about which ocean he was in. The warm seawater and the strong south-flowing current added further confirmation that they were now in the Indian Ocean. Dias was for continuing, but his crew were weary and increasingly concerned that they would run out of provisions before they could rendezvous with their supply ship. Portuguese sea captains were expected to consult their officers before making major decisions, and a compromise was negotiated: the officers agreed to continue following the coast east for two more days, but if nothing happened to change their minds on the way, they would turn back. That was time enough to sail another 70 kilometres or so to the mouth of a river, which Dias named the Rio do Infante (now the Great Fish River) in honour of Prince Henrique, where, as agreed, they turned back. The trend of the coast was clear – India and the Indies lay ahead – but Dias was destined never to see them for himself.

Now sailing with both the wind and the current, the two ships made easy progress west along the coast. After rounding

Cape Agulhas, which Dias estimated was 35° south in latitude, they were back in the Atlantic Ocean, and, after sailing another 160 kilometres further northwest, they saw ahead of them the spectacular Cape of Good Hope and behind it the iconic Table Mountain. Dias landed on the cape and erected a third *padrão*. Strong winds and the meeting of the currents of the Indian and Atlantic oceans create turbulent seas off the cape, and a (possibly apocryphal) story has it that Dias wanted to call it the Cape of Storms, but King João insisted on the more optimistic *Cabo de Boa Esperança* to celebrate the opening of the new sea route to the east. By July, Dias was back at Lüderitz Bay, where he found that six of the nine men he'd left behind with the supply ship had been killed in disputes with the local inhabitants. The survivors must have had an anxious time of it, because one of them, Fernão Colaco, was so overcome with relief at the return of the rest of the expedition that he apparently died of joy. The supply ship was now so worm-infested and rotten that it was burned as soon as its stores had been offloaded. On the return trip, Dias rescued the crew of a wrecked Portuguese ship on the island of Príncipe, picked up a chest of gold at Elmina and bought some slaves in Liberia before finally arriving back at Lisbon in December 1488 to end a voyage of sixteen months and 22,000 kilometres.

No European, let alone Portuguese, navigator had ever sailed so far as Dias. He had brought back a wealth of information about the southern oceans and their wind systems, and he had opened the way to the east. Given the scale of his achievement, the fulfilment of over fifty years of patient exploration, Dias might reasonably have expected a hero's welcome back in Lisbon. Not a bit of it. King João gave Dias no special reward or recognition: he had failed to explore the Indian Ocean and he had failed to find Prester John. What followed was an anticlimax. With the reports of both Dias and Covilhã, João knew that he was close to achieving his ambition of linking Portugal directly with India and the Indies. The king began planning a new expedition to sail directly to India, but his health began to fail and preparations were still incomplete when he died in 1495, aged only forty.

By this time, the Genoese navigator Christopher Columbus had made an audacious attempt to beat the Portuguese to the Indies by sailing west across the Atlantic, reducing Dias's achievement to a footnote in history.

17

They all laughed

1474–1508

Humble beginnings – The myth that won't die – Columbus's world view – Decision time – Landfall – The Treaty of Tordesillas – Columbus's legacy – The western Antipodes – 'One like Columbus' – The New World – Plus ultra – 'Who's got the last laugh now?'

'They all laughed at Christopher Columbus when he said the World was round' goes the old song.[51] Some people may well have laughed at Columbus, but if they did it wasn't because he said the world was round – everybody knew that. The reason Columbus found it hard to sell his plan to go to the Indies by sailing due west across the Atlantic wasn't because anyone thought he'd sail over the edge of the world, it was because he had some distinctly unorthodox ideas about how big the world actually was. These should have doomed his plan to failure had not the New World got in the way. Because his discovery of the New World was accidental, Columbus has often been portrayed as no more than a lucky fool. Luck certainly came into it, but it wasn't blind luck. By 1492, Columbus was an experienced Atlantic navigator, and his plan included a practical escape route home if the Indies turned out not to be where he thought they were. The New World being in the way certainly saved Columbus from embarrassment, but it didn't necessarily save him and his crew from a miserable death by thirst and starvation on the great global Ocean.

Humble beginnings

Born Cristoffa Corombo in the Republic of Genoa in 1451, Columbus came from a comfortably off and respected artisan family. Columbus worked with his father, a master wool weaver, until he was about twenty years old, when he got out of the wool trade and went to sea on a voyage to Tunis. In 1474, Columbus became an apprentice business agent for the wealthy Genoese Centurione merchant family, which gave him the opportunity to go on more voyages, first in the Mediterranean and then, in 1476, to the Atlantic with an armed convoy sailing to Galway in Ireland and Bristol in England. According to Columbus's biographer, his younger, illegitimate, son Fernando, in February 1477, he joined a voyage to 'Thule', most likely meaning Iceland, on a ship from Bristol, even sailing 'a hundred leagues beyond'. If the voyage really did take place – most historians are sceptical – there is no evidence from Columbus's own writings that he learned anything of the Norse Vinland voyages while we was there. Later that year, Columbus sailed in a Portuguese ship from Galway to Lisbon, where he would continue his work as an agent for the Centuriones until 1485. There, he joined his brother Bartholomew, who was working as a cartographer for the Portuguese crown. In 1478, the Centuriones sent him off on a trip to buy sugar in Madeira. While there, he married Felipa, the daughter of the Portuguese nobleman-explorer Bartolomeu Perestrello, the misguided rabbit-fancier of Porto Santo (see p. 434). Socially, this was a good marriage for a common-born merchant, but it also gained him the gift of his deceased father-in-law's sea charts and put him at the heart of the Portuguese seafaring establishment. Columbus had ample opportunities to learn about the Portuguese voyages of exploration along the African coast and became convinced that if it was possible for them to sail so far to the south that it must be equally possible to sail the same sort of distances west, perhaps even as far as the Indies.

Around 1482, Columbus went on a trading voyage to Guinea, visiting the Portuguese *feitoria* at Elmina. Returning to Madeira to find that his wife had died, Columbus moved, with their young son Diego, to Lisbon in 1484. Here he began to seek backers for a plan he had conceived, which he grandly called the 'Enterprise of the Indies', to pioneer a new trade route to Asia by sailing west across the Atlantic. Columbus first tried his powers of persuasion on the Portuguese King João II, while sending his brother Bartholomew off like a travelling salesman to hawk the idea to the kings of England and France. Bartholomew had a miserable time of it; not only did he fail to arouse any interest in his brother's plan, he was kidnapped and robbed by pirates along the way. King João was, at least, interested, but he thought Columbus's demands were excessively expensive. Instead, he accepted the rival proposal from van Olmen and Estreito, who agreed that their (unsuccessful) voyage in search of the phantom Island of the Seven Cities would be at their own expense (see Chapter 15, pp. 419–20). In 1485, Columbus secretly left Portugal for the Spanish court at Córdoba. The Duke of Medinaceli, a wealthy shipping magnate, offered Columbus generous support until Queen Isabella and King Ferdinand began to take an interest and told the duke, politely but firmly, that the sponsorship of world exploration was only appropriate for royalty. Columbus was delighted by the royal interest but years of frustration awaited him. The Catholic Monarchs were preoccupied with their war against Granada, the last Muslim stronghold in Spain, and they referred Columbus's proposal to an academic commission to assess the practicality of his proposal. Endless objections were raised, but not once was it claimed that Columbus would sail over the edge of the world.

The myth that won't die

The persistence even in the twenty-first century of the belief that medieval people thought that the world was flat is hard to explain; it certainly isn't based on evidence, because there isn't any. It's now probably part of a lazy assumption that the

Middle Ages was a time of ignorance and religious superstition so, obviously, flat-Earthism must have gone with the territory. This ingrained popular prejudice against an entire era is a tribute to the effectiveness of a propaganda campaign waged by seventeenth-century Huguenots (French Protestants) to paint their Roman Catholic persecutors as superstitious, ignorant and hostile to scientific enquiry. Their claim that the medieval church taught that the Earth was flat was uncritically accepted by Enlightenment scholars, because it confirmed their own anti-clerical prejudices, and by nineteenth-century evolutionary scientists, who deployed it to denigrate their science-denying religious opponents. However, what, in modern terms, made the myth go viral, at least in the English-speaking world, was *A History of the Life and Voyages of Christopher Columbus*, written by the American diplomat and novelist Washington Irving in 1828. Irving did his research dutifully enough in the Spanish archives but thought that what he found was rather dull, so he spiced his biography up with some fake history of his own invention to portray his hero, in a way he calculated would appeal to his fellow countrymen, as the unorthodox maverick battling an oppressive and pedantic establishment, in this case the Catholic Church, which hauled him before the Inquisition for daring to question belief in the flat Earth. The book was an international bestseller, running to a couple of hundred editions, and Irving's knowingly false claim has been endlessly repeated ever since, even in academic circles. It obviously didn't occur to Irving, or to the vast majority of his millions of readers, that Columbus didn't actually prove that the world was round because he didn't sail any further than the New World and then went back the way he'd come. Had his contemporaries actually believed in a flat Earth, all that Columbus would have proved to them was that he hadn't reached the edge of it yet.

In reality, the spherical earth was academic orthodoxy in medieval Europe's universities, all of which were controlled by the supposedly anti-science Catholic Church. Astronomy was even a compulsory subject, and it was the Ptolemaic universe, which had a spherical Earth at its centre, that was taught. The standard university astronomy textbook of the time, *De spherae mundi* ('On the Sphere of the World'), which included a long discussion of the sphericity of the Earth, was written by a French monk, Johannes de Sacrobosco. Another popular astronomical text which discussed the sphericity of the Earth was *Imago Mundi*, written by a French cardinal, Pierre d'Ailly. A full list of all the prominent churchmen who wrote about the sphericity of the Earth in the Middle Ages would be a long one, but among them were also the Venerable Bede and St Thomas Aquinas. It is hard to find anyone in the medieval Catholic Church who did not believe that the Earth was a sphere.

Belief in the spherical Earth wasn't confined to universities; it underpinned the increasingly scientific navigation methods of the age and featured in art, on public astronomical clocks, in the poetry of Dante and Chaucer among others, and in the notoriously unreliable travel writing of the time. The anonymous English author of the popular and influential *Travels of Sir John Mandeville*, written around 1366, told the story of an Englishman who accidentally found that he had circumnavigated the world. Travelling east,

> he passed India and many isles beyond India, where there are more than five thousand isles, and travelled so far by land and sea, girdling the globe, that he found an isle where he heard his own language being spoken … He had travelled so far over land and sea, circumnavigating the earth, that he had come to his own borders; if he had gone a bit further, he would have come to his own district.[52]

But there was no transport available, so the traveller returned home by the way he had come, 'so he had a long journey'. Some years afterwards, the author says, the traveller went to Norway and was blown off course to an island, which he immediately recognized as the island where he had heard his own language being spoken, and realized that he had circumnavigated the world. This proved, the author wrote, that 'if a man had adequate shipping and good company, and had moreover his health and wanted to see the world, he could traverse the whole world, above and below'. Translations of the 'Travels' were very popular in Italy, so Columbus very likely knew this encouraging tale.

The most obvious evidence that medieval Europeans believed that the Earth is round is Martin Behaim's *Erdapfel* ('Earth Apple'), the oldest surviving world globe but certainly not the first to be made. The German-born Behaim became an adviser to King João II of Portugal in 1484 and, in his service, he visited Guinea, where he experimented with the use of the cross-staff for navigation, and the Azores. Columbus certainly knew about Behaim's work and may even have met him. Following the death of his mother in 1490, Behaim returned to his home city of Nuremburg for three years to sort out his family's affairs. While he was there, the city council commissioned him to produce a display globe, the *Erdapfel*, for the town hall. It was a magnificent work, incorporating all the latest geographical knowledge gained by the Portuguese voyages of exploration, the ultimate cartographic portrayal of the pre-Columbian world with Europe, Asia and Africa standing alone in the global Ocean. Behaim completed his globe in 1492, just months before Columbus returned from his first voyage to the New World. You can really only feel sorry for him.

Columbus's world view

The consequences of Columbus's voyage were so transformative that we now talk about the pre-Columbian and post-Columbian world views, making it easy to forget that the man himself was a product of the pre-Columbian world and, even as others began to realize the true import of his discoveries, in his own mind he never left it. Columbus didn't have the educational opportunities that were available to people from wealthier backgrounds. As far as is known, he received no formal schooling during his childhood beyond somehow acquiring basic literacy and numeracy. However, Columbus was curious about the world, and once he had left the family business and started to work as an agent, he began educating himself. As well as his native Genoese dialect, he became fluent in Latin, Portuguese and Castilian, taught himself arithmetic and geometry, learned cartography and read voraciously, if uncritically, about astronomy, geography, history and philosophy. Columbus also enjoyed reading travelogues and was particularly captivated by *The Travels of Marco Polo* and its descriptions of the fabulous wealth of the Indies and China. Like many self-educated people, Columbus pursued his own lines of enquiry and showed a strong confirmatory bias, reading only what reinforced his beliefs rather than what challenged them.

Perhaps the most important influence on Columbus's thinking was the work of the Italian geographer Paolo dal Pozzo Toscanelli (1397–1482). Among the many things medieval cartographers didn't know for sure was how far east the Asian continent extended. Most tended to exaggerate its size and Toscanelli exaggerated more than most, believing it to be over 8,000 kilometres wider than it really is. By Toscanelli's calculations, this placed Japan roughly 90 degrees of longitude west of the Canary Islands (about 8,000 kilometres) rather than the 200 degrees it actually is, less than half the true distance (nearly 20,000 kilometres). This was still a long way for a fifteenth-century sailing ship, but Toscanelli believed it was possible, and in 1474 he sent a letter and a map of the Ocean to the Portuguese King Afonso V, outlining a plan to sail westwards to the Spice Islands of the East Indies. Ever cautious, Afonso rejected the proposal, but it later became known to Columbus, who wrote to Toscanelli about it, outlining his own proposal. Toscanelli wrote an encouraging reply, telling Columbus that 'the said voyage is not only possible, but it is true, and certain to be honourable and to yield incalculable profit, and very great fame among all Christians'.

Toscanelli also sent Columbus a copy of the map he had sent to King Afonso, which, it is known for certain, he took with him on his first voyage in 1492.

Another important influence of Columbus's thinking was d'Ailly's *Imago Mundi*, which introduced him to the work of the ninth-century Persian astronomer al-Farghani (known in the west as Alfraganus). Al-Farghani had calculated that a degree of latitude was 56.67 miles, from which Columbus calculated that the circumference of the Earth at the Equator must be 20,400 miles (32,860.6 kilometres). Columbus assumed that al-Farghani's calculations were based on the 4,856-foot Roman mile. Had he ever had any formal tuition in astronomy, he would have known that al-Farghani's estimate was based on the 7,091-foot Arabic mile. As a result of this basic error, Columbus underestimated the true circumference of the Earth by about 20 per cent. Combined with Toscanelli's overestimate of the size of Asia, this led Columbus to calculate that the Indies were only 68 degrees of longitude west of the Canary Islands – that is, about 5,700 kilometres, an underestimate of about 58 per cent. This was the prime cause of Columbus's difficulties in selling his plan. Most geographers accepted Eratosthenes' remarkably accurate estimate of the Earth's circumference as being approximately 39,425 kilometres, a very slight underestimate. By rights, there would be nothing but open ocean 5,700 kilometres west of the Canary Islands. Columbus would run out of supplies, or be forced to turn back, long before he got anywhere near Asia.

Columbus's convictions were not based solely on book-learning. While in Galway, Columbus saw two dead bodies which had washed ashore in a boat. He thought that they had an Asiatic appearance and so must have drifted across the ocean from China. He collected anecdotes too. The Portuguese pilot Martín Vicente told him that he had found himself 450 leagues west of Cape St Vincent and had pulled from the water a piece of strangely carved wood after several days of strong westerly winds. Pedro Correa, Columbus's brother-in-law, claimed to have found similar pieces of carved driftwood on Porto Santo island, in the Madeira archipelago. People in the Azores told him that, after prolonged westerlies, huge canes unknown in Europe and pine trees of unknown species were often washed up. On Flores, he had heard, two corpses with broad, alien faces had been washed up. All evidence, Columbus thought, that Asia was near.

The Atlantic's phantom islands also played an important part in Columbus's reasoning. Europeans knew about the vast Indonesian archipelago that lay east of China and tended to assume that the elusive phantom islands, like Antillia and Brasil, were extreme parts of it. Belief in their existence made it seem more credible to Columbus that China could be reached by sailing west. He had heard, and was encouraged by, the many stories of islands sighted in the fog during the Bristolian and Portuguese voyages searching for Brasil and Antillia, so he felt confident that he would have the opportunity to take on fresh water and food on the long voyage to Asia. In his biography of Columbus, Fernando wrote 'these fables and stories ... as they fell in with his own designs, he committed them carefully to memory'. Fernando well recognized his father's tendency to confirmatory reasoning.

Decision time

The commission of enquiry finally delivered its report on Columbus's proposal in 1490. Unsurprisingly, it took a negative view of Columbus's prospects of success and advised the Catholic Monarchs to turn him down. However, Columbus hadn't been wasting his time while the committee deliberated, he'd been building a network of supporters at court who kept his cause alive. Columbus finally got his opportunity in 1492, following the surrender of Granada in January that year. The royal treasurer, Luis de Santángel, warned the monarchs that Columbus was planning to leave Spain to seek support in France or England. This finally forced Ferdinand and Isabella to make a decision. They were well aware of Bartolomeu Dias's successful voyage around Africa and the commercial opportunities that it promised to open for Portugal. Even if its chances of success seemed slim, Columbus's proposal at least offered Spain a chance to get to the Spice Islands ahead of the Portuguese and head off any attempt by the English or French to muscle in on the spice trade.

In April 1492, the Catholic Monarchs agreed that, should he be successful, Columbus should have the grand title of 'Admiral of the Ocean Sea' and be appointed viceroy and governor of all new lands that he claimed for Spain. In addition, he would have the right to one tenth of the revenues of the new lands and the option of purchasing a one-eighth share of any commercial venture in those lands and receive one eighth of their profits. The terms were generous – so generous that the monarchs later regretted them and tried to renege on the deal. Queen Isabella also offered a lifetime pension to whoever sighted land first on the voyage.

Columbus finally set sail on the evening of 3 August from the port of Palos de la Frontera, about 13 kilometres east of Huelva. He had three ships: the largest, his flagship, was the carrack *Santa Maria*, the others were the caravels *Niña* and *Pinta*, captained by the brothers Martín Alonso and Vicente Yañez Pinzón, both of them experienced Atlantic navigators and occasional pirates. Columbus sailed first to Gomera in the Canary Islands, where he took on fresh supplies, before setting out on his ocean crossing on 9 September. Columbus's plan was to utilize the *volta do mar*, sailing west on the Trade Winds and returning on the westerlies. This was not a do-or-die mission; Columbus knew that he could at any time change course and sail north to pick up the westerlies, which would reliably take him and his fleet home. This plan wasn't quite as watertight as Columbus probably thought it was; what he didn't know was that he was sailing into the Caribbean hurricane season: had he met one, he might now be just a footnote in history, along with van Olmen and Estreito.

Two weeks out from Gomera, Columbus conferred with

Martín Alonso Pinzón. By his calculations, they should by now have sighted Antillia, which Toscanelli's chart had placed, conveniently, exactly halfway between the Canary Islands and Cipangu (Japan). Pinzón agreed that they were in the right area, and they concluded that the pilots had failed to take the ocean current properly into account and that they were too far northeast to see the non-existent island. Columbus adjusted his course accordingly. The map couldn't be wrong. After four weeks at sea, and still no land sighted, Columbus's sailors were becoming restive, fearing that they might run out of supplies before they could return home. On 9 October, Columbus, supported by the Pinzóns, headed off a mutiny by agreeing that if no land had been sighted after three more days, they would set course back to Spain. Large flocks of birds had been sighted, and Columbus was feeling confident that he wouldn't have to keep his promise; land couldn't be far off now, he thought. At two o'clock on the morning of 12 October 1492, land was sighted from the *Pinta*, but when alerted, Columbus claimed that he had already seen a light, 'like a small wax candle', on land three hours earlier, so claiming the queen's pension for himself.

Landfall

At daybreak, Columbus's fleet anchored off a low, wooded island. Naked people were seen on the shore watching the strange and unfamiliar sight. Carrying a royal standard, Columbus went ashore with the Pinzóns and an armed party and, after thanking God, he formally claimed the land for the Catholic Monarchs. Those in the crew who had doubted Columbus asked his pardon. The watching islanders could have had no idea that the brief ceremony performed by the strangers on the shore spelled disaster for them and millions of other Native Americans. Columbus found the unsuspecting islanders to be friendly, curious and delighted with the gifts of red bonnets, glass beads, hawk bells and other cheap trinkets that he handed out. Columbus thought them well-built and handsome, with the same skin colour as the Guanches but with broader faces, large eyes and long, coarse black hair. Like the Guanches, the islanders painted their bodies and wore little in the way of clothing. They carried no weapons and did not know the use of iron or, much to Columbus's disappointment, gold either. Despite their simple technology, Columbus thought the islanders intelligent and opined that they would be easily converted to Christianity. More ominously, he added that they would make good servants: Columbus would begin their enslavement in 1494 after his return to the Caribbean. After two days, Columbus set sail to continue his explorations, but only after he'd kidnapped six of the guileless islanders to take back to Spain with him to present to the Catholic Monarchs. Believing that he had discovered some outlying isles of the Indies, Columbus described them as *Indios*, or 'Indians'.

The islanders called their home island Guanahaní, but Columbus renamed it San Salvador (Holy Saviour) in thanks to God for his safe landfall. San Salvador must have been one of the smaller islands in the Bahamas archipelago, but it's never been possible to identify exactly which one. Since the late eighteenth century, it has been thought most likely that Columbus's San Salvador was Watling's Island, which has been known officially as San Salvador since 1925. However, nearly a dozen alternative locations have been proposed. Research in the 1980s, taking account of modern knowledge of Atlantic winds and currents to adjust Columbus's log, indicated a landfall over 100 kilometres further south on Samana Cay or Plana Cays. Whichever island it was, the islanders who greeted Columbus would have belonged to the Taíno-speaking Lucayan people, who were Stone Age farmers and fishers. Within thirty years of their meeting with Columbus they would be extinct as a people, victims of epidemics of introduced European diseases and Spanish slave raids that left the Bahamas completely depopulated.

Columbus spent three months exploring the Bahamas, the northeast coast of Cuba, which he thought was Cipangu, and the north coast of Hispaniola, which he thought might at last be the missing phantom island of Antillia: it lives on still as the collective name of the Caribbean archipelago, the Antilles. Columbus's journals display his complete conviction that he was in Asia, together with wonder at the beauty of the land and a real estate agent's eye to its potential value. He noted how suitable the islands' tropical environment was for growing sugar cane. On Christmas Day, the *Santa Maria* ran aground on a reef off the coast of Hispaniola. The ship could not be refloated, but a friendly local chief, Guacanagari, sent his canoes to help unload all the stores and bring them safely ashore. Informed by Guacanagari that there were gold mines inland, Columbus salvaged the timbers from the *Santa Maria* to build a fort, La Navidad, which he garrisoned with forty-three officers and men, the first European settlement in the New World since the Norse abandoned L'Anse aux Meadows nearly 500 years before.

The Treaty of Tordesillas

On 16 January 1493, Columbus left Hispaniola with his two remaining ships, setting course northeast to pick up the westerlies, and reached Santa Maria in the Azores on 18 February, where he got an unexpectedly hostile reception: the Portuguese governor threatened to seize his ships on suspicion of piracy. Two days later, Columbus was allowed to set sail again only for a storm to force him to take refuge in Lisbon on 4 March. In what must have been an uncomfortable meeting for both, King João, no doubt suffering from a bad case of sour grapes, informed Columbus that he believed that his voyage violated the terms of the 1479 Treaty of Alcáçovas. Columbus finally returned to Palos, to a hero's welcome, on 15 March and soon afterwards was received by Ferdinand and Isabella at court in Barcelona, where he was showered with honours. The threat of conflict between Spain and Portugal over Columbus's discoveries was quickly headed off with the Treaty of Tordesillas, the greatest of all European carve-ups of the rest of the world. The treaty, agreed in 1494, divided the whole of the non-Christian world between Spain and Portugal along a meridian drawn 370 leagues west of the Cape Verde Islands, which was eventually determined as being 46° of longitude west. No European had yet even seen most of the lands and the oceans that were being shared out. The doctrine of discovery did not require that non-Christians be consulted about the treaty, but no ruler in the Christian world was consulted either. While Christian rulers were prepared to recognize territorial claims based on discovery, they vehemently rejected the concept that the Spanish and the Portuguese could legitimately exclude them from the sea itself and prevent them from making their own discoveries. The determination, in particular, of France, England and the Netherlands to ignore the treaty set the stage for three centuries of bitter colonial conflict.

Columbus's legacy

Few events in human history have been more consequential than Columbus's first voyage in 1492: it marked year one of the modern age. Unlike the Norse before them, the Europeans of Columbus's time had the technology, skills, resources, ideologies and surplus population (both free and enslaved) to exploit their discoveries. They did so with extraordinary rapidity: only thirty years after Columbus's voyage, Ferdinand Magellan's Basque lieutenant Juan Sebastián Elcano successfully completed the first circumnavigation of the world in the service of Spain. Europeans would go on to explore and map every continent, so becoming the first to discover the world in its entirety. In the process, they ended the age when discrete civilizations existed in isolation or were in contact with one another only through intermediaries, as Europe and China had been. All of the world's civilizations were for the first time brought into direct maritime contact with one another. This was disruptive everywhere, but the previously completely isolated civilizations of the Americas did not survive the shock of the encounter: it isn't for nothing that the history of the Americas is starkly divided into pre- and post-Columbian periods. Old World pathogens and violence and maltreatment by the colonists devastated the indigenous population of the Americas, clearing the way for its widespread replacement by Europeans and enslaved Africans. There was an equally significant global biological transfer of domesticated plants and animals between continents which transformed diets, farming practices and natural environments globally. In Europe, the greatest rewards were reaped by those countries on the Atlantic Ocean that were geographically best placed to take advantage of the new global trade routes: Spain, Portugal, France, England and the Netherlands. Long seen in economic terms as the edge of the world, they now found themselves at the centre of the new globalized trade network and prospered accordingly. The Atlantic replaced the Indian Ocean as the economic centre of the world. The major European losers were the Baltic-centred Hanseatic League and, ironically, the Italian mercantile cities, especially Genoa and Venice: ironic because Italian navigators played such a significant role in opening up the Atlantic in the first place. They sought and found new trading opportunities but others were better placed to take advantage of them: it was an object lesson in being careful what you wish for. Much of the wealth the Europeans extracted from the Americas ultimately found its way to India and China as payment for spices, silks and other luxuries, driving their economic growth and prosperity to new heights: it was only after the Industrial Revolution that the flow of wealth was reversed in Europe's favour. The greatest losers in the new Atlantic-centred world were the Islamic powers of the Middle East and North Africa. Their role as essential middlemen in global trade made redundant, they entered a long-term relative decline which ended the Islamic challenge to Christian Europe. Prince Henrique would have felt justified.

The western Antipodes

Martin Behaim's new globe did not become a museum piece overnight, however: it would take more than a decade before it became clear what Columbus had actually discovered. Until then, the European world view remained decidedly pre-Columbian: there were still only three continents. The global Ocean had just grown a little smaller, that was all. News of Columbus's voyage travelled fast. The new medium of moveable-type printing was revolutionizing European intellectual life, enabling the rapid diffusion of new ideas and discoveries. Printed copies of Columbus's reports, published within weeks of his return, spread the news to the rest of Europe long before the end of the year. The excitement was palpable; against all expectations, it seemed that Columbus really had opened a new route to the riches of the east.

There were, however, a few doubters who thought Columbus's discoveries could not be accommodated within the existing world view. Within two months of Columbus's return, the Italian-Spanish historian Peter Martyr claimed that Columbus had discovered not Asia but the western Antipodes, one of those hypothetical continents that the Greeks had reasoned must exist to keep the world properly balanced. Columbus, he said, had entered a new and unexplored hemisphere of the world, the 'western hemisphere' (*ab occidente hemisphero*): he was the first to coin the term. The doubters would only grow in number. Columbus made three more voyages during which he fruitlessly explored most of the Caribbean archipelagos, parts of the coastline of the Central and South American continental mainland and discovered the mouth of the Orinoco river. All the time, he was convinced that China and India, and all their riches, could not be many more leagues to the west. The huge discharge flowing from the Orinoco briefly cast a shadow of doubt over Columbus's mind: it was so vast, he thought, that it must come from a great land mass. However, he easily convinced himself that this was not a fourth continent but the Earthly Paradise which medieval Europeans had long believed lay somewhere in

Asia. Columbus died an embittered man in 1506, feeling that he had been denied the credit he deserved for his discoveries. He still believed that the lands he had discovered were part of Asia, but by this time few others did. Discoveries of new lands were coming thick and fast, and the idea that they were all just outlying isles of the Indies was becoming increasingly implausible.

'One like Columbus'

In 1496, Spain's ambassador in London reported home that 'one like Columbus' had persuaded King Henry VII to support his plan to sail west across the Atlantic to 'the country of the great Khan' (China) by a route that he claimed would be shorter than Columbus's. This was the Italian navigator John Cabot (Giovanni Caboto), who had settled in Bristol the year before, probably attracted there by the city's record of sponsoring voyages of exploration in the North Atlantic. Cabot sailed from Bristol in May 1497 in a single ship, a 50-tonne carrack called the *Matthew*, and, after a month at sea made landfall somewhere on Newfoundland's Avalon Peninsula. He and his crew were the first Europeans to reach North America since the days of the Norse. Cabot landed briefly to claim ownership for Henry VII, then spent the next thirty-five days following the Newfoundland coast north, probably to within a few kilometres of the lost Norse settlement at L'Anse aux Meadows at the northern tip of the Great Northern Peninsula, before returning to England. Cabot believed that he had reached northern China, but the English simply called his discovery the 'New Found Land'. What most impressed Cabot and his crew was not the 'New Found Land' itself but the Grand Banks, which they reported were 'swarming with fish, which can be taken not only with the net but in baskets let down with a stone'. Cabot's Bristolian sponsors showed little interest in this discovery; it was new trade routes they wanted, not fish, but the Bretons, Basques and Portuguese were quick to see the commercial possibilities. Cabot disappeared on a return voyage in 1498, but by 1509, follow-up expeditions from Bristol and Portugal had traced most of the North American coast from the entrance of Hudson Bay, south to the Chesapeake, all without finding any trace of the country of the Great Khan.

In July the same year that Cabot rediscovered North America, the new Portuguese king, Manuel I (r. 1495–1521), sent a fleet of four ships under Vasco da Gama to complete what Bartolomeu Dias had begun ten years previously and sail to India. Learning from Dias's experience, da Gama made rapid passage around the tip of Africa by plotting a course that swung far west out into the Atlantic to take advantage of the *volta do mar*. As they crossed the Equator, driftwood and flocks of seabirds hinted at the presence of land not far away over the western horizon. Da Gama's fleet arrived at Calicut (Kozhikode) in southern India in May 1498 and returned in triumph to Lisbon in August or September 1499. He had beaten Columbus to it and pioneered a direct trade route to the spice lands of Asia, albeit at the cost of losing over half his crew to scurvy. Six months after da Gama's homecoming, a fleet of thirteen ships departed Lisbon for India under Pedro Álvares Cabral. Cabral charted a course south that was just a little further west than da Gama's, and, on 21 April 1500, he ran up against the forested coast of Brazil, near Monte Pascoal, just short of 17° of latitude south of the Equator. Dias's discovery of the southern hemisphere's *volta do mar* made an accidental Portuguese discovery of Brazil all but inevitable. Cabral calculated that this new land lay east of the demarcation agreed in the Treaty of Tordesillas, and he claimed it for Portugal. To begin with, Cabral believed that he'd only discovered an oceanic island, but after a week exploring the coast it was clear to him that this was a continental-size landmass. The evidence against Columbus was stacking up.

The New World

It was the Florentine explorer and navigator Amerigo Vespucci who finally made the leap of the imagination that ended the pre-Columbian world view. Between 1497 and 1504, Vespucci was employed as a pilot on a number of Spanish and Portuguese expeditions (exactly how many is disputed) which between them charted most of the coast of South America between Venezuela and Rio de Janeiro, but it isn't for these that he is mainly remembered, it's because he coined the term 'New World' and gave his name to America. The 'New World' first appears in a letter Vespucci wrote, in Latin, to a former school friend and patron, Lorenzo Pietro de' Medici, in which he described his voyage to Brazil in 1501–2. Brazil, he was sure, was not an island but an unknown continent:

> Concerning my return from those new regions which we found and explored ... These we may rightly call a New World [Novus Mondus]. Because our ancestors had no knowledge of them, and it will be a matter wholly new to all those who hear about them, for this transcends the view held by our ancients, inasmuch as most of them hold that there is no continent to the south beyond the equator, but only the sea which they named the Atlantic and if some of them did aver that a continent there was, they denied with abundant argument that it was a habitable land. But that this their opinion is false and utterly opposed to the truth ... my last voyage has made manifest; for in those southern parts I have found a continent more densely peopled and abounding in animals than our Europe or Asia or Africa, and, in addition, a climate milder and more delightful than in any other region known to us, as you shall learn in the following account.[53]

Vespucci wrote more about his voyages in another letter written to the Florentine statesman Piero Soderini in which he repeated the phrase 'New World'. Like Columbus's reports, printed copies of Vespucci's letters circulated widely, and they were quickly translated into French, Italian, Dutch and German. Among those who read Vespucci's letters and were convinced by them were the German cartographer Martin Waldseemüller and his collaborator Matthias Ringmann, who were at that time working on a new universal geography. The world map they published to accompany it in 1507 was the birth certificate of the modern Atlantic Ocean. Entitled the *Universalis Cosmographia*, this was the first world map to show the new discoveries as being unambiguously separate from Asia. For thousands of years, the Atlantic had been only a peripheral sea of the great global Ocean, its western bounds completely undefined. Waldseemüller's map began to define those bounds, turning the Atlantic into an ocean in its own right. The map also introduced a new name, 'America', although it was applied only to South America. In the introduction he wrote for their handbook, Ringmann explained, 'I do not see what right any one would have to object to calling this part [the South American mainland], after Americus who discovered it and who is a man of intelligence, Amerigen, that is, the Land of Americus, or America.' Ironically, Vespucci never knew that he'd had a continent named after him, because copies of Waldseemüller's map never made it to Spain before he died in 1512. Demoting Columbus to being merely the discoverer of the West Indies did not go down well in Spain, but after the Flemish cartographer Gerardus Mercator used 'America' to name both North and South America on his influential world map in 1538, the usage was set in stone.

Plus ultra

In 1505, the Spanish monarchs called a conference of navigators, the *Junta de Navegantes*, at Toro to discuss the new discoveries and determine their significance. It broke up without agreement, but when it reconvened at Burgos in 1508 it formally accepted that the new discoveries were not part of Asia as had been hoped. Vespucci attended both conferences and his arguments that Columbus had discovered a 'New World' seem to have been decisive. The pre-Columbian world was officially over. The aspiration to find a western route to Asia remained just as strong as ever, but it was now accepted that it would have to be either through or around the New World: the New World's transformation from unexpected obstacle to land of opportunity happened only after the discovery of the gold-rich Aztec Empire in 1517.

The discovery of the New World was more than just a geographical discovery; it was also an intellectual liberation. For centuries, Europeans had been in thrall to the learning of the ancient world. It was only because he had boldly (if misguidedly) questioned that inherited wisdom that Columbus discovered the New World and now everything else was open to question too. In *Novum Organum** (1620), in which he laid the foundations of modern scientific method, the English philosopher Francis Bacon expressed his belief that the discovery of the New World and the burgeoning Scientific Revolution went hand in hand. The Pillars of Hercules had symbolized the edge of the known world for generations of sailors, both the limit of navigation and the limit of geographical knowledge, in the same way that the revered works of the ancient philosophers, such as Plato and Aristotle, had put limits on thought and the development of a scientific understanding of the world. The Spanish and Portuguese voyages to the New World and India had metaphorically smashed the Pillars of Hercules in the same way that the new scientific methods were smashing the ancient orthodoxies and leading the way to a greater understanding of the cosmos. Bacon's inspired choice of illustration for his title page is telling: it shows a galleon sailing between two mighty pillars. At the bottom there is a quotation from the Vulgate Bible, *Multi pertransibunt et augebitur scientia*, meaning 'Many will pass through and knowledge will be the greater' (Daniel 12:4). *Non plus ultra* became *plus ultra* ('further beyond'), Bacon's personal motto and that of the Spanish king and Holy Roman Emperor Charles V (r. 1516–56), the first ruler of a truly global empire.

* The title is inspired by Aristotle's *Organon*, a collection of treatises on logic: it can be translated variously as 'method', 'instrument', 'tool' or 'organ'.

'Who's got the last laugh now?'

Columbus had his detractors even before his death, and he was hardly cold in his grave before claims were made that he was not the real discoverer of the New World. Spanish critics patriotically claimed that it was really the Spanish Pinzón brothers, not the Genoese Columbus, who discovered the New World, or that it was some unknown Spanish pilot who had previously crossed the Atlantic and given directions to Columbus on his return. Quite why this mystery pilot chose to tell no one but Columbus about his discovery, rather than take credit for it himself, was never explained. Since that time, claims for pre-Columbian discoverers of the New World have multiplied. Basques, Bretons, Bristolians, the Welsh, the Scots, the Irish, the Germans, the Venetians, the Arabs, West Africans, Romans, Greeks, Phoenicians, Ancient Egyptians, Atlanteans, lost tribes of Israelites, Neolithic megalith-builders, Ice Age mammoth hunters and even the Chinese have all been claimed by someone to have crossed the Atlantic before Columbus. If even only half of them really did, surely someone would have taken Columbus aside and told him not to bother because it had already been done? The Norse beat Columbus to it, no one else did.

Columbus had his own way of dealing with his detractors, if this anecdote told by the Italian traveller Girolamo Benzini in his 1565 book *The History of the New World* is to be believed (which it probably shouldn't):

> There were many who could not endure that a foreigner and an Italian should acquire so much honour and so much glory, not only in the kingdom of Spain but also in the other nations of the world … Columbus being at a party with many noble Spaniards, where, as was customary, the subject of conversation was the Indies: one of them undertook to say: 'Mr Christopher, even if you had not found the Indies, we should not have been devoid of a man who would have attempted the same that you did, here in our own country of Spain, as it is full of great men

clever in cosmography and literature.' Columbus said nothing in answer to these words, but having desired an egg to be brought to him, he placed it on the table saying: 'Gentlemen, I will lay a wager with any of you, that you will not make this egg stand up as I will, naked and without anything at all.' They all tried, and no one succeeded in making it stand up. When the egg came round to the hands of Columbus, by beating it down on the table he fixed it, having thus crushed a little of one end; wherefore all remained confused, understanding what he would have said: that after the deed is done, everybody knows how to do it; that they ought first to have sought for the Indies, and not laugh at him who had sought for it first, while they for some time had been laughing, and wondered at it as an impossibility.[54]

References

This book has been written in a non-academic style and its purpose has been solely to introduce the general reader to a neglected, but fascinating and important, historical subject. Anyone who would like a single-volume academic overview dedicated to the history of the pre-Columbian Atlantic will search for one in vain; however, they will find that the relevant chapters of David Abulafia's monumental *The Boundless Sea: A Human History of the Oceans* make an excellent starting place, or, for a more archaeological perspective, Barry Cunliffe's *Facing the Ocean: the Atlantic and its Peoples*. Listed below are the main works consulted in writing this book; the vast majority of the journal articles referred to are available online from JSTOR, Research Gate and Academia.

Abulafia, David, *The Discovery of Mankind: Atlantic Encounters in the Age of Columbus* (Yale University Press, New Haven, 2008).

Abulafia, David, *The Boundless Sea: A Human History of the Oceans* (Penguin, London, 2019).

Adhikari, Mohamed, 'Europe's First Colonial Incursion into Africa: The Genocide of Aboriginal Canary Islanders', *African Historical Review*, vol. 49 (2017), pp. 1–26.

Adu-Boahen, Kwabena, 'The Impact of European Presence on

Slavery in the Sixteenth to Eighteenth-Century Gold Coast', *Transactions of the Historical Society of Ghana*, vol. 14 (2012), pp. 165–99.

Almagro-Gorbea, Martín (ed.), *Iberia. Protohistory of the Far West of Europe: From Neolithic to Roman Conquest* (Universidad de Burgos, Burgos, 2014).

Arge, Símun, V., 'The Landnám in the Faroes', *Arctic Anthropology*, vol. 28, no. 2 (1991), pp. 101–20.

Arneborg, Jette, et al. (eds), 'Norse Greenland: Selected Papers from the Hvalsey Conference 2008', *Journal of the North Atlantic*, Special Volume 2 (2009).

Azurara, Gomes Eannes de, *Chronicle of the Discovery and Conquest of Guinea,* translated by Charles Raymond Beazley (Hakluyt Society, London, 1896).

Ball, Philip, 'A Viking Saga: Did Norse Seafarers Really Find Their Way Across Stormy Oceans with the Aid of a Delicate Crystal?', *New Scientist*, vol. 225 (2015), pp. 40–1.

Barkham, S., 'The Basque Whaling Establishments in Labrador 1536–1632', *Arctic*, vol. 37 (1984), pp. 515–19.

Barrett, James H. and Orton, David C. (eds), *Cod and Herring: The Archaeology and History of Medieval Sea Fishing* (Oxbow, Oxford, 2016).

Batey, Janet, and Englert, Anton, *Ohthere's Voyages: A Late 9th-Century Account of Voyages along the Coasts of Norway and Denmark* (Viking Ship Museum, Roskilde, 2007).

Bennett, Herman, L., *African Kings and Black Slaves: Sovereignty and Dispossession in the Early Modern Atlantic* (University of Pennsylvania Press, Philadelphia, 2019).

Bennett, Jim, *Navigation* (Oxford University Press, Oxford, 2017).

Bérard, Benoit and Biar, Alexandra, 'Indigenous Navigation in the Caribbean Basin', *Archaeonautica*, vol. 21 (2012), pp. 237–44.

Béthencourt, Jean de, *The Canarian, or Book of the Conquest and Conversion of the Canarians in the Year 1402*, translated by R. H. Major (Hakluyt Society, London, 1872).

Bilic, Tomislav, 'Locations of Mythical Exile', *Mnemosyne*, vol. 66 (2013), pp. 247–72.

Black, Jeremy, *A Brief History of the Atlantic* (Robinson, London, 2022).

Blench, Roger, 'The Peopling of the Canaries: New Data and New Hypotheses', *Études et Documents Berbères*, vol. 45–6 (2021), pp. 149–73.

Bowen, E. G., *Britain and the Western Seaways* (Thames and Hudson, London, 1972).

Bridges, E. Lucas, *Uttermost Part of the Earth* (London, 1947).

Bradley, Bruce, and Stanford, Dennis, 'The North Atlantic Ice-Edge Corridor: A Possible Palaeolithic Route to the New World', *World Archaeology*, vol. 36, no. 4, Debates in World Archaeology (2004), pp. 459–78.

Broodbank, C., *The Making of the Middle Sea* (Thames and Hudson, London, 2013).

Bulbeck, Chilla and Bowdler, Sandra, 'The Faroes Grindadráp or Pilot Whale Hunt', *Australian Archaeology*, vol. 67 (2008), pp. 53–60.

Burlton, Clive, *The Matthew of Bristol* (Bristol Books, Bristol, 2017).

Byock, Jesse, *Viking Age Iceland* (Penguin, London, 2001).

Campbell, I. C., 'The Lateen Sail in World History', *The Journal of World History*, vol. 6 (1995), pp. 1–23.

Carpenter, R., *Beyond the Pillars of Heracles* (Delacorte, 1963).

Carreras, C. and Morais, R. (eds), *The Western Roman Atlantic Façade*, BAR International Series 2162 (2010).

Cassidy, Lara M. et al., 'Neolithic and Bronze Age Migration to Ireland and Establishment of the Insular Atlantic Genome', *Proceedings of the National Academy of Sciences of the United States of America*, vol. 113 (2016), pp. 368–73.

Casson, Lionel, 'Speed under Sail of Ancient Ships', *Transactions of the American Philological Society*, vol. 82 (1951), pp. 136–48.

Chamorro, Javier G., 'Survey of Archaeological Research on Tartessos', *American Journal of Archaeology*, Apr. 1987, vol. 91, no. 2 (Apr. 1987), pp. 197–232.

Church, Mike, J., 'The Vikings Were Not the First Colonizers of the Faroe Islands', *Quaternary Science Reviews*, vol. 77 (2013) pp. 228–32.

Connell, Will, 'Boat Building, Navigation, and West African Indigenous Knowledge', *African Diaspora ISPs, Paper 2* (2001).

Crone, G. R., *The Voyages of Cadamosto and Other Documents on Western Africa in the Second Half of the Fifteenth Century* (Hakluyt Society, London, 1937).

Crosby, Alfred W., 'An Ecohistory of the Canary Islands: A Precursor of European Colonization in the New World and Australasia', *Environmental Review*, vol. 8 (1984), pp. 214–35.

Crosby, Alfred W., *Ecological Imperialism: The Biological Expansion of Europe 900–1900* (2nd edn, Cambridge UP, Cambridge, 2004).

Crumlin-Pedersen, Ole, *Archaeology and the Sea in Scandinavia and Britain* (The Viking Ship Museum, Roskilde, 2010).

Cummings, John, *The Voyage of Christopher Columbus: Columbus' Own Journal of Discovery Newly Restored and Translated* (Weidenfeld, London, 1992).

Cunliffe, Barry, *Facing the Ocean: the Atlantic and Its Peoples* (OUP, Oxford, 2001).

Cunliffe, Barry, *The Extraordinary Voyage of Pytheas the Greek* (Penguin, London, 2001).

Cunliffe, Barry, *Between the Oceans* (Yale University Press, New Haven, 2008).

Cunliffe, Barry and Koch, John T. (eds), *Celtic from the West: Alternative Perspectives: Archaeology, Genetics, Language and Literature* (Oxbow, Oxford, 2012).

Cunliffe, Barry and Koch, John T. (eds), *Celtic from the West 2: Rethinking the Bronze Age and the Arrival of Indo-European in Atlantic Europe* (Oxbow, Oxford, 2013).

Cunliffe, Barry, *Bretons and Britons: The Fight for Identity* (Oxford University Press, Oxford, 2021).

Darwin, Charles, *The Voyage of the Beagle* (London, 1845).

Davidson, Peter, *The Idea of North* (Reaktion, London, 2005).

Decorse, Christopher R., 'Culture Contact, Continuity, and Change on the Gold Coast, AD 1400–1900', *The African Archaeological Review*, vol. 10 (1992), pp. 163–96.

Diamond, Jared, *Collapse: How Societies Choose to Fail or Survive* (Viking Penguin, New York, 2005).

Dicuil, *Dicuili Liber de Mensura Orbis Terrae*, translated by J. J. Tierney (Dublin, 1967).

Disney, A. R., *A History of Portugal and the Portuguese Empire. Volume 2: The Portuguese Empire* (Cambridge University Press, Cambridge, 2009).

Dollinger, Philippe, *The German Hansa* (Macmillan, London, 1970).

Enterline, James Robert, *Erikson, Eskimos and Columbus: Medieval European Knowledge of America* (Johns Hopkins University Press, Baltimore, 2002).

Epstein, Jeremiah, F., 'Sails in Aboriginal Native America', *American Antiquity*, vol. 48 (1990), pp. 489–98.

Fagan, Brian, *Ancient North America* (Thames and Hudson, London, 2019).

Fear, A. T., 'The Tower of Cadiz', *Faventia*, vol. 12–13 (1990), pp. 199–211.

Fernández-Armesto, Felipe, *Before Columbus: Exploration and Colonization from the Mediterranean to the Atlantic, 1229–1492* (University of Pennsylvania Press, Philadelphia, 1987).

Fernández-Armesto, Felipe, *Columbus* (Duckworth, London, 1991).

Fiolhais, Carlos (ed.), *The Global History of Portugal: from Prehistory to the Modern World* (Sussex Academic Press, Brighton, 2022).

Fitzhugh, William and Ward, Elizabeth I. (eds), *Vikings: The North Atlantic Saga* (Smithsonian Institution Press, Washington, 2000).

Fitzpatrick, Scott M., 'Seafaring Capabilities in the Pre-Columbian Caribbean', *Journal of Maritime Archaeology*, vol. 8 (2013), pp. 101–38.

Francis, Daniel, *A History of World Whaling* (Viking, Markham, Ontario, 1990).

Fregel, Rosa, et al., 'Demographic History of the Canary Islands Male Gene-Pool: Replacement of Native Lineages by European', *BMC Evolutionary Biology*, vol. 9 (2009), pp. 167–81.

Freitag, Barbara, 'Hy Brasil: The Metamorphosis of an Island from a Cartographic Error to Celtic Elysium', *Studies in Comparative Literature* 69 (Brill, Amsterdam, 2013).

Friel, Ian, *The Good Ship: Ships, Shipbuilding and Technology in England 1200–1520* (British Museum Press, London, 1995).

Galliou, P. and Jones, M., *The Bretons* (Blackwell, Oxford, 1991).

Gannon, Angela, and Geddes, George, *St Kilda, the Last and Outermost Isle* (Historic Environment Scotland, Edinburgh, 2015).

Gardiner, M., 'The Character of Commercial Fishing in Icelandic Waters in the Fifteenth Century', in Barrett, J., and Orton, D. (eds), *Cod and Herring: The Archaeology and History of Medieval Sea Fishing*, pp. 80–90 (Oxbow Books, Oxford, 2016).

Gardiner, Robert (ed.), *Cogs, Caravels and Galleons: The Sailing Ship 1000–1650* (Conway's History of the Ship, London, 1994).

Gardiner, Robert (ed.), *The Age of the Galley: Mediterranean Oared Vessels since Pre-Classical Times* (Conway's History of the Ship, London, 1995).

Gardiner, Robert (ed.), *The Earliest Ships: The Evolution of Boats into Ships* (Conway's History of the Ship, London, 1996).

Gascoigne, John, 'Crossing the Pillars of Hercules: Francis Bacon, the Scientific Revolution and the New World', in Gal, O., and Chen-Morris, R. (eds), *Science in the Age of Baroque* (Springer Science and Business Media, Dordrecht, 2013), pp. 217–37.

Goetzmann William, H. and Williams, Glyndwr, *The Atlas of North American Exploration: From the Norse Voyages to the Race to the Pole* (Prentice Hall, New York, 1992).

Goldhahn, Joakim, 'Rethinking Bronze Age Cosmology: A North European Perspective', in Fokkens, Harry, and Harding, Anthony (eds), *Handbook of the European Bronze Age* (Oxford: Oxford University Press, 2013), pp. 248–65.

Gutscher, Marc-Andre, 'Destruction of Atlantis by a Great Earthquake or Tsunami? A Geological Analysis of the Spartel Bank Hypothesis', *Geology*, vol. 33 (2005), pp. 685–88.

Hamidullah, Mohammed, 'Muslim Discovery of America before Columbus', *Journal of the Muslim Students' Association of the United States and Canada*, vol. 4, no. 2 (Winter 1968), pp. 7–9.

Hamley, Kit M. et al., 'Evidence of Prehistoric Human Activity in the Falkland Islands', *Science Advances*, vol. 7, no. 44 (2021), eabh3803.

Haywood, John, *The Penguin Historical Atlas of the Vikings* (Penguin, Harmondsworth, 1995).

Haywood, John, *Dark Age Naval Power: Frankish and Anglo-Saxon Seafaring Activity* (2nd edn, Anglo-Saxon Books, Hockwold-Cum-Wilton, Norfolk, 1999).

Haywood, John, *The Historical Atlas of the Celtic World* (Thames and Hudson, London, 2001).

Haywood, John, *The Celts: from Bronze Age to New Age* (Pearson, 2004).

Haywood, John, *Northmen: The Viking Saga AD 793–1241* (Head of Zeus, London, 2015).

Herodotus, *The Histories*, edited by Robert B. Strassler (Quercus, London, 2008).

Holsey, Bayo, '"Watch the Waves of the Sea": Literacy, Feedback, and the European Encounter at Elmina', *History in Africa*, vol. 38 (2011), pp. 79–101.

Horn, Walter et al., *The Forgotten Hermitage of Skellig Michael* (University of California Press, Berkeley, 1990).

Hourani, Albert, *Arab Seafaring* (revised and expanded edn, Princeton University Press, Princeton, NJ, 1995).

Hughes, Thomas L., '"The German Discovery of America": A Review of the Controversy over Pining's 1473 Voyage of Exploration', *German Studies Review*, vol. 27 (2004), pp. 503–26.

Hutchinson, Gillian, *Medieval Ships and Shipping* (Leicester University Press, London, 1994).

Issawi, Charles, 'Arab Geography and the Circumnavigation of Africa', *Osiris*, vol. 10 (1952), pp. 117–28.

Javier, F., and García, G., 'The Legendary Traditions about the Tower of Hercules', *Folklore*, vol. 125 (2014), pp. 306–21.

Jensen, Jørgen, *The Prehistory of Denmark* (Gyldendal, Copenhagen, 2013).

Johnson, Donald S., *Phantom Islands of the Atlantic* (Goose Lane, Fredericton, NB, 1996).

Jones, Evan, and Condon, Margaret M., *Cabot and Bristol's Age of Discovery* (University of Bristol, Bristol, 2016).

Jones, Gwyn, *The Norse Atlantic Saga* (2nd edn, Oxford University Press, Oxford, 1986).

Julius Caesar, *The Conquest of Gaul* (trans. S. A. Handford, Penguin, 1951).

Koch, John T., *An Atlas for Celtic Studies* (Oxbow, Oxford, 2007).

Koch, John T., 'A Case for Tartessian as a Celtic Language', *Palaeohispanica* vol. 9 (2009), pp. 339–51.

Krogh, Knud J., *Viking Greenland* (Copenhagen, 1967).

Kuitems, M., Wallace, B. L., Lindsay, C. et al., 'Evidence for European Presence in the Americas in AD 1021', *Nature*, vol. 601 (2022), pp. 388–91.

Kurlansky, Mark, *Cod* (Vintage, London, 1997).

Kurlansky, Mark, *The Basque History of the World* (Vintage, London, 2000).

Lagan, Jack, *The Barefoot Navigator* (2nd edn, Bloomsbury, London, 2017).

Lainema, Matti, and Nurminen, Juha, *Ultima Thule* (John Nurminen, Helsinki, 2001).

Larson, L. M. (trans.), *The King's Mirror* (Twayne Publishers, New York, 1917).

Law, Robin, 'West Africa's Discovery of the Atlantic', *International Journal of African Historical Studies*, vol. 44, no. 1 (2011), pp. 1–25.

Lebor Gabála Érenn: The Book of the Takings of Ireland, ed. S. G. McCloskey (Celtic New Dawn Press, 2022).

Lewis, A. R. and Runyan, T. J., *European Naval and Maritime History 300–1500* (Indiana University Press, Bloomington, 1990).

Ling, J. and Koch, John, 'A Sea Beyond Europe to the North and West', in Dodd, J. and Meijer, E. (eds), *Giving the Past a Future* (Archaeopress, Oxford, 2018), pp. 96–111.

Ljungvist, Frederick Charpentier, 'The Significance of Remote Resource Regions for Norse Greenland', *Scripta Islandica*, vol. 56 (2005), p. 13–54.

Lødøen, Trond and Mandt, Gro, *The Rock Art of Norway* (Windgather Press, Oxford, 2010).

López-Ruiz, Carolina, 'Gargoris and Habis: A Tartessic Myth of Ancient Iberia and the Traces of Phoenician Euhemerism', *Phoenix*, vol. 71 (2017), pp. 286–7.

Lunde, Paul, 'Pillars of Hercules, Sea of Darkness', *Saudi Aramco World*, vol. 43 (1992), pp. 6–17.

MacKillop, James, *Myths and Legends of the Celts* (Penguin, London, 2005).

Mackley, Jude S., *The Legend of St Brendan* (Brill, Leiden, 2008).

Magnus Magnusson and Hermann Pálsson (trans.), *The Vinland Sagas: The Norse Discovery of America* (Penguin, Harmondsworth, 1965).

Mallory, J. P., *The Origins of the Irish* (Thames and Hudson, London, 2015).

Mallory, J. P., *In Search of the Irish Dreamtime* (Thames and Hudson, London, 2018).

Marcus, G. J., 'The First Discovery of Iceland', *Studies: An Irish Quarterly Review*, vol. 44 (1955), pp. 315–18.

Marcus, G. J., 'The Norse Emigration to the Faeroe Islands', *English Historical Review*, vol. 71 (1956), pp. 556–61.

Marcus, G. J., 'The Mariner's Compass: Its Influence on Navigation in the Late Middle Ages', *History*, vol. 41 (1956), pp. 16–24.

Marcus, G. J., *The Conquest of the North Atlantic* (Boydell, Woodbridge, 1980).

Marean, C. W., 'Pinnacle Point Cave 13B (Western Cape Province, South Africa) in Context: The Cape Floral Kingdom, Shellfish, and Modern Human Origins', *Journal of Human Evolution*, vol. 59 (2010), pp. 425–43.

Markham, C. R., 'On the Whale Fishery of the Basque Provinces of Spain', *Nature*, vol. 25 (1882), pp. 365–8.

Markoe, Glenn E., *The Phoenicians* (British Museum Press, London, 2000).

Martin, A. M., 'Auga dos Cebros (Pontevedra, Galicia): Un barco del Bronce Final II en la fachada atlántica de la Peníncula Ibérica (1325–1050 a. c.)', *Saguntum*, vol. 51 (2019), pp. 23–39.

McAlhany, Joseph, 'Sertorius between Myth and History: The Isles of the Blessed Episode in Sallust, Plutarch and Horace', *The Classical Journal*, vol. 112 (2016), pp. 57–76.

McGhee, Robert, 'Contact between Native North Americans and the Medieval Norse: A Review of the Evidence', *American Antiquity*, vol. 49 (1984), pp. 4–26.

McGhee, Robert, *Ancient People of the Arctic* (UBC Press, Vancouver, 1996).

McGrail, Seán, *Early Ships and Seafaring: Water Transport Beyond Europe* (Pen and Sword, Barnsley, 2015).

McGrath, Patrick, *Bristol and America 1480–1631* (Bristol Historical Association, Bristol, 1997).

Mearns, David, L., 'An Early Portuguese Mariner's Astrolabe from the Sodré Wreck Site, Al Hallaniyah, Oman', *International Journal of Nautical Archaeology* (2019), pp. 1–12.

Meier, Dirk, *Seafarers, Merchants and Pirates in the Middle Ages* (Boydell, Woodbridge, 2006).

Meijer, Fik, *A History of Seafaring in the Classical World* (Croom Helm, London, 1986).

Morillo, M., Ochoa, C. F. and Dominguez, J. S., 'Hispania and the Atlantic Route in Roman Times: New Approaches to Ports and Trade', *Oxford Journal of Archaeology*, vol. 35 (2016), pp. 267–84

Moseley, C. W. R. D. (trans.), *The Travels of Sir John Mandeville* (Penguin, Harmondsworth, 1983).

Munch, Gerd Stamsø, *Borg in Lofoten: A Chieftain's Farm in North Norway* (Tapir Academic Press, Trondheim, 2002).

Newitt, Malyn, *The Portuguese in West Africa 1415–1670* (Cambridge University Press, Cambridge, 2015).

Nicolle, David C., 'Medieval Islamic Navigation in the Atlantic', *Journal of Medieval and Islamic History*, vol. 2 (2002), pp. 3–14.

Nisbet, H. C. and Gailey, R. A., 'A Survey of the Antiquities of North Rona', *Archaeological Journal*, vol. 107 (1960), pp. 88–115.

Ochoa, C. Fernandez and Morillo, A., 'Roman Lighthouses on the Atlantic Coast in the Western Roman Atlantic Façade', *BAR International Series* 2162 (2010).

O'Connor, Ralph (trans.), 'Star-Oddi's Dream', in *Icelandic Histories and Romances* (Tempus, Stroud, 2002).

O'Sullivan, Aidan and Breen, Colin, *Maritime Ireland: An Archaeology of Coastal Communities* (Tempus, Stroud, 2007).

Olalde, Iñigo, et al., 'The Beaker Phenomenon and the Genomic Transformation of Northwest Europe', *Nature*, vol. 555 (2018), pp. 190–6.

Øye, Ingvild (ed.), *Bergen and the German Hansa* (Bryggens Museum, Bergen, 1994).

Paine, Lincoln, *The Sea and Civilization: a Maritime History of the World* (Alfred A. Knopf, New York, 2013).

Parkington, John, 'Middens and Moderns: Shellfishing and the Middle Stone Age of the Western Cape, South Africa', *South African Journal of Science*, vol. 99 (2003), pp. 243–7.

Parry, J. H., *The Spanish Seaborne Empire* (Hutchinson, London, 1966).

Patterson, N., Isakov, M., Booth, T. et al., 'Large-Scale Migration into Britain during the Middle to Late Bronze Age', *Nature*, vol. 601 (2022), pp. 588–94.

Perdikaris, S. and McGovern, T. H., Walrus, 'Cod Fish, and Chieftains: Intensification in the Norse North Atlantic', in Thurston, T. L. and Fisher, C. T. (eds), *Seeking a Richer Harvest: The Archaeology of Subsistence Intensification, Innovation, and Change* (Springer Media, New York, 2007), pp. 193–216.

Pérez, S. C. and López-Ruis,C., *Tartessos and the Phoenicians in Iberia* (OUP, 2016).

Pétillon, Jean-Marc, 'First Evidence of a Whale Bone Industry in the Western European Upper Paleolithic: Magdalenian Artifacts from Isturitz (Pyrénées-Atlantiques, France)', *Journal of Human Evolution*, vol. 54 (2008), pp. 720–6.

Phillips, Kelly M., 'Solutrean Seal Hunters? Modeling Transatlantic Migration Parameters Fundamental to the Solutrean Hypothesis for the Peopling of North America', *Journal of Anthropological Research*, vol. 70, no. 4 (2014), pp. 573–600.

Plato, *Timaeus and Critias*, trans. Desmond Lee (Penguin, Harmondsworth, 1965).

Powell, Eric A., 'Lost History of the Sheep Islands', *Archaeology*, vol. 76 (2023), pp. 55–63.

Price, Michael, 'Vikings in Paradise: Did the Norse Settle the Azores?', *Science*, vol. 374 (6564), 2021, p. 141.

Prósper, B. M., 'Some Observations on the Classification of Tartessian as a Celtic Language', *Journal of Indo-European Studies*, vol. 42 (2014), pp. 468–86.

Pumfrey, Stephen, *Latitude and the Magnetic Earth* (Icon, Cambridge, 2002).

Pye, Michael, *The Edge of the World: How the North Sea Made Us Who We Are* (Viking, London, 2014).

Ramos, Robert Sala (ed.), *Pleistocene and Holocene Hunter-Gatherers in Iberia and the Gibraltar Strait* (Universidad de Burgos, Burgos, 2014).

Ravenstein, E. G., 'The Voyages of Diogo Cão and Bartholomeu Dias, 1482–88', *Geographical Journal*, vol. 16 (1900), pp. 625–55.

Rick, T. C. et al., 'Millennial-Scale Sustainability of the Chesapeake Bay Native American Oyster Fishery', *PNAS*, vol. 113 (2016), pp. 6,568–73.

Roberts, B. W., 'Farmers in the Landscape or Heroes on the High Seas? Britain and Ireland in the Bronze Age', in Fokkens, H., and Harding, A. (eds.), *The Oxford Handbook of Bronze Age Europe* (OUP, Oxford, 2020), pp. 531–49.

Rogers, Francis M., 'The Vivaldi Expedition', *Annual Report of the Dante Society*, vol. 73 (1955), pp. 31–45.

Roller, Duane, W., *Ancient Geography: The Discovery of the World in Classical Greece and Rome* (I. B. Tauris, London, 2015).

Rozwadowski, Helen, M., *Vast Expanses: A History of the Oceans* (Reaktion, London, 2018).

Ruddock, Alwyn A., 'John Day and the English Voyages across the Atlantic before 1497', *Geographical Journal*, vol. 2 (1966), pp. 225–33.

Russell, Peter, *Prince Henry 'the Navigator': A Life* (Yale University Press, New Haven, 2001).

Salisbury, Neal, 'The Indians' Old World: Native Americans and the Coming of Europeans', *William and Mary Quarterly*, vol. 53 (1996), pp. 435–58.

Scammell, G. V., *The World Encompassed: The First European Maritime Empires c.800–1650* (Methuen, London, 1981).

Schei, L. V. and Moberg, G., *The Faroe Islands* (John Murray, London, 1991).

Schoff, W. H. (trans.), *The Periplus of Hanno* (Philadelphia, 1912).

Seaver, Kirsten A., *The Last Vikings* (I. B. Tauris, London, 2010).

Seiffert, Erik R. et al., 'A Parapithecid Anthropoid of African Origin in the Paleogene of South America', *Science*, vol. 368 (2020), pp. 194–7.

Severin, Tim, *The Brendan Voyage: A Leather Boat Tracks the Discovery of America by the Irish Sailor Saints* (Hutchinson, London, 1978).

Sharrer, Harvey L., 'The Passing of King Arthur to the Island of Brasil in a Fifteenth-Century Spanish Version of the Post-Vulgate Roman du Grall', *Romania*, vol. 92 (1971) pp. 65–74.

Sims-Williams, Patrick, 'An Alternative to "Celtic from the East" and "Celtic from the West"', *Cambridge Archaeological Journal*, vol. 30 (2020), pp. 511–29.

Smith, Christopher, *Late Stone Age Hunters of the British Isles* (Routledge, London, 1992).

Smith, Michèle Hayeur, '"Tangled up in Blue": The Death, Dress and Identity of an Early Viking-Age Female Settler from Ketilsstaðir, Iceland', *Medieval Archaeology*, vol. 63, no. 1 (2019), pp. 95–127.

Smith, Robert, 'The Canoe in West African History', *Journal of African History*, vol. 11 (1970), pp. 515–33.

Sparavigna, A. C., *The Science of al-Biruni* (Turin, 2013).

Stanford, Dennis, J. and Bradley, Bruce, A., *Across Atlantic Ice: The Origin of America's Clovis Culture* (University of California Press, Berkeley, 2013).

Starr, S. Frederick, 'So Who Did Discover America?', *History Today*, vol. 63 (2013), pp. 42–6.

Straus, Lawrence G., et al., 'Ice Age Atlantis? Exploring the

Solutrean-Clovis "Connection"', *World Archaeology*, vol. 37.4, Debates in 'World Archaeology' (2005), pp. 507–32.

Szabo, Vicki Ellen, *Monstrous Fishes and the Mead Dark Sea: Whaling in the Medieval North Atlantic* (Brill, Leiden, 2007).

Tibi, Amin, 'The Vikings in Arabic Sources', *Islamic Studies*, vol. 35 (1996), pp. 211–17.

Tooley, R. V., *Maps and Map-Makers* (Batsford, London, 1949).

Unger, Richard W., 'Dutch Herring, Technology, and International Trade in the Seventeenth Century', *Journal of Economic History*, vol. 40 (1980), pp. 253–80.

Van Duzer, C., 'The Voyage of Trezenzonio to the Great Island of the Solstice', *Folklore*, vol. 119 (2008), pp. 335–45.

Wallace, Birgitta Linderoth, *Westward Vikings: The Saga of L'Anse aux Meadows* (Historic Sites Association, St John's, NL, 2012).

Warren, William F., 'The Babylonian Universe Newly Interpreted', *Journal of the Royal Asiatic Society* (1908), pp. 977–83.

Webb, J. F. (trans.), 'The Voyage of St Brendan', in *Lives of the Saints* (Penguin, Harmondsworth, 1965).

Will, M., et al., 'An Evolutionary Perspective on Coastal Adaptations by Modern Humans during the Middle Stone Age of Africa', *Quaternary International*, vol. 30 (2016), pp. 1–19.

Williams, R. Alan and Le Carlier de Veslud, C., 'Boom and Bust in Bronze Age Britain: Major Copper Production from the Great Orme Mine and European Trade', *Antiquity*, vol. 93 (2019), pp. 1, 178–96.

Winchester, Simon, *Atlantic* (Harper Collins, London, 2010).

Wittmann, Kevin, R., '"Closest to Where the Sun Sets": The Fortunate Islands and the Limits of the World', *Medieval Geography and Cartography* (Durham University, Durham, 2016).

Zagórski, Boguslaw, R., 'Sea Names of the Arab World', *Onomastica*, vol. 57 (2013), pp. 205–28.

Zurara, Gomes Eanes de, *The Chronicle of the Discovery and Conquest of Guinea*, translated by Edgar Prestage (2 vols, Hakluyt Society, London, 1896–9).

Endnotes

1 Tacitus, *Agricola* 30: *Atque omne ignotum pro magnifico est.*
2 Abraham Ortelius, *Thesaurus Geographicus* (Antwerp, 1596), see entry for 'Gadiricus'.
3 *Polite Conversations*, 1738.
4 Charles Darwin, *The Voyage of the Beagle* (1845), 1905 John Murray edition, p. 203.
5 Quoted in Carolina López-Ruiz, 'Gargoris and Habis: A Tartessic Myth of Ancient Iberia and the Traces of Phoenician Euhemerism', *Phoenix*, vol. 71, 2017, p. 267.
6 Diodorus Siculus, *The Library of History*, Book V, ch. 19, trans. Loeb Classical Library, 1939.
7 *The Periplus of Hanno*, translated by W. H. Schoff (Philadelphia, 1912).
8 Lionel Casson, 'Speed under Sail of Ancient Ships', *Transactions of the American Philological Society*, vol. 82 (1951), pp. 136–48.
9 Herodotus, *Histories*, 4.42–3 (translated by Andrea L. Purvis in *The Landmark Herodotus*, ed. Robert B. Strassler, 2007).
10 Herodotus, *Histories*, 4.43.
11 Hesiod, *Works and Days*, line 170, translated by M. L. West (OUP, 1988).
12 Homer, *Iliad*, Book 18, lines 478–608.
13 *The Geography of Strabo*, bk IV 5.5 (Loeb Classics, 1917).
14 Plutarch, *Sertorius*, 8. 2–5. Translated by Joseph McAlhany.
15 Strabo, *Geography*, 2.3. Loeb edition, translated by Horace Leonard Jones.

16 Translated by Kenneth Jackson in *A Celtic Miscellany* (Penguin Classics, 1951), p. 279.
17 Translated by Simon Keynes and Michael Lapidge in *Alfred the Great: Asser's Life of King Alfred and Other Contemporary Sources* (Penguin, Harmondsworth, 1983), pp. 142–3.
18 *The Voyage of St Brendan*, translated by J. F. Webb, in *Lives of the Saints*, p. 36 (Penguin, Harmondsworth, 1965).
19 Translated by J. J. Tierney, *Dicuili Liber de Mensura Orbis Terrae* (Dublin, 1967).
20 Ibid.
21 *The Seafarer,* translated by S. A. J. Bradley, *Anglo-Saxon Poetry* (Dent, London, 1982).
22 *Orkneyinga Saga* (translated by Hermann Pálsson and Paul Edwards, Hogarth Press, London, 1978).
23 Genesis 8:6–12.
24 Gwyn Jones, *The Norse Atlantic Saga*, p. 157.
25 *The King's Mirror*, translated by Larson (Twayne Publishers, New York, 1917), p. 142.
26 Ditto, pp. 149–50.
27 *Erik the Red's Saga*, translated by Magnus Magnusson and Hermann Pálsson.
28 *Eyrbyggja Saga*, trans H. Pálsson and P. Edwards (Southside, Edinburgh, 1973), p. 194.
29 Trans. *Vinland Sagas*, p. 15.
30 Translated by Ole J. Benedictow, *The Complete History of Plague in Norway 1348–1645* (Cambridge Scholars Publishing, 2022), p. 173.
31 Julius E. Olson, *The Voyages of the Northmen* (New York, 1906), p. 73.
32 Translated by J. E. Turville-Petre, Viking Society for Northern Research, 1947.
33 Translated by Thomas Wright, 1863. From *De Naturis Rerum* ('On the Nature of Things').
34 Amerigo Vespucci, *Mundus Novus*, translated by George Tyler Northup (Princeton University Press, 1916), p. 4.
35 Translated by Mohammed Hamidullah, *The Muslim Discovery of America before Columbus*, p. 7.

36 Translated by Mohammed Hamidullah, *The Muslim Discovery of America before Columbus*, p. 7.

37 Translated by Paul Lunde, 'Pillars of Hercules, Sea of Darkness', *Saudi Aramco World*, May/June 1992.

38 Translation: Jim Siebold, https://www.myoldmaps.com/late-medieval-maps-1300/249-fra-mauros-mappamundi/fra-mauro-transcriptions.pdf

39 Translated by Nehemiah Levtzion and J. F. P. Hopkins, *Corpus of Early Arabic Sources for West African History* (Markus Wiener, Princeton, 2000), pp. 268–9.

40 Quoted in Ingvild Øye, *Bergen and the German Hansa* (Bryggens Museum, Bergen, 1994), p. 11.

41 Judge for yourselves. The opera can be watched on YouTube: https://www.youtube.com/watch?v=v7zdrfo4sac

42 Translated by Francis M. Rogers, 'The Vivaldi Expedition', p. 36.

43 Alfred W. Crosby, *Ecological Imperialism: The Biological Expansion of Europe 900–1900* (Cambridge UP, Cambridge, 2004), p. 81.

44 Mohamad Adhikari, 'Europe's First Colonial Incursion into Africa: The Genocide of Aboriginal Canary Islanders', *African Historical Review*, vol. 49 (2017), pp. 1–26.

45 Quoted in Schei and Moberg, *The Faroe Islands* (John Murray, London, 1991), p. 125.

46 Translated by Harvey L. Sharrer, 'The Passing of King Arthur to the Island of Brasil', p. 67.

47 *Quem quer passar além do Bojador / Tem que passar além da dor.* Fernando Pessoa, *Mensagem* (Lisbon, 1934), Mar Portuguez X, p. 64.

48 Gomes Eannes de Azurara, *Chronicle of the Discovery and Conquest of Guinea,* translated by Charles Raymond Beazley (Hakluyt Society, London, 1896), ch. XXV, pp. 81–2.

49 G. R. Crone (trans.), *The Voyages of Cadamosto and Other Documents on Western Africa in the Second Half of the Fifteenth Century* (Hakluyt Society, London, 1937), pp. 39–40.

50 From the title of Niccolò Machiavelli's notorious political treatise *Il Principe* ('The Prince'), published in 1532.

51 'They All laughed', George and Ira Gershwin (1937).
52 *The Travels of Sir John Mandeville* (Penguin, Harmondsworth, 1983), Chapter 20, translated by C. W. R. D. Moseley.
53 Amerigo Vespucci, *Mundus Novus*, translated by George Tyler Northup (Princeton University Press, Princeton 1916), p. 1.
54 *The History of the New World by Girolamo Benzoni*, translated by W. H. Smyth (Hakluyt Society, London, 1857), pp. 16–17. The anecdote may be derived from a similar story that was told about the Italian architect Filippo Brunelleschi (1377–1446).

Image Credits

1. Paul Kim / Alamy Stock Photo
2. Royal Geographical Society / Alamy Stock Photo
3. The Image Bank / Getty Images
4. iStock / Getty Images Plus
5. Luis Miguel Bugallo Sánchez / Wikimedia Commons
6. © Wessex Archaeology
7. Jose Lucas / Alamy Stock Photo
8. CNG Coins Coin from CNG coins / Wikimedia Commons
9. © Stiftung Museum Kunstpalast, Düsseldorf
10. © Castles and Fortifications of England and Wales
11. Athanasius Kircher: Mundus subterraneus, vol. 1. Amsterdam 1664 / Wikimedia Commons
12. Captain Thomas Phillips / Wikimedia Commons
13. Towel401 / Wikimedia Commons
14. imageBROKER.com GmbH & Co. KG / Alamy Stock Photo
15. De Agostini Picture Library / Getty Images
16. Photo: Steve Birrell Photography
17. Peter EA Lindström / Wikimedia Commons
18. INTERFOTO / Alamy Stock Photo
19. Author's photo
20. The Print Collector / Alamy Stock Photo
21. Author's photo
22. Author's photo
23. N3MO / Wikimedia Commons
24. © UNESCO / Wikimedia Commons
25. imageBROKER.com GmbH & Co. KG / Alamy Stock Photo
26. Gabriel de Vallseca / Wikimedia Commons

27. Livro das Armadas / Wikimedia Commons
28. © National Maritime Museum, Greenwich, London
29. Hispalois / Wikimedia Commons
30. Inventaire des sceaux de la Flandre: recueillis dans les dépôts d'archives, musées et collections particulières du Département du Nord - 1873 / Wikimedia Commons
31. © The History Blog
32. Cofiant Images / Alamy Stock Photo
33. Polylerus / Wikimedia Commons
34. Descrittione et historia del regno de l'isole Canarie gia dette le Fortvnate / Wikimedia Commons
35. Museus e Monumentos de Portugal /Arquivo e Documentação Fotográfica Saint Vincent Panels, third panel by Nuno Gonçalves
36. Gift of J. Pierpont Morgan, 1900 / Metropolitan Museum of Art
37. © Heidelberg University Library
38. Bill Gozansky / Alamy Stock Photo
39. GRANGER - Historical Picture Archive / Alamy Stock Photo

Index

A

B

C

D

E

F

I

J

K

L

M

O

P

Q

R

S

T

U

Rey de castella:
Este he o marco dantre castella, τ portugall
Rey de castella
A linha equinocialis:
Mare ocean
Pollus antarticus: